HARRAP'S

GLOSSARY OF

Spanish-English

COMMERCIAL & INDUSTRIAL TERMS

Inglés-Español

Compiled by

Louis J. Rodrigues, M.A., M.A. (Cantab), Member
American Literary Translators Association, Translators
Association (Society of Authors: Great Britain) Asociación
Profesional Española de Traductores e Intérpretes,
Institution of Translation & Interpreting

Josefina Bernet Soler, Licenciada en Filología Inglesa
(Barcelona), M.A. (Essex)

HARRAP

London

Distributed in the United States by
PRENTICE HALL
New York

First published in Great Britain 1990
by Harrap Books Ltd.
Chelsea House, 26 Market Square,
Bromley, Kent BR1 1NA

©Harrap Books Limited, 1990

ISBN 0-245-60018-3

Printed and bound in Great Britain
by The Bath Press, Avon

PREFACE

This Glossary was inspired by our sometimes frustrating experience in having to consult others available on the market that are either incomplete, incomprehensible, or simply incoherent. Our claim to originality in its compilation is, therefore, tenuous. What we have attempted to do is to provide a more accurate, more accessible guide to the most important terms pertaining to Commerce and Industry and their corresponding equivalents in English or Spanish, while at the same time, eliminating the errors (especially of orthography) that have been perpetrated by our predecessors.

A Glossary is not a Dictionary and the user desiring to know the meaning of these terms is recommended to consult one on the subject.

The arrangement is strictly alphabetical. Headwords are printed in Bold Type, qualifiers in Ordinary Type, and foreign equivalents in each case in Italics. Cross-referencing in both the English and Spanish sections, and between the two sections, is intended to be comprehensive and any omissions are unintentional.

LJR
JBS

Barcelona/Cambridge
September 1989

PROLOGO

Este Glosario es el resultado de nuestra, a veces, frustrante experiencia a la hora de consultar otros ya existentes en el mercado y que son o bien incompletos o incomprensibles o simplemente incoherentes. Nuestra pretensión de originalidad en su recopilación es, por tanto, sutil; pero, lo que hemos intentado es una guía más precisa y fácil a la que recurrir de los términos m s importantes utilizados en el lenguaje del Comercio y la Industria y sus correspondientes equivalencias al Inglés o Español, eliminando, al mismo tiempo, los errores que se han producido en nuestros antecesores, especialmente los ortográficos.

Un Glosario no es un Diccionario y el usuario que desee conocer el significado de estos términos deber consultar cualquiera especializado en el tema.

La ordenación es estrictamente alfabética. Las palabras matrices están mecanografiadas en negrita, las calificativas en mecanografiado normal y sus equivalentes a la lengua extranjera en cualquiera de los casos en letra cursiva. La comparación de términos dentro de las secciones de Inglés y Español así como entre las dos secciones, ha sido pensada para ofrecer una mejor comprensión y cualquier omisión es inintencionada.

LJR
JBS

Barcelona/Cambridge
Septiembre 1989

PART ONE

ENGLISH - SPANISH

ABBREVIATIONS

L	Latin
Am	American
Br	British
A	Argentinian
C	Cuban
Ch	Chilean
M	Mexican
PR	Puerto Rican

A

abandonment *abandono*
abate, to *rebajar, reducirse*
abatement *supresión, reducción*
–, basic *reducción básica*
abbreviated test specifications *especificación de pruebas abreviadas*
abeyance *suspensión, expectativa*
–, in *en suspenso, pendiente*
ability test, mental *prueba de capacidad mental*
–, administrative *capacidad administrativa*
–, analytical *capacidad analítica*
–, basic mental *capacidad mental básica*
–, executive *capacidad directiva*
–, financial purchasing *capacidad financiera de compra*
–, general *sagacidad*
–, intellectual *capacidad o capacitación intelectual*
–, learning *capacidad de aprender*
–, merchandising *capacidad de negociar, habilidad comercial*
–, sales *aptitud para vender*
abnormal *anormal*
above par *sobre la par, a premio*
– issue *emisión sobre la par*
abridge, to *abreviar, resumir*
abrogate, to *revocar, anular*
absence from work *falta de asistencia al trabajo*
absolute *absoluto*
– address *dirección absoluta*
– deviation *desviación absoluta*
– endorsement *endoso absoluto*
– interest *interés establecido*
– sale *venta incondicional*
– standard *patrón absoluto, atipificación absoluta*
– time *hora absoluta*
– total loss *pérdida total (efectiva)*
– value *valor absoluto*
absorb the loss, to *asumir la pérdida*
abstract *resumen, sumario, extracto*
– bulletin *boletín de resúmenes*
– of current account *extracto de cuenta corriente*
abundance, economy of *economía de abundancia*

abut, to *empalmar*
accelerated depreciation *depreciación acelerada*
– fatigue test *prueba acelerada de fatiga*
– life test *prueba acelerada de duración*
– motion *movimiento acelerado*
– performance test *pruebas aceleradas de destreza*
acceleration *aceleración*
– clause *cláusula para el vencimiento anticipado de una deuda*
– note *pagaré con opción de pago adelantado*
– principle *principio de aceleración*
– time *duración de la aceleración*
accept subject to *aceptar a reserva de*
–, to *aceptar, reconocer, comprometerse al pago de un documento*
acceptance *aceptación*
– of a draft *aceptación de una letra*
– standards *normas de aceptación*
– test or trials *pruebas de aceptación o adaptación*
–, bank *aceptación bancaria*
–, blank or uncovered *aceptación a descubierto*
–, clean *aceptación general*
–, collateral *colateral, garantía, resguardo*
–, consumer *aceptación a favor del público*
–, general *aceptación sin reservas*
–, partial *aceptación condicionada*
–, qualified *aceptación condicional*
–, to refuse *retrasar la aceptación*
–, trade *aceptación comercial*
accepted bills *efectos aceptados*
– draft *letra aceptada*
– standards *normas aprobadas*
acceptor *aceptante, aceptador*
access, rapid *acceso rápido*
accident proof a *prueba de accidentes*
– risk *riesgo de accidentes*
–, industrial *accidente de trabajo*
–, occupational *accidente de tráfico*
accidental damage *daño o deterioro accidental*
accommodation *acomodación, favor, ajuste, arreglo*
– bill of lading *conocimiento de favor*
– bill or draft *letra de favor*

- credit *crédito en descubierto*
- endorsement *endoso por aval*
- indorsement *aval de efectos comerciales*
- papers *efectos de favor*

accord *acuerdo, convenio*

account *cuenta*
- classification, expenses *clasificación de las cuentas de gastos*
- clerk *contable*
- deals, combined *ventas de cuentas combinadas*
- for, to *dar razón de*
- stated *cuenta conforme o convenida*
-, accruals *cuenta acumulativa*
-, active *cuenta activa*
-, advances *cuenta de anticipos*
-, allowance *cuenta o fondos de reserva*
-, balance *cuenta de balance*
-, blocked *cuenta controlada o congelada o bloqueada*
-, book *cuenta sin comprobantes*
-, bulk *cuenta resumida*
-, capital *cuenta de capital*
-, cash *cuenta de caja*
-, charge *cuenta corriente*
-, clear *cuenta en regla*
-, clear reckoning *cuenta clara*
-, clearance *cuenta de giros*
-, clearing *cuenta de compensación*
-, closed *cuenta saldada*
-, closing *cuenta compensadora o de cierre*
-, credit or creditor *cuenta acreedora*
-, current *cuenta corriente*
-, debit or debitor *cuenta deudora*
-, deposit *cuenta corriente o de depósito*
-, discounts *cuenta de descuentos*
-, disputed *cuenta impugnada*
-, doubtful *cuenta de cobro dudoso*
-, drawing *cuenta corriente o de anticipos*
-, expense *cuenta de gastos*
-, fixtures *cuenta de mobiliario*
-, goods or merchandise *cuenta de mercancías*
-, goodwill *cuenta de crédito o del valor prestigio*
-, government *cuenta del gobierno*
-, inactive *cuenta sin movimiento*
-, income *cuenta de ganancias*
-, itemized *cuenta detallada*
-, joint *cuenta de participación*
-, loan *cuenta de préstamo*
-, mature *cuenta vencida o pagadera*
-, net foreign investment *cuentas de inversiones extranjeras netas*
-, offset *cuenta de compensación, contracuenta*
-, on *a cuenta*

-, open *cuenta abierta*
-, outstanding *cuenta pendiente o atrasada*
-, overdrawn *cuenta en descubierto*
-, production *cuenta de producción*
-, provision *cuenta de reserva*
-, purchase *cuenta de compra*
-, sales *cuenta de ventas*
-, specified *cuenta detallada*
-, statement of *estado de cuentas*
-, status *estado de cuentas*
-, summary *cuenta centralizadora*
-, suspense *cuenta de suspenso*
-, to buy the *comprar a término (en bolsa)*
-, to open an *abrir una cuenta*
-, to pay on *pagar a cuenta*
-, to render an *rendir una cuenta, pasar facturas*
-, trading *cuenta de compraventa o explotación*
-, trust *cuenta fiduciaria*
-, value in *valor de cuenta*
-, work *cuenta de explotación*

accountability *obligación de rendir cuentas, responsabilidad*

accountable *responsable*
-, to be *rendir cuentas*

accountancy *contabilidad, contaduría, preparación de cuentas*
- business *contabilidad comercial*

accountant *contador, contable*
-, certified public *contable público titulado*
-, cost *contable de costos*
-, expert *experto en contabilidad*
-, general *jefe de contabilidad*
-, marketing *especialista o experto en mercadología*
-, production cost *contable de costes de producción*
-, public *contador o contable público*
-, sales cost *contable de costes de venta*

accounting *contabilidad, contaduría, preparación de cuentas*
- firms *empresas o agencias contables*
- machine, numerical *máquina numérica de contabilidad*
-, administrative *contabilidad administrativa*
-, business *contabilidad comercial o mercantil*
-, cost *contabilidad de costes*
-, credits *contabilidad de créditos*
-, distribution *contabilidad de la distribución*
-, distribution cost *contabilidad de costes de distribución*
-, expense-centre *contabilidad de gastos centralizados*
-, inventory *contabilidad inventarial*
-, management *contabilidad de gestión*

–, material *contabilidad de material*
–, merchandise *contabilidad de mercancías*
–, production cost *contabilidad de costes de producción*
–, sales *contabilidad de ventas*
–, shop and cost *contabilidad de talleres para determinación de costes*
accounts *cuentas*
– in arrears *cuentas atrasadas*
– overcharged *cuentas sobrecargadas o hinchadas*
– receivable *cuentas por cobrar, deudas activas cuenta de clientes*
– receivable documents *documentos de cuentas a cobrar*
– receivable ledger *libro mayor de ventas, documentos de cuentas a cobrar*
–, asset *cuentas del activo*
–, balance sheet *cuentas de balances*
–, bank *cuentas bancarias*
–, budget *cuentas de presupuesto*
–, external *cuentas de operaciones en el extranjero*
–, industrial *cuentas industriales*
–, liability *cuentas de pasivo*
–, nominal *cuentas impersonales*
–, payable *cuentas por pagar, cuenta de proveedores libro mayor de compras*
–, pledged *cuentas pignoradas*
–, recoverable *cuentas recobrables*
–, secured *cuentas garantizadas*
–, standard *cuentas tipo*
–, standardized *cuentas normalizadas o tipificadas*
–, sundry *cuentas diversas*
–, to doctor *amañar o falsificar cuentas*
–, to settle *ajustar cuentas*
–, treasury *cuentas de tesorería*
–, worthless *cuentas incobrables*
accretion *agrandamiento, aumento, acumulación*
accrual *aumento, acumulación*
– basis *base acumulativa, contabilidad por acumulación*
– of discount *incremento del descuento*
accruals account *cuenta acumulativa*
– payable *acumulaciones pagaderas*
–, tax *impuestos acumulados*
accrued interest *interés acumulado*
– liabilities *pasivo acumulado*
– taxes *impuestos causados o vencidos, por pagar*
accumulated profits *utilidades acumuladas*
– random series *serie aleatoria acumulada*
accumulative error *error acumulativo*
– record card *ficha de registro acumulativo*

– value *valor acumulativo*
accuracy *precisión*
– test, clerical speed and *prueba de precisión y rapidez administrativa*
–, survey of working speed and *encuesta de precisión y rapidez de trabajo*
achievement *logro, acabamiento, realización, ejecución, perfeccionamiento*
acid-test ratio *proporción entre el activo y pasivocirculante*
acknowledge, to *admitir, reconocer*
– receipt *acusar recibo*
acquire, to *adquirir*
acquired rights *derechos adquiridos*
acquisition, original *adquisición original*
acquittance *resguardo, recibo, carta de pago*
across the board *programa diario a la misma hora*
act *acto, hecho, derecho*
– of incorporation *escritura constitutiva*
–, companies' *ley de sociedades*
–, compensation *ley de accidentes de trabajo*
acting *interino, suplente*
– chief *jefe actuante o accidental o interino*
– director *director accidental o interino*
– manager *gerente interino o suplente o en funciones*
– order *delegación de poderes*
– partner *socio gerente*
– president *presidente interino o en funciones*
– secretary *secretario interino*
action cycle *ciclo de funcionamiento, ciclo de trabajo*
–, direct *acción directa, sabotaje*
–, punitive *medida represiva*
activation research *investigación de la activación*
active *activo*
– account *cuenta activa*
– balance *saldo acreedor*
– bonds *títulos al portador*
– buying *demanda activa*
– capital *capital efectivo*
– debt *deuda que produce interés*
– market price competition *mercado de competición activa*
– partner *socio activo*
– trade balance *balance comercial favorable*
– trust *fideicomiso, activo*
activity *actividad, trabajo, tarea*
– analysis *programación lineal*
– chart, multiple *diagrama de actividades simultáneas*
– dip *caída o descenso de la actividad*
– loss *pérdida de actividad*
– process chart, multiple *diagrama de proceso*

de actividades simultáneas
- vector analysis test *prueba o examen analítico del rumbo de la actividad*
-, collective *actividad colectiva*
-, gainful *actividad lucrativa*
-, group *actividad de grupo (social)*
-, mental *actividad mental, decisión mental*
-, multiple *actividades múltiples*
-, research *actividad investigadora*
-, sales-promotion *actividad de promoción de ventas*
actual *real, efectivo, actual, flagrante*
- attainment *producción efectiva*
- basis *gastos reales*
- behaviour *conducta real*
- capacity *capacidad real*
- cash value *valor real en mercado, costo de reposición*
- cost *coste/o efectivo o verdadero*
- employment *ocupación real*
- income *ingreso efectivo*
- liabilities *pasivo efectivo o real*
- loss *pérdida efectiva*
- markdown *rebaja efectiva*
- market value *valor real en mercado o plaza*
- markup *margen comercial efectivo o real*
- output *rendimiento efectivo, producción efectiva*
- price *precio real*
- purchases *compras efectivas*
- relationship *relación verdadera o efectiva*
- sales *ventas efectivas*
- stock *existencias efectivas*
- time *tiempo real, tiempo empleado*
- total loss *pérdida total real*
- value *valor real*
- value method *método del valor actual*
- wage *salario efectivo*
- yield *rendimiento real*
actuality, burning *actualidad inmediata*
actuarial estimate *estimación actuarial*
- profit *ganancia contable*
actuary *actuario*
ad (Am) *anuncio*
- campaign *campaña de publicidad*
- index *índice de anuncios*
- size *tamaño del anuncio*
ad lib *a voluntad*
ad valorem *ad valorem, según valor*
ads, want (Am) *anuncios por salarios, pequeños anuncios clasificados, anuncios económicos*
adaptability, clerical *adaptabilidad administrativa*
adaptation *adaptación, acomodación*
adapted *calificado*

add up, to *totalizar, sumar*
added, net value *valor agregado neto*
adder *máquina sumadora, circuito aditivo*
-, algebraic *sumadora algebraica*
-, electronic *sumadora electrónica*
adding and calculating machine *máquina de calcular y sumar*
- machine *máquina sumadora*
- machine, cash registering and *máquina registradora y sumadora*
- machine, electric *máquina eléctrica de sumar*
- machine, hand-operated *máquina de sumar a mano*
- machine, ten-key *máquina de sumar de diez teclas*
- register *registro sumador*
- roll *rollo de papel para máquina sumadora*
additional charge *gasto adicional o suplementario oaccesorio*
- cost *coste adicional o suplementario*
- debit *cargo adicioal*
- load *sobrecarga*
- markup, net *margen comercial adicional neto*
address arrangement *disposición de la dirección*
- card *ficha de dirección*
- counter, memory *contador de dirección de memoria*
- counter, program *contador de dirección de programa*
- drum *tambor de direcciones*
- generator *generador de dirección*
- group card *ficha para el grupo de dirección*
- instructions, single *instrucción de dirección sencilla*
- light *luz de dirección*
- register *registro de direcciones*
- selection switch *interruptor de selección de direcciones*
- register, storage *almacenamiento del registro de direcciones*
- system, public *sistema de comunicación directa*
-, business *dirección comercial*
-, four-digit *dirección de cuatro dígitos*
-, mailing *dirección postal*
addressee *destinatario*
addressing machine *máquina de imprimir direcciones*
addressograph *adresógrafo*
adequate compensation *compensación o remuneración equitativa*
adjust, to *ajustar, regularizar, tasar*
adjustable stop motion *movimiento regulable*

de parada
adjusted rate *tasa ajustada*
–, seasonally *reajustado según temporada*
adjuster, average *ajustador, tasador o arreglador*
–, claim *ajustador de reclamaciones*
adjusting entry *asiento de ajuste*
adjustment *arreglo, ajuste, tasación*
– bond *bono sobre ganancias o beneficios*
– entry *asiento regulador o de regulación*
– of a claim *pago de una reclamación*
–, automatic wage *ajuste automático de sueldos*
–, price *ajuste de precios*
–, salary *reajuste de salarios*
–, yearly *ajuste anual*
administer *administrar*
administration *administración*
– committee *comité de administración*
– cost *gastos de administración*
– expenses *gastos de administración*
–, budget *administración del presupuesto*
–, dynamic *administración dinámica*
–, fiscal *administración*
administrative ability *capacidad administrativa*
– accounting *contabilidad administrativa*
– agency *oficina administrativa*
– assistant *ayudante administrativo*
– expenses *gastos administrativos o de dirección*
– services *servicios administrativos*
– unit *unidad administrativa*
administrator *administrador, dirigente, gobernante, gerente, gestor*
admissible error *tolerancia*
admitted assets *activo aprobado o computable o admitido*
adumbration *bosquejo, croquis, esbozo*
advance *anticipo, avance, adelanto, alza, aumento*
– bill *letra, factura, giro*
– collections *cobros por adelantado*
– diagram *gráfico de avance*
– expense fund *fondo de anticipos para gastos*
– in blank *anticipo en descubierto*
– notice *aviso anticipado*
– order *pedido inicial*
– payment *pago adelantado, anticipo*
– payments on purchase obligations *envíos a cuenta de pedidos a servir*
–, cash *anticipo en metálico*
–, in *por adelantado*
–, price *subida de precio, encarecimiento*
advances *anticipos, adelantos, préstamos*
– account *cuenta de anticipos*

– on securities *préstamos sobre títulos*
–, reimbursable *anticipos reembolsables*
–, returnable *anticipos retornables*
adverse balance *saldo desfavorable*
– balance of payments *balanza de pagos desfavorable*
advertise, to *anunciar, avisar*
advertisement *anuncio*
– board *tablero de anuncios*
– border *línea de cierre de un anuncio*
– in feuilleton style *reportaje publicitario*
– manager *jefe del departamento de anuncios*
– page plan *maqueta publicitaria*
– rates *tarifa de anuncios*
– representative *representante de la sección de anuncios*
–, band or strip *anuncio en forma de faja o tira*
–, blind *anuncio anónimo*
–, composite *anuncio colectivo*
–, illuminated *anuncio luminoso*
–, publisher's *nota editorial, anuncio de publicaciones*
advertiser *anunciante, anunciador (A)*
advertising *publicidad, reclame (A), propaganda*
– agency *agencia de publicidad*
– agent *agente de publicidad, corredor de anuncios*
– allowance *asignación para publicidad*
– budget *presupuesto para publicidad*
– committee *comité de publicitarios*
– consultant *consejero publicitario*
– copy *texto publicitario o de un anuncio, texto de aviso (M, C, A)*
– department *departamento de publicidad*
– display *proyecto de anuncio compuesto*
– dollar *dinero invertido en publicidad*
– efforts *esfuerzos de publicidad*
– expenses *gastos de publicidad*
– media *medios de publicidad accional*
– medium *medios de publicidad*
– page *página de anuncios*
– prestige *publicidad de prestigio*
–, broadcast or radio *publicidad por radio o radiada*
–, circular *circular de publicidad*
–, cooperative *publicidad en cooperación*
–, direct *publicidad directa*
–, display *publicidad en plafones*
–, free gift *publicidad por artículos de reclamo*
–, industrial *publicidad industrial*
–, mail order *publicidad directa por correos*
–, national *publicidad nacional*
–, newspaper *publicidad en la prensa, anuncios en los periódicos*
–, novelty *publicidad por el objeto, envío de*

muestras o novedades
–, poster *publicidad por medio de carteles*
–, television *publicidad en televisión*
advice *consejo, aviso, opinión, advertencia, notificación*
–, shipping *aviso de embarque*
–, trade *asesoría comercial*
advise, to *avisar, notificar*
adviser, advisor *asesor, consejero*
–, technical *asesor técnico*
advisory *consultivo*
– board *junta consultiva*
– committee *comité consultivo*
– council *consejo consultivo o de asesoramiento, consejo asesor*
– forecast *pronóstico preventivo*
– function *función asesora*
– service *servicio de asesoramiento*
aegis *égida, auspicio, patronato*
affair *asunto, negocio*
affairs, statement of *estado estimado de liquidación*
affect, to *afectar*
affidavit *declaración, acta notarial*
affiliate *afiliada o asociada a una cadena*
affiliated company *compañía o empresa asociada, filial*
– firm *casa filial*
affinity *afinidad, semejanza, analogía, atracción*
–, constant *constante de afinidad*
affixer, stamp *pegador de sellos*
affreightment, contract of *póliza de fletamiento*
after a pattern *según modelo o plantilla*
– costs *gastos extraordinarios*
– date *fecha posterior*
– hours *horas extraordinarias*
– office hours *después de las horas de oficina*
– sales service *servicio de postventas, servicio de piezas de recambio, servicio de ayuda después de vender*
aftermath *resultados, consecuencias, repercusiones*
against documents *contra documentos*
– payment, documents *documentos contra pago*
age *edad*
– at entry *edad de ingreso*
– at withdrawal *edad de retiro*
– composition of population *composición de la población por edad*
– group *grupo de edad*
– limit *límite de edad*
–, mean *edad media, promedio de edad*
–, mental *edad mental*

–, of *mayor de edad*
–, retirement *edad de jubilación*
–, under *menor de edad*
agency *agencia, órgano, oficina, empresa, gestión*
– office *oficina de negocios*
–, administrative *oficina administrativa*
–, advertising *agencia de publicidad*
–, aircraft operating *empresa de transporte aéreo*
–, associated *agencia asociada*
–, collection *compañía agencia de cobranzas*
–, contract *contrato de agencia*
–, distributing *agencia distribuidora*
–, employment *agencia de colocaciones*
–, information *agencia de información*
–, news *agencia de noticias*
–, publicity *agencia de publicidad o de informaciones publicitarias*
agenda *orden del día, agenda*
agent *agente, representante, corresponsal, delegado*
– general *agente general*
– of exchange *agente de cambio, corredor de bolsa*
– officer *oficial pagador*
–, advertising *agente de publicidad, corredor de anuncios*
–, business *delegado del gremio o sindicato*
–, clearinghouse *agente bancario de compensaciones*
–, commission *comisionista*
–, estate *corredor de bienes raices*
–, forwarding *agente de envíos, comisionista expedidor*
–, labour *agente de colocaciones*
–, public relations *agente de relaciones públicas*
–, sales *agente de ventas*
–, selling *agente de ventas*
–, shipping *agente despachador, agente embarcador*
–, sole *agente exclusivo*
aggregate *global, total, agregado*
– demand price *precio de la demanda global*
– error *error total*
– gross liabilities *pasivo bruto global*
– imports *importaciones globales, total de importaciones*
– investment *inversión total*
– output *rendimiento total*
– principal amount *cantidad total del capital*
– supply function *función total de la oferta*
– supply price *precio de la oferta global*
– volume *volumen total*
–, statistical *conjunto estadístico*

aggressive *dinámico, agresivo, enérgico*
- competition *competición enérgica*
- sales effort *esfuerzo combativo de ventas*
agony column *sección de anuncios pequeños*
agreed price *precio convenido*
- upon, value *valor entendido*
- value *valor convenido*
agreement *contrato, arreglo*
- of service *contrato de servicios*
- to resell *pacto de retroventa*
-, binding *acuerdo obligatorio*
-, bonus *acuerdo sobre primas*
-, buying *contrato de compra*
-, clearing *convenio de compensaciones*
-, coefficient of *coeficiente de acuerdo*
-, collective bargaining *contrato colectivo de trabajo*
-, commercial *acuerdo comercial*
-, commodity *acuerdo o tratado comercial*
-, draft *proyecto de contrato*
-, factory *acuerdo de empresa*
-, gentlemen's *pacto de caballeros*
-, indemnity *pacto de indemnización*
-, labour *contrato colectivo de trabajo*
-, multilateral *convenio multilateral*
-, partnership *pacto social, contrato de asociación*
-, pooling *acuerdo o convenio consorcial*
-, salvage *contrato de salvamento*
-, union-employer *acuerdo entre el sindicato y los patronos*
-, work *acuerdo colectivo*
-, written *acuerdo por escrito*
agreements, barter *convenios de trueque*
-, international tax *acuerdos fiscales internacionales*
-, reciprocal trade *tratados comerciales recíprocos*
aid *ayuda*
-, economic *ayuda económica*
aim *ansia*
air *aire*
- charter *flete aéreo*
- express *expreso aéreo*
- freight *flete o carga aérea*
- fares *tarifas aéreas*
- traffic control *control de tránsito aéreo*
- waybill *conocimiento de embarque aéreo*
airbroker *corredor aéreo*
airbroking *corretaje aéreo*
aircraft chartering *fletamento aéreo*
- operating agent *empresa de transporte aéreo*
airlines *líneas aéreas*
airport tariffs *tarifas de aeropuerto*
algebraic adder *sumadora algebraica*
- fraction *fracción algebraica*

alien *extranjero*
alienable *enajenable*
alienate, to *enajenar, transferir*
alignment *trazado, alienación, sincronización*
all charges deducted *deducidos todos los gastos*
- domestic design *proyecto totalmente racional*
- hands *todo el personal*
- in cost *coste total*
- in policy *póliza a todo riesgo*
- in prices *precios totales*
- in time *tiempo de presencia*
- inclusive index *índice completo*
- out *a toda potencia, a pleno rendimiento*
- out effort *esfuerzo máximo*
- rights reserved *derechos de propiedad reservados*
- round price *precio global o total*
allied industries *industrias conexas*
allocation *asignación, cuota, dotación, distribución, aplicación, colocación, cupo de materiales, afijación, aprobación de gastos*
- committee *comité de cupos, dotación de personal*
- control *control de cupos*
- of labour *distribución de la mano de obra*
-, budget *asignación del presupuesto*
allot, to *repartir, distribuir*
allotment *asignación, cuota, distribución, consignación, lote*
-, budget *distribución del presupuesto*
-, original *asignación inicial*
-, primary *asignación inicial*
allotments, to comply with *quedar dentro de los límites de asignaciones fijadas*
allotted *asignado, repartido, dividido, distribuido en cupos*
allow, to *abonar en cuenta, descontar, reducir, admitir, conceder, permitir*
allowable closing error *error admisible de cierre*
- error *error admisible*
- expenses *gastos autorizables*
- return *utilidad permisible*
- variation *variación admitida*
allowance *bonificación, descuento, rebaja, retribución, prima, suplemento de jornal, ajuste*
- account *cuenta o fondos de reserva*
- for damages *indemnización por daños o perjuicios*
- for necessaries *pensión alimenticia*
-, advertising *asignación para publicidad*
-, compensating relaxation *suplemento para compensar la fatiga*

–, contingency *suplemento para imprevistos*
–, depreciation *reserva de depreciación, amortización permitida*
–, draft *rebaja por pérdida de peso*
–, excess work *suplemento por variación del método*
–, family *pensión, compensación familiar*
–, fatigue *suplemento por fatiga*
–, learner's *suplemento por aprendizaje*
–, methods variation *suplemento por variación del método*
–, personal *suplementos personales*
–, personal needs *suplementos personales*
–, redemption *amortización autorizada*
–, sales *rebaja del precio de factura*
–, tare *rebaja normalizada del peso bruto*
–, tool *gratificación por desgaste de herramientas*
–, trade *descuento comercial*
allowances reserve *reserva para bonificaciones*
allowed time *tiempo concedido*
alongside, free *libre al costado de vapor*
alphabetic accounting machine *máquina alfabética de contabilidad*
– data *datos alfabéticos*
– device *dispositivo alfabético*
– information *información alfabética*
– information machine *máquina para información alfabética*
– printing punch *perforadora impresora alfabética*
– processing *sistematización alfabética*
– summary punching *perforación de datos alfabéticos al sumarizar*
– writing *escritura alfabética*
alphabetical code *clave alfabética*
– index *índice alfabético*
– punching *perforación alfabética*
– sequence *serie alfabética*
alphanumeric key punch *perforadora alfanumérica*
alphanumerical characters *caracteres alfanuméricos*
– record *registro alfanumérico*
– translator *traductor alfanumérico*
– type bar list entry *entrada a las barras alfanuméricas para listar*
– type bar total entry *entrada a las barras alfanuméricas para totales*
– verifier *verificadora alfanumérica*
alteration, costs *modificación de costes*
alternate standard *norma alternativa o variante*
amalgamated balance sheets *balances consolidados*

amalgamation *amalgama, fusión*
amend, to *enmendar, reformar, corregir*
amendment *reforma, enmienda*
amends *recompensa, compensación, reparación*
amortization *amortización*
– factor *coeficiente de amortización*
– quota *cupo o tanto de amortización*
– schedule *programa, cuadro de amortización*
–, plant *amortización de la instalación*
amount *importe, suma, cuota, cantidad, valor, proporción*
– at risk *cantidad en riesgo*
– brought in *suma de ejercicios anteriores*
– carried over *suma y sigue*
– due *suma debida*
– of duty *adeudo*
–, aggregate principal *cantidad total del capital*
–, average *valor promedio*
–, consolidated *monto global*
–, face *valor nominal*
–, gross *importe total*
–, net *importe neto o líquido*
–, total *importe total*
amplifier, analog computing *amplificador de cálculo analógico*
analog and digital computers *computadoras o calculadoras analógicas y digitales*
– computer *calculadora analógica*
– computing amplifier *amplificador de cálculo analógico*
– to digital converter *convertidor de sistema análogo a sistema numérico*
analysis *análisis*
– by products, cost *análisis de coste por productos*
– consumer market *análisis del mercado consumidor*
– survey, work *encuesta sobre el análisis del trabajo*
–, activity *programación lineal*
–, attitudes *análisis de actitudes*
–, break-even *curva de rentabilidad*
–, child *análisis del niño*
–, data *análisis de datos*
–, differential *análisis diferencial*
–, distribution cost *análisis del coste de producción*
–, experimental stress *análisis experimental de esfuerzos*
–, factor *análisis de factores*
–, job *análisis de trabajo*
–, market *análisis del mercado*
–, operations or operational *análisis o investigaciones operativas*

–, public *análisis del público*
–, sales *análisis de ventas*
–, statistical *análisis estadístico*
–, statistical sampling *análisis estadístico de muestreo*
–, ultimate *análisis esencial o último*
analyst *analista, analizador, ensayador*
–, consultant *analista consejero*
–, forms *analista de estados o formularios*
–, market *analista del mercado*
–, marketing *analista de mercadología*
–, personnel *analizador de personal*
–, research *analista investigador*
–, sales cost *especialista en costes de venta*
–, time study *analista del estudio de tiempos*
analytical ability *capacidad analítica*
– balance sheet *hoja de balance analítico*
analyzer *analizador*
ancillary equipment *equipo variado o complementario*
– letter of credit *carta de crédito auxiliar*
angle *punto de vista, ángulo, insinuación*
–, sales *punto de vista de ventas, política de ventas*
annual *anual, anuario*
– balance *balance anual*
– cash inflow *ingresos anuales en efectivo*
– convention *convención anual*
– depreciation *depreciación anual*
– financial report *informe financiero anual*
– fiscal period *ejercicio fiscal*
– holiday *vacación anual*
– income *renta anual*
– index *índice anual*
– instalment *plazo anual*
– issue *edición anual*
– leave *permiso anual*
– load factor *factor de carga anual*
– losses *pérdidas anuales*
– maintenance *mantenimiento anual*
– redemption of debentures *reembolso anual de obligaciones*
– report *informe o memoria anual*
– return *renta o ingreso anual*
– sale *venta anual*
– statement *estado anual*
– subsidy *subvención o subsidio anual*
– survey *inspección o encuesta anual*
– training *capacitación anual, instrucción anual*
– upkeep cost *costo de entretenimiento anual*
– value *rendimiento o valor anual*
annuity *renta anual, anualidad*
– benefits *beneficios de pensión*
– bond *bono sin vencimiento*
– contract *contrato de pensión o de anualidad*

– payable *anualidad o renta pasiva*
–, deferred *anualidad o renta diferida*
–, life *anualidad o renta vitalicia*
–, perpetual *anualidad perpetua*
–, retirement *pensión de retiro*
–, temporary *anualidad temporal*
–, term *anualidad temporal*
–, terminable *anualidad temporal*
–, variable *anualidad variable*
annul, to *anular, cancelar*
annum, per *al año*
anomalous endorsement *endoso irregular*
another "first" *otra primicia*
antagonistic cooperation *cooperación por necesidad*
anticipated profits *utilidades previstas anticipadas*
antithesis, time *antítesis cronológica*
antitrust laws *leyes antimonopolistas*
appeal, to *apelar*
appliances, electrical *artículos electrodomésticos*
–, home *aparatos de menaje o del hogar*
–, household *aparatos demésticos*
applicant *solicitante*
application *solicitud, aplicación*
–, field of *campo de aplicación, alcance*
–, patent *solicitud de patente*
–, span of *campo de aplicación, alcance*
applied research *investigación aplicada*
appoint, to *nombrar*
appointment , part-time *destino o empleo no todo el año*
–, power of *facultad de nombrar*
apportion, to *prorratear, repartir*
apportionment *prorroteo, distribución, derrama*
–, scale of *escala de revaluación*
appraisal *valuación, tasación, apreciación, justiprecio valoración, aforo*
– of precision *valuación de la precisión*
– surplus *superávit de revaluación*
appraise, to *apreciar, evaluar, tasar*
appraised value *valor estimado*
appraisement *valuación, tasación, justiprecio, apreciación*
appraiser *tasador, valorador, aforador*
appreciation *apreciación, alza*
apprentice *aprendiz*
apprenticeship *aprendizaje*
–, duration of *duración del aprendizaje*
approach *enfoque, política, punto de vista, acceso*
–, conventional statistical *enfoque estadístico convencional*
–, marketing *enfoque mercadológico*

–, problem systematic *enfoque sistemático de problemas*
–, projective *enfoque proyectivo*
–, qualitative *enfoque cualitativo*
–, sales *enfoque de las ventas*
–, selective distribution *enfoque de la distribución selectiva*
–, statistical *enfoque estadístico*
–, systematic *enfoque sistemático*
appropriation *asignación, aplicación, suma presupuestada*
–, budget *asignación del presupuesto*
approval, to buy on *comprar a condición*
aptitude, clerical *aptitud administrativa*
arbitrage scheme, commodity *plan de arbitraje sobremercancías*
– scheme, multilateral *sistema de arbitraje multilateral*
– test *prueba de aptitud*
– test, differential *prueba de aptitudes diferenciales*
arbitration *arbitraje*
– process *procedimiento de arbitraje*
–, compulsory *decisión arbitral, arbitraje obligatorio*
–, industrial *arbitraje laboral*
arbitrator *árbitro, mediador*
area *área, zona*
– probability sample *muestreo por zonas y probabilidad*
– sampling *muestreo de zona, muestreo por zonas*
–, circulation *zona de difusión*
–, comparability factor *factor de comparabilidad de áreas*
–, currency *zona monetaria*
–, dollar *zona del dólar*
–, potential trading *zona potencial de comercio*
–, sterling *zona de la esfera esterlina*
–, working *zona de trabajo*
arithmetic average *promedio aritmético*
– data processing *sistematización de datos aritméticos*
– mean, weighted *media aritmética ponderada*
– or geometric rate of growth *progresión aritmética o geométrica de aumento o crecimiento*
arrangements, commodity *acuerdo sobre mercancías*
–, financial *régimen de financiación*
arrears *atrasos, retrasos*
– of interest *intereses atrasados*
–, dividend *atrasos de dividendo*
–, in *moroso, vencido, atrasado*
art, commercial *arte comercial o publicitario*

article *artículo, género, mercancía, producto, efecto*
–, mass produced *artículo o producto hecho en serie*
articled clerk *dependiente con contrato de aprendizaje*
articles of partnership *contrato de asociación*
artist, commercial *dibujante o artista comercial*
–, poster *cartelista, pintor de carteles*
as per invoice *según factura*
– per sample *según muestra*
– per voucher *según comprobante*
asking price *precio nominal, precio oferta*
assemble, to *armar, montar, ensamblar*
assembling plant *planta ensambladora o de montaje*
assembly *montaje*
– line *cadena de producción, línea de montaje, tren de ensamblaje, métodos mecanizados de producción*
– line operation *trabajo en cadena*
– line production *producción en cadena*
assess, to *tasar, valuar*
assessed taxes *impuestos directos*
– value *valor catastral*
– valuation *tasación oficial, aranceles*
assessment *tasación, impuesto, contribución, gravamen*
–, basis of *base de avalúo*
asset *partida del activo*
– accounts *cuentas del activo*
assets *activo, bienes, valores positivos, haberes*
–, admitted *activo aprobado*
–, available *activo disponible, disponibilidades*
–, capital *capital activo, valores patrimoniales*
–, cash *activo en efectivo, valores disponibles*
–, circulating *activo circulante o en circulación*
–, company's *activo social*
–, convertible *activo convertible*
–, current *activo corriente o circulante*
–, deferred *activo diferido*
–, financial *activos financieros*
–, fixed *activo fijo, valores inmovilizados*
–, fixed tangible *activo fijo tangible*
–, floating *capital, activo flotante*
–, foreign exchange *activo en divisas*
–, intangible *activo nominal*
–, interest-yielding *activo con rendimiento de intereses*
–, liquid *valores realizables*
–, net *activo neto*
–, partnership *bienes sociales*
–, passive *activo intangible*

–, permanent *capital fijo*
–, personal *bienes muebles o mobiliarios,*
  bienes personales, fortuna personal
–, physical *valores materiales*
–, pledged *activo gravado*
–, quick *activo disponible*
–, real *bienes inmuebles o raíces*
–, slow *activo disponible a largoplazo*
–, tangible *activo tangible*
–, wasting *bienes agotables, activo agotable*
–, watered *activo diluído*
–, working *activo circulante o del trabajo*
assign, to *asignar, conceder, aplicar*
assignee *cesionario*
assignment, task *señalamiento del trabajo*
assimilation *asimilación*
assistance, discriminatory *ayuda preferente*
–, mutual *ayuda mutua*
–, non-discriminatory *ayuda no selectiva*
assistant *ayudante, auxiliar*
– sales manager *jefe auxiliar de ventas*
– secretary *secretario auxiliar*
– superintendent *superintendente auxiliar*
–, administrative *ayudante administrativo*
–, executive *ayudante de dirección*
associate *socio, asociado*
associated agency *agencia asociada*
– company *compañía asociada, empresa*
  afiliada
association *sociedad, compañía, asociación*
– interviewing, free *entrevista de libre*
  asociación
– method, free *método de libre asociación*
–, clearing *asociación de compensación*
–, employers' *asociación patronal*
–, free *asociación controlada o libre o*
  inducida
–, trade *asociación de comerciantes, sociedad*
  comercial
assortment *surtido, acopio*
–, goods *surtido de géneros*
assumed liabilities *pasivo asumido*
assumption *supuesto*
attachment, machine *accesorio o aditamento*
  de máquina
attainment, actual *producción efectiva*
–, expected *ejecución prevista*
attendance card *ficha de tiempo trabajado*
– hours, overtime *horas extraordinarias de*
  asistencia al trabajo
– hours, regular *horas de asistencia normal*
– time *tiempo de presencia*
– time recording system *sistema registrador de*
  horas de trabajo
attention *atención*
– time *tiempo de atención o de vigilancia*

attitude test *prueba o test de actitud*
attitudes analysis *análisis de actitudes*
–, group *actitudes de grupo*
attorney *abogado, procurador*
– general *procurador general, fiscal general*
–, power of *carta poder*
auction *subasta, remate*
– sales *ventas en subasta*
–, public *subasta pública*
–, to *subastar*
–, to buy at *comprar por subasta*
–, to sell at *rematar, vender en subasta*
audit *auditoría, arqueo o verificación, revisión*
  o ajuste de cuentas
– procedure *procedimiento de auditoría*
– report *informe de auditoría*
–, balance sheet *auditoría de balance*
–, cash *auditoría de caja*
–, internal *revisión, intervención o ajuste*
  interior de cuentas
–, public *auditoría pública*
–, retail store *comprobación en las tiendas al*
  por menor
–, traffic *control o verificación de carteles*
  emplazados, control de carteleras
auditing department *sección de revisión de*
  cuentas
– of sales, cost *revisión del coste de ventas*
– standards *normas de auditoría*
–, cost *ajuste o intervención de costes*
–, files *comprobación y verificación de*
  ficheros
auditor *auditor, interventor, censor de cuentas*
authenticate, to *refrendar, legalizar*
authorities, government *entidades oficiales,*
  autoridades del gobierno
–, port *autoridades portuarias*
authority, housing *autoridad sobre casas*
  habitación
–, ultimate *autoridad fundamental*
authorization, budget *autorización del*
  presupuesto
–, revenue *agentes fiscales, inspectores de*
  hacienda
authorized *autorizado*
– capital *capital autorizado*
– signature *firma autorizada*
auto-start key *tecla de arranque automático*
automatic address modification *modificación*
  automática de dirección
– gain *ganancia o amplificación automática*
– gain control *control automático de ganancia*
  o ampliación
– premium loan *préstamo con primas*
  automáticas
– vending *ventas automáticas*

- wage adjustment *ajuste automático de sueldos*
automation *automatismo, automatización, cambio técnico al sistema automático*
- , factory *automatización de las fábricas*
availability *disponibilidad*
available *disponible*
- assets *activo disponible, disponibilidades*
- funds *fondos disponibles*
- labour *mano de obra disponible*
- machine time *tiempo disponible de máquina*
- process time *tiempo disponible de proceso*
- resources *recursos disponibles*
- , to make *poner a disposición*
average *promedio, término medio*
- adjuster *ajustador, tasador, arreglador*
- amount *valor promedio*
- balance *saldo medio*
- buyer *comprador medio o típico*
- circulation *tirada media*
- consumer *consumidor medio*
- earnings, gross *promedio de ingresos brutos*

- gross sale *promedio de ventas brutas*
- markup *promedio del margen comercial*
- order size *volumen promedio de apellidos*
- output *producción media*
- performance *ejecución media*
- price *precio medio*
- retail stock *promedio de existencias al detalle*
- sample number *número promedio de muestra*
- time *tiempo medio*
- unit cost *coste unitario medio*
- variable cost *coste variable medio*
- , arithmetic *promedio aritmético*
- , composite *promedio compuesto*
- , general *promedio general*
- , stock *promedio de mercancías*
- , straight *promedio directo*
- , weighted *promedio compensado o ponderado*
avoidable delay *retraso evitable*
award, cash *premio en efectivo*
azimuth co-ordinates *coordenadas acimut*

B

back page *última página*
– taxes *impuestos atrasados*
–, buying *retroventa*
–, carry *pérdida traspasada al año anterior*
–, to buy *volver a comprar*
backing, financial *respaldo económico, apoyo financiero*
backlog *acumulación reserva*
bad debts *cuentas incobrables, cuentas o deudas morosas, créditos incobrables*
bail *fianza*
bailee *depositario*
balance *saldo, balance, diferencia*
– account *cuenta de balance*
– of payments *balanza de pagos*
– of payments, adverse *balanza de pagos desfavorables*
– of trade *balanza comercial*
– of trade, unfavourable *balanza comercial desfavorable o deficitaria, saldo desfavorable*
– of trade, visible *balance visible de comercio*
– sheet *balance general, balance de situación*
– sheet, analytical *hoja de balance analítica*
– sheet, audit *auditoría de balance*
– sheet, comparative *estado de balance comparativo*
– sheet, consolidated *estado de contabilidad consolidada*
– sheet, interim *balance tentativo*
– sheets, amalgamated *balances consolidados*
–, active *saldo acreedor*
–, active trade *balanza comercial favorable*
–, adverse *saldo desfavorable*
–, annual *balance anual*
–, average *saldo medio*
–, budget *equilibrio del presupuesto*
–, cash *saldo en caja*
–, clearing *saldo no compensado*
–, credit *saldo acreedor*
–, debit *saldo deudor*
–, diminishing *amortización decreciente*
–, dormant *saldo inactivo*
–, general *balance general*
–, opening *saldo de apertura*
–, remainder *saldo remanente*
–, residual *saldo residual*
–, to show a *señalar o arrojar un saldo*
–, to strike a *hacer balance, arrastrar el saldo*

–, trade *balanza comercial*
–, trial *balanza de prueba o comprobación, extracto de comprobación (A)*
–, unallotted *saldo no asignado*
–, want of *desequilibrio*
–, working *saldo corriente*
balanced reduction *reducción equilibrada*
– sample *muestra contrabalanceada*
– system *sistema de compensación*
balances, sterling *saldos de esterlina*
balancing factor *factor de compensación*
band, advertisement *anuncios en forma de faja, anuncios en forma de tira*
–, rubber *banda de goma, goma elástica*
bank *banco*
– acceptance *aceptación bancaria*
– account *cuenta bancaria*
– branch *sucursal de banco*
– clearings *compensaciones bancarias*
– draft *letra, giro bancario*
– examiners *auditores, inspectores bancarios*
– manager *director o gerente de banco*
– money order *giro bancario*
– note *billete de banco*
– of issue *banco que emite billetes de banco*
– overdraft *sobregiro real*
– papers *valores bancarios*
– rate *tasa bancaria, tipo de interés, descuento bancario*
– reconciliation *reconciliación bancaria*
– reserves *reservas bancarias*
– statement *estado de cuenta, extracto bancario*
– transfer *transferencia bancaria*
–, cash at *efectivos en el banco*
–, clearing *banco de giro, cámara de compensación*
–, credit *banco de crédito*
–, discount *banco de descuento*
–, government *banco del estado*
–, mortgage *banco hipotecario*
–, non-member *banco no respaldado, banco fuera de la cámara de compensación*
–, postal savings *caja postal de ahorros*
–, private *banco particular*
–, savings *caja de ahorros*
banking *banca, bancario*
– department *departamento bancario*
– house *institución bancaria*

– theory *teoría de restricción de la emisión de billetes*
– warranty *garantía bancaria*
–, investment *banco de inversiones*
bankrupt *quiebra*
–, to *quebrar, ir a la quiebra*
bankruptcy *quiebra, bancarrota*
–, composition in *acuerdo, arreglo entre fallido y acreedores*
–, petition in *petición de quiebra*
bar chart *gráfico de barras*
– list entry, alphanumerical type *entrada a las barras alfanuméricas para listar*
– total entry, alphanumerical type *entrada a las barras alfanuméricas para totales*
–, tare *escala de taras*
bargain *ganga, barata, pacto, convenio*
– price *precio de ganga o de ocasión*
– sale *liquidación a precios reducidos*
–, chance *compra de ocasión*
–, to strike a *cerrar un trato, llegar a un convenio*
bargaining agreement, collective *contrato colectivo de trabajo*
– power *poder para negociar*
bargains, wage *convenios sobre salarios*
barometer, business *barómetro comercial*
barrier *barrera*
barriers, tariff *barreras fiscales*
–, trade *barreras comerciales*
barter *trueque, intercambio de mercancía*
– agreements *convenios de trueque*
– trade *comercio de trueque, comercio de operaciones compensadas*
base pay *salario base*
– price *precio básico o base*
– rate *salario base*
– rate of pay *tipo básico de pago*
–, compensation *base de retribución*
–, tariff *base de impuesto, base imponible*
basic *básico*
– abatement *reducción básica*
– crops *cultivos básicos*
– economic trends *tendencias económicas básicas*
– index *índice básico*
– investment *inversión básica*
– mental ability *capacidad mental básica*
– motivation *motivación básica*
– patent *patente primitiva u original*
– rebate *descuento básico*
– salary *salario base*
– stock *existencia mínima*
– time *tiempo básico*
– wage *salario básico*
– work week *semana básica de trabajo*

basing point *punto básico, punto de partida*
basis *base*
– for depreciation *base de depreciación*
– of assessment *base de evalúo*
– of taxation *base del impuesto*
–, accrual *base acumulativa*
–, actual *gastos reales*
–, cash *al contado*
–, commission *a comisión*
–, income *rentabilidad efectiva*
–, tax *base de tributación*
–, yield *tasación según rendimiento*
basket bidding *licitación sobre varios valores a la vez*
batch card *hoja de ruta, ficha de ruta*
– production *producción por lotes*
– size *tamaño del lote*
bear market *mercado bajista, especulación a la baja*
– sale *venta especulativa a la baja*
– speculator *especulador a la baja*
bearer *portador, tenedor*
– bond *bono o título al portador*
– debenture *obligación al portador*
– paper *documento al portador*
– securities *títulos al portador*
– share *acción al portador*
–, cheque to *cheque al portador*
–, payable to *pagadero al portador*
bearing debentures, fixed interest- *obligaciones de interés fijo*
bears *agentes bursátiles, bajistas*
behaviour *comportamiento*
– patterns *normas de conducta*
–, actual *conducta actual*
–, buying *conducta en la compra*
–, collective *conducta colectiva o de grupo*
–, human *conducta humana*
–, market *conducta del mercado*
–, personnel *conducta del personal*
–, price *comportamiento de los precios*
behavioural information *información sobre la conducta*
below cost price *precio bajo costo*
– par *bajo par*
– the line *por debajo de los precios*
belt conveyor *cinta transportadora*
bench *lugar de trabajo*
–, work *puesto de trabajo*
beneficiary *beneficiario, tenedor, portador*
benefit *beneficio, provecho*
– fund reserve *reserva para auxiliar a los empleados*
– payments *beneficios*
– programme, employee *programa a beneficio de empleados y obreros*

– society *sociedad de beneficencia o de socorros mutuos*
–, clear *beneficio líquido o neto*
benefits, annuity *beneficios de pensión*
–, family *subvención familiar*
–, fringe *prestaciones, beneficios adicionales al sueldo*
–, old-age *prestaciones por vejez*
–, superannuation *beneficios de jubilación*
–, unemployment *beneficios para desempleo*
berthage *amarraje, derechos de atraque*
best *mejor*
– bid *la mejor oferta*
– profit output *producción de utilidad máxima*
– profit point *punto de utilidad máxima*
between jobs *entre empleos sucesivos*
between time, in- *duración intermedia*
biannual *semestral, semianual*
bias *bias, parcialidad, predisposición, prejuicio, propensión, sesgo*
–, downward *sesgo por defecto*
–, sampling *bias del muestreo*
bid *propuesta, oferta, postura, proposición, puja*
– and offer *oferta y demanda*
– in, to *sobrepujar para beneficiar al vendedor*
– price *precio de oferta*
–, best *la mejor oferta*
–, sealed *propuestas selladas*
–, unit price *oferta o propuesta a precios unitarios*
bidder, highest *mejor postor*
bidding, basket *licitación sobre varios valores a la vez*
–, competitive *concurso, subasta, licitación*
bids, closed *propuestas selladas*
bilateral agreement *acuerdo bilateral*
bill *factura, cuenta, letra, giro, billete*
– of entry *declaración aduanal*
– of exchange *letra limpia o sin reservas*
– of exchange, inland *letra de cambio interna*
– of goods *partida de mercancías vendidas*
– of lading *conocimiento de embarque*
– of lading, accommodation *conocimiento de favor*
– of lading, certified *conocimiento de embarque con certificación consular*
– of lading, foul *conocimiento de embarque con reservas*
– of lading, full *conocimiento de embarque con responsabilidad del transportador*
– of lading, straight *conocimiento nominativo, conocimiento de embarque corrido o intraspasable*
– of lading, through *conocimiento de embarque directo*
– of materials *lista de materiales*

– of sale *escritura de venta, comprobante o cuenta de venta, factura*
– poster *fijador de carteles*
–, accommodation *letra de favor*
–, advance *letra factura giro*
–, demand *letra, giro a la vista*
–, domestic *letra sobre el interior*
–, foreign *letra sobre el exterior*
–, protested *letra protestada*
–, short *letra de corto plazo*
–, short-time *letra a corto plazo*
–, sight *letra a la vista*
–, time *letra a plazos*
–, to draw a *girar una letra*
–, to settle a *cancelar una factura*
–, trade *letra o giro comercial, efecto mercantil, letra de cambio*
–, usance *letra a plazo*
–, way *factura, hoja de ruta o marcha, conocimiento de embarque, carta de porte*
billing *facturación*
– department *departamento de facturación*
– machine *máquina de facturar*
–, cycle *facturación en ciclos*
bills *facturas, documentos*
– due *documentos vencidos o por pagar*
– payable *documentos por pagar, efectos a pagar*
– receivable *documentos por cobrar*
–, federal (Am) *efectos financieros*
–, finance *efectos financieros*
–, maturity of *vencimiento de las letras*
bimanual *bimanual*
bimetallism *sistema monetario bimetálico*
bin *caja, bandeja, recipiente*
– tag *etiqueta de almacén*
binding agreement *acuerdo obligatorio*
bipolar *ambivalente*
birth *nacimiento*
– control *control de natalidad*
– rate *natalidad, tasa de natalidad*
Black Friday *viernes histórico en que han ocurrido desastres financieros*
– list *lista negra*
– market *mercado negro, bolsa negra*
blank *en blanco, formulario, modelo*
– acceptance *aceptación en blanco, aceptación a descubierto*
– form *estado, formulario, modelo*
–, advance in *anticipo en descubierto*
–, in *al descubierto*
–, standard *formulario tipo*
–, weighted *formulario ponderado*
–, weighted application *solicitud de empleo ponderada*
blanket bond *fianza general*

– policy *póliza abierta*
blind advertisement *anuncio anónimo*
– entry *asiento confuso*
block of stocks *lote de acciones*
– sorting *clasificación por lotes*
–, chain *cadena sin fin*
–, emotional *bloqueo emocional*
blocked *bloqueado, controlado*
– account *cuenta bloqueada o controlada o congelada*
– currency *moneda controlada*
– funds *fondos congelados*
blocking *bloqueo*
blotter *papel secante*
blotting paper *papel secante*
blue chips *valores o acciones de primera*
– collar worker *obrero manual*
– paper *papel copia para máquina*
– print *copia heliográfica*
board *junta directiva*
– meeting *reunión de los directivos*
– of directors *junta directiva, consejo de administración*
–, across the *programa diario a la misma hora*
–, advertisement *tablero de anuncios*
–, advisory *junta consultiva*
–, chairman of the *presidente del consejo*
–, conciliation *junta de conciliación*
–, control *junta de control*
–, disposal *comisión de ventas, oficina de ventas*
–, drafting *tablero de dibujo*
–, free on *libre de gastos a bordo*
–, planning *junta de planificación*
–, status *cuadro demostrativo de la situación de material*
–, wage *junta ajustadora de sueldos*
body image *imagen física*
–, corporate *sociedad anónima*
–, public *organismo público*
bond *bono, título, obligación*
– and mortgage *escritura de préstamo e hipoteca*
– company *compañía de finanzas*
– issue *emisión de bonos*
– of idemnity *fianza de indemnización*
–, adjustment *bono sobre ganancias o beneficios*
–, annuity *bono sin vencimiento*
–, bearer *bono o título al portador*
–, blanket *fianza general*
–, callable *bono reembolsable con anticipación*
–, contract *fianza contratista*
–, corporate *bono, obligación de una sociedad*
–, customs *fianza de aduana*
–, dated *bono a plazo fijo*
–, debenture *bono sin garantía hipotecaria*
–, delivery *fianza para devolver bienes embargados* –

–, equipment *bono sobre equipo*
–, export *fianza de exportación*
–, guarantee *fianza*
–, in *afianzado, en aduana, en admisión temporal*
–, income *bono sobre ganancias*
–, indemnity *contrafianza*
–, interest *bono para pagar intereses de otros bonos*
–, irredeemable *obligación no amortizable*
–, low-yield *bono de rendimiento bajo*
–, mortgage *bono con garantía hipotecaria*
–, passive *bono sin interés*
–, payment *fianza de pago*
–, perpetual *bono sin vencimiento*
–, personal *título nominativo*
–, preference *bono privilegiado*
–, priority *bono privilegiado*
–, real-estate *bono inmobiliario*
–, registered *bono nominativo o registrado*
–, restricted *bono no transferible*
–, revenue *bono respaldado con ingresos públicos especiales*
–, saving *bono o título de ahorro*
–, secured *bono hipotecario*
–, short-term *bonos a corto plazo*
–, statutory *fianza legal*
–, yield *obligación emitida por bajo de la par*
bonded *afianzado, depositado*
– goods *géneros en depósito*
– yards and sheds *tinglados de almacenaje de artículos voluminosos y pesados*
– warehouse *almacén general de depósito, depósito aduanal*
–, customs *bajo control aduanero*
bonder of goods *depositante de mercancías*
bondholder *tenedor de bonos, obligacionista*
bondholdings *bonos en cartera*
bonding company *compañía de finanzas*
bonds, active *títulos al portador*
–, convertible *bonos convertibles en acciones*
–, deferred *obligaciones diferidas*
–, exchequer *bonos de la tesorería*
–, government *bonos o títulos del estado*
–, issue of *emisión de obligaciones*
–, refunding *bonos de reintegración*
–, serial *bonos de vencimiento en serie*
–, treasury *bonos del estado, bonos de la tesorería*
bondsman *fiador, afianzador*
bonus *premio, bonificación, incentivo, prima, aguinaldo*
– agreement *acuerdo sobre primas*
– committee man *representante de los obreros en el comité de primas*
– plan *sistema de primas*

book 17 **brought in**

- scheme *sistema de incentivos o de primas*
- share *acción gratuíta o beneficiaria*
- sheet *boletín de primas*
-, lien *prima de compensación*
-, production *prima de producción*
-, stepped *prima escalonada*
-, timeworker's *prima de compensación*
book *libro*
- account *cuenta sin comprobante*
- entry *asiento contable, partida*
- of original entry *libro diario*
- profits *utilidades aparentes en libros*
- surplus *superávit en libros*
- value *valor según libros*
- value, net *valor neto en libros*
-, cash *libro de caja*
-, invoice *libro de facturas*
-, minute *libro de actas*
-, pass *libro de banco, de depósito*
-, rate *libro de tarifas*
-, sales *libro de ventas*
-, stock *libro de existencias o de inventario, registro de acciones*
-, trial-balance *libro de balances de comprobación*
-, year *anuario*
book-keeper *tenedor de libros, contable*
book-keeping *teneduría de libros, contabilidad*
- machine *máquina de contabilidad*
- machine, cash register and *máquina registradora contable*
- machine, electronic *máquina electrónica de contabilidad*
- machine operator *operador de máquina contable*
-, double-entry *contabilidad por partida doble*
-, single-entry *contabilidad por partida simple*
books of original entry *libros de primera entrada*
boom *período de auge, bonanza*
border, advertisement *línea de cierre de un anuncio*
boss *empresario, dueño, capataz, jefe*
-, gang *jefe de equipo*
-, squad *capataz de brigada, jefe de escuadrilla*
bottleneck *embotellamiento, estrangulamiento*
bound, outward *con destino al extranjero*
bounty *bonificación, subvención*
-, export *subsidio para la exportación*
box, safe-deposit *caja de seguridad*
boycott *boicot*
bracket, income *categoría de ingreso*
brackets, salary *escalas de salarios*
brain, electronic *cerebro electrónico*
brains trust *grupo de expertos*
brainstorm *tormenta de cerebros*

branch *sucursal*
- establishment *sucursal*
- manager *director de sucursal*
- offices, network of *red de sucursales*
-, bank *sucursal de banco*
brand *marca de fábrica, clase, tipo*
- image *imagen de una marca*
- loyalty *lealtad a la marca*
- name *marca registrada, nombre de la marca*
- new *flamante, nuevo*
- ratings *apreciación de la marca*
- trend survey *encuesta sobre tendencias de marcas*
branded goods *productos o artículos de marca*
- product, consumer *producto de marca y de consumo*
breadwinner *asalariado, sostén de la familia*
break, to *quebrar, arruinarse*
- even analysis *curva de rentabilidad*
- even performance *comportamiento de la curva de rentabilidad*
- even point *punto de equilibrio*
- even, to *cubrir gastos, lograr un equilibrio entre pérdidas y ganancias*
- point *punto de separación, breakdown análisis, descomposición*
breaker, law- *infractor de la ley*
breaking *quiebra*
breakup value *valor en liquidación*
bribe, to *sobornar*
bridge *intervalo*
- toll *derechos de puente*
brief, to *informar, aleccionar, instruir*
British Commonwealth *Comunidad Británica de Naciones*
broadcast or radio advertising *publicidad por radio o radiada*
-, television *programa de televisión*
broad market *período de movimiento, período de gran variedad de acciones*
broadsheet (Br) *folleto o prospecto desplegable*
brochure *folleto*
broker *corredor, agente, comisionista*
-, buying *corredor de compras*
-, customs *agente aduanal*
-, insurance *corredor, agente de seguros*
-, merchandise *corredor de mercancías*
-, odd lot *corredor que compra y vende acciones en lotes menores de cien*
-, real-estate *corredor de bienes*
-, shift *corredor o agente marítimo*
-, spot *corredor de productos para entrega inmediata*
brokerage *corretaje*
brought in, amount *suma de ejercicios anteriores*

budget *presupuesto*
- accounts *cuentas de presupuesto*
- administration *administración del presupuesto*
- allocation *asignación del presupuesto*
- allotment *distribución del presupuesto*
- appropriation *asignación del presupuesto*
- authorization *autorización del presupuesto*
- balance *equilibrio del presupuesto*
- deficit *déficit presupuestal*
- estimates *cálculo, proyecto del presupuesto*
- form *modelo del presupuesto*
- procedures, markdown *procedimientos para rebajar el presupuesto*
-, advertising *presupuesto de publicidad*
-, capital *presupuesto de gastos de capital*
-, consolidated *presupuesto global*
-, distress *presupuesto reducido o limitado*
-, interim *presupuesto provisional*
-, operational *presupuesto de explotación*
-, ordinary *presupuesto ordinario*
-, regular *presupuesto ordinario*
-, sales *presupuesto de ventas*
-, time *tiempo estimado*
-, unbalanced *presupuesto no nivelado*
-, variable *presupuesto variable*
budgetary control *comprobación o fiscalización delpresupuesto*
- cuts *reducciones del presupuesto*
buffer pool *reserva, fondo estabilizador, amortiguador*
- stock *reserva, fondo, almacenamiento estabilizador*
- stock plan *política de existencias estabilizadoras*
build sales, to *crear ventas*
- up capital, to *crear capital*
built-in *integrante*
bulk *grueso, bulto, volumen*
- account *cuenta resumida*
- cargo *carga a granel*
-, in *en granel, al por mayor*
bull *alcista*
- market *mercado alcista*
- speculator *especulador al alza*
- the market *especular al alza*
bulletin, abstract *boletín de resúmenes*
bullion, gold coin and *oro acuñado y en barras*
bullion reserve *reserva metálica*
buoyant prices *precios con tendencia al alza*
burden *gravamen, gravar, imponer cargas excesivas, gastos generales*
-, fiscal *carga fiscal*
-, real *carga real*
-, tariff *gravamen fiscal*
-, variable *gastos generales variables*
bureau *oficina, agencia, dirección*

- of standards *oficina de normas o tipificación*
-, employment *oficina de colocación*
burning actuality *actualidad inmediata*
burst-up *quiebra comercial*
business *negocios, comercios*
- accountancy *contabilidad comercial*
- accounting *contabilidad comercial o mercantil*
- address *dirección comercial*
- agent *delegado del gremio o del sindicato*
- barometer *barómetro comercial*
- centre *centro comercial*
- concern *empresa comercial*
- contraction *contracción del mercado*
- corporation *corporación mercantil*
- cycle *ciclo económico*
- cycle policy *política de coyuntura*
- cycle, typical *ciclo económico clásico*
- day *día hábil*
- deal *transacción comercial, negocio*
- deposits *depósito para gastos de negocios*
- die *sello comercial*
- earnings *utilidades de la empresa*
- establishment *casa de comercio*
- expansion *expansión del mercado*
- figure *volumen de los negocios*
- forecast *pronóstico del mercado*
- getting *principios que proporcionan negocios*
- history *historia comercial*
- hours *horas de comercio*
- house *casa o establecimiento comercial*
- in futures *operación a término, negocio a plazo*
- income *ingresos comerciales o industriales*
- income, consolidated *cuenta consolidada de ingreso*
- income, net *ingreso mercantil neto*
- information *información mercantil*
- investment *inversión comercial*
- letterhead *membrete*
- like *sistemático, ordenado, metódico, entendido en negocios*
- machines *máquinas de oficina*
- man *comerciante, hombre de negocios*
- management *dirección comercial*
- manager *jefe o director comercial*
- motive *motivo de gastos de consumo*
- movement *giro de negocios, movimiento comercial*
- papers *efectos comerciales, revistas profesionales*
- premises *edificio u oficina comercial, almacén*
- profits *utilidades comerciales*
- prospects *coyuntura comercial*
- recession *depresión económica*
- research *investigación de la actividad comercial*

– responsibility *responsabilidad comercial*
– science *ciencias económicas*
– statistics *estadística comercial*
– trend *tendencia del mercado*
– trip *viaje comercial*
– upswing *mejoramiento comercial*
– week *semana comercial*
– year *año económico u administrativo, ejercicio anual*
–, corporate *empresa constituída en sociedad*
–, income from *ingreso mercantil*
–, line of *género de actividad comercial, ramo de negocio*
–, mail order *venta por correspondencia, negocios por correspondencia*
–, shipping *empresa de transporte marítimo*
–, to found a *establecer un negocio*
–, unsound *negocios improductivos*
busy hour *hora de mayor afluencia de tráfico*
buy, to *comprar, adquirir*
– and sell, to *cambalachear*
– at auction, to *comprar por subasta*
– at market price, to *comprar a precio del mercado*
– at sight, to *comprar a ojo*
– back, to *volver a comprar*
– by sampler, to *comprar según muestra*
– dirt cheap, to *comprar a bulto o baratísimo, comprar a precio tirado*
– for cash, to *comprar al contado*
– in, to *comprar por cuenta del dueño*
– on a fall, to *comprar a la baja*
– on approval, to *comprar a condición*
– on instalment, to *comprar a plazos*
– on tick, to *comprar al fiado*
– out, to *comprar la parte de un socio*
– outright, to *adquirir los derechos en bloque*
– over, to *sobornar, comprar a una persona*
– secondhand, to *comprar de segunda mano*
– the account, to *comprar a término*
– up, to *acaparar, comprar en masa*
– wholesale, to *comprar al por mayor*
–, a good *una ganga*
buyer *comprador, jefe o agente de compras*
– up *acaparador*
-'s choice *elección del comprador*
-'s cost, expenses at *gastos a cargo del comprador*
-'s market *mercado del comprador o consumidor, mercado bajo*

-'s option *opción del comprador*
-'s premises or department *oficina o departamento de compras*
buyers over *mayoría de compradores*
buying agreement *contrato de compra*
– back *retroventa*
– behaviour *conducta en la compra*
– broker *corredor de compras*
– calendar *calendario de compras*
– calendar year *calendario de compras*
– habits, consumer *hábitos de compra del consumidor*
– impulse *estímulo a la compra*
– in *aprovisionamiento*
– motive *motivo de compra*
– order *orden de compra*
– power *poder adquisitivo, capacidad de compra*
– power index *índice del poder adquisitivo, índice de la capacidad de compra*
– price *precio de compra*
– rate *tarifa o tipo de compra*
– up *acaparamiento*
–, active *demanda activa*
–, central *compras centralizadas*
–, comparative *compras por comparación*
–, credit *comprar a crédito*
–, foreign *compras en el extranjero*
–, group *compras agrupadas*
–, hand-to-mouth *compras improvisadas, compras al día*
–, trade *compras por las fábricas*
–, upscale *compras a precios ascendentes escalonados*
by easy payments *con facilidades de pago*
– instalments *a plazos*
– job *trabajo hecho a horas perdidas*
– product *subproducto*
– product recovery plant *instalación para recuperación de subproductos*
– profit *ganancias suplementarias*
– proxy *por poder*
– return mail *a vuelta de correo*
– sample *según muestra*
– the job *a destajo*
– trial and error *por tanteos*
bye-laws *estatutos secundarios*

C

cabinet, electronic filing- *archivador electrónico*
–, filing- *archivador*
–, steel filing- *estante de acero para archivar correspondencia*
calculating machine *calculadora, máquina de calcular*
– machine, adding and *máquina de sumar y calcular*
– machine operator *operador de máquina calculadora*
calculation, cumulative markup *cálculo del margen comercial acumulativo*
calculator *calculadora*
–, key-drive *calculadora accionada por teclado*
–, printing *calculadora por impresión*
–, rotary *calculadora rotativa*
calendar year *año civil*
–, buying *calendario de compras*
calibrated stopwatch *cronómetro de precisión*
calibrating factor *factor de calibración, factor para rectificar*
call *visita, comunicación, retiro*
– and sales reports *informes de visitas y ventas*
– date *fecha de reembolso*
– loan *préstamo reembolsable a la vista*
– money *dinero prestado exigible a la vista*
– off, to *dar por terminado*
– slip *volante o formulario de visitas*
–, money at *disponibilidades a la vista*
–, port of *puerto de escala*
callable bond *bono reembolsable con anticipación*
calling in of currency *retiro de moneda*
calls *sesiones especiales de bolsa*
campaign, ad *campaña de publicidad*
–, local *campaña local*
cancellation, markdown *rebaja o reducción de precio*
–, markup *anulación del margen comercial*
candid *franco*
canned goods *conservas alimenticias*
– meat *carne en conserva*
cannery *fábrica de conservas*
canons of taxation *estipulaciones en política impositiva*

canvass, to *buscar órdenes*
canvasser *corredor*
capacity *capacidad de producción*
–, actual *capacidad real*
–, idle *capacidad inactiva*
–, individual taxpaying *capacidad contributiva tributaria*
–, plant *capacidad de producción*
–, productive *capacidad de producción*
–, profit-earning *capacidad lucrativa*
–, taxpaying *capacidad tributaria*
capita income, per *renta por habitante*
capital *capital*
– account *cuenta de capital*
– assets *activo fijo, capital activo, bienes patrimoniales*
– budget *presupuesto de gastos de capital*
– cost *gastos de instalación o de fundación*
– development fund *fondos para equipo de producción*
– dividend *dividendo de capital*
– expenditures *gastos de capital*
– flow *movimiento de capital*
– formation *formación de capital*
– formation, net *formación neta de capital*
– gains *utilidades de capital, ganancias por enajenación de bienes*
– gains tax *impuestos sobre las ganancias de capital*
– goods *bienes de capital o de producción, equipo industrial, elementos o medios de producción*
– goods industries *industrias de artículos de capital*
– inflow *afluencia de capital*
– investment *inversión de capital*
– levy *impuesto sobre capital*
– liabilities *pasivo fijo, obligaciones de capital*
– market *mercado de capitales o financiero*
– outflow *salida de capitales al exterior*
– payment *pago de cuenta de capital*
– renewal *reinversión de capital*
– resources *bienes de equipo, infraestructura*
– share *acción de capital*
– stock *capital social, acciones de capital*
– stock tax *impuesto sobre capital en acciones*
– structure *estructura de capital*

– surplus *excedente o superávit de capital*
– transactions *transacciones de capital*
– transfer *transferencia de capital*
– turnover *giro de capital, movimiento*
–, active *capital activo*
–, authorized *capital autorizado*
–, circulating *activo circulante, liquidez*
–, company's issued *capital emitido por la compañía*
–, consumption *capital de consumo*
–, corporate *capital social*
–, declared *capital declarado o escriturado*
–, fixed *activo fijo*
–, floating *capital circulante o flotante*
–, idle *capital inactivo o improductivo*
–, instrument *capital instrumental*
–, invested *capital aportado*
–, marginal efficiency of *eficacia marginal del capital*
–, movements of *movimientos de capital*
–, nominal *capital social*
–, obligated *capital suscrito*
–, operating *capital de explotación*
–, original *capital original*
–, outstanding *capital suscrito*
–, paid-in *capital exhibido o pagado*
–, registered *capital autorizado o social*
–, return of *rendimiento del capital*
–, share *capital en acciones*
–, stated *capital declarado de acciones*
–, subscribed *capital suscrito*
–, to build up *crear capital*
–, trade *capital comercial*
–, uncalled *capital de reserva o no reembolsado, capital suscrito pero no exhibido*
–, unproductive *capital improductivo*
–, venture *capital de especulación*
–, watered *capital inflado*
–, working *capital en giro, capital de trabajo, activo circulante, capital activo*
capitalized profits *utilidades capitalizadas*
capitation tax *impuesto por persona, capitación*
carbon paper *papel carbón*
card accounting machine, electric punched- *máquina eléctrica contable de fichas perforadas*
card file *fichero*
– file, permanent *fichero permanente*
–, accumulative record *ficha de registro acumulativo*
–, address *ficha de dirección*
–, address group *ficha para el grupo de dirección*
–, attendance *ficha de tiempo trabajado*

–, batch *ficha u hoja de ruta*
–, client cost *ficha de costos del cliente*
–, clock *ficha de reloj*
–, inspección *boletín de verificación*
–, job *bono de trabajo, hoja de trabajo*
–, merged *ficha intercalada*
–, order information *ficha de información de órdenes*
–, pattern *muestrario*
–, pledge *ficha de garantía*
–, reminder *ficha recordativa o recordatoria*
–, route *ficha de ruta*
–, stock control *ficha de control de existencias*
–, time *ficha de tiempos*
–, window *cartel de escaparate*
cargo insurance *seguro de mercancía*
– liner *barco de carga*
– vessel, dry *barco de carga seca*
–, bulk *carga a granel*
carried over, amount *suma y sigue*
carrier *empresa transportadora*
–, contract *empresa transportadora por contrato*
–, sea *empresa naviera*
-'s risk *riesgo del transportador*
carry *cargar, llevar*
– back *pérdida traspasada al año anterior*
– over *suma y sigue, remanente de una mercancía*
–, cash and *pago al contado*
carrying cost *coste de almacenamiento*
cartage *acarreo*
cartel *cartel, monopolio*
–, regional *monopolio regional*
cartelized commodity *producto cartelizado, controlado por cartel*
case history *historia o exposición de casos*
–, copyright *proceso por plagio o falsificación*
–, glass *escaparate, vitrina, aparador*
–, show *expositor, aparador, vitrina, vidriera*
–, upper *capital*
cash *efectivo*
– account *cuenta de caja*
– advance *anticipo en metálico*
– and carry *pago al contado*
– assets *activo en efectivo, valores disponibles*
– at bank *efectivo en el banco*
– audit *auditoría de caja*
– award *premio en efectivo*
– balance *saldo en caja*
– basis *al contado*
– book *libro de caja*
– control record *libro de caja*
– count *arqueo de caja*
– deal *operación al contado*
– deficit *déficit de caja*

– discount *descuento por pronto pago*
– dividend *dividendos en efectivo*
– economy *economía monetaria*
– entry *asiento de caja*
– funds *fondos en efectivo*
– funds, imprest *fondos para gastos menores*
– holdings *disponibilidades en efectivo*
– imprest *fondo fijo de caja*
– in advance *pago adelantado*
– in hand *efectivo disponible, existencia en caja*
– inflow *entrada en efectivo*
– inflow, annual *ingresos anuales en efectivo*
– journal *libro, diario de caja*
– market *mercado de productos disponibles*
– on delivery *pago contra reembolso*
– or collect on delivery *cóbrese a la entrega, pago contra reembolso*
– outgoings and income *entradas y salidas de caja*
– payment *pago al contado*
– position *situación líquida*
– position, consolidated *situación de caja global*
– price *precio al contado*
– register *caja registradora*
– register and book-keeping machine *máquina registradora contable*
– registering and adding machine *máquina registradora sumadora*
– reserve, compulsory *reserva obligatoria en metálico*
– reserves *reservas líquidas en efectivo*
– sale *venta al contado*
– shorts and overs *déficit y excedentes de caja*
– store *tienda de ventas al contado*
– value *valor efectivo*
– value, fair *valor justo del mercado*
– voucher *comprobante de caja*
–, in *al contado, en efectivo*
–, petty *caja para gastos menores, caja chica*
–, prompt *pago al contado*
–, ready *disponibilidades de caja, fondos disponibles*
–, spot *pago al contado*
–, to buy for *comprar al contado*
–, to withdraw *retirar efectivo*
cashier *cajero*
-'s cheque *cheque de caja, de ventanilla*
casual income *utilidad accidental*
– profits *utilidades extraordinarias*
– worker *obrero provisional o migratorio*
catalogue, price *catálogo de precios, lista de precios*
categories, specific income *categorías de ingresos específicos*

ceiling price *precio tope, precio máximo permitido*
– wage *salario máximo o tope*
census, distributing *censo de distribución*
cent, per *por ciento*
central buying *compras centralizadas*
– files *ficheros centrales*
centre of location *centro de ubicación*
– spread *anuncio de doble página central*
–, business *centro comercial*
–, distributing *centro distribuidor*
–, documentation *centro de documentación*
–, population *centro de población*
–, research *centro de investigaciones*
–, shipping *centro de ventas, zona comercial*
certificate *certificado, dictamen, reporte, acta*
– of conformity *certificado de conformidad*
– of deposit *certificado de depósito*
– of indebtedness *certificado de adeudo*
– of origin *certificado de origen*
–, inventory *confirmación de inventario*
–, mortgage *cédula hipotecaria*
–, progress *certificación de buena cuenta*
–, qualified *certificado con salvedades*
–, share *certificado de acciones*
–, stock *certificado de acciones*
–, tax *certificado de compra de bienes raíces o inmuebles*
–, unqualified *certificado sin salvedades*
certified *certificado*
– bill of lading *conocimiento de embarque con certificación consular*
– cheque *cheque certificado*
– public accountant *contador o contable público titulado*
certify, to *certificar, dar fe*
chain *cadena*
– block *cadena sin fin*
– discount *rebajas en cadena*
– reaction *reacción en cadena*
– stores *cadena de tiendas, tiendas en cadena*
chair *presidente, ponente*
chairman *presidente*
– of the board *presidente del consejo*
chamber of commerce *cámara de comercio*
–, cold storage *cámara frigorífica*
chance bargain *compra de ocasión*
change *cambio*
– in cost *cambio en los costos*
– in expectation *cambio en las previsiones*
–, exogenus *alteración económica debida a factores no económicos*
changeover time *cambio de turno*
changes, fashion *cambio de modas*
–, impending *cambios inminentes*
–, price *cambios de precio*

–, seasonal *variaciones o cambios estacionales*
channel *canal, vía*
– of distribution *vía o canal de distribución*
–, television *canal de televisión*
character loan *préstamo sin garantía colateral*
–, national *carácter nacional*
characteristic *característica, factor de trabajo*
characters, alphanumerical *caracteres alfanuméricos*
charge *cargo, cargar, cobrar*
– account *cuenta corriente*
– sales *ventas a crédito*
–, additional *gasto suplementario, gasto adicional*
–, free of *libre de cargos*
chargeable *cargable, adeudable*
–, expenses *gastos reembolsables*
chargehand *jefe de equipo*
charges *cargos, débitos, gastos*
– deducted, all *deducidos todos los gastos*
–, collection *gastos de cobros, cargos por cobros*
–, deferred *cargos diferidos*
–, finance *gastos financieros*
–, inclusive of all *todos los gastos deducidos*
–, overhead *sobrecarga, gastos indirectos*
–, protest *gastos de protesto*
–, salvage *cargos de salvamento*
–, shipping *gastos de embarque*
–, standing *cargos permanentes*
–, storage *derechos de embalaje*
–, superintending *gastos de inspección*
–, survey *gastos de inspección*
–, warehousing *gastos de almacenaje*
charitable trust *fideicomiso caritativo*
chart, comparative rating *cuadro comparativo de capacidades*
–, bar *gráfico de barras*
–, duty *asignación de las horas*
–, flow *diagrama de circulación*
–, forms distribution *diagrama de distribución de impresos*
–, forms procedure *diagrama del uso de impresos*
–, forms distribution process *diagrama de distribución de impresos*
–, forms or papers procedure *diagrama de procedimiento de formularios o estados*
–, gang process *diagrama de proceso del equipo*
–, light *diagrama de alumbrado*
–, machine process *diagrama de procedimientos a máquina*
–, man-machine *diagrama hombre máquina*
–, multiple activity *diagrama de actividades simultáneas*

–, multiple activity process *diagrama de proceso de actividades simultáneas*
–, operation *diagrama operativo*
–, operation flow *diagrama de flujo de operaciones*
–, operation process *diagrama de procedimiento de operación*
–, operation-machine process *diagrama de procedimiento de máquina y operación*
–, organization *organigrama, diagrama de organización*
–, process *diagrama de procedimientos*
–, profile *diagrama o psicograma caracterológico*
–, progress *gráfico de la marcha del trabajo*
–, resolution *pruebas de ajuste*
–, right and left hand *diagrama de ambas manos*
–, scatter *gráfica de dispersión*
–, simo *simograma, diagrama de movimientos simultáneos*
–, simultaneous motion-cycle *simograma, diagrama de ciclo de movimientos simultáneos*
–, strata *diagrama de estratos*
–, stress- *monograma para cálculo de esfuerzos*
–, superimposed curve *diagrama de curvas superpuestas*
–, test *modelo de prueba, ficha de prueba*
–, two-handed process *diagrama de ambas manos-, work distribution diagrama de distribución del trabajo*
charter *escritura de constituación, contrato de fletamiento de un barco*
–, air *flete aéreo*
–, time *fletamiento por tiempo*
chartered *autorizado, contratado*
chartering, aircraft *fletamiento aéreo*
chaser, progress *seguidor de pieza*
cheap, to buy dirt *comprar baratísimo, comprar a precio tirado, comprar a bulto*
cheat *artificio, engaño*
–, to *engañar, estafar*
check *comprobación, verificación, control*
– data *datos comprobatorios*
– list *lista de comprobación*
– mark *punto de referencia*
– study *estudio de comprobación*
– test *contraprueba*
– up, to *cotejar, verificar, confrontar*
–, spot *comprobación en el sitio*
–, to *comprobar, revisar*
checking copy *ejemplar comprobante*
checks, test *pruebas selectivas, tanteos*
cheque *cheque, talón*

– clearings *compensaciones de cheques o bancarias*
– stub *talón de cheque*
– to bearer *cheque al portador*
–, cash *cheque de caja*
–, certified *cheque certificado*
–, registered *cheque de administración*
–, soiled *cheque inutilizado*
–, stale *cheque caducado*
–, to draw a *extender un cheque*
–, to raise a *aumentar el importe de un cheque*
–, traveller's *cheque de viajero*
–, voided *cheque anulado*
–, voucher *cheque con comprobante*
chequebook *talonario de cheques*
cheques for collection *cheques al cobro*
–, outstanding *cheques pendientes*
–, returned *cheques devueltos*
chest, community *fondos de socorro, fondos para ayuda asistencial*
chief *jefe*
– executives *altos directivos*
–, acting *jefe interino, jefe accidental*
–, department *jefe de departamento*
child analysis *análisis del niño*
– labour *trabajo de menores*
chips, blue *valores, acciones de primera*
choice, buyer *elección del comprador*
– technique, error *técnica de selección de errores*
–, free *libre elección*
chronograph *cronógrafo*
chronological study *estudio cronológico*
circular letter *circular de publicidad*
–, advertising *circular de publicidad*
circularize *enviar circulares*
circulating *circulación, circulante*
– assets *activo circulante, activo en rotación, activo realizable*
– capital *capital circulante*
circulation area *zona de difusión*
– manager *jefe de ventas*
–, average *tirada media*
–, net sales *tirada neta*
citizenship *ciudadanía*
civil law *derecho civil*
claim *reclamación, demanda, reivindicación*
– adjuster *ajustador de reclamaciones*
– damages, to *reclamar daños*
– established *reclamación reconocida*
– for short delivery *reclamación por envío incompleto*
–, adjustment of a *pago de una reclamación*
–, indirect *demanda por daño emergente*
–, secured *reclamación garantizada*
–, to *reclamar, demandar*

claims, part settlement of *ajuste parcial de reclamaciones*
class *clase social, clase económica-social*
– conscious *conciencia de clase*
– rate *clase de salario, clase de tarifa*
–, working *clase obrera, proletariado*
classes, labouring *clases obreras*
–, mutually exclusive *clases mutuamente exclusivas*
classical economics *economía clásica*
classification, documentary *clasificación de documentos*
–, expenses account *clasificación de las cuentas de gastos*
–, job *clasificación del trabajo*
–, standard *clasificación uniforme*
classified ads *anuncios clasificados*
clause *cláusula, disposición*
–, acceleration *cláusula para el vencimiento anticipado de una deuda*
–, competition *cláusula contractual*
–, employment *cláusula de empleo*
–, escalator *cláusula sobre el tipo graduable de salario*
–, escape *cláusula de escape*
–, most favoured nation *cláusula de la nación más favorecida*
–, penalty *cláusula penal*
–, peril point *cláusula de punto crítico*
–, sliding-scale *cláusula de revisión de precios*
–, variation *cláusula de variación de precios*
clean *limpio, sin reservas, simple*
– acceptance *aceptación general*
– bill of exchange *letra limpia, letra sin reservas*
– bill of lading *conocimiento de embarque sin observaciones*
– credit *crédito simple*
– draft *letra simple, giro simple, giro sin documentos*
– letter of credit *carta de crédito simple*
– paper *papel blanco*
– profit *beneficio líquido*
– receipt *recibo sin reservas*
– states *bienes no hipotecados*
– value *valor líquido*
clear account *cuenta en regla*
– benefit *beneficio líquido o neto*
– expenses *gastos cubiertos*
– goods, to *saldar o liquidar géneros*
– of all expenses *libre de todo gasto*
– profit *beneficio líquido, ganancia líquida*
– reckoning account *cuenta clara*
– the market, to *dejar desprovisto el mercado*
– the rights, to *comprobar los derechos literarios*

– value *valor neto*
–, free and *libre de gravamen*
clearance *saldo, liquidación, beneficio
líquido, compensación de cheques, despacho
aduanal*
– account *cuenta de giros*
– inwards *declaración de entrada en aduana*
– loan *préstamo de un día*
– outwards *declaración de salida en aduana*
– prices *precios de liquidación*
– procedure *proceso de depuración del
personal*
– sales *ventas por liquidación*
–, customs *despacho aduanal*
–, slum *supresión de barrios bajos malsanos*
clearing *compensación, canje (A)*
– account *cuenta de compensación*
– agreement *convenio de compensaciones*
– association *asociación de compensación*
– balance *saldo no compensado*
– bank *banco de giro, cámara de
compensación*
clearing-house *cámara de compensación,
banco de liquidación*
– agent *agente bancario de compensaciones*
–, commodity *cámara de compensación de
productos*
clearings, bank *compensaciones bancarias*
–, cheque *compensaciones de cheques,
compensaciones bancarias*
clerical adaptability *adaptabilidad
administrativa*
– aptitude *aptitud administrativa*
– competence *competencia administrativa,
aptitud administrativa*
– costs *costes administrativos*
– efficiency test *eficiencia administrativa*
– force *personal administrativo*
– routine *tramitación burocrática*
– speed and accuracy test *prueba de precisión
y rapidez administrativas*
– test, general *prueba administrativa general*
– work *trabajo administrativo*
clerk, accounts *contable*
–, articled *dependiente con contrato de
aprendizaje*
–, cost *calculista de costos*
–, file *archivero, clasificador (persona)*
–, general *oficinista*
–, mail *encargado del correo*
–, pay *empleado pagador*
–, payroll *pagador, cajero*
–, sales order *receptor de órdenes de venta*
–, stock *encargado de existencias*
–, stock room *encargado de almacén*
–, voucher *encargado de los comprobantes*

–, retail *dependiente al por menor*
clever merchant *comerciante experto*
cleverness *sagacidad*
client cost card *ficha de costos del cliente*
clipping, newspaper *reporte de periódico,
cabecera de periódico*
clock card *ficha de reloj*
– stamp *reloj fechador*
– time *tiempo real, tiempo empleado*
–, work round the *trabajo continuo*
clog *entorpecer*
close copy *copia exacta*
– corporation *sociedad anónima controlada
por pocos*
– down, to *cerrar una fábrica, terminar la
emisión*
– examination *examen minucioso, examen
atento*
– focussed operation *operación
cuidadosamente preparada*
– investigation *investigación minuciosa*
– market *mercado estable*
– price *precio estable, precio sin beneficio*
– translation *traducción fiel o exacta*
closed *cerrado*
– account *cuenta saldada*
– bids *propuestas selladas*
– end investment company *empresa
inversionista de capital limitado*
– market *mercado reservado, mercado
exclusivo*
– set *conjunto cerrado*
– system *sistema cerrado*
– union *gremio obrero que hace difícil la
entrada de nuevos miembros*
closing account *cuenta compensadora o de
cierre*
– date *fecha de cierre*
– entries *partidas o asientos de cierre*
– error, allowable *error admisible de cierre*
– inventory valuation *valoración del cierre de
inventario*
– price *precio de cierre*
– quotation or rate *cotización final, precio de
cierre en bolsa*
– rate of exchange *cambio de precio de cierre*
– stock inventory *cierre del inventario de
existencias*
closure *cierre*
coalition *coalición, alianza*
c.o.d. shipment *envío contra reembolso*
code *código, clave, principios*
– word *palabra clave, palabra convencional*
–, alphabetical *clave alfabética*
–, commercial *código comercial, derecho
mercantil, clave comercial*

–, labour *ley de trabajo, derecho obrero*
coding, reverse *codificación inversa*
coefficient of agreement *coeficiente de acuerdo*
– efficiency *rendimiento comercial*
– of distribution *coeficiente de distribución*
–, input-output *coeficiente insumo producto*
–, scatter *coeficiente de dispersión*
–, statutory *coeficiente legal*
–, work *coeficiente de trabajo*
coin and bullion, gold *oro acuñado y en barra*
– counter *máquina contadora de monedas*
– operated vending machine *máquina de vender accionada por introducción de moneda*
coined word *palabra inventada o acuñada*
coining *acuñación de moneda*
cold storage *almacenaje refrigerado*
– storage chamber *cámara frigorífica*
– storage warehouse or store *almacén frigorífico*
column *columna*
– diagram *diagrama de columnas*
–, agony *sección de anuncios pequeños*
collapse, to *derrumbarse*
collar worker, blue- *obrero manual*
collateral *colateral, garantía, resguardo*
– acceptance *aceptación de garantía*
– contract *contrato de prenda*
– loan *préstamo con garantía*
– note *pagaré prendario, colateral*
– security *garantía prendaria, colateral*
–, lend on *prestar con respaldo colateral*
collect on delivery *pago contra reembolso, cóbrese a la entrega*
–, freight *flete por cobrar*
–, to *cobrar, recaudar*
collected *cobrado, colectado*
– unearned interest *intereses cobrados y no vencidos*
collective data, methods of *métodos para reunir datos*
collection *cobro, recaudación*
– agency *compañía, agencia de cobranzas*
– charges *gastos de cobros, cargos por cobro*
– draft *giro de cobro*
– expenses *gastos de cobranza*
– expenses, credit and *gastos de crédito y cobro*
– fees *gastos de recaudación, honorarios por cobro*
– items *efectos por cobrar*
– letter *letra girada, carta de cobro*
– ratio *índice de cobros*
– techniques, data *técnicas de recogida de datos*

–, cheques for *cheques al cobro*
–, documents for *documentos por cobrar*
–, stay of *suspensión de pago*
–, tariff *recaudación fiscal*
collections, advance *cobros por adelantado*
–, direct *cobros directos*
–, indirect *cobros, recaudaciones indirectas*
collective activity *actividad colectiva*
– bargaining *contrato o convenio colectivo*
– bargaining agreement *contrato colectivo de trabajo*
– behaviour *conducta colectiva, conducta de grupo*
– goods *bienes públicos*
– reward *recompensa colectiva*
– security *seguridad colectiva*
– training *capacidad o instrucción colectiva*
collector *coleccionista, recaudador*
– of customs *administrador de aduana*
– of internal revenue *recaudador de rentas*
–, tariff *recaudador fiscal*
-'s office *administrador de rentas*
collisions *tropiezos*
combination in restraint of trade *acuerdo para restringirla*
competencia
combine *cartel, unión de organizaciones o empresas, consorcio*
combined accounts deals *ventas de cuentas combinadas*
– work *trabajo en colaboración*
commencing salary *salario inicial*
commentator *locutor*
commerce *comercio, negocios, relaciones sociales*
–, chamber of *cámara de comercio*
–, domestic *comercio interior*
commercial *comercial, mercantil*
– agreement *acuerdo comercial*
– art *arte comercial, arte publicitario*
– artist *dibujante o artista comercial*
– code *código comercial, derecho mercantil, clave comercial*
– commodities *artículos comerciales*
– commodity *acuerdo o tratado comercial*
– company *sociedad mercantil*
– credit company *sociedad financiera o de crédito comercial*
– director or manager *director comercial*
– documentary credit *crédito documentario comercial*
– documents *papeles de negocios, documentos*
– draft *giro comercial*
– efficiency *rendimiento económico o industrial*
– enterprises *razón social, empresa o casa*

comercial
- feasibility *posibilidad comercial*
- grades *calidades comerciales*
- intercourse *relaciones comerciales,*
  intercambio comercial
- invoice *factura comercial*
- law *derecho mercantil*
- package *embalaje, empaquetado comercial*
- papers *papeles de negocios, documentos*
  negociables
- partnership *sociedad mercantil en comandita*
- processing methods *métodos comerciales de*
  elaboración
- report *informe comercial, boletín*
  informativo comercial
- research *investigación comercial*
- secretariat *secretaría comercial*
- secretary *secretario comercial*
- standard *norma o patrón comercial*
- standing *crédito mercantil*
- television *televisión comercial o publicitaria*
- terms *términos comerciales*
- transaction *operación comercial*
- traveller *viajante comercial*
- undertaking *empresa auxiliar o filial*
- usage *usos o costumbres comerciales*
- value *valor de venta, valor en plaza, valor*
  industrial
commercialese *jerga comercial,*
  comercialismos
commercialism *comercialismo*
commercialization *comercialización*
commercials *anuncios*
commissar *comisario*
commission *comisión*
- agent *agente a comisión, comisionista*
- basis *a comisión*
- merchant *comisionista*
- rate, progressive *tipo de comisión*
  progresiva
- rate, regressive *tipo de comisión regresiva*
- rate, sliding-scale *tipo de comisión a escala*
  gradual
-, on *a comisión*
-, public service *comisión de servicio público*
-, selling *comisión de ventas*
-, tariff *agencia administrativa para recaudar*
  impuestos
commissions, split *comisiones repartidas*
commitment *compromiso*
committee *comité, junta*
-, administration *comité o junta de*
  administración
-, advertising *comité de publicitarios*
-, advisory *comité consultivo*
-, allocation *comité de dotación de personal*

-, drafting *comité de redacción*
-, executive *comité ejecutivo*
-, finance *comité financiero*
-, joint *comisión mixta*
-, joint production *consejo de producción de*
  la empresa
-, shop *comité de empresa*
-, standing *comisión permanente*
-, steering *junta de gobierno, comité de*
  organización
-, works *comité de empresa*
commodities, commercial *artículos*
  comerciales
-, domestic *productos nacionales*
-, miscellaneous *mercancías varias*
-, staple *géneros de consumo corriente*
commodity *artículo, mercancía, producto*
- agreement *acuerdo comercial, sobre*
  mercancías
- arbitrage scheme *plan de arbitraje sobre*
  mercancías
- arrangements *acuerdos sobre mercancías*
- clearing-house *cámara de compensación de*
  productos
- draft *letra para compraventa de productos*
- exchanges *bolsa de productos*
- flow *corriente de mercancías*
- futures *productos para entregas futuras*
- index *índice de precios de mercancías*
- line sale *venta en el ramo de mercancías*
- management *reglamentación en materia de*
  productos
- paper *efectos respaldados por productos*
- rates *tarifas para mercancías*
- standard *mercancía patrón*
-, cartelized *producto cartelizado, controlado*
  por cartel
-, composite *mercancía compuesta*
-, luxury *artículo de lujo, producto suntuario*
-, primary *artículo básico*
common *común*
- denominator *denominador común*
- ownership *propiedad común*
- sense *sentido común*
- share *acción común u ordinaria*
- stock *acciones comunes u ordinarias*
Commonwealth, British *Comunidad*
  Británica de Naciones
communication *comunicación*
- network *red de transmisiones*
-, means of *medios de comunicación*
community chest *fondos de socorro, fondos*
  para asistencia social
companies act *ley de sociedades*
company *compañía, empresa, sociedad*
  mercantil, corporación

– deeds *actas de la sociedad*
– promoter *promotor de empresa*
– union *sindicato formado por empleados de una sola empresa*
–, affiliated *compañía filial*
–, allied *compañía asociada*
–, associated *compañía asociada, empresa afiliada*
–, bonding *compañía de finanzas*
–, closed-end investment *empresa inversionista de capital limitado*
–, commercial *sociedad mercantil*
–, commercial credit *sociedad financiera, sociedad de crédito comercial*
–, controlled *compañía filial*
–, finance *sociedad financiera*
–, guarantee *compañía de fianzas*
–, holding *"holding", compañía principal propietaria de las acciones*
–, incorporated *sociedad anónima*
–, insurance *compañía de seguros, aseguradora*
–, investment *compañía inversionista*
–, joint *sociedad en comandita*
–, joint-stock *sociedad anónima, compañía por acciones*
–, limited *compañía, sociedad de responsabilidad limitada*
–, limited liability *compañía de responsabilidad limitada*
–, merged *compañía fusionada*
–, open-end investment *empresa inversionista de capital variable*
–, operating *empresa de explotación*
–, parent *compañía matriz, compañía principal o propietaria*
–, resident *compañía que funciona en el lugar de incorporación*
–, shipping *empresa naviera*
–, stock *compañía por acciones, sociedad anónima*
–, subsidiary *compañía filial*
–, trust *compañía fiduciaria*
-'s assets *activo social*
-'s issued capital *capital emitido por la compañía*
-'s liabilities *pasivo social*
comparability factor, area *factor de comparabilidad de áreas*
comparative balance sheet *estado de balance comparativo*
– costs, theory of *teoría de costos comparativos*
– data *datos comparativos*
– mortality, index of *índice de mortalidad comparativa*

– rating chart *cuadro comparativo de capacidades*
– test *prueba comparativa*
comparison buying *compras por comparación*
– system, factor *sistema de comparación de factores*
compensating error *error de compensación*
– relaxation allowance *suplemento para compensar la fatiga*
compensation *compensación, indemnización, remuneración, salario*
– act *ley de accidentes del trabajo*
– base *base de retribución*
– deals *ventas por compensación*
– insurance *seguro de compensación*
– level *nivel de remuneración*
–, adequate *compensación equitativa, remuneración equitativa*
–, unemployment *compensación por desempleo*
–, workmen's *compensación por accidentes de trabajo*
compensatory duty *impuesto compensatorio*
– time off *descanso de compensación*
competence, clerical *competencia o aptitud administrativa*
competition *competencia, concurrencia*
– clause *cláusula contractual*
– clause, exclusivity stipulation *cláusula contractual de exclusividad*
–, active market price *mercado de competición activa*
–, aggressive *competencia enérgica*
–, direct price *competencia directa de precios*
–, free *libre competencia*
–, unfair *competencia desleal*
competitive bidding *concurso, subasta, licitación*
– cost *precio de competencia*
– price *precio competitivo, precio de competencia*
complaint *queja*
complementary works *trabajos complementarios*
completed products *productos terminados*
– transactions *transacciones consumadas*
completion *terminación, término*
– method, percentage of *método de porcentaje de terminación*
–, stage of *etapa de acabado*
complex *complejo*
– fraction *quebrado compuesto*
– personality *personalidad compleja*
comply with allotments, to *quedar dentro de los límites de asignaciones fijadas*

component *componente, pieza*
– method *método de los componentes*
–, output *componente de producción*
composite advertisement *anuncio colectivo*
– average *promedio compuesto*
– commodity *mercancía compuesta*
– depreciation *depreciación colectiva o combinada*
– hypothesis *hipótesis compuesta*
composition in bankruptcy *acuerdo, arreglo entre fallido y acreedores*
– of population, age *composición de la población por edad*
– tax *impuesto a tanto alzado*
compound fraction *fracción de fracción*
– interest *interés compuesto*
comprehensive economic control *control económicocomprensivo*
– evaluation programme *programa de evaluación completa*
compression of demand *compresión de la demanda*
comptroller *registrador, interventor, controlador*
compulsion *compulsión*
compulsory *obligatorio*
– arbitration *decisión arbitral, arbitraje obligatorio*
– cash reserve *reserva obligatoria en metálico*
– currency *moneda en curso forzoso*
– insurance *seguro obligatorio*
– purchase *compra obligatoria, expropiación*
– reserves of banks *reservas bancarias obligatorias*
– retirement *retiro forzoso*
– return *declaración obligatoria*
– sale *venta obligatoria, adjudicación forzosa, expropiación*
computation *cómputo, cálculo, cuenta, estimación, avaluo, evaluación*
–, seasonal *cálculo estacional*
–, statistical *cálculo estadístico, cómputo estadístico*
computator *calculista, calculador*
computed stress *esfuerzo calculado*
computer *calculadora, computador, ordenador*
– memory *memoria de máquina calculadora*
–, analog *calculadora analógica*
–, digital *calculadora de teclas, computador electrónico digital*
–, electronic *calculadora electrónica*
–, electronic numerical integrator and *calculadora e integradora numérica electrónica*
computers, analog and digital *computadoras*

analógicas y digitales
computing *cómputo, cálculo*
– amplifier, analog *amplificador de cálculo analógico*
– gear *mecanismo calculador*
– machine *máquina de calcular*
– rule *regla de cálculo*
concealment of profits *ocultación de utilidades*
concept *concepto*
concern *empresa, casa comercial*
–, business *empresa comercial*
–, going *empresa en funcionamiento*
–, rated *empresa clasificada por agencias de crédito*
–, wholesale *casa o firma mayorista*
concerns, domestic *empresas nacionales*
concession *concesión, privilegio*
– in price *precio especial, rebajado*
–, pooled *concesión mancomunada*
concessionaire *concesionario*
concessions, schedule of *lista de concesiones*
conciliation board *junta de conciliación*
conciliator *mediador, árbitro*
condemnation *expropiación, enajenación obligatoria*
condition, in saleable *en estado de venta*
–, statement of *estado de situación*
–, statement of financial *balance general, balance de situación*
conditional endorsement *endoso condicional*
conditioned reflex *reflejo condicionado*
conditions, labour *condiciones laborales*
–, to meet *sujetarse a condiciones*
–, working *condiciones de trabajo*
confabulation *confabulación*
conference *conferencia, sindicato, consorcio*
–, press *conferencia de prensa*
–, shipping *asociación de empresa de transportes marítimos*
confidence, self- *seguridad en sí mismo, confianza en símismo*
–, vote of *voto de confianza*
confiscatory taxation *tributación confiscatoria*
configuration *configuración*
conflict *conflicto, oposición, competición*
conflicting tendencies *tendencias en conflicto*
conformity, certificate of *certificado de conformidad*
congress *congreso, convención*
conscience *conciencia*
–, corporate *conciencia corporativa o social*
conscious *consciente*
–, class *conciencia de clase*
consensus *consentimiento*
consequential damages *daños emergentes*

conservation retención, conservación
– programme programa de conservación
–, soil conservación de suelos o tierras
consideration precio, prestación
consign, to consignar, traspasar
consignee destinatario, consignatario, comisionista
consignment consignación, envío
–, on en consignación
–, shipment on embarque a consignación
–, to sell on vender en consignación
consignor remitente
consistency uniformidad, estabilidad
consolidate, to consolidar, unir, combinar
consolidated consolidado
– amount monto global
– balance sheet estado de contabilidad consolidado
– budget presupuesto global
– business income cuenta consolidada de ingreso
– cash position situación de caja global
– debt deuda consolidada
consolidating of a tariff consolidación de una tarifa
– statement estado de consolidación
consolidation consolidación, concentración
–, surplus from superávit de consolidación
conspicuous consumption consumo debido a lo visible del precio y llamativo del producto
constant cantidad constante
– currency moneda de valor constante
– percentage depreciation method método de amortización de porcentaje constante
–, affinity constante de afinidad
–, testing constante del aparato medidor
constitution constitución
constrained movement movimiento controlado
consular consular
– fees derechos consulares
– invoice factura consular
consultant consejero
– analyst analista consejero
–, advertising consejero publicitario
–, management asesor de dirección
–, sales asesor sobre métodos de ventas
consulting experts expertos en consultas, consultores
consumables bienes consumibles
consume, marginal propensity to propensión marginal a consumir
–, propensity to propensión a consumir
consumer acceptance aceptación a favor del público
– branded product producto de marca y

consumo
– buying habits hábitos de compra del consumidor
– credit crédito al consumidor
– durables bienes durables de consumo
– economics aspectos económicos del consumo
– education educación del consumidor
– goods artículos de consumo
– market mercado de consumo
– market analysis análisis del mercado consumidor
– panel panel de consumidores
– preferences preferencias del consumidor
– purchaser consumidor-comprador
– relations relaciones con los consumidores
– research investigación sobre el consumidor
– research, quantitative investigación cuantitativa del consumidor
– stimulants estímulos del consumidor
– study estudio del cliente o consumidor
–, average consumidor medio
–, potential consumidor potencial
consumption consumo
– capital capital de consumo
– duties derechos de consumo
– function función de consumo
– goods bienes de consumo
– habits hábitos de consumo
–, conspicuous consumo debido a lo visible del precio y llamativo del producto
–, home consumo nacional
–, private consumo privado
–, per capita consumo por persona
contact man agente de contacto
container, reusable envase reutilizable
contend disputar, pleitar
content, work valor del trabajo
contents, table of índice
contest concurso, competición
contingency eventualidad
– allowance suplemento por imprevistos
– fund fondo para imprevistos
contingent eventual, contingente
– fund fondo de contingencia
– liabilities pasivo contingente
– profits utilidades contingentes
– reserve reserva de contingencia
continuing guarantee garantía contínua
continuity continuidad
continuous continuo
– population register registro continuo de la población
– production producción continua
– random variable variable aleatoria continua
– rating rendimiento continuo

–, reading method *método de lectura continua*
continuum *continuo*
contract *contrato, convenio, escritura*
– bond *fianza de contratista*
– carrier *empresa transportadora por contrato*
– labour *trabajadores, braceros contratados*
– of affreightment *póliza de fletamiento*
– of hire *contrato de trabajo*
– of sale *contrato de compraventa*
– price *precio acordado según contrato*
– time *lapso de terminación*
–, agency *contrato de agencia*
–, annuity *contrato de pensión o de anualidad*
–, collateral *contrato de prenda*
–, cost-plus *coste más honorarios, coste más porcentaje*
–, dependent *contrato condicional*
–, employment *contrato de trabajo*
–, lumpsum *contrato a precio alzado, en cantidad global*
–, maritime *contrato marítimo*
–, open-end *contrato exclusivo*
–, partnership *contrato social de asociación*
–, publishing *contrato de edición o publicación*
–, purchase *contrato de compraventa*
–, reciprocal *contrato bilateral o recíproco*
–, sliding-scale *contrato de precio revisable*
–, spot *contrato al contado*
–, to execute a *firmar un contrato*
–, under *bajo contrato*
–, underwriting *contrato de suscripción de valores*
–, yellow-dog *promesa por parte del obrero de no sindicalizarse*
contracting parties *partes contractantes*
contraction, business *contracción del mercado*
contracts, outstanding *contratos en curso*
contra-cyclical policy *política anticíclica*
control board *junta de control*
– record, cash *libro de caja*
– record, stock *registro de verificación de existencias*
– room *sala de control*
–, air traffic *control de tráfico aéreo*
–, automatic gain *control automático de ganancia o ampliación*
–, birth *control de natalidad*
–, budgetary *comprobación o fiscalización del presupuesto*
–, committee *control de cupos*
–, comprehensive economic *control económico comprensivo*
–, cost *control de costos*
–, credit *control de crédito*

–, exchange *control de cambios*
–, expenditure *control de gastos*
–, form sales *formulario de verificación de ventas*
–, inventory *control de existencias*
–, material *control de materiales*
–, production *control de producción*
–, quality *control de calidad*
–, sales *control de ventas*
–, statistical *verificación estadística*
–, steering *control o mando de la dirección*
–, step *regulación gradual*
–, stock *control de existencias*
–, unit stock *comprobación en unidades de las existencias*
–, waste *control de desperdicios*
controlled *controlado, dirigido*
– company *compañía filial*
– economy *economía dirigida*
– exchange *cambio controlado*
– machine time *tiempo controlado por la máquina*
– prices *precios controlados o regulados*
– sample *muestra controlada*
controller *controlador*
–, sales *verificador de ventas*
controlling interest *participación de control, inversión dominante*
controls, trade *restricciones al comercio*
convenience goods *artículos de primera necesidad*
convention *convención, congreso*
–, annual *convención anual*
–, draft *proyecto de convenio*
–, tariff *convención fiscal*
conventional statistical approach *enfoque estadístico convencional*
conversion *conversión, canje*
converter, analog to digital *convertidor de sistema análogo o sistema numérico*
convertible *convertible*
– assets *activo convertible*
– bonds *bonos convertibles en acciones*
conveyance *título de traspaso o de traslación de dominio*
conveyor *transportador*
– belt *cinta transportadora*
cooling-off period *tregua*
co-operation *cooperación*
–, antagonistic *cooperación por necesidad*
–, employee *cooperación de los empleados u obreros*
–, employee-employer *cooperación entre patronos y obreros*
–, employer-union *cooperación entre patronos y obreros*

co-operative advertising *publicidad en
cooperación*
– society *sociedad cooperativa de consumo*
–, buying *cooperativa de compras*
co-ordinates, azimuth *coordenadas acimut*
co-ordination *coordinación*
co-owner *copropietario*
copy, advertising *texto publicitario, texto de
un anuncio*
–, checking *ejemplar comprobante*
–, close *copia exacta*
–, file *copia para archivo*
–, loose *número o ejemplar suelto*
–, sample *ejemplar de muestra*
–, voucher *ejemplar comprobante de un
anuncio*
copying *transcripción, acción de copiar,
copiador*
– ink *tinta de copiar*
– lamp *lámpara de hacer copias*
– paper *papel fino para copias de cartas, papel
cebolla*
– paste *pasta de copiar*
– pencil *lápiz tinta*
– press *prensa de copiar*
– process *tiraje de películas*
– template *plantilla copiadora*
copyman *redactor publicitario*
copyright *derechos de reproducción, derechos
de autor*
– case *proceso por plagio o falsificación*
– infringement *infracción, lesión o violación
de los derechos del autor*
– laws *leyes sobre propiedad intelectual*
– practice *ejercicio del derecho de autor*
– protection *protección de la propiedad
intelectual*
– reserved *derechos de publicación reservados*
–, to *registrar un libro o una obra*
copyrighted material *material, temas y obras
registradas*
– name *nombre o seudónimo registrado*
copyrighting *depósito legal, registro de
publicación*
copywriter *redactor publicitario*
corollary *corolario*
corporate *incorporado, social*
– body *sociedad anónima*
– bond *bono, obligación de una sociedad*
– business *empresa construída en sociedad*
– capital *capital social*
– conscience *conciencia social o corporativa*
– name *razón social*
– person *persona corporativa*
– personality *personalidad social*
– profits *utilidades de sociedad anónima*

– property *propiedad corporativa*
– saving *ahorro social*
– taxes *impuestos de sociedad anónima*
– trust *fideicomiso de sociedad anónima*
corporation *sociedad anónima por acciones*
–, business *corporación mercantil*
–, close *sociedad anónima controlada por
pocos*
–, domestic *cooperación o compañía nacional*
–, non-profit-making *asociación ño lucrativa*
–, non-stock *sociedad sin acciones*
–, public service *empresa de servicio público*
–, trading *sociedad mercantil*
correlation *correlación*
correspondents, crop *corresponsales
agrícolas*
cost *costo*
– accountant *contable de costos o costes*
– accountant, production *contable de costes de
producción*
– accountant, sales *contable de costes de venta*
– accounting *contabilidad de costos o costes*
– accounting, production *contabilidad de
costes de producción*
– accounting, shop and *contabilidad de
talleres para determinación de costes*
– analysis by products *análisis de coste por
productos*
– analysis distribution *análisis del coste de
distribución*
– analyst, sales *especialista en costes de venta*
– auditing *ajuste o intervención de costes*
– auditing of sales *revisión del coste de ventas*
– clerk *calculista de costos*
– control *control de costos*
– curve *curva de costos*
– distribution *repartición de costos*
– free *libre de gastos*
– insurance and freight *costo, seguro y flete*
– insurance, freight and exchange *costo,
seguro, flete y cambio*
– of living *coste de la vida*
– of living differential *tasa diferencial del coste
de la vida*
– or market (whichever is lower) *el menor
precio ya sea de costo o de mercado*
– price *precio de coste*
– price, below *precio bajo costo*
– standards *normas de costos*
– standards distribution *módulos o normas de
costes de distribución*
– value *valor de costo*
– value method *método del valor de costo*
–, actual *coste efectivo o verdadero*
–, additional *coste adicional, coste
suplementario*

–, administration *gastos de administración*
–, all-in *coste total*
–, annual upkeep *coste de entretenimiento anual*
–, average variable *coste variable medio*
–, capital *gastos de instalación o fundación*
–, carrying *coste de almacenamiento*
–, change in *cambio en los costos*
–, competitive *precio de competencia*
–, current *coste actual*
–, delivery *coste de entrega*
–, depreciation *costo de depreciación*
–, direct *coste directo*
–, expenses at buyer's *gastos a cargo del comprador*
–, factor *coste de factores*
–, fixed *coste fijo*
–, gross *coste total*
–, historical *coste inicial*
–, increased *aumento del costo*
–, indirect *costos indirectos*
–, interest *coste por pago de intereses*
–, joint *costo de producción común a dos o más productos*
–, marginal *costo marginal*
–, marginal user *costo marginal de utilización*
–, operating *coste de producción*
–, original *costo inicial*
–, prime *coste de fabricación, coste primario*
–, production *coste de fabricación o producción*
–, relevant *costo pertinente*
–, replacement *costo de reposición*
–, reproduction *costo de reproducción o reposición*
–, sales *coste de ventas*
–, standard *coste tipo*
–, to underwrite the *asegurar el coste*
–, unit *coste unitario*
–, user *coste de uso o de utilización*
–, value at factor *valor al costo de los factores*
cost-plus contract *coste más honorarios, coste más porcentaje*
costing, sales *fijación del coste de las ventas*
costs alteration *modificación de costes*
–, after *gastos extraordinarios*
–, clerical *costes administrativos*
–, distribution of *reparto de costes*
–, distributors' *costes de los distribuidores*
–, drafting *gastos de estudio*
–, economic *costos económicos*
–, external *costes de distribución*
–, maintenance *costes de mantenimiento*
–, overall distribution *costes adjuntos o globales de distribución*
–, overhead *gastos generales*

–, schedule *costos proyectados*
–, standing *costos o gastos permanentes*
–, storage *gastos de almacenaje*
–, training *gastos o costes de capacitación*
–, variable *costes variables*
council, advisory *consejo consultivo, consejo de asesoramiento o asesor*
–, works *comisión de obreros*
counselling interview *entrevista de asesoramiento*
count, cash *avance de caja*
counter, bargain *baratillo*
–, coin *máquina contadora de monedas*
–, display *exposición de mostrador, expositor*
–, memory address *contador de dirección de memoria*
–, program address *contador de dirección de programa*
counteract, to *contrarrestar*
counterclaim *contrademanda*
counterfeit *falsificación*
– money *dinero falso*
counterfoil *talón*
countervailing *compensatorio*
country, dollar-hungry *país escaso de dólares*
–, single crop *país de monocultivo*
–, source *país de origen*
coupon bonds *bonos al portador*
court *tribunal, juzgado*
–, labour *tribunal de trabajo*
cover page *página de la cubierta*
covering letter *carta de presentación*
– note *aval o garantía comercial*
crash programme *programa de urgencia*
credit *crédito*
– account *cuenta acreedora*
– against taxes *deducción por impuestos pagados*
– and collection expenses *gastos de crédito y cobro*
– balance *saldo acreedor*
– bank *banco de crédito*
– buying *compras a crédito*
– company, commercial *sociedad financiera, sociedad de crédito comercial*
– control *control de créditos*
– department *sección de crédito*
– entry *asiento de abono*
– extension *extensión o ampliación de créditos*
– instrument *documento o instrumento de crédito*
– manager *director o jefe de créditos*
– note *nota de crédito*
– policy *política de crédito*
– rating *grado o límite de crédito, estimación o valoración crediticia*

– references *referencias de crédito*
– report *informe de crédito*
– statement *estado financiero*
– underwriters *aseguradores de créditos*
–, accommodation *crédito en descubierto*
–, ancillary letter of *carta de crédito auxiliar*
–, clean *crédito simple*
–, clean letter of *carta de crédito simple*
–, consumer *crédito al consumidor*
–, deferred *crédito diferido*
–, documentary *crédito documentario*
–, foreign tax *deducción por impuestos pagados en el extranjero*
–, irrevocable letter of *carta de crédito irrevocable, letra de crédito irrevocable*
–, letter of *carta de crédito*
–, on *a crédito*
–, open *crédito abierto*
–, reinbursement *crédito de reembolso*
–, revolving *crédito renovable*
–, sale on *venta al fiado*
–, straight *crédito irrevocable*
–, straight letter of *letra de crédito a la vista*
–, time letter of *carta o letra de crédito a plazo*
–, to *acreditar*
–, to grant *conceder crédito*
–, to relax *facilitar crédito*
–, trade *crédito mercantil o comercial*
–, unconfirmed *crédito no confirmado*
creditor *acreedor*
– account *cuenta acreedora*
–, lien *acreedor embargador*
–, preferred *acreedor privilegiado*
–, unsecured *acreedor sin caución*
creditors, sundry *acreedores diversos*
–, joint *coacreedores*
credits accounting *contabilidad de créditos*
–, frozen *créditos congelados*
–, rationing of *restricción de créditos*
crisis, money *crisis monetaria*
critical materials *materiales estratégicos*
crop *cosecha, producción agrícola*
– correspondents *corresponsales agrícolas*
– country, single- *país de monocultivo*
– index *índice, coeficiente de producción agrícola*
– insurance *seguro contra la pérdida de las cosechas*
crops, basic *cultivos básicos*
–, rotation of *rotación de cultivos*
cross entry *asientos cruzados*
– licensing *concesión recíproca de licencias, de patente*
– sample *muestra cruzada*
– section *sección cruzada, grupo representativo*

– section data *datos de sección cruzada*
crossfoot, to *sumar horizontalmente*
crossfooter *aditamiento para suma y resta horizontal*
crowd *multitud, masa*
cue *referencia*
cumulative *acumulativo, acumulable*
– dividend *dividendo acumulable*
– effect *efecto acumulativo*
– markup calculation *cálculo del margen comercial acumulativo*
– preferred stock *acciones privilegiadas de dividendo acumulable*
– timing *método de lectura continua, cronometraje por lecturas acumuladas*
currencies, readjustment of *reajuste monetario*
currency *moneda de un país, circulación (dinero)*
– area *zona monetaria*
– devaluation *devaluación de la moneda*
–, blocked *moneda controlada*
–, calling of *retiro de moneda*
–, compulsory *moneda en curso forzoso*
–, constant *moneda de valor constante*
–, domestic *moneda del país*
–, fall of *devaluación de la moneda*
–, foreign *divisas, moneda extranjera*
–, hard *divisas convertibles, divisas estables*
–, soft *moneda de valor inestable*
–, unit of *unidad monetaria*
–, unsound *moneda inestable*
current *corriente*
– account *cuenta corriente*
– account, abstract of *extracto de cuenta corriente*
– assets *activo corriente, activo en acción*
– cost *coste actual*
– data *informaciones corrientes*
– expectations *previsiones actuales*
– expenditures *gastos corrientes*
– input *insumo corriente*
– liabilities *pasivo, circulante, exigible*
– life table *tabla de mortalidad actual*
– payment *pagos corrientes*
– physical output *producción física corriente*
– price *precio corriente o actual del mercado*
– revenue *ingreso ordinario*
– services *servicios habituales*
– supplementary cost *costo suplementario actual*
– surplus *excedente, superávit*
– value *valor actual, precio corriente*
– yield *rendimiento corriente*
curtailment *restricción*
curve, cost *curva de los costos*

–, demand *curva de la demanda*
–, distribution *curva de distribución*
–, earnings *curva de ganancia o de salarios*
–, frequency *curva de frecuencia, curva de distribución de frecuencia*
–, production *curva de producción*
–, sales *curva o gráfico de ventas*
–, supply *curva de la oferta*
–, wage *curva de ganancia o de salarios*
–, work *curva de producción*
custom *costumbre, hábito*
customary price *precio acostumbrado*
customer *cliente*
– service *servicio para los consumidores o clientes*
–, steady *cliente fijo*
customs *aduana*
– bond *fianza de aduana*
– bonded *bajo control aduanal*
– broker *agente aduanal*
– clearance *despacho aduanal*
– declaration *declaración aduanal*
– duty *derechos de aduana*
– exempt *exento de derechos aduanales*
– free *libre de derechos de aduana*
– manifest *manifiesto de aduana*
– quotas *cupos arancelarios*
– rebate *rebaja en los derechos de aduana*
– receipts *ingresos de aduana*
– regulations *reglamento de aduana*
– tariffs *aranceles aduaneros*
– union *unión, asociación de aduanas*

– value *valor en aduana*
–, collector of *administrador de aduana*
–, local *costumbres de la plaza o del lugar*
cut *rebaja*
– prices *precios pelados*
– rate *precio o tarifa reducido por rebaja*
–, tax *reducción de impuestos*
–, to *cortar, reducir*
cuts, budgetary *reducciones del presupuesto*
cutting, price- *reducción de precios*
–, rate- *reducción de tarifas*
cycle *ciclo*
– action *ciclo de funcionamiento, ciclo de trabajo*
– length *duración del ciclo*
– policy, business *política de coyuntura*
– time *duración del ciclo*
–, billing *facturación en ciclos*
–, business *ciclo económico*
–, economic *ciclo económico*
–, savings *ciclo de ahorros*
–, trade *ciclo económico*
–, typical business *ciclo económico clásico*
–, work *ciclo de trabajo*
cyclic element *elemento regular o cíclico o repetitivo*
– time *duración del ciclo*
cyclical fluctuations *fluctuaciones cíclicas*
– fluctuations, season *fluctuaciones cíclicas de temporada*
cyclograph *ciclógrafo*

D

daily *diario, cotidiano*
– paper *diario, periódico*
damage *daño, avería, deterioro*
– survey *inspección de avería*
–, accidental *daño accidental, deterioro accidental*
damages, allowance for *indemnización por averías o daños*
–, consequential *daños emergentes*
–, double *indemnización doble*
–, indirect *daños indirectos*
–, liquidated *daños liquidados*
–, nominal *indemnización nominal*
–, property *daños materiales*
–, prospective *daños anticipados*
–, to claim *reclamar por daños*
–, unliquidated *daños no liquidados*
danger situation *situación de peligro*
data *datos, información*
– analysis *análisis de datos*
– collection techniques *técnicas de recogida de datos*
– design, engineering *datos técnicos para proyectos*
– display system *sistema de presentación de datos*
– file *lote de datos*
– handling device *dispositivo de manejo de datos o utilización de datos*
– handling system *sistema de manejo de datos*
– information *información sobre datos*
– processing *clasificación, elaboración o proceso de datos*
– processing equipment *equipo de sistematización de datos*
– processing equipment, electronic integrated *equipo electrónico de elaboración e integración de datos*
– processing machine, electronic *equipo electrónico de elaboración e integración de datos*
– processing, arithmetic *sistematización de datos aritméticos*
– processing, electronic *elaboración electrónica de datos*
– programme, integrated *programa de integración de datos*
– recorder *registrador de datos*

– sheet, technical *hoja de datos técnicos*
–, alphabetic *datos alfabéticos*
–, check *datos comprobatorios*
–, comparative *datos comparativos*
–, current *informaciones corrientes*
–, expanded *datos inflados*
–, job *datos laborales*
–, methods of collecting *métodos para reunir datos*
–, normative *datos normativos o normalizados*
–, objective *datos objetivos*
–, pre-test sample *datos de muestra de pruebas previas*
–, primary *datos de origen o primarios*
–, printed output for *documentos impresos como norma de información*
–, sales *datos sobre las ventas*
–, secondary *datos secundarios*
–, standard time *datos de tiempos normalizados*
–, statistics *datos estadísticos*
–, subjective *datos subjetivos*
–, survey *datos de una encuesta*
–, tabulation of *tabulación de datos*
–, transmission *transmisión de datos*
–, working *datos de funcionamiento*
date bond *bono a plazo fijo*
– of delivery *fecha de entrega*
–, after *fecha posterior*
–, call *fecha de reembolso*
–, closing or press *fecha de cierre*
–, delivery *fecha de entrega*
–, equated *fecha media de vencimiento*
–, load *fecha de carga o de fabricación*
–, maturity *fecha de vencimiento*
–, out of *caducado*
–, publication *fecha de publicación, fecha de salida*
–, sales to *ventas a crédito*
dating *vencimiento*
– stamp *fechador de sellos*
–, e.o.m. *vencimiento a fin de mes*
day *día*
– labourer *jornalero, trabajador, peón*
– rate *jornal*
– work *trabajo a jornal*
–, business *día hábil*

–, order of the *orden del día*
–, pay *día de pago*
–, settling *día de liquidación*
–, week *día de trabajo, día laboral*
–, working *día de trabajo, día util*
daybook *libro diario*
daylight saving *avance de la hora*
days of grace *días de gracia*
dead freight *falso flete*
deadline *término, límite del plazo fijado*
deadlock *estancamiento*
dead time *tiempo muerto*
– weight capacity *tonelaje*
deal *negociación, operación, transación*
–, business *transacción comercial, negocio*
–, cash *operación al contado*
–, package *estabilización económica*
–, to *negociar*
dealer *comerciante, negociante, distribuidor*
– margin *margen del comerciante*
–, wholesale *mayorista, comerciante al por mayor*
deals, combined accounts *ventas de cuentas combinadas*
–, compensation *ventas por compensación*
death duties *impuestos de sucesión*
– rate *mortalidad, tasa de mortalidad*
– rate, occupational *tasa de mortalidad por profesiones*
– tax *impuesto de sucesión*
debasement *depreciación de la moneda*
debenture *obligación, título de crédito, orden de pago*
– bond *bono sin garantía hipotecaria*
– issue *emisión de obligaciones*
–, bearer *obligación al portador*
–, floating *obligación flotante, obligación no consolidada*
–, mortgage *obligación de hipoteca o hipotecaria*
–, simple *obligación simple, sin garantía específica*
debentures, annual redemption of *reembolso anual de obligaciones*
–, fixed interest-bearing *obligaciones de interés fijo*
–, loan on *préstamo en obligaciones*
–, registered *obligaciones nominativas*
debit *cargo, débito, adeudar, cargar*
– account *cuenta deudora*
– balance *saldo deudor*
– deferred *cargo diferido*
– entry *asiento de cargo*
– note *nota de cargo*
– or debtor account *cuenta deudora*
–, additional *cargo adicional*

debitor account *cuenta deudora*
debt *deuda, adeudo, obligación*
– at sight *deuda a la vista*
–, active *deuda que produce interés*
–, consolidated *deuda consolidada*
–, deferred *deuda diferida*
–, domestic *deuda interior*
–, external *deuda exterior*
–, fixed *deuda consolidada*
–, floating *deuda flotante*
–, foreign *deuda exterior o en el extranjero*
–, funded *deuda consolidada, obligaciones a largo plazo, pasivo a largo plazo, deuda a largo plazo*
–, gross national *deuda nacional bruta*
–, internal *deuda interior*
–, liquidated *deuda liquidada*
–, long-term *crédito a largo plazo*
–, national *deuda nacional*
–, partnership *deudas sociales*
–, passive *deuda sin interés*
–, permanent *deuda permanente*
–, preferred *deuda de la prioridad*
–, privileged *deuda privilegiada, deuda preferida*
–, public *deuda pública*
–, redeemable *deuda amortizable*
–, stale *deuda caducada*
–, to recognize a *admitir una deuda*
–, unfunded *deuda no consolidada, deuda flotante*
–, unliquidated *deuda no determinada, deuda por pagar*
–, unsecured *deuda sin caución*
–, unsinkable *deuda no amortizable*
debtor *deudor*
– account *cuenta deudora*
debtors, joint *codeudores, deudores mancomunados*
–, doubtful *deudor dudoso*
debts, bad *cuentas malas, deudores morosos*
–, outstanding *deudas existentes, deudas pendientes*
debut *estreno*
declaration of trust *declaración de fideicomiso*
–, customs *declaración aduanal*
–, export *declaración de exportación*
–, import *declaración de importación*
declared capital *capital declarado, escriturado*
– dividend *dividendo decretado*
decline *baja*
–, price *baja de precios*
decrease, planned stock *disminución de existencias previstas*
deducted, all charges *deducidos todos los*

gastos
deductible *deducible*
deduction *deducción, descuento*
–, personal *deducción personal o individual*
–, tariff *deducción, rebaja del impuesto*
deed *escritura, contrato*
– of gift *escritura de donación*
– of sale *contrato de compraventa*
– of transfer *escritura de traspaso*
– of trust *escritura de fideicomiso*
–, title *título de propiedad*
deeds, company *actas de la sociedad*
defalcation *desfalco*
defective goods *mercancías defectuosas*
deferred *diferido*
– annuity *anualidad diferida, renta diferida*
– assets *activo diferido*
– bonds *bonos de interés diferido,*
    obligaciones diferidas
– charges *cargos diferidos*
– credit *crédito diferido*
– debit *carga diferida*
– debt *deuda diferida*
– dividend *dividendo diferido*
– liabilities *pasivo diferido*
– payment *pago aplazado*
– profits *utilidades por realizar*
– quantity discount *descuento por cantidades*
    acumuladas
–, pension *pago diferido de pensión*
deficiency payment *pago para cubrir un*
    déficit
deficit *déficit*
– economy *economía deficitaria*
– financing *financiamiento deficitario*
– spending *gastos deficitarios*
–, budget *déficit presupuestal*
–, cash *déficit de caja*
–, operating *pérdida, déficit de explotación*
–, trade *balanza de pagos desfavorable*
deflate, to *desinflar*
deflated *deflacionado, reducido*
deflation *deflación*
degree *grado*
delay *retraso, demora, interrupción, espera*
– method, ratio *método de observaciones*
    instantáneas
–, avoidable *retraso evitable*
delinquent tax *impuesto no pagado a tiempo*
delivery *entrega, despacho*
– bond *fianza para devolver bienes*
    embargados
– cost *coste de entrega*
– date *fecha de entrega*
– service, poor *servicio de entrega deficiente*
–, cash on *pago contra reembolso*

–, claim for short *reclamación por envío*
    incompleto
–, collect on *pago contra reembolso*
–, date of *fecha de entrega*
–, home *entrega a domicilio*
–, order *entrega de pedidos*
–, port of *puerto terminal*
–, short *entrega incompleta*
–, spot *entrega inmediata*
–, time of *plazo de entrega*
demand *demanda*
– bill *letra, giro a la vista*
– curve *curva de la demanda*
– deposits *depósitos a la vista*
– draft *letra, giro a la vista*
– for labour *demanda de trabajadores,*
    demanda de mano de obra
– function *función demanda*
– note *pagaré a la vista*
– price, aggregate *precio a la demanda global*
– schedule *tabla, curva de demanda*
–, compression of *compresión de la demanda*
–, effective *demanda efectiva*
–, elastic *demanda elástica*
–, intermittent *intermitencias en la demanda*
–, on *a la vista, a la presentación*
–, pay on *pagadero a la presentación*
–, seasonal *demanda de temporada*
–, supply and *oferta y demanda*
–, to *demandar, cobrar*
demarcation dispute *conflicto intergremial*
    sobre responsabilidades
demography, mathematical *demografía*
    matemática
demonstration worker *demostrador*
demonstrator *demostrador*
demurrage *demora*
denominator, common *denominador común*
denounce, to *denunciar, dar por terminado*
density *densidad*
–, population *densidad de población o*
    demográfica
–, potential *densidad potencial*
department chief *jefe de departamento*
– head *jefe de departamento*
– manager *jefe de departamento*
– schedule *programa de departamento*
– stores *grandes almacenes*
– superintendent *jefe de departamento*
–, advertising *departamento de publicidad*
–, auditing *sección de revisión de cuentas*
–, banking *departamento bancario*
–, billing *departamento de facturación*
–, credit *sección de crédito*
–, distribution *servicio de expediciones*
–, export *sección de exportación*

–, foreign exchange *sección de cambio extranjero*
–, import *sección de importación*
–, issue *departamento emisor*
–, loan *sección de préstamos*
–, publicity *departamento de información publicitaria*
–, purchasing *sección de compras*
–, sales *sección de ventas, departamento de ventas*
–, staff training *departamento asesor de capacitación*
–, time study *oficina de tiempos*
–, wages *departamento de salarios*
departure, time of *hora de salida*
dependability *sentido de la responsabilidad*
dependency *dependencia*
dependent *dependiente*
– contract *contrato condicional*
– variable *variable dependiente*
deplete, to *agotar*
depletion *agotamiento*
deposit *depósito*
– account *cuenta de depósito, cuenta de ahorro*
–, certificate of *certificado de depósito*
–, derivative *depósito derivado*
–, on *en depósito, en el banco*
–, time *depósito a plazo o a término*
deposits, business *depósitos para gastos de negocio*
–, demand *depósitos a la vista*
–, savings *depósitos de ahorros*
–, trust *depósitos especiales, depósitos en fideicomiso*
depot, distribution *depósito para distribución*
depreciated value *valor depreciado*
depreciation *depreciación*
– allowance *reserva de depreciación, amortización permitida*
– cost *costo de depreciación*
– factor, effective *factor real de la demanda*
– of currency *depreciación de la moneda*
–, accelerated *depreciación acelerada*
–, accrued *depreciación acumulada*
–, annual *depreciación anual*
–, appraisement method *depreciación por tasación*
–, basis for *base de depreciación*
–, composite *depreciación combinada, depreciación colectiva*
–, straight-line *depreciación en línea recta*
–, unit cost *depreciación a base del coste unitario de producción*
depressing influence *influencia depresiva*
depth *profundidad, fondo*

derivative deposit *depósito derivado*
describe, to *exponer*
description, job *descripción del trabajo*
design *boceto, croquis, designio, dibujo, diseño, empresa, fin, idea, intención, intento, objetivo, patrón, plan, plano, propósito, proyecto*
– covered by patents pending *diseño protegido por patentes en tramitación*
– engineering data *datos técnicos para proyectos*
– engineering staff *personal de estudios de proyectos*
– office *oficina de proyectos*
– rate *gasto normal*
– research *investigación dirigida*
– staff *personal de proyectos*
– standardization programme *programa de normalización de diseños*
– team *equipo de proyecto*
– technique *técnica de diseños*
– time *tiempo previsto*
–, all-domestic *proyecto totalmente racional*
–, experimental *sistema de experiencias, plan experimental*
–, forms *diseño de estados o formularios*
–, process *proyecto del proceso, preparación del trabajo*
–, product *diseño, presentación del producto*
–, questionnaire *preparación del cuestionario*
–, sample *diseño o enfoque de una muestra*
designer *dibujante, delineante, bocetista, proyectista, constructor, realizador, autor, inventor*
–, poster *cartelista, dibujante o pintor de carteles*
designing *estudio, proyecto, creación de modas*
designs registered and world patents pending *modelos registrados y patentes mundiales en trámite*
desk research *investigación en la oficina*
–, information *cuadro de información*
detail shortage *falta de piezas*
deterioration *deterioro, evolución desfavorable*
determinism *determinismo económico*
devaluation *devaluación*
–, currency *devaluación de la moneda*
–, exchange *pérdida por conversión de moneda*
develop a product, to *crear o propagar un producto*
development engineer *técnico proyectista*
– fund *fondo de expansión*
– fund, capital *fondos para equipo de*

producción
- schedule, engineering *programa técnico del desarrollo de fabricación*
- unit, product *unidad de desarrollo de un producto*
- work *labor de crear y perfeccionar y propagar*
-, economic *desarrollo económico*
-, research and *investigación y desarrollo*
developmental test *ensayo evolutivo*
deviation *desviación*
-, absolute *desviación absoluta*
-, squared *desviación cuadrática*
-, standard *desviación normal*
device *recurso, artificio, dispositivo, ingenio, mecanismo*
-, alphabetic *dispositivo alfabético*
-, data handling *sistema de manejo de datos*
-, pre-test *proyecto propio de prueba*
-, safety *dispositivo de seguridad*
devices, offsetting *dispositivos de desplazamiento*
-, testing *dispositivo de pruebas*
devise, to *idear*
- a method, to *idear un sistema*
diagram, advance *gráfico de avance*
-, column *diagrama de columnas*
-, distribution *diagrama de distribución*
-, flow *diagrama de circulación*
-, form flow *gráfico de la serie de impresos*
-, frequency *diagrama de frecuencia, histograma*
-, process *diagrama gráfico de procedimiento o elaboración*
-, scatter *diagrama múltiple o de difusión*
-, traffic *diagrama de tráfico*
dial *esfera*
dichotomy *dicotomía*
dictating machine *máquina de dictar*
- machine, electronic *máquina de dictar electrónica*
dictatorship *dictadura*
die, business *sello comercial, sello de la casa*
diem, per *por día, diario*
differential analysis *análisis diferencial*
- piecework *salario diferencial por piezas*
- timing *medida de tiempos por diferencia*
digit address, four- *dirección de cuatro dígitos*
digital computer *calculadora de teclas, computador electrónico digital*
- computers, analog and *calculadoras analógicas y digitales*
dimensions, standardized *dimensiones o medidas normalizadas*
diminishing *decreciente*
- balance *amortización decreciente*

- productiveness *productividad decreciente*
- returns *rendimiento decreciente*
dip, activity *caída o descanso de la actividad*
direct *directo*
- action *acción directa, sabotaje*
- advertising *publicidad directa*
- collections *cobros directos*
- cost *coste directo*
- duplicator *multicopista de líquido*
- interviewing *interrogatorio directo*
- investment *inversión directa*
- mail campaign *campaña por correspondencia*
- price competition *competencia directa de los precios*
- production *producción directa*
- sale *venta directa*
- selling expenses *gastos de la venta directa*
- tax *impuesto directo*
- work *trabajo directo*
direction measurement, error *medición de la dirección del error*
director, acting *director interino*
-, commercial *director comercial*
-, managing *director gerente*
-, technical *director técnico*
-, traffic *director o jefe de tráfico*
-, training *director de información o entretenimiento*
directors, board of *junta directiva, consejo de administración*
directory, trade *guía comercial*
dirt cheap, to buy *comprar baratísimo, comprar a precio tirado, comprar a bulto*
disability income *ingreso, renta por incapacidad*
-, permanent partial *incapacidad parcial permanente*
-, permanent total *incapacidad absoluta permanente*
-, personal *incapacidad individual*
-, physical *incapacidad física*
-, total *invalidez total*
disburse, to *desembolsar*
discontinue, to *suspender, descontinuar*
discount *descuento, bonificación*
- bank *banco de descuento*
- factor *factor de descuento*
- house *tienda de rebajas, saldista*
- policy *sistema de descuento*
- price *precio de descuento o rebajado*
- rate *tasa, tipo de descuento*
-, accrual of *incremento del descuento*
-, cash *descuento por pronto pago*
-, chain *rebajas en cadena*
-, cumulative quantity *descuento por*

cantidades acumuladas
–, deferred quantity *descuento por cantidades acumuladas*
–, exchange *pérdida por conversión de moneda*
–, expressive *descuento grande*
–, lapsed *descuento caducado*
–, quantity *descuento por cantidades*
–, time *descuento por pago dentro del plazo señalado*
–, trade *descuento comercial*
–, true *descuento real, descuento externo (M)*
–, volume *descuento por volumen*
discounts account *cuenta de descuentos*
–, sales *descuentos de pronto pago*
–, scale of *tarifa escalonada*
discrepancy *discrepancia, diferencia*
discrimination *discriminación*
–, tariff *discriminación fiscal*
discriminatory assistance *ayuda preferente*
– pricing *fijación discriminatoria de precios*
disease, occupational *enfermedad profesional*
dishonour, to *no aceptar, no pagar*
dishonoured bill *letra rechazada*
dismissal *despido*
– wage *indemnización por despido*
disorder, functional *desorden funcional*
dispatch *envío, expedición*
dispatcher *lanzador*
dispatching *lanzamiento*
dispense with, to *renunciar a*
displacement, population *desplazamiento de población*
display *exposición, exhibición, despliegue*
– advertising *publicidad en plafones*
– material, window *material para exposición de escaparates, disposición de cosas en escaparates*
– poster *pancarta de publicidad*
– system, data *sistema de presentación de datos*
–, advertising *proyecto de anuncio compuesto*
–, counter *exposición de mostrador, expositor*
–, mass *exposición masiva*
–, merchandise *exposición de mercancías*
–, poor *exposición inadecuada o deficiente*
–, sample *exposición de muestras*
–, window *exposición o composición de escaparates*
disposable income *ingreso disponible, ingreso neto*
disposal *disposición, cesión*
– board *comisión de ventas, oficina de ventas*
dispose of *deshacerse de una cosa*
disposition *aplicación, arreglo, disposición*
dispute *conflicto*

–, demarcation *conflicto intergremial sobre responsabilidades*
–, industrial *conflicto de trabajo*
–, labour *conflicto de trabajo*
–, wage *controversia o desacuerdo sobre sueldos*
disputed account *cuenta impugnada*
disqualified *incapacitado, incompetente*
dissenting stockholder *accionista disidente*
dissolve *desvanecimiento*
distance freight *flete por distancia*
– time graph *diagrama de tiempos*
distort, to *distorsionar, tergiversar, falsear*
distress *remate, urgencia*
– budget *presupuesto reducido o limitado*
– prices *precios de remate*
– selling *ventas de embargo*
– warrant *orden de embargo*
distributed profits *utilidades pagadas o distribuidas*
distributing agency *agencia distribuidora*
– centre *centro distribuidor*
– network *red de distribución*
– zone *zona de reparto o distribución*
distribution accounting *contabilidad de la distribución*
– approach, selective *enfoque de la distribución selectiva*
– census *censo de distribución*
– chart, form *diagrama de distribución de impresos*
– chart, form process *diagrama de distribución de impresos*
– chart, work *diagrama de distribución del trabajo*
– cost accounting *contabilidad de costes de distribución*
– cost analysis *análisis del coste de distribución*
– cost information *información sobre el coste de distribución*
– cost standards *módulos o normas de costes de distribución*
– costs, over-all *costes globales de distribución*
– curve *curva de frecuencia, curva de distribución de frecuencia*
– department *servicio de expediciones*
– depot *depósito para distribución*
– diagram *diagrama de distribución*
– expenses, general *gastos generales de distribución*
– of costs *reparto de costes*
– zone *zona de abastecimiento*
–, channel of *vía o canal de distribución*
–, cost *repartición de costos*
–, frequency *distribución de frecuencia*
distributive profits *utilidades repartibles*

- tax *impuesto de repartición*
- trade *comercio de distribución*
distributor *concesionario, comerciante distribuidor*
-'s costs *costes de los distribuidores*
- maximum price *precio máximo del concesionario*
- selling price *precio de venta para los distribuidores*
diversion of profits *desviación ilícita de utilidades*
divest, to *despojar*
dividend *dividendo*
- arrears *atrasos de dividendo*
- in kind *dividendo en especie*
- warrant *cédula de dividendo*
-, capital *dividendo de capital*
-, cash *dividendo en efectivo*
-, cumulative *dividendo acumulable*
-, declared *dividendo decretado*
-, deferred *dividendo diferido*
-, interim *dividendo parcial*
-, irregular *dividendo ocasional*
-, liquidating *dividendo de liquidación*
-, passed *dividendo omitido*
-, preferred *dividendo preferente, dividendo sobre acciones privilegiadas*
-, property *dividendo de bienes o en especie*
-, stock *dividendo en acciones*
-, unclaimed *dividendo no reclamado*
-, year-end *dividendo a fin de año*
division *división, ramo, negocio, sección, departamento*
- manager *director o gerente de una división industrial o mercantil*
- of labour *división del trabajo*
- of production *negociado de producción*
- of work *división del trabajo*
-, industrial *distribución de actividades económicas*
-, personnel *departamento o sección de personal*
divisional merchandise manager *director comercial desección*
-, dock, ex- *puesto en el muelle, franco en el muelle*
docket *rótulo, minuta, sumario, etiqueta, ficha*
- file *expediente*
-, inquiry *ficha o letrero de información*
-, to *rotular, clasificar documentos*
doctor accounts, to *falsificar cuentas*
document *documento, acta*
-, commercial *papeles de negocios*
-, public *escritura pública*
documentary *documental*

- classification *clasificación de documentos*
- credit *crédito documentario*
- credit, commercial *crédito documentario comercial*
- film *película documental*
- reproduction service *servicio de reproducción de documentos*
documentation centre *centro de documentación*
- service *servicio de documentación*
documents *documentos*
- against payment *documentos contra pago*
- for collection *documentos de embarque*
-, against *contra documentos*
-, commercial *papeles de negocios, documentos*
-, shipping *documentos de embarque*
dodging, tariff *evasión de impuestos*
dole *socorro pecuniario*
-, unemployment *indemnización por desempleo*
dollar *dólar*
- area *zona del dólar*
- gap *déficit o escasez de dólares*
- shortage *escasez de dólares*
-, advertising *dinero invertido en publicidad*
domestic *nacional, del país*
- bill *letra sobre el interior*
- commerce *comercio interior o nacional*
- commodities *productos nacionales*
- concerns *empresas nacionales*
- corporation *corporación o compañía nacional*
- currency *moneda del país*
- debt *deuda interior*
- investment *inversión interior*
- market *mercado nacional*
- or home trade *comercio interior*
- order *pedido para el interior*
- price *precio para venta interior*
- product, gross *producto bruto interno*
- products *productos nacionales o internos*
- purchases *compras en el país*
domination *dominación*
domicile *domicilio, residencia*
donate, to *donar, contribuir*
donation *donación*
done, work *trabajo realizado*
donor *donador*
dormant balance *saldo inactivo*
- partner *socio comanditario*
double *doble*
- damages *indemnización doble*
- dealing *falsedad, engaño*
- entry *partida doble*
- entry book-keeping *contabilidad por partida*

doble
- indemnity *doble indemnización*
- liability *doble responsabilidad*
- page spread *anuncio a doble página*
- standard *patrón doble*
- taxation *doble tributación*
doubt *duda, indecisión*
doubtful account *cuenta de cobro dudoso*
- debt *deudor dudoso*
down payment *pago al contado*
- period *período de cierre por reparaciones*
- rated output *producción disminuída*
- swing *fase descendente*
- tools, to *cerrar en el trabajo, declararse en huelga*
- turn *receso económico, fase de depresión*
-, laid *entregado, puesto*
-, to close *cerrar una fábrica, terminar la emisión*
-, write *rebajar el valor*
downgrading *depreciación de productos*
downing of tools *cesación del trabajo*
downward bias *sesgo por defecto*
- motion *movimiento descendente*
- trend *tendencia a la baja*
draft *plano, dibujo, diseño, trazado, borrador, esquema, minuta, anteproyecto, letra de cambio, orden de pago, libramiento*
- agreement *proyecto de contrato*
- allowance *rebaja por pérdida de peso·*
- at sight *letra o efecto a la vista*
- convention *proyecto de convenio*
- maturity *vencimiento del giro o efecto*
- payment *pago por letra*
- register *registro de giros librados*
- specification *proyecto de especificación*
-, acceptance of a *aceptación de una letra*
-, accepted *letra aceptada*
-, accommodation *letra de favor*
-, bank *giro bancario*
-, clean *giro sin documentos*
-, collection *giro de cobro*
-, commercial *giro comercial*
-, commodity *letra para compraventa de productos*
-, demand *letra, giro a la vista*
-, local *letra de plaza*
-, rough *borrador*
-, sight *letra a la vista*
-, time *giro a plazo*
-, trade *giro comercial*
drafting board *tablero de dibujo*
- committee *comité de redacción*
- costs *gastos de estudio*
- equipment *equipo de dibujo*

- machine *máquina de dibujar*
- room *sala de dibujo*
- table *mesa de dibujo*
- tool *útil de dibujo*
drafts and estimates *planos y presupuestos*
draftsman *delineante, jefe de dibujantes, redactor*
drag *rémora, avanzar lentamente*
draw, to *girar*
- a bill *girar una letra*
- a cheque *extender un cheque*
- interest *producir intereses*
drawback *devolución*
drawee *girado, librado*
drawer *girador*
drawing account *cuenta de anticipos*
-, specifications *diseño o esquema de especificaciones*
dresser, window- *escaparatista, decorador de escaparates, aparadorista (A)*
dressing, window- *componer escaparates, decoración de escaparates*
drive *campaña publicitaria, impulso, instinto*
-, export *campaña en favor de la exportación*
drives, motivation *impulsos de motivación*
drugstore (Am) *farmacia, drugstore*
drum, address *tambor de direcciones*
drummer (Am) *viajante comercial*
dry cargo vessel *barco de carga seca*
- goods store *paquetería*
due amount *suma debida*
- data *fecha prevista de terminación*
-, bills *documentos vencidos, documentos por pagar*
-, to fall *vencer*
dummy stock *acciones de propiedad simulada*
- stockholder *tenedor ficticio de acciones de otros*
dumping *depósito, venta bajo coste, rebaja desleal de precios*
-, obnoxious *dumping ofensivo y activo*
-, to offset *neutralizar el dumping*
duplicating machine operator *operador de máquina multicopista*
-, stencil *multicopista de estarcido*
duplicator *multicopista, duplicadora*
-, direct *multicopista de líquido*
-, fluid *multicopista de fluido*
-, offset *multicopista offset*
-, spirit *multicopista de azográfica*
-, stencil *multicopista de estarcido*
durable goods *mercancías duraderas*
durables, consumer *bienes durables de consumo*
duration of apprenticeship *duración del aprendizaje*

duties, consumption *derechos de consumo*
–, death *impuestos de sucesión*
–, excise *impuestos indirectos*
–, fixed *derechos fijos*
–, port *derechos portuarios*
–, revenue *derechos fiscales*
–, rights and *derechos y deberes*
–, schedule of *arancel*
–, seasonal *derechos arancelarios de temporada*
–, stamp *impuesto del timbre*

–, succession *impuestos de sucesión*
–, transit *derechos de tránsito*
duty chart *asignación de las horas*
–, amount of *adeudo*
–, compensatory *impuesto compensatorio*
–, customs *derechos de aduana*
–, export *derechos de exportación*
–, import *derechos de importación*
–, protective *derechos proteccionistas*
dynamic administration *administración dinámica*

E

earmarked *reservado*
- gold *oro en consignación, oro en custodia*
- sale *venta reservada*
- for *destinado a*
earn one's keep, to *ganarse la vida*
earned *ganado, devengado*
- income *ingreso devengado*
- interest *interés devengado, interés acumulado*
- rate *ganancia por hora o por unidad de tiempo*
- surplus *beneficios acumulados*
earner, wage *asalariado*
earnest money *dinero en garantía, dinero en prenda*
earning, hourly *ganancia por hora o por unidad de tiempo*
-, retained *beneficios no distribuidos*
earnings *ingresos, ganancias, utilidades, haberes*
- curve *curva de ganancia, curva de salarios*
- sheet *boletín de primas*
- statement *estado de pérdidas y ganancias*
-, business *utilidades o ganancias de la empresa*
-, expected *ganancias previstas*
-, gross *ganancias brutas*
-, gross average *promedio de ingresos brutos*
-, incentive *prima, bonificación*
-, net *ganancias o utilidades netas*
-, pooled *ganancias puestas a fondo común*
-, potential *ganancias potenciales, ganancias previstas*
-, pre-tax *ganancias antes de los impuestos*
-, total piecework *ingresos globales en salarios por piezas*
easy *fácil*
- market *mercado fácil, mercado en baja*
- money *crédito fácil, mercado fácil de dinero*
- payments *facilidades de pago*
- payments, by *con facilidades de pago*
- terms *facilidades de pago*
econometrics *econometría*
economic *económico, de economía*
- aid *ayuda económica*
- control, comprehensive *control económico comprensivo*
- costs *costos económicos*

- cycle *ciclo económico*
- determinism *determinismo económico*
- development *desarrollo económico*
- education *educación económica*
- events, sequence of *serie de fenómenos económicos*
- flow *corriente económica*
- growth *crecimiento económico*
- ignorance *ignorancia económica*
- pattern *estructura económica*
- policy *política económica, coyuntura económica, sistema económico*
- process *proceso económico*
- sanctions *sanciones económicas*
- stability *estabilidad económica*
- stagnation *estanamiento económico*
- system *sistema económico*
- trends, basic *tendencias económicas básicas*
- warfare *guerra económica*
economics *economía*
-, classical *economía clásica*
-, consumer *aspectos económicos del consumo*
-, welfare *economía para el bienestar familiar*
economy *economía*
- of abundance *economía de abundancia*
- of scarcity *economía de escasez*
-, cash *economía monetaria*
-, controlled *economía dirigida*
-, deficit *economía deficitaria*
-, home *economía doméstica*
-, managed *economía dirigida*
-, motion *economía de movimientos*
-, non-cash *economía no monetaria*
-, one-crop *economía de monocultivo*
-, planned *economía dirigida*
-, subsistence *economía de subsistencia*
edition *edición*
editor *director, editor*
editorial *editorial, artículo de fondo*
education *formación, enseñanza, instrucción*
-, consumer *educación de consumidor*
-, economic *educación económica*
-, industrial *enseñanza vocacional*
-, public *educación pública*
effect *producción, efecto*
- payment, to *efectuar el pago*
-, accumulative *efecto acumulativo*

–, inflationary *efecto inflacionista*
effective *efectivo*
– demand *demanda efectiva*
– depreciation factor *factor real de la demanda*
– rate *tasa real*
effectiveness *rendimiento*
–, evaluation of training *valoración de la eficacia en el adiestramiento*
effects *bienes, efectos*
efficiency of capital, marginal *eficacia marginal delcapital*
–, test *prueba de eficiencia*
–, clerical *eficiencia administrativa*
–, coefficient of *rendimiento comercial*
–, commercial *rendimiento económico o industrial*
–, gross *rendimiento bruto, rendimiento total*
–, marketing *eficacia mercadológica*
effort *esfuerzo*
–, aggressive sales *esfuerzo combativo de ventas*
–, all-out *esfuerzo máximo*
–, selling *esfuerzo de ventas*
efforts, advertising *esfuerzos de publicidad*
–, marketing *esfuerzos de exploración mercadológica*
elapsed time *tiempo trascurrido, período de observación*
elastic demand *demanda elástica*
electric adding machine *máquina eléctrica de sumar*
– punched-card accounting machine *máquina eléctrica contable de fichas perforadas*
electrical applicances *artículos electrodomésticos*
electronic adder *sumadora electrónica*
– book-keeping machine *máquina electrónica de contabilidad*
– brain *cerebro electrónico*
– computer *calculadora electrónica*
– data processing *elaboración electrónica de datos, sistematización electrónica de datos*
– data-processing machine *máquina electrónica de elaboración de datos*
– dictating machine *máquina electrónica de dictado*
– engineer *técnico electrónico*
– filing-cabinet *archivador electrónico*
– integrated data-processing equipment *equipo electrónico de elaboración e integración de datos*
– numerical integrator and computer *calculadora e integradora numérica electrónica*
– sorter *clasificadora electrónica*

electronics *electrónica*
element *elemento*
– breakdown *descomposición de elementos*
–, cyclic *elemento cíclico, regular, o repetitivo*
–, external *elemento externo*
–, foreign *elemento extraño*
–, incidental *elemento irregular o extraño*
–, intermittent *elemento irregular o extraño*
–, motion *elemento de movimiento*
–, non-cyclic *elemento no cíclico, elemento extraño*
–, occasional *elemento irregular o extraño*
–, repetitive *elemento cíclico, regular o repetitivo*
–, work *elemento de trabajo*
embargo *embargo, prohibición*
embezzle, to *desfalcar*
embezzlement *desfalco*
emergency funds *fondo para casos imprevistos, fondos de previsión*
emotional block *bloqueo emocional*
empirical test method *método de prueba empírico*
employee *empleado, dependiente, obrero*
– benefit programme *programa a beneficio de empleados y obreros*
– co-operation *cooperación de los empleados y obreros*
– employer co-operation *cooperación entre patronos y obreros*
– handbook *manual del empleado*
– manual *manual del empleado*
– participation in management *participación obrera en la dirección, jurado de empresa*
– rating form *formulario para valorar los méritos del obrero*
– relations, employer- *cooperación entre patronos y obreros*
employees, government *empleados públicos, funcionarios*
–, part-time *empleados sólo parte de la jornada*
-'s earnings ledger *libro mayor de devengos de empleados*
– settlement *liquidación para los empleados*
– training *adiestramiento de los empleados*
– welfare expenses *gastos para servicio social de los obreros*
employer *patrón, empresario, dueño, propietario, jefe, contratista*
– co-operation, employee- *cooperación entre patronos y obreros*
– employee relations *relaciones entre empresario y obrero*
– of labour *contratista de trabajo*
– union co-operation *cooperación entre*

patronos y obreros
-'s liability *responsabilidad del patrono*
-'s liability insurance *seguro contra responsabilidades patronales*
employers' association *asociación patronal*
– representative *representante de los patronos*
employment *empleo, contrato de trabajo*
– agency *agencia de colocaciones*
– bureau *oficina de colocación*
– clause *cláusula de empleo*
– contract *contrato de trabajo*
– exchange *bolsa de trabajo*
– exchange register *registro o inscripción de bolsa de trabajo*
– function *función de empleo*
– index number *índice de ocupación*
– interviews *entrevistas de colocación*
– legislation *legislación laboral*
– offered *oferta de trabajo, empleo vacante*
– register *registro de colocaciones*
–, actual *ocupación real*
–, full *empleo total*
–, full-time *empleo de jornada completa*
–, gainful *ocupación lucrativa o provechosa*
–, part-time *jornada reducida*
–, volume of *volumen de ocupación*
emporium *gran establecimiento de venta*
empty set *conjunto vacío*
enclosure *anexo*
encumbrance *gravamen, carga*
end of period *fin de ejercicio*
– product *producto final*
– investment company, closed- *empresa inversionista de capital limitado*
–, open *de capital variable, sin límite de importe, programa abierto*
endeavour *esfuerzo*
–, to *esforzarse*
endorsable *endosable*
endorse, to *endosar*
endorsement *endoso*
–, absolute *endoso absoluto*
–, accommodation *endoso por aval*
–, anomalous *endoso irregular*
–, conditional *endoso condicional*
–, liability for *responsabilidad por endoso o aval*
–, non-restrictive *endoso sin restricciones*
–, previous *endoso anterior*
–, qualified *endoso condicional*
endow, to *dotar*
endowment *dote, fundación*
– policy *póliza dotal*
enforcement *ejecución de una ley*
engineer *ingeniero, técnico, experto, maquinista*

–, development *técnico proyectista*
–, electronic *técnico electrónico*
–, freelance *ingeniero que trabaja por su cuenta*
–, information *técnico de información*
–, lighting *ingeniero luminotécnico*
–, methods *ingeniero encargado del estudio de métodos*
–, planning *ingeniero encargado del planeamiento*
–, project *ingeniero proyectista*
–, radio *técnico en radio*
–, research *técnico investigador*
–, sales *técnico de ventas*
–, standards *ingeniero de normalización o tipificación*
–, television *técnico en televisión*
–, valuation *técnico tasador*
engineering data design *datos técnicos para proyectos*
– development schedule *programa técnico del desarrollo de fabricación*
– research *investigación industrial*
– staff, design *personal de estudios*
–, administration *técnica administrativa*
–, production *estudio de métodos*
–, radio *técnica radiofónica*
–, television *técnica televisiva*
engross, to *monopolizar, acaparar*
enlarge, to *aumentar*
enrol, to *inscribir, inscribirse*
entente *convenio, pacto*
enterprise *empresa*
–, free *libertad de empresa, iniciativa privada*
–, government *empresa estatal*
–, profitable *empresa rentable*
–, private *empresa privada, iniciativa privada*
–, retail *empresa o tienda al detalle*
enterprises, commercial *razón social, empresa o casa comercial*
enterprising merchant *comerciante emprendedor*
entity, legal *persona moral*
entrepreneur *empresario*
entries, closing *partidas de cierre, asientos de cierre*
entry *entrada, asiento, anotación*
– book-keeping, double- *contabilidad por partida doble*
– book-keeping, single- *contabilidad por partida simple*
– permit *permiso de entrada, permiso de declaración aduanal*
–, adjusting *asiento de ajuste*
–, adjustment *asiento regulador o de regulación*

–, age at *edad de ingreso*
–, bill of *declaración aduanal*
–, blind *asiento confuso*
–, book *asiento contable, partida*
–, book of original *libro diario o de primera entrada*
–, cash *asiento de caja*
–, credit *asiento de abono*
–, cross *asiento cruzado*
–, debit *asiento de cargo*
–, double *partida doble*
–, journal *asiento de diario*
–, ledger *asiento de mayor*
–, original *asiento en el diario, primera entrada*
–, port of *puerto de entrada, puerto fiscal*
–, readjusting *contrapartida*
–, simple *partida simple*
envelope sealer *cierra-sobres*
–, pay *sobre con la paga*
e.o.m. dating *vencimiento a fin de mes*
equal pay for equal work *igual renumeración por igual trabajo*
equalization fund *fondo de estabilización, caja decompensación*
equate, to *igualar*
equated date *fecha media de vencimiento*
equation, human *factor humano*
equilibrium *equilibrio*
– profit *ganancia normal o de equilibrio*
– value *valor de equilibrio*
equipment *equipo, medios de producción*
– bond *bono sobre equipo*
– standards, office *normalización de equipos de oficina*
– trust *escritura fiduciaria sobre equipo*
–, ancillary *equipo variado o complementario*
–, data-processing *equipo de sistematización de datos*
–, drafting *equipo de dibujo*
–, electronic integrated data-processing *equipo electrónico de elaboración e integración de datos*
–, non-expendable *equipo permanente*
–, permanent *equipo fijo*
–, office *equipo de oficinas*
–, stationery *equipo de material de escritorio*
–, used *planta de segunda mano, equipo usado*
equitable *equitativo*
equities *acciones, derechos sobre el activo*
equitiy *patrimonio neto, capital propio, fondos o recursos económicos*
– funds *fondos en títulos*
eraser *borrador*
errand-boy *recadero*
error *error*

– choice technique *técnica de selección de errores*
– direction measurement *medición de la dirección del error*
–, accumulative *error acumulativo*
–, administrative *tolerancia*
–, admissible *tolerancia*
–, aggregate *error total*
–, allowable *error admisible*
–, allowable closing *error admisible de cierre*
–, by trial and *por tanteos*
–, compensating *error de compensación*
–, mean square *error cuadrático medio*
–, non-sampling *error ajeno al muestreo*
–, normal sampling *error normal de muestreo*
–, prescribed *error prescrito*
–, prescribed range of *amplitud de error prescrito*
–, random *error de azar*
–, sampling *error de muestreo*
–, standard *error típico*
–, systematic *error constante*
–, trial and *método de tanteos*
errors, pooling of *combinación de errores*
escalator *escalera rodante, escalera mecánica*
– clause *cláusula sobre el tipo graduable de salario*
escape clause *cláusula de escape*
– clause, wage *cláusula de revisión de salarios*
escrow *garantía, plica*
established claim *reclamación reconocida*
establishment, branch *sucursal*
–, business *casa de comercio*
–, staff *plantilla de personal asesor*
estate *propiedad, hacienda, bienes*
– agent *corredor de bienes inmuebles raices*
– tax *impuesto sobre sucesiones*
–, personal *bienes, muebles, bienes personales*
–, improved real- *predio edificado*
–, joint *propiedad mancomunada*
estimate, actuarial *estimación actuaria*
–, rough *presupuesto aproximado*
estimated ratio *razón estimativa*
– time *tiempo estimado*
estimates *cálculos, estimaciones*
–, budget *cálculo, proyecto del presupuesto*
–, drafts and *planos y presupuestos*
–, expenditure *cálculos de gastos*
–, income *cálculos de ingreso*
–, main *cálculos básicos*
–, supplementary *cálculos adicionales*
estimator *estimador, calculador*
–, maximum likelihood *estimador del máximo de verosimilitud*
evade, to *evadir*
evader *evasor*

evaluate, to *valuar, tasar*
evaluated rate *tarifa de valoración*
evaluation *avalúo, valoración*
– of training effectiveness *valoración de la eficacia en el adiestramiento*
– programme, comprehensive *programa de evaluación completa*
– scale, job *escala de valoración del trabajo*
–, function *valoración de funciones*
–, job *valoración de trabajos*
evaluator, job *encargado de la valoración de trabajos*
even number *número par*
– point, break- *punto de equilibrio*
–, to break *cubrir gastos, lograr un equilibrio entre pérdidas y ganancias*
ex-dock *puesto en el muelle, franco en el muelle*
examination, close *examen minucioso, examen atento*
examiners, bank *auditores, inspectores bancarios*
exceed, to *exceder*
excess profit tax *impuesto sobre beneficios extraordinarios,impuesto sobre exceso de utilidades*
– work allowance *suplemento por variación del método*
exchange *cambio, bolsa*
– assets, foreign *activo en divisas*
– at par *cambio a la par*
– control *control de cambios*
– department, foreign *sección de cambio extranjero*
– devaluation *pérdida por conversión de la moneda*
– discount *pérdida por conversión de la moneda*
– margin *margen de cambio*
– permit *permiso, autorización de cambio*
– permit, foreign *permiso para operar con divisas*
– premium *beneficio de cambio*
– rate *tipo de cambio*
– rates, multiple *tasas múltiples*
– register, employment *registro o inscripción de bolsa de trabajo*
– standard, gold *patrón cambio oro*
– value *valor en cambio*
–, agent of *agente de cambio, corredor de bolsa*
–, bill of inland *letra de cambio interna*
–, closing rate of *cambio de precio de cierre*
–, controlled *cambio controlado*
–, employment *bolsa de trabajo*
–, first of *primera de cambio*

–, fixed rate of *tipo de cambio fijo*
–, foreign *cambio extranjero*
–, labour *oficina de colocación*
–, quotations stock *boletín de cambios en bolsa*
–, rate of *tipo de cambio*
–, real rate of *tipo de cambio real*
–, sight rate of *cambio a la vista*
–, spot *cambio del día*
–, sterling *divisas en libras esterlinas*
–, stock *bolsa de comercio o de valores, bolsa de corredores*
exchanges, commodity *bolsa de productos*
exchequer bonds *bonos de la tesorería*
excise duties *impuestos indirectos*
– tax *impuestos sobre ventas*
exclusive *exclusivo, reservado*
– classes, mutually *clases mutualmente excluyentes*
– rights *derechos exclusivos*
– territory *territorio, mercado reservado*
exclusivity stipulation competition clause *cláusula contractual de exclusividad*
execute a contract, to *firmar un contrato*
executed trust *fideicomiso formalizado*
executive *ejecutivo, funcionario*
– ability *capacidad directiva*
– assistant *ayudante de dirección*
– committee *comité ejecutivo*
– judgement *criterio de los directivos*
– session *sesión ejecutiva*
–, market *jefe comercial, jefe de ventas*
–, pricing *directivo que fija los precios*
executives, chief *altos directivos*
–, marketing *directivos de la distribución*
executor *albacea*
exempt *exento, libre*
–, tax- *exento o libre de impuestos*
exemption *exención, franquicia*
–, personal *exención personal*
–, reciprocal *exención recíproca*
exertion *esfuerzo*
exogenous change *alteración económica debida a factores no económicos*
expand, to *aumentar, inflar*
expanded data *datos inflados*
expansible market *mercado extensible*
expansion, business *expansión del mercado*
–, vertical *expansión vertical*
expectancy, life *probabilidad de vida*
expectation of gain, mathematical *previsión matemática de ganancias*
–, change in *cambio de las previsiones*
expectations, current *previsiones actuales*
expected attainment *ejecución prevista*
– earnings *ganancias previstas*

– performance *ejecución prevista*
– salary *salario deseado*
– sales *ventas en expectativa, ventas esperadas*
expedients, financial *expedientes financieros*
expendable *gastable, desechable*
expended work *trabajo consumido*
expenditure *gasto, inversión, desembolso*
– control *control de gastos*
– estimates *cálculos de gastos*
–, government *gastos públicos*
expenditures, capital *gastos de capital*
–, current *gastos corrientes*
–, family living *gastos de mantenimiento de la familia*
–, marginal *gastos marginales*
–, net *gastos netos*
–, operating *gastos de explotación*
–, revenue *desembolsos de ingresos*
–, to pare down *reducir los gastos*
expense *gasto, coste, desembolso, pérdida*
– account *cuenta de gastos*
– centre, accounting *contabilidad de gastos centralizados*
– fund, advance *fondo de anticipo para gastos*
– voucher *comprobante de gasto*
–, non-recurring *gastos ocasionales*
expenses account classification *clasificación de las cuentas de gastos*
– at buyer's cost *gastos a cargo del comprador*
– chargeable *gastos reembolsables*
– incurred *gastos ocasionados*
– involved *gastos a prever, gastos incluídos*
– report *informe sobre los gastos*
–, administration *gastos de administración*
–, administrative *gastos administrativos o de dirección*
–, advertising *gastos de publicidad*
–, allowable *gastos autorizables*
–, chargeable *gastos reembolsables*
–, clear *gastos cubiertos*
–, clear of all *libre de todo gasto*
–, collection *gastos de cobranza*
–, credit and collection *gastos de crédito y cobro*
–, direct selling *gastos de la venta directa*
–, extraordinary *gastos extraordinarios*
–, family *gastos familiares*
–, financial *gastos de financiación*
–, general *gastos generales*
–, general distribution *gastos generales de distribución*
–, handling *gastos de manipulación*
–, incidental *gastos accesorios*
–, living *gastos de manutención*
–, manufacturing *gastos de fabricación*
–, marketing *gastos de distribución*

–, miscellaneous *gastos varios*
–, operating *gastos de funcionamiento o de explotación*
–, overhead *gastos generales o indirectos*
–, packing *gastos de embalaje*
–, petty *gastos menores*
–, running *gastos ordinarios o de operación*
–, sundry *gastos varios*
–, transportation *gastos de transporte*
–, travelling *gastos de viaje, viáticos*
–, unforeseen *gastos imprevistos o inesperados*
–, warehousing *gastos de almacenaje*
expensive discount *descuento grande*
expensive-to-make product *producto costoso de fabricar*
experience, line *experiencia funcional y jerárquica*
–, office *experiencia de oficinas*
experiment *experimento*
experimental design *sistema de experiencias, planexperimental*
– research *investigación experimental*
– stress analysis *análisis experimental de esfuerzos*
– work *trabajo experimental*
expert accountant *experto en contabilidad*
–, marketing *especialista o perito en mercadología*
experts, consulting *expertos en consultas, consultores*
–, fashion *especialistas en modas, modistas creadores*
expiration *vencimiento*
export *exportación*
– bond *fianza de exportación*
– bounty *subsidio para la exportación*
– declaration *declaración de exportación*
– declaration, shipper's *declaración de exportación*
– department *departamento o sección de exportación*
– drive *campaña en favor de la exportación*
– duty *derechos de exportación*
– house *casa exportadora*
– licence *licencia de exportación*
– manager *gerente o director de exportación*
– permit *permiso de exportación*
– price *precio de exportación*
– quota *cuota de exportación*
– subsidies *subsidios para la exportación*
– surplus *excedentes portables*
– trade *comercio exterior o de exportación*
–, to *exportar*
exports, quantum of *volumen físico de las exportaciones*
express, air *expreso aéreo*

expropriate, to *expropiar, confiscar*
extend, to *extender*
extension *ampliación, extensión*
–, credit *extensión o ampliación de créditos*
external *externo*
– accounts *cuentas de operaciones en el extranjero*
– costs *costes de distribución*
– debt *deuda exterior*
– element *elemento externo*

– flow *corriente externa*
– imbalance *desequilibrio de la balanza de pagos*
– trade *comercio exterior*
– variance *variancia externa*
– work *trabajo externo*
extra *suplemento, extra*
extraordinary expenses *gastos extraordinarios*
– profits *utilidades extraordinarias*
extrapolation *extrapolación*

F

face amount *valor nominal*
– value *valor nominal*
facilities *instalaciones, facilidades*
–, production *medios de producción, grupo de trabajo*
–, research *medios de investigación*
factor *factor, agente*
– analysis *análisis de factores*
– comparison system *sistema de comparación de factores*
– cost *coste de factores*
– cost, marginal *costo marginal de los factores*
– cost, value at *valor al costo de los factores*
–, amortization *coeficiente de amortización*
–, annual load *factor de carga anual*
–, area comparability *factor de comparabilidad de áreas*
–, balancing *factor de compensación*
–, calibrating *factor de calibración, factor para rectificar*
–, discount *factor de descuento*
–, effective depreciation *factor real de la demanda*
–, human *factor humano*
–, job *factor de trabajo, característica, requisito*
–, load *grado de saturación, carga de trabajo*
–, motivation *factor de motivación*
–, output *factor de producción*
–, tolerance *factor de tolerancia*
–, work *factor de trabajo*
-'s lien *gravamen de factor*
factors, offsetting *factores compensatorios*
–, prime *factores primos*
–, production *factores de producción*
–, rent *factores de renta*
factory *fábrica, industria, planta industrial*
– agreement *acuerdo de empresa*
– automation *automatización de las fábricas*
– limits *tolerancia de fabricación*
– manager *director de fábrica*
– order *orden de fabricación o de trabajo*
– overheads *gastos de fábrica*
– price *precio de fábrica*
– process *proceso de fabricación*
– supplies *suministros de fábrica*
– worker *obrero industrial*
factual information *información sobre los hechos del día*

fail, to *quebrar, fallar, fracasar*
failure *quiebra, omisión*
fair *justo, equitativo*
– cash value *valor justo del mercado*
– market value *valor justo del mercado*
– price *precio justo o leal*
– return *beneficio justo*
– sampling *muestreo correcto*
– value *valor o precio justo*
fall *caída, baja*
– due, to *vencer*
– in prices *baja de precios*
– of currency *devaluación de la moneda*
–, to buy on a *comprar a la baja*
false return *declaración de impuestos falsa*
familiarism *solidaridad familiar, familiarismo*
family *familia*
– allowance *pensión, compensación familiar*
– benefits *subvención familiar*
– expenses *gastos familiares*
– income *ingreso familiar*
– living expenditures *gastos de mantenimiento de la familia*
– partnership *sociedad familiar*
–, mean size of *tamaño medio de las familias*
–, medium size *familia de tamaño medio*
fancy goods *artículos de fantasía*
far-reaching *de gran alcance*
fares, air *tarifas aéreas*
farm operator *productor agrícola*
fashion *moda*
– changes *cambio de modas*
– experts *especialistas de modas, modistos creadores*
– goods *artículos de moda*
– paper or magazine *periódico o revista de modas*
– parade *desfile de modas*
– show *exposición de modas*
– trends *tendencias de la moda*
fastidious *escrupuloso, exigente, quisquilloso, delicado*
fatigue *fatiga*
– allowance *suplemento por fatiga*
– test, accelerated *prueba acelerada de fatiga*
–, surface *fatiga leve, fatiga superficial*
favoured nation clause, most *cláusula de la*

nación más favorecida
feasible *visible*
feasibility, commercial *posibilidad comercial*
feather-bedding *empleo de personal innecesario debido a exigencias de los trabajadores*
feature *artículo, característica*
–, structural *característica estructural*
federal *federal*
– bills (Am) *efectos financieros*
– funds(Am) *fondos federales*
– income tax (Am) *impuesto federal sobre ingresos*
federation, employers' *sociedad patronal, federación patronal*
–, labour *federación de trabajadores*
fee *retribución, gratificación, emolumento, estipendio, honorarios, cargo, comisión*
–, retaining *pago anticipado con que se ajusta el servicio de una persona*
feed, to *alimentar*
feeling *sentimiento*
fees *honorarios*
–, collection *gastos de recaudación, honorarios por cobro*
–, consular *derechos consulares*
–, licence *derechos de licencia*
–, registration *derechos de registro*
–, variable *honorarios variables*
feuilleton style, advertisement in *reportaje publicitario*
feverish market *mercado febril*
fidelity, high *alta fidelidad*
fiduciary *fiduciario*
– income tax returns, taxable *ingresos por impuestos sobre la renta fiduciaria imponible*
– money *moneda fiduciaria*
– value *valor fiduciario*
field manager *inspector de entrevistadores*
– of application *campo de aplicación, alcance*
– survey *encuesta mediante entrevista, encuesta en campaña*
fieldwork *trabajo en campaña*
figure *cifra*
–, business *volumen de los negocios*
–, sales *cifra de ventas*
file *archivo, fichero, legajo, registro, clasificación*
– away, to *archivar*
– clerk *archivero, clasificador (persona)*
– copy *copia para archivo*
– procedure *procedimiento de archivo*
– the information, to *registrar la información*
–, card *fichero*
–, data *lote de datos*
–, docket *expediente*

–, information *lote de informaciones, archivo de informaciones*
–, letter *archivador*
–, live *fichero de movimiento*
–, master *fichero maestro o clave*
–, merged *archivo embrollado*
–, mobile *archivo móvil*
–, permanent card *fichero permanente*
–, plan *archivo de planos o dibujos, planoteca*
–, resource *fichero de proveedores*
–, storage *archivador o fichero inactivo*
–, suspense *fichero de trámite*
–, term-card *fichero de condiciones de venta*
–, to have on *tener en cartera*
–, visible *archivo visible*
–, voucher *clasificador o archivador de comprobantes*
files auditing *comprobación o verificación de ficheros*
–, central *ficheros centrales*
–, transfer *ficheros inactivos*
filing-cabinet *fichero*
–, electronic *archivador electrónico*
–, steel *estante de acero para archivar correspondencia*
filing indexes *índices de archivos*
– system *sistema de archivos*
– system, wheel-type *fichero giratorio*
–, hand *clasificación manual*
–, index *índice de archivos o clasificadores*
fill, to *rellenar*
film, documentary *película documental*
final balance *saldo o balance final*
– output *producción final*
– product *producto final*
finance *finanzas*
– bills *efectos financieros*
– charges *gastos financieros*
– company *sociedad financiera*
– economy, personal *sociedad para préstamos menores*
– law *legislación financiera*
–, to *financiar, costear, solventar (M)*
finances *finanzas*
– committee *comité financiero*
–, public *finanzas públicas*
financial *financiero*
– arrangement *régimen de financiación*
– assets *activos financieros*
– backing *respaldo económico (Am), apoyo financiero*
– condition, statement of *balance general o de situación*
– expedients *expedientes financieros*
– expenses *gastos de financiación*
– incentive *estímulo financiero*

- interests *intereses financieros (Am)*, *intereses económicos*
- liability *responsabilidad económica*
- management *administración o dirección financiera*
- partner *socio capitalista*
- period *ejercicio financiero o económico*
- position *situación financiera*
- position, statement of *estado financiero*
- purchasing ability *capacidad financiera de compra*
- records *documentos financieros*
- report, annual *informe financiero anual*
- resources *recursos financieros, posibilidades fiscales (Am)*
- reward *recompensa monetaria*
- specialist *especialista en finanzas*
- stabilization *regularización económica (Am), estabilización financiera*
- standing *solvencia, grado de solvencia*
- statement *estado o balance financiero, balance general (Am)*
- stringency *situación financiera difícil*
- system *sistema financiero*
- year *ejercicio económico, año económico*

financier *financiero, economista, hacendista, rentista*

financing *financiamiento, financiación*
-, deficit *financiamiento deficitario*

findings *resultados de una encuesta o investigación*

finished goods inventory *existencia de productos acabados*
- products *productos acabados o terminados*

finite multiplier *multiplicador finito*

firm *casa, empresa, firma, firme*
- prices *precios firmes*
- signature *firma social*
-, affiliated *casa filial*
-, member of the *socio de la firma o empresa*
-, retail *empresa o tienda al detalle*
-, wholesale *empresa o casa al por mayor*

firms, accounting *empresas o agencias contables*

first *primero*
- lien *primer gravamen o hipoteca*
- mortgage *primera hipoteca*
- of exchange *primera de cambio*
- performance *estreno*
-, industrial *estreno o primicia industrial*

first-sample showing *exhibición de primeros modelos*

fiscal administration *administración fiscal*
- period, annual *ejercicio fiscal*
- burden *carga fiscal*
- information service *servicio de información*

en material fiscal
- measures *medidas fiscales*
- period *período contable, período fiscal*
- policy *política fiscal*
- year *año fiscal*

fixed *fijo, determinado*
- assets *activo fijo, valores inmovilizados*
- capital *activo fijo*
- cost *coste fijo*
- debt *deuda consolidada*
- duties *derechos fijos*
- income securities *valores de renta fija*
- interest-bearing debentures *obligaciones de interés fijo*
- investment *inversión de renta fija*
- liabilities *pasivo fijo, pasivo consolidado*
- rate of exchange *tipo de cambio fijo*
- selling price *precio fijo de venta*
- tangible assets *activo fijo tangible*
- term *plazo fijo*

fixture *dispositivo de fijación, plantilla, utillaje*
-, rotary *montaje rotativo*

fixtures *instalaciones, enseres*
- account *cuenta de mobiliario*
-, furniture and *mobiliario y equipo*
-, permanent *instalaciones fijas*

flat market *mercado flojo*
- money *moneda de curso forzoso*
- price *precio redondo o de compra*
- rate *tasa uniforme, precio global*
- ratings *valoración estimada de la actuación*

float time *tiempo de circulación de una pieza o trabajo*

floating *flotante*
- assets *capital, activo flotante*
- capital *capital circulante, capital flotante*
- debentures *obligaciones no consolidadas, obligaciones flotantes*
- debt *deuda flotante*
- liabilities *pasivo circulante*
- policy *póliza abierta*

floor manager *jefe de escena*
- prices *precios mínimos*
- stand *puesto expositivo interior*
-, selling *sección o lugar de venta*

floorwalker *vigilante o supervisor*

flow *corriente, circulación*
- chart *diagrama de circulación*
- chart, operation *diagrama de flujo de operaciones*
- chart, work *diagrama de flujo de trabajo*
- diagram *diagrama de circulación*
- diagram, form *gráfico de la serie de impresos*
- line *cadena de producción*
- process chart *diagrama del proceso*
- sheet *diagrama de avance, plantilla de*

operaciones sucesivas
–, capital *movimiento de capital*
–, commodity *corriente de mercancías*
–, economic *corriente económica*
–, external *corriente externa*
–, traffic *volumen del tráfico*
fluctuation, long-term *fluctuación a largo plazo*
–, short-term *fluctuación a corto plazo*
fluctuations, cyclical *fluctuaciones cíclicas*
–, season cyclical *fluctuaciones cíclicas de temporada*
–, secular *fluctuaciones, variaciones a largo plazo*
–, statistical *oscilaciones estadísticas*
–, stock *fluctuaciones de existencias*
fluid, duplicator *multicopista de fluído*
fly-leaf *guarda de un libro*
focal point *punto focal*
focussed group interviewing *interrogatorio de grupos limitados*
– operation, close *operación cuidadosamente preparada*
fold-over *desdoblado*
folder *folleto desplegable*
follow-up *insistencia, continuación*
– letter *cartas de insistencia*
– reminder *cartas de insistencia*
– research *investigación permanente*
– sales *ventas continuadas*
– system *sistema de continuidad, sistema de cartas de insistencia*
foodstuffs *productos alimentícios*
force, clerical *personal administrativo*
–, labour *personal obrero*
–, sales *equipo de vendedores, personal de ventas*
–, task *personal operante, fuerza para misión especial*
–, work *personal obrero*
forced *forzado, forzoso*
– frugality *frugalidad forzosa*
– sale *venta forzosa*
– saving *ahorro forzado*
force down prices, to hacer bajar los precios
forecast *previsión, pronóstico*
–, advisory *pronóstico preventivo*
–, business *pronóstico del mercado*
–, long-range sales *previsión de ventas a largo plazo*
–, producer's *pronóstico de los productores*
–, sales *previsión de ventas*
–, seasonal *pronóstico de la temporada*
forecasting, sales *previsión de ventas*
foreign *extranjero*
– bill *letra sobre el exterior*

– buying *compras en el extranjero*
– currency *divisas, moneda extranjera*
– debt *deuda exterior o en el extranjero*
– element *elemento extraño*
– exchange *divisas, cambio exterior o extranjero*
– exchange assets *activo en divisas*
– exchange department *sección de cambio extranjero*
– exchange permit *permiso para operar con divisas*
– grant *subvención extranjera*
– investment *inversión extranjera*
– investment account, net *cuenta de inversiones extranjeras netas*
– products *productos extranjeros*
– sales manager *jefe de ventas para el exterior*
– securities *valores extranjeros*
– tax credit *deducción por impuestos pagados en el extranjero*
– trade (Br) *comercio exterior*
foreman *jefe, contramaestre*
–, labour *jefe de operarios, capataz*
–, petty *contramaestre adjunto*
forerunner *precursor*
foreseen *previsto*
foresight *previsión*
forge, to *falsificar*
forgery *falsificación*
fork-lift truck *carretilla elevadora con horquilla*
form *formulario, forma*
– distribution chart *diagrama de distribución de impresos*
– flow diagram *gráfico de la serie de impresos*
– list *lista de impresos*
– or paper distribution chart *diagrama de distribución de impresos*
– procedure chart *diagrama del uso de impresos*
– process distribution chart *diagrama de distribución de impresos*
–, blank *formulario, modelo, estado*
–, budget *modelo de presupuesto*
–, employee rating *formulario para valorar los méritos del obrero*
–, order *formulario de pedidos*
–, requisition *impreso para pedidos*
–, set *formulario*
–, standard *formulario tipo*
format *formato*
formation, capital *formación de capital*
–, habit *formación de costumbre*
–, net capital *formación neta de capital*
forms *estados, cuadros*
– analyst *analista de estados o formularios*

– design *diseño de estados o formularios*
–, sales control *formularios de verificación de ventas*
forward, to sell *vender para entrega futura*
forwarding agent *agente, expedidor aduanal, comisionista expedidor*
– receipt *recibo de expedición*
foul bill of lading *conocimiento de embarque con reservas*
found a business, to *establecer un negocio*
founder's shares *acciones de fundador*
founding stockholders *socios fundadores*
fountain pen *estilográfica, pluma*
four-digital address *dirección de cuatro dígitos*
fraction, algebraic *fracción algebraica*
–, complex *quebrado compuesto*
–, compound *fracción de fracción*
fractional shares *cupones de acción*
frame *esquema, campo visual*
–, to *formar, forjar*
franchise *franquicia, privilegio, patente*
franking machine *máquina franqueadora*
fraud *fraude, estafa*
free *libre, gratuito*
– alongside *libre al costado del vapor*
– and clear *libre de gravamen*
– association *asociación controlada*
– association interviewing *entrevista de libre asociación*
– association method *método de libre asociación*
– choice *libre elección*
– competition *libre competencia*
– enterprise *libertad de empresa, iniciativa privada*
– gift advertising *publicidad por artículos de reclamo*
– gift offers *oferta de envíos gratuítos*
– goods *mercancías exentas de derechos*
– labour *trabajo libre*
– list *lista de artículos exentos de derechos, lista de personas exentas de pago*
– lunch *degustación*
– market *mercado libre*
– of charges *libre de cargos*
– on board *libre de gastos, franco a bordo*
– on rail *puesto sobre vagón*
– port *puerto libre*
– press *libertad de prensa o imprenta*
– publicity *información publicitaria gratuita*
– speech *libertad de palabra o de oratoria*
– trade *libre cambio*
– trade area *zona de cambio libre*
– trader *librecambista*
–, cost- *libre de gastos*

–, customs- *libre de derechos de aduana*
–, tax- *libre de impuestos*
freeholder *propietario*
freelance engineer *ingeniero que trabaja por su cuenta*
freeze a credit, to *suspender un crédito*
–, price- *congelación de precios*
–, wage- *congelación de sueldos*
freight and exchange, cost insurance *costo, seguro, flete y cambio*
– collect *flete por cobrar*
– prepaid *flete pagado*
– rates *tarifas de flete*
–, air *flete aéreo, carga aérea*
–, cost insurance and *costo, seguro y flete*
–, dead *falso flete*
–, distance *flete por distancia*
–, home *flete de retorno o de vuelta*
–, labour *flete terrestre*
–, ocean *flete marítimo*
–, rate of *tarifa de flete*
–, return *flete de retorno*
frequency *frecuencia*
– curve *curva de frecuencia*
– diagram *diagrama de frecuencia, histograma*
– distribution *distribución de frecuencia*
Friday, Black *Viernes histórico en que han ocurrido desastres financieros*
fringe benefits *prestaciones, beneficios adicionales al sueldo*
front page *primera página*
frozen credits *créditos congelados*
frugality, forced *frugalidad forzosa*
full *completo, total*
– bill of lading *conocimiento de embarque con responsabilidad del transportador*
– employment *empleo total*
– endorsement *endoso completo, endoso a la orden*
– pay *sueldo completo*
– price *precio íntegro o de venta al detalle*
– settlement *saldo final, finiquito*
– swing, in *plena actividad, plena producción*
–, in *por saldo de cuentas*
–, paid in *liquidado, totalmente pagado*
–, payment in *saldo, finiquito, liquidación*
full-time employment *empleo de jornada completa*
fully-paid shares *acciones cubiertas, exhibidas*
fumbling *pruebas, tanteo*
function *función*
– evaluation *valoración de funciones*
–, advisory *función asesora*
–, aggregate supply *función total de la oferta*
–, consumption *función consumo*
–, demand *función demanda*

–, employment *función de empleo*
–, intensity *función de intensidad*
–, marketing *función mercadológica*
–, risk *función del riesgo*
functional disorder *desorden funcional*
fund *fondo*
–, advance expense *fondo de anticipo para gastos*
–, capital development *fondo para equipo de producción*
–, contingency *fondo por imprevistos*
–, contingent *fondo de contingencia*
–, development *fondo de expansión*
–, equalization *fondo de estabilización, caja de compensación*
–, guarantee *fondo de garantía*
–, imprest *fondo fijo*
–, industrial insurance *fondo para accidentes industriales*
–, insurance *fondo de seguro propio*
–, mutual *fondo mutualista*
–, pension *fondo de pensión*
–, preferred stock sinking *fondo de amortización de acciones preferentes*
–, provident *fondo de previsión*
–, redemption *fondo de redención o amortización*
–, renewal *fondo de reposición*
–, reserve *fondo de reserva*
–, retirement *fondo de pensión*
–, retiring *caja de retiros*
–, revolving *fondo renovable*
–, sinking *fondo de amortización*
–, stabilization *fondo de estabilización*
–, strike *fondo de huelga*
–, superannuation *fondo de pensiones de vejez*

–, trading *fondo comercial*
–, trust *fondo en fideicomiso, fondo de fideicomiso, fondo fiduciario*
–, welfare *fondo de previsión social*
fundable *consolidable*
funded *consolidado*
– debt *deuda consolidada, obligaciones a largo plazo, pasivo a largo plazo, deuda a largo plazo*
– liabilities *pasivo fijo*
– trust *fideicomiso con depósito de fondos*
funding operation *operación de consolidación*
funds *fondos, dinero*
–, available *fondos disponibles*
–, blocked *fondos congelados*
–, cash *fondos en efectivo*
–, emergency *fondos de previsión*
–, equity *fondos en títulos*
–, federal *fondos federales*
–, imprest cash *fondos para gastos menores*
–, invested *fondos invertidos*
–, management of *administración o manejo de fondos*
–, public *fondos públicos, hacienda pública*
–, sterilized *fondos improductivos*
–, surplus *fondos sobrantes*
–, to raise *conseguir fondos*
–, working *fondos de habilitación*
furnish money, to *financiar, refaccionar*
furniture and fixtures *mobiliario y equipo*
futures *futuros*
– market *mercado de futuros*
–, business in *operación a término, negocio a plazo*
–, commodity *productos para entrega futura*
–, trading in *operaciones de futuro*

G

gag law *ley restrictiva de la libertad de opiniones o de prensa*
gain control, automatic *control automático de ganancia o ampliación*
– sharing *participación en las ganancias*
–, automatic *ampliación o ganancia automática*
–, overall *ganancia total*
gainful *lucrativo, provechoso, ganancioso*
– activity *actividad lucrativa*
– employment *ocupación lucrativa o provechosa*
gains tax, capital *impuestos sobre las ganancias de capital*
–, capital *utilidades de capital, ganancias por enajenación de bienes*
–, mathematical expectation of *previsión matemática de ganancias*
–, offsetting *ganancias o beneficios compensativos*
gang *equipo, grupo*
– boss *jefe de equipo*
– process chart *diagrama de proceso del equipo*
ganger *jefe de equipo*
gap *diferencia, déficit, brecha*
–, dollar *déficit o escasez de dólares*
–, trade *déficit comercial*
gauging *calibrado*
gear, computing *mecanismo calculador*
–, in *en marcha*
–, testing *aparato de pruebas, mecanismo comprobador*
general ability *sagacidad*
– acceptance *aceptación sin reservas*
– accountant *jefe de contabilidad, contador general*
– agent *agente, apoderado general*
– average *avería común o gruesa, promedio general*
– balance *balance general*
– clerical test *prueba administrativa general*
– clerk *oficinista*
– distribution expenses *gastos generales de distribución*
– expenses *gastos generales*
– meeting *reunión general*
– mortgage *hipoteca colectiva*

– partnership *sociedad colectiva*
– rate *impuesto general*
– shop *bazar*
– stores *grandes almacenes*
– strike *huelga general*
–, attorney *procurador general, fiscal general*
generation life tables *tablas de mortalidad de generaciones*
generator, address *generador de dirección*
gentlemen's agreement *pacto de caballeros*
genuine *genuino, legítimo*
geographic stratification *estratificación geográfica*
geometric mean, weighted *media geométrica ponderada*
getting, business- *principios que proporcionan negocios*
gift advertising, free *publicidad por el objeto, envío de muestras o novedades*
– offers, free *oferta de envíos gratuitos*
– tax *impuesto sobre donaciones*
–, deed of *escritura de donación*
gimmick *idea o artículo útil para un fin*
glamour *encanto*
glass case *escaparate, vitrina, aparador*
global progression, scale of *escala de progresión*
glut *exceso, superabundancia*
goal *meta, objetivo*
going concern *empresa en funcionamiento*
– value *valor de negocio en marcha*
gold *oro*
– coin and bullion *oro acuñado y en barras*
– exchange standard *patrón cambio oro*
– payments *pagos en oro*
– point *punto oro, límite del oro*
– prices *precios oro*
– ratio *proporción de la moneda de oro en relación con la circulación*
– reserve *reserva de oro, encaje de oro*
– standard *patrón oro, talón*
– stock, monetary *existencias de oro acuñado*
– subsidy programme *programa de subsidio del oro*
–, earmarked *oro en consignación o en custodia*
good buy *una ganga*
–, make- *inserción o emisión gratuitas*

goods *bienes mercancía, productos, artículos*
- account *cuenta de mercancías*
- and services *bienes y servicios*
- assortment *surtido de géneros*
- in process *productos en elaboración*
- in transit *mercancías en tránsito*
- inventory, finished *existencia de productos acabados*
- or merchandise account *cuenta de mercaderías o mercancías*
- partly-processed *productos semiacabados*
-, bill of *partida de mercancías vendidas*
-, bonded *géneros en depósito*
-, bonder of *depositante de mercancías*
-, branded *productos de marca*
-, canned *conservas alimenticias*
-, capital *bienes de capital o de producción, equipo industrial, elementos o medios de producción*
-, collective *bienes públicos*
-, consumer *artículos de consumo*
-, consumption *bienes de consumo*
-, convenience *artículos de primera necesidad*
-, defective *mercancías defectuosas*
-, durable *bienes duraderos*
-, fancy *artículos de fantasía*
-, fashion *artículos de moda*
-, free *mercancías exentas de derecho*
-, investment *bienes de inversión*
-, light *mercancías o productos ligeros*
-, line of *serie o línea de artículos, partida*
-, luxury *artículos de lujo*
-, non-essential *bienes no esenciales, bienes no necesarios*
-, non-monetary *bienes no monetarios*
-, piece *artículos sueltos*
-, quality *mercancías de calidad*
-, sale *saldos, mercancías de poco valor*
-, seasonal *artículos de temporada*
-, secondhand *artículos de segunda mano, artículos usados*
-, slow moving *mercancías de salida lenta o difícil*
-, to clear *saldar géneros, liquidar géneros*
-, transit *mercancías en tránsito*
goodwill *crédito, plus valía, valor extrínseco, clientela*
-, latent *plus valía latente*
government *gobierno*
- account *cuenta del gobierno*
- agency *oficina, dependencia del gobierno*
- authorities *entidades oficiales, autoridades del gobierno*
- bank *banco del estado*
- bonds *bonos o títulos del estado*
- employees *empleados públicos, funcionarios*

- enterprise *empresa estatal*
- expenditure *gastos públicos*
- loans *préstamos, créditos otorgados por el gobierno*
- monopoly *monopolio del estado*
- revenues *ingresos fiscales*
- sinking fund *fondo de reserva del gobierno*
grace period *período de gracia*
-, days of *días de gracia*
gradation *graduación*
grade rate *grado o clase de salario, clase de tarifa*
grades, commercial *calidades comerciales, normas*
grading *graduación, calibración, clasificación por grados*
graft *soborno*
grant *subvención, concesión*
- a patent, to *conceder una patente*
- credit, to *conceder crédito*
-, foreign *subvención extranjera*
-, land *concesión o donación de tierras*
-, to *conceder*
graph, distance-time *diagrama de aceleraciones y tiempos*
graphico-numerical method *método numérico gráfico*
graphology *grafología*
graphs *gráficas*
grasp *agarrar*
gratuity *propina, gratificación*
grievance *queja*
gross *en bruto, grueso, total, sin deducciones*
- amount *importe total*
- average earnings *promedio de ingresos brutos*
- cost *coste total*
- domestic product *producto bruto interno*
- earnings *beneficios totales, ganancias brutas*
- efficiency *rendimiento bruto o total*
- for net *bruto por neto*
- income *ingreso bruto, utilidad*
- laden weight *peso total cargado*
- liabilities, aggregate *pasivo bruto global*
- loss *pérdida bruta*
- margin *beneficio bruto*
- margin, maintained markup *margen comercial sostenido o total*
- markdown *rebaja total*
- national debt *deuda nacional bruta*
- national product *producto nacional bruto*
- output *producción bruta*
- premium *prima total*
- price *precio de venta al público, precio de venta total*
- proceeds *ingresos totales, producto bruto*

– profit *beneficios totales, utilidad bruta, ganancias íntegras*
– profit margin *margen de beneficio bruto*
– receipts *ingresos brutos, ganancia total*
– returns *rendimiento bruto*
– revenue *ingreso bruto*
– sale price *precio de venta al público, precio de venta total*
– sale, average *promedio de ventas brutas*
– sales *ventas brutas*
– saving *ahorro bruto*
– weight *peso bruto, peso total*
–, power in *poder sin interés del operado*
group *grupo*
– activity *actividad de grupo*
– attitudes *actitudes de grupo*
– buying *compras agrupadas*
– card, address *ficha para el grupo de dirección*
– interviewing, focussed *interrogatorio de grupo limitados*
– work *trabajo de equipo*
–, age *grupo de edades determinadas*
–, low-income *grupo de personas de ingresos reducidos*
–, socio-economic *grupo socio económico o económico social*
–, steering *grupo director*

–, task *comité de trabajo*
–, working *equipo, grupo de trabajo, medios de producción*
grouping *clasificación*
– interval *intervalo de agrupamiento*
groups, labour *grupos de trabajadores*
–, pressure *grupos de presión*
–, user *grupos de usuarios*
growth-rate, population *índice de aumento de población*
–, economic *crecimiento económico*
–, rate of *tasa de crecimiento*
guage, standard *plantilla, calibre patrón*
guarantee *garantía*
–, continuing *garantía continua*
–, letter of *carta de garantía*
–, to *garantizar*
guaranteed wage *sueldo garantizado*
guarantor *fiador*
guaranty bond *fianza*
– company *compañía de fianzas*
– fund *fondo de garantía*
guessing *adivinación*
guidance, vocational *orientación profesional*
guild *asociación, hermandad, gremio, corporación*
–, merchant *asociación de comerciantes*
–, trade (Br) *corporación, gremio, sindicato*

H

habit formation *formación de costumbre*
– training *hábitos o modo de portarse en
sociedad*
habits, consumer buying *hábitos de compra
del consumidor*
–, consumption *hábitos de consumo*
–, personal *hábitos personales*
hand filing *clasificación manual*
– -to-mouth buying *compras improvisadas,
compras al día*
– -to-mouth working *trabajo o funcionamiento
a producción al día*
–, leading *jefe de equipo*
–, on *disponible, en existencia*
–, stock in *mercancías en almacén*
–, to buy second *comprar de segunda mano*
hand-operated adding machine *máquina de
sumar a mano*
handbill *prospecto*
handbook, employee *manual del empleado*
handicap *obstáculo, desventaja*
handicraftsman *artesano*
handling device, data- *dispositivo de manejo
de datos o utilización de datos*
– expenses *gastos de manipulación*
– time *tiempo de transporte o movimiento de
materiales*
–, information *utilización de datos*
–, in-process *transporte interprocesal*
–, materials *movimiento de materiales*
hands, all *todo el personal*
handwriting *escritura a mano*
hard currency *divisas convertibles, divisas
estables*
– money *dinero efectivo, en metálico*
harmonic mean, weighted *media armónica
ponderada*
have on file, to *tener en cartera*
hawker, street *vendedor ambulante*
hazard, occupational *riesgo profesional*
head *cabeza*
– office *oficina principal o central*
–, department *jefe de departamento*
heading *anuncio mancheta*
headline *título*
–, newspaper *titular*
headquarters *oficina central o principal,
cuartel general*

health insurance *seguro de enfermedad*
–, industrial *vitalidad industrial*
heaviness *pesadez*
hedge *resguardo*
–, to *ponerse a cubierto, cubrirse*
hedging *operaciones para entrega futura*
heir *heredero*
heirs, joint *coherederos*
helper *ayudante*
herd instinct *instinto de rebaño*
hidden reserve *reserva oculta*
hi-fi *alta fidelidad*
high fidelity *alta fidelidad*
– or low sales level *nivel alto o bajo de ventas*
– or medium or low productivity indexes
*coeficientes o índices de alta, media o baja
productividad*
– rating *alta puntuación*
– turnover rate *porcentaje elevado de cambios
de personal*
high-pressure salesmanship *habilidad para
forzar las ventas*
high-speed punched-card machine *máquina
de perforación de fichas a gran velocidad*
– selling *esfuerzo intenso de ventas*
highest bidder *mejor postor*
highlights, news *noticias más importantes*
highway systems *sistemas de carreteras*
highways *carreteras principales*
hindrance *rémora, obstáculo*
hire, to *compra a plazos, compra en abonos*
–, contract of *contrato de trabajo*
historical cost *costo inicial*
history, business *historia comercial*
–, case *exposición de casos, historia de casos*
–, work *historial laboral*
hoard *atesorar, acumular*
–, propensity to *propensión a atesorar*
hoarding *acaparamiento*
–, poster (Br) *cartelera, valla anunciadora*
hold *sostener*
holder *tenedor, portador, poseedor*
–, label *portamarbeta*
–, proxy *apoderado*
holders, security *tenedores de títulos*
holding company *compañía principal,
propietaria de acciones*
holdings *haberes disponibles*

–, cash *disponibilidades en efectivo*
–, security *títulos en portafolio*
holiday, annual *vacaciones anuales*
home *hogar, domicilio, residencia*
– appliances *aparatos de menaje o del hogar*
– commerce *comercio interior*
– consumption *consumo nacional*
– delivery *entrega a domicilio*
– economics *economía doméstica*
– freight *flete de retorno o vuelta*
– market *mercado interior, mercado nacional*
– market prices *precios de mercado nacional*
– office *oficina principal*
– patent *patente nacional*
– prices *precios nacionales*
– produce *productos domésticos o nacionales*
– products *productos domésticos o nacionales*
– sales manager *director o jefe de ventas para el interior del país*
– trade *comercio interior*
–, permanent *lugar de residencia permanente*
honest *honrado, probo*
hot money *dinero adquirido por medio de transacciones monetarias ilegales*
hour, busy *hora de mayor afluencia de tráfico*
hourly earning *ganancia por hora o por unidad de tiempo*
– wage *salario por hora*
hours, after *horas extraordinarias*
–, business *horas de comercio*
–, office *horas de oficina*
–, overtime attendance *horas extraordinarias de asistencia al trabajo*

–, regular attendance *horas de asistencia normal*
–, spare *horas libres o disponibles*
–, working *horas laborables*
house port *puerto de matrícula*
– rent *alquiler de casa*
–, banking *institución bancaria*
–, business *casa comercial, establecimiento comercial*
–, clearing *cámara de compensación, banco de liquidación*
–, discount *tienda de rebajas, saldista*
–, export *casa exportadora*
–, import *casa importadora*
–, mail order *firma que anuncia y vende por correo*
–, parent *casa matriz, compañía controladora*
–, publishing *casa editora*
–, wholesale *casa o firma mayorista*
house-to-house salesmen *vendedores a domicilio*
household appliances *aparatos domésticos*
housing authority *autoridad sobre casas habitación*
– shortage *escasez de viviendas*
human behaviour *conducta humana*
– equation *factor humano*
– factor *factor humano*
hungry country, dollar- *país escaso de dólares*
hypothesis, composite *hipótesis compuesta*

I

idea *idea*
ideas, marketing *ideas mercadológicas*
idle *ocioso, inactivo*
– capacity *capacidad inactiva*
– capital *capital inactivo o improductivo*
– machine time *tiempo de máquina parada*
– market *mercado desanimado*
– time *tiempo inactivo*
idleness *ociosidad, desocupación*
ignorance, economic *ignorancia económica*
illegal *ilegal*
– interest *usura, interés ilícito*
– strike *huelga no autorizada*
illuminated advertisement *anuncio luminoso*
image *imagen*
–, body *imagen física de uno mismo*
–, brand *imagen de una marca*
imbalance, external *desequilibrio de la balanza de pagos*
imitation *imitación, falso*
immovables *inmuebles, bienes raíces*
impact *impacto*
impair, to *empeorar, deteriorar*
impending changes *cambios inminemtes*
implement *herramienta*
implementation *estructuración*
implication *implicación, deducción, contradicción*
import *importación*
– declaration *declaración de importación*
– department *sección de importación*
– duty *derechos de importación*
– house *casa importadora*
– licence *licencia o permiso de importación*
– permit *permiso de importación*
– quota *cuota de importación*
– restrictions *restricciones a la importación*
– restrictions, non-discriminatory *restricciones no selectivas a la importación*
– restrictions, policy of non-discriminatory *política de restricciones no selectivas a la importación*
– tariff *arancel de importación*
– trade *comercio de importación*
imports *importaciones*
–, aggregate *importaciones globales, total de importaciones*
–, restricted *importaciones restringidas o controladas*

impose a tax, to *imponer un impuesto o tasa*
impossibility, physical *imposibilidad material*
impost *impuesto, contribución*
imprest *adelanto, préstamo*
– cash funds *fondo para gastos menores*
– fund *fondo fijo*
–, cash *fondo fijo de caja*
improve, to *mejorar, perfeccionar*
improved real-estate *predio edificado*
improvement *mejora*
–, plant *mejora de la instalación o planta*
impulse *impulso*
– buying *estímulo a la compra*
– items *artículos atractivos o llamativos*
– process, random *proceso de impulso aleatorio*
in abeyance *en suspenso*
– advance *por adelantado*
– advance, cash *pago adelantado*
– arrears *moroso, vencido*
– arrears, accounts *cuentas atrasadas*
– between time *duración intermedia*
– blank *al descubierto*
– bond *afianzado, en aduana, en admisión temporal*
– bulk *a granel, al por mayor, en masa, bruto*
– buy *comprar por cuenta del dueño*
– cash *al contado, en efectivo*
– cost, all- *coste total*
– feuilleton style, advertisement *reportaje publicitario*
– full *por saldo de cuentas*
– full swing *en plena actividad o producción*
– full, paid *liquidado, totalmente pagado*
– full, receipt *finiquito*
– futures, business *operación a término, negocio a plazo*
– gear *en marcha*
– hand, cash *efectivo disponible, existencia en caja*
– kind *en especie*
– kind, payment *pago en especie*
– prices, all- *precios totales*
– print *impreso, publicado, en existencia*
– progress *en vías de, en curso de fabricación*
– saleable condition *en estado de venta*
– stock or store *en existencia o reservas*

– surplus, paid- *excedente de capital*
– the market *en el mercado, dispuesto a compra*
– the red *en números rojos, con déficit*
– time, all- *tiempo de presencia*
– working order *en actividad normal, en buen estado de funcionamiento, en condiciones de servicio*
–, buying *aprovisionamiento*
inability *incapacidad*
inactive *cuenta sin movimiento*
inadequacy *insuficiencia*
inalienable *inajenable*
incentive *incentivo, prima*
– earnings *prima, bonificación*
– system *sistema de prima*
– time *tiempo concedido, tiempo primado*
– wage *prima de producción*
– wage system *sistema de salario incentivo*
–, financial *estímulo financiero*
–, monetary *prima en metálico*
–, weak *incentivo amortiguado o reducido*
incentives, psychological *incentivos psicológicos*
incidence *incidencia*
incidental *concomitante, irregular*
– element *elemento irregular o extraño*
– expenses *gastos accesorios o varios*
– powers *poderes concomitantes*
incidentals *gastos imprevistos*
inclusive *todos los gastos comprendidos*
– index, all- *índice completo*
– of all charges *todos los gastos deducidos*
– rate *tarifa a tanto alzado*
– sum *suma global*
income *ingreso, entradas o rédito (A)*
– account *estado de ingresos, cuenta de ganancias*
– basis *rentabilidad efectiva*
– bond *bono sobre ganancias, contrato de renta de retiro*
– bracket *categoría de ingreso*
– categories, specific *categorías de ingresos específicos*
– estimates *cálculos de ingreso*
– from business *ingresos mercantiles*
– from securities, tax on *impuesto sobre la venta de valores inmobiliarios*
– liable to tax *ingreso gravable*
– ratio, parity *razón de partida de ingresos*
– statement *declaración de ingresos*
– tax *impuesto sobre la renta*
– tax returns, taxable fiduciary *ingresos por impuestos sobre la renta fiduciaria imponible*
– tax, federal(Am) *impuesto federal sobre ingresos*

– tax, individual *impuesto individual sobre ingresos personales*
– tax, personal *impuesto sobre ingresos personales*
–, actual *ingreso efectivo*
–, annual *renta anual*
–, business *ingresos comerciales, ingresos industriales*
–, casual *utilidad accidental*
–, disability *ingreso o renta por incapacidad*
–, disposable *ingreso disponible, ingreso neto*
–, earned *ingreso devengado*
–, family *ingreso familiar*
–, gross *ingreso bruto, utilidad*
–, marginal *ingreso marginal*
–, motive *motivo de gastos de consumo*
–, national *renta nacional*
–, net *beneficio neto*
–, net business *ingreso mercantil neto*
–, non-operating *ingresos no provenientes de la operación*
–, normal *ingreso normal*
–, operating *ingresos de explotación*
–, per capita *renta por habitante*
–, personal *ingreso personal*
–, private *ingreso particular*
–, probable *ingreso probable*
–, real *ingreso real*
–, realized *ingresos vencidos*
–, statement of *estado de ingresos*
–, taxable *bienes tributarios, renta o utilidad imponible*
–, tax-free *ingreso libre de impresos*
–, unearned *renta de inversiones, haberes diferidos*
–, unemployment *seguro de desempleo*
–, yearly *renta anual*
incorporate, to *incorporar, costituir*
incorporated company *sociedad anónima*
incorporation *incorporación, identificación*
–, act of *escritura constitutiva*
increase *incremento, aumento*
–, planned stock *aumento de existencias previstas*
–, rate of *tasa de aumento o de crecimiento*
–, to show an *arrojar o denotar un aumento*
increased cost *aumento del costo*
– production *aumento de producción*
increment, unearned *plus valía*
incurred, expenses *gastos ocasionados*
indebted *obligado, adeudado*
indebtedness *adeudo, deuda*
–, certificate of *certificado de adeudo*
indefeasible *irrevocable*
indemnity *indemnización*
– agreement *pacto de indemnización*

– bond *contrafianza*
– insurance *seguro de indemnización*
–, double *indemnización*
–, letter of *carta de indemnización*
indenture *escritura, partida, documento*
indentured labour *mano de obra contada a largo plazo*
independent variables *variables independientes*
indeterminacy, quantitative *indeterminación cuantitativa*
index *índice*
– filing *índice de archivos, índice de clasificadores*
– number *número índice*
– number, employment *índice de ocupación*
– of comparative mortality *índice de mortalidad comparativa*
– of physical production *índice de la producción física*
–, ad *índice de anuncios*
–, all-inclusive *índice completo*
–, alphabetical *índice alfabético*
–, annual *índice anual*
–, basic *indice básico*
–, buying power *índice del poder adquisitivo, índice de la capacidad de compra*
–, commodity *índice de precios de mercancías*
–, crop *índice, coeficiente de producción agrícola*
–, market *índice de mercados*
–, performance *nivel de rendimiento*
–, population *índice de población*
–, price *índice de precios*
–, production *índice de producción*
–, productivity *coeficiente o índice de productividad*
–, sales *índice de ventas*
–, sort *índice de clasificación o selectivo*
–, total population *índice total de población*
–, urban population *índice de población urbana*
–, unit value *índice de valores unitarios*
–, unweighted *índice no ponderado*
–, weighted *índice ponderado*
indexes, filing *índices de archivo*
indexing *preparación y puesta en posición*
– jig *preparación o puesta en posición de la herramienta, utillaje o máquina*
indictment *denuncia*
indirect *indirecto*
– claim *demanda por daño emergente*
– collections *cobros, recaudaciones indirectas*
– cost *costos indirectos*
– damages *daños indirectos*
– labour *mano de obra indirecta, trabajo*

indirecto
– liabilities *pasivo directo o contingente*
– production *producción indirecta*
– tax *impuesto indirecto*
– work *trabajo indirecto, mano de obra indirecta*
individual *individual, individuo, personal*
– income tax *impuesto individual sobre ingresos personales*
– investor *inversionista individual*
– order *pedido individual*
– schedule *programa o plan personal, cédula personal*
– tax-paying capacity *capacidad contributiva individual*
– work *trabajo individual*
-'s response *conducta del individuo*
inducement to invest *incentivo para invertir*
inductive method *método inductivo*
industrial *industrial*
– accident *accidente de trabajo*
– accounts *cuentas industriales*
– advertising *publicidad industrial*
– arbitration *arbitraje laboral*
– dispute *conflicto de trabajo*
– division *distribución de actividades económicas*
– education *enseñanza vocacional*
– first *estreno industrial, primicia industrial*
– health *vitalidad industrial*
– information *información industrial*
– injuries *accidentes de trabajo*
– insurance *seguro industrial*
– insurance fund *fondo para accidentes industriales*
– output *producción industrial*
– partner *socio industrial*
– partnership *participación de utilidades, participación obrera en los beneficios*
– planning *planeación industrial*
– relations *relaciones industriales o laborables*
– safety *seguridad industrial*
– securities *títulos industriales*
– society *sociedad industrial*
– union *gremio industrial*
– user *consumidor industrial*
industrialize *industrializar*
industries, allied *industrias conexas*
–, capital goods *industrias de artículos de capital*
–, key *industrias esenciales*
industry *industria*
–, staple *industria de productos básicos*
inefficiency *ineficacia, incompetencia*
inefficient *ineficaz, incompetente*
inequitable *injusto*

infant industry *industria naciente*
inferiority *inferioridad*
inflated prices *inflación de precios*
– profits *utilidades infladas*
inflation *inflación*
–, price *inflación de precios*
–, runaway *inflación desmedida*
inflationary effect *efecto inflacionista*
inflow, annual cash *ingresos anuales en efectivo*
–, capital *afluencia de capital*
–, cash *entrada en efectivo*
influence, depressing *influencia depresiva*
informal *oficioso, no oficial*
informant *informante*
information *informción, datos*
– agency *agencia de información*
– desk *cuadro de información*
– engineer *técnico de información*
– file *lote de informaciones, archivo de informaciones*
– handling *utilización de datos*
– handling equipment *aparatos de utilización de datos*
– machine, alphabetic *máquina para información alfabética*
– processing *sistematización de datos, proceso de obtención de datos*
– record *registro de datos o de informaciones*
– register *registro de informaciones*
– service, fiscal *servicio de información en material fiscal*
– source *fuente de información*
– storage *compilación de datos*
– test *prueba o test de información*
–, alphabetic *información alfabética*
–, behavioural *información sobre la conducta*
–, business *información mercantil*
–, data *información sobre datos*
–, factual *información sobre los hechos del'día*
–, industrial *información industrial*
–, market research *información en la investigación de mercados*
–, marketing *información, información mercadológica*
–, merchandising *información sobre la técnica de mercancías, información sobre la distribución en el mercado*
–, recorded *datos registrados*
–, required *información conveniente*
–, sales *información de ventas*
–, selective *información selectiva o selecta*
–, statistical *información estadística*
–, to file the *registrar la información*
–, to store *acumular información*
–, unit sales *información sobre las unidades vendidas*

informed opinion *opinión informada*
infringement, copyright *infracción, lesión o violación de los derechos de autor*
–, patent *infracción o violación de patentes*
inheritance tax *impuesto sobre herencias*
inhibition *inhibición*
initial markup *margen comercial inicial*
injuries, industrial *accidentes de trabajo*
–, occupational *accidente de trabajo, lesión*
injury *daño*
ink, copying *tinta de copiar*
inked ribbon *cinta entintada*
inland bill of exchange *letra de cambio interna*
inner page *página interior*
in-process handling *transporte interprocesal*
input *alimentación, consumo, inyección, compras, gasto, potencia, importación*
–, current *insumo corriente*
input-output *insumo producto*
input-output coefficient *coeficiente insumo producto*
inquiries *informaciones, datos*
inquiry *investigación, encuesta, demanda, pedido*
– docket *ficha de información, letrero de información*
– office *oficina de información*
–, market *indagación sobre el mercado*
–, statistical *investigación estadística*
insecurity *inseguridad*
inside work *trabajo interno*
insight *conciencia de la propia vida interior*
insolvency *insolvencia*
inspect, to *inspeccionar, revisar*
inspection *inspección*
– card *boletín de verificación*
instability *inestabilidad*
instalment plan *plan de venta en abonos*
– sales *ventas en abonos, ventas a plazos*
–, annual *plazo anual*
–, to buy on *comprar a plazos*
instalments, by *a plazos*
–, to pay by *pagar a plazos*
instinct, herd *instinto de rebaño*
instruct, to *dar instrucciones*
instruction sheet, job *hojas de instrucciones laborales*
instruction, single-address *instrucción de dirección sencilla*
–, technical *instrucción técnica*
instructions, shipping *instrucciones de embarque*
–, under *con órdenes de*
instrument *documento, escritura*
– capital *capital instrumental*

–, credit *documento o instrumento de crédito*
instruments, negotiable *instrumentos negociables*
insurable risks *riesgos asegurables*
insurance *seguro*
– and freight, cost *costo, seguro y flete*
– broker *corredor, agente de seguros*
– company *compañía de seguros, aseguradora*
– freight and exchange, cost *costo, seguro, flete y cambio*
– fund *fondo para seguros*
– fund, industrial *fondo para accidentes industriales*
– policy *póliza de seguro*
– policy, life *póliza de seguro de vida*
– premium *prima de seguro*
– trust *fideicomiso de seguro*
–, cargo *seguro de mercancía*
–, compensation *seguro de compensación*
–, compulsory *seguro obligatorio*
–, crop *seguro contra la pérdida de las cosechas*
–, health *seguro de enfermedad*
–, indemnity *seguro de indemnización*
–, industrial *seguros industriales*
–, obligatory *seguro obligatorio*
–, unemployment *seguro contra el desempleo*
–, workmen's *seguro obrero*
insure, to *asegurar, asegurarse*
insured *asegurado*
insurer *asegurador*
intangible assets *activo nominal*
intangibles *activo intagible*
integral, probability *integral de probabilidad*
integrated data program *programa de integración de datos*
– data-processing equipment, electronic *equipo electrónico de elaboración e integración de datos*
integrator *integradora*
– and computer, electronic numerical *calculadora e integradora numérica electrónica*
intellectual ability *capacidad o capacitación intelectual*
intelligence *noticia, aviso, informe, inteligencia*
– test *prueba de inteligencia*
intensity function *función de intensidad*
intensive sampling *muestreo intensivo*
interact, to *reaccionar entre sí*
interblock variance *varianza interbloque*
intercourse, commercial *relaciones comerciales, intercambio comercial*
interest *interés, rédito, participación*
– bearing debentures, fixed *obligaciones de*

interés fijo
– bond *bono para pasar intereses de otros bonos*
– collected, unearned *intereses cobrados y no vencidos*
– cost *coste por pago de intereses*
– rate *tasa de interés*
–, absolute *interés establecido*
–, accrued *interés acumulado*
–, arrears of *interés atrasado*
–, compound *interés compuesto*
–, controlling *participación de control, inversión dominante*
–, earned *interés devengado, interés acumulado*
–, human *interés humano*
–, illegal *usura, interés ilícito*
–, legal *interés legal, interés al tipo legal*
–, life *usufructo vitalício*
–, minority *interés minoritario*
–, rate of *tasa de interés*
–, to draw *producir intereses*
interest dividend *interés dividendo*
interest-free loan *empréstito sin interés*
interest-yielding assets *activo con rendimiento de intereses*
interests, merger of *fusión de intereses*
–, financial *intereses financieros (Am) intereses económicos*
–, vected *intereses establecidos*
–, vested *intereses creados*
interfere, to *interferir*
interim balance sheet *balance tentativo*
– budget *presupuesto provisional*
– dividend *dividendo parcial*
intermediary *intermediario*
intermittent demand *intermitencias en la demanda*
– element *elemento irregular o extraño*
internal audit *revisión de cuentas, ajuste interior de cuentas*
– debt *deuda interior*
– revenue *ingreso interior*
– revenue, collector of *recaudador de rentas*
– revenue tax *impuesto fiscal*
– work *trabajo interno*
international *internacional*
– tax agreements *acuerdos fiscales internacionales*
– values, theory of *teoría de los valores internacionales*
interpretation, statistical *interpretación estadística*
interruption *interrupción, espera, retraso, demora*
interval, grouping *intervalo de agrupamiento*

intervene, to *intervenir*
intervention *intervención*
interview reports *informes de revistas*
–, counselling *entrevista de asesoramiento*
–, oral *entrevista personal*
–, telephone *entrevista por teléfono*
interviewer *entrevistador, interrogador*
interviewing *acción o sistema de entrevistar o interrogar*
–, direct *interrogatorio directo*
–, focussed group *interrogatorio de grupos limitados*
interviews, employment *entrevistas de colocación*
introspection *introspección*
introversion *introversión*
introvert *introverto*
intuition *intuición*
invalidate, to *anular*
invalidity *invalidez, nulidad*
inventory *inventario, existencias*
– accounting *contabilidad inventarial*
– certificate *confirmación de inventario*
– control *control de existencias*
– records *libro de almacén o bodega*
– requirements *requisitos del inventario*
– shortage *mermas en el inventario o en las existencias*
– turnover *movimiento, rotación de existencias*
– valuation *valoración de las existencias*
– valuation, closing *valoración del cierre del inventario*
–, base-stock method of pricing *inventario a precio fijo para existencias básicas, método de precio básico*
–, closing stock *cierre del inventario de existencias*
–, finished goods *existencias de productos acabados*
–, merchandise *existencias*
–, unit *inventario por unidades*
–, valued *inventario valorado, existencias valoradas*
invest capital *capital aportado*
– demand schedule *curva de la demanda de inversión*
– funds *fondos invertidos*
–, inducement to *incentivo para invertir*
–, propensity to *propensión a invertir*
–, to *invertir*
investment *inversión*
– account, net foreign *cuentas de inversiones extranjeras netas*
– company, open-end *empresa inversionista de capital variable*
– in kind *inversión en especie*

– policy *política de inversión*
–, basic *inversión básica*
–, business *inversión comercial*
–, capital *inversión de capital*
–, direct *inversión directa*
–, domestic *inversión interior*
–, fixed *inversión de renta fija*
–, foreign *inversión extranjera*
–, gross *inversión bruta*
–, net *inversión neta*
–, productive *inversión productiva*
investments, temporary *inversiones transitorias*
investigation, close *investigación minuciosa*
–, market *investigación sobre el mercado*
–, preliminary *investigación preliminar*
investor *inversionista*
–, individual *inversionista individual*
invisible trade *comercio invisible*
– transactions *transacciones u operaciones invisibles*
invoice *factura*
– book *libro de facturas*
– price *precio de factura*
– procedure *tramitación de facturas*
– register *registro de facturas*
–, as per *según factura*
–, commercial *factura comercial*
–, consular *factura consular*
–, itemized *factura detallada*
–, proforma *factura proforma, factura simulada*
invoicing, order *facturación de pedidos*
involuntary unemployment *desempleo o paro involuntario*
involved, expenses *gastos a prever, gastos incluídos*
inwards, clearance *declaración de entrada en aduana*
irredeemable bond *obligación no amortizable*
irregular dividend *dividendo ocasional*
irrevocable letter of credit *letra o carta de crédito irrevocable*
issue *emisión de valores*
– above par *emisión sobre la par*
– below par *emisión bajo la par*
– department *departamento emisor*
– of bonds *emisión de obligaciones*
– price *precio de emisión*
–, annual *edición anual*
–, bank of *banco que emite billetes de banco*
–, bond *emisión de bonos*
–, debenture *emisión de obligaciones*
–, rate of *curso de emisión*
–, stock *emisión de acciones*
–, shares *emisión de acciones, emisión de*

valores
issued capital, company's *capital emitido por la compañía*
item *artículo, elemento, partida, concepto, suelto, renglón*
− shortage or shrinkage *merma o pérdida de mercancía*
itemize, to *detallar*

itemized account *cuenta detallada*
− invoice *factura detallada*
items, collection *efectos para cobrar*
−, impulse *artículos atractivos o llamativos*
−, par *efectos cobrables sin comisión*
−, staple *artículos de consumo corriente*
−, uncollected *artículos no cobrados, artículos por cobrar*

J

jargon, technical *jerga técnica*
jig, indexing *preparación o puesta en posición de la herramienta utillaje o máquina*
job *trabajo, tarea, actividad, corretaje*
– analysis *análisis del trabajo*
– card *bono de trabajo, hoja de trabajo*
– classification *clasificación del trabajo*
– data *datos laborables*
– description *descripción del trabajo*
– evaluation *valoración de trabajos, clasificación del trabajo según calidad*
– evaluation scale *escala de valoración del trabajo*
– evaluator *encargado de la valoración de trabajos*
– factor *factor, requisito o característica de trabajo*
– instruction sheet *hojas de instrucciones laborales*
– lot *lote de mercancías, partida de saldo*
– manual *manual laboral*
– merchant *vendedor de saldos o retales*
– order *orden de trabajo*
– planning *plan de trabajo, plan de tareas*
– performance *ejecución o rendimiento del trabajo*
– rating *valoración de trabajo*
– requirements *requisitos del trabajo*
– rotation *rotación de trabajos*
– satisfaction *satisfacción en el trabajo*
– specification *especificación del trabajo*
– ticket *bono de trabajo, hoja de trabajo*
– training *adiestramiento en el trabajo*
– value *valor del trabajo*
–, by- *trabajo hecho a horas perdidas*
–, by the *a destajo*
–, key *trabajo clave*
–, standard *trabajo tipo*
jobber *intermediario, corredor, agente de bolsa, comisionista*
–, stock- *agiotista, corredor de bolsa o acciones*
jobbery *agiotaje*
jobbing, stock- *agiotaje*

John Bull (Br) *Inglaterra*
John Doe (Am) *fulano de tal*
joint *mancomunado, colectivo*
– account *cuenta de participación o mancomunada*
– committee *comisión mixta*
– company *sociedad en comandita*
– cost *costos de producción común a dos o más productos*
– creditors *coacreedores*
– debtors *codeudores, deudores mancomunados*
– estate *propiedad mancomunada*
– heirs *coherederos*
– liability *obligación mancomunada, responsabilidad solidaria*
– owner *copropietario*
– production committee *consejo de producción de la empresa*
– property *propiedad indivisa*
– session *sesión plenaria*
– stock *capital social, fondo social*
– stock company *sociedad anónima o en comandita, compañía por acciones*
– study *estudio conjunto*
– transactions *transacciones comunes*
jointly *mancomunadamente*
journal *libro diario, diario, periódico*
– entry *asiento de diario*
– receipts *libro diario de entradas*
–, cash *libro diario de caja*
–, trade *periódico o revista de ramo comercial, industrial o profesional*
journalese *periodístico*
journalism *periodismo*
journalist *periodista*
journeyman *jornalero*
judgement *juicio, criterio*
–, executive *criterio de los directivos*
–, merchandising *criterio comercial*
junior *el menor o auxiliar*
junk value *valor de desechar*
– partner *socio menor*

K

keep *manutención, subsistencia*
– up *mantener, conservar*
–, to *guardar, conservar*
–, to earn one's *ganarse la vida*
keeping, book- *teneduría de libros, contabilidad*
key *clave*
– drive calculator *calculadora accionada por teclado*
– exports *exportaciones clave*
– industries *industrias clave o esenciales*
– job *trabajo clave*
– process *proceso clave*
– punch, alphanumeric *perforadora alfanumérica*

– punch machine operator *operador de máquina perforadora*
– station *estación principal*
–, auto-start *tecla de arranque automático*
kickback *pago que un empleado debe dar a su jefe para poder conservar su empleo*
kind, dividend in *dividendo en especie*
–, in *en especie*
–, investment in *inversión en especie*
–, payment in *pago en especie*
kiosk (Br) *kiosco*
kiting *circulación de cheques sin fondos*
knock-down price (Br) *precio muy rebajado*
know-how *destreza, habilidad, pericia, experiencia, conocimientos prácticos*

L

label *etiqueta, rótulo, marbete*
- holder *portamarbete*
- , route *ficha de ruta*
- , work *ficha de ruta, hoja de ruta*
labelling machine *máquina de etiquetar*
labour *trabajo, tarea, actividad*
- agent *agente de colocaciones*
- agreement *contrato colectivo de trabajo*
- code *ley de trabajo, derecho obrero*
- conditions *condiciones laborales*
- court *tribunal de trabajo*
- dispute *conflicto de trabajo*
- exchange (Br) *bolsa de trabajo, oficina de colocación*
- federation *federación de trabajadores*
- force *personal obrero*
- foreman *jefe de operaciones, capataz*
- groups *grupos de trabajadores*
- layoff *cese del empleo, despido del trabajo*
- laws *legislación laboral, derecho obrero*
- leaders *directivos de organizaciones obreras, oficiales de los gremios, sindicatos obreros*
- market *mercado de mano de obra*
- relations *relaciones laborales, relaciones obrero-patronales*
- saving *ahorro de trabajo*
- statistics *estadísticas de trabajo*
- stoppage *paralización del trabajo*
- troubles *cuestión obrera*
- turnover *personal de reemplazo, movimiento, rotación de obreros, cambios en el personal para mantener un número fijo*
- union *gremio, sindicato, asociación obrera*
- , allocation of *distribución de la mano de obra*
- , available *mano de obra disponible*
- , contract *trabajadores, braceros contratados*
- , demand for *demanda de trabajadores, demanda de mano de obra*
- , division of *división del trabajo*
- , employer of *contratista de trabajo*
- , free *trabajo libre*
- , indentured *mano de obra contratada a largo plazo*
- , indirect *mano de obra indirecta, trabajo indirecto*
- , migration of *migración de mano de obra*
- , mobility of *movilidad de trabajo*

- , productive *mano de obra directa*
- , union *trabajadores sindicalizados*
- , unskilled *trabajadores no clasificados, trabajadores no especializados*
labour-management cooperation *colaboración obrero-patronal*
labour-management relations *relaciones entre obreros y directivos*
labour-saving *el que ahorra trabajo, economizador de mano de obra*
labour-saving devices *dispositivos o aparatos para ahorrar mano de obra*
labourer *trabajador, jornalero, peón, obrero, operario, bracero*
- , day- *jornalero, trabajador, peón*
labouring classes *clases obreras*
laden weight, gross *peso total cargado*
lading *cargamento, conocimiento de embarque*
- , accommodation bill of *conocimiento de favor*
- , bill of *conocimiento de embarque*
- , foul bill of *conocimiento de embarque en reservas*
- , full bill of *conocimiento de embarque con responsabilidad del transportador*
- , straight bill of *conocimiento de embarque corrido o intraspasable*
lag *retraso*
- , time *retraso, retardo*
- , to *retrasarse*
laid down *entregado (en transporte)*
lamp, copying *lámpara de hacer copias*
land *tierra, terreno*
- freight *flete terrestre*
- grant *concesión, donación de tierras*
- office *oficina del catastro*
- reform *reforma agraria*
- tax *impuesto sobre terrenos, predial*
- under lease *terreno arrendado*
landholder *terrateniente*
landless *sin tierra*
landowner *terrateniente*
landslide *derrumbe, mayoría de votos abrumadora*
lapsed discount *descuento caducado*
large sample *muestra grande*
- scale *en gran escala, grande*

latent goodwill *plus valía latente*
launch on the market *presentar en el mercado*
law *ley, derecho*
– breaker *infractor de la ley*
– of diminishing returns *ley del rendimiento decreciente*
– of nations *derecho internacional*
– of nature *derecho natural, ley natural*
–, civil *derecho civil*
–, commercial *derecho mercantil*
–, finance *legislación financiera*
–, gag *ley restrictiva de la libertad de opiniones de prensa*
–, mercantile *derecho mercantil*
–, natural *ley natural, derecho natural*
–, patent *ley de patentes, derecho de patentes*
laws, antitrust *leyes antimonopolistas*
–, copyright *leyes sobre propiedad intelectual*
–, labour *legislación laboral*
–, poor *leyes de beneficencia*
–, revenue *leyes fiscales*
–, sumptuary *leyes suntuarias*
lawsuit *litigio, acción judicial*
lawyer *abogado*
lay in a stock, to *surtir sus almacenes, proveerse, almacenar*
lay out, to *proyectar*
lay-days *días de estadía, días de demora*
lay-off/layoff *despido, paro forzoso*
–, labour *cese del empleo, despido del trabajo*
lead, additional *sobrecarga*
leader *caudillo, dirigente, guiador*
–, loss *artículos de reclamo, objeto reclamo*
–, price *fijador de precios, precio piloto*
leaders, labour *directivos de organizaciones obreras,oficiales de los gremios o sindicatos obreros*
leadership *don de mando, jefatura, caudillaje, dirección, mando*
– potential *capacidad de mando*
–, price *conducción o primacía de precios*
leading hand *jefe de equipo*
– question *pregunta directa*
leadman *jefe de equipo*
leaf *hoja*
–, loose *hojas sueltas o móviles*
leaflet *octavilla*
leakage *derrame, merma*
lean year *año magro, año pobre*
leap year *año bisiesto*
learner's allowance *suplemento por aprendizaje*
learning *asimiliación*
– ability *capacidad de aprender*
lease *arrendamiento, arriendo*
–, land under *terreno arrendado*

leave, annual *permiso anual*
lecture *conferencia, sermón*
ledger *libro mayor*
– entry *asiento en el mayor*
– value *valor en libros*
–, accounts receivable *documentos de cuentas a cobrar, libro mayor de ventas*
–, employees' earnings *libro mayor de devengos de empleados*
–, receivables *libro mayor de cuentas por cobrar*
–, sales *libro mayor de ventas*
–, statistical *mayor estadístico*
–, stock *libro de acciones, auxiliar (libro) de acciones*
–, stores *libro de existencias*
–, subsidiary *auxiliar del mayor (libro)*
legacy tax *impuesto sobre sucesiones*
legal *legal, lícito*
– entity *persona moral*
– interest *interés legal, interés al tipo legal*
– reserve *reserva legal*
– strike *huelga autorizada*
– tender *moneda de curso legal, moneda corriente o legal*
– weight *peso legal*
legislation, employment *legislación laboral*
–, unilateral *leyes unilaterales*
lend, to *prestar*
– on collateral *prestar con respaldo colateral*
– on mortgage *prestar sobre hipoteca*
letter *carta, letra*
– file *archivador*
– of credit *carta de crédito*
– of credit, ancillary *carta o letra de crédito auxiliar*
– of credit, clean *carta o letra de crédito simple*
– of credit, irrevocable *carta o letra de crédito irrevocable*
– of credit, sight *letra de crédito a la vista*
– of credit, time *carta o letra de crédito a plazo*
– of guarantee *carta de garantía*
– of indemnity *carta de indemnización*
– opener *abrecartas*
–, circular *circular de publicidad*
–, collection *letra girada, carta de cobro*
–, covering *carta de presentación*
–, sales *carta de prospección*
letterhead *membrete*
–, business *membrete*
letters, follow-up *cartas de insistencia*
level *nivel, plano, etapa*
– out, to *nivelar*
–, compensation *nivel de remuneración*
–, motivation *nivel de motivación, estímulo psíquico*

–, price *nivel de precio*
–, significance *nivel de significación*
–, subsistence *nivel de subsistencia*
–, wage *nivel de sueldos*
levelling *nivelación*
levy *impuesto, contribución*
– taxes, to *imponer impuestos*
–, capital *impuesto sobre capital*
liabilities *obligaciones, pasivo, deudas, masa pasiva*
–, accrued *pasivo acumulado*
–, actual *pasivo real*
–, aggregate gross *pasivo bruto global*
–, assumed *pasivo asumido*
–, capital *pasivo fijo, obligaciones de capital*
–, company's *pasivo social*
–, contingent *pasivo contingente*
–, current *pasivo flotante*
–, deferred *pasivo diferido*
–, fixed *pasivo fijo, pasivo consolidado*
–, floating *pasivo circulante*
–, funded *pasivo fijo*
–, indirect *pasivo indirecto, pasivo contingente*
–, matured *pasivo vencido*
–, passive *pasivo fijo*
–, reserve *reserva de pasivo*
–, secured *pasivo garantizado*
–, trade *pasivo comercial*
–, total *pasivo total*
–, unsecured *pasivo no garantizado*
liability *obligación, pasivo, responsabilidad*
– accounts *cuentas de pasivo*
– company, limited *compañía de responsabilidad limitada*
– for endorsement *responsabilidad por endoso o aval*
– insurance, employers' *seguro contra responsabilidades patronales*
–, double *doble responsabilidad*
–, employer's *responsabilidad del patrono*
–, financial *responsabilidad económica*
–, joint *responsabilidad solidaria*
–, limited *responsabilidad limitada*
–, personal *pasivo u obligación personal*
–, primary *responsabilidad directa*
–, tax *activo no imponible*
–, unlimited *responsabilidad ilimitada*
liable for tax *gravable, sujeto a impuesto*
– to *susceptible de*
liaison *coordinación*
liberalization *liberalización*
licence *licencia, patente*
– fees *derechos de licencia*
–, export *licencia o permiso de exportación*
–, import *licencia o permiso de importación*
–, patent *licencia de patentes*

licences, ration out *restringir las licencias*
licensee *concesionario, permisionario*
licensing, cross- *concesión recíproca de licencias*
lien *gravamen, embargo precautorio*
– bonus *prima de compensación*
– creditor *acreedor embargador*
–, factor's *gravamen de factor*
–, first *primer gravamen o hipoteca*
–, preferred *gravamen preferente*
–, tax *gravamen por impuestos no pagados*
life *vida, efectividad*
– annuity *anualidad, pensión vitalicia, renta vitalicia*
– expectancy *duración media de vida, probabilidad de vida*
– insurance policy *póliza de seguro de vida*
– interest *usufructo vitalicio*
– member *socio vitalicio*
– of a patent *plazo, vigencia de una patente*
– table *tabla de mortalidad actual*
– test, accelerated *prueba acelerada de duración*
–, standard of *nivel de vida*
–, working *período de actividad, vida útil*
light chart *diagrama de alumbrado*
– filter *filtro de luz*
– goods *mercancías o productos ligeros*
–, address *luz de dirección*
lighting engineer *ingeniero luminotécnico*
like product *producto similar*
likelihood method, maximum *método del máximo de verosimilitud*
limit, age *límite de edad*
–, time *plazo*
limitations, statute of *estatuto de limitaciones o de prescripciones*
limited *limitado*
– company *compañía, sociedad de responsabilidad limitada*
– liability *responsabilidad limitada*
– liability company *compañía de responsabilidad limitada*
– partnership *sociedad limitada, sociedad en comandita*
– price store *tienda a precios únicos*
limited-response question *pregunta de respuestas limitadas*
limits, factory *tolerancia de fabricación*
–, tolerance *límites de tolerancia*
line *línea, renglón, especialidad, método, plan, conocimiento ocupación, empleo, serie, ramo, negocio, compañía comercial*
– depreciation, straight- *depreciación proporcional*

– experience *experiencia funcional y jerárquica*
– of business *género de actividad comercial, ramo de negocio*
– of goods *serie o línea de artículos, partida*
– of products *serie de productos*
– of samples *muestrario*
– operation *operación lineal*
– operation, assembly- *trabajo en cadena*
– organization *organización lineal*
– production, assembly- *producción en cadena*
– production, straight- *producción continua*
– sale, commodity *venta en el ramo de mercaderías*
– sampling *muestreo de líneas, muestrario*
–, assembly- *cadena de producción, línea de montaje, tren de ensamblaje*
–, below the *por debajo de los precios*
–, flow *cadena de producción*
–, picket *cordón de huelguistas*
–, price *precio límite*
–, product- *cadena o serie de producción*
–, waiting *línea de espera, cola*
linear programming *programación lineal*
liner, cargo *barco de carga*
liquid *líquido, disponible, realizable*
– assets *líquido, activo circulante, valores realizables*
– market *mercado activo*
– resources *recursos líquidos, recursos realizables*
liquidate, to *liquidar, pagar*
liquidated *liquidado, pagado*
– damages *daños liquidados*
– debt *deuda liquidada*
liquidating dividend *dividendo de liquidación*
liquidation value *valor de liquidación*
liquidator *liquidador, ajustador*
liquidity *liquidez, disponibilidad*
– preference *preferencia por la liquidez*
– premium *prima de liquidez*
–, standard of *patrón de liquidez*
list entry, alphanumerical type bar *entrada a las barras alfanuméricas para listar*
– price *precio de lista, precio de catálogo*
– price, retail *lista de precios al detalle*
–, black *lista negra*
–, check *lista de comprobación*
–, form *lista de impresos*
–, free *lista de artículos exentos de derecho, lista de personas exentas de pago*
–, mailing *lista de direcciones*
–, packing *especificaciones de embalaje*
–, price *lista de precios o tarifas*
–, routine *lista ordinaria*
–, temporary price *lista provisional de precios*

listed securities *valores bursátiles*
literature, trade *impresos de publicidad*
litigate, to *litigar, pleitar, contender*
litigation *litigio, pleito, contienda, litigación*
live file *fichero de movimiento*
living *vivo, activo*
– expenditures, family *gastos de mantenimiento de la familia*
– expenses *gastos de manutención*
–, cost of *coste de la vida*
–, differential cost of *tasa diferencial del coste de la vida*
–, standard of *nivel de vida*
load *carga, saturación*
– date *fecha de carga o de fabricación*
– factor *grado de saturación, carga de trabajo*
– factor, annual *factor de carga anual*
–, additional *sobrecarga*
–, machine *carga de máquina*
–, release *dejar carga*
–, traffic *carga de explotación*
–, work *carga de trabajo*
loading *carga*
loan *préstamo, empréstito*
– account *cuenta de préstamo*
– department *departamento o sección de préstamos*
– on debentures *préstamo en obligaciones*
– refunded *préstamo amortizado o reembolsado*
–, automatic premium *préstamo con primas automáticas*
–, call *préstamo reembolsable a la vista*
–, character *préstamo sin garantía colateral*
–, clearance *préstamo de un día*
–, collateral *préstamo con garantía*
–, interest-free *empréstito sin interés*
–, monetary stabilization *empréstito para estabilizar la moneda*
–, non-amortizable *préstamo no amortizable*
–, perpetual *empréstito no amortizable perpetuo*
–, pledge *préstamo pignoraticio*
–, secured *préstamo garantizado*
–, tied *préstamo condicionado*
–, time *préstamo a plazo*
–, to raise a *conseguir un préstamo*
–, unsecured *préstamo a descubierto o sin caución*
loans, government *préstamos, créditos otorgados*
–, low-interest *préstamos a bajo interés*
lobbyist *negociador, intrigante*
local *local, regional*
– campaign *campaña local*
– customs *costumbres de la plaza o del lugar*

– draft *letra de plaza*
– taxes *impuestos locales*
location, centre of *centro de ubicación*
lock out *cierre, dejar sin trabajo a los obreros*
log, test *registro de pruebas*
long-range *de gran alcance*
– planning *planificación de largo alcance, programación a largo plazo*
– sales forecast *previsión de ventas a largo plazo*
long-term *a largo plazo*
– debt *crédito a largo plazo*
– fluctuation *fluctuación a largo plazo*
loose copy *número o ejemplar suelto*
– leaf *hojas sueltas o móviles*
– sheet *prospecto*
loss *pérdida*
– leader *artículos de reclamo, objeto reclamo*
– statement, profit and *estado de pérdidas y ganancias*
–, absolute total *pérdida total efectiva*
–, activity *pérdida de actividades*
–, actual *pérdida efectiva*
–, actual total *pérdida total real*
–, gross *pérdida bruta*
–, net *pérdida neta*
–, operating *pérdida de explotación*
–, partial *pérdida parcial*

–, profit and *pérdidas y ganancias*
–, seasonal *pérdidas de la temporada*
–, to absorb the *asumir la pérdida*
–, to sell at a *vender con pérdida*
–, total *pérdida total*
–, unavoidable *pérdidas inevitables*
losses, annual *pérdidas anuales*
–, to offset the *compensar las pérdidas*
lost time *tiempo perdido*
lot *lote*
– size *tamaño del lote*
–, job *lote o partida de saldo*
–, stray *lote o partida aislada*
–, wholesale *lote al por mayor*
low price *precio bajo*
low-income group *grupo de personas de ingresos reducidos*
low-interest loans *préstamos a bajo interés*
low-yield bond *bono de rendimiento bajo*
loyalty, brand *lealtad a la marca*
lumpsum contract *contrato a precio alzado, en cantidad global*
lunch, free *degustación*
luxuries *artículos de lujo*
luxury commodity *artículo de lujo, producto suntuario*
– goods *artículos de lujo, bienes suntuarios*

M

machine attachment *accesorio o aditamento de máquina*
- load *carga de máquina*
- operator, book-keeping *operador de máquina contable*
- operator, calculating *operador de máquina calculadora*
- operator, duplicating *operador de máquina multicopista*
- operator, key punch *operador de máquina perforadora*
- process chart *diagrama de procedimiento a máquina*
- time *tiempo de utilización de la máquina*
- time, available *tiempo disponible de máquina*
- time, controlled *tiempo controlado por la máquina*
- time, idle *tiempo de máquina parada*
-, adding *máquina sumadora*
-, adding and calculating *máquina de sumar y calcular*
-, addressing *máquina de imprimir direcciones*
-, alphabetic accounting *máquina alfabética de contabilidad*
-, billing *máquina de facturar*
-, book-keeping *máquina de contabilidad*
-, calculating *máquina de calcular, calculadora*
-, cash register and book-keeping *máquina registradora contable*
-, cash registering and adding *máquina registradora sumadora*
-, coin-operated vending *máquina de vender accionada por introducción de moneda*
-, computing *máquina de calcular*
-, dictating *máquina de dictado*
-, drafting *máquina de dibujar*
-, electric adding *máquina eléctrica de sumar*
-, electronic book-keeping *máquina electrónica de contabilidad*
-, electronic data-processing *máquina electrónica de elaboración de datos*
-, electronic dictating *máquina de dictar electrónica*
-, franking *máquina franqueadora*
-, hand-operated adding machine *máquina de sumar a mano*
-, high-speed punched-card *máquina de perforación de fichas a gran velocidad*
-, labelling *máquina de etiquetar*
-, numbering *máquina numeradora*
-, numerical accounting *máquina numérica de contabilidad*
-, standing *máquina inactiva, máquina parada*
-, stapling *grapadora*
-, ten-key adding *máquina de sumar de diez teclas*
-, vending *máquina de venta automática*
-, wrapping *máquina para envolver*
machinery and equipment *maquinaria y equipo*
machines, business *máquinas de oficina*
magazine or review *revista*
- section *sección especial*
- supplement *revista suplemento de un periódico*
-, fashion *revista de modas*
-, monthly *revista mensual*
-, quarterly *revista trimestral*
mail campaign, direct *campaña por correspondencia*
- clerk *encargado del correo*
- order *pedido hecho por correo, venta por correo*
- order advertising *publicidad directa por correo*
- order business *venta por correspondencia, negocios por correspondencia*
- order house *firma que anuncia y vende por correo*
- order selling *venta por correspondencia, negocios por correspondencia*
-, by return *vuelta de correo*
-, registered *correo certificado*
-, regular *correo ordinario*
mailing address *dirección postal*
- list *lista de direcciones*
main estimates *cálculos básicos*
- office *oficina central*
maintenance *conservación, mantenimiento*
- costs *costes de mantenimiento*
-, annual *mantenimiento anual*
maintained markup *margen comercial sostenido o total*

make available, to *poner a disposición*
–, standard *marca corriente, tipo corriente*
make-good *inserción o emisión gratuita*
make-up *compaginación, ajuste de las páginas*
make-up pay *renumeración complementaria hasta el salario garantizado*
–, mental *carácter mental, configuración de la mentalidad*
–, payroll *confección de nóminas*
maker *autor, fabricante*
-'s price *precio de fábrica*
makeshift *improvisado, provisional*
maladjustment *inadaptación o desajuste*
man, bonus committee *representante de los obreros en el comité de primas*
–, contact *agente decontacto*
–, sandwich *hombre anuncio*
man-hours *hora de mano de obra*
–, output *producción por hora por mano de obra*
–, productive *mano de obra productiva*
man-machine chart *diagrama hombre-máquina*
manage, to *administrar, dirigir*
managed economy *economía dirigida*
management *dirección, gerencia, administración, jefatura*
– accounting *contabilidad de gestión*
– consultant *asesor de la dirección*
– of funds *manejo de fondos, administración de fondos*
– shares *acciones de administración, acciones de fundador*
– strategy, market *estrategia en la dirección del mercado*
–, business *dirección comercial*
–, commodity *reglamentación en materia de productos*
–, employee participation in *participación obrera en la dirección*
–, financial *administración o dirección financiera*
–, personnel *dirección del personal*
–, sales *dirección de ventas*
–, top *alto mando*
manager *administrador, gerente, director*
–, acting *director, jefe interino o suplente*
–, advertising *jefe de publicidad*
–, assistant sales *jefe auxiliar de ventas*
–, bank *director o gerente de banco*
–, branch *director de sucursal*
–, business *director o jefe comercial*
–, circulation *jefe de ventas*
–, commercial *jefe comercial*
–, credit *director o jefe de créditos*

–, department *jefe de departamento*
–, division *director o gerente de división industrial o mercantil*
–, divisional *director comercial de sección*
–, export *director o gerente de exportación*
–, factory *director de fábrica*
–, field inspector *de entrevistadores*
–, floor *jefe de escena*
–, foreign sales *jefe de ventas para el exterior*
–, home sales *director de ventas para el interior del país*
–, market *director o jefe de mercado*
–, market research *director de investigaciones del mercado*
–, marketing *director comercial de mercadización*
–, merchandise *jefe comercial, jefe de almacén*
–, office *jefe de oficinas*
–, personnel *director o jefe de personal*
–, plant *director de planta o fábrica*
–, product planning *adaptación de un producto a las necesidades del mercado*
–, public relations *director de relaciones públicas*
–, regional sales *director o jefe de ventas de zona*
–, sales *director comercial, jefe de ventas*
–, sales promotion *jefe de promoción de ventas*
–, store *director, jefe o encargado de tienda*
–, traffic *jefe de tráfico*
–, works *director de fábrica*
managing director *director gerente*
– partner *socio gerente o administrador*
manifest *manifiesto*
–, customs *manifiesto de aduana*
manpower *mano de obra, personal obrero*
manual, employee *manual del empleado*
–, job *manual laboral*
–, standard practice *manual de prácticas tipificadas*
manufacturer *fabricante, industrial*
-'s price *precio de fábrica*
manufacturing expenses *gastos de fabricación*
– order *orden de fabricación, orden de trabajo*
– process *procedimiento o proceso de fabricación*
– schedule *programa de fabricación*
margin *margen*
– dealer *margen del comerciante*
– of preference *margen de preferencia*
– of profits *margen de utilidades*
–, exchange *margen de cambio*
–, gross *beneficio bruto*
–, gross profit *margen de beneficio bruto*

–, price *margen de utilidad*
marginal *marginal*
– cost *costo marginal*
– efficiency of capital *eficacia marginal del capital*
– expenditures *gastos marginales*
– factor cost *costo marginal de los factores*
– income *ingreso marginal*
– proceeds *importe marginal de ventas*
– product *producto marginal*
– propensity to consume *propensión marginal a consumir*
– supplies *abastecimientos marginales*
– unit *unidad marginal*
– user cost *costo marginal de utilización*
marine *marítimo, marino*
– risk *riesgo marítimo*
– underwriters *aseguradores contra riesgos marítimos*
maritime contract *contrato marítimo*
mark, check *punto de referencia*
markdown *rebaja, reducción de precios*
– cancellation *rebaja o reducción de precio*
– price *precio de rebaja*
–, actual *rebaja efectiva*
–, budget procedures *procedimientos para rebajar el presupuesto*
–, gross *rebaja total*
markdowns, planned *rebajas previstas*
marked price *precio marcado o fijado*
market *mercado*
– analysis *análisis del mercado*
– analysis, consumer *análisis del mercado consumidor*
– analyst *analista del mercado*
– behaviour *conducta del mercado*
– executive *jefe comercial o de ventas*
– expectations *previsiones del mercado*
– index *índice de mercados*
– inquiry *indagación sobre el mercado*
– investigation *investigación sobre el mercado*
– manager *director o jefe de mercado*
– management strategy *estrategia en la dirección del mercado*
– measurement *medición del mercado*
– method *método de precios del mercado*
– price *precio corriente*
– price competition, active *mercado de competición activa*
– price method *método del precio del mercado*
– price, at *a precio de mercado, a precio de plaza*
– price, to buy at *comprar a precio de mercado*
– prices, home *precios de mercado nacional*
– rate *tipo del mercado*

– rate of interest *tasa de interés del mercado*
– report *informe del mercado*
– research *investigación del mercado*
– research information *información en la investigación de mercados*
– research manager *director de investigaciones del mercado*
– research reports *informes de investigación de mercados*
– survey *examen o encuesta sobre el mercado*
– trends *tendencias del mercado*
– value *valor de mercado, valor en plaza*
– value, actual *valor real en mercado*
– value, fair *valor justo del mercado*
–, bear *mercado bajista, especulación a la baja*
–, buyer's *mercado del comprador o consumidor, mercado bajo*
–, bull *mercado alcista*
–, bull the *especular al alza*
–, black *mercado negro*
–, broad *período de movimiento de gran variedad de acciones*
–, capital *mercado de capitales, mercado financiero*
–, cash *mercado de productos disponibles*
–, close *mercado estable*
–, closed *mercado reservado, mercado exclusivo*
–, consumer *mercado de consumo*
–, domestic *mercado nacional*
–, easy *mercado fácil, mercado en baja*
–, expansible *mercado extensible*
–, feverish *mercado febril*
–, flat *mercado flojo*
–, free *mercado libre*
–, futures *mercado de futuros, mercado a término*
–, home *mercado interior o nacional*
–, idle *mercado desanimado*
–, in the *en el mercado, dispuesto a compra*
–, labour *mercado de mano de obra*
–, liquid *mercado activo*
–, open *mercado libre, mercado abierto*
–, potential *mercado potencial*
–, quiet *mercado encalmado*
–, restricted *mercado reservado*
–, sagging *mercado flojo*
–, saturated *mercado saturado*
–, securities *mercado de valores, mercado bursátil*
–, seller's *mercado del vendedor*
–, spot *mercado de productos disponibles*
–, steady *mercado sostenido, mercado de poca fabricación*
–, stiff *mercado firme*
–, stock *mercado o bolsa de valores, bolsa*

comercial
–, strong *mercado firme*
–, thick *mercado de gran consumo*
–, thin *mercado de poco consumo*
–, weak *mercado flojo*
–, wholesale *mercado al por mayor*
–, world *mercado mundial*
marketability *negociabilidad*
marketable *negociable, comerciable, vendible*
– title *título negociable*
marketing *mercadología, técnica comercial*
– analyst *analista de mercadología*
– approach *enfoque mercadológico*
– efficiency *eficacia mercadológica*
– efforts *esfuerzos de exploración
mercadológica*
– executives *directivos de la distribución*
– expenses *gastos de distribución*
– expert *especialista o perito en mercadología*
– function *función mercadológica*
– ideas *ideas mercadológicas*
– information *información mercadológica*
– manager *director comercial de
mercadización*
– mix *síntesis de los elementos del mercado*
– process *procedimiento de distribución*
– research *investigación mercadológica,
investigación distributiva*
– situation *situación mercadológica*
– strategy *estrategia mercadológica*
markup *margen comercial, beneficio*
– cancellation *anulación del margen comercial*
– price *diferencia entre el precio y el costo*
–, actual *margen comercial efectiva o real*
–, average *promedio del margen comercial*
–, initial *margen comercial inicial*
–, maintained *margen comercial sostenido o
total*
–, net additional *margen comercial adicional
neto*
mart *mercado*
Mary Doe (Am) *fulana de tal*
mass display *exposición masiva*
– produced article *artículo hecho en serie*
– production *producción en serie o en masa*
master file *fichero maestro o clave*
– schedule *programa básico*
mat, matrix *matriz, cliché, molde*
matched samples *muestras concordantes*
material accounting *contabilidad de material*
– control *control de materiales*
– standardization *tipificación de materiales*
–, copyrighted *material o temas y obras
registradas*
–, window display *material para exposición de
escaparates*

–, working *material de explotación*
materials handling *movimiento de materiales*
–, bill of *lista de materiales*
–, critical *materiales estratégicos*
–, primary *materiales*
–, raw *materias primas*
mathematical demography *demografía
matemática*
– expectation of gain *previsión matemática de
ganancias*
matter, printed *impresos*
matters, money *cuestiones o temas
monetarios*
mature account *cuenta vencida, cuenta
pagadera*
–, to *vencer, cumplirse el plazo*
matured liabilities *pasivo vencido*
maturity *vencimiento, cumplimiento, plazo*
– date *fecha de vencimiento*
– of bills *vencimiento de las letras*
– value *valor al vencimiento*
–, draft *vencimientos del giro o efecto*
–, value at *valor al vencimiento*
–, yield to *rendimiento al vencimiento*
maximize, to *elevar al máximo*
maximum likelihood estimator *estimador del
máximo de verosimilitud*
– likelihood method *método del máximo de
verosimilitud*
– price, distributor's *precio máximo del
concesionario*
mean *promedio aritmético*
– size of family *tamaño medio de las familias*
– square error *error cuadrático medio*
– wage *salario máximo, salario tope*
–, age *edad media, promedio de edad*
–, provisional *promedio provisional*
–, weighted *media ponderada*
–, weighted arithmetic *media aritmética
ponderada*
–, weighted geometric *media geométrica
ponderada*
–, weighted harmonic *media armónica
ponderada*
means of communication *medios de
comunicación*
– of production *medios de producción, equipo
de trabajo*
measure *medida, recurso*
–, standard *medida legal*
measurement *medición*
–, error direction *medición de la dirección del
error*
–, market *medición del mercado*
–, performance *medición del rendimiento*
–, productivity *medición de la productividad*

–, work *medición del trabajo*
measures, fiscal *medidas fiscales*
meat, canned *carne en conserva*
mechanization *mecanización*
media *medio, medios*
–, advertising *medios de publicidad*
median *valor medio, mediana*
medium *mediano, medio*
– size family *familia de tamaño medio*
meet conditions, to *sujetarse a condiciones*
– specifications, to *cumplir con las especificaciones*
– the price, to *aceptar el precio*
meeting *junta, reunión, asamblea, convención, conferencia*
– of shareholders *asamblea general de accionistas*
–, board *sesión del consejo de administración, reunión de los directivos*
–, general *reunión general*
–, ordinary *junta ordinaria*
–, plenary *sesión plenaria*
–, regular *asamblea ordinaria*
member of the firm *socio de la firma o empresa*
–, life *socio vitalício*
–, ordinary *miembro titular*
–, part-time *miembro que solo trabaja parte del día*
–, regular *miembro titular*
memory *memoria*
– address counter *contador de dirección de memoria*
–, computer *memoria de máquina calculadora*
mensuration *medición*
mental *mental*
– ability test *prueba de capacidad mental*
– activity *actividad mental*
– age *edad mental*
– make-up *carácter mental, configuración de la mentalidad*
– work *trabajo mental*
– ability, basic *capacidad mental básica*
mentality *mentalidad*
mercantile *mercantil, comercial*
– law *derecho mercantil*
merchandise *mercancía, mercadería*
– account *cuenta de mercancías, mercaderías*
– accounting *contabilidad de mercancías*
– broker *corredor de mercancías*
– display *exposición de mercancías*
– inventory *existencias*
– manager *jefe comercial o de almacén*
– manager, divisional *director comercial de sección*
– pricing *fijación del precio de la mercancía*

–, retail *mercancías al por menor, mercancías de menudeo*
–, slow-selling *mercancía de venta lenta o difícil*
–, staple *mercancía de consumo corriente*
merchandising *comercialización, política o técnica de mercancías, puesta de mercancías en el mercado*
– ability *capacidad de negociar, habilidad comercial*
– information *información sobre la técnica de mercancías, información sobre la distribución en el mercado*
– judgement *criterio comercial*
– profit *utilidad comercial*
– sense *instinto de vendedor, sentido de comerciante*
merchant *comerciante, negociante, mercader, tratante*
– guild *asociación de comerciantes*
–, clever *comerciante experto*
–, commission *comisionista*
–, enterprising *comerciante emprendedor*
–, job *vendedor de saldos o retales*
–, wholesale *comerciante al por mayor*
merge, to *fusionarse, unir, combinar, intercalarse*
merged card *ficha intercalada*
– company *compañía fusionada*
– file *archivo embrollado*
merger *fusión, incorporación, unión*
– of interests *fusión de intereses*
merit rating *valoración de méritos*
message *mensaje, comunicación*
messenger *meritorio, mensajero, botones*
method *método, procedimiento*
– of selected points *método de los puntos elegidos*
–, actual value *método del valor actual*
–, component *método de los componentes*
–, cost value *método del valor de coste*
–, empirical test *método de prueba empírico*
–, free-association *método de libre asociación*
–, graphico-numerical *método numérico gráfico*
–, inductive *método inductivo*
–, market *método de precios del mercado*
–, market price *método del precio del mercado*
–, maximum likelihood *método del máximo de verosimilitud*
–, percentage of completion *método de porcentaje de terminación*
–, presumptive *método de probabilidad*
–, price of last purchase *método del precio de la última compra*
–, ranking *método de jerarquización*

–, ratio delay *método de observaciones instantáneas*
–, retail *método de la venta al por menor*
–, sampling *método de muestreo*
–, standard *método normalizado*
–, to devise a *idear un sistema*
methods engineer *ingeniero encargado del estudio de métodos*
– of collecting data *métodos para reunir datos*
– study *estudio de métodos, análisis de movimientos*
– variation, allowance *suplemento por variación del método*
–, commercial processing *métodos comerciales de elaboración*
–, statistical *métodos estadísticos*
metric system *sistema métrico*
microcard *microficha, microcopia*
microcopy *microcopia*
microcopying *microcopiaje, microcopiado*
microfile equipment *equipo de microrregistro*
microfilm *microfilm, micropelícula*
–, to *microfilmar, microfotografiar*
microfilming *microfilmación, microfilmado*
microsample *micromuestra*
microsampling *micromuestreo*
middleman *intermediario, revendedor*
migration of labour *migración de mano de obra*
– statistics *estadísticas de migración*
migratory worker *emigrante*
mill *fábrica, taller, molino*
mimeograph *mimeógrafo*
mind *mente*
minimize, to *reducir al mínimo*
minimum wage *salario mínimo*
minor *menor de edad*
minority *minoría*
– interest *interés minoritario*
– stockholders *accionistas de la minoría*
mint *casa de moneda*
minus *menos, negativo*
minute book *libro de actas*
–, standard *minuto tipo*
minutes *actas, minutas*
misappropiation *malversación de fondos*
miscalculation *error de cálculo*
miscellaneous commodities *mercancías varias*
– expenses *gastos varios*
miserliness *avaricia*
misleading *engañoso*
misprint *errata tipográfica*
mix, marketing *síntesis de los elementos del mercado*
mixed model *modelo mixto*

– sampling *muestreo mixto*
mob *multitud excitada*
mobile file *archivo móvil*
mobility of labour *movilidad del trabajo*
model, mixed *modelo mixto*
moderate price *precio módico, precio razonable*
modification, automatic address *modificación automática de dirección*
mogul *gran personaje, patrón*
monetary *monetario*
– gold stock *existencias de oro acuñado*
– incentive *prima en metálico*
– stabilization loan *empréstito para estabilizar la moneda*
– supply *oferta monetaria, disponibilidad monetaria*
money *dinero*
– at call *disponibilidades a la vista*
– crisis *crisis monetaria*
– matters *cuestiones o temas monetarios*
– order *giro postal o bancario*
– order, bank *giro bancario*
–, call *dinero prestado exigible a la vista*
–, counterfeit *dinero falso*
–, earnest *dinero en garantía, dinero en prenda*
–, easy *crédito fácil, mercado fácil de dinero*
–, fiduciary *moneda fiduciaria*
–, flat *moneda de curso forzoso*
–, hard *dinero efectivo, en metálico*
–, hot *dinero adquirido por medio de transacciones monetarias ilegales*
–, paper *papel moneda*
–, ready *efectivo, fondos disponibles, dinero constante*
–, spare *ahorros*
–, till *efectivo en ventanilla*
–, uncontrolled *moneda no intervenida*
–, unsound *moneda inestable*
–, to furnish *financiar, refaccionar*
–, to print *imprimir dinero*
–, to raise *conseguir dinero o fondos*
–, to waste *malgastar dinero*
–, token *moneda divisionaria*
money-commodity *dinero mercancía*
moneylender *prestamista*
monopolist *monopolista, acaparador*
monopolize, to *monopolizar, acaparar*
monopoly *monopolio, acaparamiento*
– prices *precios de monopolio*
–, government *monopolio del estado*
–, qualified *monopolio limitado*
monopsony *monopolio del comprador*
monthly magazine *revista mensual*
– (news)paper *periódico mensual*

moratorium *moratoria*
moratory *moratorio*
mortality *mortalidad*
–, index of comparative *índice de mortalidad comparativa*
mortgage *hipoteca*
– bank *banco hipotecario*
– bond *bono con garantía hipotecaria*
– certificate *cédula hipotecaria*
– debenture *obligación hipotecaria*
–, bond and *escritura de préstamo e hipoteca*
–, first *primera hipoteca*
–, general *hipoteca colectiva*
–, lend on *prestar sobre hipoteca*
–, open-end *hipoteca sin límite de importe*
–, to *hipotecar*
–, to pay off a *redimir una hipoteca*
–, unified *hipoteca consolidad*
mortgagee *acreedor hipotecario*
mortgagor *deudor hipotecario*
most favoured nation clause *cláusula de la nación más favorecida*
– powerful test *prueba más poderosa*
motel *motel*
motion *movimiento*
– analysis *análisis de movimientos*
– economy *economía de movimientos*
– element *elemento de movimiento*
– pattern *diagrama de movimientos*
– plane *plano de movimiento*
– study *estudio de movimientos*
–, accelerated *movimiento acelerado*
–, adjustable stop *movimiento regulable de parada*
–, downward *movimiento descendente*
motivating drives *impulsos de motivación*
motivation *motivación*
– analysis *análisis de motivaciones*
– drives *impulsos de motivación*
– factor *factor de motivación*
– level *nivel de motivación*
– techniques *técnicas de motivación*
– theory *teoría de la motivación*

–, basic *motivación básica*
motive *motivo*
– income *motivo de gasto de consumo*
–, business *motivo de negocios*
–, buying *motivo de compra*
–, precautionary *motivo precaución*
–, profit *motivo de lucro, con fines de lucro*
–, speculative *motivo especulativo*
–, transactions *motivo transacción*
motto *divisa, lema*
mouth, word of *comunicación oral*
movable property *bienes muebles*
movement *movimiento*
– pattern *trayectoria del movimiento*
–, business *giro de negocios, movimiento comercial*
–, constrained *movimiento controlado*
–, upward *movimiento de alza*
movements, capital *movimientos de capital*
multilateral *multilateral*
– agreement *convenio multilateral*
– arbitrage scheme *sistema de arbitraje multilateral*
– trade *comercio multilateral*
multiple *múltiple*
– activity *actividades múltiples*
– activity chart *diagrama de actividades simultáneas*
– activity process chart *diagrama de proceso de actividades simultáneas*
– exchange rates *tasas múltiples*
– rate of exchange *tasa de cambio múltiple*
– store *empresa con gran número de sucursales*
– stratification *estratificación múltiple*
– taxation *imposición múltiple*
multiple-phase process *proceso multifásico*
multiplier *multiplicador*
–, finite *multiplicado finito*
mutual assistance *ayuda mutua*
– fund *fondo mutualista*
mutually exclusive classes *clases mutuamente excluyentes*

N

name, brand *marca registrada, nombre de la marca*
–, copyrighted *nombre registrado*
–, corporate *razón social*
–, trade *nombre comercial, marca de comercio, nombre o dibujo registrado como marca*
national advertising *publicidad nacional*
– advertising media *medios de publicidad nacional*
– character *carácter nacional*
– debt *deuda nacional*
– debt, gross *deuda nacional bruta*
– income *renta nacional*
– output *producción nacional*
– product, gross *producto nacional bruto*
– road *carretera nacional*
nationalize, to *nacionalizar*
nations, law of *derecho internacional*
–, under-developed *países subdesarrollados*
native produce *productos domésticos nacionales*
natural law *ley natural, derecho natural*
– resources *recursos naturales*
nature, law of *derecho natural, ley natural*
need *necesidad*
needs allowance, personal *suplemento por necesidades personales, suplementos personales*
negligence *negligencia, imprudencia*
negotiable *negociable, transmisible*
– instruments *instrumentos negociables*
– paper *efectos negociables*
– securities *valores transmisibles*
negotiate, to *negociar, tratar*
neon *neón, tubo neón*
– sign *rótulo luminoso de neón*
net *neto, líquido*
– additional markup *margen comercial adicional neto*
– amount *importe líquido o neto*
– assets *activo neto*
– book value *valor neto en libros*
– business income *ingreso mercantil neto*
– capital formation *formación neta de capital*
– earnings *ganancias o utilidades netas*
– expenditures *gastos netos*
– foreign investment account *cuentas de inversiones extranjeras netas*
– income *beneficio neto, ingreso neto*
– investment *inversión neta*
– loss *pérdida neta*
– price *precio neto*
– process time *tiempo neto de transformación*
– profits *beneficios netos, utilidades netas*
– reproduction *tasa neta de reproducción*
– revenue *beneficio neto, ingreso neto*
– sales *ventas netas*
– sales circulation *tirada neta*
– savings *ahorro neto*
– taxes *impuestos netos*
– value added *valor agregado neto*
– weight *peso neto*
– worth *activo o capital o valor neto*
–, gross for *bruto por neto*
–, tangible *activo neto tangible*
network *cadena, red, circuito, sistema, cadena de emisoras*
– of branch offices *red de sucursales*
–, communication *red de transmisiones*
–, distributing *red de distribución*
–, supply *red de distribución*
–, television *red de emisoras de televisión*
new, brand *flamante, nuevo*
news agency *agencia de noticias*
– highlights *noticias más importantes*
–, picture *ilustración de prensa*
–, shopping *noticiarios o folletos colectivos*
–, stop-press *últimas noticias*
newscast *noticiario, programa de noticias*
newscaster *cronista de radio*
newspaper *periódico*
– advertising *publicidad en la prensa, anuncios en los periódicos*
– clipping *recorte de periódico, cabecera de periódico*
– headline *titular*
– serial *folletín*
–, monthly *periódico mensual*
nominal *nominal*
– accounts *cuentas impersonales*
– capital *capital autorizado, capital social*
– damages *indemnización nominal*
– partner *socio nominal*
nominate, to *nombrar, designar*
non-acceptance *falta de aceptación*

non-amortizable loan *préstamo no amortizable*
non-assenting stockholders *accionistas disidentes*
non-assessable stock *acciones no gravables*
non-cash economy *economía no monetaria*
non-commercial *no comercial*
non-cyclic element *elemento no cíclico, elemento extraño*
non-discriminatory assistance *ayuda no selectiva*
non-discriminatory import restrictions *política de restricciones no selectivas a la importación*
non-dutiable *franco de impuestos*
non-essential goods *bienes no esenciales o no necesarios*
non-expendable equipment *equipo permanente*
non-factor services *servicios no correspondientes a los factores de producción*
non-import restrictions *restricciones no selectivas a la importación*
non-interest-bearing *que no devenga interés*
non-market product *producto no comercializado*
non-member bank *banco no comercializado*
non-monetary goods *bienes no monetarios*
non-negotiable *no negociable, intransferible*
non-operating income *ingresos no provenientes de la operación*
non-par-value stock *acciones sin valor nominal*
non-payment *falta de pago*
non-profit-making corporation *asociaciación no lucrativa*
non-recurring expense *gastos ocasionales*
non-renewable *no renovable, no prorrogable*
non-resident *no residente*
non-restrictive endorsement *endoso sin restricciones*
non-sampling error *error ajeno de muestreo*
non-static *dinámico*
non-stock corporation *sociedad sin acciones*
non-taxable *exento de impuestos, no gravable*
non-voting stock *acciones sin derecho a voto*
non-wage-goods *artículos para asalariados*
normal *normal*
– income *ingreso normal*
– performance *actuación normal*

– residence *residencia permanente*
– sampling error *error normal de muestreo*
– sorting *clasificación normal*
– tax *impuesto normal o básico*
– time *tiempo normal*
normative data *datos normativos o normalizados*
notary *notarío*
-'s office *notaría*
note *nota, pagaré, documento*
–, acceleration *pagaré con opción de pago adelantado*
–, bank *billete de banco*
–, collateral *pagaré prendario, colateral*
–, covering *aval, garantía comercial*
–, credit *nota de crédito*
–, debit *nota de cargo*
–, demand *pagaré a la vista*
–, promissory *pagaré, nota de pago*
notebook, stenographer's *cuaderno de taquigrafía*
notes payable *documentos por pagar*
– receivable *efectos a cobrar, documentos por cobrar*
–, treasury *obligaciones del estado*
notice *noticia, información*
–, advance *aviso anticipado*
–, written *aviso escrito*
notify, to *notificar, avisar, participar*
novelty advertising *publicidad por el objeto o por artículos de reclamo, envío de muestras o novedades*
null and void *nulo y sin valor*
nullify, to *anular, invalidar*
number, average sample *número muestral promedio*
–, back *número atrasado*
–, even *número par*
–, index *número índice*
–, odd *número impar*
–, optimum *número óptimo*
–, registration *número de registro o matrícula*
–, serial *número de serie*
numbering machine *máquina numeradora*
numerical accounting machine *máquina numérica de contabilidad*
– integrator and computer, electronic *calculadora e integradora numérica electrónica*
numerical value *valor numérico*

O

object *objeto*
objective data *datos objetivos*
obligated capital *capital suscrito*
obligation *obligación, título*
obligations, advance payments on purchase
envíos a cuenta de pedidos a servir
obligatory insurance *seguro obligatorio*
obnoxious dumping *dumping ofensivo y
activo*
obsolescence *caída en desuso, vejez técnica
de las máquinas*
obsession *obsesión*
occasional element *elemento irregular o
extraño*
occupation tax *impuesto de empleo o
profesión*
occupational *relativo a la profesión u oficio*
– accident *accidente de tráfico*
– death rate *tasa de mortalidad por
profesiones*
– disease *enfermedad profesional*
– hazard *riesgo profesional*
– injury *lesión, accidente de trabajo*
– status *categoría profesional*
occurrence *frecuencia*
ocean freight *flete marítimo*
odd lot broker *corredor que compra y vende
acciones en lotes menores a cien*
– sample *muestra suelta*
of age *mayor de edad*
off, to call *dar por terminado*
off-print *tirada aparte*
off-season sales *ventas fuera de temporada*
offer *oferta, ofrecer*
–, bid and *oferta y demanda*
offered price *precio de oferta*
–, employment *oferta de trabajo, empleo
vacante*
offers, free gift *oferta de envíos gratuitos*
office *oficina, despacho, agencia*
– equipment *equipo de oficinas*
– equipment standards *normalización de
equipos de oficina*
– experience *experiencia de oficinas*
– hours *horas de oficina*
– hours, after *después de las horas de oficina*
– manager *jefe de oficinas*
– services *servicios de oficina*

– supervisor *supervisor de oficinas*
– training programme *programa de
capacitación de oficinas*
– work *trabajo de oficina*
– worker *oficinista*
–, agency *oficina de negocios*
–, collector's *administración de rentas*
–, copyright *registro de la propiedad
intelectual*
–, design *oficina de proyectos*
–, head *oficina principal o central*
–, home *oficina principal*
–, inquiry *oficina de información*
–, land *oficina de catastro*
–, main *oficina central*
–, notary's *notaría*
–, patent *oficina de patentes*
–, patent and trademark *oficina de patentes y
marca*
–, secretary's *secretaría*
–, tax *oficina recaudadora, recaudación de
impuestos*
–, tax-collector's *administración de impuestos,
recaudación de impuestos*
officer *oficinista, oficial, funcionario*
–, agent *oficial pagador*
offices, network of branch *red de sucursales*
official *oficial*
offset *cancelación, compensación,
contrapartida*
– account *cuenta de compensación,
contracuenta*
– dumping, to *neutralizar el dumping*
– duplicator *multicopista offset*
– printing *impresión offset*
– process *procedimiento offset*
– reserves *reservas de tasación*
– scale *escala de desviaciones*
– the losses, to *compensar las pérdidas*
offsetting devices *dispositivos de
desplazamiento*
– factors *factores compensatorios*
– gains *ganancias o beneficios compensativos*
old-age benefits *prestaciones por vejez*
– pension *pensión por vejez*
oligopoly *monopolio parcial o de unos pocos*
omission *omisión*
omit, to *omitir, suprimir*

on account *a cuenta*
– commission *a comisión*
– consignment *en consignación*
– credit *a crédito*
– demand *a la vista, a la presentación*
– deposit *en depósito, en el banco*
– hand *disponible, en existencia*
– rail, free *puesto sobre vagón*
– receipt *al recibo de*
– relief *viviendo de ayuda estatal o de la beneficencia*
on-the-job training *formación sobre la marcha, capacitación mientras se trabaja*
one-crop economy *monocultura*
one-price *precio único*
– policy *política de precio único*
one-sided test *prueba unilateral*
open account *cuenta abierta*
– an account, to *abrir una cuenta*
– credit *crédito abierto*
– population *población abierta*
– question *pregunta abierta o de respuesta libre*
– system *sistema abierto*
open-country population *población rural*
open-door policy *política de puerta abierta*
open-end *de capital variable, sin límite de importe, programa abierto*
– contract *contrato exclusivo de un material, contrato para suministro de cantidad indefinida*
– investment company *empresa inversionista de capital variable*
– mortgage *hipoteca sin límite de importe*
open-market *mercado abierto o libre*
– operations *operaciones en el mercado abierto*
opener, letter *abrecartas*
opening balance *saldo de apertura*
– price *precio de apertura*
operating agency aircraft *empresa de transporte aéreo*
– capital *capital de explotación*
– company *empresa de explotación*
– cost *costo de explotación*
– deficit *pérdida, déficit de explotación*
– expenditures *gastos de explotación*
– expenses *gastos de explotación*
– income *ingresos de explotación*
– loss *pérdida de explotación*
– statement *estado de resultados de operación*
– surplus *excedente de explotación*
operation *operación, fase*
– chart *diagrama operativo*
– flow chart *diagrama de flujo de operaciones*

– machine process chart *diagrama de procedimiento de máquina y operación*
– process chart *diagrama de procedimiento de operación*
–, assembly line *trabajo en cadena*
–, closed focussed *operación cuidadosamente preparada*
–, funding *operación de consolidación*
–, line *operación lineal*
–, overall *funcionamiento general*
operational analysis *análisis o investigaciones operativas*
– budget *presupuesto de explotación*
operations, analysis *análisis o investigaciones operativas*
–, open-market *operaciones en el mercado abierto*
–, sampling *operaciones de muestreo*
operative *operario*
operator *operario*
–, book-keeping machine *operador de máquina contable*
–, computer *operador de máquina calculadora, operador de ordenador*
–, duplicating machine *operador de máquina multicopista*
–, farm *productor agrícola*
–, key punch machine *operador de máquina perforadora*
–, telephone *telefonista*
opinion polls, public *escrutinio de la opinión pública*
–, informed *opinión informada*
–, public *opinión pública*
optimum *óptimo*
– number *número óptimo*
– performance *actuación óptima*
– sum *suma más favorable*
option to purchase *opción de compra*
–, buyer's *opción del comprador*
–, seller's *opción del vendedor*
oral interview *entrevista personal*
order *orden, pedido, decreto*
– delivery *entrega de pedidos*
– information card *ficha de información de órdenes*
– invoicing *facturación de pedidos*
– of the day *orden del día*
– of, to pay to the *pagar a la orden de*
– size *volumen de pedidos*
–, size, average *volumen promedio de pedidos*
–, acting *delegación de poderes*
–, advance *pedido inicial, pedido de tanteo*
–, bank money *giro bancario*
–, buying *orden de compra*
–, domestic *pedido para el interior*

–, factory *orden de fabricación o trabajo*
–, in working *actividad normal, en condiciones de servicio*
–, individual *pedido individual*
–, job *orden de trabajo*
–, mail *pedido hecho por correo*
–, manufacturing *orden de fabricación o trabajo*
–, money *giro postal, libranza postal*
–, payable to *pagadero a la orden*
–, processing *proceso de elaboración*
–, purchase *orden o nota de compra*
–, random *orden aleatorio*
–, rank *jerarquía*
–, rush *pedido urgente*
–, spot *orden para entrega y pago inmediato*
–, standing *pedido pendiente, orden vigente*
–, stop-loss *orden de pérdida limitada, orden de compra o venta de acciones*
–, to place an *hacer un pedido*
–, trial *pedido de ensayo o prueba*
–, unrated *pedido no preferente*
–, work *orden de trabajo*
order-form *formulario de pedidos*
ordinary *normal, corriente*
– budget *presupuesto ordinario*
– meeting *junta ordinaria*
– member *miembro titular*
– session *sesión ordinaria, junta ordinaria*
– term *período ordinario*
organization chart *diagrama de organización, organigrama*
–, line *organización lineal*
orientation *orientación*
origin, certificate of *certificado de origen*
original *original*
– acquisition *adquisición original*
– allotment *asignación inicial*
– capital *capital inicial*
– cost *costo inicial*
– entry *asiento en el diario, primera entrada*
– entry, book of *libro diario*
– stock *acciones primitivas*
out of date *caducado*
– of stock *agotado*
–, all *a toda potencia, a pleno rendimiento*
–, to buy *comprar la parte de un socio*
outdoor sign *rótulo exterior*
outfitter *abastecedor, proveedor*
outflow *salida, exportación*
–, capital *salida de capitales al exterior*
outgoing *saliente*
outlay *desembolso, salida, expendido*
outlet *salida, mercado*
outline *croquis, esquema, esbozo, diseño, argumento, sigla*

output *producción, producto*
– coefficient, input- *coeficiente insumo producto*
– component *componente de producción*
– factor *factor de producción*
– standardization *tipificación del rendimiento o producción*
–, actual *rendimiento efectivo, producción efectiva*
–, aggregate *rendimiento total*
–, average *producción media*
–, best profit *producción de utilidad máxima*
–, current physical *producción física corriente*
–, down-rated *producción disminuída*
–, final *producción final*
–, gross *producción bruta*
–, industrial *producción industrial*
–, input- *insumo producto*
–, man-hour *producción por hora por mano de obra*
–, national *producción nacional*
–, net *producción neta*
–, plant *producción o rendimiento de planta o fábrica*
–, potential *producción potencial*
–, rate of *rendimiento*
–, reduced *producción disminuída o reducida*
–, valuation of *valuación de la producción*
outright *cesión por un tanto alzado de los derechos de autor*
–, to buy *adquirir los derechos en bloque*
outsell, to *competir en ventas, vender más barato*
outside work *trabajo externo*
outstanding account *cuenta pendiente o atrasada*
– capital *capital suscrito*
– cheques *cheques pendientes*
– contracts *contratos en curso*
– debts *deudas existentes o pendientes*
– securities *acciones o títulos emitidos*
– stock *capital suscrito, acciones en manos del público*
outward bound *con destino al extranjero*
outwards, clearance *declaración de saldo en aduana*
over, buyers *mayoría de compradores*
–, carry *saldo anterior, remanente de una mercancía*
–, to buy *sobornar, comprar a una persona*
overall distribution costs *costes conjuntos o globales de distribución*
– gain *ganancia total*
– operation *funcionamiento general*
– performance *rendimiento total*
– probability *probabilidad total*

overcharge, to *cobrar demasiado,*
  sobrecargar
overcharged, accounts *cuentas sobrecargadas*
overcredit, to *abonar de más*
overdebit, to *debitar de más*
overdraft *giro en descubierto*
–, bank *sobregiro real*
overdraw *girar en descubierto*
–, to *sobrecargar, girar en descubierto*
overdrawn account *cuenta en descubierto*
overdue *vencido, atrasado*
overhead *sobrecarga, gastos indirectos*
– charges *gastos indirectos*
– costs *gastos generales*
– expenses *gastos generales o indirectos*
overheads, factory *gastos de fábrica*
overlap *traslapación*
–, to *traslapar*
overload *sobrecarga*
overloaded *sobrecargado*
overloading *sobrecarga*
overlook, to *pasar por alto*
overpayment *pago excesivo*

overseer *superintendente, supervisor, regente*
  de imprenta
overstate, to *exagerar, abultar*
overstock *exceso de existencias*
overstocking *almacenamiento excesivo*
overtime *horas extraordinarias, tiempo extra*
– attendance hours *horas extraordinarias de*
  asistencia al trabajo
– work *trabajo a horas extras*
overvalue, to *valuar en exceso*
over-exposure *sobreexposición*
over-investment *inversión excesiva,*
  sobreinversión
over-issue *emisión excesiva*
over-production *superproducción*
over-supply *superabundancia de la oferta*
owner *propietario, dueño*
–, joint *copropietario*
–, part *copropietario*
–, prescriptive *propietario por prescripción*
–, qualified *tenedor de interés limitado*
ownership *propiedad, pertenencia*
–, common *propiedad en común*

P

pace *ritmo, velocidad*
package *paquete*
– deal *estabilización económica*
–, commercial *embalaje o empaquetado comercial*
packer *embalador, empaquetador*
packing *embalaje, envase, empaque*
– expenses *gastos de embalaje*
– list *especificaciones de embalaje*
– paper *papel de embalaje*
pact *acuerdo, pacto, convenio*
pad, stamp *almohadilla para tintar*
page plan, advertisement *maqueta publicitaria*
– spread, double *anuncio a doble página*
–, advertising *página de anuncios*
–, back *última página*
–, cover *página de la cubierta, cubierta de libro*
–, front *primera página*
–, inner *página interior*
–, title *portada de libros, primera página de un periódico*
paid in full *liquidado, totalmente pagado*
–, part *pagado parcialmente*
paid-in surplus *excedente de capital*
paid-up capital *capital exhibido, pagado*
– stock *acciones cubiertas*
pallet *plataforma*
panel *panel*
–, consumer *panel de consumidores*
–, test *cuadro o equipo panel de pruebas*
paper money *papel moneda*
– profits *utilidades no realizadas*
– punch *punzadora para papel*
– size *formato de periódico*
–, bearer *documento al portador*
–, blotting *papel secante*
–, blue *papel copia para máquina*
–, carbon *papel carbón*
–, clean *papel blanco*
–, commodity *efectos respaldados por productos*
–, copying *papel cebolla, papel fino para copia de cartas*
–, daily *diario, periódico*
–, fashion *periódico de modas*
–, monthly *periódico mensual*

–, negotiable *efectos negociables*
–, packing *papel de embalaje*
–, to read a *presentar una comunicación, dar una conferencia*
–, wrapping *envoltura, envoltorio, faja*
papers, accommodation *efectos de favor*
–, bank *valores bancarios*
–, business *papeles de negocios, efectos comerciales, revistas profesionales*
–, commercial *papeles de negocios, papeles comerciales*
–, ship's *documentación del barco*
par *par, paridad*
– items *efectos cobrables sin comisión*
– value *valor a la par*
–, values, schedule of *tabla de valores a la par*
–, above *sobre par*
–, below *bajo par*
–, exchange at *cambio a la par*
parade *exposición, desfile, parada, cabalgata*
–, fashion *desfile de modas*
parcel post *paquete postal*
pare down expenditures, to *reducir los gastos*
parent company *compañía matriz, empresa principal*
– house *casa matriz, compañía controladora*
parity income ratio *razón de paridad de ingresos*
– price *precio de paridad*
part *papel, pieza, componente*
– owner *copropietario*
– paid *pagado parcialmente*
– payment *pago a cuenta*
– settlement of claims *ajuste parcial de reclamaciones*
part-time *parcial, durante parte del día*
– appointment *destino o empleo no todo el año*
– employees *empleados solo parte de la jornada*
– employment *jornada reducida*
– member *miembro que solo trabaja parte del día*
– worker *trabajador en jornada incompleta*
part-timer *empleado que trabaja por cuenta de varios patronos*

partial disability, permanent *incapacidad parcial permanente*
 – payment *pago parcial, pago a cuenta*
 – acceptance *aceptación condicionada*
 – loss *pérdida parcial*
 – replacement *reposición parcial*
participating stock *acciones preferentes participantes*
participation in management, employee *participación obrera en la dirección, jurado de empresa*
particulars *conceptos, detalles*
parties, contracting *partes contratantes*
partner *socio, asociado*
 –, acting *socio gerente*
 –, active *socio activo*
 –, dormant *socio comanditario*
 –, financial *socio capitalista*
 –, industrial *socio industrial*
 –, junior *socio menor*
 –, managing *socio gerente o administrador*
 –, nominal *socio nominal*
partnership *sociedad, compañía, asociación*
 – agreement *pacto social, contrato de asociación*
 – articles *escrituras de sociedad*
 – assets *bienes sociales*
 – at will *asociación sin plazo fijo de duración*
 – contract *contrato social de asociación*
 – debt *deudas sociales*
 – property *bienes sociales*
 –, articles of *contrato de asociación*
 –, commercial *sociedad mercantil en comandita*
 –, family *sociedad familiar*
 –, general *sociedad colectiva*
 –, industrial *participación de utilidades, participación obrera en los beneficios*
 –, limited *sociedad limitada, sociedad en comandita*
 –, senior *socio principal, socio más antiguo*
 –, sleeping *socio comanditario*
 –, working *socio activo*
parts, standard *piezas normalizadas*
party, working *consejo industrial mixto*
pass, to *pasar, aprobar, transmitir*
 – book *libro de banco, libro de depósitos*
passed dividend *dividendo omitido*
passive *pasivo*
 – assets *activo intangible*
 – bond *bono sin interés*
 – debt *deuda sin interés*
 – liabilities *pasivo fijo*
 – trust *fideicomiso pasivo*
passport *pasaporte*
paste, copying *pasta de copiar*

pasteboard *cartón*
patent *patente*
 – and trademark office *oficina de patentes y marcas*
 – application *solicitud de patente*
 – infringement *infracción o violación de patentes*
 – law *ley de patentes, derecho de patentes*
 – licence *licencia de patentes*
 – office *oficina de patentes*
 – pending *patente en tramitación o pendiente*
 – rights *derechos de patentes*
 – royalties *derechos de patente*
 –, basic *patente primitiva, patente original*
 –, home *patente nacional*
 –, life of a *plazo, vigencia de una patente*
 –, take out a *sacar una patente, patentar*
 –, to grant a *conceder una patente*
patented process *proceso patentado*
patentee *inventor, poseedor de patente*
patents pending, design covered by *diseño protegido por patentes en tramitación*
 – pending, designs registered and world *modelos registrados y patentes mundiales en trámite*
path, flow *recorrido*
patrimony *patrimonio*
pattern *patrón, modelo, prototipo, forma, estructura, esquema, configuración*
 – card *muestrario*
 – of trade *situación comercial*
 –, after a *según modelo o plantilla*
 –, economic *estructura económica*
 –, motion *diagrama de movimientos*
 –, movement *trayectoria del movimiento*
 –, price *comportamiento de los precios*
 –, test *pruebas de ajuste*
patterns, behaviour *normas de conducta*
pawn, to *dar en prenda, empeñar*
pay *paga, sueldo, salario*
 – back *restituir*
 – by instalments, to *pagar a plazos*
 – clerk *empleado pagador*
 – day *día de pago*
 – envelope *sobre con la paga*
 – in full *pagar por completo, pagar la totalidad*
 – off, to *pagar y despedir a un empleado*
 – off a mortgage *redimir una hipoteca*
 – on account *pagar a cuenta*
 – to the order of *pagar a la orden de*
 – warrant *autorización, orden de pago*
 –, base *salario base*
 –, full *sueldo completo*
 –, make-up *remuneración complementaria hasta el salario garantizado*
 –, severance *pago de despido, indemnización*

de despido
–, strike *pago a huelguistas*
–, take-home *sueldo después de deducciones*
pay-as-you-go policy *pago de impuestos a medida que el contribuyente recibe sus ingresos*
payable *pagadero, por pagar*
– accounts *cuentas por pagar, cuenta de proveedores, libro mayor de compras*
– at sight *pagadero a la vista o a la presentación*
– on demand *pagadero a la presentación*
– to bearer *pagadero al portador*
– to order *pagadero a la orden*
–, accruals *acumulaciones pagaderas*
–, annuity *anualidad o renta pasiva*
–, bills *efectos a pagar*
–, notes *documentos por pagar*
–, vouchers *comprobantes a cobrar*
payee *beneficiario, portador, cobrador*
payer *pagador*
–, tax- *contribuyente*
paymaster *pagador*
payment *pago, paga*
– bond *fianza de pago*
– in full *pago total, saldo, finiquito, liquidación*
– in kind *pago en especie*
– refused *pago rehusado, pago negado*
–, advance *pago anticipado, anticipo*
–, capital *pago de cuenta de capital*
–, cash *pago al contado*
–, deferred *pago aplazado*
–, deficiency *pago para cubrir un déficit*
–, down *pago al contado*
–, draft *pago por letra*
–, part *pago a cuenta*
–, partial *pago parcial, pago a cuenta, plazo*
–, prompt *pago al contado*
–, received *recibí*
–, retroactive *pago de sueldos atrasados*
–, social security *pago por previsión social*
–, suspend *suspender el pago*
–, tender of *oferta de pago*
–, token *adelanto a cuenta de pago de una obligación*
–, to effect *efectuar el pago*
–, to present for *presentar al pago*
–, to refuse *rehusar el pago*
–, to stop *suspender el pago, detener el pago*
payments on purchase obligations, advance *envíos o cuenta de pedidos a servir*
–, adverse balance of *balanza de pagos desfavorable*
–, balance of *balanza de pagos*
–, benefit *beneficio, provecho*

–, by easy *con facilidades de pago*
–, current *pagos corrientes*
–, easy *facilidades de pago*
–, gold *pagos en oro*
–, progress *pagos escalonados*
payroll *nómina*
– clerk *pagador*
– make-up *confección de nóminas*
– tax *impuesto sobre sueldos*
peak *punto máximo*
– period *período agudo, período máximo*
– production *producción máxima*
– sales *ventas máximas*
peculation *peculado, desfalco*
peg *clavija*
pegged price *precio de estabilización*
pen, fountain *estilográfica, pluma*
penalties *multas, sanciones, recargos*
penalty clause *cláusula penal*
pencil, copying *lápiz tinta*
– sharpener *sacapuntas*
pending, design covered by patents *diseño protegido por patentes en tramitación*
–, patent *patente en tramitación o pendiente*
pension *pensión, jubilación*
– deferred *pago diferido de pensión*
– fund *fondo de pensión*
– rights *derechos de pensión o jubilación*
– trust *fideicomiso de pensiones*
–, old-age *pensión por vejez*
–, widow's *viudedad, pensión de viudedad*
per annum *al año*
– capita *por cabeza, por persona*
– capita consumption *consumo por habitante*
– capita income *renta por habitante*
– cent *por ciento*
– diem *por día, diario*
– diem rates *tarifas por día*
– invoice, as *según factura*
– sample, as *según muestra*
– voucher, as *según comprobante*
percentage *porcentaje, por ciento*
– depreciation method, constant *método de amortización de porcentaje constante*
– of completion method *método de porcentaje de terminación*
– of profit *porcentaje de utilidades*
perception *percepción*
perforator *perforadora*
performance *actuación, ejecución, rendimiento*
– index *nivel de rendimiento*
– measurement *medición del rendimiento*
– rating *apreciación de la actuación, valoración de la actuación*
– standard *norma de rendimiento*

– test, accelerated *prueba acelerada de destreza*
–, average *ejecución media*
–, break-even *comportamiento de la curva de rentabilidad*
–, expected *ejecución prevista*
–, first *estreno*
–, job *ejecución del trabajo, rendimiento del trabajo*
–, measurement *medición del rendimiento*
–, normal *actuación normal*
–, optimum *actuación óptima*
–, overall *rendimiento total*
–, planned *ejecución o actuación prevista*
–, sales *rendimiento de ventas*
–, substandard *rendimiento inferior al normal*
perfunctorily *superficialmente*
peril point clause *cláusula de punto crítico*
period *período*
–, annual fiscal *ejercicio fiscal*
–, cooling-off *tregua*
–, down *período de cierre por reparaciones*
–, end of *fin del ejercicio*
–, financial *ejercicio financiero, ejercicio económico*
–, fiscal *período contable, período fiscal*
–, grace *período de gracia*
–, peak *período agudo, período máximo*
–, trial *período de prueba*
permanent *permanente*
– assets *capital fijo*
– debt *deuda permanente*
– equipment *equipo fijo*
– fixtures *instalaciones fijas*
– home *lugar de residencia permanente*
– partial disability *incapacidad parcial permanente*
– total disability *incapacidad absoluta permanente*
permeated with *permeado de*
permissive use *uso pasivo*
permit *licencia, permiso*
–, entry *permiso de entrada, permiso de declaración aduanal*
–, exchange *permiso o autorización de cambio*
–, export *permiso de exportación*
–, foreign exchange *permiso para operar con divisas*
–, import *permiso de importación*
permittee *tenedor de permiso de patente*
perpetual *perpetuo*
– annuity *anualidad perpetua*
– bond *bono sin vencimiento*
– loan *empréstito no amortizable, perpetuo*
– trust *fideicomiso perpetuo*
person, corporate *persona corporativa*

personal *personal, particular*
– allowance *suplementos personales*
– assets *bienes muebles o mobiliarios, bienes personales, fortuna personal*
– bond *título nominativo, fianza particular*
– deduction *deducción personal o individual*
– disability *incapacidad individual*
– estate *bienes muebles o personales*
– exemption *exención personal*
– finance economy *sociedad para préstamos menores*
– habits *hábitos personales*
– income *ingreso personal*
– income tax *impuesto sobre ingresos personales*
– liability *responsabilidad personal de accionistas*
– needs allowance *suplemento por necesidades personales, suplementos personales*
– property *bienes muebles*
– saving *ahorro personal*
– security *garantía personal o mobiliaria*
– tax *impuesto personal*
personality, corporate *personalidad social*
–, complex *personalidad compleja*
personnel analyst *analizador de personal*
– behaviour *conducta del personal*
– division *departamento o sección de personal*
– management *dirección del personal*
– manager *director o jefe de personal*
– policies *política con respecto a personal*
– roster *nómina de personal*
– selection *selección del personal*
– tests *pruebas de personal*
– training *capacidad del personal*
–, plant *personal de fábrica*
persuasion *persuasión*
petition in bankruptcy *petición de quiebra*
petty cash *caja para gastos menores, caja chica*
– expenses *gastos menores*
– foreman *contramaestre adjunto*
phase *fase, operación*
photocopy *fotocopia*
photostat *fotocopia*
physical *físico*
– assets *valores materiales*
– disability *incapacidad física*
– impossibility *imposibilidad material*
– output, current *producción física corriente*
– production, index of *índice de la producción física*
pick-up in demand *aumento de demanda*
picket *piquete de huelga*
– line *cordón de huelguistas*
picnic *jira campestre*
picture, news *ilustración de prensa*

piece goods *artículos sueltos*
- rate *precio unitario o por pieza*
- worker *operario a contrato o por tarea*
piecework *trabajo a destajo o por pieza*
- price *precio por pieza o unitario*
- system *sistema de salario por pieza*
-, differential *salario diferencial por piezas*
piercing *agudo, penetrante*
pilferage *hurto, sisa*
pilot *muestra piloto, muestra de orientación*
- study *estudio de orientación*
- survey *encuesta piloto*
place an order, to *hacer un pedido*
- of business *domicilio social, local del negocio*
-, work *puesto de trabajo*
plan file *archivo de planos o dibujos, planoteca*
-, bonus *sistema de primas*
-, instalment *plan de venta en abonos*
-, retirement *plan de retiro*
-, to *planear*
plane, motion *plano de movimiento*
planned economy *economía dirigida*
- markdowns *rebajas previstas*
- performance *ejecución o actuación prevista*
- purchases *compras previstas*
- sales *ventas previstas*
- stock decrease *disminución de existencias previstas*
- stock increase *aumento de existencias previstas*
- stocks *existencias previstas*
planning *planeamiento, programación*
- board *junta de planificación*
- engineer *ingeniero encargado del planeamiento*
- manager, product *jefe de programación de productos*
-, economic *planeación, programación económica*
-, industrial *planeación industrial*
-, job *plan de trabajo o tareas*
-, long-range *planificación de largo alcance, programación a largo plazo*
-, product *adaptación de un producto a las necesidades del mercado*
-, sales *planeamiento de las ventas*
plant amortization *amortización de la instalación*
- capacity *capacidad de producción*
- improvement *mejoría de la instalación o planta*
- manager *director de fábrica*
- personnel *personal de fábrica*
- schedule *amortización de la instalación*

-, assembling *planta ensambladora, planta de montaje*
plate, step *plataforma de trabajo*
pledge *garantía, prenda, señal, colateral*
- loan *préstamo prendario o pignoraticio*
pledged accounts *cuentas pignoradas*
- assets *activo grabado*
- securities *valores dados en garantía*
plenary meeting *sesión plenaria*
plough back profits, to *reinvertir las utilidades*
plural-voting stock *acciones de voto plural*
plurality *pluralidad*
point clause, peril *cláusula de punto crítico*
-, basing *punto básico, punto de partida*
-, best profit *punto de utilidad máxima*
-, break *punto de separación*
-, break-even *punto de equilibrio*
-, focal *punto focal*
-, gold *punto oro, límite del oro*
-, resting *punto de reposo*
-, starting *punto de arranque o partida*
-, vanishing *punto de desvanecimiento*
points, method of selected *método de los puntos elegidos*
policies, personnel *política con respecto al personal*
policy *política, práctica, póliza*
- of non-discriminatory import restrictions *política de restricciones no selectivas a la importación*
- of restraint *política de austeridad*
-, all-in *póliza a todo riesgo*
-, blanket *póliza abierta*
-, contracyclical *política anticíclica*
-, credit *política de crédito*
-, discount *sistema de descuento*
-, economic *política económica, coyuntura*
-, endowment *póliza dotal*
-, fiscal *política fiscal*
-, floating *póliza abierta*
-, insurance *póliza de seguro*
-, investment *política de inversión*
-, one-price *política de precio único*
-, open-door *política de puerta abierta*
-, pay-as-you-go *pago de impuestos o medida que el contribuyente recibe sus ingresos*
-, population *política demográfica*
-, price support *política de sostenimiento de precios*
-, public *política pública*
-, purchasing *política de compras*
-, sales *sistema de ventas*
-, single price *sistema de precios únicos*
-, wage *política en materia de salarios*
policy-maker *el que determina la política*

policyholder *tenedor de póliza*
politics *política*
poll *votación, sondeo de opinión pública*
– tax *impuesto por persona*
polling *voto, votación, elecciones, escrutinio*
polls, public opinion *escrutinio de la opinión pública*
pool *consorcio, convenio, concentración o mancomunidad de empresas, sindicato industrial*
–, buffer *reserva, fondo estabilizador, amortiguador*
pooled concession *concesión mancomunada*
– earnings *ganancias puestas a fondo común*
pooling agreement *acuerdo o convenio consorcial*
– of errors *combinación de errores*
– principle *principio de concentración industrial*
poor delivery service *servicio de entrega deficiente*
– display *exposición inadecuada o deficiente*
– laws *leyes de beneficiencia*
population *población*
– centre *centro de población*
– density *densidad de población o demográfica*
– displacement *desplazamiento de población*
– growth rate *índice de aumento de población*
– index *índice de población*
– index, total *índice total de población*
– index, urban *índice de población urbana*
– policy *política demográfica*
– pyramid *pirámide de población*
– recorded *población registrada*
– register, continuous *registro continuo de la población*
– samples *muestras de población*
– trend *tendencia demográfica*
–, age composition of *composición de la población por edad*
–, open *población abierta*
–, stationary *población estacionaria*
port *puerto*
– authorities *autoridades portuarias*
– duties *derechos portuarios*
– of call *puerto de escalas*
– of delivery *puerto terminal*
– of entry *puerto de entrada, puerto fiscal*
– of shipment *puerto de embarque*
–, free *puerto libre*
–, house *puerto de matrícula*
–, shipping *puerto de embarque*
portfolio *lista de valores que se tienen, cartera*
position *posición, emplazamiento, situación económica*

–, cash *situación líquida*
–, financial *situación financiera*
–, statement of financial *balance general*
possess, to *poseer, tener*
possessor *poseedor*
possessory title *título posesorio*
post, parcel *paquete postal*
–, vacant *puesto, empleo, cargo vacante*
postal savings bank *caja postal de ahorros*
postdated *posfechado*
posted price *precio impuesto, tarifa oficial*
poster *cartel, letrero*
– advertising *publicidad por medio de carteles*
– artist *cartelista, pintor de carteles*
– designer *cartelista, pintor o dibujante de carteles*
–, bill *fijador de carteles*
–, display *pancarta de publicidad*
–, hoarding (Br) *cartelera, valla anunciadora*
postpone, to *posponer, aplazar*
post-quota surplus *excedente de cuota*
postwar *postguerra*
potential consumer *consumidor potencial*
– density *densidad potencial*
– earnings *ganancias potenciales o previstas*
– market *mercado potencial*
– output *producción potencial*
– sales *ventas potenciales*
–, leadership *capacidad de mando*
poundage *comisión*
poverty *pobreza, indigencia*
power *autoridad, poder, fuerza, capacidad, facultad*
– in gross *poder sin interés del apoderado*
– of appointment *facultad de nombrar*
– of attorney *carta poder, para transar*
–, bargaining *poder para negociar*
–, buying *poder adquisitivo, capacidad de compra*
–, purchasing *poder de compra, poder adquisitivo*
–, spending *poder para gastar*
powerful test, most *prueba más poderosa*
powers, incidental *poderes concomitantes*
practicability *posibilidad de ejecución*
practicable *viable, factible*
practice *adiestramiento, formalización*
– procedure, standard *procedimiento de prácticas normalizadas*
–, copyright *ejercicio del derecho de autor*
–, standard *sistema tipo*
precautionary motive *motivo precaución*
precision, appraisal of *valuación de la precisión*
–, sampling *precisión del muestreo*
prediction, statistical *predicción estadística*

predisposition *predisposición*
prefer, to *dar preferencia, preferir*
preference *preferencia, prioridad*
– bond *bono privilegiado*
– share *acción privilegiada o preferente*
– stock *acciones privilegiadas*
–, liquidity *preferencia por la liquidez*
–, margin of *margen de preferencia*
preferences, consumer *preferencias del consumidor*
preferential *preferente, privilegiado*
– price *precio preferencial*
– tariff *tarifa preferencial*
– trading systems *sistemas de comercio preferenciales*
preferred *preferido, preferente*
– creditor *acreedor privilegiado*
– debt *deuda de la prioridad*
– dividend *dividendo sobre acciones privilegiadas*
– lien *gravamen preferente*
– procedure *procedimiento preferente*
– stock *acciones preferidas o preferentes*
– stock sinking fund *fondo de amortización de acciones preferentes*
– stock, cumulative *acciones privilegiadas de dividendo acumulable*
– stock, prior *acciones preferidas superiores*
– stockholder *accionista preferido*
preliminary investigation *investigación preliminar*
– study *estudio preliminar*
premises *local, establecimiento, posesiones*
–, business *almacén, oficina o edificio comercial*
–, buyer's *oficinas o departamento de compras*
premium *prima, bonificación*
– loan, automatic *préstamo con primas automáticas*
– system *sistema de primas*
–, exchange *beneficio de cambio*
–, gross *prima total*
–, insurance *prima de seguro*
–, liquidity *prima de liquidez*
–, share *prima de emisión*
–, stipulated *prima estipulada*
–, stock *prima de emisión*
prepaid, freight *flete pagado*
preparation *preparación*
prepayment *pago adelantado*
prescribe, to *prescribir*
prescribed error *error prescrito*
– range of error *amplitud de error prescrito*
prescriptive owner *propietario por prescripción*
present, to *presentar, dar*

– for payment *presentar al pago*
– worth *valor actual*
president *presidente*
–, acting *presidente interino, presidente en funciones*
–, vice- *vicepresidente, subdirector*
press conference *conferencia de prensa*
– date *fecha de cierre*
– release *comunicado de prensa*
–, copying *prensa de copiar*
–, free *libertad de prensa, libertad de imprenta*
–, printing *máquina de imprimir*
–, rotary *rotativa*
–, yellow *prensa sensacionalista*
pressure groups *grupos de presión*
prestige advertising *publicidad de prestigio*
presumptive method *método de probabilidad*
pre-tax earnings *utilidades antes de los impuestos*
pre-test *prueba previa*
– device *proyecto previo de prueba*
– sample data *datos de muestra de pruebas previas*
prevailing price *precio dominante, precio en vigor*
preventive rights *derechos preventivos o precautorios*
previous endorsement *endoso anterior*
price *precio*
– adjustment *ajuste de precios*
– advance *subida de precio, encarecimiento*
– as provided in the contract *precio según contrato*
– behaviour *comportamiento de los precios*
– catalogue *catálogo o lista de precios*
– changes *cambios de precio*
– competition, active market *mercado de competición activa*
– competition, direct *competencia directa de precios*
– control *control de precios*
– cutting *reducción de precios*
– decline *baja de precios*
– freeze *congelación de precios*
– index *índice de precios*
– inflation *inflación de precios*
– leader *fijador de precios, precio piloto*
– leadership *conducción o primacia de precios*
– level *nivel de precios*
– line *precio límite*
– list *lista de precios, tarifa*
– list, temporary *lista provisional de precios o tarifas*
– margin *margen de utilidad*
– method, market *método del precio del mercado*

– pattern *comportamiento de los precios*
– quotation *cotización de precios*
– regulation *reglamentación de precios*
– subsidy *subsidio de precios*
– support policy *política de sostenimiento de precios*
– war *guerra de precios*
–, actual *precio real*
–, agreed *precio convenido*
–, aggregate demand *precio de la demanda global*
–, aggregate supply *precio de la oferta global*
–, all-round *precio global*
–, asking *precio nominal, precio de oferta*
–, average *precio medio*
–, bargain *precio de ganga o de ocasión*
–, base *precio base o básico*
–, below cost *precio bajo costo*
–, bid *precio de oferta*
–, budget *precio módico*
–, buying *precio de compra*
–, cash *precio al contado*
–, ceiling *precio máximo permitido, precio tope*
–, close *precio estable, precio sin beneficio*
–, closing *precio de cierre*
–, competitive *precio competitivo o de competencia*
–, concession in *precio especial, rebajado*
–, cost *precio de costo*
–, current *precio actual o corriente*
–, customary *precio acostumbrado*
–, discount *precio de descuento, precio rebajado*
–, distributor's maximum *precio máximo del concesionario*
–, distributor's selling *precio de venta para distribuidor*
–, domestic *precio para venta interior*
–, export *precio de exportación*
–, factory *precio de fábrica*
–, fair *precio justo o leal*
–, fixed selling *precio fijo de venta*
–, flat *precio redondo o de compra*
–, full *precio íntegro o de venta al detalle*
–, gross *precio de venta al público, precio de venta total*
–, gross sale *precio de venta al público, precio de venta total*
–, invoice *precio de factura*
–, issue *precio de emisión*
–, knock-down (Br) *precio muy rebajo*
–, low *precio bajo*
–, manufacturer's *precio de fábrica*
–, markdown *precio de rebaja*
–, market *precio corriente*

–, markup *diferencia entre precio y costo*
–, moderate *precio módico o razonable*
–, net *precio neto*
–, offered *precio de oferta*
–, opening *precio de apertura*
–, parity *precio de paridad*
–, piecework *precio por pieza, precio a destajo*
–, pledged *precio de estabilización*
–, posted *precio impuesto, tarifa industrial*
–, preferential *precio preferencial*
–, prevailing *precio dominante, precio en vigor*
–, producer's *precio de fábrica*
–, prospective *precio probable*
–, purchase *precio de compra*
–, real *precio real*
–, remunerative *buen precio*
–, resale *precio de reventa*
–, reserve *precio mínimo fijado en subasta*
–, retail *precio al detalle*
–, retail list *lista de precios al detalle*
–, retail selling *precio de venta al detalle*
–, ruling *precio en vigor, precio predominante*
–, sale *precio de venta*
–, selling *precio de venta*
–, set *precio fijo o establecido*
–, spot *precio en plaza, precio inmediato*
–, standard *precio regulador*
–, stock-taking *precio de inventario*
–, supply *precio de oferta*
–, test *precio de lista o catálogo*
–, to buy at market *comprar a precio de mercado*
–, to meet the *aceptar el precio*
–, to set a *fijar un precio*
–, top *precio máximo*
–, trade *precio neto, comercial o corriente*
–, unit *precio unitario*
–, upset *precio de primera oferta, precio o tipo de subasta*
–, wholesale *precio mayorista*
prices *precios*
– down, to force *hacer bajar los precios*
–, all-in *precios totales*
–, buoyant *precios con tendencia al alza*
–, clearance *precios de liquidación*
–, contract *precio acordado según contrato*
–, controlled *precios controlados o regulados*
–, cut *precios pelados*
–, distress *precios de remate*
–, fall in *baja de precios*
–, firm *precios firmes*
–, floor *precios mínimos*
–, gold *precios oro*
–, home *precios nacionales*
–, inflated *inflación de precios*

–, monopoly *precios de monopolio*
–, prohibitive *precios prohibitivos*
–, rising *precios de alza*
–, slashed *precios deducidos*
–, stable *precios estables*
–, steady *precios firmes o sostenidos*
–, stiffening *precios firmes*
–, street *precios fuera de bolsa*
–, subscription *precio de emisión de nuevas acciones*
pricing *fijación de precios*
– executive *directivo que fija los precios*
–, discriminatory *fijación selectiva o discriminatoria de precios*
–, merchandise *fijación del precio de la mercancía*
primary *primario*
– allotment *asignación inicial*
– commodity *producto primario*
– data *datos de origen, datos primarios*
– liability *responsabilidad directa*
– materials *materias primas*
– products *productos primarios*
– rights *derechos primarios*
– wants *artículos de primera necesidad*
prime cost *costo de fabricación, coste primario*
– factors *factores primos*
– rate *tasa preferencial*
principal amount, aggregate *cantidad total del capital*
principle *principio*
–, acceleration *principio de aceleración*
–, pooling *principio de concentración industrial*
–, reciprocity *principio de reciprocidad*
principles, sampling *principios de muestreo*
print, blue- *copia heliográfica*
– money, to *imprimir dinero*
–, in *impreso, publicado, en existencia*
printed matter *impreso*
– output for data *documentos impresos como norma de información*
printer *impresor*
printing *impresión*
– calculator *calculadora con impresión*
– press *máquina de imprimir*
– process *procedimiento de impresión*
– punch, alphabetic *perforadora impresora alfabética*
–, offset *impresión offset*
prior preferred stock *acciones preferidas superiores*
priority bond *bono privilegiado*
private *particular, privado*
– bank *banco particular*
– consumption *consumo privado*

– enterprise *empresa privada, iniciativa privada*
– income *ingreso particular o privado*
– property *propiedad privada, bienes particulares*
– rights *derechos individuales o particulares*
– sale *venta directa*
– secretary *secretaria particular*
– trust *fideicomiso particular o privado*
privilege *privilegio, concesión*
privileged debt *deuda privilegiada, deuda preferida*
probabilities, quantitative *probabilidades cuantitativas*
probability *probabilidad*
– integral *integral de probabilidad*
– range *recorrido de probabilidad*
– rate *tasa de probabilidad*
– ratio test *prueba de la razón de la probabilidad*
– sample *muestra de la probabilidad*
– sample, area *muestreo por zonas y probabilidad*
– sampling *muestreo de probabilidad*
–, overall *probabilidad total*
probable income *ingreso probable*
probing questions *preguntas de sondeo*
– techniques *técnicas de sondeo*
problem systematic approach *enfoque sistemático de problemas*
procedure *procedimiento, método de trabajo*
– chart, forms or paper *diagrama de procedimiento de formularios o estados*
–, audit *procedimiento de auditoría*
–, clearance *proceso de depuración del personal*
–, file *procedimiento de archivo*
–, invoice *tramitación de facturas*
–, preferred *procedimiento preferente*
–, sampling *procedimiento de muestreo*
–, standard practice *procedimiento de prácticas normalizadas*
–, standardized *procedimiento normalizado*
procedures, markdown budget *procedimientos para rebajar el presupuesto*
proceeds *productos*
– of sales *producto de ventas*
–, gross *ingresos totales, producto bruto*
–, marginal *importe marginal de ventas*
process *elaboración, procedimiento*
– chart *diagrama de procedimiento*
– chart, flow *diagrama del proceso*
– chart, gang *diagrama de proceso del equipo*
– chart, machine *diagrama de procedimientos a máquina*
– chart, multiple activity *diagrama de proceso*

de actividades simultáneas
- chart, operation *diagrama de procedimiento de máquina y operación*
- chart, two-handed *diagrama de ambas manos*
- design *proyecto del proceso, preparación de trabajo*
- diagram *diagrama gráfico de procedimiento o elaboración*
- time, available *tiempo disponible de proceso*
-, arbitration *procedimiento de arbitraje*
-, copying *tiraje de películas*
-, economic *proceso económico*
-, factory *proceso de fabricación*
-, goods in *productos en elaboración*
-, key *proceso clave, procedimiento clave*
-, manufacturing *producción o proceso de fabricación*
-, marketing *procedimiento de distribución*
-, multiple-phase *proceso multifásico*
-, net time *tiempo neto de transformación*
-, offset *proceso offset, procedimiento offset*
-, patented *proceso patentado*
-, printing *procedimiento de impresión*
-, roundabout *proceso directo*
-, random impulse *proceso de impulso aleatorio*
-, stationary *proceso estacionario*
-, work in *manufactura en proceso*
processed goods, partly *productos semiacabados*
processing equipment, data- *equipo de sistematización de datos*
- error *error de procedimiento, error de elaboración*
- machine, electronic data- *equipo electrónico de elaboración de datos*
- methods, commercial *métodos comerciales de elaboración*
- of products *elaboración de productos*
- order *proceso de elaboración*
- tax *impuesto por elaboración*
-, alphabetic *sistematización alfabética*
-, arithmetic data *sistematización de datos aritméticos*
-, data- *proceso de datos, clasificación, elaboración*
-, electronic data- *elaboración electrónica de datos*
-, information *sistematización de datos, proceso de obtención de datos*
processor *elaborador, preparador, manipulador*
produce *producto, producción, provisiones, víveres*
-, home *productos domésticos o nacionales*

-, native *productos domésticos nacionales*
-, residual *subproducto*
-, semi-finished *producto semielaborado*
produced article, mass- *artículo hecho en serie, producto hecho en serie*
producer *productor*
-'s forecast *pronóstico de los productores*
- price *precio de fábrica*
product *producto, artículo, género, mercancía*
- design *diseño o presentación de producto*
- development unit *unidad de desarrollo de un producto*
- line *cadena o serie de producción*
- planning *adaptación de un producto a las necesidades del mercado*
- planning manager *jefe de programación de productos*
-, by- *subproducto*
-, consumer branded *producto de marca y de consumo*
-, end *producto final*
-, expensive to make *producto costoso de fabricar*
-, final *producto final*
-, gross domestic *producto bruto interno*
-, gross national *producto nacional bruto*
-, marginal *producto marginal*
-, non-market *producto no comercializado*
-, substitutive *producto de sustitución, sucedáneo*
-, to develop a *crear o propagar un producto*
production *producción*
- account *cuenta de producción*
- bonus *prima de producción*
- control *control de producción*
- cost *coste de fabricación o de producción*
- cost accountant *contable de costes de producción*
- cost accounting *contabilidad de costes de producción*
- curve *curva de producción*
- facilities *medios de producción, grupo de trabajo, equipo*
- factors *factores de producción*
- index *índice de producción*
- line *cadena de producción*
- profit *beneficio, utilidades de producción*
- record *registro de producción*
- schedules *esquemas o programas de producción*
- standard *norma de producción*
- statistics *estadísticas de producción*
- subsidy *subsidio a la producción*
- tax *impuesto sobre producción*
- value, unit *unidad de valor productivo*

–, assembly-line *cadena de producción, línea de montaje, tren de ensamblaje*
–, batch *producción por lotes*
–, continuous *producción continua*
–, direct *producción directa*
–, division of *negociado de producción*
–, increased *aumento de la producción*
–, index of physical *índice de la producción física*
–, indirect *producción indirecta*
–, mass *producción en serie o en masa*
–, means of *medios de producción, equipo de trabajo*
–, peak *producción máxima*
–, quantity *producción en serie*
–, regular *producción en serie*
–, seasonal *producción de temporada*
–, series *producción en serie*
–, standardized *producción en serie, producción normalizada o tipificada*
productive capacity *capacidad de producción*
– investment *inversión productiva*
– labour *mano de obra directa*
– man-hours *hombre-horas productivos*
– potential *potencial de producción*
– time *tiempo productivo*
– work *trabajo productivo*
productiveness, diminishing *productividad decreciente*
productivity *productividad*
– index *coeficiente de productividad, índice de productividad*
– measurement *medición de la productividad*
– test *prueba de productividad*
products, cost analysis by *análisis de coste por productos*
–, completed *productos terminados*
–, domestic *productos nacionales*
–, finished *productos acabados o terminados*
–, foreign *productos extranjeros*
–, home *productos domésticos o nacionales*
–, line of *serie de productos*
–, primary *productos primarios*
–, processing of *elaboración de productos*
–, quality of *calidad de los productos*
–, semi-manufactured *productos semielaborados*
–, waste *desperdicios, productos de desecho*
profile *psicograma, diagrama*
– chart *diagrama caracterológico*
–, progress *perfil de avance del trabajo*
profit *utilidad, ganancia, lucro*
– and loss *pérdidas y ganancias*
– and loss statement *estado de pérdidas y ganancias*
– margin, gross *margen de beneficio bruto*

– motive *motivo de lucro*
– output, best *producción de utilidad máxima*
– point, best *punto de utilidad máxima*
– sharing *reparto, participación en los beneficios*
– sharing reserve *reserva para participación de utilidades*
– tax *impuesto sobre beneficios*
–, actuarial *ganancia contable*
–, by- *ganancias suplementarias*
–, clean *beneficio líquido*
–, clear *beneficio o ganancia líquida*
–, equilibrium *ganancia normal, ganancia de equilibrio*
–, gross *beneficios totales, ganancias íntegras*
–, merchandising *utilidad comercial*
–, net *beneficio neto*
–, percentage of *porcentaje de utilidades*
–, production *beneficios, utilidades de producción*
–, to sell at a *vender con ganancia*
–, to show a *denotar o arrojar una ganancia*
–, to yield a *producir un beneficio o ganancia*
profit-earning capacity *capacidad lucrativa*
profitable *provechoso, beneficioso, productivo*
– enterprise *empresa rentable*
profiter *acaparador, agionista*
profits *utilidades*
–, accumulated *utilidades acumuladas*
–, anticipated *utilidades anticipadas*
–, book *utilidades aparentes*
–, business *utilidades comerciales*
–, capitalized *utilidades capitalizadas*
–, casual *utilidades extraordinarias*
–, concealment of *ocultación de utilidades*
–, contingent *utilidades contingentes*
–, corporate *utilidades de sociedad anónima*
–, deferred *utilidades por realizar*
–, distributed *utilidades pagadas o distribuidas*
–, distributive *utilidades repartibles*
–, diversion of *desviación ilícita de utilidades*
–, extraordinary *utilidades extraordinarias*
–, inflated *utilidades infladas*
–, margin of *margen de utilidades*
–, net *utilidades netas*
–, paper *utilidades no realizadas*
–, taxable *utilidades gravables, beneficios gravables*
–, to plough back *reinvertir las utilidades*
–, undistributed *beneficios no pagados, beneficios no repartidos*
proforma invoice *factura simulada, proforma*
– statement *estado en proforma*
prognosis *prognosis*
programme address counter *contador de*

dirección de programa
–, conservation *programa de conservación*
–, crash *programa de urgencia*
–, design standardization *programa de normalización de diseño*
–, employee benefit *programa a beneficio de empleados y obreros*
–, office training *programa de capacitación de oficinas*
–, integrated data *programa de integración de datos*
–, television *programa de televisión*
–, training *programa de capacitación o aprendizaje*
programming *elaboración de programas, programación*
–, linear *programación lineal*
programmer *programador*
progress certificate *certificación de buena cuenta*
– chart *gráfico de la marcha del trabajo*
– chaser *seguidor de piezas*
– payments *pagos escalonados*
– profile *perfil de avance del trabajo*
– report *informe del avance de una obra*
–, in *en vías de, en curso de fabricación*
progressing *progreso*
progression, scale of global *escala de progresión global*
progressive commission rate *tipo de comisión progresiva*
– surtax *sobretasa*
– tariff *tarifa progresiva*
– taxation *tributación progresiva*
– wage *salario progresivo*
prohibitive prices *precios prohibitivos*
project *proyecto, plan, empresa*
– engineer *ingeniero proyectista*
–, research *proyecto de investigación*
–, unsound *proyecto improductivo*
projective approach *enfoque proyectivo*
promissory note *nota de pago, pagaré*
promote, to *fomentar, promover*
promoter, company *promotor de empresa*
promotion *promoción, fomento*
– manager, sales *jefe de promoción de ventas*
–, sales *promoción de ventas*
–, trade *fomento del comercio*
prompt cash *pago al contado*
– payment *pago al contado*
proof *prueba, comprobación*
–, accident- a *prueba de accidentes*
proof-reader *corrector de pruebas*
proof-reading *corrección de pruebas*
propaganda, psychological *propaganda psicológica*

propensity *propensión*
– to consume *propensión a consumir*
– to consume, marginal *propensión marginal a consumir*
– to hoard *propensión a atesorar*
– to invest *propensión a invertir*
– to save *propensión a ahorrar*
property *bienes, haberes, propiedad*
– damage *daños materiales*
– dividend *dividendo de bienes*
– rights *derechos de propiedad*
– tax *impuesto sobre bienes o inmuebles*
–, corporate *propiedad corporativa*
–, joint *propiedad indivisa*
–, movable *bienes muebles*
–, partnership *bienes sociales*
–, personal *bienes muebles*
–, private *propiedad privada, bienes particulares*
–, public *bienes de dominio público*
–, real *bienes muebles, bienes raíces*
–, right of *derechos de dominio*
–, tangible *bienes tangibles*
proprietorship net worth *capital neto*
pro-rata *prorrata, en proporción*
prorogation *prórroga*
prospective *probable, esperado, anticipado*
– damages *daños anticipados*
– price *precio probable*
– yield *rendimiento probable*
prospects, business *coyuntura comercial*
protection, copyright *protección de la propiedad intelectual*
protective duty *derechos proteccionistas*
– tariff *tarifa proteccionista*
protest *protesto*
– charges *gastos de protesto*
–, to *protestar*
–, under *bajo protesta*
protested bill *letra protestada*
protestee *protestado*
protester *protestador*
provided in the contract, price as *precio según contrato*
provident fund *fondo de previsión*
provision *disposición*
– account *cuenta de reserva*
–, statutory *disposición legal*
provisional mean *promedio provisional*
proxy *poder, carta poder*
– holder *apoderado*
–, by *por poder*
–, vote by *voto por poder*
psychological incentives *incentivos psicológicos*
– propaganda *propaganda psicológica*

psychologist *psicólogo*
psychology *psicología*
public *público*
– accountant *contador o contable público*
– accountant, certified *contable público titulado*
– address system *sistema de comunicación directa*
– analysis *análisis del público*
– auction *subasta pública*
– audit *auditoría pública*
– body *organismo público*
– debt *deuda pública*
– debt, redemption of the *amortización de la deuda pública*
– document *escritura pública*
– education *educación pública*
– finances *finanzas públicas*
– funds *fondos públicos, hacienda pública*
– opinion *opinión pública*
– opinion polls *escrutinio o sondeos de la opinión pública, encuestas*
– policy *política pública*
– property *bienes de dominio público*
– relations *relaciones públicas, relaciones generales*
– relations agent *agente de relaciones públicas*
– relations manager *director de relaciones públicas*
– relations officer *encargado de las relaciones públicas*
– revenue *renta fiscal, ingresos públicos*
– sale *subasta con aviso anticipado*
– sector *sector público*
– securities *valores públicos*
– service commission *comisión de servicio público*
– service corporation *empresa de servicio público*
– service utilities *servicios públicos*
– treasury *tesorería, erario*
– trust *fideicomiso público*
– undertaking *empresa pública*
– utility *servicio público, empresa de servicio público*
– utility securities *títulos de empresas de servicio público*
– welfare *bienestar público*
– works *obras públicas*
publication date *fecha de publicación, fecha de salida*

publicity agency *agencia de publicidad, de informaciones publicitarias*
– department *departamento de información publicitaria*
–, free *información publicitaria gratis*
publisher's advertisement *nota editorial, anuncio de publicaciones*
publishing *editorial*
– contract *contrato de edición o publicación*
– house *casa editora*
punch machine operator, key *operador de máquina perforadora*
–, alphanumeric key *perforadora alfanumérica*
–, alphabetic printing *perforadora impresora alfabética*
–, paper *punzadora para papel*
–, to *perforar*
punching *perforación de fichas*
–, alphabetic *perforación alfabética*
–, alphabetic summary *perforación de datos alfabéticos al sumarizar*
punitive action *medida represiva*
purchase *comprar*
– account *cuenta de compra*
– contract *contrato de compraventa*
– obligations, advance payments on *envíos a cuenta de pedidos a servir*
– order *orden de compra, nota de compra*
– price *precio de compra*
– requisition *petición de compra*
– tax *impuesto sobre ventas*
–, compulsory *compra obligatoria, expropiación*
–, hire *comprar a plazos, comprar en abonos*
–, option to *opción de compra*
purchaser, consumer *consumidor comprobador*
purchases, actual *compras efectivas*
–, domestic *compras en el país*
–, planned *compras previstas*
purchasing ability, financial *capacidad financiera de compra*
– department *sección o departamento de compras*
– policy *política de compras*
– power *poder de compra, poder adquisitivo*
purge *purga*
put in a bid, to *licitar*
pyramid, population *pirámide de población*

Q

qualifications *requisitos, cualidades, calificaciones, salvedades, títulos*
qualified *limitado, condicionado, calificado*
– acceptance *aceptación condicionada o condicional*
– certificate *certificado con salvedades*
– endorsement *endoso condicional*
– monopoly *monopolio limitado*
– owner *tenedor de interés limitado*
– worker *obrero o trabajador calificado*
qualifying shares *acciones habilitantes*
qualitative *cualitativo*
– approach *enfoque cualitativo*
– standards *normas cualitativas*
quality control *control de calidad*
– goods *mercancías de calidad*
– of products *calidad de los productos*
–, top *calidad superior*
quantitative *cuantitativo*
– consumer research *investigación cuantitativa del consumidor*
– indeterminacy *indeterminación cuantitativa*
– probabilities *probabilidades cuantitativas*
– standards *normas cuantitativas*
quantities, significant *cantidades importantes*
quantity discount *descuento por cantidades*
– discount, cumulative *descuento por cantidades acumuladas*
– discount, deferred *descuento por cantidades acumuladas*
– production *producción en serie*
quantum of exports *volumen físico de las exportaciones*
quarter *trimestre*
quarterly *trimestralmente*

– magazine or review *revista trimestral*
quasi-rent *cuasi-renta*
quay *muelle, embarcadero*
queries, technical *consultas técnicas*
question, leading *pregunta directa*
–, limited-response *pregunta de respuestas limitadas*
–, open *pregunta de respuesta libre, pregunta de respuesta abierta*
questioning technique *método interrogativo o analítico*
questionnaire *cuestionario*
– design *preparación del cuestionario*
questions, probing *preguntas de sondeo*
quick assets *activo disponible*
quiet market *mercado encalmado*
quiz *examen oral o escrito*
quota *cuota*
– sampling *muestreo por cupos o cuotas*
– system *sistema de cuotas*
–, amortization *cuota o cupo de amortización*
–, export *cuota de exportación*
–, factor *tanto o cupo de amortización*
–, import *cuota de importación*
–, sales *cuota de ventas, cupo de ventas*
quotable *cotizable*
quotas, custom *cupos arancelarios*
quotation *cotización*
– closing *cotización final, precio de cierre en bolsa*
–, price *cotización de precios*
quotations, stock exchange *cotizaciones, precios bursátiles*
quote, to *cotizar*

R

race *raza*
radio advertising *publicidad radiada*
– advertising, broadcast or *publicidad por radio o radiada*
– engineer *técnico en radio*
– engineering *técnica radiofónica*
– release *comunicado de radio*
– report *radiorreportaje*
– silence *suspensión de emisión*
– station *estación radiofónica*
– transmission *transmisión por radio, transmisión radiofónica*
rail, free on *puesto sobre vagón o railes*
railroad transportation *transporte ferroviario*
raise, to *alzar, levantar, cultivar*
– a cheque *aumentar el importe de un cheque*
– a loan *conseguir un préstamo*
– funds *conseguir fondos*
– money *conseguir fondos*
random *azar, aleatorio, fortuito*
– error *error al azar*
– impulse process *proceso de impulso aleatorio*
– order *orden aleatoria*
– sample *muestra al azar*
– sampling *muestreo al azar*
– sampling error *error de azar en el muestreo*
– sequence *sucesión aleatoria*
– series *serie aleatoria*
– series, accumulated *serie aleatoria acumulada*
– start *comienzo al azar*
– variable, continuous *variable aleatoria continua*
randomization *aleatorización*
range of error, prescribed *amplitud de error prescrito*
– of values *escala de valores*
–, long- *de gran alcance*
–, probability *recorrido de probabilidad*
–, salary *escala de salarios*
–, standard *capacidad normal*
–, yearly *precios máximos y mínimos del año*
rank order *jerarquía*
ranking method *método de jerarquización*
rapid access *acceso rápido*
rateable *valuable, tasable*
rate *tasa, tipo, coeficiente, tarifa, precio,*

valoración, valorización
– book *libro de tarifas*
– cutting *reducción de tarifas*
– of exchange *tipo de cambio*
– of exchange, closing *cambio de precio de cierre*
– of exchange, fixed *tipo de cambio fijo*
– of exchange, multiple *tasa de cambio múltiple*
– of exchange, real *tipo de cambio real*
– of exchange, sight *cambio a la vista*
– of freight *tarifa de flete*
– of growth *tasa de crecimiento*
– of increase *tasa de crecimiento, tasa de aumento*
– of interest *tasa de interés*
– of interest, market *tasa de interés del mercado*
– of issue *curso de emisión*
– of output *rendimiento*
– of return *tasa de rendimiento*
– of speed or turnover *movimiento de ventas, tiempo de la distribución*
– regulation *control de tarifas*
– setting *fijación de tarifas*
–, adjusted *tasa ajustada*
–, bank *tipo de interés bancario, descuento bancario*
–, base *salario base*
–, birth *natalidad, tasa de natalidad*
–, buying *tarifa o tipo de compras*
–, class *clase de salario o de tarifa*
–, closing *cotización final, precio de cierre en bolsa*
–, cut *precio o tarifa reducidos por rebaja*
–, day *jornal*
–, death *mortalidad, tasa de mortalidad*
–, design *gasto normal*
–, discount *tasa, tipo de descuento*
–, earned *ganancia por hora, por unidad de tiempo*
–, effective *tasa real*
–, evaluated *tarifa de valoración*
–, exchange *tipo de cambio*
–, flat *tasa uniforme, precio global*
–, general *impuesto general*
–, grade *grado o clase de salario, clase de tarifa*

–, inclusive *tarifa a tanto alzado*
–, interest *tasa de interés*
–, market *tipo del mercado*
–, net reproduction *tasa neta de reproducción*
–, occupational death *tasa de mortalidad por profesiones*
–, piece *precio unitario, precio por pieza*
–, population growth *índice de aumento de población*
–, prime *tasa preferencial*
–, probability *tasa de probabilidad*
–, progressive commission *tipo de comisión progresiva*
–, reduced *tarifa reducida*
–, regressive commission *tipo de comisión regresiva*
–, revenue *impuesto sobre la venta*
–, sliding scale *tipo de comisión a escala gradual*
–, stock turnover *giro de existencias (promedio)*
–, starting *salario o sueldo inicial*
–, straight *tarifa constante*
–, wage *tarifa de salarios*
–, yield *tipo de rendimiento*
rated concern *empresa clasificada por agencias de crédito*
– output, down- *producción disminuída*
rates, advertisement *tarifas de anuncios*
– card, advertisement *tarifas de publicidad*
–, commodity *tarifas para mercancías*
–, freight *tarifas de flete*
–, multiple exchange *tasas múltiples*
–, per diem *tarifas por día*
rating *tasación, valor asignado, clasificación de una empresa*
– chart, comparative *cuadro comparativo de capacidades*
– form, employee *formulario para valorar los méritos del obrero*
–, continuous *rendimiento continuo*
–, credit *estimación o valoración crediticia*
–, high *alta puntuación*
–, job *valoración del trabajo*
–, merit *valoración de méritos*
–, performance *apreciación de la actuación, valoración de la actuación*
ratings, brand *apreciación de la marca*
–, flat *valoración estimada de la actuación*
–, security *clasificación de valores*
ratio *razón, coeficiente, índice*
– acid-test *proporción entre el activo y pasivo circulante*
– delay method *método de observaciones instantáneas*
– of solvency *índice de solvencia*

– test, probability *prueba de la razón de la probabilidad*
–, collection *índice de valores*
–, estimated *razón estimada*
–, gold *proporción de la moneda de oro en relación con la circulación*
–, parity income *razón de paridad de ingresos*
–, reserve *relación de reserva*
–, sales *índice de ventas*
–, standard *razón estándar o normal*
–, stock-sales *proporción entre existencias y ventas*
–, stock-turnover *proporción entre existencias y giro*
ration, to *racionar*
– out licences *restringir las licencias*
rationalization *racionalización*
rationing *racionamiento*
– of credits *restricción de créditos*
raw materials *materias primas*
– materials turnover *movimiento de materias primas*
– materials, strategic *materias primas estratégicas*
re-acceptance *reaceptación*
reaction *reacción*
–, chain *reacción en cadena*
–, self-sustaining *reacción automantenida*
read a paper, to *presentar una comunicación, dar una conferencia*
reader *corrector de pruebas, consultor técnico de un editor, anuncio en forma de texto*
–, proof- *corrector de pruebas*
reading method, continuous *método de lectura contínua*
– room *sala de lectura, sala de corrección de pruebas*
–, proof- *corrección de pruebas*
readout *lectura*
readjusting entry *contrapartida*
readjustment of currencies *reajuste monetario*
ready cash *fondos disponibles, disponibilidades de caja*
– money *efectivo, fondos disponibles, dinero contante*
real assets *bienes inmuebles o raíces*
– burden *carga real*
– estate *bienes raíces*
– estate bond *bono inmobiliario*
– estate broker *corredor de bienes raíces*
– estate tax *impuesto sobre inmuebles, predial*
– estate, improved *predio edificado*
– income *ingreso real*
– price *precio real*
– property *bienes inmuebles o raíces*

– rate of exchange *tipo de cambio real*
– securities *garantías hipotecarias*
– wages *salarios reales*
reality *realidad*
realization value *valor en liquidación*
realized income *ingresos vencidos*
– results *resultados obtenidos*
realtor *corredor de bienes raíces o fincas*
reappraisal *reavalúo*
reappraise, to *evaluar*
reappraisement *revaluación*
rearrangement *disposición nueva*
rearranging *reclasificación*
reasoning *razonamiento*
rebate *rebaja, deducción, bonificación, descuento*
–, basic *descuento básico*
–, customs *rebaja en los derechos de aduana*
rebuilt *reconstruida*
receipt *recibo, abono, talón*
– in full *finiquito*
–, clean *recibo sin reservas*
–, forwarding *recibo de expedición*
–, on *al recibo de*
–, to acknowledge *admitir, reconocer*
–, warehouse *recibo de almacén*
receipts *ingresos, entradas, rentas, recibos*
– journal *libro diario de entradas*
–, customs *ingresos de aduana*
–, gross *ingresos brutos, ganancia total*
–, tax *ingresos fiscales*
–, total *ingresos íntegros, ingresos totales*
receivable documents, accounts *documentos de cuentas acobrar*
– ledger, accounts *libro mayor de ventas, documentos de cuentas a librar*
–, accounts *cuenta de clientes, deudas activas, cuentas por cobrar*
–, bills *documentos por cobrar*
–, notes *efectos a cobrar, documentos por cobrar*
receivables *cuentas por cobrar*
receive, to *recibir, percibir*
received payment *recibí*
–, value *valor recibido*
receiver *receptor, liquidador, síndico, administrador*
receiving teller *recibidor, cajero recibidor*
receptacle *caja, bandeja, recipiente*
recession *depresión*
–, business *depresión económica*
re-charter, to *refletar*
recipient *recibidor, recipiente*
reciprocal *recíproco*
– contract *contrato bilateral o recíproco*
– exemption *exención recíproca*

– trade agreements *tratados comerciales recíprocos*
reciprocity principle *principio de reciprocidad*
reckon, to *calcular*
reckoner *calculador*
reckoning *cálculo, ajuste de cuentas*
– account, clear *cuenta clara*
reclamation *recuperación, aprovechamiento de tierras*
recognize a debt, to *admitir una deuda*
recollection *recuerdo*
reconciliation, bank *reconciliación bancaria*
reconditioned *reconstruida*
re-consignment *cambio de destinatario de una mercancía*
record *registro, acta*
–, alphanumerical *registro alfanumérico*
–, information *registro de datos, registro de informaciones*
–, production *registro de producción*
–, registration *alta de registro*
–, returns *registro de devoluciones*
–, sales *registro estadístico de ventas*
–, stock *registro de existencias*
–, stock-control *registro de verificación de existencias*
recorded information *datos registrados*
–, population *población registrada*
recorder, data *registrador de datos*
recording secretary *secretario de actas*
– system, attendance time *sistema registrador de horas de trabajo*
records *registros, archivos*
–, financial *documentos financieros*
–, inventory *libro de almacén o bodega*
recount *recuento*
recover, to *recuperar, cobrar, recobrar*
recoverable accounts *cuentas recobrables*
recovery *recuperación, cobranza*
– plant, by-product *instalación para recuperación de subproductos*
– value *valor de recuperación*
recurring *recurrente*
– samples *muestras que se repiten*
red tape *papeleo, formulismo*
–, in the *en números rojos, con déficit*
re-date, to *poner fecha nueva*
redeem, to *redimir, rescatar, amortizar*
redeemable *redimible, rescatable, amortizable*
– debt *deuda amortizable*
redeemed *redimido, rescatado, amortizado*
redemption *rescate*
– allowance *amortización autorizada*
– fund *fondo de rescate, caja de amortización*
– of the public debt *amortización de la deuda*

pública
– of debentures, annual *reembolso anual de obligaciones*
– price *precio de rescate*
re-discount *redescuento*
reduce, to *reducir*
reduced output *producción disminuída, reducida*
– rate *tarifa reducida*
reducing-balance method of depreciation *método de saldo decreciente*
reducing-charge method *método de depreciación con cargos decrecientes*
reduction, balanced *reducción equilibrada*
redundancy *sobrante, redundancia*
redundant stock *existencias sobrantes, existencias redundantes*
reference, trade *referencia comercial*
references, credit *referencias de crédito*
reflex *reflejo*
–, conditioned *reflejo condicionado*
reform, land *reforma agraria*
refund *devolución, reembolso*
–, to *devolver, reembolsar, consolidar, amortizar*
refundable tax *impuesto reembolsable*
refunded, loan *préstamo amortizado o reembolsado*
refunding bonds *bonos de reintegración*
refusal *negativa, rechazo*
refuse *desecho*
– acceptance, to *rehusar la aceptación*
– payment, to *rehusar el pago*
refused, payment *pago rehusado, pago negado*
regimentation *regimentación*
regional cartel *monopolio regional*
– sales manager *director o jefe de ventas de zona*
register *registro*
– and book-keeping machine, cash *máquina registradora contable*
– a trademark, to *registrar una marca de fábrica*
– a vessel, to *abanderar un barco*
–, adding *registro sumador*
–, address *registro de direcciones*
–, cash *caja registradora*
–, draft *registro de giro librador*
–, employment *registro de colocaciones*
–, information *registro de informaciones*
–, invoice *registro de facturas*
–, security *registro de valores*
–, stock *registro de acciones o existencias*
–, storage address *almacenamiento del registro de direcciones*

–, voucher *registro de comprobantes*
registered *registrado, titulado*
– bond *bono nominativo*
– capital *capital social*
– cheque *cheque de administración*
– debentures *obligaciones nominativas*
– mail *correo certificado*
– securities *títulos nominativos o registrados*
– shares *acciones nominativas o registradas*
– stock *acciones nominativas o registradas*
– trademark *marca registrada*
registering and adding machine, cash *máquina registradora sumadora*
registration *registro*
– fees *derechos de registro*
– number *número de registro o matrícula*
– record *acta de registro*
registry *registro*
– of vital statistics *registro demográfico*
regressive commission rate *tipo de comisión regresiva*
regular *corriente, ordinario*
– attendance hours *horas de asistencia normal*
– budget *presupuesto ordinario*
– mail *correo ordinario*
– meeting *asamblea ordinaria*
– member *miembro titular*
– production *producción en serie*
– session *sesión o junta ordinaria*
– term *período ordinario*
regulation *reglamento, reglamentación*
–, price *reglamentación de precios*
–, rate *control de tarifas*
regulations, customs *reglamento de aduana*
reimbursable advances *anticipos reembolsables*
reimburse, to *reembolsar, reintegrar*
reimbursement credit *crédito de reembolso*
reinstate, to *restablecer, reincorporar*
reissue *reimpresión, reedición*
reject, to *rehusar, rechazar*
rejection *fracaso*
relations manager, public *director de relaciones públicas*
– officer, public *encargado de las relaciones públicas*
–, consumer *relaciones con los consumidores*
–, employer-employee *relaciones entre empresario y empresa*
–, industrial *relaciones industriales o laborales*
–, labour *relaciones laborales, relaciones obrero-patronales*
–, public *relaciones públicas, relaciones generales*
relationship *relación*
–, actual *relación verdadera, relación efectiva*

relax credit, to *facilitar el crédito*
relaxation *relajamiento, reposo, descanso*
– allowance, compensating *suplemento para compensar la fatiga*
– of restrictions *disminución de restricciones*
relay, television *retransmisión televisiva*
release *comunicado, finiquito, descargo*
– load *dejar cargar*
–, press *comunicado de prensa*
–, radio *comunicado de radio*
–, to *descargar, librar*
re-lease, to *rearrendar*
relet, to *recontratar*
relevant cost *costo pertinente*
reliability *confiabilidad*
reliable *confiable, fidedigno*
– source *de buena fuente*
relief *asistencia, socorro, beneficencia*
– works *obras para reducir el desempleo*
–, on *viviendo de ayuda estatal, de la beneficencia*
–, unemployment *auxilio de desempleo*
relieve shortages, to *remediar la escasez*
remainder balance *saldo remanente*
remake, to *rehacer*
reminder card *ficha recordatoria o recordativa*
–, follow-up *cartas de insistencia*
remission *remesa, remisión*
– of a tax *reducción de un importe, cancelación de un importe*
remit, to *remitir, enviar*
remittance *envío, remesa*
remunerate, to *remunerar*
remuneration *remuneración, salario*
remunerative price *buen precio*
render, to *rendir, hacer*
– an account, to *rendir una cuenta, pasar facturas*
renegotiate, to *reajustar, renegociar*
renew, to *renovar, prorrogar*
renewal *renovación, prórroga*
– fund *fondo de reposición*
–, capital *reinversión de capital*
renewals and replacements reserve *reserva para renovación y reposición*
rent *alquiler, arriendo*
– factors *factores de renta*
rental *arriendo, alquiler*
– value *valor por concepto de alquiler*
repay, to *reembolsar*
repayment *reembolso*
repeal, to *derogar*
repetitive element *elemento regular, cíclico o repetitivo*
replacement *reposición, reemplazo*
– cost *costo de reposición*

–, partial *reposición parcial*
report *informe, relación*
– writing *redacción de informes*
–, annual *informe anual, memoria anual*
–, annual financial *informe financiero anual*
–, audit *informe de auditoría*
–, commercial *informe o boletín comercial*
–, credit *informe de crédito*
–, expenses *informe sobre los gastos*
–, market *informe del mercado, revista del mercado*
–, progress *informe del avance de una obra*
–, radio *radiorreportaje*
–, tax *impreso de declaración de renta*
–, to *informar*
reporter *periodista, informador, reportero*
reports, call and sales *informes de visitas y ventas*
–, interview *informes de revistas*
–, research *informes de investigación de mercados*
represent, to *representar*
representative *representante, representativo*
– sample *muestra representativa*
– sample selection *selección de muestras representativas*
–, advertisement *representante de la sección de anuncios*
–, employers' *representante de los patronos*
–, sales *agente de ventas*
reprint *separata, reimpresión, tirada aparte*
reproduction cost *costo de reposición, costo de reproducción*
– service, documentary *servicio de reproducción de documento*
request *solicitud, demanda*
required information *información conveniente*
requirement *requisito, característica, estipulación*
requirements, inventory *requisitos del inventario*
–, job *requisitos de trabajo*
requisites *requisitos*
requisition form *impreso para pedidos*
–, purchase *petición de compra*
resale price *precio de reventa*
rescind, to *rescindir*
research *investigación*
– activity *actividad investigadora*
– analyst *analista investigador*
– and development *investigación y desarrollo*
– centre *centro de investigaciones, centro investigador*
– engineer *técnico investigador*
– facilities *medios de investigación*
– information, market *información en la*

investigación de mercados
- manager, market *director de investigaciones del mercado*
- project *proyecto de investigación*
- scientist *investigador científico*
- staff *cuerpo o grupo de investigadores*
- team *investigación en equipo*
- techniques *técnicas de investigación*
- work *trabajo de investigación*
-, activation *investigación de la actividad*
-, applied *investigación aplicada*
-, business *investigación de la actividad comercial*
-, commercial *investigación comercial*
-, consumer *investigación sobre el consumidor*
-, design *investigación dirigida*
-, desk *investigación en la oficina*
-, engineering *investigación industrial*
-, experimental *investigación experimental*
-, follow-up *investigación permanente*
-, market *investigación del mercado*
-, marketing *investigación mercadológica, investigación distributiva*
-, quantitative consumer *investigación cuantitativa del consumidor*
-, sales *investigación de ventas*
-, scientific *investigación científica*
-, statistical *investigación estadística*
-, technological *investigación tecnológica*
researcher, statistical *investigador estadístico*
resell, agreement to *pacto de retroventa*
reservations and safeguards *reservas y garantías*
reserve *reserva*
- above normal *reserva superior a lo normal, excedente*
- fund *fondo de reserva*
- liabilities *reserva de pasivo*
- price *precio mínimo fijado en subasta*
- ratio *relación de reserva*
-, allowances *reserva para bonificaciones*
-, benefit-fund *reserva para auxilios a empleados*
-, bullion *reserva metálica*
-, compulsory cash *reserva obligatoria en metálico*
-, contingent *reserva de contingencia*
-, gold *encaje de oro, reserva de oro*
-, hidden *reserva oculta*
-, legal *reserva legal*
-, profit-sharing *reserva para participación de utilidades*
-, renewals and replacements *reserva para renovación y reposición*
-, sinking fund *reserva para amortización*
reserved, copyright *derechos de publicación*

reservados
reserves of banks, compulsory *reservas bancarias obligatorias*
-, bank *reservas bancarias*
-, cash *reservas líquidas en efectivo*
-, offset *reservas de tasación*
residence *residencia, domicilio*
-, normal *residencia permanente*
resident *habitante, residente, vecino*
- company *compañía que funciona en el lugar de incorporación*
residual balance *saldo residual*
- product *subproducto*
resign, to *renunciar, dimitir*
resignation *resignación, dimisión*
resolution *acuerdo, decisión*
- chart *pruebas de ajuste*
resolve, to *acordar, resolver*
resource file *fichero de proveedores*
resources *medios, recursos*
-, available *recursos disponibles*
-, capital *bienes de equipo, infraestructura*
-, financial *recursos financieros, posibilidades fiscales (A)*
-, liquid *recursos líquidos o realizables*
-, natural *recursos naturales*
respite *plazo, prórroga*
respondent *interrogado*
response, individual's *conducta del individuo*
responsibility, business *responsabilidad comercial*
responsible *responsable, solvente*
rest *resta, resto, diferencia, saldo, descanso, reposo*
resting point *punto de reposo*
restoration of stock *restauración de las existencias*
restrain, to *restringir*
restraint of trade, combination in *acuerdo para restringir la competencia*
-, policy of *política de austeridad*
restricted *restringido, reservado*
- bond *bono no transferible*
- imports *importaciones restringidas, controladas*
- market *mercado reservado*
restrictions, import *restricciones a la importación*
-, non-discriminatory *restricciones no selectivas a la importación*
-, policy of non-discriminatory import *política de restricciones no selectivas a la importación*
-, relaxation of *disminución de restricciones*
results *éxito publicitario*
-, realized *resultados obtenidos*

retail *detalle, menudeo*
- clerk *dependiente al por menor*
- enterprise *empresa o tienda al detalle*
- firm *empresa o tienda al detalle*
- list price *lista de precios al detalle*
- merchandise *mercancías al por menor, mercancías de menudeo*
- method *método de la venta al por menor*
- price *precio al detalle, precio al por menor*
- sales *ventas al detalle*
- sales tax *impuesto sobre las ventas al por menor*
- selling price *precio de venta al detalle o por menor*
- stock average *promedio de existencias al detalle*
- store *tienda*
- store audit *comprobación en las tiendas al por menor*
- trade *comercio al por menor*
retailer *detallista, tendero, comerciante, vendedor al por menor, almacenero (M)*
retained earning *beneficios no distribuidos*
-, value *valor retenido*
retaining fee *pago anticipado con que se ajusta el servicio de una persona*
retaliatory tariff *impuestos de represalia*
retention *retención*
retirement *retiro, jubilación*
- age *edad de jubilación*
- annuity *pensión de retiro*
- fund *fondo de pensión*
- plan *plan de retiro*
-, compulsory *retiro forzoso*
retiring fund *caja de retiros*
retraining *reeducación*
re-transfer *retransmisión*
retroactive payment *pago de sueldos atrasados*
return *producto, rendimiento, beneficio*
- freight *flete de retorno*
- mail, by a *vuelta de correo*
- of capital *rendimiento del capital*
-, allowable *utilidad permisible*
-, annual *ingreso o renta anual*
-, compulsory *declaración obligatoria*
-, fair *beneficio justo*
-, false *declaración falsa de impuestos*
-, rate of *tasa de rendimiento*
-, sales *devolución de artículos vendidos*
-, tax *impreso de declaración de renta*
returnable advances *anticipos reembolsables*
returned cheques *cheques devueltos*
returns *producto, ingreso, utilidades*
- record *registro de devoluciones*
-, diminishing *rendimiento decreciente*

-, taxable fiduciary income tax *ingresos por impuestos sobre la renta fiduciaria imponible*
re-usable container *envase reutilizable*
revaluation *revaloración, revaluación*
revenue *ingresos, entrada, crédito, renta, tesoro, aduanas*
- authorities *fisco, administración fiscal, agentes fiscales, inspectores de hacienda*
- bond *bono del estado*
- duties *derechos fiscales*
- expenditures *desembolsos de ingresos*
- laws *leyes fiscales*
- rate *impuesto sobre la renta*
- stamp *timbre fiscal*
- tariff *arancel fiscal*
- tax, internal *impuesto fiscal*
-, current *ingreso ordinario*
-, gross *ingreso bruto*
-, internal *ingreso interior*
-, net *ingreso o beneficio neto*
-, public *renta fiscal, ingresos públicos*
reversal *inversión, cambio, revocación*
reverse coding *codificación inversa*
reversion *reversión, retroventa, revendición*
review *revista*
-, monthly *revista mensual*
revise, to *enmendar, codificar*
revision *modificación, revisión*
revival *reestreno*
revolving credit *crédito renovable*
- fund *fondo renovable*
reward *gratificación, premio*
-, collective *recompensa colectiva*
-, financial *recompensa monetaria*
ribbon, inked *cinta entintada*
right *derecho, título, privilegio*
- and left hand chart *diagrama de ambas manos*
- of property *derecho de dominio*
- to strike *derecho de huelga*
-, sole *derecho exclusivo*
rights reserved, all *derechos de propiedad reservados*
-, acquired *derechos adquiridos*
-, exclusive *derechos exclusivos*
-, patent *derechos de patente*
-, pension *derechos de pensión o jubilación*
-, preventive *derechos preventivos o precautorios*
-, primary *derechos primarios*
-, private *derechos individuales o particulares*
-, property *derechos de propiedad*
-, to clear the *comprobar los derechos literarios*
-, vested *derechos adquiridos*

rigidity *rigidez, inflexibilidad*
ring *sindicato*
–, shipping *asociación de empresas de transporte marítimo*
rise *alza, aumento*
rising prices *precios de alza*
risk function *función del riesgo*
–, accident *riesgo de accidentes*
–, amount at *cantidad en riesgo*
–, carrier's *riesgo de trasportador*
–, marine *riesgo marítimo*
–, spread of *diversificación de los riesgos*
risks, insurable *riesgos asegurables*
road selling *venta en ruta*
– sign *rótulo anunciador en carretera*
– tax *impuesto para conservación de camiones*
–, national *carretera nacional*
roll, adding *rollo de papel para máquina sumadora*
room, control *sala de control*
–, drafting *sala de dibujo*
–, reading *sala de lectura, sala de corrección de pruebas*
–, sales *lonja de ventas*
root *radical, raíz*
roster, personnel *nómina de personal*
rotary calculator *calculadora rotativa*
– fixture *montaje rotativo*
– press *rotativa*
rotation of crops *rotación de cultivos*
– of stocks *rotación de existencias*
–, job *rotación de trabajos*

rough *basto, en bruto, aproximado*
– draft *borrador*
– estimate *presupuesto aproximado*
– sorting *clasificación aproximada*
round price, all- *precio global*
– the clock, work *trabajo continuo*
roundabout process *proceso indirecto*
route *ruta*
– card *hoja o ficha de ruta*
– label *hoja o ficha de ruta*
– sheet *hoja de ruta*
routine *rutina, rutinario*
– list *lista ordinaria*
–, clerical *tramitación burocrática*
royalties, patent *derechos de patente*
royalty *derechos de autor, derechos de patente*
rubber band *banda de goma, goma elástica*
– stamp *sello o timbre de goma*
rule *regla, reglamento*
–, computing *regla de cálculo*
ruling price *precio en vigor, precio predominante*
run low, to *agotarse*
–, test *test práctico, prueba práctica*
runaway inflation *inflación desmedida*
running expenses *gastos ordinarios, gastos de operación*
– time *tiempo de utilización de la máquina, tiempo de máquina*
ruse *subterfugio*
rush order *pedido urgente*

S

sabotage *sabotaje*
sacrifice *sacrificio*
–, at *con pérdida*
safe *caja de seguridad, seguro*
– deposit box *caja de seguridad*
safeguard *resguardo, garantía*
–, to *proteger*
safeguards, reservations and *reservas y garantías*
safety *seguridad*
– device *depósito de seguridad*
– stock *existencia de seguridad*
–, industrial *seguridad industrial*
sagging market *mercado flojo*
salary *sueldo, salario, remuneración*
– adjustment *reajuste de salarios*
– brackets *escalas de salarios*
– range *escala de salarios*
– scales *escalas de salarios*
– stipulations *estipulaciones de salarios*
–, basic *salario base*
–, commencing *salario inicial*
–, expected *salario deseado*
–, stated *salario establecido*
sale *venta*
– goods *saldos*
– on credit *venta al fiado*
– price *precio de venta*
– price, gross *precio de venta al público, precio de venta total*
–, absolute *venta incondicional*
–, annual *venta anual*
–, auction *subasta, remate*
–, average gross *promedio de ventas brutas*
–, bargain *liquidación a precios reducidos*
–, bear *venta especulativa a la baja*
–, bill of *escritura de venta, comprobante o cuenta de venta, factura*
–, cash *venta al contado*
–, compulsory *venta obligatoria, adjudicación forzosa, expropiación*
–, contract of *contrato de compraventa*
–, deed of *contrato de compraventa*
–, earmarked *venta reservada*
–, forced *venta forzada*
–, private *venta directa*
–, public *subasta con aviso anticipado*
saleability *capacidad o facilidad de venta,*
vendibilidad
saleable *vendible*
– condition, in *en estado de venta*
sales *ventas*
– ability *aptitud para vender*
– account *cuenta de ventas*
– accounting *contabilidad de ventas*
– agent *agente de ventas*
– allowance *rebaja del precio de factura*
– analysis *análisis de ventas*
– angle *punto de vista de ventas, política de ventas*
– approach *enfoque de las ventas, política de ventas*
– book *libro de ventas*
– budget *presupuesto de ventas, gastos de ventas*
– circulation, net *tirada neta*
– consultant *asesor sobre métodos de ventas*
– control *control de ventas, fiscalización de ventas*
– control forms *formularios de verificación de ventas*
– controller *verificador de ventas*
– cost *coste de ventas*
– cost accountant *contable de costes de venta*
– cost analyst *especialista en costes de venta*
– costing *fijación del coste de ventas*
– curve *curva o gráfico de ventas*
– data *datos sobre las ventas*
– department *departamento o sección de ventas*
– discounts *descuentos por pronto pago*
– effort, aggressive *esfuerzo combativo de ventas*
– engineer *técnico de ventas*
– figure *cifra de ventas*
– force *personal de ventas, equipo de vendedores*
– forecast *previsión de ventas*
– forecast, long-range *previsión de ventas a largo plazo*
– forecasting *previsión de ventas*
– index *índice de ventas*
– information *información de ventas*
– information, unit *información sobre las unidades vendidas*
– ledger *libro mayor de ventas*

– letter *carta de prospección*
– management *dirección de ventas*
– manager *director comercial, jefe de ventas*
– manager, assistant *jefe auxiliar de ventas*
– manager, foreign *jefe de ventas para el extranjero*
– manager, home *jefe de ventas para el interior del país*
– manager, regional *director o jefe de ventas de zona*
– order clerk *receptor de órdenes de venta*
– performance *rendimiento de ventas*
– planning *planeamiento de las ventas*
– policy *sistema de ventas*
– promotion *promoción de ventas*
– promotion manager *jefe de promoción de ventas*
– promotional activity *actividad de promoción de ventas*
– quota *cuota de ventas, cupo de ventas*
– ratio *índice de ventas*
– record *registro estadístico de ventas*
– reports, call and *informes de visitas y ventas*
– representative *agente de ventas*
– research *investigación de ventas*
– return *devolución de artículos vendidos*
– room *lonja de ventas*
– service, after- *servicio de postventas, servicio de piezas de recambio*
– statistics *estadística de ventas*
– tax *impuesto sobre el precio de ventas*
– tax, retail *impuesto sobre las ventas al por menor*
– team *equipo de ventas*
– to date *ventas a crédito*
– volume *volumen de ventas*
–, actual *ventas efectivas*
–, auction *ventas en subasta*
–, budget *presupuesto de ventas*
–, charge *ventas a crédito*
–, clearance *ventas por liquidación*
–, cost auditing of *revisión del coste de ventas*
–, direct *venta directa*
–, expected *ventas en espectativa o esperados*
–, follow-up *ventas continuados*
–, gross *ventas brutas*
–, instalment *ventas en abonos, ventas en plazos*
–, net *ventas netas*
–, off *ventas fuera de temporada*
–, peak *ventas máximas*
–, planned *ventas previstas*
–, potential *ventas potenciales*
–, proceeds of *producto de ventas*
–, retail *ventas al detalle*
–, to build *crear ventas*

salesman, travelling (Br) *viajante comercial, vendedorviajante*
– house-to-house *vendedores a domicilio*
salesmanship *aptitud o técnica de vender*
–, high-pressure *habilidad para forzar las ventas*
salvage *salvamento, recuperación*
– agreement *contrato de salvemento*
sample *muestra, testigo*
– copy *ejemplar de muestra*
– data, pre-test *datos de muestra de pruebas previas*
– design *diseño de una muestra*
– display *exposición de muestras*
– number, average *número muestral promedio*
– selection *selección de muestras*
– selection, representative *selección de muestras representativas*
– size *tamaño de la muestra*
– statistics *estadística de la muestra*
– survey *encuesta por muestra*
– variation *variación de las muestras*
–, area probability *muestreo por zonas y probabilidad*
–, as per *según muestra*
–, balanced *muestra contrabalanceada*
–, by *según muestra*
–, controlled *muestra controlada*
–, cross *muestra cruzada*
–, large *muestra grande*
–, odd *muestra suelta*
–, probability *muestra de probabilidad*
–, random *muestra al azar*
–, representative *muestra representativa*
–, self-correcting *muestra de autocorrección*
–, self-weighted *muestra autoponderada*
–, sequential *muestra sucesiva*
–, simple *muestra simple*
–, stratified *muestra estratificada*
–, standard *muestra tipo*
–, systematic *muestra sistemática*
–, take a *sacar una muestra*
–, to buy by *comprar según muestra*
–, weighted *muestra ponderada*
sampler *tomador o sacador de muestras*
samples, line of *muestrario*
–, matched *muestras concordantes*
–, population *muestras de población*
–, recurring *muestras que se repiten*
sampling *muestreo*
– analysis, statistical *análisis estadístico de muestreo*
– bias *bias del muestreo*
– error *error de muestreo*
– error, normal *error normal de muestreo*
– error, random *error de azar en el muestreo*

– method *método de muestreo*
– operations *operaciones de muestreo*
– precision *precisión del muestreo*
– principles *principios de muestreo*
– procedure *procedimiento de muestreo*
– survey *encuesta por muestreo*
– technique *técnica de muestreo*
– theory *teoría del muestreo*
– variance *variancia del muestreo*
–, area *muestreo por zonas*
–, fair *muestreo correcto*
–, mixed *muestreo mixto*
–, probability *muestreo de probabilidad*
–, quota *muestreo por cupos*
–, random *muestreo al azar, muestreo aleatorio*
–, statistical *muestreo estadística*
–, systematic *muestreo sistemático*
sanctions *sanciones*
–, economic *sanciones económicas*
sandwich man *hombre-anuncio*
satisfaction *satisfacción, placer*
–, job *satisfacción en el trabajo*
saturated market *mercado saturado*
save, to *ahorrar*
–, propensity to *propensión a ahorrar*
saving *ahorro, economía*
–, corporate *ahorro social*
–, daylight *avance de la hora*
–, forced *ahorro forzado*
–, gross *ahorro bruto*
–, labour *ahorro de trabajo*
–, personal *ahorro personal*
–, to show a *presentar una economía*
savings *ahorros*
– bank *banco, caja de ahorros*
– bank, postal *caja postal de ahorros*
– bond *títulos o bonos de ahorro*
– cycle *ciclo de ahorros*
– deposits *dépositos de ahorro*
–, net *ahorro neto*
scale *escala*
– commission rate, sliding *tipo de comisión a escala gradual*
– of apportionment *escala de repartición*
– of discounts *tarifa escalonada*
– of global progression *escala de progresión*
– of wages *escala de sueldos, escalafón*
–, job evaluation *escala de valoración de trabajo*
–, large *en gran escala, grande*
–, offset *escala gradual de salarios, escala de aumentos*
–, wage *escalafón, escala de salarios*
scales, salary *escalas de salarios o sueldos*
scarcely populated area *área escasamente poblada*

scarcity, economy of *económico de escasez*
scatter chart *gráfica de dispersión*
– coefficient *coeficiente de dispersión*
– diagram *diagrama de dispersión*
schedule *programa, plan, honorario, tabla*
– of concessions *lista de concesiones*
– of duties *arancel*
– of par values *tabla de valores a la par*
–, demand *tabla, curva de demanda*
–, department *programa de departamento*
–, engineering development *programa técnico del desarrollo de fabricación*
–, factor *programa, cuadro de amortización*
–, individual *programa o plan personal, cédula personal*
–, management *programa de fabricación*
–, master *programa básico*
–, supply *tabla de oferta*
–, time *programa de tiempo*
–, training *programa de instrucción*
–, work *programa de trabajo*
scheduled costs *costos proyectados*
schedules, production *exámenes o programas de producción*
scheduling *programación*
scheme *proyecto, plan*
–, bonus *sistema de primas o incentivos*
–, commodity arbitrage *plan de arbitraje sobre mercancías*
–, suggestion *sistema de sugerencias*
schemer *proyectista*
science, business *ciencias económicas*
scientific research *investigación científica*
scientist, research *investigador científico*
score *tanteo, puntos, cómputo*
scrap *chatarra, desperdicios*
scrip *vale, certificado*
scrutiny *escrutinio*
sea carrier *empresa naviera*
sealed bid *propuestas selladas*
sealer, envelope *cierra sobres*
search, to *buscar*
season *temporada, estación*
– cyclical fluctuations *fluctuaciones cíclicas de temporada*
–, slack *temporada de depresión*
seasonal *estacional, de estación o temporada*
– changes *vacaciones o cambios estacionales*
– computation *cálculo estacional*
– demand *demanda de temporada*
– duties *derechos arancelarios de temporada*
– forecast *pronóstico de la temporada*
– goods *artículos de temporada*
– loss *pérdidas de la temporada*
– production *producción de temporada*

– unemployment *desempleo estacional*
– variation *variación estacional*
– worker *trabajador de temporada*
seasonally adjusted *reajustado según temporada*
secondhand goods *artículos de segunda mano, artículos usados*
– shop *tienda de segunda mano, tienda de baratillo o lance*
–, to buy *comprar de segunda mano*
secondary data *datos secundarios*
secret, trade *secreto industrial*
secretariat, commercial *secretaría comercial*
secretary, acting *secretario interino*
–, assistant *secretario auxiliar*
–, commercial *secretario comercial*
–, private *secretaria particular*
–, recording *secretario de actas*
-'s office *secretaría*
section data, cross- *datos de sección cruzada*
–, cross- *grupo representativo, sección cruzada*
–, magazine *sección especial*
sector, public *sector público*
secular fluctuations *fluctuaciones, variaciones a largo plazo*
– stagnation *baja actividad económica en largo plazo de tiempo*
– trend *curso, tendencia a largo plazo*
secured *asegurado, garantizado*
– accounts *cuentas garantizadas*
– bond *bono hipotecario*
– claim *reclamación garantizada*
– liabilities *pasivo garantizado*
– loan *préstamo garantizado*
–, value *valor en garantía, valor en prenda*
securities *obligaciones, títulos, valores*
– market *mercado bursátil o de valores*
–, advances on *préstamos sobre títulos*
–, bearer *títulos al portador*
–, fixed-income *valores de renta fija*
–, foreign *valores extranjeros*
–, industrial *títulos industriales*
–, listed *valores bursátiles*
–, negotiable *valores transmisibles*
–, outstanding *acciones o títulos emitidos*
–, pledged *valores dados en garantías*
–, public *valores públicos*
–, public utility *títulos de empresas de servicio público*
–, unlisted *valores no inscritos en bolsa*
–, unsound *valores especulativos*
security holders *tenedores de títulos*
– holdings *títulos en portafolio*
– payments, social *pago por previsión social*
– ratings *clasificación de valores*
– register *registro de valores*

– tax, social *impuesto de seguro social*
–, collateral *garantía prendaria, colateral*
–, collective *seguridad colectiva*
–, personal *garantía personal o mobiliaria*
–, social *previsión social, seguridad social*
seizure *embargo*
select, to *seleccionar*
selected points, method of *método de los puntos elegidos*
selection *selección*
– switch, address *interruptor de selección de direcciones*
– with arbitrary probability *selección con probabilidad arbitraria*
– with equal probability *selección con igual probabilidad*
– with probability proportional to size *selección con probabilidad proporcional al tamaño*
–, personnel *selección del personal*
–, sample *selección de muestras*
selective distribution approach *enfoque de la distribución selectiva*
– information *información selectiva*
self *yo, ego*
– adjusting *que se ajusta en forma automática*
– confidence *seguridad en sí mismo, confianza en sí mismo*
– confident *confianza o seguridad en sí mismo*
– consumption *autoconsumo*
– correcting sample *muestra de autocorrección*
– financed *autofinanciado*
– liquidating *autoliquidable, automortizable*
– service stores *tiendas de autoservicio*
– sufficiency *independencia económica, autosuficiencia*
– sustaining reaction *reacción automantenida*
– weighted sample *muestra autoponderada*
sell at auction *rematar, vender en subasta*
– at loss *vender con pérdida*
– at profit *vender con ganancia*
– at the closing market *vender a precio de cierre*
– at the opening market *vender a precio de apertura*
– forward *vender para entrega futura*
– off *liquidar*
– on consignment *vender en consignación*
– short *vender en descubierto, operar en descubierto*
– up *liquidar*
–, to buy and *cambalachear*
seller *vendedor*
–, street *vendedor ambulante*
-'s market *mercado del vendedor*
-'s option *opción del vendedor*

selling agent *agente de ventas*
– commission *comisión de venta*
– effort *esfuerzo de ventas*
– expenses, direct *gastos de la venta directa*
– floor *sección o lugar de venta*
– off *liquidación*
– price *precio de venta*
– price, distributor's *precio de ventas para los distribuidores*
– price, fixed *precio fijo de venta*
– price, retail *precio de venta al detalle o por menor*
– terms *condiciones de venta*
–, distress *ventas de urgencia*
–, high-pressure *esfuerzo intenso de ventas*
–, mail order *venta o negocio por correspondencia*
–, road *venta en ruta*
semi-finished *semiacabado, semielaborado*
semi-manufactured products *productos semielaborados*
semi-product *producto semielaborado*
semi-skilled *semiespecializado*
senior partner *socio principal, socio más antiguo*
seniority *antigüedad*
sense, common- *sentido común*
sensible *sensato, prudente*
sensory *sensorio*
sentient *ente, ser sensible*
sequence *secuencia*
– of economic events *serie de fenómenos económicos*
–, alphabetical *serie alfabética*
–, random *sucesión aleatoria*
–, timed *secuencia cíclica*
–, timing *secuencia cronizada o temperizada*
sequential sample *muestra sucesiva*
serendipity *facultad de descubrir casualmente*
serial *serial, de serie*
– bonds *bonos de vencimiento en serie*
– number *número de serie*
–, newspaper *folletín*
series *serie*
– production *producción en serie*
–, accumulated random *serie aleatoria acumulada*
–, random *serie aleatoria*
–, time *serie cronológica*
service fees *honorarios*
– stores, self- *tiendas de autoservicio*
–, advisory *servicio de asesoramiento*
–, after-sales *servicio de post-venta, servicio de piezas de recambio*
–, agreement of *contrato de servicios*
–, customer *servicio para los clientes o*

consumidores
–, documentation *servicio de documentación*
–, fiscal information *servicio de información en material fiscal*
–, poor delivery *servicio de entrega deficiente*
services, administrative *servicios administrativos*
–, current *servicios habituales*
–, goods and *bienes servicios*
–, non-factor *servicios no correspondientes a los factores de producción*
–, office *servicios de oficina*
–, supply *servicios de abastecimiento, créditos financieros*
servitude *servidumbre*
session, executive *sesión ejecutiva*
–, joint *sesión plenaria*
–, ordinary *sesión ordinaria, junta ordinaria*
set *dispuesto, predispuesto, :eceptor, escenario*
– a price, to *fijar un precio*
– aside, to *reservar, apartar*
– form *formulario*
– of bills of lading *juego de conocimientos de embarque*
– price *precio fijo o establecido*
– up, to *vender a subasta, componer*
–, closed *conjunto cerrado*
–, empty *conjunto vacío*
setback *retroceso, contratiempo*
setter, type- *máquina para componer tipos*
set-off *compensación, disminución progresiva*
set-up *preparación*
setting, rate *fijación de tarifas*
–, type- *composición de tipos*
settle a bill, to *cancelar una factura*
– a strike, to *solucionar una huelga*
– accounts, to *ajustar cuentas*
– up, to *apagar*
–, to *ajustar, arreglar, resolver*
settlement *ajuste, arreglo, saldo, finiquito, liquidación*
– of claims, part *ajuste parcial de reclamaciones*
–, employees' *liquidación para los empleados*
–, full *saldo final, finiquito*
settling day *día de liquidación*
severance pay *pago de despido, indemnización de despido*
share *acción, participación*
– capital *capital en acciones*
– certificate *certificado de acciones*
– premium *prima de emisión*
– without par value *acción sin valor nominal*
–, bearer *acción al portador*
–, bonus *acción gratuita, acción beneficiaria*

–, capital *acción de capital*
–, common *acción común, acción ordinaria*
–, preference *acción privilegiada o preferente*
shareholder *accionista*
shareholders, meeting of *asamblea general de accionistas*
shares *acciones*
– issue *emisión de acciones, emisión de valores*
–, founder's *acciones de fundador*
–, fractional *cupones de acción*
–, fully-paid *acciones cubiertas, exhibidas*
–, management *acciones de administración o de fundador*
–, preference *acciones preferentes*
–, qualifying *acciones habilitantes*
–, registered *acciones nominativas o registradas*
–, to split *dividir las acciones*
sharing, gain- *participación en las ganancias*
–, profit- *reparto, participación en los beneficios*
sharpener, pencil *sacapunta*
sheds, bonded yards and *tinglado de almacenaje de artículos voluminosos y pesados*
sheet accounts, balance *cuentas de balance*
–, analytical balance *hoja de balance analítico*
–, balance *balance de situación, balance general*
–, bonus *boletín de primas*
–, comparative balance *estado de balance comparativo*
–, earnings *boletín de primas*
–, flow *diagrama del avance, plantilla de operaciones sucesivas*
–, interim balance *balance tentativo*
–, job instruction *hojas de instrucciones laborales*
–, loose *prospecto*
–, route *hoja de ruta*
–, tally *hoja de cuentas*
–, tear *página o recorte comprobante de anuncio*
–, technical data *hoja de datos técnicos*
–, time *hoja de jornales devengado*
–, work *hoja de repartición, hoja de computaciones, póliza de contabilidad (M), hoja de trabajo(C), hoja preparatoria del cierre, papel de trabajo (M), estado constructivo (C)*
sheets, amalgamated balance *balances consolidados*
shift *movimiento, cambio, desplazamiento*
–, work *trabajo a tornas*
shipment *embarque, envío*
– on consignment *embarque a consignación*

–, c.o.d. *envío contra reembolso*
＊–, port of *puerto de embarque*
shipper *embarcador, remitente*
shipper's export declaration *declaración de exportación*
shipping *embarque, envío*
– advice *aviso de embarque*
– agent *agente despachador, agente embarcador*
– broker *corredor, agente marítimo*
– business *empresa de transportes marítimos*
– charges *gastos de embarque*
– company *empresa naviera*
– conference *asociación de empresas de transportes marítimos*
– documents *documentos de embarque*
– instructions *instrucciones de embarque*
– marks *marcas de embarque*
– port *puerto de embarque*
– ring *asociación de empresas de transporte marítimo*
ship's papers *documentación del barco*
shop *taller, fábrica, tienda*
– and cost accounting *contabilidad de talleres para determinación de costes*
– committee *comité de empresa*
– steward *representante del personal*
– union *empresa en la que se puede ẽmplear obreros sindicalizados o no pero que en plazo corto se sindicalizarán*
– window *escaparate*
–, general *bazar*
–, secondhand *baratillo, tienda de lance, tienda de segunda mano*
–, work- *taller, obrador, oficina*
shopping centre *centro de ventas, zona comercial*
– news *noticiarios colectivos, folletos colectivos*
short *corto, escaso*
– bill *letra a corto plazo*
– delivery *entrega incompleta*
– delivery, claim for *reclamación por envío incompleto*
– supply *escasez*
– wave *onda corta*
–, sell *vender en descubierto, operar en descubierto*
short-date *a corto plazo*
short-period *de períodos cortos*
short-term bond *bono a corto plazo*
– fluctuation *fluctuación a corto plazo*
short-time bill *letra a corto plazo*
shortage *déficit, escasez, merma*
–, detail *falta de piezas*

–, dollar *escasez de dólares*
–, housing *escasez de viviendas*
–, inventory *mermas en las existencias o en el inventario*
–, item *pérdida de mercancía, merma de mercancía*
–, stock *mermas en las existencias*
shortages, to relieve *remediar la escasez*
shorthand *taquigrafía*
shortsightedness *imprevisión*
shorts and overs, cash *déficit y excedentes de caja*
show *muestra, pequeña exposición*
– a balance, to *señalar un saldo, arrojar un saldo*
– a profit, to *denotar o arrojar una ganancia*
– a saving, to *presentar una economía*
– an increase, to *arrojar un aumento*
–, fashion *exposición de modas*
showcard *cartel para escaparate o vitrina, aparador*
showcase *vitrina, vidriera*
showing, first-sample *exhibición de primeros modelos*
showroom *local de exhibición, sala de muestras*
show-window *vitrina, aparador, ventanal*
shrinkage *merma, déficit, pérdida, contracción*
–, item *pérdida de mercancía*
shutdown time *tiempo de actividad*
sight bill *letra a la vista*
– draft *giro, letra a la vista*
– letter of credit *letra de crédito a la vista*
– rate of exchange *cambio a la vista*
–, at *a la vista, a la presentación*
–, debt at *deuda a la vista*
–, draft at *letra o efecto a la vista*
–, pay at *pagadero a la vista, pagadero a la presentación*
–, to buy at *comprar a ojo*
sign *rótulo, letrero, placa, signo*
–, neon *rótulo luminoso de neón*
–, outdoor *rótulo exterior*
–, road *rótulo anunciador en carretera*
–, sky *rótulo anunciador en azoteas*
–, storage *señal de almacenamiento*
–, wall *rótulo mural, rótulo en pared*
signature *firma, sintonía*
–, authorized *firma autorizada*
–, firm *firma social*
signboard *letrero o rótulo en establecimiento*
significance level *nivel de significación*
– test *prueba de significación*
significant quantities *cantidades importantes*
silence, radio *suspensión de emisión*

similar terms *condiciones comerciales*
simo chart *simograma, diagrama de movimientos simultáneos*
simple cost functions *funciones de costo simple*
– debenture *obligación simple*
– sample *muestra simple*
simultaneous motion-cycle chart *simograma, diagrama de ciclo de movimientos simultáneos*
sinecure *canonjía, sinecura*
single address instruction *instrucción de dirección sencilla*
– crop country *país de monocultivo*
– entry *partida simple*
– entry book-keeping *contabilidad por partida simple*
– tax *impuesto único*
single-price policy *sistema de precios únicos*
sink, to *amortizar, colocar a fondo perdido*
sinking fund *fondo de amortización*
– fund reserve *reserva para amortización*
– fund, government *fondo de reserva del gobierno*
– fund, preferred stock *fondo de amortización de acciones preferentes*
sitdown strike *huelga de brazos caídos, huelga con ocupación*
site *sitio, lugar*
–, test *campo de experiencias*
sitting *sesión, junta, reunión*
situation *colocación, puesto, empleo, ocupación*
–, danger *situación de peligro*
–, marketing *situación mercadológica*
–, vacant *cargo vacante, puesto, empleo*
size *formato, medida*
– family, medium *familia de tamaño medio*
– of family, mean *tamaño medio de las familias*
–, ad *tamaño del anuncio*
–, average order *volumen promedio de pedidos*
–, batch *tamaño del lote*
–, lot *tamaño del lote*
–, order *volumen de pedidos*
–, paper *formato de periódico*
–, sample *tamaño de la muestra*
–, standard *tamaño normalizado*
–, stock *tamaño corriente*
skill *destreza, habilidad*
skilled trade *oficio calificado*
– worker *trabajador u obrero calificado*
sky-sign *rótulo anunciador en azoteas*
slack season *temporada de depresión*
slashed prices *precios reducidos*

sleeping partner *socio comanditario*
slide *diapositiva*
– rule *regla de cálculo*
– transparency *diapositiva en transparencia*
sliding-scale *escala móvil*
– clause *cláusula de revisión de precios*
– commission rates *tipos de comisión a escala gradual*
– contract *contrato de precio revisable*
– salary *escala gradual de salarios, escala de aumentos*
slip *volante, talón, formulario, ticket, etiqueta*
–, call *volante de visitas, formulario de visitas*
–, work *hoja de trabajo, bono de trabajo*
slips, want- *artículos necesarios, artículos convenientes*
slogan *lema, slogan, frase publicitaria*
slope *pendiente*
slow *lento*
– assets *activo disponible a largo plazo*
slow-moving goods *mercancías de salida lenta o difícil*
slow-selling merchandise *mercancía de venta lenta o difícil*
slum clearance *supresión de barrios bajos malsanos*
slump *depresión económica*
smuggle, to *contrabandear*
social *social*
– security *previsión social, seguridad social*
– security payment *pago por previsión social*
– security tax *impuesto de seguro social*
– welfare *bienestar social*
– work *trabajo o servicio social*
society *sociedad*
–, benefit *sociedad de socorros mutuos*
–, co-operative *sociedad cooperativa de consumo*
–, industrial *sociedad industrial*
socio-economic group *grupo económico social*
sociogram *sociograma*
sociologist *sociólogo*
sociology *sociología*
soft currency *moneda de valor inestable*
soil conservation *conservación de suelos o tierras*
sold *vendido*
sole agent *agente exclusivo*
– right *derecho exclusivo*
solvency *solvencia*
sort index *índice de clasificación, índice selectivo*
– tray *casillero de clasificación*
–, standard *tipo de norma, clasificación de normas*

sorter *clasificador*
–, electronic *clasificador electrónico*
sorting, block *clasificación por lotes*
–, normal *clasificación normal*
–, rough *clasificación aproximada*
source *origen, providencia*
– country *país de origen*
–, information *fuente de información*
–, reliable *de buena fuente*
space *espacio en blanco*
span of application *campo de aplicación, alcance*
spare hours *horas libres, horas disponibles*
– money *ahorros*
– time *tiempo libre*
spares *reservas, recambios, reservas*
specialist, financial *especialista en finanzas*
specific *específico, determinado*
– income categories *categorías de ingresos específicos*
specification, draft *proyecto de especificación*
–, job *especificación del trabajo*
–, work *especificación de trabajo*
specifications drawing *diseño de especificaciones, esquema de especificaciones*
–, abbreviated test *especificación de pruebas abreviadas*
–, to meet *cumplir con las especificaciones*
specified account *cuenta detallada*
specimen *espécimen, muestra, testigo*
speculate, to *especular*
speculative motive *motivo especulativo*
speculator *especulador, agiotista*
–, bear *especulador a la baja*
–, bull *especulador al alza*
speech, free *libertad de palabra, libertad de oratoria*
speed *velocidad*
– of turnover *movimiento de ventas, tiempo de la distribución*
– up *aumento de producción por hora o día*
spending power *poder para gastar*
–, deficit *gastos deficitarios*
spirit duplicator *multicopista de azográfica*
–, team *espíritu de equipo*
split commissions *comisiones repartidas*
– shares, to *dividir las acciones*
spoil, to *deteriorar, descomponerse*
spoiled cheque *cheque inutilizado*
sponsor *patrocinador, fiador, auspiciador*
spot broker *corredor de productos para entrega inmediata*
– cash *pago al contado*
– check *comprobar, revisar*
– contract *contrato al contado*

- delivery *entrega inmediata*
- exchange *cambio del día*
- market *mercado de productos disponibles*
- order *orden para entrega y pago inmediato*
- price *precio inmediato, precio en plaza*
spread *divulgación, propagación, diferencia entre los precios de oferta y demanda*
- of risk *diversificación de los riesgos*
-, centre *anuncio de doble página central*
-, double page *anuncio a doble página*
-, wage *rango de salarios*
squad boss *jefe de cuadrilla, capataz de brigada*
square error, mean *error cuadrático medio*
- measure *medida de superficie*
squared deviation *desviación cuadrática*
squeeze *falta de productos entregables contra contratos*
stability *estabilidad, constancia, firmeza, solidez*
- test *prueba de estabilidad*
-, economic *estabilidad económica*
stabilization fund *fondo de estabilización*
- loan, monetary *empréstito para estabilizar la moneda*
-, financial *regularización económica (Am), estabilización financiera*
-, wage *estabilización de tipos de sueldo*
stabilize, to *estabilizar*
stabilizer *fuerza estabilizadora*
stable *estable*
- prices *precios estables*
staff *miembros de la administración, equipo asesor, personal*
- establishment *plantilla de personal asesor*
- structure *estructura funcional*
- training department *departamento asesor de capacitación*
-, design *personal de proyectos*
-, design engineering *personal de estudios de proyectos*
-, research *cuerpo o grupo de investigadores*
-, supervisory *cuadro de personal supervisor*
staffed *con personal suficiente, bien dotado de personal*
stage *etapa*
- of completion *etapa de acabado*
stagnation, business *paralización de los negocios*
-, economic *estanamiento económico*
-, secular *baja actividad económica en largo plazo de tiempo*
stale bill of lading *conocimiento de embarque tardío*
- cheque *cheque caducado*
- debt *deuda caducada*

stale-dated *de fecha atrasada*
stamp *timbre, sello*
- affixer *pegador de sellos*
- duties *impuesto del timbre*
- pad *almohadilla para tintar*
- tax *impuesto del timbre*
-, clock *reloj fechador*
-, dating *fechador de sellos*
-, revenue *timbre fiscal*
-, rubber *sello de goma, timbre de goma*
-, time *reloj fechador, marcador de fecha y hora*
stand, floor *puesto expositivo interior*
standard *patrón, norma, tipo, modelo*
- accounts *cuentas tipo*
- blank *formulario tipo*
- classification *clasificación uniforme*
- costs *costo tipo, coste prefijado*
- deviation *desviación normal*
- error *error típico*
- form *formulario tipo*
- gold *oro de ley*
- guage *plantilla, calibre patrón*
- job *trabajo tipo*
- make *marca corriente*
- measure *medida legal*
- method *método normalizado*
- minute *minuto tipo*
- of liquidity *patrón de liquidez*
- of living *nivel de vida*
- parts *piezas normalizadas*
- practice *sistema tipo*
- practice manual *manual de prácticas tipificadas*
- practice procedure *procedimiento de prácticas normalizadas*
- price *precio regulador*
- range *capacidad normal*
- ratio *razón standard, razón normal*
- sample *muestra tipo*
- size *tamaño normalizado*
- sort *tipo de norma, clasificación de normas*
- time *hora oficial*
- time data *datos de tiempos normalizados*
- wage *salario base*
- weight *peso legal, peso patrón*
-, absolute *patrón absoluto, tipificación absoluta*
-, alternate *norma alternativa, norma variante*
-, commercial *norma o patrón comercial*
-, commodity *mercancía patrón*
-, double *patrón doble*
-, gold exchange *patrón cambio oro*
-, performance *norma de rendimiento*
-, production *norma de producción*
-, temporary *norma provisional*

–, unified *norma unificada*
–, up to *dentro de las normas, al nivel de norma*
–, work *norma de trabajo*
standardization *normalización, unificación, tipificación*
– programme, design *programa de normalización de diseños*
–, material *tipificación de materiales*
–, performance *tipificación del rendimiento*
standardized accounts *cuentas normalizadas, cuentas tipificadas*
– dimensions *dimensiones o medidas normalizadas*
– procedure *procedimiento normalizado*
– production *producción en serie, producción normalizada o tipificada*
– questionnaire *cuestionario normativo*
standardizer *normalizador, tipificador*
standards distribution, costs *módulos o normas de costes de distribución*
– engineer *ingeniero o técnico de normalización*
–, acceptances *normas de aceptación*
–, accepted *normas aprobadas*
–, advertising *normas publicitarias*
–, auditing *normas de auditoría*
–, bureau of *oficina de normas o tipificación*
–, cost *normas de costos*
–, international *normas internacionales*
–, office equipment *normalización de equipos de oficina*
–, qualitative *normas cualitativas*
–, quantitative *normas cuantitativas*
standing *solvencia, reputación, crédito, permanente, vigente*
– charges *cargos permanentes*
– committee *comisión permanente*
– costs *costos o gastos permanentes*
– machine *máquina inactiva o parada*
– order *pedido pendiente, orden vigente*
–, commercial *crédito mercantil*
–, financial *solvencia, grado de solvencia*
standpoint *punto de vista*
staple *materia prima, producto básico o principal, principal, prominente, establecido, introducido*
– commodities *productos básicos, géneros de consumo corriente*
– industry *industria de productos básicos*
– items *artículos de consumo corriente*
– merchandise *mercancía de consumo corriente*
staples *grapas, broches*
stapling machine *grapadora*
start key, auto- *tecla de arranque automático*

starting point *punto de arranque o partida*
– rate *salario o sueldo inicial*
state tax *impuesto estatal*
stated capital *capital declarado*
– salary *salario establecido*
–, account *cuenta conforme o convenida*
statement *estado de cuenta, relación, estado, presentación, relato, memoria, informe*
– of account *estado de cuentas, extracto de cuenta*
– of affairs *estado financiero*
– of assets and liabilities *balance financiero, estado de pasivo y activo*
– of condition *estado de situación*
– of financial condition *balance general o de situación*
– of financial position *balance general*
– of income *estado de ingresos*
–, annual *estado anual*
–, bank *estado de cuenta, extracto bancario*
–, commission *estado de comisión*
–, consolidating *estado de consolidación*
–, credit *estado financiero*
–, earnings *estado de pérdidas y ganancias*
–, financial *estado o balance financiero, balance general (Am)*
–, income *declaración de ingresos*
–, operating *estado de resultados de operación*
–, profit and loss *estado de pérdidas y ganancias*
–, pro-forma *estado en proforma*
–, supporting *estado demostrativo contable*
states, clean *bienes no hipotecados*
station, radio *estación radiofónica*
–, key *estación principal*
–, work *lugar de trabajo*
stationary population *población estacionaria*
– process *proceso estacionario*
stationery *papelería, artículos de escritorio, material de oficina*
– equipment *equipo de material de escritorio*
– store *tienda de papelería*
statism *economía dirigida, control de la economía por el gobierno*
statistical *estadístico*
– aggregate *conjunto estadístico*
– analysis *análisis estadístico*
– approach *enfoque estadístico*
– approach, conventional *enfoque estadístico convencional*
– computation *cálculo estadístico, cómputo estadístico*
– control *verificación estadística*
– information *información estadística*
– inquiry *investigación estadística*
– interpretation *interpretación estadística*

– ledger *mayor estadístico*
– methods *métodos estadísticos*
– prediction *predicción estadística*
– research *investigación estadística*
– researcher *investigador estadístico*
– sampling *muestreo estadístico*
– sampling analysis *análisis estadístico de muestreo*
– test *ensayo estadístico*
– theory *teoría estadística*
statistician *estadístico*
statistics *estadística, datos estadísticos*
– data *datos estadísticos*
–, business *estadística comercial*
–, labour *estadística de trabajo*
–, migration *estadística de migración*
–, production *estadística de producción*
–, sales *estadística de ventas*
–, sample *estadística de la muestra*
–, vital *estadísticas vitales, estadísticas demográficas*
status *estado, posición, rango social*
– board *cuadro demostrativo de la situación del material*
–, account *estado de cuentas*
–, occupational *categoría profesional*
statute *estatuto, ley*
– of limitations *estatuto, escrituras*
statutory *estatutario*
– bond *fianza legal*
– coefficient *coeficiente legal*
– provision *disposición legal*
stay of collection *suspensión de pago*
steadiness *estabilidad, uniformidad*
steady customer *cliente fijo*
– market *mercado de poca fluctuación*
– prices *precios firmes o sostenidos*
steerage *control, mando, gobierno, dirección*
steering committee *junta de gobierno*
– control *control o mando de la dirección*
– group *grupo director*
stencil duplicating *multicopias por estarcido*
– duplicator *multicopista de estarcido*
– work *trabajo de estarcido*
stenographer *taquígrafo, estenógrafo*
-'s notebook *cuaderno de taquigrafía*
stenographer-typist *taquimecanógrafo, taquidactilógrafo*
stenography *estenografía*
step control *regulación gradual*
– plate *plataforma de trabajo*
stepped bonus *prima escalonada*
stereotype *estereotipo, estereotipia*
sterilize, to *neutralizar, esterilizar*
sterilized funds *fondos improductivos*
sterling area *zona esfera esterlina*

– balances *saldos de esterlinas*
– exchange *divisas en libras esterlinas*
steward, shop *representante del personal*
sticker *etiqueta engomada*
stiff market *mercado firme*
stiffening prices *precios firmes*
stimulants, consumer *estímulos del consumidor*
stimulus *estímulo*
–, subliminal *estímulo subliminal*
stipulated premium *prima estipulada*
stipulation, clause exclusivity *cláusula contractual de exclusividad*
–, exclusivity *cláusula contractual de exclusividad*
stipulations, salary *estipulaciones de salarios*
stock *capital comercial, acciones, fondos públicos, existencias, mercancías, provisión, repuesto, papel en general, papel para ser impreso*
– average *promedio de mercancías*
– book *libro de existencias, libro de inventario, registro de acciones*
– capital *capital social, acciones de capital*
– certificate *certificado de acciones*
– clerk *encargado de existencias*
– company *sociedad anónima, compañía por acciones*
– control *control de existencias*
– control card *ficha control de existencias*
– control record *registro de verificación de existencias*
– control, unit *comprobación en unidades de las existencias*
– decrease, planned *disminución de existencias previstas*
– dividend *dividendo en acciones*
– exchange *bolsa de comercios o de valores, bolsa de corredores*
– exchange quotations *boletín de cambios en bolsa*
– exchange securities *valores bursátiles*
– fluctuations *fluctuaciones de existencias*
– in hand *mercancías en almacén*
– in trade *bienes comerciales*
– increase, planned *aumento de existencias previstas*
– inventory, closing *cierre del inventario de existencias*
– issue *emisión de acciones*
– keeping *almacenaje*
– ledger *libro de acciones, auxiliar (libro) de acciones*
– market *mercado o bolsa de valores, bolsa comercial*
– plan, buffer *política de existencias*

estabilizadoras
- premium *prima de emisión*
- record *registro de existencias*
- register *registro de existencias o acciones*
- room clerk *encargado de almacén*
- sales ratio *proporción entre existencias y ventas*
- shortage *mermas de las existencias*
- sinking fund, preferred *fondo de amortización de acciones preferentes*
- size *tamaño corriente*
- speculation *especulación, juego de bolsa*
- taking price *precioo de inventario*
- trading *juego de bolsa*
- tax, capital *impuesto sobre capital en acciones*
- turnover *giro de existencias, renovación de existencias*
- turnover rate *giro de existencias (promedio)*
- turnover ratio *proporción entre existencias y giro*
-, actual *existencias efectivas*
-, average retail *promedio de existencias al detalle*
-, basic *existencia mínima*
-, buffer *reserva, fondo, almacenamiento estabilizador*
-, common *acciones comunes, acciones ordinarias*
-, cumulative preferred *acciones privilegiadas de dividendos acumulables*
-, dummy *acciones de propiedad simulada*
-, in *en existencia, en reserva*
-, joint *capital o fondo social*
-, monetary gold *existencias de oro acuñado*
-, non-assessable *acciones no gravables*
-, non-voting *acciones sin derecho a voto*
-, original *acciones primitivas*
-, out of *agotado*
-, outstanding *capital suscrito*
-, paid-up *acciones cubiertas*
-, participating *acciones preferentes participantes*
-, plural-voting *acciones de voto plural*
-, preference *acciones privilegiadas*
-, preferred *acciones preferentes*
-, redundant *existencias sobrantes o redundantes*
-, registered *acciones nominativas o registradas*
-, restoration of *restauración de las existencias*
-, safety *existencia de seguridad*
-, speculation *especulación, juego de bolsa*
-, surplus *existencias sobrantes*
-, to lay in a *proveerse, almacenar, surtir los almacenes*

-, to take *hacerse el inventario*
-, voting *acciones con derecho a voto*
stockbroker *corredor de acciones, agente de cambio y bolsa*
stockholder *accionista*
-, dissenting *accionista disidente*
-, dummy *acciones de propiedad simulada*
-, preferred *accionista preferido*
stockholders, founding *socios fundadores*
-, minority *accionistas de la minoría*
-, non-assenting *accionistas disidentes*
stockjobber *corredor de bolsa o acciones*
stockjobbing *agiotaje*
stockowner *accionista*
stockpile *almacenamiento*
stockroom *almacén de repuesto*
- clerk *encargado del almacén*
stocks *valores públicos, acciones*
-, block of *lote de acciones*
-, planned *existencias previstas*
-, rotation of *rotación de existencias*
-, warehouse *existencias en almacén*
-, watered *acciones diluídas, capital inflado (M)*
stop-loss order *orden de pérdida limitada, orden de compra o venta de acciones*
stop motion, adjustable *movimiento regulable de parada*
- payment, to *detener el pago, suspender el pago*
- press news *últimas noticias*
- work *abandono de trabajo*
stoppage *retención, suspensión, parada, espera, demora, retraso, interrupción*
-, labour *paralización del trabajo*
stopwatch *cronómetro*
-, calibrated *cronómetro de precisión*
storage *almacenaje, almacenamiento*
- address register *almacenamiento del registro de direcciones*
- chamber, cold *cámara frigorífica*
- charges *derechos de embalaje*
- costs *gastos de almacenaje*
- file *archivador o fichero inactivo*
- sign *señal de almacenamiento*
- system *sistema de almacenamiento, memorizador calculador electrónico*
- warehouse or store, cold- *almacén frigorífico*
-, cold *almacenaje refrigerado*
-, information *compilación de datos*
store *tienda, almacén*
- information, to *acumular información, memorizar con calculador electrónico*
- manager *director, jefe o encargado de tienda*
- window *escaparate de tienda*

–, cash *tienda de ventas al contado*
–, drug (Am) *farmacia*
–, dry-goods *paquetería*
–, in *en existencia, en reserva*
–, multiple *empresa con gran número de sucursales*
–, retail *tienda*
–, stationery *tienda de papelería*
–, wholesale *almacén mayorista*
stores *previsiones, pertrechos*
– ledger *libro de existencias*
–, chain *cadena de tiendas, tiendas en cadena*
–, department *grandes almacenes*
–, general *grandes almacenes*
–, self-service *tiendas de auto servicio*
–, variety *bazares*
storing *almacenamiento*
stowage *estilba, bodega marítima*
straight average *promedio directo*
– bill of lading *conocimiento nominativo, conocimiento de embarque intraspasable*
– credit *crédito irrevocable*
– line depreciation *depreciación en línea recta*
– line production *producción continua*
– rate *tarifa constante*
– time *horas ordinarias trabajo, sueldo constante, sueldo por horas*
– work *trabajo directo, trabajo sencillo*
strain *tensión, esfuerzo, dificultad*
strata chart *diagrama de estratos*
strategic raw materials *materias primas estratégicas*
strategy, market management *estrategia en la dirección del mercado*
–, marketing *estrategia mercadológica*
stratification *estratificación*
–, geographic *estratificada geográfica*
–, multiple *estratificación*
stratified sample *muestra estratificada*
stratify, to *estratificar*
straw vote *voto no oficial*
stray lot *lote o partida aislada*
street hawker *vendedor ambulante*
– prices *precios fuera de bolsa*
– seller *vendedor ambulante*
– vendor *vendedor ambulante*
strength of test *potencia de una prueba*
stress *esfuerzo, tensión, fatiga, coeficiente de trabajo, importancia, penosidad*
– analysis, experimental *análisis experimental de esfuerzos*
– chart *monograma para cálculo de esfuerzo*
–, computed *esfuerzo calculado*
strike *huelga, paro, ganga, éxito, golpe*
– a balance, to *hacer balance, arrastrar el saldo*

– a bargain, to *cerrar un trato, llegar a un convenio*
– an average, to *arrojar un promedio*
– breaker *esquirol, rompehuelgas (C, PR)*
– breaking *rotura de huelga*
– fund *fondo de huelga*
– pay *pago a huelguistas*
–, general *huelga general*
–, illegal *huelga no autorizada*
–, legal *huelga autorizada*
–, right to *derecho de huelga*
–, settle a *solucionar una huelga*
–, sitdown *huelga con ocupación, huelga de brazos caídos*
–, sympathetic *huelga por solidaridad*
–, token *disposición de ánimo*
–, wildcat *huelga no sancionada por el sindicato*
striker *huelguista*
strikes riots and civil commotions clause *cláusula sobre huelgas, tumultos y disturbios civiles*
stringency *penuria, escasez monetaria*
–, financial *situación financiera difícil*
strip, advertisement *anuncio en forma de banda, anuncio en forma de tira*
strong *firme, pujante, con tendencia al alza*
– market *mercado firme*
structure, capital *estructura de capital*
–, staff *estructura funcional*
–, systematic *esquema sistemático*
structural feature *característica estructural*
stub, cheque *talón de cheque*
study analyst, time *analista del estudio de tiempo*
– department, time *oficina de tiempos*
–, check *estudio de comprobación*
–, chronological *estudio cronológico*
–, consumer *estudio del cliente o consumidor*
–, joint *estudio conjunto*
–, methods *estudio de métodos, análisis de movimientos*
–, motion *estudio de movimientos*
–, pilot *estudio de orientación*
–, preliminary *estudio preliminar*
– time *estudio de tiempos*
–, work *estudio del trabajo*
stump *tribuna pública, arenga electoral, reto, desafío*
style *estilo, tipo, clase, dicción, género, especie, modo, uso*
–, advertisement in feuilleton *reportaje publicitario*
sublease *subarriendo, subalquiler*
sublet, to *subarrendar, subalquilar*
substandard *subtipo, inferior*

– performance *rendimiento inferior al normal*
– work *trabajo deficiente o inferior*
subtenant *subinquilino*
subject *sujeto, súbdito, asunto*
subjective data *datos subjetivos*
sublimation *sublimación, superación*
subliminal stimulus *estímulo subliminal*
subscribed capital *capital suscrito*
subscription price *precio de emisión de nuevas acciones*
subsidiary company *compañía filial*
– ledger *auxiliar del mayor (libro)*
subsidies, export *subsidios para la exportación*
subsidize, to *subvencionar*
subsidy *subvención, subsidio*
– programme, gold *programa de subsidio del oro*
–, annual *subvención anual, subsidio anual*
–, price *subsidio de precios*
–, production *subsidio a la producción*
subsistence *subsistencia*
– economy *economía de subsistencia*
– level *nivel de subsistencia*
– wages *salarios mínimos para subsistir*
substitute *sustituto, sustituir, sustitutivo*
substitutes *sucedáneos*
substitution, to curtail *sustituir un producto por otro*
substitutive product *producto de sustitución, sucedáneo*
succession *sucesión*
– duties *impuestos de sucesión*
– tax *impuesto de sucesión*
sue, to *demandar, procesar*
suggestion *sugestión*
– scheme *sistema de sugerencias*
sum, inclusive *sumo global*
–, optimum *suma más favorable*
summarize, to *resumir*
summary account *cuenta centralizadora*
– punching, alphabetic *perforación de datos alfabéticos al sumarizar*
summation *acumulación, adición, suma*
sumptuary laws *leyes suntuarias*
sundries *artículos varios, gastos varios*
sundry accounts *cuentas diversas*
– creditors *acreedores diversos*
– expenses *gastos varios*
superannuated *incapacitado*
superannuation *jubilación, pensión de retiro*
– benefits *beneficios de jubilación*
– fund *fondo de pensión*
superfluous *superfluo*
superimposed-curve chart *diagrama de curvas superpuestas*

superintendent *superintendente, jefe administrativo, director técnico*
–, assistant *superintendente auxiliar*
–, department *jefe de departamento*
superintending charges *gastos de inspección*
supermarket *supermercado*
supersede, to *reemplazar*
supersensivity *hipersensibilidad*
supervise, to *supervisar, revisar, fiscalizar, inspeccionar*
supervision *supervisión, fiscalización*
supervisor *supervisor, revisor, interventor, superintendente*
–, office *supervisor de oficinas*
–, training *supervisor de capitación*
supervisory staff *cuadro de personal supervisor*
supplement, magazine *revista suplemento de un periódico*
suplementary cost, current *costo suplemento actual*
– estimates *cálculos adicionales*
– tax *impuesto adicional*
supplier *proveedor, abastecedor, distribuidor*
supplies *abastecimientos, suministros, materiales, provisiones, víveres, efectos, pertrechos, enseres*
–, factory *suministros de fábrica*
–, marginal *abastecimientos marginales*
supply *suministro, oferta*
– and demand *oferta y demanda*
– curve *curva de la oferta*
– function, aggregate *función total de la oferta*
– network *red de distribución*
– price *precio de oferta*
– price, aggregate *función total de la oferta*
– schedule *tabla de oferta*
– services *créditos financieros, servicios de abastecimiento*
–, monetary *oferta monetaria, disponibilidad monetaria*
–, short *escasez*
–, to *aprovisionar, surtir, abastecer, proveer, suministrar, proporcionar, reemplazar*
support policy, price *política de sostenimiento de precios*
– price *precio sostenido*
supporting statement *estado demostrativo contable*
suppression *evasión*
surcharge *recargo, sobreprima*
surety *fianza, garantía, caución, seguridad, certeza*
surface fatigue *fatiga leve, fatiga superficial*
surplus *sobrante, superávit, excedente, exceso*
– from consolidation *superávit de*

consolidación
- funds *fondos sobrantes*
- stock *existencias sobrantes*
-, appraisal *superávit de revaluación*
-, book *superávit en libros*
-, capital *superávit de capital, excedente de capital*
-, current *superávit disponible*
-, earned *beneficios acumulados*
-, export *excedentes portables*
-, operating *excedente de explotación*
-, paid in *excedente de capital*
-, port-quota *excedente de cuota*
surrender value *valor de rescate, valor entregado*
surrogate *substituto*
surtax *recargo, sobretasa, impuesto adicional*
survey *estudio, encuesta, inspección, investigación*
- charges *gastos de inspección*
- data *datos de una encuesta*
- of working speed and accuracy *encuesta de precisión y rapidez de trabajo*
- techniques *técnicas de encuesta, técnicas de sondeo*
-, annual *inspección anual, encuesta anual*
-, brand trend *encuesta sobre tendencias de marcas*
-, damage *inspección de avería*
-, field *encuesta mediante entrevista, encuesta en campaña*
-, market *examen o encuesta sobre el mercado*
-, pilot *encuesta piloto*
-, sample *encuesta por muestra*
-, sampling *encuesta por muestreo*
-, work analysis *encuesta sobre el análisis del trabajo*
survival *supervivencia*
suspend payment, to *suspender el pago*
suspense account *cuenta en suspenso*
- file *fichero trámite*
sweat *fatiga, trabajo agotador*
sweating *explotación de obreros*
swindle *estafa*
swindler *estafador*
swing of trade *fluctuación del mercado*
-, down *fase descendente*
-, in full *plena actividad, plena producción*

switch, to *cambiar, canjear*
symbol *símbolo*
sympathetic *comprensivo, amable*
- strike *huelga por solidaridad*
sympathy *simpatía*
symptom *síntoma*
syndicate *sindicato*
system *sistema*
- of taxation *sistema fiscal*
-, attendance time recording *sistema registrador de horas de trabajo*
-, balanced *sistema de compensación*
-, banking *sistema bancario*
-, closed *sistema cerrado*
-, data display *sistema de presentación de datos*
-, data handling *sistema de manejo de datos*
-, economic *sistema económico*
-, factor comparison *sistema de comparación de factores*
-, filing *sistema de archivos*
-, follow-up *sistema de continuidad, sistema de cartas de insistencia*
-, financial *sistema financiero*
-, incentive *sistema de primas*
-, metric *sistema métrico*
-, open *sistema abierto*
-, piecework *sistema de salario por pieza*
-, premium *sistema de primas*
-, public address *sistema de comunicación directa*
-, quota *sistema de cuotas*
-, storage *sistema de almacenamiento, memorizador calculador electrónico*
-, tax *sistema tributario*
-, warehousing *sistema de depósitos*
systematic analysis *análisis sistemático*
- approach *enfoque sistemático*
- approach, problem *enfoque sistemático de problemas*
- error *error constante*
- sample *muestra sistemática*
- structure *esquema sistemático*
- sampling *muestreo sistemático*
systems, highway *sistemas de carreteras*
-, preferential trading *sistemas de comercio*

T

table of contents *índice*
–, current life *tabla de mortalidad actual*
–, drafting *mesa de dibujo*
–, yield *tabla de rendimiento*
tabulation of data *tabulación de datos*
tag bin *etiqueta de almacén*
take a sample, to *sacar una muestra*
– account of stock, to *hacer inventario*
– home pay *sueldo neto, sueldo después de deducciones*
– out a patent, to *sacar una patente*
– stock, to *hacer recuento de existencias, hacerse el inventario*
taken, time *tiempo empleado, tiempo real*
takings *ingresos, recaudaciones*
tally *anotación, talón, resguardo*
– sheet *hoja de cuentas*
–, to *llevar la cuenta, confrontar, cuadrar la cuenta*
tangible assets *activo tangible*
– assets, fixed *activo fijo tangible*
– net worth *activo neto tangible*
– property *bienes tangibles*
tape, red *papeleo, formulismo*
tare *tara*
– allowance *rebaja normalizada del peso bruto*
– and tret *tara y merma*
– bar *escala de taras*
target *objetivo, meta, producción, cantidad total*
– time *tiempo pretendido*
tariff *tarifa, arancel*
- barriers *barreras fiscales*
– base *base de impuesto, base imponible*
– burden *gravamen fiscal*
– collection *recaudación fiscal*
– collector *recaudador fiscal*
– commission *agencia administrativa para recaudar impuestos*
– convention *convención fiscal*
– deduction *deducción, rebaja del impuesto*
– discrimination *discriminación fiscal*
– dodging *evasión de impuestos*
– exemption *exención de impuestos*
– free income *ingreso libre de impuestos*
– free interest *intereses libres de impuestos*
– jurisdiction *jurisdicción fiscal*
– laws *leyes fiscales*

– on profits *impuesto sobre utilidades*
– rebate *bonificación fiscal*
– reduction *bonificación, reducción del impuesto*
– refund *devolución de impuesto pagado*
– report *declaración de ingresos gravables*
– return *declaración de ingresos gravables*
– revenue *ingresos fiscales, arancel fiscal*
– union *unión aduanera*
– year *año gravable, año fiscal*
–, consolidating of a *consolidación de una tarifa*
–, import *arancel de importación*
–, preferential *tarifa preferencial*
–, progressive *tarifa progresiva*
–, property *impuesto predial*
–, protective *tarifa proteccionista*
–, retaliatory *impuestos de represalia*
–, sales *impuesto sobre ingresos mercantiles*
tariffs, airport *tarifas de aeropuerto*
–, customs *aranceles aduaneros*
taring *determinación de la tara*
task *tarea, deber, trabajo, faena, labor*
– assignment *señalamiento del trabajo*
– force *personal operante, fuerza para misión especial*
– group *comité de trabajo*
tax accruals *impuestos acumulados*
– agreements, international *acuerdos fiscales*
– basis *base de tributación*
– certificate *certificado de compra de bienes raíces o inmuebles*
– collector *recaudador de impuestos, cobrador de impuestos*
– collector's office *administración de impuestos, recaudación de impuestos*
– credit, foreign *deducción por impuestos pagados en el extranjero*
– cut *reducción de impuestos*
– exempt *exento o libre de impuestos*
– exemption *exención de impuestos*
– free *libre de impuestos*
– inspector *inspector de hacienda*
– liability *activo no imponible*
– lien *gravamen por impuestos no pagados*
– office *oficina recaudadora de impuestos*
– paying capacity *capacidad tributaria*
– paying capacity, individual *capacidad*

contributiva individual
- payer contribuyente
- receipts ingresos fiscales
- receiver recaudador o cobrador de impuestos
- report impreso de declaración de renta
- return impreso de declaración de renta
- returns, taxable fiduciary income ingresos por impuestos sobre la renta fiduciaria imponible
- system sistema tributario
-, capitation impuesto por persona, capitación
-, composition impuesto a tanto alzado
-, death impuesto de sucesión
-, delinquent impuesto no pagado a tiempo
-, direct impuesto directo
-, distributive impuesto de repartición
-, estate impuesto sobre sucesiones
-, excess-profit impuesto sobre beneficios extraordinarios, impuesto sobre exceso de utilidades
-, excise impuesto sobre ventas
-, gift impuesto sobre donaciones
-, income impuesto sobre la renta
-, indirect impuesto indirecto
-, inheritance impuesto sobre herencias
-, land impuesto sobre tierras, predial
-, legacy impuesto sobre sucesiones
-, liable for gravable, sujeto a impuesto
-, normal impuesto normal o básico
-, occupation impuesto de empleo o profesión
-, payroll impuesto sobre sueldos
-, personal impuesto personal
-, poll impuesto por persona
-, processing impuesto por elaboraciones
-, production impuesto sobre producción
-, profit impuesto sobre beneficios
-, property impuesto sobre bienes o inmuebles
-, purchase impuesto sobre ventas
-, real-estate impuesto sobre inmuebles, predial
-, refundable impuesto reembolsable
-, remission of a reducción o cancelación de un importe
-, road impuesto para conservación de caminos
-, sales impuesto sobre el precio de ventas
-, single impuesto único
-, social security impuesto de seguro social
-, stamp impuesto del timbre
-, state impuesto estatal
-, succession impuesto de sucesión
-, supplementary impuesto adicional
-, to impose a imponer un impuesto o tasa
taxability imponibilidad
taxable gravable

- income bienes tributarios, renta o utilidad imponible
- profits beneficios o ganancias gravables
- value valor imponible o tributario
taxation imposición de impuestos
-, basis of base del impuesto
-, canons of estipulaciones en política impositiva
-, confiscatory tributación confiscatoria
-, double doble tributación
-, multiple imposición múltiple
-, progressive tributación progresiva
-, system of sistema fiscal
taxes, accrued impuestos causados o vencidos, impuestos por pagar
-, assessed impuestos directos
-, back impuestos atrasados
-, corporate impuestos de sociedad anónima
-, credit against deducción por impuestos pagados
-, local impuestos locales
-, net impuestos netos
-, property impuestos sobre inmuebles
-, to levy imponer impuestos
taxpayer contribuyente
team equipo, grupo de trabajo, medios de producción
- research investigación en equipo
- spirit espíritu de equipo
- work trabajo en equipo
-, design equipo de proyecto
-, sales equipo de venta
tear sheet página o recorte comprobante de anuncio
-, wear and desgaste, depreciación
technical adviser asesor técnico
- data sheet hoja de datos técnicos
- director director técnico
- instruction instrucción técnica
- jargon jerga técnica
- queries consultas técnicas
- training formación o preparación técnica
technicality tecnicismo, término técnico
technician técnico
technique técnica, tecnicismo
-, design técnica de diseños
-, error choice técnica de selección de errores
-, questioning método interrogativo o analítico
-, sampling técnica de muestreo
techniques, data collection técnicas de recogida de datos
-, motivation técnicas de motivación
-, probing técnicas de sondeo
-, research técnicas de investigación
-, survey técnicas de encuesta o sondeo

technocracy *tecnocracia*
technological research *investigación*
  tecnológica
telecast *programa de televisión*
 –, to *emitir por televisión, televisar*
telephone interview *entrevista por teléfono*
 – operator *telefonista*
teleprinter *teleimpresor, teletipista*
teleview, to *televisar*
televise, to *televisar*
televising *televisivo, televisual*
television *televisión*
 – advertising *publicidad en televisión, anuncio*
 – broadcast *programa de televisión*
 – channel *canal de televisión*
 – commercials *anuncios por televisión*
 – engineer *técnico en televisión*
 – engineering *técnica televisiva*
 – network *red de emisoras de televisión*
 – programme *programa de televisión*
 – relay *retransmisión de televisión*
 –, commercial *televisión comercial o*
  publicitaria
teller *cajero, pagador*
 –, receiving *recibidor, cajero recibidor*
temperament *temperamento*
template *patrón, plantilla, modelo, molde*
 –, copying *plantilla copiadora*
tempo *ritmo, velocidad*
temporary *temporal, temporero*
 – annuity *anualidad temporal*
 – investments *inversiones transitorias*
 – price list *lista provisional de precios*
 – standard *norma provisional*
ten-key adding machine *máquina de calcular*
  de diez teclas
tenant *inquilino, arrendatario*
tendencies, conflicting *tendencias en conflicto*
tender *propuesta, oferta*
 – of payment *oferta de pago*
 –, legal *moneda de curso legal, moneda legal o*
  corriente
tension *tensión*
tenure *tendencia, posesión*
term annuity *anualidad temporal*
 – card file *fichero de condiciones de venta*
 – debt, long- *crédito a largo plazo*
 – of patent *duración de una patente*
 –, fixed *plazo fijo*
 –, long *largo plazo*
 –, ordinary *período ordinario*
 –, regular *período ordinario*
terminable annuity *anualidad temporal*
terminal wage *indemnización por despido*
terminogenesis *génesis terminológica*
terminology *terminología*

terms of sale *condiciones de venta*
 –, commercial *términos comerciales*
 –, easy *facilidades de pago*
 –, selling *condiciones de venta*
 –, similar *términos semejantes*
 –, trade *condiciones comerciales*
territory, exclusive *territorio, mercado*
  reservado
test *prueba, ensayo, examen, experimento,*
  test
 – chart *modelo o ficha de prueba*
 – checks *pruebas selectivas, tanteos*
 – log *registro de pruebas*
 – method, empirical *método de prueba*
  empírico
 – panel *cuadro o panel de pruebas*
 – pattern *pruebas de ajuste*
 – run *test práctico, prueba práctica*
 – sample *muestra para prueba o ensayo*
 – site *campo de experiencias*
 – specifications, abbreviated *especificación de*
  pruebas abreviadas
 –, accelerated fatigue *prueba acelerada de*
  fatiga
 –, accelerated life *prueba acelerada de*
  duración
 –, accelerated performance *pruebas*
  aceleradas de destreza
 –, acceptance *prueba de aceptación*
 –, activity vector analysis *prueba analítica del*
  rumbo de la actividad
 –, aptitude *prueba de aptitud o capacidad*
 –, attitude *prueba o test de actitud*
 –, check *contraprueba*
 –, clerical speed and accuracy *prueba de*
  precisión y rapidez administrativas
 –, comparative *prueba comparativa*
 –, developmental *ensayo evolutivo*
 –, differential aptitude *prueba de aptitudes*
  diferenciales
 –, efficiency *prueba de eficiencia*
 –, general clerical *prueba administrativa*
  general
 –, information *prueba o test de información*
 –, intelligence *prueba de inteligencia*
 –, most powerful *prueba más poderosa*
 –, one-sided *prueba unilateral*
 –, personnel *pruebas de personal*
 –, probability ratio *prueba de la razón de la*
  probabilidad
 –, productivity *prueba de productividad*
 –, significance *prueba de significación*
 –, stability *prueba de estabilidad*
 –, statistical *ensayo estadístico*
 –, strength of *potencia de una prueba*
 –, trial *método de prueba, contraste de prueba*

tester *probador, medidor, encargado de las pruebas*
testing *prueba, verificación, comprobación, experimento, ensayo*
– devices *dispositivos de pruebas*
– gear *aparato de pruebas, mecanismo comprobador*
test, personnel *pruebas de personal*
text *texto*
theory of comparative costs *teoría de costos comparativos*
– of international values *teoría de los valores internacionales*
–, banking *teoría de restricción de la emisión de billetes*
–, information *teoría de la información*
–, motivation *teoría de la motivación*
–, sampling *teoría del muestreo*
–, statistical *teoría estadística*
thick market *mercado de gran consumo*
thin market *mercado de poco consumo*
thinking *pensamiento*
thrift *economía, frugalidad*
through bill of lading *conocimiento de embarque directo*
throughput *cantidad tratada, producción o rendimiento total*
tick, to buy on *comprar al fiado*
ticket, job *bono de trabajo, hoja de trabajo*
–, tool *boletín de petición de utillaje y herramientas*
tied loan *préstamo condicionado*
tight-money policy *política de restricción de créditos*
till money *efectivo de ventanilla*
time *tiempo*
– antithesis *antítesis cronológica*
– bill *letra a plazo*
– budget *tiempo estimado*
– card *ficha de tiempos*
– charter *fletamiento por tiempo*
– deposit *depósito a plazo*
– discount *descuento por pago dentro del plazo señalado*
– draft *giro a plazo*
– graph, distance *diagrama de espacios y tiempos*
– lag *retraso, retardo*
– letter of credit *carta de crédito a plazo*
– limit *plazo*
– loan *préstamo a plazo fijo*
– of delivery *plazo de entrega, término de entrega*
– of departure *hora de salida*
– off, compensatory *descanso de compensación*

– recording system, attendance *sistema registrado de horas de trabajo*
– schedule *programa de tiempo*
– selling *venta de plazos*
– series *serie cronológicsa*
– sheet *hoja de jornales devengados*
– stamp *estudio de tiempos*
– study analyst *analista del estudio de tiempo*
– taken *tiempo empleado, tiempo real*
– used *tiempo empleado, tiempo real*
– wage *tarifa por tiempo*
– work *trabajo por unidad de tiempo*
– worker, part- *trabajador en jornada incompleta*
–, absolute *hora absoluta*
–, acceleration *duración de la aceleración*
–, actual *tiempo real, tiempo empleado*
–, adjustment *tiempo de adaptación*
–, all-in *tiempo de presencia*
–, allowed *tiempo concedido*
–, attendance *tiempo de presencia*
–, attention *tiempo de atención o de vigilancia*
–, available machine *tiempo disponible de máquina*
–, available process *tiempo disponible de proceso*
–, average *tiempo medio*
–, basic *tiempo básico*
–, changeover *cambio de torno*
–, clock *tiempo real, tiempo empleado*
–, contract *lapso de terminación*
–, cyclic *duración del ciclo*
–, dead *tiempo muerto*
–, design *tiempo previsto*
–, elapsed *tiempo transcurrido, período de observación*
–, estimated *tiempo estimado*
–, float *tiempo de circulación de una pieza o trabajo*
–, handling *tiempo transporte o movimiento de materiales*
–, idle *tiempo inactivo*
–, idle machine *tiempo de máquina parada*
–, incentive *tiempo concedido o privado*
–, lost *tiempo perdido*
–, machine *tiempo de utilización de la máquina*
–, normal *tiempo normal*
–, process *tiempo neto de transformación*
–, productive *tiempo poductivo*
–, running *tiempo de utilización de la máquina*
–, shutdown *tiempo de actividad*
–, spare *tiempo libre*
–, standard *hora oficial, hora legal*
–, straight *hora ordinaria trabajo, sueldo constante, sueldo por horas*

–, target *tiempo pretendido*
–, training *tiempo de aprendizaje*
–, waiting *tiempo de espera*
timed sequence *secuencia cíclica*
timeworker's bonus *prima de compensación*
timing *cronometraje*
– sequence *secuencia cronizada o temperizada*
–, cumulative *método de lectura continua, cronometraje por lecturas acumuladas*
–, differential *medida de tiempos por diferencia*
title *título*
– deed *título de propiedad*
– page *portada de libro, primera página de un periódico*
–, marketable *título negociable*
to-order bill of lading *conocimiento a la orden*
token *disposición de ánimo*
– payment *adelanto a cuenta de pago de una obligación*
– strike *disposición de ánimo*
tolerance factor *factor de tolerancia*
– limits *límites de tolerancia*
toll *peaje, impuesto por uso de algo*
–, bridge *derechos de puente*
tonnage *tonelaje*
tool *instrumento, elemento, herramienta, medio*
– allowance *gratificación por desgaste de herramientas*
– ticket *boletín de petición de utillaje y herramientas*
–, drafting *útil de dibujo*
tools, downing of *cesación del trabajo*
–, to down *cesar en el trabajo, declararse en huelga*
top management *alto mando*
– price *precio máximo*
– quality *calidad superior*
topnotch *de calidad inmejorable, renombrado o eminente muy bien hecho*
total *total*
– amount *importe total*
– disability *invalidez total*
– entry, alphanumerical type bar *entrada a las barras alfanuméricas para totales*
– liabilities *pasivo total*
– loss *pérdida total*
– loss, absolute *pérdida total efectiva*
– loss, actual *pérdida total real*
– piecework earnings *ingresos globales en salarios por piezas*
– population index *índice total de población*
– receipts *ingresos totales*
totalize, to *totalizar*
trade *comercio, negocio, industria, gremio*

– acceptance *aceptación comercial*
– advice *asesoría comercial*
– agreements, reciprocal *tratados comerciales recíprocos*
– allowance *descuento comercial*
– area, free *zona de cambio libre*
– association *asociación de comerciantes, sociedad comercial*
– balance *balanza comercial*
– balance, active *balanza comercial favorable*
– barriers *barreras comerciales*
– bill *letra o giro comercial, efecto mercantil letra de cambio*
– buying *compras por las fábricas*
– capital *capital comercial*
– controls *restricciones al comercio*
– credit *crédito mercantil o comercial*
– cycle *ciclo económico*
– deficit *balanza de pagos desfavorable*
– directory *guía comercial*
– discount *descuento comercial*
– draft *giro comercial*
– gap *déficit comercial*
– guild (Br) *corporación, gremio, sindicato*
– in *cambio, trueque, canje, entrega a cuenta*
– journal *periódico o revista de ramo comercial o industrial*
– liabilities *pasivo comercial*
– literature *impresos de publicidad*
– name *nombre comercial, marca de comercio, nombre o dibujo registrado como marca*
– price *precio neto o comercial o corriente*
– promotion *fomento del comercio*
– reference *referencia comercial*
– secret *secreto industrial*
– terms *condiciones comerciales*
– union *sindicato obrero, gremio profesional, asociación profesional obrera (Ch)*
– value *valor de venta*
–, balance of *balanza comercial*
–, barter *comercio de trueque, comercio de operaciones compensadoras*
–, distributive *comercio de distribución*
–, domestic *comercio interior*
–, export *comercio de exportación*
–, external *comercio exterior*
–, foreign (Br) *comercio exterior*
–, free *libre cambio*
–, home *comercio interior*
–, import *comercio de importación*
–, invisible *comercio invisible*
–, multilateral *comercio multilateral*
–, pattern of *situación comercial*
–, retail *comercio al por menor*
–, skilled *oficio calificado*

–, stock in *bienes comerciales*
–, swing of *fluctuación del mercado*
–, to *comerciar, negociar, cambiar, traficar*
–, visible items of *elementos visibles de comercio*
–, wholesale *comercio al por mayor, venta al por mayor*
trademark *marca comercial, marca industrial (M)*
– office, patent and *oficina de patentes y marcas*
–, registered *marca registrada*
–, to register a *registrar una marca de fábrica*
trader *tratante, comerciante, traficante, negociante*
–, free *librecambista*
trading *compraventa*
– account *cuenta comercial*
– area, potential *zona potencial de comercio*
– corporation *sociedad mercantil*
– fund *fondo comercial*
– in futures *operaciones de futuro*
– systems, preferential *sistemas de comercio preferenciales*
–, stock *juego de bolsa*
traffic *tráfico, circulación, negocio, comercio movimiento de mercancías*
– credit *control o verificación de carteles emplazados, control de carteles*
– control, air *control de tránsito aéreo*
– diagram *diagrama de tráfico*
– director *director o jefe de tráfico*
– flow *volúmen del tráfico*
– load *carga de explotación*
– manager *jefe de tráfico*
–, to *comerciar, negociar, traficar*
trainee *aprendiz*
trainer *instructor, entrenador, profesor*
training *instrucción, entrenamiento, adiestramiento, formación*
– costs *costes de aprendizaje*
– department, staff *departamento asesor de capacitación*
– director *director de formación o entrenamiento*
– effectiveness, evaluation of *valoración de la eficacia en el adiestramiento*
– programme *programa de capacitación o formación*
– programme, office *programa de capacitación de oficinas*
– schedule *programa de instrucción*
– supervisor *supervisor de capacitación*
– time *tiempo de aprendizaje*
–, annual *capacitación anual, instrucción anual*

–, collective *capacidad o instrucción colectiva*
–, employees' *adiestramiento de los empleados*
–, habit *hábitos o modo de portarse en sociedad*
–, job *adiestramiento en el trabajo*
–, on-the-job *formación sobre la marcha, capacitación mientras se trabaja*
–, personnel *capacidad del personal*
–, technical *formación técnica*
–, vocational *formación profesional*
transaction *negocio, transacción, operación mercantil*
–, commercial *operación comercial*
transactions, capital *transacciones de capital*
–, completed *transacciones consumadas*
–, invisible *transacciones u operaciones invisibles*
–, joint *transacciones comunes*
transfer *transferencia, traspaso*
– files *ficheros inactivos*
–, bank *transferencia bancaria*
–, capital *transferencia de capital*
–, deed of *escritura de traspaso*
transferable *transferible*
transmission, radio *transmisión por radio, transmisión radiofónica*
transhipment *transbordo*
transit duties *derechos de tránsito*
– goods *mercancías en tránsito*
–, goods in *mercancías en tránsito*
translator, alphanumerical *traductor alfanumérico*
translation, close *traducción fiel o exacta*
transmission data *transmisión de datos*
transparency, slide *diapositiva en transparencia*
transportation expenses *gastos de transporte*
–, railroad *transporte ferroviario*
traveller, commercial (Am) *viajante comercial*
traveller's cheque *cheque de viajero*
travelling expenses *gastos de viaje, viáticos*
– salesman (Br) *vendedor viajante, viajante comercial*
tray, sort *casillero de clasificación*
treasury *tesorería*
– accounts *cuentas de tesorería*
– bonds *bonos del estado, bonos de la tesorería*
– notes *obligaciones del estado*
–, public *tesorería, erario*
treaty *tratado, convenio*
trend *tendencia, rumbo, curso, dirección*
–, business *tendencia del mercado*
–, downward *tendencia a la baja*
–, fashion *tendencias de la moda*
–, population *tendencia demográfica*

–, secular *curso, tendencia a largo plazo*
trends, basic economic *tendencias económicas
básicas*
–, market *tendencias del mercado*
tret *rebaja o deducción por merma*
–, tare and *tara y merma*
trial and error, by *por tanteos*
– balance *balanza de prueba o comprobación,
extracto de comprobación (A)*
– balance book *libro de balances de
comprobación*
– order *pedido de ensayo, pedido de prueba*
– period *período de pruebas*
– test *análisis de prueba, contraste de prueba*
trials, acceptance *pruebas de adaptación*
tribute *tributo, impuesto*
trimming, window- *componer escaparates,
decoración de escaparates*
trip, business *viaje comercial*
troubles, labour *cuestión obrera*
truck, fork-lift *carretilla elevadora con
horquilla*
true discount *descuento real, descuento
externo (M)*
trust *trust, fideicomiso, consorcio*
– account *cuenta fiduciaria*
– company *compañía fiduciaria*
– deposits *depósitos especiales, depósitos en
fideicomiso*
– fund *fondo fiduciario, fondo en fideicomiso*
–, charitable *fideicomiso caritativo*
–, brains *grupo de expertos*
–, corporate *fideicomiso de sociedad anónima*
–, declaration of *declaración de fideicomiso*
–, deed of *escritura de fideicomiso*
–, equipment *escritura fiduciaria sobre equipo*
–, executed *fideicomiso formalizado*
–, funded *fideicomiso con depósito de fondos*
–, insurance *fideicomiso de seguro*
–, passive *fideicomiso pasivo*
–, pension *fideicomiso de pensiones*
–, perpetual *fideicomiso perpetuo*
–, private *fideicomiso particular o privado*

–, public *fideicomiso público*
trustee *administrador de un trust,
fideicomisario*
turnout *concurrencia, producción en tiempo
determinado*
turnover *rotación, entrada, ingresos totales,
giro, ganancia total, inversión*
– rate, high *porcentaje elevado de cambios de
personal*
– rate, stock *giro de existencias (promedio)*
– ratio, stock *proporción entre existencias y
giro*
–, capital *capital social en acciones*
–, inventory *movimiento, rotación de
existencias*
–, labour *personal de reemplazo, movimiento
o rotación de obreros*
–, rate *tasa, precio, tarifa, rotación, entrada,
giro, ganancia total*
–, raw materials *movimiento de materias
primas*
–, speed of *movimiento de ventas, tiempo de la
distribución total*
–, stock *renovación de existencias, giro de
existencias*
two-handed process chart *diagrama de
ambas manos*
tycoon *magnate industrial*
type *clase, figura, tipo, emblema, letra*
– bar list entry, alphanumerical *entrada a las
barras alfanuméricas para listar*
– bar total entry, alphanumerical *entrada a las
barras alfanuméricas para totales*
– setter *máquina para componer tipos*
– setting *composición de tipos*
types, information *clases o tipos de
información*
typesetter *cajista, máquina para componer
tipos*
typewriter *máquina de escribir*
typical business cycle *ciclo económico clásico*
typist, stenographer- *taquimecanógrafo,
taquidactilógrafo*

U

ultimate *último, final, máximo, fundamental*
- analysis *análisis esencial o último*
- authority *autoridad fundamental*
unadjusted *no ajustado, pendiente*
unallotted balance *saldo no asignado*
unambiguous *inequívoco*
unappropriated *no asignado, no consignado*
unauthorized *no autorizado, desautorizado*
unavoidable loss *pérdidas inevitables*
unbalanced budget *presupuesto no nivelado*
unbiased *sin desviación, insesgado*
unbusinesslike *inhábil para los negocios, no metódico, poco práctico, poco formal*
uncertainty *incertidumbre*
uncalled capital *capital de reserva o no reembolsable, capital suscrito pero no exhibido*
unclaimed *sin reclamar, sin cobrar*
- dividend *dividendo no reclamado*
unclassified *no clasificado, sin clasificar*
uncollectable *incobrable, irrecuperable*
uncollected items *artículos no cobrados, por cobrar*
unconfirmed credit *crédito no confirmado*
uncontrolled money *moneda no intervenida*
uncovered *descubierto, en descubierto*
- acceptance *aceptación a descubierto*
undated *sin fecha*
undeclared *no declarado*
undelivered *no entregado*
under age *menor de edad*
- contract *bajo contrato*
- instructions *con órdenes de*
- lease, land *terreno arrendado*
- protest *bajo protesta*
- way *en camino, en curso*
underbid *oferta baja, oferta en baja*
-, to *hacer una propuesta más baja*
undercharge, to *cobrar de menos*
undercut, to *ofrecer mercancías a precio más bajo*
underdeveloped nations *países subdesarrollados*
underestimate *valuación, estimación baja*
underpaid *con sueldo insuficiente*
underproduction *producción insuficiente*
underscore, to *subrayar*
undersell, to *vender a bajo precio, malbaratar*

underselling *venta a bajo precio, reducción de precios*
undersigned *infrascrito, suscrito*
undertake, to *emprender*
undertaking *compromiso, empresa*
-, commercial *empresa auxiliar, empresa filial*
-, public *empresa pública*
undervalue, to *valuar en menos, estimar bajo*
underwrite, to *suscribir, asegurar*
- the cost, to *asegurar al costo*
underwriter *suscriptor de valores, asegurador o compañía aseguradora*
underwriters, credit *aseguradores de créditos*
-, marine *aseguradores contra riesgos marítimos*
underwriting contract *contrato de suscripción de valores*
undeveloped *no desarrollado, no explotado*
undistributed *no repartido*
- profits *beneficios no pagados, beneficios no repartidos*
undivided *no dividido, no repartido*
unearned *no ganado*
- income *renta de inversiones, haberes diferidos*
- increment *plus valía*
- interest collected *intereses cobrados y no vencidos*
uneconomic *antieconómico*
unemployed *desocupado, cesante*
unemployment *desempleo, paro laboral, paro forzoso, desocupación*
- benefits *beneficios para desempleo*
- compensation *compensación por desempleo*
- dole *indemnización por desempleo*
- income *seguro de desempleo*
- insurance *seguro contra el desempleo*
- relief *auxilio de desempleo*
-, involuntary *desempleo o paro involuntario*
-, seasonal *desempleo estacional*
unencumbered *sin gravámenes, saneado, libre de gravamen*
uneven *impar, desigual*
unfair *injusto*
- competition *competencia desleal*
unfavourable *desfavorable*
- balance of trade *balanza comercial desfavorable, balanza deficitaria, saldo*

desfavorable
unfeasible *impracticable*
unfit *incapaz, inhábil, impropio*
unforeseen expenses *gastos imprevistos, gastos inesperados*
unfriendly *poco amistoso*
unfunded debt *deuda no consolidada, deuda flotante*
unified mortgage *hipoteca consolidada*
– standard *norma unificada*
unilateral legislation *leyes unilaterales*
unincorporated *no incorporado*
union *sindicato, gremio obrero, asociación*
– co-operation, employer- *cooperación entre patronos y obreros*
– employer agreement *acuerdo entre el sindicato y los patronos*
– labour *trabajadores sindicalizados*
– shop *empresa en la que se puede emplear obreros sindicalizados o no pero que en plazo corto se sindicalizarán*
– wage *salario sindical*
–, closed *gremio obrero que hace difícil la entrada de nuevos miembros*
–, company *sindicato formado por empleados de una sola empresa*
–, customs *unión, asociación de aduanas*
–, industrial *gremio industrial*
–, labour *gremio, sindicato, asociación obrera*
–, tariff *unión aduanera*
–, trade *sindicato obrero, gremio profesional, asociación profesional obrera (Ch)*
union-employer agreement *acuerdo entre el sindicato y los patronos*
unionize, to *agremiarse, sindicalizarse*
unit *unidad, elemento unitario*
– cost *costo unitario*
– cost, average *coste unitario medio*
– cost depreciation *depreciación a base del coste unitario de producción*
– inventory *inventario por unidades*
– of currency *unidad monetaria*
– price *precio unitario*
– price bid *oferta o propuesta a precios unitarios*
– production value *unidad de valor productivo*
– sales information *información sobre las unidades vendidas*
– stock control *comprobación en unidades de las existencias*
– value index *índice de valores unitarios*
– vector *vector unidad*
– weight *peso unitario*
–, administrative *unidad administrativa*
–, marginal *unidad marginal*
–, product development *unidad de desarrollo*

de un producto
unlawful *ilegal*
unlicensed *no autorizado*
unlimited *ilimitado, sin límites*
– liability *responsabilidad ilimitada*
– wants *necesidades económicas*
unliquidated *no liquidado*
– damages *daños no liquidados*
– debt *deuda no determinada, deuda por pagar*
unlisted securities *valores no inscritos en bolsa*
unmarketable *incomerciable*
unnegotiable *innegociable*
unofficial *extraoficial*
unpaid *sin pagar, por pagar*
unpredictable *incierto, imposible de predecir*
unproductive *improductivo*
– capital *capital improductivo*
unprofitable *antieconómico*
unqualified certificate *certificado sin salvedades*
unrated *no clasificado*
– order *pedido no preferente*
unrefundable *no restituible*
unrestricted work *trabajo no restringido*
unsecured creditor *acreedor sin caución*
– debt *deuda sin caución*
– liabilities *pasivo no garantizado*
– loan *préstamo a descubierto o sin caución*
– trade *negocio no garantizado*
unsinkable debt *deuda no amortizable*
unskilled labour *trabajadores no clasificados, trabajadores no especializados*
unsound business *negocios improductivos*
– currency *moneda inestable*
– money *moneda inestable*
– project *proyecto improductivo*
– securities *valores especulativos*
unstable *inestable*
unsuitable *inapropiado*
unwarranted *no garantizado, injustificado*
unweighted index *índice no ponderado*
unworked *inexplotado, sin aprovechar*
up to standard *dentro de las normas, al nivel de norma*
–, buyer- *acaparador*
–, buying- *acaparamiento*
–, to buy *acaparar, comprar en masa*
up-to-the-minute *el último grito de la moda*
upkeep *conservación*
– cost, annual *coste de entrenamiento anual*
upper case *capital*
upscale buying *compras a precios ascendentes escalonados*
upset price *precio de primera oferta, precio o*

tipo de subasta
upswing *aumento, alza, mejora*
–, business *mejoramiento comercial*
upturn *aumento, alza, mejora*
upward movement *movimiento en alza*
urban population index *índice de población
urbana*
usage, commercial *usos comerciales*
usance *usanza, uso, condiciones de pago*
– bill *letra a plazo*
use, permissive *uso pasivo*
used equipment *planta de segunda mano,
equipo usado*

–, time *tiempo empleado o real*
user *consumidor, usuario, parroquiano*
– cost *coste de utilización*
– cost, marginal *costo marginal de utilización*
– groups *grupos de usuarios*
–, industrial *consumidor industrial*
utilities, public service *servicios públicos*
utility *utilidad, empresa de servicio público*
–, public *servicio público, empresa de servicio
público*

V

vacancy *empleo vacante, vacación*
vacant *post puesto vacante, empleo, plaza o*
  cargo libre
  – situation *cargo vacante, puesto, empleo*
vacation *vacaciones*
vagueness *vaguedad*
validate, to *validar, legalizar*
validity *validez*
valuation *valuación, tasa, justiprecio, avalúo,*
  apreciación, estimación
  – engineer *técnico tasador*
  – of output *valuación de la producción*
  –, assessed *tasación oficial, aranceles*
  –, inventory *valoración de las existencias*
value *valor, estimación*
  – added *valor agregado*
  – added, net *valor agregado neto*
  – agreed upon *valor entendido*
  – at factor *cost valor al costo de los factores*
  – at maturity *valor al vencimiento*
  – in account *valor en cuenta*
  – index, unit *índice de valores unitarios*
  – method, actual *método del valor actual*
  – method, cost *método del valor de coste*
  – received *valor recibido*
  – retained *valor retenido*
  – secured *valor en garantía, valor en prenda*
  –, absolute *valor absoluto*
  –, accumulative *valor acumulativo*
  –, actual *valor real*
  –, actual cash *valor real en mercado, costo de*
  reposición
  –, agreed *valor convenido*
  –, annual *rendimiento anual, valor anual*
  –, appraised *valor estimado*
  –, assessed *valor catastral*
  –, book *valor en libros*
  –, breakup *valor en liquidación*
  –, cash *valor efectivo*
  –, clean *valor líquido*
  –, clear *valor neto*
  –, commercial *valor de venta o en plaza, valor*
  industrial
  –, cost *valor de costo*
  –, current *valor actual, precio corriente*
  –, customs *valor en aduana*
  –, depreciated *valor depreciado*
  –, equilibrium *valor de equilibrio*

  –, exchange *valor en cambio, valor de cambio*
  –, face *valor nominal*
  –, fair *valor o precio justo*
  –, fair cash *valor justo del mercado*
  –, fair market *valor justo del mercado*
  –, fiduciary *valor fiduciario*
  –, going *valor de negocio en marcha*
  –, job *valor del trabajo*
  –, junk *valor de desechar*
  –, ledger *valor en libras*
  –, liquidation *valor de liquidación*
  –, market *valor de mercado, valor en plaza*
  –, maturity *valor al vencimiento*
  –, numerical *valor numérico*
  –, par *valor a la par*
  –, realization *valor en liquidación*
  –, recovery *valor de recuperación*
  –, rental *valor por concepto de alquiler*
  –, surrender *valor de rescate*
  –, taxable *valor imponible, valor tributario*
  –, trade *valor de venta*
  –, unit production *unidad de valor productivo*
  –, weighted *valor ponderado*
valued *inventory inventario valorado,*
  existencias valoradas
values, *range of escala de valores*
  –, schedule of par *tabla de valores a la par*
vanishing *point punto de desvanecimiento*
variable *variable*
  – annuity *anualidad variable*
  – budget *presupuesto variable*
  – burden *gastos generales variables*
  – cost, average *coste variable medio*
  – costs *costes variables*
  – fees *honorarios variables*
  – yield debenture *obligación de ingresos*
  variables
  –, dependent *variable dependiente*
  –, independent *variable independiente*
variance *varianza, separación tipo*
  –, external *varianza externa*
  –, interblock *varianza interbloque*
  –, sampling *varianza del muestreo*
variation *allowance, methods suplemento por*
  variación del método
  – clause *cláusula de variación de precios*
  –, allowable *variación admitida*
  –, sample *variación de las muestras*

–, seasonal *variación estacional*
variety stores *bazares*
varying-interval prediction *pronósticos a intervalos variables*
vected interests *intereses establecidos*
vector random variable *variable vectorial aleatoria*
–, unit *vector unidad*
vendee *cesionario, comprador*
vending machine *máquina de venta automática*
– machine, coin-operated *máquina de vender accionada por introducción de moneda*
–, automatic *ventas automáticas*
vendor *vendedor*
–, street *vendedor ambulante*
venture *empresa, riesgo, especulación*
– capital *capital de especulación*
verifier, alphanumerical *verificadora alfanumérica*
verify, to *verificar*
vertical expansion *expansión vertical*
vessel, dry cargo *barco de carga seca*
–, to register a *abanderar un barco*
vested interests *intereses creados*
– rights *derechos adquiridos*
veto *veto*
–, to *vetar, prohibir*
vice-president *vicepresidente, subdirector*
visible balance of trade *balance visible de comercio*
– file *archivo visible*
– items of trade *elementos visibles de*

comercio, exportaciones e importaciones de mercancías
vital statistics *estadísticas vitales, estadísticas demográficas*
vocation *vocación, carrera, profesión, oficio*
vocational guidance *orientación profesional*
– training *formación profesional*
void, null and *nulo y sin valor*
voided cheque *cheque anulado*
volume discount *descuento por volumen*
– of employment *volumen de ocupación*
–, aggregate *volumen total*
–, sales *volumen de ventas*
vote *voto*
– by proxy *voto por poder*
– of confidence *voto de confianza*
–, straw *voto no oficial*
–, to *votar*
voting stock *acciones con derecho a voto*
vouch, to *comprobar, certificar*
voucher *comprobante de pago, justificante, documento probatorio resguardo, póliza*
– cheque *cheque con comprobante*
– clerk *encargado de los comprobantes*
– copy *ejemplar comprobante de un anuncio*
– file *clasificador o archivador de comprobantes*
– register *registro de comprobantes*
–, as per *según comprobante*
–, cash *comprobante de caja*
–, expense *comprobante de gasto*
vouchers payable *comprobantes a cobrar*

W

wage *salario, sueldo, jornal, paga, renumeración*
– adjustment, automatic *ajuste automático de sueldos*
– bargains *convenios sobre salarios*
– board *junta ajustadora de sueldos*
– ceiling *salario máximo o tope*
– curve *curva de ganancia*
– dispute *controversia o descuento sobre sueldos*
– earner *asalariado*
– escalator clause *cláusula de revisión de salarios*
– freeze *congelación de sueldos*
– level *nivel de sueldos*
– policy *política en materia de salarios*
– range *rango de salarios*
– rate *tarifa de salarios*
– scale *escala de salarios o sueldos, escalafón*
– spread *rango de salarios*
– stabilization *estabilización de tipos de sueldo*
– system, incentive *sistema de salario incentivo*
–, actual *salario efectivo*
–, basic *salario básico*
–, dismissal *indemnización por despido*
–, guaranteed *sueldo garantizado*
–, hourly *salario por hora*
–, incentive *prima de producción*
–, maximum *salario máximo o tope*
–, minimum *salario mínimo*
–, progressive *salario progresivo*
–, standard *salario base*
–, terminal *indemnización por despido*
–, time *tarifa por tiempo*
–, union *salario sindical*
wages department *departamento de salarios*
–, real *salarios reales*
–, scale of *escala de sueldos, escalafón*
, subsistence *salarios mínimos para substituir*
waiting line *línea de espera, cola*
– time *tiempo de espera*
waiver *renuncia*
walkout (Am) *huelga, paro con abandono del puesto de trabajo*
wall-sign *rótulo mural, rótulo en pared*
want *necesidad, carencia*
– ads *anuncios por palabras, pequeños*

anuncios clasificados, anuncios económicos
– of balance *desequilibrio*
– slips *artículos necesarios, artículos convenientes*
–, to be in *estar necesitado*
wants, primary *artículos de primera necesidad*
–, unlimited *necesidades económicas*
war, price *guerra de precios*
warehouse *almacén, depósito, bodega (C), hangar (A), barraca (Ch)*
– receipt *recibo de almacén*
– stocks *existencias en almacén*
–, bonded *almacén general de depósito aduanal*
warehouseman *almacenista, almacenador (M), almacenero (C)*
warehousing charges *gastos de almacenaje*
– expenses *gastos de almacenaje*
– system *sistema de depósitos*
warfare, economic *guerra económica*
warrant *vale, garantía, certificado de depósito*
–, distress *orden de embargo*
–, dividend *cédula de dividendo*
–, pay *autorización, orden de pago*
warranty, banking *garantía bancaria*
wastage *desgaste, desperdicio*
waste *desperdicio*
– control *control de desperdicios*
– money, to *malgastar dinero*
– products *desperdicios, productos de deshecho*
wasteful *antieconómico*
wasting assets *bienes agotables, activo agotable*
watered assets *activo diluído*
– capital *capital inflado*
– stock *capital inflado (M), acciones diluídas*
wave, short *onda corta*
way, under *en camino, en curso*
waybill *hoja de ruta, factura, conocimiento de embarque, hoja de marcha*
–, air *conocimiento de embarque aéreo*
weak incentive *incentivo amortiguado, incentivo reducido*
– market *mercado flojo*
weaken, to *debilitarse*
wealth *caudal, dineral, riqueza, plata (Am)*
wear and tear *desgaste, depreciación*

week, business *semana comercial, semana laboral*
week-day *día de trabajo*
weight *peso, coeficiente de ponderación*
– capacity, dead *tonelaje*
–, gross *peso total*
–, gross laden *peso total cargado*
–, legal *peso legal*
–, net *peso neto*
–, standard *peso legal, peso patrón*
–, unit *peso unitario*
weighted *ponderado*
– application blank *solicitud de empleo ponderado*
– arithmetic mean *media aritmética ponderada*
– average *promedio ponderado*
– blank *formulario ponderado*
– geometric mean *media geométrica ponderada*
– index *índice ponderado*
– mean *media ponderada*
– sample *muestra ponderada*
– value *valor ponderado*
weighting *ponderación*
welfare *bienestar social, asistencia pública, previsión social*
– economics *economía para el bienestar familiar*
– expenses, employees' *gastos para servicio social de los obreros*
– fund *fondo de previsión social*
– work *prestaciones asistenciales*
–, public *bienestar público*
–, social *bienestar social*
well-being *bienestar*
wharf *muelle, embarcadero*
wharfage *derechos de muelles, muellaje*
wheel-type filing system *fichero giratorio*
wholesale *venta al por mayor*
– concern *casa o firma mayorista*
– dealer *mayorista, comerciante al por mayor*
– firm *empresa o casa al por mayor*
– house *casa o firma mayorista*
– lot *lote al por mayor*
– market *mercado al por mayor*
– merchant *comerciante al por mayor*
– price *precio mayorista, precio de al por mayor*
– store *almacén mayorista*
– trade *comercio al por mayor, venta al por mayor*
–, to buy (at) *comprar al por mayor*
wholesaler *vendedor mayorista, almacenista, mayorista*
widow's pension *viudedad, pensión de viudedad*

wildcat strike *huelga no sancionada por el sindicato*
will, partnership at *asociación sin plazo fijo de duración*
willingness *buena disposición*
windfall loss *pérdidas imprevistas*
window card *cartel de escaparate*
– display *exposición de escaparate, disposición cosas en escaparate*
– display material *material para exposición de escaparates*
– dresser *decorador de escaparates, escaparatista, aparadorista (Am)*
– dressing *componer escaparates, decoración de escaparates*
– trimming *componer escaparates, decoración de escaparates*
–, store *escaparate de tienda*
withdraw, to *retirar, retirarse*
– cash, to *retirar efectivo*
withdrawal *retiro de fondos, retirada de mercancías*
–, age at *edad de retiro*
withheld *retenido*
word of mouth *comunicación oral*
–, code *palabra convencional, palabra clave*
–, coined *palabra acuñada, palabra inventada*
work *trabajo, tarea, faena, labor, obra, empleado, actividad*
– account *cuenta de explotación*
– agreement *acuerdo colectivo*
– analysis survey *encuesta sobre el análisis del trabajo*
– at a loss, to *trabajar con pérdidas*
– allowance, excess *suplemento por variación del método*
– bench *puesto de trabajo*
– coefficient *coeficiente de trabajo*
– content *valor del trabajo*
– curve *curva de producción*
– cycle *ciclo de trabajo*
– distribution chart *diagrama de distribución del trabajo*
– done *trabajo realizado*
– element *elemento de trabajo*
– factor *factor de trabajo*
– flow chart *diagrama de flujo del trabajo*
– force *personal obrero*
– history *historial laboral*
– in process *manufactura en proceso*
– label *ficha de ruta*
– load *faena, carga de trabajo*
– measurement *medición del trabajo*
– order *orden de trabajo*
– out, to *ejecutar, efectuar, llevar a cabo, poner en práctica*

- place *puesto de trabajo*
- round the clock *trabajo continuo*
- schedule *programa de trabajo*
- sheet *hoja de repartición, papel de trabajo (M), póliza de contabilidad (M), hoja de trabajo (C), estado constructivo (C), hoja de computaciones*
- shop *taller, obrador, oficina*
- slip *hoja de trabajo, bono de trabajo*
- specification *especificación de trabajo*
- standard *norma de trabajo*
- station *lugar de trabajo*
- study *estudio del trabajo*
- system, piece- *trabajo por pieza, a por medida*
- week, basic *semana básica de trabajo*
-, absence from *falta de asistencia al trabajo*
-, combined *trabajo en colaboración*
-, day *trabajo a jornal*
-, development *labor de crear, perfeccionar y propagar*
-, direct *trabajo directo*
-, division of *división del trabajo*
-, expended *trabajo consumido*
-, experimental *trabajo experimental*
-, external *trabajo externo*
-, group *trabajo en equipo*
-, indirect *mano de obra indirecta, trabajo indirecto*
-, inside *trabajo interno*
-, internal *trabajo interno*
-, mental *trabajo mental*
-, office *trabajo de oficina*
-, outside *trabajo externo*
-, overtime *trabajo a horas extras*
-, piece- *trabajo por pieza o por tarea*
-, productive *trabajo productivo*
-, research *trabajo de investigación*
-, shift *trabajo a turnos*
-, social *trabajo social, servicio social*
-, stencil *trabajo de estarcio*
-, stop *abandono de trabajo*
-, straight *trabajo directo, trabajo sencillo*
-, substandard *trabajo deficiente o inferior*
-, team *trabajo en equipo*
-, time *trabajo por unidad de tiempo*
-, unrestricted *trabajo no restringido*
-, welfare *prestaciones asistenciales*
workable *laborable, factible, viable, explotable*
workbench *puesto de trabajo*
workday *día laborable*
worker *trabajador, obrero, operario, jornalero*
-, casual *obrero provisional, obrero migratorio*

-, demonstration *demostrador*
-, factory *obrero industrial*
-, migratory *emigrante*
-, office *trabajo de oficina*
-, part-time *trabajador en jornada incompleta*
-, piece- *operario a contrato*
-, qualified *obrero o trabajador calificado*
-, seasonal *trabajador de temporada*
-, semi-skilled *obrero o trabajador semicalificado*
-, skilled *obrero o trabajador calificado*
workflow *circuito de producción*
working *funcionamiento, operación, maniobra*
- area *zona de trabajo*
- assets *activo circulante*
- balance *saldo corriente*
- capital *capital circulante, capital activo, capital en giro, capital de trabajo*
- class *clase obrera, proletariado*
- conditions *condiciones de trabajo*
- data *datos de funcionamiento*
- day *día laborable, día útil*
- funds *fondos de habilitación*
- group *equipo de trabajo, grupo de trabajo, medios de producción*
- hours *horas laborables*
- life *período de actividad, vida útil*
- order, in *en actividad normal, en condiciones de servicio en buen estado de funcionamiento*
- partner *socio activo*
- party *consejo industrial mixto*
- speed and accuracy, survey of *encuesta de precisión y rapidez de trabajo*
-, hand-to-mouth *funcionamiento o trabajo a producción al día*
-, individual *trabajo individual*
workman *trabajador*
workmanlike *bien hecho, bien realizado*
workmanship *mano de obra, manufactura, ejecución*
workmen's compensation *compensación por accidentes de trabajo*
- insurance *seguro obrero*
workpiece *pieza*
workroom *taller de reparaciones, obrador*
works *fábrica, taller, trabajos, obras*
- committee *comité de empresa*
- council *comisión de obreros*
- manager *director de fábrica*
-, complementary *trabajos complementarios*
-, public *obras públicas*
-, relief *obras para reducir el desempleo*
workshop *taller*
world market *mercado mundial*

worsening *evolución desfavorable, empeorando*
worth *valor, valía*
–, net *valor neto, capital neto, activo neto*
–, present *valor actual*
–, tangible net *activo neto tangible*
worthless *inútil, sin valor*
– accounts *cuentas incobrables*
wrapper *envoltorio, faja de periódico*
wrapping *envoltura, faja, envoltorio*
– machine *máquina para envolver*
– paper *papel de embalaje*
write down, to *rebajar el valor*

– in *nombre manuscrito*
– in, to *intercalar, insertar*
– off *cargo por depreciación, cancelación*
– off, to *anular, eliminar, suprimir*
– up *revaluación, aumento de valor en los libros, aumento injustificable del valor nominal del activo*
writer *escritor, autor*
writing, alphabetic *escritura alfabética*
writing, report *redacción de informes*
written *escrito*
– agreement *acuerdo por escrito*
– notice *aviso escrito*

Y

yards and sheds, bonded *tinglados de almacenaje de artículos voluminosos y pesados*
year book *anuario*
– end dividend *dividendo a fin de año*
–, business *ejercicio anual, año administrativo, año económico*
–, calendar *año civil*
–, financial *ejercicio económico, año económico*
–, fiscal *año económico*
–, lean *año pobre o magro*
–, leap *año bisiesto*
yearly adjustment *ajuste anual*
– income *ingreso o renta anual*
– range *precios máximos y mínimos del año*
yellow press *prensa sensacionalista, periódicos sensacionales*

– dog contract *promesa por parte del obrero de no sindicalizarse*
yield *rendimiento, producto, producción, cosecha, renta, rédito*
– a profit *producir un beneficio o ganancia*
– basis *tasación según rendimiento*
– bond *obligación emitida por bajo de la par*
– rate *tipo de rendimiento*
– table *tabla de rendimiento*
– to maturity *rendimiento al vencimiento*
–, actual *rendimiento real*
–, current *rendimiento corriente*
–, prospective *rendimiento probable*
–, to *producir*
yielding *productivo*

Z

zone *zona*
—, distributing *zona de distribución, zona de reparto*

—, distribution *zona de abastecimiento*

SELECT LIST OF ABBREVIATIONS AND ACRONYMS
ENGLISH

a/c	account current	cuenta corriente	c/c
acc.	acceptance	aceptación	acept.
admin.	adminstration	administración	admón.
ad.val.	L. ad valorem: according to value	conforme a su valor	
AGM	Annual General Meeting	asamblea general anual	
a.m.	L. ante meridiem: before noon	antemeridiano, antes del mediodía	a.m.
A/R	against all risks	seguro marítimo contra todo riesgo	
a.r.	account receivable	cuenta por cobrar	
a.s.a.p.	as soon as possible	tan pronto como sea posible	
ASTMS	Association of Scientific, Technical and Managerial Staffs	Asociación de Directivos Administrativos, Técnicos y Científicos	
avdp.	avoirdupois	sistema de pesas inglés	
BIS/BIZ	Bank for International Settlements	Banco Internacional de Pagos	BIP
b/f	brought forward	suma y sigue	
B/L	Bill of Lading	conocimiento de embarque, guía de embarque, carta de porte, guía aérea	
bl.	bale	bola, paca, fardo	
BSI	British Standards Institution	Institución Británica de Normalización	
b.v.	book value	valor según los libros	
CACM/MICA	Central American Common Market	Mercado Común Centroamericano	MCCA
CAF	Cost, Assurance, Freight	coste/o, seguro y flete	
CARICOM	Caribbean Community and Common Market	Comunidad y Mercado Común del Caribe	
cart	cartage	carretaje, acarreo, porte	
C.B.D.	Cash Before Delivery	pago antes de la entrega, pago en efectivo con el pedido	
cc.	cubic centimetre	centímetro cúbico	cc
CCC	Customs Co-operation Council	Consejo de Cooperación Aduanera	CCA
cf.	confer, compare	comparar, confrontar, cotejar	cf.
c/f	carried forward	a la venta, al frente	
cge.pd. carriage paid	porte pagado		
C.I.	Consular Invoice	factura consular	
C.I.F.	cost, insurance and freight	coste, seguro y flete	CSF
CIFE	cost, insurance, freight and exchange	coste, seguro, flete y cambio	
cm.	centimetre	centímetro	cm.
CMEA	Council for Mutual Economic Assistance	Consejo de Asistencia Económica Mútua	CAEM

Co.	Company	Compañía	Cía.
c/o	carried over	suma y sigue	
C.O.D.	Cash On Delivery/Collect On Delivery	entrega contra reembolso pago contra entrega	C.O.D.
COPAL	Cocoa Producers' Alliance	Alianza de Productos de Cacao	
CPA	Certified Public Accountant	Contador Público Titulado	
cr.	credit, creditor	crédito, haber, acreedor	
CWS	Co-operative Wholesale Society	Sociedad Cooperativa deMayoristas	
dis.	discount	descuento	dto.
doz/dz.	dozen	docena	doc.
dr.	debit, debtor	débito, deudor, debe	
D/s	Days after sight	días vista	d/v
dy	day	día	
ECGD	Export Credits Guarantee Department	Departamento de Garantía de Crédito a la Exportación	
ECLA	Economic Commission for Latin America	Comisión Económica para América Latina	CEPAL
e.e.	error excepted	salvo error	
EEC	European Economic Community	Comunidad Económica Europea	CEE
EFTA	European Free Trade Association	Asociación Europea de Libre Intercambio	AELI
E&OE	errors and omissions excepted	salvo error u omisión	s.e.u.o.
e.g.	L. exempli gratia: for example	por ejemplo	por ej.
encl.	enclosure	anexo	
et al.	L. et alii: and others	y otras	
f.b.	freight bill	factura de flete	
FIFO	First-In-First-Out	primero en entrar, primero en salir	FIFO
f.o.b.	free on board	libre a bordo, franco bordo, presto a bordo, libre de gastos a bordo	l.a.b./f.a.b
f.o.c.	free on car	libre sobre vagón, libre de gastos	
f.o.q.	free on quay	libre sobre muelle	
FRB	Federal Reserve Bank	Banco de Reserva Federal	
ft.	foot, feet	pie, pies	
f.t.	full term	condiciones completas	
gal.	gallon	galón	
GATT	General Agreement on Tariffs and Trade	Acuerdo General sobre Tarifas y Comercio	GATT
GIGO	Garbage in, garbage out	Basura entra, basura sale	BEBS
GDP	Gross Domestic Product	Producto bruto interno	
GNP	Gross National Product	Producto nacional bruto	PNB
gr.wt.	gross weight	peso bruto	
HP	hire purchase	arrendamiento con opción a comprar	
hr.	hour	hora	h.
IAEA	International Atomic Energy Agency	Organismo Nacional Energía Atómica	OIEA
IBRD	International Bank for Reconstruction and Development/World Bank	Banco Internacional de Reconstrucción y Fomento	BIRF
I.C.C.	International Chamber of Commerce	Cámara de Comercio Internacional	CCI

ICJ	International Court of Justice	Tribunal Internacional de Justicia	TIJ
IDA	International Development Association	Asociación Internacional de Desarrollo	AID
i.e.	L. id est: that is	es decir	
IEA	International Energy Agency	Agencia Internacional de la Energía	AIE
IFAD	International Fund for Agricultural Development	Fondo Internacional de Desarrollo Agrícola	FIDA
IFC	International Finance Corporation	Corporación Financiera Internacional	CFI
IMF	International Monetary Fund	Fondo Monetario Internacional	FMI
inst.	instant	del corriente	
INTELSAT	International Telecommunications Satellite Organization	Organización Internacional de Telecomunicaciones por Satélite	
inv.	invoice	factura	
I.O.U.	I Owe You	pagaré, vale, abonaré	
JP	Justice of the Peace	Juez de Paz	
Jnt.Stk	joint stock	acciones de sociedad anónima	
Jr.	Junior	Hijo	
Kg.	Kilogram(me)	Kilogramo	Kg.
Kl.	Kilolitre	Kilolitro	Kl.
Km.	Kilometre	Kilómetro	Km.
l.	litre	litro	l.
lb.	pound	libra	lb.
L/C	Letter of Credit	carta de crédito	
LIFO	Last In-First Out	último en entrar, primero en salir	ueps
Ltd.	Limited Company	Compañía o Sociedad Limitada	
m.	metre	metro	m.
MCCA/CACM	Central American Common Market	Mercado Común Centroamericano	MCCA
min.	minute	minuto	min.
mm.	millimetre	milímetro	mm.
MS	manuscript	manuscrito	
mth.	month	mes	
m.v.	market value	valor de mercado	
NATO	North Atlantic Treaty Organization	Organización del Tratado del Atlántico Norte	OTAN
NCV	no commercial value	sin valor comercial	
NEB (UK)	National Enterprise Board	Junta Empresa Nacional	
n/f	no funds	sin fondos	
NHS (UK)	National Health Service	Servicio Nacional de Salud	
nt.wt.	net weight	peso neto	
o/a	on account (of)	a cuenta (de)	
OAPEC	Organization of Arab Petroleum Exporting Countries	Organización de los Países Arabes Exportadores de Petróleo	OPAEP
OAS	Organization of American States	Organización de los Estados Americanos	OEA
OAV	Organization of African Unity	Organización de la Unidad Africana	OUA
OECD/OCDE	Organization for Economic Cooperation and Development	Organización para la Cooperación y Desarrollo Económico	OCDE

O & M	Organization and Methods	Organización y métodos	
OPEC	Organization of Petroleum Exporting Countries	Organización de los Países Exportadores de Petróleo	OPEP
OR	Operational research/ Operations research	investigación operativa	
p.a.	L. per anuum: per year, yearly	al año	
P.A.Y.E.	Pay As You Earn	pague a medida que gane	
p.c.	per cent	tanto por ciento, por ciento, porcentaje	
PLC	Public Limited Company	Sociedad Anónima	S.A.
p.m.	L. Post meridiem: after noon	por la tarde, de la tarde	p.m.
P.O.	Postal Order	giro postal	
P.O.B.	Post Office Box	apartado de correos	
P.O.D.	Pay On Delivery	pago a la entrega	
P.P.	Parcel Post	servicio de paquetes postales	
p.p.	L. per procurationem: for and on behalf of	por orden	p.p.
PR	Public Relations	relaciones públicas	
P.S.	L. postscriptum: postscript	posdata	PD.
R.	Registered	certificado	
R & D	Research & Development	Investigación y Desarrollo	
S.D.	L. sine die: without day	Sin fecha fijada, hasta nueva orden	
sec.	second	segundo	s./seg.
Sr.	Senior	Padre	
tab.	tabulator	tabulador	
T.T.	telegraphic transfer	transferencia telegráfica	
UNCTAD	United Nations Conference on Trade and Development	Conferencia de las Naciones Unidas sobre Comercio y Desarrollo	
UNO	United Nations Organization	Organización de las Naciones Unidas	ONU
VAT	Value Added Tax	Impuesto sobre el valor añadido	IVA
vol.	volume	volumen	
vs.	L. versus: against	en contraposición, en pro y en contra, contra, en comparación con, en contraste con	
viz.	L. videlicet: namely	a saber, es decir, o sea	
yd.	yard	yarda	
yr.	year	año	

PART TWO

ESPAÑOL - INGLES

ABREVIATURAS

L	Lat
Am	Inglés (Norteamericano)
Ing	Inglés (Británico)
A	Argentina
AC	América Central
C	Cuba
Ch	Chile
M	México
PR	Puerto Rico

A

a cuenta *on account*
a granel *in bulk*
abandono *abandonment*
– de trabajo *stop work*
abaratar *to lower the price*
abarcar *to cover or include*
abarrotado *congested, jammed*
– de mercancías *overstocked*
abarrotes, almacenista de *wholesale grocer*
abastecedor *outfitter, supplier*
– de comestibles al por mayor *wholesale grocer, supplier*
abastecer *to furnish or supply*
abastecimiento principal *main supply*
–, servicios de *supply services*
–, zona de *distribution zone*
abastecimientos *supplies, stock, stores*
–, mercado de *provision market*
abatir *to lower*
abierta, cuenta *open account, running account*
–, población *open population*
–, póliza *blanket policy*
abierto, crédito *open credit*
–, mercado *open market*
–, programa *open end*
–, sistema *open system*
abogado *attorney, lawyer*
abogados, barra de *bar association*
abogar *to advocate*
abolir *to revoke or annul*
abonable *payable*
abonado *subscriber*
abonar *to credit*
– en cuenta *to allow*
– la cuenta *to credit the account*
– los derechos de aduana *to pay duty*
abono *allowance, credit entry, instalment*
– o recibo *receipt*
abonos, compras en *instalment buying*
–, ventas en *instalment sales*
abrecartas *letter opener*
abreviar *to abridge*
abrir *to open*
– propuestas *to open bids*
– un crédito *to open a credit*
– una cuenta *to open an account*
abrogar *to annul or repeal*
absentismo *absenteeism*

absoluta permanente, capacidad *permanent total disability*
–, hora *absolute time*
absoluto *absolute*
–, aval *full endorsement*
–, endoso *absolute endorsement*
–, valor *absolute value*
absorber la pérdida *to absorb the loss*
absorción de la atención *engrossing of the attention*
acaparador *buyer-up, monopolist, profiteer*
acaparamiento *monopoly*
acaparar *to buy up, monopolize, hoard or engross*
– el mercado *to corner the market*
acarrear *to transport or carry*
acarreo *cartage, transportation*
acceso *approach*
accesorio de máquina *machine attachment*
–, gasto *additional change, incidental expense*
accidental, director *acting director*
–, jefe *acting chief*
–, utilidad *casual income*
accidente de trabajo *industrial accident, occupational injury*
accidentes industriales, fondo para *industrial insurance fund*
– de trabajo, ley de *compensation act*
– de trabajo, seguro contra compensación legal por *workmen's compensation insurance*
– laborales, compensación por *workmen's compensation*
–, a prueba de *accident-proof*
–, frecuencia de *accident frequency*
–, índice de *accident rate*
–, porcentaje de *accident rate*
–, porcentaje de gravedad de los *accident severity rate*
–, porcentaje de mortalidad por *accident death rate*
–, proporción de *accident rate*
–, repetición de *accident sequence*
–, riesgo de *accident risk*
–, seguro contra *casualty insurance*
acción *action, share of stock*
– bancaria *bank share*
– hipotecaria *foreclosure*

– irredimible *debenture stock*
– nominativa *registered share*
accionada por teclado, calculadora *key-drive calculator*
acciones *shares of stock*
– acumulativas *cumulative stock*
– al portador *bearer shares*
– autorizadas *authorized stock*
– comunes *common stock*
– con derecho de voto *voting stock*
– cubiertas *fully-paid shares*
– de administración *management stock*
– de capital *capital stock*
– de fundador *founder's shares*
– de voto plural *plural-voting stock*
– diferidas *deferred stock*
– emitidas *issued stock*
– en circulación *outstanding stock*
– inscritas *listed stock*
– integralmente, asignar las *to allot the shares in full*
– ordinarias *common stock equities*
– por emitir, compraventa de *when-issued trading*
– preferentes *preferred stock*
– preferentes participantes *participating stock*
– preferidas *preferred stock*
– primitivas *original stock*
– privilegiadas *preference shares, preferred stock*
– sin derecho a voto *non-voting stock*
– sin valor nominal *non-par-value stock*
– suscritas *subscribed capital stock*
–, capital en *stock*
–, certificado de *stock certificate*
–, comandita por *stock association*
–, comisionista de *stockbroker*
–, compañía por *stock company, chartered company*
–, corredor de *stockbroker*
–, dividendos en *stock dividends*
–, emisión de *shares issue*
–, fraccionamiento de *share split*
–, mercado bursátil de *stock market*
–, registro de *stock register*
–, sociedad por *joint-stock company*
–, tenedor de *stockholder*
accionista *stockholder, shareholder*
– disidente *dissenting stockholder*
accionistas *stockholder*
–, acuerdo de *stockholder's resolution*
–, asamblea general de *meeting of shareholders*
–, junta de *stockholders' meeting*
aceleración *speed-up*
acelerada, depreciación *accelerated*

depreciation
acelerado, movimiento *accelerated motion*
aceptación *acceptance*
– a descubierto *blank or uncovered acceptance*
– a favor del público *consumer acceptance*
– bancaria *bank acceptance*
– comercial *trade acceptance*
– condicionada *qualified acceptance*
– contra documentos *acceptance against documents*
– de favor *accommodation acceptance*
– de una letra *acceptance of a draft*
– de una marca, valor de *goodwill*
– del público *consumer acceptance*
– sin reservas *general acceptance*
–, documentos contra *documents against acceptance*
–, línea de *acceptation line*
–, normas de *acceptance standards*
aceptada, letra *accepted draft*
aceptador *acceptor*
aceptados, efectos *accepted bills*
aceptante *acceptor*
aceptar *to accept or honour*
– a reserva de *to accept subject to*
acero para archivar correspondencia, estante de *steel filing cabinet*
acomodación *accommodation*
acopio *assortment*
acreedor *creditor*
– hipotecario *mortgagee*
– ordinario *general creditor*
– privilegiado *preferred creditor*
– sin caución *unsecured creditor*
–, saldo *active or credit balance*
acreedora, cuenta *credit account, creditor account*
acreedores diversos *sundry creditors*
acta de acción *deed of release*
– de constitución *deed of settlement*
actas *minutes of a meeting*
–, libro de *minute book*
activa, demanda *active demand*
–, mercado de competencia *active market price competition*
activas, deudas *accounts receivable*
actividad *activity, job, task, work*
– comercial, investigación de la *business research*
– investigadora *research activity*
– múltiple *multiple activity*
– simultánea *multiple activity*
–, caída de la *activity dip*
–, campo de *field of activity*
–, esfera de *field of activity*
–, investigación de la *activation research*

–, pérdida de *activity loss*
–, período de *working life*
activo *assets, active assets*
– acumulado *accrued assets*
– admisible *admissible assets*
– agotable (C) *wasting assets*
– aparente *intangible assets*
– aprobado *admitted assets*
– capital *capital assets*
– circulante *circulating or working assets*
– comercial *current assets*
– corriente *current assets*
– de trabajo *working assets*
– diferido *deferred assets*
– diluído *watered assets*
– disponible *available or liquid assets, funds available, cash in hand*
– dudoso *doubtful assets*
– en divisas *foreign-exchange assets*
– fijo *capital assets, fixed capital*
– gravado *pledged assets*
– inmovilizado *fixed assets*
– intangible *intangibles*
– líquido *net value*
– neto *net value*
– neto tangible *tangible net worth*
– no imponible *tax liability*
– oculto *concealed assets*
– permanente *permanent assets*
– realizable *tangible assets*
– social *company's assets, partnership assets*
– tangible *tangible assets*
– y pasivo *assets and liabilities*
–, cuentas del *asset accounts*
–, derechos sobre el *equities*
–, partida del *asset*
–, socio *active partner*
activos *assets*
– comprometidos *committed assets*
– sociales *corporate assets*
acto mercantil *commercial transaction*
actuación del sistema *system performance*
– normal *normal performance*
– óptima *optimum performance*
– tipo *standard performance*
–, apreciación de la *performance or speed rating*
–, valoración de la *performance or speed rating*
–, valoración estimada de la *flat ratings*
actual *current, present*
–, cambio *spot exchange*
–, estado *present status*
actuante, jefe *acting chief*
actuario *actuary*
acuerdo *agreement, resolution*

– colectivo *collective agreement, work agreement*
– comercial *commercial agreement*
– comercial de intercambio *trade agreement*
– comercial de reciprocidad *reciprocal trade agreement*
– consorcial *pooling agreement*
– de accionistas *stockholder's resolution*
– de compensación *clearing agreement*
– de empresa *factory agreement*
– entre el sindicato y los patronos *union-employer agreement*
– o tratado comercial *commodity agreement*
– por escrito *written agreement*
–, coeficiente de *coefficient of agreement*
acumula, interés que se *accruing interest*
acumulable *cumulative, accumulative*
acumulaciones *accruals*
– pagaderas *accruals payable*
–, cuenta de *accruals account*
acumulada, anualidad *accumulated annuity*
–, depreciación *accrued depreciation*
–, renta *accrued income*
acumuladas, utilidades *accumulated profits*
acumulado, activo *accrued assets*
–, capital *accumulated worth*
–, interés *accrued interest*
–, pasivo *accrued liabilities*
acumulados, ingresos *accrued income*
acumular *to accrue*
acumulativa, base *accrual basis*
acumulativas, acciones *cumulative stock*
acumulativo *cumulative*
–, cálculo de margen comercial *cumulative-markup calculation*
–, efecto *cumulative effect*
–, valor *accumulative value*
acuñación de moneda *coining*
acuñar moneda *to mint, to coin*
acusar recibo *to acknowledge receipt*
acuse de recibo *acknowledgement of receipt*
adaptabilidad administrativa *clerical adaptability*
adaptación *adjustment*
–, tiempo de *adaptation time*
adelantado, cobro por *advanced collections*
–, pago *advance payment, cash in advance, prepayment*
–, por *in advance*
adelantar *to pay in advance*
adelanto *advance*
– sobre valores *advance upon collateral (security)*
adeudar *to owe, to debit*
adeudo *indebtedness, debit*
–, certificado de *indebtedness certificate*

adición *addition*
adicional, cláusula *rider*
–, coste *additional cost*
–, gasto *additional expense*
–, impuesto *surtax*
adicionales, ingresos *additional income*
adicionar *to add*
adiestramiento *training, practice*
– de agentes vendedores *training salesmen*
– de aprendices *training apprentices*
– de los empleados *employees' training*
– en el trabajo *job instruction or training*
–, director de *training director*
–, programas de *training programmes*
adiestrar *to train*
adinerado *wealthy*
aditamento *apron, rider*
– de máquina *machine attachment*
adjudicación *award, adjudication*
adjuntar *to attach or enclose*
adjunto, contramaestre *petty foreman*
–, secretario *assistant secretary*
administración *administration, management*
– de rentas *collector's office*
– dinámica *dynamic administration*
– financiera *financial management*
– judicial *receivership*
–, acciones de *management stock*
–, asesor sobre *management consultant*
–, comité *administration committee*
–, contrato por *cost-plus contract*
–, consejo de *board of directors*
–, gastos de *administration cost*
–, mala *mismanagement*
administrador *administrator*
– de tienda *store manager*
– interino *acting manager*
– o fideicomisario de trust *trustee*
– síndico *receiver*
–, ayudante *assistant manager*
administrar *to manage or administer*
administrativa general, prueba *general clerical test*
–, adaptabilidad *clerical adaptability*
–, contabilidad *administrative accounting*
–, eficacia *clerical efficiency*
–, unidad *administrative unit*
administrativo *administrative, executive*
–, año *business year*
–, ayudante *administrative assistant*
–, cargo *executive position*
–, comité *executive committee*
–, jefe *overseer*
–, papeleo *red tape*
administrativos, costes *clerical costs*
–, gastos *administrative expenses*

–, servicios *administrative services*
admisible, activo *admissible assets*
admitida, variación *allowable variation*
adoptada, nomenclatura *adopted nomenclature*
adquirido, superávit *acquired surplus*
adquiridos, derechos *vested rights or interests*
adquirir *to acquire*
– los derechos en bloque *to buy rights outright*
adquisición *acquisition*
adquisitiva, capacidad *purchasing power*
–, paridad *parity in purchasing power*
adquisitivo, poder *purchasing power*
aduana *customshouse*
–, abonar los derechos de *to pay duty*
–, agente de *customshouse broker, forwarding agent*
–, aranceles de *customs tariffs*
–, derechos de *customs duties*
–, exento de derechos de *customs-exempt*
–, fianza de *customs bond*
–, imponer derechos de *to assess customs duty*
–, ingresos de *customs receipts*
–, libre de derechos de *customs-free*
–, manifiesto de *customs manifest*
–, vista de *customs inspector*
aduanal, declaración *bill of entry*
–, impuesto *customs duties*
aduanera, zona *customs area*
aduanero, tasador *apparaiser*
advertencias, huelga de *token strike*
aérea, carga *air-freight*
–, carta *airmail letter*
aéreas, tarifas *air fares*
aéreo, conocimiento de embarque *air waybill*
–, control de tránsito *air traffic control*
–, corredor *air-broker*
–, correo *airmail*
–, corretaje *airbroking*
–, fletamiento *aircraft chartering, aircraft time-charter*
–, flete *air-freight*
–, seguro *airplane insurance*
aeropuerto, tarifas de *airport tariffs*
aeropuertos, control del tráfico de *airport traffic control*
afianzado *bonded*
afijación *allocation*
– por valores *value allocation*
afiliación a un gremio, tarjeta de *working card*
afiliada *affiliated*
–, compañía *subsidiary company*
afiliar *to affiliate*
afiliarse a sindicato obrero, contrato que prohibe *yellowdog contract*

afines, compañías *related companies*
afluencia de capitales *inflow of capital*
aforador *appraiser*
aforo *appraisal, appraisement*
agencia *agency, bureau*
– de colocaciones *employment agency*
– de proyectos *design agency*
– distribuidora *distributing agency*
–, contrato de *agency contract*
agencias contables *accounting firms*
agenda *agenda*
agente *agent*
– bancario de compensaciones *clearinghouse agent*
– de aduana *customshouse broker, forwarding agent*
– de bolsa *stockbroker*
– de colocaciones *labour agent*
– de envíos, comisionista expedidor *forwarding agent*
– de negocios *business agent*
– de seguros *insurance broker*
– de ventas *sales agent*
– de viajes *travel agent*
– exclusivo *sole agent*
– general *general agent*
– viajero *travelling salesman (Br), commercial traveller (Am)*
agentes bursátiles bajistas *bears*
– fiscales *revenue authorities*
– vendedroes, adiestramiento de *training salesmen*
agio *usury, speculation*
agiotaje *usury, speculation, stock-jobbing*
agiotista *usurer, speculator, stock-jobber*
agotable, activo (C) *wasting assets*
agotables, beneficios *wasting assets*
agotado *out-of-stock*
agotador, trabajo *sweat, fatigue*
agotamiento *depletion*
agotar *to deplete*
agraria, reforma *land reform*
agregado, valor *value added*
agregar *to add*
agrícola, cooperativismo *agricultural cooperation*
–, economía *agricultural economics*
agrupadas, compras *group buying*
agujas, cronómetro con dos *two-handed stopwatch*
agudo, período *peak period*
ahorrar *to save or economize*
–, propensión a *propensity to save*
ahorro *saving, economy*
– de trabajo *labour saving*
– negativo *non-saving*

–, banco de *savings bank*
–, bono de *savings bond*
–, caja de *savings bank*
–, ciclo de *savings cycle*
–, cuentas de *savings account*
ajustar *to adjust or settle*
– cuentas *to settle accounts*
ajuste *adjustment, settlement*
– automático de sueldos *automatic wage adjustment*
– de compaginación *page layout (Am), page make-up (Br)*
– de costes *cost auditing*
– de cuentas *audit, auditing*
– de precios *price adjustment*
–, asiento de *adjusting entry*
–, pruebas de *test pattern*
ajustes (C) *taskwork*
al azar *at random*
al contado *in cash*
al descubierto *in blank*
albacea *executor*
alcance, de gran *long range*
alcista *bull, bullish*
–, mercado *bull market*
–, tendencia *upward trend*
aleatoria continua, variable *continuous random variable*
–, muestra *random sample*
–, muestra no *non-random sample*
–, variable *aleatory or random variable*
–, variable vectorial *vector random variable*
aleatorio *random*
–, comienzo *random start*
–, error del muestreo *random sampling error*
alfabética de contabilidad, máquina *alphabetic accounting machine*
–, clave *alphabetical code*
–, perforación *alphabetical punching*
–, serie *alphabetical sequence*
alfabético, índice *alphabetic index*
alfanumérica, barra *alphanumerical type bar*
–, perforadora *alphanumerical key punch*
alfanumérico, registro *alphanumerical record*
alfanuméricos, caracteres *alphanumerical characters*
algebraica, sumadora *algebraic adder*
aliciente *incentive*
alienar *to alienate*
alimentación (de aparato o máquina) *input*
alimentar *to feed*
alimenticias, conservas *canned goods*
alimenticios, productos *foodstuffs*
alineación *alignment*
almacén *store, stock-room, warehouse*
– comercial *business premises*

- de repuesto *stock-room*
- frigorífico *cold-storage warehouse*
- general de depósito *bonded warehouse*
- mayorista *wholesale store*
-, en *in stock*
-, encargado de *stock-room clerk*
-, etiqueta de *bin tag*
-, gran *department store*
-, jefe de *merchandise manager*
-, libro de *stock-book*
-, mercancías en *stock in bond*
-, rotación de existencias en *stock turnover*
almacenadas, mercancías *capital comercial*
almacenador (M) *warehouseman*
almacenaje o almacenamiento *storage,*
stock-keeping
-, derechos de *storage charges*
almacenar *to store*
-, operación de *storage operation*
almacenes, grandes *general or department*
stores
-, reposición de *replenishment of stores*
-, surtir sus *to lay in a stock*
almacenista o mayorista (A, C) *wholesaler*
- de abarrotes *wholesale grocer*
- de comestibles (C) *wholesale grocer*
- de víveres (C) *wholesale grocer*
- o almacenero *warehouseman*
almohadilla (para tintar) *stamp pad*
almoneda *auction*
alquilar *to rent*
alquiler *rent*
alquileres cobrados y no devengados
unearned rent collected
alta fidelidad *high fidelity*
- puntuación *high rating*
altas finanzas *high finance*
alternación de esfuerzos *alternation of stress*
alternativa, norma *alternate standard*
alto funcionario *high official*
- mando *top-management*
- rendimiento *high yield*
altos directivos *chief executives*
alza *rise*
- artificial de precio *ballooning*
- de impuestos *increase of taxes*
- de precios *boom*
- de salarios *wage increase*
-, movimiento de *upward movement*
-, precio en *rising price*
alzado, contrato a precio *lumpsum contract*
amañar o falsificar cuentas *to doctor*
accounts
amarraje *berthage*
ambiente, medio *environment, milieu*
ambulante, vendedor *street hawker, street*

seller
aminorar *to reduce*
amistoso *friendly*
amonedar *to coin*
amortiguador, incentivo *weak or reduced*
incentive
amortiguamiento *damper*
amortizable *amortizable, redeemable*
-, deuda *redeemable debt*
amortización *amortization, redemption*
- constable *straight-line depreciation*
- de una deuda *debt redemption*
- decreciente, método de *declining balance*
method
-, bonos de *sinking-fund bonds*
-, caja de *sinking fund*
-, coeficiente de *amortization factor*
-, cupo de *amortization quota*
-, empréstito de *amortization loan, sinking-*
fund loan
-, fondo de *sinking fund*
amortizar *to amortize, redeem or sink*
- un deuda *to sink a debt*
amplia, tarifa *loose rate, loose piece rate*
amplísimo *full power*
análisis *analysis*
- de cuentas *account analysis*
- de datos *data analysis*
- de escalabilidad *scaleability analysis*
- de factores *factor analysis*
- de insumos y productos *input-output*
analysis
- de la curva de la rentabilidad *break-even*
analysis
- de la estructura latente *latent structure*
analysis
- de mercados *market research or analysis*
- de movimientos *motion analysis*
- de operaciones *operational analysis or*
research
- de series de tiempos *time-series analysis*
- de temperamento *temperament analysis*
- de tiempos y deberes *time-and-duty analysis*
- de ventas *sales analysis*
- del coste de distribución *distribution cost*
analysis
- del ingreso nacional *national income*
analysis
- del mercado consumidor *consumer market*
analysis or research
- del rendimiento anterior *past performance*
analysis
- del trabajo *job analysis*
- del trabajo, encuesta sobre el *work analysis*
survey
- diferencial *differential analysis*

– escalar *scale analysis or research*
– escalogramático *scalogram analysis*
– estadístico *statistical analysis*
– o recuento de tráfico *traffic count*
– y mejora de métodos *methods or production engineering*
analista *analyst, scanner*
– consejero *consultant analyst*
– de estados *forms analyst*
– de formularios *forms analyst*
– de mercadología *marketing analyst*
– de publicidad *advertising analyst*
– del mercado *market analyst*
– investigador *research analyst*
analítico, balance *analytical balance*
–, método *questioning technique*
analizador de personal *personnel analyst*
analógica, calculadora *analog computer*
analógicas y digitales, computadoras *analog and digital computers*
anexo *enclosure, rider*
angustia *anxiety*
animar el comercio *to stimulate trade*
anónima, compañía *stock company*
–, sociedad *chartered company*
anónimas, deudas de sociedades *corporate debts*
anormal *abnormal*
anotación *tally*
anotador de tiempos *time-keeper*
anotados, datos *recorded data*
anotar un pedido *to book an order*
antedicho *above-mentioned*
antefechar *to foredate or antedate*
anteproyecto *draft, draught, projection*
anterior, análisis de rendimiento *past performance analysis*
–, cierre *previous close*
–, endoso *previous endorsement*
antes mencionado *above-mentioned*
anticíclica, política *contra-cyclical policy*
anticipación, con *in advance*
anticipada, programación *advance programming*
anticipadamente *in advance*
anticipadas, utilidades *anticipated profits*
anticipado, dividendo *advanced dividend*
–, pago *advance payment*
anticipar *to advance or anticipate*
anticipo *advanced payment, balance sheet*
– del estado a sus proveedores *imprest*
– en descubierto *advance in blank*
– en metálico *cash advance*
anticipos reembolsables *returnable advances*
–, cuenta de *drawing or advances account*
antigüedad *seniority*

–, escala de *seniority list*
antiguo, cliente *old customer*
antimonopolio *antitrust*
antimonopolítico *antitrust*
anual *annual, yearly*
– de aumento, porcentaje *annual percentage increase*
–, aumento medio *average annual increase*
–, balance *annual balance*
–, capacitación o instrucción *annual training*
–, convención *annual convention*
–, depreciación *annual depreciation*
–, edición *annual issue*
–, ejercicio *calendar or business year*
–, encuesta *annual survey*
–, estado *annual report*
–, índice *annual index*
–, información *annual report*
–, informe *annual report*
–, mantenimiento *annual maintenance*
–, permiso *annual leave*
–, plazo *annual instalment*
–, progresión *annual average*
–, renta *yearly or annual income*
–, reporte *annual report*
–, subsidio *annual subsidy*
–, venta *annual sale*
anuales, pérdidas *annual losses*
anualidad *annuity, annual income*
– acumulada *accumulated annuity*
– diferida *deferred annuity*
– pasiva *annuity payable*
– vencida *annuity due*
– vitalicia *life annuity*
anualmente *yearly, annually*
anulación del margen comercial *markup cancellation*
anular *to annul, cancel or invalidate*
anuncia y vende por correo, firma que *mail order house*
anunciadora, valla *posting, bill posting*
anuncio *advertisement*
– compuesto, proyecto de *advertising display, layout*
–, hombre *sandwich man*
–, tamaño del *ad size*
anuncios, corredor de *advertising canvasser, advertising salesman*
–, jefe del departamento de *advertisement manager*
–, página de *advertising page*
–, sección de *advertising department*
–, valla de *posting, bill posting*
añadidura *rider*
año *year*
– administrativo *business year*

– bisiesto *leap year*
– comercial *commercial year*
– económico *fiscal year*
– fiscal *fiscal year*
– magro *lean year*
apaciguamiento *appeasement*
aparato doméstico *household appliance*
aparente, activo *intangible assets*
aparentes, utilidades *book profits*
aparte, tirada *off-print*
apelación *appeal*
apelar *to appeal*
apertura, asiento de *opening entry*
–, cotizaciones de *opening prices*
–, hora de *time on*
–, precios de *opening prices*
–, saldo de *opening balance*
aplazado, pago *deferred payment*
aplazar *to defer or postpone*
aplicable *applicable*
aplicación, campo de *field or span of application*
aplicada, investigación *applied research*
aplicar *to apply or allocate*
– impuestos *to impose taxes*
apoderado *empowered, authorized, proxy, power of attorney*
aportación *contribution*
aportaciones en especie *assets in kind*
aportado, capital *invested capital*
aportar fondos *to finance*
apoyar *to support or back*
apoyo financiero *financial backing*
apreciación *appraisal, rating*
– de la actuación *speed or performance rating*
– de la velocidad *speed or performance rating*
– preferida *preferred rating*
apreciar *to appraise or value*
aprecio *appraisal, valuation*
aprendices, adiestramiento de *training apprentices*
aprendiz *apprentice, trainee*
aprendizaje *apprenticeship*
–, contrato de *contract of apprenticeship*
–, curva de *learning or training curve*
–, dependiente con contrato de *articled clerk*
–, suplemento por *learner's allowance, training allowance*
–, tiempo de *learning or training time*
apresurar *to expedite*
aprobación *approval, authorization*
– de un gasto *allocation, allotment*
–, sujeto a *on approval*
aprobadas, normas *accepted standards*
aprobado, activo *admitted assets*
–, cheque *certified cheque*

aprobar *to approve or pass*
apropiar *to assign or allocate*
aprovechable *usable*
aprovisionar *to supply*
aproximado, presupuesto *rough estimate*
aptitud para vender *sales ability*
–, programa de pruebas laborales de *aptitude job-test programme*
–, test de *aptitude test*
aptitudes diferenciales, prueba de *differential aptitude test*
apto *fit, able*
apuestas, corredor de *bookmaker*
apuntatiempo (C) *timekeeper*
arancel *tariff*
– de exportación *duties on exports*
– diferencial *differential duties*
– fiscal *revenue tariff*
– proteccionista *protective tariff*
arancelaria, concesión *tariff concession*
–, política *tariff policy*
–, protección *tariff protection*
–, reforma *tariff reform*
–, tarifa *schedule of customs duties*
arancelarias, barreras *tariff barriers*
arancelarios de temporada, derechos *seasonal duties*
–, cupos *custom quotas*
aranceles de aduana *customs tariffs*
arbitración *arbitration*
arbitraje *arbitration*
–, procedimiento de *arbitration process*
arbitral, decisión *arbitral decision*
archivador *letter file*
– electrónico *electronic filing-cabinet*
– inactivo *storage file*
archivadores, índice de *index filing*
archivar *to file away*
– correspondencia, estante de acero para *steel filing-cabinet*
archivero *file clerk*
archivista *file clerk*
archivo *file, filing-cabinet*
– movil *mobile file*
– o lote de informaciones *information file*
– visible *visible file*
–, copia para *file copy*
–, departamento de *file department*
–, procedimiento de *file procedure*
archivos de publicidad *advertising records*
–, índices de *filing indexes*
–, problema de *filing problem*
–, sistema de *filing system*
–, supervisión de los *filing supervision*
área de ventas *sales territory or area*
– geográfica *geographical or land area*

áreas comerciales *trade or trading areas*
aritmética o geométrica de aumento o crecimiento, progresión *arithmetic or geometric rate of growth*
aritmético, promedio *arithmetic average or mean*
armar *to assemble*
arqueo *audit, appraisal of assets, cash count*
arranque automático, tecla de *auto-start key*
–, punto de *starting point*
arrastrar el saldo *to strike a balance*
arreglada, conducta *steadiness*
arreglar una cuenta *to settle an account*
arreglo *accommodation*
arrendador *landlord, lessor*
arrendamiento *lease, rent*
–, contrato de *lease*
arrendar *to rent, lease or let*
arrendatario *tenant, lessee*
arriendo *rental, lease*
–, tomar en *to lease or rent*
arrojar el balance *to yield a balance*
– un aumento *to show an increase*
– un promedio *to strike an average*
– un saldo *to show a balance*
– una ganancia *to show a profit*
arte de vender *salesmanship*
artesanado *artisanship*
artesano *artisan, craftsman*
artículo *article, commodity, goods, merchandise, product*
– de reclamo *loss leader*
– hecho en serie *mass-produced article*
– patentado *proprietary article*
artículos *goods, products*
– comerciales *commercial commodities*
– de consumo *consumer goods*
– de consumo corriente *staple items*
– de escritorio *stationery*
– de exportación *export commodities or goods*
– de fantasía *fancy goods*
– de importación *import goods*
– de lujo *luxuries, luxury goods*
– de menaje *household or home appliances*
– de moda *fashion goods*
– de primera necesidad *primary or convenience goods*
– de temporada *seasonal goods*
– exentos de derechos, lista de *tax-free list*
– electrodomésticos *electrical appliances*
– o productos de marca *branded goods*
– sueltos *piece goods*
–, serie de *article series*
artífice *artificer, artist, maker, craftsman*
artificial de precio, alza *ballooning*
artificio *cheat*

artístico, estudio *studio*
asalariado *wage-earner*
asamblea *meeting*
– general de accionistas *meeting of shareholders*
– ordinaria *regular meeting*
–, presidir la *to preside over the meeting*
asegurable *insurable*
asegurables, riesgos *insurable risks*
asegurado *insured, covered*
–, valor *amount value*
asegurador *insurer, underwriter*
aseguradores contra riesgos marítimos *marine underwriters*
asegurar *to underwrite*
– el costo *to underwrite the cost*
asentar *to enter*
– una partida *to make an entry*
asesor *adviser, advisor*
– comercial *business or commercial counsellor*
– de capacitación, departamento *staff training department*
– de carreras *vocational counsellor*
– directivo *management consultant*
– sobre administración *management consultant*
– técnico *technical adviser*
–, equipo *staff*
asesora, función *advisory function*
asesoramiento, entrevista de *counselling interview*
–, servicio de *advisory service*
asesorar *to advise*
asesoría comercial *trade assessorship*
asiento *entry*
– confuso *blind entry*
– cruzado *cross entry*
– de abono *credit entry*
– de ajuste *adjusting entry*
– de apertura *opening entry*
– de caja *cash entry, cash item*
– de cargo *debit entry*
– de crédito *debit item*
– de diario *journal entry*
– de traspaso *transfer entry*
– del mayor *ledger entry*
asientos de cierre *closing entries*
–, pasar los *to increase the nominal value*
–, resumen de *abstract of posting*
asignación *allowance, allotment, assignment*
– de fondos *allocation, allotment*
asignado, valor *rating*
asignar *to allocate, assign or allot*
– fondos a *to appropriate funds to*
– las acciones integralmente *to allot the shares in full*

asistencia *assistance, relief*
- al trabajo, falta de *absence from work*
- pública *public welfare work*
- social *relief, social welfare*
- técnica *technical assistance*
asociación *association, company, union*
- de comerciantes *trade association*
- obrera *labour union*
- profesional obrera *trade union*
-, artículos de *articles of partnership*
-, contrato de *articles of partnership*
asociada *affiliate*
asociadas, compañías *associated companies*
asociado *associate, partner*
asociarse *to form a partnership*
asumido, pasivo *assumed liabilities*
asumir la pérdida *to absorb the loss*
asunto *matter, business, subject*
atención, absorción de la *engrossing of the attention*
atenciones, programa de *requirements schedule*
atender *to take care of, to handle*
atento, examen *close examination*
atesorar, propensión a *propensity to hoard*
atmósfera *atmosphere*
atraer clientela *to attract customers*
atrasado *late, delinquent*
- o vencido *in arrears*
atrasados, impuestos *back taxes*
atrasarse *to be late, to be in arrears*
atraso *delay*
atrasos *arrears*
auditar *to audit*
auditor *auditor*
auditoría *audit, auditing*
- de balance *balance-sheet audit*
- de caja *cash audit*
- interna *internal audit*
- parcial *partial audit*
- privada *internal audit*
- pública *public audit*
-, certificado de *audit certificate*
-, dictamen de *auditor's certificate*
-, informe de *audit report*
-, normas de *auditing standards*
-, reporte de *auditor's report*
auge *peak, boom*
- económico *prosperity*
aumentar *to increase*
aumento *increase*
- de demanda *pick-up demand*
- de población, índice de *population growth rate*
- de precio *increased price*
- de producción *increased production*

- de producción sin aumento de sueldo *speed-up*
- de sueldo *raise in salary*
- del descuento *advance of discount rate*
- del número de acciones sin aumentar el capital *stock split-up*
- injustificable del valor nominal del activo *write-up*
- medio anual *average annual increase*
-, arrojar un *to show an increase*
-, denotar un *to show an increase*
-, factor de *raising factor*
-, porcentaje anual de *annual percentage increase*
-, recorte de *tear sheet*
-, tipo medio de *average of increase*
aumentos, escala de *sliding scale*
ausencia, tiempo de *absent time*
ausentismo *absenteeism*
auspiciar *to sponsor or back*
austeridad, política de *austerity programme, policy of restraint*
auténtico *authentic, certified*
autoconsumo *self-consumption*
autocorrección, muestra de *self-correcting sample*
automación *automation*
automantenida, reacción *self-sustaining reaction*
automática, ganancia *automatic gain*
-, venta *automatic vending*
automático *automatic*
- de ganancia, control *automatic gain control*
- de sueldos, ajuste *automatic wage adjustment*
-, sistema *automatic system*
automatismo *automation*
automatización *automation*
- de la industria *industrial automation*
- de las fábricas *factory automation*
- de las oficinas *office automation*
automatizar *to automatize*
automóviles, exposición de *motor show, automobile show*
autonomía *autonomy*
- económica *economic self-sufficiency*
autónomo *autonomous*
autor, derechos de *copyright, royalties*
-, infracción de derechos de *copyright infringement*
autoridad *authority*
autoridades portuarias *port authorities*
autorizables, gastos *allowable expenses*
autorización *authorization*
- global *overall authorization*
autorizada, firma *authorized signature*

autorizadas, acciones *authorized stock*
autorizado *authorized*
−, capital *authorized capital*
autorizar *to authorize or empower*
autoservicio, tiendas de *self-service stores*
autosuficiencia *self-sufficiency*
autosuficiente *self-sufficient*
auxiliar *assistant, auxiliary, helper*
− de caja *auxiliary cash-book*
− de ventas, jefe *assistant sales manager*
− del gerente *assistant manager*
− del mayor *auxiliary ledger*
− en investigaciones *research fellow*
−, cuenta *adjunct account*
−, empresa *ancillary undertaking*
−, negocio *side business*
−, secretario *assistant secretary*
−, superintendente *assistant superintendent*
auxiliares, libros *subsidiary book*
aval *endorsement*
− absoluto *full endorsement*
− comercial *covering note*
− de efectos comerciales *accommodation endorsement*
− limitado *qualified endorsement*
avalar *to endorse or back*
avalúo *appraisal, valuation, evaluation*
− catastral *assessed valuation*
− fiscal *appraisal for taxation*
−, base de *basis of assessment*
−, precio de *assessed valuation*
avance de la hora *daylight saving*
− del trabajo, perfil de *progress profile*
− del trabajo, plan del *progress schedule*
−, diagrama de *flow sheet*

avenencia *compromise, deal*
avenimiento *agreement*
avería *damage, average*
− gruesa *gross average*
averiado, material *spoilage*
averías, fianza de *average bond*
−, indemnización por *allowances for damages*
−, póliza de *average policy*
avisar *to notify or advise*
aviso *advice, notice*
− de embarque *shipping notice*
− de llegada *arrival notice*
− de protesto *notice of protest*
−, luces de *warning lights*
−, texto de (M, C, A) *advertising copy*
ayuda *assistance, aid*
− después de vender, servicio de *after-sales service*
− mutua *mutual assistance*
− no selectiva *non-discriminatory assistance*
ayudante *assistant, helper*
− administrador *assistant manager*
− administrativo *administrative assistant*
− cajero *assistant cashier*
− de dirección *executive assistant*
−, contador *junior accountant*
ayudar *to help or assist*
ayuntamiento *city council, city hall, municipal government*
azar *risk, accident, random*
−, al *at random*
−, error de *random error*
−, muestreo al *random sampling*
−, números al *random numbers*
−, selección al *random selection*

B

bagaje *baggage (Am)*
baja *fall, drop, decline*
– de la ocupación *decreasing employment*
– de precios *price decline*
– del mercado *drop in prices*
– económica *business depression*
– violenta *crash*
–, comprar a la *to buy on a fall*
–, especulación a la *bear market*
–, oferta en *underbid*
–, tendencia a la *downward trend*
bajar el valor *to decline in value*
bajista *bear, bearish*
–, mercado *bear market*
bajistas, agentes bursátiles *bears*
bajo *low, below, under*
– contrato *under contract*
– costo, precio *below cost price*
– de la par, obligación emitida por *yield bond*
– fianza *under bond*
– par *below par*
– precio, venta *underselling*
–, precio *low price*
balance *balance, balance sheet*
– analítico *analytical balance*
– anual *annual balance*
– comparativo *comparative balance sheet*
– consolidado *consolidated balance sheet*
– de comprobación (A) *trial balance*
– de números (A, C) *trial balance*
– de operación *profit and loss statement*
– del banco *bank statement*
– del mayor *ledger balance*
– negativo *minus balance*
– sinóptico *working sheet*
– tentativo *tentative balance sheet*
–, arrojar el *to take a balance*
–, auditoría de *balance sheet audit*
–, cuenta de *balance account*
–, en *in balance*
–, hacer *to strike a balance*
–, hoja de *balance sheet*
–, venta de *inventory sale*
balancear *to balance*
– el presupuesto *to balance the budget*
balances consolidados *amalgamated balance sheets*
– de comprobación, libro de *trial balance book*
–, compensación de *clearing*
balanza *balance*
– comercial *trade balance*
– comercial desfavorable *adverse trade balance*
– comercial favorable *active trade balance*
– de cambios *balance of trade*
– de comprobación *trial balance*
– de pagos *balance of payments*
– de pagos al exterior *balance of external payments*
– de pagos desfavorables *adverse balance of payments*
– de pagos negativa *unfavourable balance of payments*
– de pagos positiva *favourable balance of payments*
– de pagos, déficit en la *deficit in the balance of payments*
– de prueba *trial balance*
– deficitaria *unfavourable balance of trade*
– económica *balance of international payments*
– visible de comercio *visible balance of trade*
banca *banking*
– central *central banking*
– privada *private banking*
– unitaria *unit banking*
bancaria anónima, sociedad *joint-stock company*
–, acción *bank share*
–, aceptación *bank acceptance*
–, compañía *banking company*
–, cuenta *bank account*
–, letra *bank draft*
–, referencia *bank reference*
–, reserva *bank reserve*
–, transferencia *bank transfer*
bancarias, compensaciones *clearings*
–, cuentas *bank account*
–, operaciones *banking operations*
bancario de compensaciones, agente *clearinghouse agent*
–, descuento *bank discount, bank rate*
–, giro *bank draft*
–, préstamo *bank loan*
–, sistema *bank reference*

–, tipo *bank rate*
–, tipo de interés *bank rate*
bancarios, cargos *bank charges*
–, depósitos *bank deposits*
–, gastos *bank charges*
–, giros *bank drafts*
–, valores *bank paper*
bancarrota *bankruptcy*
banco *bank*
– de ahorros *savings bank*
– de compensación *clearing bank*
– de emisión *bank of issue*
– de fomento *development bank*
– de liquidación *clearing bank, clearinghouse*
– del estado *government bank*
– emisor *bank of issue*
– estatal *government bank*
– fiduciario *trust company*
– hipotecario *mortgage bank*
– no respaldado *non-member bank*
–, balance del *bank statement*
–, billete de *bank note*
–, emisión de billetes de *banknotes issue*
bancos, depósitos en *bank deposits*
banda de goma o caucho *rubber band*
barata *bargain, bargain sale*
barómetro comercial *business barometer*
barra alfanumérica *alphanumerical type bar*
– de abogados *bar association*
–, oro en *bar gold*
barraca (Ch) *warehouse*
barrera *barrier*
barreras *barriers*
– arancelarias *tariff barriers*
– comerciales *trade barriers*
báscula *scale*
base *base, basis*
– acumulativa *accrual basis*
– de avalúo *basis of assessment*
– de depreciación *basis for depreciation*
– de pagos limitados *limited payment basis*
– de tiempos *time base*
– de tributación *tax basis*
– del impuesto *tax base*
– impositiva *tax base*
–, inversión *basic investment*
–, precio *base price*
–, programa *master schedule*
–, reducción *basic abatement*
–, salario *base pay, base rate, basic wage*
–, sueldo *base pay, base rate, basic wage*
–, tarifa *base rate*
básica, tasa *base rate*
básicas, industrias *key industries*
–, tendencias económicas *basic economic trends*

básico, descuento *basic rebate*
–, índice *basic index*
–, producto *staple, consumer product*
–, tiempo *basic time*
–, tipo *normal rate*
básicos, datos *basic information*
–, productos *staple commodities*
–, tiempo de movimientos *basic motion time*
beneficencia *social service, welfare*
beneficiado *beneficiary*
beneficiario *beneficiary*
beneficio *gain, profit, benefit, markup*
– bruto *gross margin*
– bruto, margen de *gross profit margin*
– de los empleados y obreros, programa a *employee benefit programme*
– de operación *revenue profit*
– justo *fair return*
– líquido *clear benefit, net income or profit*
– neto *clear benefit, net income or profit*
– normal planeado *planned normal profit*
–, dar un *yield a profit*
–, precio sin *close price*
beneficios *benefit payments*
– compensativos *offsetting gains*
– de explotación *operating profit*
– extraordinarios, impuesto de *excess profits tax*
– gravables *taxable profits*
– saldados *paid-up benefits*
– totales *gross earnings or profit*
–, participación en los *profit sharing*
beneficioso *profitable*
bias *bias*
– del muestreo *sample bias*
–, muestra sin *unbiased sample*
bienes *property, assets*
– agotables *wasting assets*
– capitales *capital goods*
– circulantes *circulating assets*
– comerciales *stock in trade*
– de capital fijo *fixed capital assets*
– de capital industriales *industrial capital (goods)*
– de consumo *consumer goods*
– durables *durable goods*
– embargados, venta de *distress-sale*
– gravables, lista de *tax roll*
– inmuebles *real-estate*
– intangibles *intangible assets*
– muebles *movables, chattels, personal assets*
– por impuestos no pagados, venta de *tax sale or title*
– públicos *public goods*
– raíces *real assets, realty, immovables*
– raíces, certificado de compra de *tax*

certificate
- raíces, corredor de *real-estate broker*
- tangibles *tangible property*
- tributarios *taxable income*
- y servicios *goods and services*
bilateral, contrato *indenture*
billete *bill, ticket*
- de banco *bank note*
billetes de banco, emisión de *banknotes issue*
bimestral *bimonthly*
bimestre *two months*
bimetalismo *bimetallism, double standard*
blanca, carta *carte blanche, full power*
blanco, cheque en *blank cheque*
-, endoso *blank endorsement*
-, firma en *blank signature*
-, formulario en *blank form*
-, papel *clean paper*
blanda, moneda *soft currency*
bloque *block*
-, adquirir los derechos en *to buy rights outright*
bloqueado, superávit *surplus*
bloquear *to freeze funds*
boicot *boycott*
boicotear *to boycott*
boleta *ticket*
- de pago predial *real-estate tax receipt*
boletín *voucher, bonus*
- de cambios en bolsa *stock-exchange quotations*
- de petición de utillaje y herramientas *tool ticket*
- de primas *bonus or earnings sheet*
- de resúmenes *abstract bulletin*
- de verificación *inspection card*
bolsa comercial *stock market*
- de compensación *clearing house*
- de corredores (Ch) *stock exchange*
- de trabajo *labour or employment agency*
- de valores *stock exchange*
- negra *black market*
-, agente de cambio y *stockholder, stockbroker*
-, boletín de cambios en *stock exchange quotations*
-, corredor de *stockbroker*
-, juego de *stock speculation*
-, maniobras de *stock speculation*
bonanza *prosperity*
-, período de *boom*
bonificación *bonus, allowance, premium, incentive earnings*
- tributaria *tax rebate*
bonificaciones de obreros *employees' bonus*
- sobre ventas *sales discounts*

-, devoluciones y *returns and allowances*
-, plan de *bonus plan*
bono *bond, bonus*
- a interés fijo *active bond*
- de ahorro *savings bond*
- de plazo largo *long-term bond*
- de rendimiento bajo *low-yield bond*
- de trabajo *job card, job ticket, work slip*
- del estado *government or state bond*
- hipotecario *mortgage bond*
- inmobiliario *real-estate bond*
- no transferible *restricted bond*
- nominal *registered bond*
- perpetuo *annuity bond*
- privilegiado *priority bond*
- redimible *callable bond*
- sin garantía hipotecaria *debenture bond*
bonos *bonds*
- al portador *coupon bonds*
- convertibles en acciones *convertible bonds*
- de amortización *sinking-fund bonds*
bordo, a *on board*
-, franco a *free on board*
-, libre a *free on board*
-, puesto a *free on board*
borrador *rough draft, daybook (Br), draft, eraser*
-, libro *daybook*
brazos caídos, huelga de *sitdown strike*
-, fuerza de *manpower, working force*
brigada, capataz de *squad boss, labour foreman*
bruta, ganancia *gross profit*
-, inversión *gross investment*
-, producción *gross output*
-, utilidad *gross profit*
brutas, entradas *gross income, revenue*
-, ventas *gross sales*
bruto *gross, in bulk*
- del detallista, margen *retailer's gross margin*
- nacional, producto *gross national product*
- por neto *gross for net*
- total *gross*
-, beneficio *gross margin*
-, importe *gross amount*
-, ingreso *gross revenue*
-, lucro *gross profit*
-, margen *gross margin*
-, peso *gross weight*
-, producto *gross proceeds*
-, rebaja normalizada del peso *tare allowance*
-, rendimiento *gross return*
brutos, datos *raw data*
-, ingresos *gross receipts or earnings*
buenos oficios *good offices*
bulto *package, parcel*

–, comprar a *to buy in bulk*
buró *agency, bureau*
burocracia *bureaucracy*
burócrata *bureaucrat*
burocrática, tramitación *clerical routine*
bursátil de acciones, mercado *stock market*

bursátiles bajistas, agentes *bears*
–, precios *stock-exchange quotations*
–, valores *stock-exchange securities, listed securities*
buscar órdenes *to canvass*

C

caballeros, pacto de *gentlemen's agreement*
cablegrafiar *to send a cable*
cablegráfica, dirección *cable address*
cabo, llevar a *to work out*
cabotaje *coastwise shipping*
–, comercio de *coastwise trade*
cadena *chain*
– de montaje *assembly line*
– de producción *flow production or assembly line, product line*
–, fabricación en *flow or line production*
–, montaje en *in-line assembly*
–, producción en *assembly line, line or flow production*
–, reacción en *chain reaction*
–, rebajas en *chain discount*
–, tiendas en *chain stores*
–, trabajo en *assembly-line operation*
caducado, cheque *stale cheque*
–, descuento *lapsed discount*
caducar *to expire or lapse*
caducidad *lapse*
– de un permiso *expiry of a permit*
caída de la actividad *activity dip*
– de precios *drop in prices*
caja *safe, cashier's office, bin, receptacle*
– chica *petty cash*
– chica, fondo de *petty-cash fund*
– chica, libro de *petty-cash book*
– chica, vale de *petty-cash voucher*
– chica, verificación de *petty-cash voucher*
– de ahorros *savings bank*
– de amortización *sinking fund*
– de caudales *safe*
– de retiros *retiring fund*
– de seguridad *safe, safe-deposit box*
– para gastos menores *petty cash*
– para muestras *sample case*
– registradora *cash register*
–, asiento de *cash entry, cash item*
–, auditoría de *cash audit*
–, auxiliar de *auxiliary cash book*
–, comprobante de *cashbook voucher*
–, corte de *closing and balancing the cash*
–, cuenta de *cash account*
–, diario de (M) *cashbook*
–, efectivo en *cash-on-hand*
–, entradas a *cash receipts*

–, faltante en *cash shortage*
–, informe de *cash report*
–, libro de *cashbook*
–, registro de (C) *cashbook*
–, saldo en *cash balance*
–, salidas de *cash disbursements*
cajas, envase en *boxing*
cajero *cashier, teller*
– cobrador *receiving teller*
– menor *petty cashier*
– principal *head teller*
– recibidor *receiving teller*
–, ayudante *assistant cashier*
calculador *calculator, estimator, reckoner*
calculadora *calculator, computer*
– accionada por teclado *key-drive calculator*
– analógica *analog computer*
– con impresión *printing calculator*
– de teclas *digital computer*
– de teclas impulsadas *key-driven calculator*
– digital *digital computer*
– electrónica *electronic computer*
calcular *to compute or figure*
–, máquina de *computing or calculating machine*
–, máquina de sumar y *adding and calculating machine*
calculista *estimator, calculator*
– de costos *cost clerk*
cálculo *estimate, calculus*
– de compras *calculation of purchases*
– del margen comercial acumulativo *cumulative markup calculation*
– estacional *seasonal computation*
– prudencial *estimate*
–, error de *miscalculation*
–, regla de *slide rule, computing rule*
calibración *gradation, classification, grading, grouping*
– fiscal *assessment*
calidad de los productos *quality of products*
– inmejorable, de *topnotch*
–, control de *quality control*
–, control estadístico de *statistical quality control*
–, mercancías de *quality goods*
–, norma de *norma de calidad*
–, voto de *deciding vote*

calificación *qualification, rating*
– del mérito *merit rating*
– del trabajo *job rating*
– fiscal *assessment*
calificado *qualified, competent*
–, endoso *qualified endorsement*
–, obrero *skilled worker*
–, trabajador *skilled tradesman or worker, craftsman*
callejera, cotización *street price*
cámara *chamber, board*
– de comercio *chamber of commerce*
– de compensación *clearinghouse*
cambiable *exchangeable*
cambiar *to change, exchange or cash*
– cheques *to cash cheques*
– una letra *to negotiate a bill*
cambiaria, paridad *par of exchange*
cambio *change, exchange*
– a la par *exchange at par*
– a la vista *sight rate of exchange*
– actual *spot exchange*
– de cierre *closing rate of exchange*
– de personal, porcentaje elevado de *high turnover rate*
– de trabajo, tiempo de *changeover time*
– de turno *shift changeover*
– del día *spot exchange*
– extranjero *foreign exchange*
– extranjero, sección de *foreign exchange department*
– oro, patrón *gold exchange standard*
– y bolsa, agente de *stockbroker, stockholder*
–, documento de *bill of exchange*
–, letra de *draft, bill of exchange*
–, libre *free trade*
–, licencia de *exchange permit*
–, primera de *first of exchange*
–, tarifa del *rate of exchange*
–, tipo de *conversion rate*
–, valor en *exchange value*
cambios de precio *price changes*
– en bolsa, boletín de *stock exchange quotations*
– en las modas *fashion changes*
– estacionales *seasonal changes*
–, balanza de *balance of trade*
–, casa de *money exchange office*
–, comité de dirección de los *steering board of trade*
–, mercado de *exchange market*
cambista *money changer*
campaña de ensayo *try-out or test campaign*
– de publicidad *advertising campaign*
– de prueba *try-out or test campaign*
– de ventas *selling campaign*

–, director de *account executive, contact executive*
–, encuesta en *field survey*
–, trabajo en *fieldwork*
campestre, gira *picnic*
campo *field, country*
– de actividad *field of activity*
– de aplicación *coverage, field or span of application*
– de experiencias *test size*
– de influencia *range of influence*
–, trabajador del *farm hand*
canal *channel*
cancelación *cancellation, annulment, payment*
– de rebajas *markdown cancellation*
– de una deuda *to wipe out a debt*
cancelado, cheque *cancelled cheque*
cancillería *Ministry of Foreign Affairs*
canje *conversion, trade-in*
canjeable *convertible*
canjear *to convert*
cansancio de comprar *buying fatigue*
cantidad *quantity*
– constante *constant*
– de trabajo *work load*
– en riesgo *amount at risk*
– nula *magnitude nil*
– total de capital *aggregate principal amount*
–, determinación de *amount determination*
–, rebaja por *quantity discount*
cantidades acumuladas, descuento por *cumulative quantity discount, deferred quantity discount*
–, descuento por *quantity discount*
capacidad *capacity, ability*
– administrativa *administrative ability*
– adquisitiva *purchasing power*
– analítica *analytical ability*
– crediticia *lending capacity*
– de aprender *learning ability*
– de compra *buying power*
– de compra, índice de la *buying power index*
– de mando *leadership potential*
– de negociar *merchandising ability*
– de pago *ability to pay*
– de producción *plant or productive capacity*
– directiva *executive ability*
– económica *financial standing*
– en el oficio, prueba de *trade test*
– financiera de compra *financial purchasing ability*
– inactiva *idle capacity*
– intelectual *intellectual ability*
– mental básica *basic mental ability*
– mental, prueba de *mental ability test*

– normal *standard range*
– potencial de compra *potential buying power*
– real *actual capacity*
– tributaria *tax-paying capacity*
–, prueba de *aptitude test*
capacidades, cuadro comparativo de *comparative rating chart*
capacitación de oficinas, programa de *office training programme*
– del personal *personnel training*
– en la industria, programa de *twin programme, training with industry programme*
– para vender *sales ability*
– psicológica *psychological training*
– o formación del personal de servicio detallista *retail service training*
– o instrucción anual *annual training*
– o instrucción colectiva *collective training*
–, departamento asesor de *staff training department*
–, director de *training director*
–, gastos de *training expenses*
–, períodos de *training periods*
–, programa de *training programme*
–, supervisor de *training supervisor*
capataz *foreman*
– de brigada *squad boss, labour foreman*
capaz *able, competent*
capita, ingreso per *per capita income*
capitación *per capita tax*
capital *capital*
– activo *working capital, capital assets*
– acumulado *accumulated worth*
– aportado *invested capital*
– autorizado *authorized capital*
– circulante *circulating or working capital*
– comercial *stock*
– de explotación *working capital*
– de operación *working capital*
– de producción *producer's capital*
– de reserva *uncalled capital*
– declarado *stated or declared capital*
– declarado de acciones sin valor nominal *stated capital*
– desembolsado *paid-up capital*
– disponible *active capital*
– emitido por la compañía *company's issued capital*
– en acciones *stock*
– exhibido *paid-in capital*
– fijo, bienes de *fixed capital assets*
– inactivo *idle capital*
– industriales, bienes de *industrial capital (goods)*
– inflado (M) *watered stock or capital*

– inicial *original capital*
– invertido *invested capital*
– limitado, empresa inversionista de *closed-end investment company*
– neto *net worth, proprietorship*
– real *capital assets*
– social *capital or joint stock*
– subscrito *subscribed capital*
– variable de *open-end capital*
–, acciones de *capital stock*
–, afluencia de *capital inflow*
–, aumento del número de acciones sin aumentar el *stock split-up*
–, consumo de *capital consumption*
–, cuenta de *capital account*
–, desembolsos de *capital expenditure*
–, dilución del *stock watering*
–, eficacia marginal del *marginal efficiency of capital*
–, estructura del *capital structure*
–, excedente de *capital surplus*
–, ganancias de *capital gains*
–, gastos de *capital expenditure*
–, giro de *capital turnover*
–, inmovilización del *lockup capital*
–, inversión de *capital investment*
, movimiento de *capital turnover*
–, movimientos de *capital movements*
–, pasivo de *capital liabilities*
–, rendimiento de *return on capital*
–, renta del *interest, return on capital*
–, superávit de *capital surplus*
capitales, bienes *capital goods*
–, escasez de *scarcity of capital*
–, huída de *flight of capital*
–, imposición de *investment of capital*
–, sociedad dedicada a la inversión de *investment trust*
capitalismo *capitalism*
capitalista *capitalist*
–, socio *financial partner*
capitalización *capitalization*
– de intereses *compounding of interest*
capitalizado, valor *capitalized value*
capitalizar *to capitalize*
caracteres alfanuméricos *alphanumerical characters*
característica estructural *structural feature*
– del sistema de ventas *selling points*
caracterológico, diagrama *profile chart*
carbón, papel *carbon paper*
carga *load, loading, freight, cargo*
– a granel *bulk cargo*
– aérea *air freight*
– completa *full load*
– de explotación *traffic load*

– de máquina *machine load*
– de retorno *return-cargo*
– de trabajo *load factor, work opportunity, work load*
– de trabajo de ventas *sales workload*
– del peso de pago, coeficiente de *revenue weight load factor*
– marítima *cargo, ocean freight*
– máxima admisible *ultimate allowance stress*
– muerta *dead load*
– por depreciación *write-off load*
– seca *dry cargo*
– útil *useful load*
–, dejar *release load*
–, factor de *load factor*
–, guía de *waybill, cargo receipt*
–, transporte en *transport loaded*
cargamento o conocimiento de embarque *lading*
cargar a la cuenta *to debit the account*
cargo *job, position, debit*
– administrativo *executive position*
– de contador *accountant*
– por cobro *collection*
– por depreciación *depreciation charges*
– y abono *debit and credit*
–, asiento de *debit entry*
–, cualidades para el *qualifications for position*
–, cumplimiento en el *position performance*
–, nota de *debit note*
cargos *charges*
– bancarios *bank charges*
– diferidos *deferred charges*
– fijos *fixed charges*
– por cobro *collection charges*
carpeta *folder*
carrera *vocation*
carreras, asesor *vocational counsellor*
carretera nacional *national road*
–, valla de *highway billboard*
carreteras principales *highways*
carretilla elevadora con horquilla *forklift truck*
carro entero, flete por *carload rate*
carta *letter, charter, map*
– aérea *airmail letter*
– blanca *carte blanche, full power*
– certificada *registered letter*
– comercial de crédito *commercial letter of credit*
– con membrete comercial *business letterhead*
– constitutiva *corporation charter*
– de cobro *collection letter*
– de crédito *letter of credit*
– de crédito a plazo *time letter of credit*

– de crédito auxiliar *ancillary letter of credit*
– de crédito irrevocable *irrevocable letter of credit*
– de crédito simple *clean letter of credit*
– de entrega inmediata *special-delivery letter*
– de insistencia *follow-up letter or reminder*
– de pago *acquittance*
– de porte *waybill, railway bill*
– de presentación *covering letter, letter of introduction*
– de prospección *sales letter*
– de recomendación *letter of recommendation*
– marina *chart, ocean chart*
– poder *proxy, power of attorney*
–, sigue *letter follows*
cartel *cartel, bill, poster, placard*
– de escaparate *window card*
– de precios *cartel for price fixing*
– regional *regional cartel*
cartelera *posting, bill posting, poster hoarding (Br)*
–, en *billing*
carteleras, control de *traffic audit*
carteles emplazados, control de *traffic audit*
–, fijador de *bill poster*
cartelización *cartelization*
cartera *portfolio*
– bancaria *list of bills discounted*
–, en *on hand*
–, tener en *to have on file*
cartón *pasteboard, cardboard*
– pasta *millboard*
cartoné, en *in paper boards*
casa *house, firm, concern, company*
– central *headquarters*
– comercial *business house*
– de banca *banking house*
– de cambios *money-exchange office*
– de comercio *business establishment*
– de moneda *mint*
– de valores, títulos u obligaciones *security house*
– editora *publishing house*
– exportadora *export house*
– filial *affiliated firm*
– importadora *import house*
– matriz *parent house, main or head office*
– mayorista *wholesale house or concern*
– principal *headquarters*
casilla o apartado de correos *post-office box*
casos, exposición de *case history*
–, historia de *case history*
castas, sistema de *caste system*
catalogar *to catalogue or list*
catálogo *catalogue, list*
– de cuentas *list of accounts*

catastral, avaluo *assessed valuation*
–, valor *assessed valuation*
catastro *real-estate register*
categoría *category, quality*
categorías de salarios *salary range*
–, progresión por *bracket progression*
caución *guarantee, security*
–, acreedor sin *unsecured creditor*
–, deuda sin *unsecured debt*
–, préstamo sin *unsecured load*
caudales, caja de *safe*
causa *cause, case, lawsuit*
–, radicar la *to bring a suit*
causado, impuesto *tax incurred*
causante moroso *delinquent taxpayer*
causar impuesto *to be subject to tax*
cebolla, papel *copying paper*
cedido, crédito *assigned claim*
cédula *schedule, official document*
– fiscal *income-tax schedule*
– hipotecaria *mortgage bond*
cédulas emitidas *warrants issued*
celebrar un contrato *to enter into a contract*
censar *to take a census*
censo *census*
– comercial *business census*
– de negocios *census of business*
– por muestreo *sample census*
–, datos del *census data*
–, verificar un *to take a census*
censor de cuentas *auditor*
censura *censorship*
centena *hundred*
centígramo *centigram*
centilitro *centilitre*
centímetro *centimetre*
central, banca *central banking*
–, casa *headquarters*
–, fichero *central file*
–, oficina *main or head office, headquarters*
–, sede *headquarters*
centralización funcional *functional centralization*
centralizados, contabilidad de gastos *expense-centre accounting*
centro comercial *business, trading or shopping centre*
– de costes *cost centre*
– de ventas *shopping centre*
– distribuidor *distributing centre*
– investigador *research centre*
cerebral, lavado *brainwashing*
cerebro electrónico *electronic brain*
cero, cronómetro con vuelta a *single pressure or snapback stopwatch*
cerrada, economía *closed economy*

cerrado, sistema *closed system*
cerrar la cuenta *to close the account*
– un trato *to strike a bargain*
– una fábrica *to close down*
cerrazón *closure*
certeza *surety*
certificación a buena cuenta en pagos de obras *progress certificate*
certificada, carta *registered letter*
–, copia *certified copy*
certificado *certificate*
– con salvedades *qualified certificate*
– consular *consular certificate*
– de acciones *stock certificate*
– de adeudo *indebtedness certificate*
– de auditoría *audit certificate*
– de compra de bienes raíces *tax certificate*
– de depósito *certificate of deposit*
– de fabricación *certificate of manufacture*
– de origen *certificate of origin*
–, correo *registered mail*
–, cheque *certified cheque*
–, extender un *to issue a certificate*
certificar *to certify*
cesación del trabajo *downing of tools*
cesante *unemployed*
cesar *to cease, stop or discharge*
– en el trabajo *to down tools*
cese *layoff, dismissal*
– de empleo *labour layoff*
cesión, acta de *deed of release*
cesionario *vendee*
cíclica, facturación *cycle billing*
–, secuencia *timed sequence*
cíclicas, fluctuaciones *cyclical fluctuations*
cíclico *cyclic*
–, elemento *cyclic or repetitive element*
ciclo *cycle*
– de ahorros *savings cycle*
– de funcionamiento *action cycle*
– de tiempos, control de *time cycle control*
– de trabajo *work cycle*
– de utilización de mercancías *turnover*
– económico *economic or trade cycle*
ciclos, facturación en *cyclic billing*
cien por cien, prima *hundred per cent incentive, straight piecework*
científica, dirección *scientific management*
–, investigación *scientific research*
–, muestra *scientific sample*
científico, investigador *research scientist*
ciento, signo de por *percentage sign*
cierrasobres *envelope sealer*
cierre *closing*
– anterior *previous close*
– de cuentas *closing of accounts*

– de los libros *closing the books*
–, asientos de *closing entries*
–, cambio de *closing rate of exchange*
–, cotización de *closing price*
–, entradas de *closing entries*
–, inventario de *closing inventory*
–, partidas de *closing entries*
–, precio de *closing quotation or rate*
cifra de los negocios *turnover*
– de ventas *sales figure*
– indicitaria *ratio*
– global *lumpsum*
– o volumen de negocios *turnover*
cifrado *in code*
cifras ajustadas *adjusted figures*
cinta *tape, ribbon*
– de máquina *typewriter ribbon*
– del indicador eléctrico *ticker tape*
– entintada *inked ribbon*
– magnética *magnetic tape*
– magnética del indicador electrónico *ticker tape*
– magnetofónica *magnetic tape*
– para máquina sumadora *adding-machine ribbon*
– perforada *punched tape*
– transportadora *belt conveyor*
circuito *chain, circuit*
– de producción *workflow*
– de transferencia de informaciones *information path*
circulación *flow, circulating*
– de la prensa *press circulation*
– monetaria, sistema de *currency*
–, acciones en *outstanding stock*
–, diagrama de *flow diagram or chart*
–, diagrama del progreso *flow process chart*
–, moneda en *outstanding money*
–, retirar de la *to withdraw from circulation*
circulante *circulating, current*
–, activo *working assets*
–, capital *capital assets*
circulantes, bienes *circulating assets*
circular *form letter*
– de publicidad *advertising circular*
círculos financieros *financial circles*
circunstancias financieras *financial conditions*
cita *appointment*
– previa, con *by appointment*
citar a junta *to call a meeting*
clara, cuenta *clear reckoning account*
clase *class, grade, type*
– económico-social *class*
– obrera *working class*
– social *class*

–, correo de primera *first-class mail (Br)*
–, correo de segunda *second-class mail (Br)*
clases obreras *labouring classes*
– mutuamente excluyentes *mutually exclusive classes*
–, lucha de *class struggle*
clasificable *classifiable*
clasificación *classification, file*
– de documentos *documentary classification*
– de las cuentas de gastos *expenses account classification*
– de normas *standard sort*
– de personal, escalas de *personnel rating scales*
– de productos por clases o tamaños *grading*
– del trabajo *job classification or evaluation*
– gradual *grading, grouping*
– múltiple *multiple sorting*
– por lotes *block sorting*
–, impulso de *sort impulse*
–, índice de *sort index*
clasificada, empresa *rated concern*
clasificado, no *unrated*
– para crédito *rated*
clasificador *sorter, file clerk*
– de comprobantes *voucher file*
clasificar *to classify, grade or docket*
cláusula *clause*
– adicional *rider*
– contractual de exclusividad *competition clause, exclusivity speculation*
– de empleo *employment clause*
– de escape *escape clause*
– de exclusión *exclusion clause, closed-shop provision*
– de la nación más favorecida *most favoured nation clause*
– de punto crítico *peril point clause*
– de revisión de precios *variation clause*
– para el vencimiento anticipado de una deuda *acceleration clause*
– penal *penalty clause*
clausura *closing, closure*
– de los libros *closing the books*
– de sesiones *adjournment*
–, sesión de *closing session*
clausurar *to close or adjourn*
clave *code, key*
– alfabética *alphabetical code*
– comercial *commercial code*
–, exportaciones *key exports*
–, industrias *key industries*
–, números *key numbers*
–, palabra *code word*
–, proceso *key process*
–, puesto *key position*

–, trabajo *key job*
cliente *client, customer*
– antiguo *old customer*
– en expectativa *prospective client*
– en perspectiva *prospective client*
– fijo *steady customer*
– potencial *prospective client*
– probable *prospective client*
clientela *clientele, customers, goodwill*
–, atraer *to attract customers*
–, descuento a la *patronage discount*
–, valor de *goodwill*
clientes, cuenta de *accounts receivable*
–, relaciones con los *consumer relations*
–, servicio para los *customer service*
coacreedor *co-creditor*
coadministrador *co-administrator*
coalición *association, coalition*
coasegurado *co-insured*
coasociación *partnership, co-partnership*
cobertura *cover*
cobrador *collector*
–, cajero *receiving teller*
cobrados y no devengados, alquileres
   unearned rent collected
–, impuestos *taxes collected*
cobranza *collection*
–, premio de *collection fee*
–, valores en *bills for collection*
cobrar *to collect*
– a la entrega *to collect on delivery*
– de más *to overcharge*
– de menos *to undercharge*
–, comprobantes a *vouchers payable*
–, cuentas por *accounts receivable*
–, dividendos por *dividends receivable*
–, documentos de cuentas a *accounts
   receivable document*
–, documentos por *notes receivable*
–, efectos a *notes receivable*
–, filete por *freight collect*
–, letras a *bills receivable*
–, plazos a *instalments receivable*
cóbrese a la entrega *collect on delivery*
cobro de créditos *collection of credits*
– directo *direct collection*
– dudoso, cuenta de *doubtful account*
– por adelantado *advanced collections*
–, cargo por *collection*
–, cargos por *collection charges*
–, carta de *collection letter*
–, gastos de *collection fees*
–, gastos de crédito y *credit and collection
   expenses*
–, honorarios por *collection fees*
–, valor al *value for collection*

–, valores al *receivables*
cobros, índice de *collection ratio*
cociente *ratio*
codeudor *co-debtor*
codeudores *joint debtors*
codificar *to code or codify*
código *code*
– de comercio *commercial code*
– de ética *code of ethics*
– de quiebras *bankruptcy laws*
– del trabajo *labour laws*
– fiscal *tax laws*
– mercantil *commercial law*
coeficiente *coefficient, factor*
– de acuerdo *coefficient of agreement*
– de amortización *amortization factor*
– de dispersión *scatter coefficient*
– de distribución *coefficient of distribution*
– de elasticidad *coefficient of elasticity*
– de liquidez *current ratio*
– de mortalidad *death rate*
– de natalidad *birth rate*
– de productividad *productivity index*
– de repartición *coefficient of apportionment*
– de seguridad *factor of safety*
– de trabajo *stress, work coefficient*
– insumo producto *input-output coefficient*
cofirmante *co-signer*
cogirador *co-drawer*
cohechar *to bribe*
cohecho *bribe, bribery*
coherederos *joint heirs*
coincidir, hacer *to bring into conformity*
colaboración, de trabajo en *combined work*
colaborador, investigador *research associate*
colapso *collapse*
colateral *collateral*
colección *collection*
coleccionista *collector*
colectar *to collect*
colectiva, capacitación *collective training*
–, conducta *collective behaviour*
–, depreciación *composite depreciation*
–, hipoteca *general mortgage*
–, instrucción *collective training*
–, póliza *group policy*
–, recompensa *collective reward*
–, seguridad *collective security*
colectivas, compras *combined buying*
colectivo de trabajo, contrato *collective
   bargaining agreement*
–, acuerdo *collective agreement*
–, contrato *collective bargaining, collective
   contract*
–, seguro *group insurance*
–, trato *collective bargaining*

colector de rentas *collector of internal revenue*
colegio de corredores *brokers' association*
colisión *collision*
colocación *position, employment, situation*
– a prueba *trial employment*
– de personal *allocation*
– en oficinas *office employment*
–, entrevistas de *employment interviews*
–, oficina de *employment bureau, labour exchange*
colocaciones, agencia de *employment agency*
–, agente de *labour agent*
–, departamento de *employment department*
–, registro de *employment register*
colocar *to place or allocate*
– a interés *to place at interest*
– dinero *to invest money*
– un pedido *to place an order*
color, papel de *coloured paper*
columnas, medida para altura de *column inch*
comandita *silent partnership*
– por acciones *stock association*
– por acciones, sociedad *joint-stock company*
–, sociedad en *joint company, limited or silent partnership*
comanditado *active partner*
comanditario *silent partner*
–, socio *dormant or sleeping partner*
combinación de errores *pooling of errors*
– para especular en fondos públicos *pool*
combinada, depreciación *composite depreciation*
combinado industrial *pool*
combinar *to combine or merge*
comerciabilidad *marketability*
comerciable *marketable*
comercial *commercial*
– acumulativo, cálculo del margen *cumulative markup calculation*
– acumulativo, porcentaje del margen *cumulative markup percentage*
– adicional neto, margen *net additional markup*
– de intercambio, acuerdo *trade agreement*
– de reciprocidad, acuerdo *reciprocal trade agreement*
– desfavorable, balanza *adverse trade balance*
– efectivo, margen *actual markup*
– favorable, balanza *active trade balance*
– inicial, margen *initial markup*
– sostenido, margen *gross margin, maintained markup*
–, aceptación *trade acceptance*
–, activo *current assets*
–, acuerdo *commercial agreement*
–, almacén *business premises*

–, anulación del margen *markup cancellation*
–, año *commercial year*
–, asesor *business counsellor*
–, asesoría *trade assessorship*
–, aval *covering note*
–, balanza *trade balance*
–, barómetro *business barometer*
–, bolsa *stock market*
–, capital *stock*
–, carta con membrete *business letterhead*
–, casa *commercial enterprise*
–, censo *business census*
–, centro *business or trading centre*
–, clave *commercial code*
–, contabilidad *business accounting or accountancy*
–, costumbre *business practice*
–, criterio *merchandising judgement, business judgement*
–, derecho *commercial law*
–, descuento *trade allowance, trade discount*
–, dirección *business address, business management*
–, director *commercial director or manager*
–, edificio *business premises*
–, empresa *commercial enterprise*
–, escuela *business school*
–, factura *commercial invoice*
–, firma *commercial house*
–, garantía *covering note*
–, gestión *marketing, commercial service*
–, giro *trade draft*
–, guía *trade directory*
–, habilidad *merchandising ability*
–, historia *business history*
–, información *merchandising information*
–, informe *commercial report*
–, intercambio *commercial intercourse*
–, intermediario *broker*
–, investigación *commercial research*
–, jefe *market executive, market manager*
–, marca *trademark*
–, margen *mark-on*
–, mejoramiento *business upswing*
–, nombre *trade name*
–, oficina *business premises*
–, operación *commercial transaction*
–, pasivo *current liabilities*
–, posibilidad *commercial feasibility*
–, posición *commercial standing*
–, práctica *commercial wage, trading*
–, precio *trade price*
–, prosperidad *boom*
–, publicación *business publication*
–, quiebra *burst-up, bankruptcy*
–, reciprocidad *reciprocal trade*

–, referencia *trade reference*
–, rendimiento *coefficient of efficiency*
–, responsabilidad *business responsibility*
–, sección *business district*
–, secretária *commercial secretary*
–, secretario *commercial secretary*
–, sello *business die*
–, semana *business week*
–, sistema *business system*
–, sociedad *trade association*
–, sociedad de crédito *commercial credit company*
–, técnica *marketing*
–, técnico *commercial practitioner*
–, televisión *commercial television*
–, texto *commercial text*
–, viajante *travelling salesman*
–, viaje *business trip*
–, zona *business district, shopping centre*
comerciales, áreas *trade or trading areas*
–, artículos *commercial commodities*
–, aval de efectos *accommodation endorsement*
–, barreras *trade barriers*
–, bienes *stock in trade*
–, cotejar *trading customs*
–, exposiciones *trade shows*
–, girar efectos *to trade*
–, papeles *commercial or business papers, commercial documents*
–, relaciones *business relations*
–, términos *commercial terms*
–, transacciones *commercial transactions*
comercialismo *commercialism*
comercialización *merchandising, commercialization*
comercializar *to commercialize or market*
comerciante *merchant, business dealer, trader, tradesman*
– al por mayor *wholesale merchant, wholesaler*
– al por menor *retailer*
– comisionista *commission merchant*
–, entrevista con *dealer interview*
–, margen del *dealer margin*
–, viajante *travelling salesman*
comerciantes, asociación de *trade association*
comerciar *to trade*
comercio *commerce, trade, business*
– al detalle *retailing*
– al menudeo *retail trade*
– al por mayor *wholesale, wholesale trade*
– de cabotaje *coastwise trade*
– de distribución *distributive trade*
– de exportación *export trade*
– de importancia *import trade*

– exterior *foreign or export trade*
– exterior, equilibrio del *balance of trade*
– interestatal *inter-state commerce*
– interior *domestic or home trade*
– invisible *invisible trade*
– libre *free trade*
– marítimo *shipping trade*
– mayorista *wholesale trade*
–, animar el *to stimulate trade*
–, balanza visible de *visible balance of trade*
–, cámara de *chamber of commerce*
–, casa de *business establishment*
–, código de *commercial code*
–, fomento del *trade promotion*
–, horas de *business hours*
–, libertad de *free trade*
–, marca de *trade name*
–, restricción de *restraint of trade*
–, zona potencial de *potential trading area*
comestibles, almacenista de *wholesale grocer*
comienzo aleatorio *random start*
comisión *commission*
– consultiva *advisory commission*
– de compra *buying commission*
– de operarios *works council*
– mixta *joint committee*
– para dictaminar sobre conducta comercial *business conduct committee*
– permanente *standing committee*
– progresiva o en escala ascendente, tiempo de *progressive or stepped-up commission rate*
– y gastos *fees and expenses*
–, comprar a *to buy on commission*
–, negociante a *commission merchant*
–, vender a *to sell on commission*
comisionar *to commission*
comisiones, liquidación de *commission statement*
comisionista *commission agent or broker*
– de acciones *stockbroker*
– expedidor *forwarding agent*
–, comerciante *commission merchant*
–, viajante *commission traveller (Am) or salesman (Br)*
comité *committee*
– administrativo *executive committee*
– de administración *administration committee*
– de cupos *allocation committee*
– de dirección de los cambios *steering board of trade*
– de dotación de personal *allocation committee*
– de empresa *works committee, shop committee*
– de orientación *steering committee*

– de trabajo *task group*
– ejecutivo *executive committee*
– financiero *finance committee*
compaginación, ajuste de *page layout (Am) or make-up (Br)*
compañía *company, corporation*
– afiliada *subsidiary company*
– anónima *stock company*
– bancaria *banking company*
– de responsabilidad limitada *limited liability company*
– de seguros *insurance company*
– filial *affiliated company*
– fusionada *merged company*
– inactiva *non-operating company*
– inmobiliaria *real-estate company*
– inversionista *investing company*
– matriz *parent or holding company*
– por acciones *stock or chartered company*
– propietaria *close corporation*
– reaseguradora *re-insuring company*
– subsidiaria *underlying company*
–, capital emitido por la *company's issued capital*
compañías afines *related companies*
– asociadas *associated companies*
–, cuenta entre *inter-company account*
comparación, compras por *comparison buying*
comparativo de capacidades, cuadro *comparative rating chart*
–, balance *comparative balance sheet*
–, estado *comparative statement*
–, estado de balance *comparative balance sheet*
comparativos, datos *comparative data*
compendio *syllabus, abstract*
compensable *balancing, equalizing*
compensación *reward, compensation*
– bancaria *clearings*
– de cheques *settlement, clearance*
– legal por accidentes de trabajo, seguro contra *compensation insurance*
– obligatoria *compulsory compensation*
– por accidentes laborales *workmen's compensation*
– progresiva *set-off*
– o liquidación de balances *clearing*
–, acuerdo de *clearing agreement*
–, banco de *clearing bank*
–, bolsa de *clearinghouse*
–, cámara de *clearinghouse*
–, descanso de *compensatory time off*
–, factor de *balancing factor*
–, liquidación por *clearing*
–, prima de *lien bonus, timeworkers' bonus*

–, seguro de *compensation insurance*
–, sistema de *balanced system*
–, ventas por *compensation deals*
compensaciones, agente bancario de *clearinghouse agent*
–, convenio de *clearing agreement*
–, diario de *clearinghouse blotter*
compensado, promedio *weighted average*
compensador, error *counter error*
compensadora, cuenta *closing account*
compensados, errores *compensating errors*
compensar *to clear*
compensativos, beneficios *offsetting gains*
compensatorio *complementary*
–, financiamiento *compensatory financing*
–, impuesto *compensatory duty*
compensatorios, factores *offsetting factors*
competencia *competition*
– activa, mercado de *active market-price competition*
– desleal *unfair competition*
– extranjera *foreign competition*
– injusta *unfair competition*
– leal *fair trade*
–, precio de *competitive price*
competente *competent, capable*
competición *contest, competition, rivalry*
competitivo, precio *competitive price*
compilación de datos *information storage*
compleja, personalidad *complex personality*
complejo *complex*
complementario *complementary*
complemento *complement*
completo, cargamento *full load*
–, índice *all-inclusive index*
–, pagar por *to pay in full*
–, sueldo *full pay*
componedor, amigable *conciliator*
componentes, método de los *method of selected points*
comportamiento *behaviour*
– de los precios *price behaviour*
composición *breakdown*
compra *purchase, buying*
– a plazos *instalment buying, hire purchase*
– de bienes raíces, certificado de *tax certificate*
– directa *direct buy*
– para cubrir ventas al descubierto *short covering*
– premeditada *pre-meditated purchase*
–, capacidad de *buying power*
–, capacidad financiera de *financial purchasing ability*
–, capacidad potencial *potential buying ability*
–, comisión de *buying commission*
–, conducta en la *buying behaviour*

–, contratos de *buying agreement*
–, motivos *buying motives*
–, nota de *purchase order*
–, opción de *option to purchase*
–, orden de *draft*
–, pedido de *purchase order*
–, precio de *buying price*
–, receptor de órdenes de *sales order clerk*
–, registro de la capacidad de *buying power survey*
comprador *buyer, purchaser*
–, gastos a cargo del *expenses at buyer's cost*
–, mercados del *buyer's market*
–, opción del *buyer's option*
–, riesgo del *buyer's risk*
comprar *to buy*
– a bulto *to buy in bulk*
– a comisión *to buy on commission*
– a condición *to buy on approach*
– a crédito *to buy on credit*
– a la baja *to buy on a fall*
– a ojo *to buy at sight*
– a precio del mercado *to buy at market price*
– a precio tirado *to buy dirt cheap*
– a tanto alzado *to buy outright*
– a término *to buy the account*
– a una persona *to buy over*
– al contado *to buy for cash*
– al fiado *to buy on credit*
– al por mayor *to buy wholesale*
– con rebaja *to buy at a discount*
– de segunda mano *to buy second hand*
– en mano *to buy up*
– la parte de un socio *to buy out*
– por cuenta del dueño *to buy in*
– por subasta *to buy at auction*
– según muestra *to buy by sample*
–, cansancio al *buying fatigue*
–, resistencia a *sales resistance*
–, volver a *to buy back*
compras a precios ascendentes *upscale buying*
– agrupadas *group buying*
– colectivas *group or combined buying or purchasing*
– efectivas *actual purchases*
– en abonos *instalment buying*
– en el extranjero *foreign buying*
– en el país *domestic purchases*
– excesivas *overbuying*
– improvisadas *hand-to-mouth buying*
– necesarias *open to buy*
– por comparación *comparison buying*
– por las fábricas *trade buying*
– previstas *planned purchases*
–, cálculo de *purchases calculation*

–, cooperativa de *buying co-operative*
–, cuenta de *purchase account*
–, departamento de *purchasing department, buyer's department or premises*
–, diario de *journal of purchases*
–, jefe de *buyer*
–, libro de *journal of purchases*
–, libro mayor de *accounts payable ledger*
–, política de *purchasing policy*
–, sección de *purchasing department*
compraventa *bargain and sale trading*
– de acciones por emitir *when-issued trading*
– de valores no inscritos *unlisted trading*
–, contratos de *contract of sale*
–, cuenta de *trading account*
–, escritura de *bill of sale*
–, impuesto sobre *sales tax*
–, lista de *check list*
–, título de *bill of sale*
comprensivo, control económico *comprehensive economic control*
comprobación *verification, tentative*
– de facturas *invoice checking*
– en el sitio *spot check*
– en las tiendas al por menor *retail store audit*
– en unidades de las existencias *unit stock control*
– o fiscalización del presupuesto *budgetary control*
– o verificación de ficheros *files auditing*
–, balance de *trial balance*
comprobante *voucher*
– de anuncio, página o recorte *tear sheet*
– de caja *cashbook voucher*
– de caja chica *petty-cash voucher*
– de gastos *expense voucher*
– de pago *receipt*
– de retiro de fondos *withdrawal voucher*
– de venta *bill of sale*
– en ejemplar completo *complete voucher copy*
–, cheque con *voucher cheque*
–, ejemplar *checking copy*
–, según *as per voucher*
comprobantes a cobrar *vouchers payable*
–, clasificador de *voucher file*
–, cuenta sin *book account*
–, encargado de los *voucher clerk*
–, registro de *voucher register*
comprobar *to check or verify*
comprometerse al pago de un documento *to accept*
comprometidos, activos *committed assets*
compromiso para comprar valores no vendidos *stand-by underwriting*
–, sin *without obligation*

compuesta, hipótesis *composite hypothesis*
–, mercancía *composite commodity*
compuesto *compound, composite*
–, interés *compound interest*
–, promedio *composite average*
computable *computable*
computadora *computer*
– electrónica *digital computer*
computadoras analógicas y digitales *analog and digital computers*
computar *to compute or calculate*
cómputo *computation, computing*
comun, sentido *common sense*
comunes, acciones *common stock*
comunicación *message*
– de orden de producción *notice of production*
– de retraso en el programa *behind-schedule notice*
– directa, sistema de *public address system*
– oral *word of mouth*
–, medio de *means of communication*
–, presentar una *to read a paper*
comunicado *release*
– de prensa *press release*
– gratuito *free publicity*
– por radio *radio release*
comunicados publicitarios *publicity releases*
comunidad *community*
con dividendo incluído *cum dividend*
conceder *to grant, allow or accord*
– crédito *to extend credit*
– interés *to allow interest*
– un descuento *to allow a discount*
– un préstamo *to grant a loan*
concedido, tiempo *allowed or incentive time*
concejo *council, board*
– municipal *city council*
concentración *recapitulation*
concepto *concept, item*
conceptos *particulars*
concertar un contrato *to make a contract*
concesión *concession, franchise, grant*
– arancelaria *tariff concession*
– mancomunada *pooled concession*
concesionario *concessionaire, licensee*
–, venta por *concession sale*
conciliación, junta de *conciliation board*
conciliar *to conciliate*
– las cuentas *to reconcile accounts*
conclusión *scoring*
concordantes, muestras *matched samples*
concurrencia *competition, turnout*
concurso *contest*
condensación *condensation*
condición, comprar a *to buy on approach*
condicionado *qualified*

condicional, aceptación *qualified acceptance*
–, endoso *conditional endorsement*
–, probabilidad *conditional probability*
condiciones *conditions*
– de crédito *credit terms*
– de pago *terms of sale, usance*
– de trabajo *working conditions*
– de venta *sales terms*
– laborales *labour conditions*
–, sujetar a *to meet conditions*
condominio *joint ownership*
conducción de precios *price leadership*
conducta arreglada *steadiness*
– colectiva *collective behaviour*
– comercial, comisión para dictaminar sobre *business conduct committee*
– del mercado *market behaviour*
– en la compra *buying behaviour*
– profesional *professional conduct*
conexas, industrias *allied industries*
conexos, costos de *joint costs*
conferencia *conference, syndicate, lecture*
– de prensa *press conference*
– marítima *shipping conference*
–, dar una *to read a paper*
conferir *to confer or consult*
– poderes *to empower*
confiabilidad *reliability*
confiable *reliable, dependable*
confianza *confidence, trust*
–, voto de *vote of confidence*
confirmación *confirmation, acknowledgment*
confirmar *to confirm or ratify*
confiscar *to seize or expropriate*
conflicto *dispute, conflict*
– de trabajo *labour dispute*
–, tendencias en *conflicting tendencies*
conflictos sociales *social conflicts*
confrontar *to check*
confuso, asiento *blind entry*
congeladas, cuentas *frozen accounts*
congelado *frozen*
–, crédito *frozen credit*
congreso *convention, congress*
conjunto, dirección del *supervision*
–, estudio *joint study*
–, sistema de *overall system*
conocimiento de embarque *bill of lading*
– de embarque aéreo *air waybill*
– de favor *accommodation bill of lading*
– innegociable *straight bill of lading*
consciente *conscious*
consecuencias *results*
conseguir a fuerza de trabajo *to work out*
consejero *adviser, consultant*
–, analista *consultant analyst*

consejo advice, commission, council, counsel
– consultivo consulting board
– de administración board of directors
– de administración, reunión del board meeting
– de empresa working council
– de producción de la empresa joint production committee
– directivo board of directors
– industrial mixto working council
–, junta del board meeting
consentimiento consensus
conservación maintenance
– de suelos soil conservation
–, costos de maintenance charges
–, programas de conservation programme
conservar to maintain or keep
conservas alimenticias canned goods
–, fábrica de cannery
consideraciones conjuntas overall considerations
consignación de fondos allocation, allotment
–, a on consignment
consignar to consign
consignatario consignee
conjuntas, consideraciones overall considerations
consolidable fundable
consolidación consolidation
consolidada, deuda funded debt, bonded debt
–, hipoteca unified mortgage
consolidado funded
–, pasivo funded debt
consolidados, balances amalgamated balance sheets
consolidar to consolidate, to sink
consorcial, acuerdo pooling agreement
consorcio consortium, syndicate, pool
constable, amortización straight-line depreciation
constancia consistency, steadiness
constante, cantidad constant
–, error systematic error
–, jornal horario straight time
–, multiplicador constant multiplier
–, sueldo straight time
constantes, precios constant prices
constitución constitution
–, acta de deed of settlement
constituir to establish or organize
constitutiva, comisión advisory commission
–, escritura corporation charter, incorporation papers
constitutivo, título charter
consular, certificado consular certificate
–, factura consular invoice

consultas técnicas technical queries
consultiva, comisión advisory commission
–, junta advisory board
consultivo, consejo consulting board
consultor economista economic adviser
– técnico de un editor reader
consumadas, transacciones completed transactions
consumido, trabajo expended work
consumidor consumer
– final ultimate consumer
– medio average consumer
– potencial potential consumer
–, análisis del mercado consumer market analysis or research
–, crédito al consumer credit
–, índice de precios al consumer price index
–, investigación sobre el consumer research
consumidor-comprador consumer-purchaser
consumidores, entrevista a los consumer interview
–, panel de consumer panel
consumir to consume
consumo supply, consumption
– corriente, artículos de staple items
– corriente, género de staple commodities
– de capital capital consumption
– en el país, valor de material consumption value
– interno domestic consumption
– nacional home consumption
– por habitante per capita consumption
–, artículos de consumption goods
–, bienes de consumer goods
–, cooperativa de consumer cooperative
–, cuenta de consumer account
–, de gran consumer product, stapler
–, educación del consumer education
–, función del consumption function
–, hábitos de consumption habits
–, mercado de consumer market
–, mercado de gran thick market
–, mercado de poco thin market
–, mercancía de staple merchandise
–, préstamo de loan for consumption
–, producto de consumer product, staple
–, sector de consumer sector
–, unidades de consumer units
contabilidad accounting, book-keeping, accountability
– administrativa administrative accounting
– comercial business accounting or accountancy
– de costes accounting costs
– de costes de distribución distribution cost accounting

– de costes de producción *production cost accounting*
– de costos *cost accounting*
– de créditos *credits accounting*
– de gastos centralizados *expense-centre accounting*
– de gastos de distribución *distribution cost accounting*
– de gestión *management accounting*
– de la distribución *distribution accounting*
– de material *material accounting*
– de mercancías *merchandise accounting*
– de partida doble *double entry book-keeping*
– de partida simple *single entry book-keeping*
– de sociedades *corporation accounting*
– de sucesiones *estate accounting*
– de talleres para determinación de costes *shop and cost accounting*
– de ventas *sales accounting*
– fiscal *government accounting*
– inventarial *inventory accounting*
– por partida doble *double-entry book-keeping*
– por partida simple *single-entry book-keeping*
–, instructivo de *plan of accounts*
–, jefe de *general accountant*
–, máquina alfabética de *alphabetic accounting machine*
–, máquina eléctrica de *electric accounting machine*
–, pruebas de *accounting evidence*
–, reglas de *accounting measures*
–, sistema de *accounting system*
contabilidades, inspector de *chartered accountant*
contabilística *accounting*
contable *accountant, accountable*
– de costes de producción *production cost accountant*
– de costes de venta *sales cost accountant*
– de costos *cost accountant*
– público titulado *certified public accountant*
–, depreciación *accounting depreciation*
–, operador de máquina *book-keeping machine operator*
–, período *accounting period*
–, práctica *accounting practice*
–, sistema *accounting system*
–, técnica *expert accountancy*
–, trabajo *accounting work*
contables, agencias *accounting firms*
–, datos *accounting data*
–, empresas *accounting firms*
–, normas *accounting standards*
–, operaciones *accounting transactions*
contacto, jefe de *account or contact executive*

contado *cash*
–, comprar al *to buy for cash*
–, pago al *cash and carry, cash or prompt payment*
–, precio al *cash price*
–, precio de venta al *cash price*
–, vender al *to sell for cash*
–, venta al *cash sale*
contador *accountant, teller*
– ayudante *junior accountant*
– de costos *cost accountant*
– en jefe *chief accountant*
– fiscal *government accountant*
– general *general accountant*
– público titulado *certified public accountant*
–, cargo de *accountant*
contadora *calculator*
contaduría *accounting, accountancy*
contante, dinero *ready money*
contar *to account*
contencioso, proceso *lawsuit*
contesta, no *non-response*
contingencia *contingency, risk*
–, fondo de *contingent fund*
–, seguro de *casuality insurance*
contingencias, tabla de *contingency table*
contingente, pasivo *contingent liabilities*
contingentes, utilidades *contingent profits*
continua, fabricación *straight line production, continuous production*
–, producción *straight line or continuous production*
–, variable aleatoria *continuous random variable*
continuación *follow-up*
continuadas, ventas *follow-up sales*
continuidad *follow-up, continuity*
–, sistema de *follow-up system*
continuo *continuum*
–, rendimiento *continuous rating*
–, trabajo *non-stop work, work round the clock*
contra reembolso *against payment*
contrabando *smuggling*
contracción *contraction*
– del mercado *business contraction*
contractual de exclusividad, cláusula *competition clause, exclusivity speculation*
contracuenta *offset account*
contrademanda *counter-claim*
contradicción *contradiction, contrariness*
contraloría *auditor's office*
contramaestre *foreman*
– adjunto *petty foreman*
contramedia *counter-measure*
contraoferta *counter-offer, counter-proposal*

contraparte *counterpart*
contrapartida *balancing or readjusting entry*
contraprueba *check test*
contrarrestar *to counteract*
contraste *contrast*
contratación *transaction*
 – de personal *employment, hiring*
contratante *contracting party*
contratantes, partes *contracting parties*
contratar *to make a contract*
contratista *contractor*
contrato *contract*
 – a precio alzado *lumpsum contract*
 – a precio determinado *fixed-price contract*
 – a precios unitarios *unit-price contract*
 – bilateral *indenture*
 – colectivo *collective bargaining, collective contract*
 – colectivo de trabajo *collective bargaining agreement*
 – de agencia *agency contract*
 – de aprendizaje, dependiente con *articled clerk*
 – de arrendamiento *lease*
 – de asociación *articles of partnership*
 – de compra *buying agreement*
 – de compraventa *contract of sale*
 – de edición *publishing contract*
 – de empleo *employment contract, contract of hire*
 – de fletamiento *contract of affreightment*
 – de precio revisable *sliding-scale contract*
 – de servicios *agreement of services*
 – de sociedad *partnership contract, incorporation papers*
 – de trabajo *employment contract*
 – de una mercancía determinada *open-end contract*
 – implícito *implied agreement*
 – marítimo *maritime contract*
 – mundial *world contract*
 – para suministro de cantidad indefinida *open-end contract*
 – por administración *cost-plus contract*
 – que prohibe afiliarse a sindicato obrero *yellowdog contract*
 – renta de retiro *income bond*
 –, bajo *under contract*
 –, celebrar un *to enter into a contract*
 –, concertar un *to make a contract*
 –, costo de *cost of contract*
 –, proyecto de *draft contract, draft agreement*
 –, violación de *breach of contract*
contratos colectivos de trabajo, reglamentación para *collective bargaining provisions*

 – de venta en firme *contracts of sale*
contribución *tax, quota, assessment*
 – inmobiliaria *real-estate tax*
 – sobre ingreso *income tax*
contribuciones, tarifa de *tax rate*
contribuyente *taxpayer*
 – evasor *tax-evader*
 – moroso *delinquent taxpayer*
contribuyentes, lista de *tax list*
control *check, checking*
 – automático de ganancia *automatic gain control*
 – de carteleras *traffic audit*
 – de ciclo de tiempos *time cycle control*
 – de cupos *allocation control*
 – de existencias, ficha de *stock control card*
 – de la calidad *quality control*
 – de la producción *production control*
 – de las tiradas *circulation control*
 – de materiales *material control*
 – de trabajo, reloj de *time clock*
 – de tránsito aéreo *air traffic control*
 – de tiempo de trabajo, reloj de *job-time recording clock*
 – del tráfico de aeropuertos *airport traffic control*
 – económico comprensivo *comprehensive economic control*
 – equilibrado *balanced or co-ordinated control*
 – estadístico de calidad *statistical quality control*
 – o fiscalización de existencias *stock control*
 – o fiscalización de ventas *sales control*
 – o verificación de carteles emplazados *traffic audit*
 –, participación de *controlling interest*
 –, sala de *control room*
controlada, corporación *controlled company*
 –, muestra *controlled sample*
controlado, movimiento *constrained movement*
 –, trabajo *controlled or restricted work*
controlador *tester*
controladora, cuenta *controlling account*
controlar *to control*
 – la inflación *to curb inflation*
controversia sobre sueldos *wage dispute*
convención *convention, congress*
 – anual *annual convention*
convenida, cuenta *account settled or stated*
convenido, precio *agreed price*
 –, valor *agreed value*
convenio *agreement, contract, accord*
 – colectivo *collective bargaining*
 – de compensaciones *clearing agreement*
 – de trabajo *collective agreement, work*

agreement
–, llegar a un *to strike a bargain*
–, proyecto de *draft convention*
convenios colectivos de trabajo *collective bargaining*
conversión *conversion*
–, derecho de *conversion option*
convertibilidad *convertibility*
convertible, moneda *convertible or hard currency*
convertibles en acciones, bonos *convertible bonds*
convocar *to call or summon*
convocatoria *notice of a meeting*
cooperación *co-operation*
– de los empleados y obreros *employer-employee co-operation*
– de un trabajo *team work*
– entre patronos y obreros *employer-employee co-operation*
cooperar *to co-operate*
cooperativa de compras *buying co-operative*
– de consumo *consumer co-operative*
–, sociedad *co-ooperative society*
cooperativismo agrícola *agricultural co-operation*
copia *copy, transcript*
– certificada *certified copy*
– exacta *close copy*
– heliográfica *blue-print*
– para archivo *file copy*
copias de cartas, papel fino para *copying paper*
coproducto *joint product*
copropiedad *joint ownership*
copropietario *part-owner*
corchetes *brackets*
cordón huelguista *picket line*
corolario *corollary*
corporación *corporation, company, trade guild*
– controlada *controlled company*
– filial *subsidiary company*
– mercantil *business corporation*
– nacional *domestic corporation*
– no lucrativa *non-profit organization*
corporativa, propiedad *corporate property*
corrección, error de *correction error*
corredor *canvasser, broker, jobber*
– aéreo *airbroker*
– de acciones *stockbroker*
– de anuncios *advertising canvasser, advertising salesman*
– de apuestas *bookmaker*
– de bienes raíces *real-estate broker*
– de bolsa *stockbroker*
– de compras *buying broker*
– de fincas *real-estate broker*

– de seguros *insurance broker*
– de ventas *selling broker*
corredores, bolsa de (Ch) *stock exchange*
–, colegio de *brokers' association*
corregido, texto *revised text*
correlativa, valoración *appraisal, rate, rating*
correo *mail, post office*
– aéreo *airmail*
– certificado *registered mail*
– de entrega inmediata *special-delivery mail*
– de primera clase *first-class mail (Br)*
– de segunda clase *second-class mail (Br)*
– ordinario *regular mail*
–, a vuelta de *by return mail*
–, encargado del *mail clerk*
–, encuesta por *postal survey*
–, firma que anuncia y vende por *mail order house*
–, pedido hecho por *mail order*
–, publicidad directa por *mail order advertising*
–, venta por *mail order business*
correos, casilla o apartado de *post-office box*
–, oficina de *post office*
–, porte de *postage*
correspondencia, estante de acero para archivar *steel filing-cabinet*
–, venta por *mail order business, mail order selling*
corresponsal *correspondent, agent*
corretaje *brokerage*
– aéreo *airbroking*
corriente *flow*
– económica *economic flow*
–, activo *current assets*
–, cuenta *current account, charge account, drawing account*
–, extracto de cuenta *abstract of current account*
–, insuma *current input*
–, interés *current interest*
–, marca *standard make*
–, moneda *legal tender*
–, precio *market price*
–, producto *current product*
–, superávit *current surplus*
–, tamaño *stock size*
–, tipo *current rate*
corta, tonelada *short ton*
corte de caja *closing and balancing the cash*
– representativo *cross section*
Corte Suprema *Supreme Court*
corto plazo, interés a *short-term interest*
– plazo, letra a *short bill*
– plazo, obligaciones a *short-term liabilities*
– plazo, préstamo a *short-term loan*
cosecha *production, output, yield*
cosechar *to harvest*

costado del vapor, entregado al *delivered alongside*
– del vapor, libre al *free alongside*
–, puesto al *free alongside*
costas *costs*
coste *expense*
– adicional *additional cost*
– anual por persona *annual cost per head*
– de distribución, análisis del *distribution cost analysis*
– de entrega *delivery cost*
– de entretenimiento anual *annual upkeep cost*
– de fabricación *production cost*
– de funcionamiento *plant operating cost*
– de inversión de instalaciones *plant investment cost*
– de los factores *factor cost*
– de producción *production cost*
– de utilización *user cost*
– de ventas *sales cost*
– de ventas, revisión del *cost auditing of sales*
– de vida, índice del *cost-of-living index*
– efectivo *actual cost*
– fijo *fixed cost*
– más porcentaje *cost plus*
– monetario *money cost*
– primario *prime cost*
– total *all-in cost, gross cost*
– unitario *unit cost*
– unitario de producción, depreciación a base del *unit cost depreciation*
– verdadero *actual cost*
–, valor de *cost value*
costeable *profitable*
costear *to finance*
costes *costs*
– administrativos *clerical costs*
– conjuntos o globales de distribuición *overall distribuition costs*
– de distribución, contabilidad de *distribution cost accounting*
– de distribución, normas de *distribution cost standards*
– de producción, contabilidad de *production cost accounting*
– de producción, contable de *production cost accountant*
– de los distribuidores *distributor's costs*
– de venta, contable de *sales accountant*
– prefijados *standard costs*
– tipo *standard costs*
– variables *variable costs*
–, ajuste de *cost auditing*
–, centro de *cost centre*
–, contabilidad de *accounting costs*
–, modificación de *cost alteration*

–, reducción de *cost reduction*
–, reparto de *distribution of costs*
costo *cost, price*
– de contrato *cost of contract*
– de fabricación *prime cost*
– de factores *factor cost*
– de montaje *assembly cost*
– de operación *operation cost*
– de producción *operating cost*
– de reposición *replacement cost*
– de sustitución *replacement cost*
– de vida *cost of living*
– directo *direct cost*
– efectivo *actual cost*
– en plaza *market price*
– estimado *estimated cost*
– inicial *historical cost*
– marginal *marginal cost*
– marginal de los factores *marginal factor cost*
– marginal de uso *marginal user cost*
– o mercado, el que sea más bajo *cost or market whichever is lower*
– por unidad *unit cost*
– primo *prime cost*
– real *actual cost*
– reducido *low or reduced cost*
– según factura *invoice cost*
– seguro, flete y cambio *cost, insurance, freight and exchange*
– unitario *unit cost*
– unitario, índice de *index of unit cost*
– variable promedio *age-variable cost*
–, asegurar el *to underwrite the cost*
–, curvas de *cost curves*
–, función del *cost function*
–, precio bajo *below cost price*
–, precio de *cost price*
–, unidad de *cost unit*
costos *expenses*
– de conexos *joint costs*
– de conservación *maintenance charges*
– de embalaje *packing expenses*
– de expedición *shipping charges*
– de operación *operating expenses*
– económicos *economic costs*
– indirectos *indirect costs*
– presupuestos *estimated cost*
– reducidos *trim costs*
–, calculista de *cost clerk*
–, contabilidad de *cost accounting*
–, contable de *cost accountant*
–, contador de *cost accountant*
–, inflación de los *cost inflation*
–, normas de *cost standards*
–, repartición de *cost distribution*
–, teoría de *theory of comparative costs*

costoso *expensive, high-priced*
costumbre *custom, buying*
– comercial *business practice*
cotejar *to compare*
– comerciales *trading customs*
cotejo, prueba de *call-back proof*
cotidiano *daily*
cotizable *quotable*
cotización *quotation, list of prices*
– callajera *street price*
– de cierre *closing price*
– de valores *listing securities*
–, demanda de *inquiry*
–, padrón de *inquiry*
–, solicitud de *request for quotation*
cotizaciones de apertura *opening prices*
cotizar *to quote*
coyuntura comercial *business prospects*
– económica *economic policy*
–, política de *business cycle policy*
creados, intereses *vested interest*
crear un producto *to develop a product*
– ventas *to build sales*
creciente, rendimiento *increasing return*
–, utilidad *increasing returns*
crecimiento económico *economic growth*
–, tasa de *rate of growth*
credibilidad *credibility*
crediticia, capacidad *lending capacity*
–, estimación *credit rating*
–, expansión *credit expansion*
–, política *credit policy*
crediticias, relaciones *credit relations*
crédito *credit, financial standing*
– a corto plazo *short-term credit*
– a largo plazo *long-term credit*
– a plazo *time letter of credit*
– abierto *open credit*
– al consumidor *consumer credit*
– cedido *assigned claim*
– congelado *frozen credit*
– de emergencia *stop-gap loan*
– documentario *documentary credit*
– documentario comercial *commercial documentary credit*
– dudoso *doubtful credit*
– en descubierto *accommodation credit*
– en moneda extranjera *credit in foreign exchange*
– irrevocable *straight or irrevocable credit*
– irrevocable, carta de *irrevocable letter of credit*
– mercantil *goodwill, reputation*
– por la experiencia *experience credit*
– rotativo *revolving credit*
– simple, carta de *clean letter of credit*
– y cobro, gastos de *credit and collection*

expenses
–, 'abrir un *to open a credit*
–, asiento de *debit item*
–, carta comercial de *commercial letter of credit*
–, carta de *letter of credit*
–, clasificado para *rated*
–, comprar a *to buy on credit*
–, conceder *to extend credit*
–, condiciones de *credit terms*
–, cuenta de *goodwill account*
–, documento de *credit instrument*
–, escasez de *credit squeeze*
–, índice de *credit rating*
–, inflación del *credit inflation*
–, informe de *credit report*
–, límite de *line of credit, loan ceiling*
–, nota de *credit note*
–, partida de *credit item*
–, política de *credit policy*
–, promesa de *credit commitment*
–, requisitos de la información de *credit information requirement*
–, restricción del *credit restriction*
–, sección de *credit department*
–, sociedad de *credit institution or company*
–, suplemento de *supplementary appropriation*
–, venta a *credit sale, sales to date*
créditos financieros *supply services*
– fallidos, pérdidas por *expenses for bad debts*
– incobrables *bad debts*
–, cobro de *collection of credits*
–, contabilidad de *credits accounting*
–, director de *credit manager*
–, extensión de *credit extension*
crisis económica *depression, economic crisis*
– monetaria *money crisis*
criterio *judgement, criterion, policy*
– comercial *merchandising or business judgement*
– de los directivos *executive judgement*
– impositivo *system of taxation*
crítico, cláusula de punto *peril point clause*
cronizada, secuencia *timing sequence*
cronógrafo *chronograph*
– o reloj registrator *time recorder*
cronológica, estadística *chronologic statistics*
cronológico, estudio *chronological study*
cronomedidor *time measurer*
cronometradas de producción, normas *stop-watch production standards*
cronometrador *time and motion study man, timekeeper*
cronometraje por lecturas acumuladas *cumulative timing, continuous reading method*
–, hoja de *time observation sheet, time study sheet*

cronómetro *stopwatch, timekeeper*
- con dos agujas *two-handed stopwatch*
- con vuelta a cero *single pressure or snapback stopwatch*
- de precisión *calibrated stopwatch*
-, estudio de tiempos por *stopwatch time study*
croquis *outline*
cruzada, datos de sección *cross section data*
-, muestra *cross sample*
-, muestreo por sección *cross section sampling*
-, sección *cross section*
-, tabulación *cross tabulation*
cruzado, asiento *cross entry*
-, índice *cross reference*
cruzados, tipos *cross rates*
cuaderno de taquigrafía *stenographer's notebook*
cuadrada, milla *square mile*
-, raíz *square root*
cuadrado de la desviación media *variance*
cuadrática media, desviación *squared deviation*
cuadrilla, jefe de *squad boss, labour foreman*
cuadro comparativo de capacidades *comparative rating chart*
- de demanda *demand schedule*
- de información *information desk*
- de la marcha del trabajo *speed schedule*
- de la oferta *supply schedule*
- de mandos *staffing*
- demostrativo de situación de material *status board*
cuadros *forms*
cuadruplicado *quadruplicate*
cualidades de mando *leadership qualities*
- para el cargo *qualifications for position*
cualitativas, normas *qualitative standards*
cualitativo, enfoque *qualitative approach*
cuantificación estadística *statistical quantificition*
- prosecutiva *quantifying follow-up*
cuantitativas, normas *quantitative standards*
cuantitativo *quantitative*
cuantitativos, datos *quantifiable or quantitative data*
cuarto de herramientas *tool store or crib*
- de muestras (Am) *showroom*
cubierta, página de la *cover page*
cubiertas, acciones *fully-paid shares*
cubrir *to cover or pay*
- los gastos *to pay expenses*
- ventas al descubierto, compra para *short covering*
cubrirse *to hedge*
cuenta *account, bill, computation, reckoning*
- abierta *open account, running account*
- acreedora *credit or creditor account*

- atrasada *outstanding account*
- auxiliar *adjunct account*
- bancaria *bank account*
- clara *clear reckoning account*
-· compensadora *closing account*
- conforme o convenida *account stated or settled*
- controladora *controlling account*
- corriente *current, charge or drawing account*
- corriente, extracto de *abstract of current account*
- de acumuladores *accruals account*
- de ahorros *savings account*
- de anticipos *drawing or advances account*
- de balance *balance account*
- de capital *capital account*
- de caja *cash account*
- de cierre *closing account*
- de clientes *accounts receivable*
- de cobro dudoso *doubtful account*
- de compensación *clearing account, offset account*
- de compras *purchase account*
- de compraventa *trading account*
- de consumo *consumer account*
- de crédito *goodwill account*
- de cheques *current account*
- de descuentos *discounts account*
- de explotación *work or trading account*
- de ganancias *income account*
- de gastos *expense account*
- de ingresos *income account*
- de inventario *inventory account*
- de mercaderías *goods or merchandise account*
- de mobiliario *fixtures account*
- de pérdidas y ganancias *profit and loss account*
- de pérdidas y gastos *account of outlays and costs*
- de proveedores *accounts payable*
- de reserva *allowance or provision account*
- de suspensión *clearing account*
- de ventas *sales account*
- del dueño, comprar por *to buy in*
- del valor prestigio *goodwill account*
- detallada *specified account*
- deudora *debit or debtor account*
- en descubierto *overdrawn account*
- en participación *joint account*
- en regla *clear account*
- entre compañías *inter-company account*
- fiduciaria *trust account*
- impugnada *disputed account*
- mancomunada *joint account*
- pagada *account settled*
- pagadera *mature account*
- particular *private account*

– pendiente *outstanding account*
– resumida *bulk account*
– saldada *account settled*
– sin comprobantes *book account*
– sin movimiento *inactive account*
– subsidiaria *sub-account*
– vencida *mature account*
–, a *on account*
–, abonar a la *to credit the account*
–, abonar en *to allow*
–, abrir una *to open an account*
–, arreglar una *to settle an account*
–, cargar a la *to debit the account*
–, cerrar la *to close the account*
–, estado o estracto de *statement*
–, liquidar una *to settle an account*
–, pagar a *to pay on account*
–, pago a *part payment, payment on account, down payment, advance cash*
–, unidad de *accounting unit*
cuentas *accounts*
– a pagar *accounts payable*
– atrasadas *accounts in arrears*
– bancarias *bank accounts*
– congeladas *frozen accounts*
– de gastos, clasificación de *expenses account classification*
– de pasivo *liability accounts*
– del activo *assets accounts*
– diversas *sundry accounts*
– generales *general accounts*
– hinchadas *accounts overcharged*
– incobrables *irrecoverable accounts, bad debts*
– mixtas *mixed accounts*
– morosas *bad debts*
– normalizadas *standardized accounts*
– pendientes *outstanding accounts*
– pignoradas *pledged accounts*
– por cobrar *accounts receivable*
– sobrecargadas *accounts overcharged*
–, ajustar *to settle accounts*
–, ajuste de *audit, auditing*
–, amañar *to doctor accounts*
–, análisis de *accounts analysis*
–, catálogo de *list of accounts*
–, censor de *auditor*
–, cierre de *closing of accounts*
–, conciliar las *to reconcile accounts*
–, estado de *statement, statement of accounts*
–, falsificar *to doctor accounts*
–, interventor de *auditor*
–, libro de *account book, ledger*
–, llevar *to keep accounts*
–, por saldo de *in full*
–, rendir *to be accountable*

–, revisión de *audit*
–, revisor de *auditor*
–, ventas a *account sales*
cuestión obrera *labour troubles*
cuestionario *questionnaire*
– normativo *standardized questionnaire*
–, precio del *questionnaire design*
cuestiones monetarias *money matters*
cultivos, rotación de *crop rotation*
cumplimiento *maturity*
– en el cargo *position performance*
–, seguro de *performance bond*
cumplir, hacer *to enforce*
cumulativo, seguro *accumulation insurance*
cuota *quota*
– de exportación *export quota*
– de importación *import allotment*
– mensual *monthly rate*
cupo *quota*
– de amortización *amortization quota*
– de gastos *expense quota*
– de materias primas *allocation*
– de ventas *sales quota*
– estimado *judgement quota*
cupos arancelarios *custom quotas*
–, control de *allocation control*
–, muestreo por *quota sampling*
curso *trend*
– de fabricación, en *manufacture in progress*
– de fabricación, materiales en *in-process materials*
– forzoso, moneda de *compulsory currency, flat money*
curva *curve*
– de aprendizaje *learning or training curve*
– de distribución de frecuencia *frequency distribution curve*
– de frecuencia *frequency or distribution curve*
– de ganancia *earnings or wages curve*
– de gastos *rating curve*
– de rentabilidad *break-even curve*
– de rentabilidad, análisis de la *break-even curve analysis*
– de producción *output, production or work curve*
– de respuesta *overall response curve*
– de salarios *wages or earnings curve*
– de salida-entrada *output-input curve*
– de ventas *sales curve*
– legal, moneda de *legal tender*
– normal de probabilidad *normal probability curve*
– total *overall curve*
curvas de costo *cost curves*

CH

charlatán *windbag*
chatarra *scrap, spoliage, wastage, waste*
chelín *shilling*
cheque *cheque*
- al *portador cheque to bearer*
- aprobado *certified cheque*
- caducado *stale cheque*
- cancelado *cancelled cheque*
- certificado *certified cheque*
- con comprobante *voucher cheque*
- de ventanilla *counter cheque*
- de viajero *traveller's cheque*
- en blanco *blank cheque*

- pendiente de pago *outstanding cheque*
- posfechado *postdated cheque*
-, girar un *to draw a cheque*
cheques, cambiar *to cash cheques*
-, compensación de *settlement, payment in full, clearance*
-, cuenta de *current account*
-, libreta de *cheque book*
-, libro de *cheque book*
-, protectora de *cheque writer*
-, talonario de *cheque book*
chica, caja *petty cash*
-, libro de caja *petty cash book*

D

daño *injury, damage*
– accidental *accidental damage*
– por choque, seguro contra *collision insurance*
daños dobles *double damages*
– emergentes *consequential damages*
– materiales *property damage*
– y perjuicios, demanda por *claim for damages*
–, reclamar *to claim damages*
dar razón de *to account for*
– un beneficio *to yield a profit*
– una conferencia *to read a paper*
datos *data, information*
– alfabéticos al sumarizar, perforación *alphabetic summary punching*
– anotados *recorded data*
– básicos *basic information, bench-mark data*
– brutos *raw data*
– comparativos *comparative data*
– contables *accounting data*
– cuantitativos *quantifiable or quantitative data*
– de funcionamiento *working data*
– de nómina *payroll data*
– de origen *primary data*
– de sección cruzada *cross section data*
– de tiempos normalizados *standard time data*
– de una encuesta *survey data*
– del censo *census data*
– estadísticos *statistics, statistical data*
– globales *overall data*
– laborales *job data*
– primarios *primary data*
– registrados *recorded information, information*
– secundarios *secondary data*
– sobre las ventas *sales data*
– técnicos, hoja de *technical data sheet*
–, análisis de *data analysis*
–, compilación de *information storage*
–, elaboración electrónica de *electronic data processing*
–, máquina electrónica de *electronic data machine*
–, proceso de *data processing*
–, recolección de *data collection, collecting data*

–, registrador de *data recorder*
–, registro de *information record*
–, sistema de manejo de *data handling system*
–, sistematización de *data processing*
–, tabulación de *tabulation of data*
–, transmisión de *data transmission*
–, utilización de *information handling*
de gran alcance *long range*
debate *moot*
debe *debit, charge*
– y haber *debit and credit*
–, entrada en el *debit entry*
–, pasar al *to debit*
deber *to owe*
debitar *to debit*
débito *debit, charge*
decenio *ten years*
decifrar *to decode*
décimo *one tenth*
decisión arbitral *compulsory arbitration*
decisiones económicas *economic decisions*
– gubernamentales *governmental decisions*
declaración *statement*
– aduanal *bill of entry*
– de exportación *export declaration*
– de ingresos *income statement*
– falsa *false return*
– fiscal *income-tax report*
declarado, capital *stated or declared capital*
–, valor *stated value*
declarar *to declare*
– una huelga *to call a strike*
declararse en huelga *to down tools*
decomisar *to confiscate*
decomiso *seizure*
decorador de escaparates *window-dresser*
decreciente, productividad *diminishing productiveness*
–, producto *diminishing returns*
–, rendimiento *diminishing returns*
–, utilidad *diminishing returns*
decretado, dividendo *declared dividend*
decretar *to decree*
deducción *deduction*
deducciones, sueldo después de *take-home pay*
deducidos todos los gastos *all charges deducted*

deducible *deductible*
deducir *to deduct*
defecto, sesgo por *downward bias*
defectuoso *defective*
defectuosos, rectificación de *rectification of rejects*
deficiencia *deficiency, want*
deficiente, exposición *poor display*
–, trabajo *substandard work*
déficit *deficit, shortage*
– de dólares *dollar gap or shortage*
– en la balanza de pagos *deficit in the balance of payments*
deficitaria, balanza *unfavourable balance of trade*
–, economía *deficit economy*
deficitario, financiamiento *deficit financing*
deficitarios, gastos *deficit spending*
definitiva, factura *final invoice*
deflación *deflation*
deflacionado *deflated*
deformada, moneda *coin biased*
degustación *free lunch*
dejar carga *release load*
– desprovisto el mercado *to clear the market*
delectación *delectation, pleasure*
delegado del gremio *business agent, walking delegate (Am)*
– sindical *business agent*
delicado *fastidious*
demanda *demand, petition*
– activa *active demand*
– de cotización *inquiry*
– de empleo *demand for labour*
– de trabajo *demand for labour*
– efectiva *effective demand*
– floja *sluggish demand*
– por daños y perjuicios *claim for damages*
–, aumento de *pick-up demand*
–, cuadro de *demand schedule*
–, diferencia entre los precios de oferta y *spread*
–, falta de *sales resistance*
–, función *demand function*
–, ley de la oferta y *law of supply and demand*
–, oferta y *supply and demand*
–, satisfacer la *to meet the demand*
–, tabla de la *demand schedule*
demandado *defendant*
demandante *plaintiff*
demandar *to demand or claim*
demográfico, registro *registry of vital statistics*
demora *delay, interruption, stoppage*
–, sin *without delay*
demostración *demonstration*
demostrador *demonstration worker,*

demonstrator
–, obrero *demonstration worker, demonstrator*
demostrativo de situación de material, cuadro *status board*
denotar un aumento *to show an increase*
– una ganancia *to show a profit*
densidad potencial *potential density*
–, función de *density function*
dentro de las normas *up to standard*
denunciar *to report, to file a claim*
departamento *department, division*
– asesor de capacitación *staff training department*
– de anuncios, jefe del *advertisement manager*
– de archivo *file department*
– de colocaciones *employment department*
– de compras *purchasing or buyer's department or premises*
– de facturación *billing department*
– de información publicitaria *publicity department*
– de publicidad *advertising department*
– de salarios *wages department*
– de servicio *service department*
– de ventas *sales department*
– o sección de personal *personnel division*
–, jefe de *department chief or head or manager*
dependencia *dependency*
dependiente *sales clerk*
– con contrato de aprendizaje *articled clerk*
– vendedor *sales person*
–, variable *dependent variable*
depositante *depositor, pledger*
– de garantía *pledger*
depositar *to deposit*
depositario *trustee, bailee, receiver*
– judicial *receiver*
depósito *warehouse, deposit*
– a plazo *time deposit*
– a término *time deposit*
– de reparto *warehouse*
– derivado *derivate deposit*
– para distribución *distribution deposit*
–, certificado de *certificate of deposit*
–, en *on deposit*
–, gastos de *warehouse rent*
–, géneros en *bonded goods*
–, mercancías de *bonded goods*
depósitos bancarios *bank deposits*
– en bancos *bank deposits*
–, sistema de *warehousing system*
depreciación *depreciation*
– a base del coste unitario de producción *unit cost depreciation*

– acelerada *accelerated depreciation*
– acumulada *accrued depreciation*
– anual *annual depreciation*
– colectiva *composite depreciation*
– combinada *composite depreciation*
– contable *accounting depreciation*
– de la moneda *depreciation of currency*
– de productos *downgrading*
– física *physical depreciation*
– por porcentaje anual constante *straight-line depreciation*
– por tasación *appraisement method of depreciation*
– proporcional *straight-line depreciation*
– real *actual depreciation*
–, base de *basis for depreciation*
–, carga por *write-off load*
–, cargo por *depreciation charges*
–, factor real de la *effective depreciation factor*
–, fondo de *depreciation fund*
–, razón de *depreciation rate*
–, tasa de *depreciation rate*
depreciado, valor *depreciated value*
depreciar *to depreciate or devalue*
depresión *depression, business depression, recession*
depuración del personal, proceso de *clearance procedure*
derecho *right*
– comercial *commercial law*
– de autor *copyright*
– de conversión *conversion option*
– de gentes *international law*
– de huelga *right to strike*
– de marca registrada *trade mark rights*
– de voto, acciones con *voting stock*
– de voto, acciones sin *non-voting stock*
– de patente *patent rights*
– exclusivo *sole right*
– internacional de autor *international copyright*
– mercantil *business or commercial law*
– obrero *labour law*
derechos *rights, taxes, duties*
– adquiridos *vested rights*
– arancelarios de temporada *seasonal duties*
– de aduana *customshouse duties, customs*
– de aduana, abonar los *to pay duty*
– de aduana, imponer *to assess customs duty*
– de aduana, libre de *customs-free*
– de almacenaje *storage charges*
– de autor *copyright, royalties*
– de autor, infracción de *copyright infringement*
– de exclusividad *exclusive rights*
– de exportación *export duties*

– de importación *import duties*
– de propiedad *property rights*
– de propiedad reservados *all rights reserved*
– de puente *bridge toll*
– de puerto *harbour duties*
– de registro *registration fees*
– en bloque, adquirir los *to buy rights outright*
– exclusivos *exclusive rights*
– individuales *individual rights*
– portuarios *port duties*
– precautorios *preventive rights*
– primarios *primary rights*
– registrados *copyrighted*
– sobre el activo *equities*
–, exento de *duty-free*
–, lista de artículos exentos de *tax-free list*
–, franco de *duty-free*
–, libre de *duty-free*
derivado, depósito *derivate deposit*
derogar *to revoke*
desanimado, mercado *idle market*
desarrollo *development*
– de un producto, unidad de *product development unit*
– económico *economic development*
desautorizado *unauthorized*
descanso *rest, relaxation*
– de compensación *compensatory time off*
–, períodos de *rest periods*
–, tiempo de *relaxation or rest time*
descargar *to unload or discharge*
descartar *to discard*
descendente, fase *downswing*
–, movimiento *downward motion*
descendentes, precios *falling prices*
descompensado *unbalanced*
desconfianza *distrust*
descongelar *to unfreeze*
descontable *discountable*
descontar *to allow, to discount or deduct*
descripción del trabajo *job description*
descubierto, al *in blank*
–, anticipo en *advance in blank*
–, compra para cubrir ventas al *short covering*
–, cuenta en *overdrawn account*
–, en *overdrawn*
–, girar en *overdraw*
–, giro en *overdraft*
–, operar en *to sell short*
–, préstamo a *unsecured loan*
–, vender en *to sell short*
–, venta al *short selling*
descuento *discount, rebate*
– a la clientela *patronage discount*
– bancario *bank discount or rate*
– básico *basic rebate*

– caducado *lapsed discount*
– comercial *trade allowance or discount*
– externo *true discount (M)*
– por cantidades *quantity discount*
– por cantidades acumuladas *cumulative or deferred quantity discount*
– por pronto pago *cash or sales discount*
– real *true discount*
–, aumento del *advance of discount rate*
–, conceder un *to allow a discount*
–, factor de *discount factor*
–, incremento del *accrual of discount*
–, precio con *discount price*
–, tasa de *discount rate*
–, tipo de *discount rate*
descuentos, cuenta de *discounts account*
deseado, salario *expected salary*
desecho, producto de *waste product*
desembarcar *to unload*
desembolsable *expendable*
desembolsado, capital *paid-up capital*
desembolsar *to disburse*
desembolso *outlay*
desembolsos de capital *paid-up capital*
– de ingresos *revenue expenditures*
desempleo *unemployment*
– estacional *seasonal unemployment*
–, indemnización por *unemployment dole*
–, seguro contra el *unemployment insurance*
deseo *wish, desire*
desfalco *embezzlement, defalcation*
–, seguro contra *embezzlement insurance*
desfavorable *unfavourable*
–, evolución *worsening*
–, saldo *adverse balance*
desfile *parade*
desgaste de herramientas, gratificación por *tool allowance*
–, uso y *wear and tear*
designio *design*
desinflar *to deflate*
desinterés *lack of interest*
desistirse de la demanda *to abandon a suit*
desleal *unfair*
– de precios, rebaja *underselling, price cutting*
–, competencia *unfair competition*
desmontaje *stripping*
desobedecer *to disobey*
desocupación *unemployment, idleness*
– involuntaria *involuntary unemployment*
desocupado, tiempo *spare time*
desorden funcional *functional disorder*
despachadas, órdenes no *backlog*
despacho *office, shipment, message*
– u oficina de equipajes *receiving office*
despedir un empleado, pagar y *to pay off*

desperdicio *scrap, waste, wastage, spoilage*
desperdicios industriales *industrial wastes*
despido *dismissal, layoff*
– del trabajo *labour layoff*
– temporal de obreros *layoff*
–, indemnización por *dismissal or terminal wage*
desplegable, folleto *folder*
–, prospecto *folder*
desplome de precios *collapse of prices*
despojo *plunder, dispossession*
desprovisto el mercado, dejar *to clear the market*
después de las horas de oficina *after-office hours*
destajista *pieceworker*
destajo *piecework, by the job*
–, operario a *pieceworker*
–, precio a *flat rate*
–, salario a *taskwork wages*
–, trabajo a *piecework, taskwork*
destinatario *consignee*
destino *part-time appointment*
–, puerto de *port of destination*
destreza *adroitness, skill*
desuso *obsolescence, disuse*
desvanecimiento, punto de *vanishing point*
desventajoso *unfavourable, disadvantageous*
desviación *deviation, bias*
– absoluta *absolute deviation*
– cuadrática *squared deviation*
– media, cuadrado de la *variance*
detallada, cuenta *specified account*
–, factura *itemized invoice*
detallado, informe *long-form report*
detallar *to itemize*
detalle *detail, retail*
–, comercio al (M) *retailing*
–, lista de precios al *retail list price*
–, precio al *retail price*
–, precio de venta al *retail selling price*
–, ventas al *retail sales*
detallista *retailer*
–, precio de *retail price*
detallistas, tarifa rebajada para *open retail rate*
detener la inflación *to check inflation*
– pagos *to stop payment*
deterioro *deterioration, damage, wear and tear*
– accidental *accidental damage*
– de cantidad *amount determination*
determinación de costes, contabilidad de talleres para *shop and cost accounting*
– de la tara *taring*
determinado, contrato a precio *fixed-price*

contract
determinismo económinco *economic
determinism*
deuda *debt*
– a corto plazo *short-term debt*
– amortizable *redeemable debt*
– consolidada *funded or bonded debt*
– diferida *deferred debt*
– exterior *external or foreign debt*
– hipotecaria *debt on mortgage*
– incobrable *bad debt*
– interior *domestic or internal debt*
– nacional *national debt*
– pendiente *unpaid debt, unpaid balance*
– privilegiada *preferred debt*
– sin caución *unsecured debt*
–, amortización de una *debt redemption*
–, amortizar una *to sink a debt*
–, cancelación de una *to wipe out a debt*
–, saldar una *to discharge a debt*
deudas *liabilities*
– activas *accounts receivable*
– pasivas *accounts payable*
– de sociedades anónimas *corporate debts*
deudor *debtor*
– de un préstamo *pledger*
– dudoso *doubtful debtor*
– moroso *delinquent debtor*
–, lado *debt side*
–, saldo *debit balance*
deudora, cuenta *debit or debtor account*
devaluación *devaluation*
devengada, nómina *accrued payroll*
devengadas, utilidades *accrued income*
devengado *earned, accrued*
devengados, alquileres cobrados y no
unearned rent collected
–, dividendos *dividend income*
–, hoja de jornales *time sheet*
–, intereses *interest income*
devengo de empleados, libro mayor de
employees' earnings ledger
devolución *refund*
– de artículos vendidos *sales return*
– de impuestos *tax refund*
devoluciones y bonificaciones *returns and
allowances*
–, registro de *returns record*
devolver *to return or refund*
día de pago *value date, pay day*
– de trabajo *working day*
– hábil *business day*
–, cambio del *spot exchange*
–, información al *factual information*
–, orden del *order of the day, agenda*
–, préstamo de un *clearance loan*

diagrama de circulación *flow diagram or chart*
– de distribución del trabajo *work distribution
chart*
– de flujo del trabajo *work flow chart*
– de operación *operation chart*
– de organización *organization chart*
– de procedimiento de formularios *forms or
papers procedure chart*
– de procedimientos *process diagram*
– de procedimientos a máquina *machine
process chart*
– del avance *flow sheet*
– del proceso *process chart*
– del proceso de circulación *flow process chart*
– del uso de impresos *forms procedure chart*
– gráfico de procedimiento *process diagram*
diapositiva *slide, diapositive, transparency*
diaria, producción *stock*
diario *journal, book of original entry,
daybook*
– de caja (M) *cashbook*
– de compensaciones *clearinghouse blotter*
– de compras *purchases journal*
– de ventas *sales journal*
–, asiento de *journal entry*
–, libro *journal*
–, salario *daily wage*
–, trabajo *journey work*
días de gracia *days of grace*
dibujo de marca *brand image*
dictado, tomar *to take dictation*
dictamen *report, affidavit*
– de auditoría *auditor's certificate*
dictaminar sobre conducta comercial,
comisión para *business conduct committee*
– dictar, máquina de *dictating machine*
diestro *adroit*
diferencia de precio *markup*
– entre el precio y el costo *markup price*
– entre los precios de oferta y demanda
spread
–, tiempo por *subtracted time*
diferencial por piezas, salario *differential
piecework*
–, análisis *differential analysis*
–, arancel *differential duties*
diferida, anualidad *deferred annuity*
–, deuda *deferred debt*
–, emisión *delayed broadcast*
–, pensión *deferred annuity*
diferidas, acciones *deferred stock*
–, obligaciones *deferred bonds*
–, utilidades *deferred income, deferred credits*
diferido *deferred*
–, activo *deferred assets*
–, dividendo *deferred dividend*

–, ingreso *deferred income*
–, pasivo *deferred liabilities*
diferidos, cargos *deferred charges*
difícil, venta *close bargain*
difusión, zona de *circulation area*
digital, calculadora *digital computer*
digitales, computadoras analógicas y *analog and digital computers*
dilación *delay*
dilución del capital *stock watering*
dimensiones normalizadas *standardized or standard dimensions*
– o tamaños corrientes en almacén *stock sizes*
dimisión *resignation*
dinámica, administración *dynamic administration*
dinámico *non-static*
dinero *money*
– contante *ready money*
– efectivo *hard money*
– efectivo, en *in cash*
– en garantía *earnest money*
– en metálico *hard money*
– en prenda *earnest money*
– mercancía *money commodity*
– o especie *currency, specie*
–, colocar *to invest money*
–, imprimir *to print money*
–, oferta de *supply of money*
dirección *management*
– absoluta *absolute address*
– cablegráfica *cable address*
– científica *scientific management*
– comercial *business address, business management*
– de los cambios, comité de *steering board of trade*
– de ventas *sales management*
– del conjunto *supervision*
– del personal *personnel management*
– postal *mailing address*
–, ayudante de *executive assistant*
–, disposición de la *address arrangement*
–, ficha de *address card*
–, ficha para el grupo de *address group card*
–, gastos de *administrative expenses*
–, información de *straight information*
–, mando de la *steering control*
–, modificación automática de *automatic address modification*
–, publicidad *direct advertising*
direcciones, lista de *mailing list*
–, registro de *address register*
–, tambor de *address drum*
directa, compra *direct buy*
–, información *straight information*

–, pregunta *open-ended question*
–, responsabilidad *primary liability*
directiva *board of directors*
–, capacidad *executive ability*
–, junta *board of directors*
directivo que fija los precios *pricing executive*
–, asesor *management consultant*
–, consejo *board of directors*
directivos de organizaciones obreras *labour leaders*
– de la distribuición *marketing executives*
–, altos *chief executives*
–, criterio de los *executive judgement*
–, relaciones entre obreros y *labour-management relations*
directo, cobro *direct collection*
–, costo *direct cost*
–, interrogatorio *direct interviewing or questioning*
–, pasivo *direct liabilities*
–, promedio *straight average*
–, trabajo *straight or direct work*
director *director, manager, editor*
– accidental *acting director*
– comercial *commercial director or manager*
– comercial de división *divisional merchandise manager*
– comercial o jefe de ventas *sales or marketing manager*
– de campaña *account or contact executive*
– de capacitación *training director*
– de créditos *credit manager*
– de equipo de proyectos *project leader*
– de establecimiento *store manager*
– de fábrica *factory, plant or works manager*
– de formación *training director*
– de investigaciones del mercado *market research manager*
– de sucursal *branch manager*
– de tienda *store manager*
– en funciones *acting manager*
– financiero *comptroller*
– interino *acting manager*
– o jefe de créditos *credit manager*
– o jefe de personal *personnel manager*
– o jefe de ventas de zonas *regional sales manager*
– o jefe de ventas para el exterior *foreign sales manager*
– o jefe de ventas para el interior *home sales manager*
– o jefe de tráfico *traffic director or manager*
– técnico *technical director*
–, grupo *steering group*
directores, junta de *board of directors*
directos, impuestos *assessed taxes*

dirigente *manager, leader*
–, personal *supervisory staff*
dirigida, economía *centrally planned economy, direct economy*
–, pregunta *leading question*
discontinuar *to discontinue*
discrepancia *discrepancy, disagreement*
discutir *to discuss*
diseño *design*
– de muestreo *sampling design*
– de productos *product design*
– de una muestra *sample design*
– o esquema de especificación *specification drawings*
– protegido por patentes en tramitación *design covered by patents pending*
diseños, técnica de *design technique*
disidente, accionista *dissenting stockholder*
disidentes *dissenting*
disminución progresiva *set-off*
disminuida, producción *down-rated output*
disminuir *to decrease*
disolver *to dissolve*
dispersión *scatter*
–, coeficiente de *scatter coefficient*
–, gráfica de *scatter chart*
disponibilidad *availability, liquidity*
–, en *on hand*
disponible *available, on hand*
– de máquina, tiempo *available machine time*
–, activo *available assets, liquid assets, funds available, cash in hand*
–, capital *active capital*
–, mano *available labour*
disponibles, fondos *available funds, ready cash, cash and bank deposits*
–, horas *spare hours*
–, obreros *labour market*
–, valores (A) *cash assets*
disposición de la dirección *address arrangement*
dispositivo *device*
– de seguridad *safety device*
dispositivos de pruebas *testing devices*
dispuesto *set*
distribución *distribution allotment, breakdown, layout*
– de frecuencia *frequency distribution*
– de frecuencia, curva de *frequency curve, distribution curve*
– de la mano de obra *allocation of labour*
– normal *normal distribution*
– selectiva, enfoque de la *selective distribution approach*
–, análisis del coste de *distribution cost analysis*

–, coeficiente de *coefficient of distribution*
–, comercio de *distributive trade*
–, contabilidad de coste de *distribution cost accounting*
–, contabilidad de la *distribution accounting*
–, depósito para *distribution deposit*
–, gastos de *marketing expenses*
–, investigación de la *distribution research, marketing research*
–, plan de *bonus plan*
–, procedimiento de *marketing process*
–, red de *distribution, distributing or supply network*
distribuidor *supplier, caterer*
–, centro *distributing centre*
–, margen del *distributor margin*
distribuidora, agencia *distributing agency*
distribuidores, coste de los *distributor's costs*
distributiva, investigación *marketing research*
diurno, trabajo *daytime work*
diversificación de los riesgos *spread of risk*
diversas, cuentas *sundry accounts*
diversos *miscellaneous, sundries*
–, acreedores *sundry creditors*
dividendo *dividend*
– a fin de año *year-end dividend*
– anticipado *advanced dividend*
– de liquidación *liquidating dividend*
– decretado *declared dividend*
– diferido *deferred dividend*
– en especie *dividend in kind*
– incluído, con *cum dividend*
– no reclamado *unclaimed dividend*
– ocasional *irregular dividend*
– omitido *passed dividend*
– parcial *interim dividend*
– preferente *preferred dividend*
dividendos *dividends*
– devengados *dividend income*
– en acciones *stock dividends*
– en efectivo *cash dividends*
– por cobrar *dividends receivable*
– por pagar *dividends payable*
–, pago de *payment of dividends*
divisa o lema *motto, slogan*
divisas *foreign exchange*
– de valor estable *hard currency*
–, activo en *foreign-exchange assets*
división *division, distribution, department*
– del trabajo *division of labour, division of work*
–, director comercial de *divisional merchandise manager*
–, signo de *division sign*
divisional, moneda *subsidiary money*
divulgación *spread*

divulgador *spreader*
doble *double*
– tributación *double taxation*
–, contabilidad por partida *double-entry book-keeping*
–, indemnización *double damages*
–, jornada *double shift*
–, partida *double entry*
–, patrón *double standard*
–, responsabilidad *double liability*
–, tiempo *double time*
docimador *tester*
documentación, servicio de *documentation service*
documental *documentary*
documentario comercial, crédito *commercial documentary credit*
–, crédito *documentary credit*
documento de cambio *bill of exchange*
– de crédito *credit instrument*
documentos *documents*
– contra aceptación *documents against acceptance*
– de cuentas a cobrar *accounts receivable documents*
– de embarque *shipping documents*
– impresos como salida de información *printed output for data*
– por cobrar *notes payable*
–, aceptación contra *acceptance against documents*
–, clasificación de *documentary classification*
–, giro sin *clean draft*
–, pago contra *cash against documents*
–, servicio de reproducción de *documentary reproduction service*
dólar publicitario *advertising dollar*
–, zona del *dollar area*
dólares, déficit de *dollar gap, dollar shortage*
–, escasez de *dollar gap*
–, mercancías pagaderas en *dollar commodities*

dolo *fraud*
doméstica, economía *home economics*
doméstico *address*
– social *place of business*
domésticos, productos *home goods*
domicilio, libre de gastos a *delivered free*
–, entrega a *home delivery*
–, puesto a *delivered free*
–, trabajador a *homeworker*
–, vendedor a *canvasser, peddler*
dominante, precio *prevailing price*
dominio *eminent domain*
don de mando *leadership*
donaciones, impuesto sobre *gift tax*
donador *donor*
donar *to donate*
dotación de personal *allocation*
– de personal, comité *allocation committee*
dotal, póliza *endowment policy*
–, seguro *endowment insurance*
dote *endowment*
duda *doubt*
dudoso, activo *doubtful assets*
–, crédito *doubtful credit*
–, cuenta de cobro *doubtful account*
–, deudor *doubtful debtor*
dueño *owner*
–, comprar por cuenta del *to buy in*
dumping ofensivo *obnoxious dumping*
–, rebaja del *margin of dumping*
duplicado *duplicate*
duplo *double*
durables, bienes *durable goods*
duración de la aceleración *acceleration time*
– de funcionamiento *time rating*
– de la puesta a punto *adjustment time*
– del funcionamiento *tool life*
– del turno *shift time*
– media de vida *life expectancy*
duradero *durable*

E

economía *economy, savings, economics*
- agrícola *agricultural economics*
- cerrada *closed economy*
- de mano de obra *labour*
- de monocultivo *one-crop economy*
- de tiempo *timesaving*
- deficitaria *deficit economy*
- dirigida *centrally planned economy, directed economy*
- doméstica *home economics*
- no monetaria *non-cash economy*
- planificada *planned economy*
- política *political economy*
-, licenciado en *economist*
económica *economic*
-, autonomía *economic self-sufficiency*
-, baja *business depression*
-, balanza *balance of international payments*
-, capacidad *financial standing*
-, corriente *economic flow*
-, coyuntura *economic policy*
-, crisis *depression, economic crisis*
-, educación *economic education*
-, estabilización *package deal*
-, estructura *economic pattern*
-, guerra *economic warfare*
-, ignorancia *economic ignorance*
-, planeación *economic planning*
-, política *economic policy*
-, potencialidad *economic possibilites*
-, programación *economic planning*
-, recuperación *business recovery*
-, renta *economic profit*
-, responsabilidad *financial liability*
-, solvencia *financial responsibility*
-, vida *economic life*
económicas básicas, tendencias *basic economic trends*
-, decisiones *economic decisions*
-, necesidades *economic needs*
-, sanciones *economic sanctions*
económico *economic*
- comprensivo, control *comprehensive economic control*
-, año *fiscal year*
-, auge *prosperity*
-, ciclo *trade cycle*
-, crecimiento *economic growth*

-, desarrollo *economic development*
-, determinismo *economic determinism*
-, período *accounting period*
-, proceso *economic process*
-, receso *business depression*
-, rendimiento *commercial efficiency*
-, respaldo *financial backing*
-, sistema *economic system*
económico-social, clase *socio-economic class*
económicos, costos *economic costs*
-, intereses *financial interests*
-, problemas *economic problems*
-, recursos *financial resources*
economista *economist*
- doméstico *home economist*
-, consultor *economic adviser*
economizador de mano de obra *labour-saving*
economizar *to economize, to save*
ecos *advertising news*
edad *age*
- de jubilación *retirement age*
-, límite de *age limit*
-, mayor de *of age*
-, menor de *minor*
edades determinadas, grupo de *age group*
edición *edition, issue*
- anual *annual issue*
-, contrato de *publishing contract*
edificio comercial *business premises*
editor, consultor técnico de un *reader*
editora, casa *publishing house*
editorialista *columnist*
educación económica *economic education*
efectiva, demanda *effective demand*
-, fecha *value date, pay day*
-, pérdida *actual loss*
-, pérdida total *absolute total loss*
-, producción *actual attainment, actual output*
-, rebaja *actual markdown*
-, rentabilidad *income basis*
efectivas, compras *actual purchases*
-, existencias *actual stock*
-, ventas *actual sales*
efectividad de las ventas *selling effectiveness*
efectivo en caja *cash-on-hand*
-, activo en *cash assets*
-, coste *actual cost*

–, costo *actual cost*
–, dinero *hard money*
–, dividendos en *cash dividends*
–, fondos en *cash funds, monies*
–, hacer *to cash, to collect*
–, pagadero en *payable in cash*
–, pagar en *to pay cash*
–, pasivo *actual liabilities*
–, premio en *cash award*
–, rendimiento en *actual output*
–, reserva en *cash reserve*
–, retirar *to draw cash*
–, retiro en *cash withdrawal*
–, valor *cash value*
–, saldo en *cash balance*
efecto *effect*
– a cobrar *notes receivable*
– a pagar *bills payable*
– a la vista *sight draft*
– acumulativo *cumulative effect*
– mercantil *trade bills*
efectos comerciales, aval de *accommodation endorsement*
– de favor *accommodation papers*
– inflacionistas *inflationary effects*
efectuar el pago *to effect payment*
eficacia de la formación *training effectivenesss*
– marginal del capital *marginal efficiency of capital*
– publicitaria *advertising effectiveness*
–, prueba de *efficiency test*
eficiencia administrativa *clerical efficiency*
égida *aegis*
ejecución *performance*
– del trabajo *job performance*
– media *average performance*
–, promedio de *average performance*
ejecutivo *executive*
–, comité *executive committee*
–, secretario *executive secretary*
ejemplar *copy*
– completo, comprobante en *complete voucher copy*
– comprobante *checking copy*
– de muestra *sample copy*
ejercicio *business year, annual fiscal period*
– anual *calendar year, annual fiscal period*
– fiscal *fiscal year, annual fiscal period*
–, fin del *end of period*
elaboración *process, processing*
– de datos, máquina electrónica de *electronic data-processing machine*
– electrónica de datos *electronic data processing*
–, equipo de *processing equipment*
–, error de *processing error*

–, impuesto por *processing tax*
–, proceso de *processing order*
elaborador *processor*
elasticidad de la oferta *elasticity of supply*
–, coeficiente de *coefficient of elasticity*
elección del comprador *buyer's choice*
–, libre de *free choice*
elecciones *polling*
electoral, plataforma *electoral platform*
eléctrica de contabilidad, máquina *electric accounting machine*
– de sumar, máquina *electric adding machine*
eléctrico, cinta del indicador *ticker tape*
electrodomésticos, artículos *appliances*
electrónica, calculadora *electronic calculator*
– de contabilidad, máquina *electronic bookkeeping machine*
– de datos, máquina *electronic data machine*
– de dictados, máquina *electronic dictating machine*
– de elaboración de datos, máquina *electronic data-processing machine*
–, computadora *digital computer*
–, sumadora *electronic adder*
electrónico, cerebro *electronic brain*
–, cinta del indicador *ticker tape*
–, elemento *electronic element*
elemental, movimiento *elemental movement*
elemento *element*
– cíclico *cyclic or repetitive element*
– de trabajo *work element*
– externo *external element*
– extraño *incidental or occasional element*
– irregular *incidental or occasional element*
– reiterativo *repetitive or cyclic element*
– repetitivo *repetitive or cyclic element*
elementos visibles de comercio *visible items of trade*
– de producción *capital goods*
elevadora con horquilla, carretilla *forklift truck*
elevar *to raise or increase*
– al máximo *to maximize*
eliminar *to write off*
embalador *packer*
embalaje *packing*
– normal *standard packing*
– para exportación *export packing*
– tipo *standard packing*
–, costos de *packing expenses*
–, especificaciones de *packing list*
–, gastos de *packing expenses*
–, instrucciones para *packing instructions*
–, papel de *wrapping paper*
embarcar *to load or ship*
embargados, venta de bienes *distress sale*

embargo *embargo, seizure*
– precautorio *lien*
–, orden de *distress warrant*
embarque *shipment*
– aéreo, conocimiento de *air waybill*
–, aviso de *shipping notice*
–, conocimiento de *lading*
–, documentos de *shipping documents*
–, gastos de *shipping charges*
–, puerto de *port of origin, port of shipment*
embotellamiento *bottleneck*
emergencia, crédito de *stopgap loan*
–, puerto de *distress port*
emergentes, daños *consequential damages*
emigrante *migratory worker*
eminente *topnotch*
–, dominio *eminent domain*
–, personaje *luminary*
emisión *issue*
– de acciones *shares issue*
– de billetes de banco *banknotes issue*
– de obligaciones *bonds issue*
– de radio *radio broadcast*
– de últimas noticias *newscast*
– diferida *delayed broadcast*
– excesiva *overissue*
– monetaria *money issue*
–, banco de *bank of issue*
–, precio de *issue price*
–, prima de *stock premium*
–, valor de *issue price*
emisor, banco *bank of issue*
emisoras de televisión, red de *televisión network*
emitidas, acciones *issued stock*
–, cédulas *warrants issued*
emitido por la compañía, capital *company's issued capital*
emitir, compraventa de acciones por *when-issued trading*
emoción *emotion*
emolumento *salary, fee*
empacar *to pack*
empadronamiento *census, tax list*
empalmar *to abut*
empaquetado *packing*
empaquetador *packer*
empeñar *to pawn*
empeorar *to impair*
empírico *empirical*
–, método de prueba *empirical test method*
empirismo *empiricism*
emplazados, control de carteles *traffic audit*
emplazamiento *position*
– de huelga *strike call*
empleado *employee, clerk*

– administrativo de oficina *office clerk*
– de oficina *white-collar worker*
– pagador *pay clerk*
– que trabaja para varios patronos *part-timer*
–, manual del *employee handbook or manual*
–, pagar y despedir un *to pay off*
–, relaciones entre empresario y *employer-employee relations*
empleados de oficina, selección de *office employees' selection*
– solo parte de la jornada *part-time employee*
– y obreros, cooperación por o para los *employee cooperation*
–, adiestramiento de los *employee training*
–, liquidación por o para los *employees' settlement*
–, manual para *employee handbook*
–, sugerencias de los *employee suggestion*
emplear *to employ or hire*
empleo *employment, job*
– reducido *part-time employment*
– solicitado *employment wanted*
– total *full employment*
–, cese de *labour layoff*
–, cláusula de *employment clause*
–, condiciones de *labour market*
–, contrato de *employment contract, contract of hire*
–, demanda de *labour demand*
–, oferta de *employment offers*
–, separación de *dismissal*
–, solicitar *to look for a job*
–, solicitud de *application for employment*
empleos sucesivos, entre *between jobs*
empresa *enterprise, company*
– al por mayor *wholesale enterprise, wholesale firm*
– auxiliar *ancillary undertaking*
– clasificada *rated concern*
– comercial *business house*
– de servicio público *utility*
– estatal *government enterprise*
– filial *ancillary undertaking*
– inversionista de capital limitado *closed-end investment company*
– matriz *parent company*
– o tienda al detalle *retail enterprise*
– o tienda al por mayor *wholesale enterprise*
– rentable *profitable enterprise*
–, acuerdo de *factory agreement*
–, comité de *works or shop committee*
–, consejo de *working council*
–, consejo de producción de la *joint production committee*
–, jurados de *employee participation in management*

–, libertad de *free enterprise*
–, libre *free enterprise*
empresas contables *accounting firms*
–, mancomunidad de *pool*
–, utilidades de las *corporate earnings*
empréstito *loan*
– de amortización *amortization or sinking-fund loan*
– de guerra *war loan*
– exterior *foreign loan*
– interior *domestic loan*
en actividad normal *in working order*
– almacén *in stock*
– cartelera *billing*
– cartoné *in paper boards*
– curso de fabricación *in progress*
– depósito *on deposit*
– descubierto *overdraw*
– dinero efectivo *in cash*
– disponibilidad *on hand*
– el mercado *in the market*
– especie *in kind*
– estado de nuevo *in mint condition*
– estado de venta *in saleable condition*
– existencia *in stock or store*
– existencia o venta *in print*
– letras grandes *in black print*
– plena actividad *in full swing*
– proceso *work in process*
– rama *in quires or sheets*
– serie *assembly line*
– suspenso *in abeyance*
– tela *in cloth boards*
enajenación *abalienation*
enajenar *to alienate*
encaje de oro *gold reserve*
encalmado, mercado *quiet market*
encarecer *to raise the price*
encarecimiento *rise in price*
encargado *foreman*
– de almacén *stockroom clerk*
– de existencias *stock clerk*
– de la valoración de trabajos *job evaluator*
– de las relaciones públicas *public relations officer*
– de los comprobantes *voucher clerk*
– de los ficheros *file clerk*
– de pruebas *tester*
– de tienda *store manager*
– del correo *mail clerk*
encartonado *in boards*
encuesta *survey*
– anual *annual survey*
– de opiniones *opinion survey*
– en campaña *field survey*
– mediante entrevistas *field survey*

– piloto *pilot survey*
– por correo *postal survey*
– por muestras *sample survey*
– sobre el análisis del trabajo *work analysis survey*
– sobre el mercado *market survey*
– sobre el personal *personnel survey*
– sobre tendencias de marca *brand trend survey*
–, datos de una *survey data*
–, investigación por *survey research*
encuestas masivas por muestreo *massive sampling survey*
– sobre el terreno *field surveys*
–, error de *error in surveys*
–, investigación por *survey research*
endosar *to endorse*
endoso *endorsement*
– absoluto *absolute endorsement*
– anterior *previous endorsement*
– calificado *qualified endorsement*
– condicional *conditional endorsement*
– en blanco *blank endorsement*
– por aval *accommodation endorsement*
enfermedad profesional *occupational disease*
–, seguro de *health insurance*
enfocada, zona *coverage*
enfoque *approach*
– cualitativo *qualitative approach*
– de la distribución selectiva *selective distribution approach*
– de la publicidad *advertising approach*
– de ventas *sales approach*
– estadístico *statistical approach*
– mercadológico *marketing approach*
– sistemático *systematic approach*
enganche *down payment, deposit*
engañar *to defraud*
engaño *fraud*
engañoso *misleading*
engomada, etiqueta *sticker*
enjuiciar *to bring a suit*
enlace del personal *shop steward*
enmienda *amendment*
enriquecerse *to get rich*
ensambladora, planta *assembling plant*
ensamblaje, tren de *assembly or production line*
ensayador *tester, scanner*
ensayo *assay, test sample*
–, campaña de *try-out campaign, test campaign*
–, muestra para *test sample*
–, pedido de *trial order*
–, prueba *prediction test*
–, test de *prediction test*

enseñanza *education, instruction, practice*
–, material de *training aid*
enseres *fixtures*
entendido en negocios *businesslike*
–, valor *value agreed upon*
entendimiento *understanding, agreement*
entero, número *whole number*
entidad *entity*
entintada, cinta *inked ribbon*
entrada *entrance revenue*
– en el debe *debit entry*
–, señal de *cue*
entradas *receipts, turnover*
– a caja *cash receipts*
– brutas *gross income, revenue*
– de cierre *closing entries*
– y salidas *receipts and expenditures*
entre empleos sucesivos *between jobs*
entrega *delivery*
– a domicilio *home delivery*
– de pedidos *order delivery*
– futura *future delivery*
– futura, productos para *commodity futures*
– inmediata *special or spot delivery*
– inmediata, correo de *special-delivery mail*
– y pago inmediato, orden para *spot order*
–, cobrar a la *to collect on delivery*
–, coste de *delivery cost*
–, fecha de *delivery date*
–, hacer *to deliver*
–, orden de *delivery order*
–, pago contra *cash on delivery*
–, plazo de *time of delivery*
–, términos de *time of delivery*
entregado al costado del vapor *delivered alongside*
–, valor *surrender value*
entregar, pagadero al *cash on delivery*
entrenamiento *training, instruction, education*
– anual, coste de *annual upkeep cost*
entrevista a los consumidores *consumer interview*
– a los detallistas *dealer interview*
– con el comerciante *dealer interview*
– de asesoramiento *counselling interview*
– no preparada *non-structured interview*
– personal *oral interview*
– por teléfono *telephone interview*
entrevistador *interviewer*
entrevistar *interviewing*
entrevistas de colocación *enployment interviews*
– no estructuradas *unstructured interviews*
–, encuesta mediante *field surveys*

–, informes de *interview reports*
envasar *to can or pack*
envase *packing, container*
– en cajas *boxing*
– ficticio *dummy package*
– normal *standard packing*
–, prototipo de *standard packing*
enviada, información *release*
enviar fondos *to remit funds*
envío contra reembolso *c.o.d. shipment, cash on delivery shipment*
– o remesa *sending*
envíos a cuenta de pedidos a servir *advance payments on purchase obligations*
–, agente de *forwarding agent*
envoltorios *wrappers*
envoltura *wrapping*
envolver, máquina para *wrapping machine*
–, papel de *wrapping paper*
epígrafe *caption*
equilibrado *balanced*
–, control *balanced or coordinated control*
equilibrio *equilibrium*
– del comercio exterior *balance of trade*
–, nivel de *equilibrium level*
–, punto de *break-even point*
–, valor de *equilibrium value*
equipajes, despacho u oficina de *receiving office*
–, oficina de *receiving office*
equipo *equipment, team, working group, plant*
– asesor *staff*
– de elaboración *processing equipment*
– de fábrica, modernización del *plant modernization*
– de material de escritorio *stationery equipment*
– de ocasión *used equipment*
– de oficina *office equipment*
– de perforación de fichas *punched card equipment*
– de proyectos, director *project leader*
– industrial *capital goods*
–, jefe de *ganger, leading hand, leadman, charge hand*
–, maquinaria y *machinery and equipment*
–, mobiliario y *furniture and fixtures*
–, trabajo de *group work, team work*
equipos de oficina, normalización de *office equipment standards*
equitativa, remuneración *adequate compensation*
equitativo *equitable*
equivocación *fluff*
erario *public treasury*

erogación *expenditure*
error *error*
- compensador *counter error*
- constante *systematic error*
- cuadrático medio *mean-square error*
- de azar *random error*
- de azar en el muestreo *random sampling error*
- de cálculo *miscalculation*
- de elaboración *processing error*
- de muestreo *sampling error*
- de primera especie *error of first kind*
- del muestreo aleatorio *random sampling error*
- en encuestas *error in surveys*
- medio *mean error*
- normal de muestreo *normal sampling error*
- prescrito *prescribed error*
- probable *probable error*
- u omisión, salvo *error and omissions excepted*
-, zona de *error band*
errores compensados *compensating errors*
-, combinación de *pooling errors*
escala *scale*
- comercial, producción en *commercial scale production*
- de aumentos *sliding scale*
- de liquidez *scale of liquidity*
- de progresión *scale of progression*
- de repartición *scale of apportioment*
- de salarios *salary range or scale*
- de sueldos *wage scale*
- de sueldos según productividad *incentive wages*
- de taras *tare bar*
- de valoración *rating scale*
- de valoración del trabajo *job evaluation scale*
- de valores *range of values*
- graudal de salarios *sliding scale*
- móvil *sliding scale*
-, puerto de *port of call*
-, viaje sin *non-stop trip*
escalabilidad, análisis de *scalability analysis*
escalado *scaling*
escalafón de antigedad *seniority list*
escalafones de mando inferiores *lower executive echelons*
escalar, análisis *scale analysis, scale research*
escalas de clasificación de personal *personnel rating scales*
escalogramático, análisis *scalogram analysis*
escalonada, prima *stepped bonus*
-, tarifa *step rate, sliding scale, scale of discounts*

escaparate *shop-window*
- de tienda *store window*
-, cartel de *window card*
escaparates, decorador de *window dresser*
-, material para exposición de *window display material*
escaparatista *window dresser*
escape, cláusula de *escape clause*
escasa demanda *little demand*
- ganancia *small profit*
escasez *scarcity, shortage*
- de capitales *scarcity of capital*
- de crédito *credit squeeze*
- de dólares *dollar gap*
- de especialistas *talent shortage*
- de viviendas *housing shortage*
escaso *scarce*
escena, jefe de *floor manager*
escote *quota*
escribir de nuevo *re-write*
-, máquina de *typewriter*
escrito, acuerdo por *written agreement*
-, por *in writing*
escritor *writer*
escritorio *desk*
-, artículos de *stationery*
-, equipo de material de *stationery equipment*
-, objetos de *office equipment*
escritura *legal instrument, contract, indenture*
- a mano *handwriting*
- constitutiva *corporation charter, incorporation papers*
- constitutiva y estatutos *constitution and bylaws*
- de asociación *articles of partnership*
- de compraventa *bill of sale*
- de hipoteca *mortgage deed*
- de sociedad *incorporation papers*
- de ventas *bill of sale*
escrutinio *polls*
- de la opinión pública *public opinion polls*
escuela comercial *business school*
esenciales, industrias *key industries*
esfera *sphere, area*
- de actividad *field of activity*
- esterlina *sterling area*
esforzarse *to endeavour*
esfuerzo *endeavour, effort, exertion, strain, stress*
- de ventas *selling effort*
- máximo *all-out effort*
esfuerzos de exploración mercadológica *marketing efforts*
- de publicidad *advertising efforts*
espacio de muestreo *sample space*
- en blanco *space*

–, alternación de *alternation of stress*
especialista en finanzas *financial specialist*
– en previsión de ventas *sales forecaster*
– en relaciones públicas *public relations specialist*
– o perito en mercadología *market expert*
especialistas, escasez de *talent shortage*
especie, aportación en *assets in kind*
–, dinero o *currency or specie*
–, dividendo en *dividend in kind*
–, en *in kind*
–, inversión en *investment in kind*
–, pago en *payment in kind*
especificación de pruebas abreviadas *abbreviated test specifications*
– del trabajo *job or work specification*
–, proyecto de *draft specification*
especificaciones de embalaje *packing list*
específico *specific*
espécimen *specimen*
espectáculos, impuesto sobre *admissions tax*
especulación a la baja *bear market*
especulador *speculator, dealer*
especular *to speculate*
– en fondos públicos, combinación para *pool*
especulativo *speculative, for profit*
–, motivo *speculative motive*
espera *delay, interruption, stoppage*
– evitable *avoidable delay*
– inevitable *unavoidable delay*
–, tiempo de *waiting time*
esperadas, utilidades *anticipated profits*
espiral de costos y precios *cost-price spiral*
esqueleto *blank*
esquema *plan, diagram, pattern, frame*
– de especificaciones, diseño o *specifications drawing*
– sistemático *systematic structure*
esquematizar *to outline*
estabilidad *stability, steadiness, consistency*
– de precios *price steadiness*
– financiera *financial stabilization*
–, prueba de *stability test*
estabilización *stabilization, equalization*
– de precios *price strengthening*
– económica *package deal*
–, fondo de *equalization fund*
estable *stable*
–, mercado *close market*
–, moneda *sound money, hard currency*
–, precio *close price*
establecido *stable*
–, salario *stated salary*
establecimiento *works*
– de valores, títulos u obligaciones *security house*

– de venta, gran *emporium*
–, director de *store manager*
estación *season*
estacional *seasonal*
–, cálculo *seasonal computation*
–, desempleo *seasonal unemployment*
estacionales, cambios *seasonal changes*
–, variaciones *seasonal changes*
estadística *statistics*
– cronológica *chronological statistics*
– de ventas *sales statistics*
–, cuantificación *statistical frequency*
–, información *statistical information*
–, investigación *statistical research*
estadísticas de producción *production statistics*
– vitales *vital statistics*
estadísticos *statistical*
– de calidad, control *statistical quality control*
–, análisis *statistical analysis*
–, enfoque *statistical approach*
–, extensímetro *statistical strain gauge*
–, investigador *statistical researcher*
–, mayor *statistical ledger*
–, muestreo *statistical sampling*
estado *condition, status, stage, state, rank*
– a sus proveedores, anticipo del *imprest*
– anual *annual report*
– comparativo *comparative statement*
– de balance comparativo *comparative balance sheet*
– de cuentas *statement of account, bank statement, statement*
– de ingresos *statement of income*
– de liquidación *liquidation statement*
– de nuevo, en *in mint condition*
– de operación *operating statement*
– de pérdidas y ganancias *profit and loss statement*
– financiero *financial statement*
–, banco del *government bank*
–, bono del *government bond, state bond*
–, secretaría de *ministry*
–, valores del *government bonds*
estados, analista *forms analyst*
estafa *fraud*
estafar *to defraud*
estaje (AC) *taskwork*
estanco *forestalling, engrossing, cornering*
estándar de vida *standard of living*
estante de acero para archivar correspondencia *steel filing-cabinet*
estante *shelf*
estantería *shelf*
estarcio, multicopista de *duplicator stencil*
estarcir *to stencil*

estatal, banco *government bank*
–, empresa *government enterprise*
–, impuesto *state tax*
estatales, impuestos *state taxes*
estatuarios, miembros *standing-request members*
estatuto de limitaciones *statute of limitations*
estatutos *articles of association, bylaws*
estenografía *stenography*
esterlina *sterling*
–, esfera *sterling area*
–, libra *pound sterling*
estilo *style*
estilográfica *fountain pen*
estimación *appraisal, estimate*
– crediticia *credit rating*
– de lineal *lineal estimation*
estimado, costo *estimated cost*
–, tiempo *estimated time*
estimador *estimator*
estimativo *estimated*
estímulo *inventive*
– subliminal *subliminal stimulus*
estipulaciones *stipulations*
– de salarios *salary stipulations*
– en política impositiva *canons of taxation*
estipulada, prima *stiuplated premium*
estrategia en la dirección del mercado *market management strategy*
– mercadológica *marketing strategy*
estrato *stratum*
estratos *strata*
estraza, papel de *kraft paper*
estrecha, tarifa *tight rate, tight piece rate*
estreno *debut, premiere, first performance*
estructura *pattern, structure*
– de capital *capital structure*
– de la estructura latente *latent structure analysis*
– de organización *organization structure*
– de salarios *wage structure*
– del capital *capital structure*
– del muestreo *sampling structure*
– económica *economic pattern*
– funcional *staff structure*
estructuración *implementation*
estructuradas, entrevistas no *unstructured interviews*
estructural, característica *structural feature*
estudio *survey*
– artístico *studio*
– conjunto *joint study*
– cronológico *chronological study*
– de métodos, ingeniero encargado del *methods engineer*
– de orientación *pilot study*

– de tiempos de fabricación *time study*
– de tiempos por cronómetro *stopwatch time study*
– del mercado *market study*
– del trabajo *work study*
– general *overall study*
– o taller *studio*
– preliminar *preliminary study or investigation*
estudios de proyectos, personal de *design engineering staff*
etapa piloto *pilot stage*
ética, código de *code of ethics*
etiqueta *ticket, slip, docket, label*
– de almacén *bin tag*
– engomada *sticker*
etiquetas, máquina de *labelling machine*
evadir impuestos *to evade taxes*
evaluación *rating, appraisal*
evaluar *to appraise or evaluate*
evasión *evasion, suppression*
– de impuestos *tax evasion, tax dodging*
– fiscal *tax evasion*
evasor, contribuyente *tax evader*
eventual, personal *temporary workers*
–, trabajador *casual worker*
evidente *apparent*
evitable, espera *avoidable delay*
–, retraso *avoidable delay*
evolución desfavorable *worsening*
ex muelle *ex-dock*
exacta, copia *close copy*
–, suma *amount certain*
–, traducción *close translation*
examen *exam, survey*
– atento *close examination*
excedente *surplus*
– de capital *capital surplus*
– resultante de la retasación de bienes *appraisal surplus*
–, utilidades *excess profits*
excesiva, emisión *ove-rissue*
–, inversión *over-investment*
excesivas, compras *overbuying*
excesivo *excessive*
exceso *excess, surplus*
– de existencias *overstock*
– de peso *overweight*
– de producción *glut*
excitada, multitud *mob*
exclusión, cláusula de *exclusion clause, closed-shop provision*
exclusividad, cláusula contractual de *competition clause, exclusivity speculation*
exclusivo, agente *sole agent*
–, derecho *sole right*
excluyentes, clases mutuamente *mutually*

exclusive classes
exención *exemption*
– de impuestos *tax exemption*
exentas de pago, lista de personas *tax-free list*
– de derechos, mercancías *free goods*
exento *exempt, free*
– de derechos *duty-free*
exentos de derechos, lista de artículos *tax-free list*
exhibición de primeros modelos *first-sample showing*
–, sala de *showroom*
exhibido, capital *paid-in capital*
exigente *fastidious*
existencia al detalle, promedio de *average retail stock*
– inicial *initial inventory*
– mínima *basic stock*
–, en *on hand, in stock*
–, falto de *out of stock*
–, ficha de *store record card*
existencias *stock, merchandise inventory*
– efectivas *actual stock*
– en almacén, rotación de *stock turnover*
– estabilizadas, política de *buffer stock plan*
– y giro, proporción entre *stock-turnover ratio*
– y ventas, proporción entre *stock-sales ratio*
–, comprobación en unidades de las *unit stock control*
–, control de *stock control*
–, encargado de *stock clerk*
–, exceso de *overstock*
–, ficha de control de *stock control card*
–, giro de *stock turnover*
–, hacer recuento de *to take stock*
–, libro de *stock book*
–, merma de las *stock shortage*
–, movimiento de *inventory turnover*
–, promedio de giro de *stock turnover rate*
–, registro de *stock record*
expansión *expansion*
– crediticia *credit expansion*
– vertical *vertical expansion*
–, cliente en *prospective client*
–, fondo de *development*
expansionista del mercado, tendencia *increasing share of market*
expectativa, ventas en *expected sales*
expedición, costos *shipping charges*
–, recibo de *forwarding receipt*
expediciones, servicio de *distribution department*
expediente *file, record, docket file*
expeditar *to expedite or facilitate*
expeditor *shipper, forwarder*
expensar *to finance*

expensión *financing*
experiencia, crédito por la *experience credit*
experiencias, cambio de *test size*
experimental, investigación *experimental research*
–, trabajo *experimental work*
experto *expert*
expertos, grupo de *brains trust*
exploración mercadológica, esfuerzos de *marketing efforts*
explorador *scanner, analyser*
explotable *workable*
explotación de obreros *sweating*
–, beneficios de *operating profit*
–, capital de *working capital*
–, carga de *traffic load*
–, cuenta de *work account, trading account*
–, gastos de *operating expenses, working expenses*
–, material de *working material*
explotar a obreros *to sweat*
exponer *to describe*
exportación *export, output*
–, arancel de *duties on exports*
–, artículos de *export commodities or goods*
–, comercio de *export trade*
–, cuota de *export quota*
–, declaración de *export declaration*
–, derechos de *export duty*
–, embalaje de *export packing*
–, gerente de *export manager*
–, impuesto a la *export duty*
–, licencia de *export permit*
–, permiso de *export permit*
–, precio de *export price*
–, prima de *drawback*
–, sección de *export department*
–, subsidios para la *export subsidies*
exportaciones clave *key exports*
– invisibles *invisible exports*
exportador *exporter*
exportadora, casa *export house*
exportar *to export*
exposición *display, exposition, fair, parade, exhibition*
– de automóviles *motor or automobile show*
– de casos *case history*
– de escaparates, material para *window display material*
– de mercancías *merchandise display*
– de modas *fashion show*
– de mostrador *counter display*
– de muestras *sample display*
– deficiente *poor display*
– inferior *interior display*
exposiciones comerciales *trade shows*

–, material para *material for exhibitions*
expositivo interior, puesto *floor stand*
expositor *showcase, gondola*
– interior, puesto *floor stand*
exprés *express*
expropiar *to expropriate*
extensible, mercado *expansible market*
extensímetro estadístico *statistical strain guage*
extensión de créditos *credit extension*
– de la muestra *sample size*
– de onda *wave length*
exterior, balanza de pagos al *balance of external payments*
–, comercio *foreign trade*
–, deuda *external or foreign debt*
–, empréstito *foreign loan*
–, equilibrio del comercio *balance of trade*
externo, descuento *true discount*
–, elemento *external element*
–, trabajo *outside or external work*
extra *extra*

–, comercio *foreign trade*
extracto *syllabus, abstract*
– de cuenta *statement of account*
– de cuenta corriente *abstract of current account*
extranjera, competencia *foreign competition*
–, crédito en moneda *credit in foreign exchange*
–, moneda *foreign exchange*
–, compras en el *foreign buying*
extranjeros, productos *foreign products*
extraño, elemento *incidental or occasional element*
extraoficial *unofficial*
extraordinarias, horas *overtime, after hours*
–, sesión *special meeting*
extraordinario, trabajo *overtime work*
extraordinarios, impuesto sobre beneficios *excess profits tax*
extrapolarización *extrapolation*
extras, obras *variations*
–, trabajo a horas *overtime work*

F

fábrica *factory, mill, plant, works*
- con obreros sindicados *closed shop*
- de conservas *cannery*
-, cerrar una *to close down*
-, director de *factory, plant or works manager*
-, franco en *ex-factory, ex-mill*
-, marca de *trade mark*
-, personal de *plant personnel*
-, precios de *manufacturer's price*
-, producción de *plant output*
fabricación *manufacture*
- continua *straight-line or continuous production*
- de utillaje, taller de *tool room*
- en cadena *flow or line production*
- en proceso *goods in process*
- en serie *mass production*
-, certificado de *certificate of manufacture*
-, coste de *production cost*
-, costo de *prime cost*
-, en curso de *in process, in progress*
-, estudios de tiempos de *time study*
-, gastos de *manufacturing expenses*
-, gerencia de *production department*
-, materiales en curso de *in-process materials*
-, orden de *factory order, work order*
-, precio de *factory price*
-, procedimiento de *manufacturing process*
-, proceso de *factory process*
-, programa de *manufacturing schedule*
-, tiempo de *task time, production time*
-, tiempo total de *total process time*
-, tolerancia de *factory limits*
fabricante *manufacturer*
fabricar *to manufacture*
fábricas, automatización de las *factory automation*
fácil, mercado *easy market*
facilidades *facilities*
- de pago *easy terms of payment, easy payments*
- de pago, con *by easy payments*
factible *workable, feasible*
factor *factor*
- de aumento *raising factor*
- de compensación *balancing factor*
- de descuento *discount factor*
- de motivación *motivation factor*

- de producción *output factor*
- de tolerancia *tolerance factor*
- de trabajo *work or job factor*
- determinante del precio *price-determining factor*
- humano *human factor*
- para rectificar *calibrating factor*
- producto *input-output*
- real de la depreciación *effective depreciation factor*
-, gravamen de *factor's lien*
factores *factors*
- compensatorios *offsetting factors*
- de producción *production factors*
- de producción, ingreso de los *factor income*
-, análisis de *factor analysis*
-, coste de *factor cost*
-, costo marginal de los *marginal factor set*
factura *bill, invoice*
- comercial *commercial invoice*
- consular *consular invoice*
- de publicidad *advertising bill or invoice*
- de venta *bill of sale*
- definitiva *final invoice*
- detallada *itemized invoice*
-, costo según *invoice cost*
-, precio de *invoice price*
-, rebaja del precio de *sales allowance*
-, según *as per invoice*
-, tara según *invoice tax*
-, valor de *invoice value*
facturación *billing*
- cíclica *cycle billing*
- de pedidos *order invoice*
- en ciclos *cycle billing*
-, departamento de *billing department*
-, procedimiento de *invoice procedure*
facturar *to bill or invoice*
-, máquina de *billing machine*
facturas, comprobación de *invoice checking*
-, libro de *invoice book*
-, registro de *invoice register*
-, tramitación de *invoice procedure*
facultad *power*
faena *work*
faja o envoltorio *wrapper*
falsa, declaración *false return*
-, moneda *counterfeit currency*

falsificación *forgery*
falsificar *to forge*
– cuentas *to doctor accounts*
falso *false*
–, filete *dead freight*
falta *fault, deficiency, lack*
– de asistencia al trabajo *absence from work*
– de demanda *sales resistance*
– de pago *non-payment*
– de peso *short weight*
– de productos entregables contra contratos *squeeze*
falto de existencia *out of stock*
fama *character*
familia, ingresos por *income per family*
familiar, ingreso *family income*
–, pensión *family allowance*
–, seguro *family insurance*
–, sociedad *family partnership*
familiares, gastos *family expenses*
fanega *bushel*
fantasía, artículos de *fancy goods*
fase *phase, operation*
– descendente *downswing*
fascículo *tract*
fatiga *sweat, fatigue*
–, suplemento por *fatigue allowance, rest allowance*
favor *accommodation*
–, aceptación de *accommodation acceptance*
–, conocimiento de *accommodation bill of lading*
–, letra de *accommodation bill or draft*
favorable *favourable, advantageous*
favorecida, cláusula de la nación más *most favoured nation clause*
febril, mercado *feverish market*
fecha *date*
– de entrega *delivery date, date of delivery*
– de vencimiento *maturity date, due date*
– efectiva *value date, pay day*
– media de vencimiento *equated date*
– prevista de terminación *due date*
– y hora, marcador de *time or clock stamp*
–, sin *undated*
fechador de sellos *date stamp*
–, reloj *time or clock stamp*
feria *fair, market*
– universal *world fair*
fiado, comprar al *to buy on credit*
fiador *bondsman, surety, backer*
fianza *bond, bail, surety*
– de aduana *customs bond*
– de averías *average bond*
– hipotecaria *mortgage*
–, bajo *under bond*

–, otorgar *to put up a bond*
–, seguro y *insurance and bond*
fiar *to give credit*
ficticio, envase *dummy package*
– de acciones de otros, tenedor *dummy-stock holder*
ficha *card, slip, ticket, docket*
– de control de existencias *stock control card*
– de dirección *address card*
– de existencia *store record card*
– de garantía *pledge card*
– de información *inquiry docket*
– de información de órdenes *order information card*
– de registro acumulativo *accumulative record card*
– de reloj *clock or time card*
– de ruta *route or batch card, work label*
– de salida de almacén *stores issued card*
– de tarifas *rate card*
– de tiempo trabajo *attendance card*
– para el grupo de dirección *group address card*
– recordativa *reminder card*
–, perforar una *to punch*
fichas perforadas, máquina de *punched-card machine*
– a gran velocidad, perforación de *high speed punched-card machine*
– perforadas, máquina de *punched-card machine*
–, perforación de *punching*
–, sistema de *filing system*
fichero *file, card file, filing-cabinet*
– central *central file*
– de condiciones de venta *term-card or term-discount file*
– de movimiento *live file*
– de proveedores *resource file*
– de trámite *suspense file*
– giratorio *wheel-type filing system*
– inactivo *storage file*
– maestro *master file*
– permanente *permanent card file*
ficheros, comprobación de *files auditing*
–, encargado de los *file clerk*
fideicomisario de un trust *trustee*
fideicomiso *trust*
– pasivo *passive or dry trust*
–, fondo en *trust fund*
–, póliza de *fidelity bond*
fidelidad, alta *high fidelity*
–, seguro de *fidelity insurance*
fiduciaria, cuenta *trust account*
–, moneda *fiduciary or token money*
fiduciario *fiduciary*

–, banco *trust company*
–, valor *fiduciary value*
fiduciarios, títulos *bonds*
fiel, traducción *close translation*
fija los precios, directivo que *pricing executive*
–, regla *standard*
–, valores de renta *fixed-income securities*
fijación de tarifas *rate fixing, rate setting*
– del precio de la mercancía *merchandise pricing*
– selectiva de precios *discriminatory pricing*
fijador de carteles *bill poster*
– de precios *price leader, price setter*
fijeza *stability, steadiness, consistency*
fijo *fixed*
– de caja, fondo *cash imprest*
– de ventas, precio *fixed selling price*
–, activo *capital assets, fixed capital*
–, cliente *steady customer*
–, coste *fixed cost*
–, pasivo *fixed liabilities*
–, plazo *fixed term*
–, rendimiento *fixed income*
fijos, cargos *fixed charges*
filial *branch, subsidiary*
–, casa *affiliated firm*
–, compañía *affiliated company*
–, corporación *subsidiary company*
–, empresa *ancillary undertaking*
–, sociedad *subsidiary company*
fin *design*
– de año, dividendo a *year-end dividend*
– del ejercicio *end of period*
final *ultimate*
–, consumidor *ultimate consumer*
–, inventario *closing inventory*
–, producto *end product*
–, uso *end use*
finalidad *purpose*
financiación *financing*
–, gastos de *financial expenses*
–, régimen de *financial arrangement*
financiamiento *financing*
– compensatorio *compensatory financing*
– deficitario *deficit financing*
financiar *to finance*
financiera, administración *financial management*
– de compra, capacidad *financial purchasing ability*
–, estabilidad *financial stabilization*
–, situación *financial standing*
–, sociedad *finance company, commercial credit company*
–, táctica *financial policy*
financieras, circunstancias *financial*

conditions
financiero *financial, financier*
– anual, informe *annual financial report*
–, apoyo *financial backing*
–, comité *finance committee*
–, director *controller*
–, estado *financial statement*
–, indicador *financial index, stock market averages*
–, sistema *financial system*
financieros, círculos *financial circles*
–, intereses *financial interest*
–, recursos *financial resources*
financista *financier*
finanzas *finance*
–, altas *high finance*
–, especialista en *financial specialist*
fincas, corredor de *real-estate broker*
finiquitar *to settle and close an account*
finiquito *full settlement, clearance*
finito, multiplicador *finite multiplier*
fino para copias de cartas, papel *copying paper*
firma *firm, signature*
– autorizada *authorized signature*
– comercial *commercial house*
– en blanco *blank signature*
– que anuncia y vende por correo *mail order house*
firmante *signatory*
firmar *to sign*
– mancomunadamente *to sign jointly*
firme, mercado *strong or stiff market*
–, oferta en *firm offer*
–, pedido en *firm order*
firmes, precios *steady prices*
fiscal *auditor, controller, district attorney (Am), fiscal*
–, año *fiscal year*
–, arancel *revenue tariff*
–, avaluo *appraisal for taxation*
–, calibración *assessment*
–, calificación *assessment*
–, cédula *for income-tax*
–, código *tax laws*
–, contabilidad *government accounting*
–, contador *government accountant*
–, declaración *income-tax report*
–, ejercicio *fiscal year, annual fiscal period*
–, evasión *tax evasion*
–, imposición *federal tax (Am)*
–, impuesto *internal revenue tax*
–, inspector *tax examiner*
–, ley *tax law*
–, período *accounting period*
–, tarifa *schedule of import duties*

–, timbre *revenue stamp*
–, tributación *federal tax (Am)*
fiscales, agentes *revenue authorities*
–, posibilidades *financial resources*
–, valores *government bonds*
fiscalización de existencias *stock control*
– de ventas *sales control*
– del presupuesto *budgetary control*
fisco *national treasury*
física, depreciación *physical depreciation*
–, índice de la producción *index of physical production*
físico *physical*
–, inventario *physical inventory*
–, recuerdo *physical inventory*
fletamento aéreo *aircraft chartering, aircraft time-charter*
–, contrato de *contract of affreightment*
fletar *to charter*
flete *freight, freight rate*
– aéreo *air freight*
– de retorno *home freight, return freight*
– falso *dead freight*
– marítimo *ocean freight*
– pagable a destino *freight collect*
– pagado *freight prepaid*
– por carro entero *carload rate*
– por cobrar *freight collect*
– y cambio, costo, seguro, *cost, insurance, freight and change*
floja, demanda *sluggish demand*
flojo, mercado *weak or dull or sagging market*
flotante *floating*
–, deuda *floating debt*
–, pasivo *current liabilities*
fluctuaciones *fluctuations*
– cíclicas *cyclical fluctuations*
– del mercado *market fluctuation*
fluido, multicopista de *duplicator fluid*
flujo de impresos, gráfico del *form flow diagram*
focal, punto *focal point*
folio *folio, page*
folletín *newspaper serial*
folleto *brochure*
– desplegable *folder*
– pequeño *booklet*
fomento *development*
– del comercio *trade promotion*
–, banca del *development bank*
fondo *background, fund*
– de amortización *sinking fund*
– de caja chica *petty-cash fund*
– de contingencia *contingent fund*
– de depreciación *depreciation fund*
– de estabilización *equalization fund*

– de expansión *development fund*
– de huelga *strike fund*
– de pensión *pension fund*
– de pensiones de vejez *superannuation fund*
– de previsión *provident or emergency fund*
– de reserva *reserve fund*
– de seguro propio *insurance fund*
– en fideicomiso *trust fund*
– fijo de caja *cash imprest*
– mutualista *mutual fund*
– para accidentes industriales *industrial insurance fund*
– para imprevistos *contingency fund*
– renovable *revolving fund*
– revolvente *rotary fund*
fondos *funds*
– a, asignar *to appropiate funds to*
– de reserva *account allowances*
– disponibles *available funds, ready cash, cash and bank deposits*
– en efectivo *cash funds, monies*
– insuficientes *no funds, insufficient funds*
– invertidos *invested funds*
– malversados *misapplied funds*
– públicos *government bonds, stock*
– públicos, combinación para especular en *pool*
–, aportar *to finance*
–, asignación de *allocation, allotment*
–, comprobante de retiro de *withdrawal voucher*
–, consignación de *allocation, allotment*
–, enviar *to remit funds*
–, situación de *remittance payment*
forma *pattern, model, form*
– de pago *terms of payment*
–, utilidad de *form utility*
formación *training, practice, education, instruction*
– del personal de servicio detallista *retail-service training*
– profesional *vocational training*
– sobre la marcha *on-the-job training*
– técnica *technical training*
– universitaria *academic training*
–, director de *training director*
–, eficacia de la *training effectiveness*
formulario *blank, set form*
– de necesidades *want slip*
– de pedidos *order form*
– de ventas perdidas *lost-sale slip*
– para valorar los méritos del obrero *employee-rating form*
– tipo *standard blank, standard form*
formularios de verificación de ventas *sales-control forms*

–, analista de *forms analyst*
–, diagrama de procedimiento de *forms or papers procedure chart*
fortuna personal *personal assets, personal estate*
forzar las ventas, habilidad para *high-pressure salesmanship*
forzosa, venta *forced sale*
forzoso, moneda de curso *compulsory currency, flat money*
–, paro *unemployment*
–, retiro *compulsory retirement*
fotocopias, máquina de *photocopy machine*
fotografía profesional *professional photography*
fracaso *rejection*
fraccionamiento *subdivision, development*
– de acciones *share split*
fraccionar *to subdivide*
franco *free, exempt*
– a bordo *free on board*
– de derechos *duty-free*
– de porte *postage-free*
– en el muelle *free on dock*
– en fábrica *ex-factory, ex-mill*
franqueadora, máquina *franking machine*
franqueo *postage*
franquicia *exemption, franchise*
frase central publicitaria *slogan*
fraude *fraud*
fraudulenta, quiebra *fraudulent bankruptcy*
frecuencia *frequency, occurrence*
– de accidentes *accident frequency*
– estadística *statistical frequency*
–, curva de *frequency curve*
–, distribución de *frequency distribution*
frenesí *brainstorm*
freno a la producción *restriction of output*
frialdad *affective rigidity*
frigorífico, almacén *cold storage warehouse*
fuente de información *information source*
fuera de temporada, ventas *off-season sales*
fuerte, precio *published price*
fuerza *force, power, strength*
– de brazos *manpower, work force*
– de trabajo *work force*
– de trabajo, conseguir a *to work out*

– de ventas *sales force*
– mayor *force majeure, act of God*
fulana de tal *Mary Doe (Am)*
fulano de tal *John Doe (Am)*
función *function, operation*
– asesora *advisory function*
– característica operante *operating characteristic function*
– consumo *consumption function*
– de densidad *density function*
– de ponderación *weight function*
– del costo *cost function*
– del riesgo *risk function*
– demanda *demand function*
– mercadológica *marketing function*
funcional, desorden *functional disorder*
–, estructura *staff structure*
–, organización *staff organization*
funcionamiento *working*
– general *overall operation*
– o producción al día *hand-to-mouth working*
–, ciclo de *action cycle*
–, coste de *plant operating cost*
–, datos de *working data*
–, duración de *time rating*
–, duración del *toll life*
–, gastos de *operating expenses*
funcionario *official*
–, alto *high official*
funciones mercadológicas *marketing functions*
–, director en *acting manager*
–, presidente en *acting president*
–, valoración de *function evaluation*
fundación *endowment*
fundador, acciones de *founder's shares*
fundamental, investigación *basic research*
fundo *land property*
furgón *freight car, boxcar*
fusión *merger, merging*
– de intereses *merger of interests*
fusionada, compañía *merged company*
futura, entrega *future delivery*
–, productos para entrega *commodity futures*
futuros *futures*
–, mercado de *futures market*

G

galerada *proof, slip*
ganancia *profit*
– automática *automatic gain*
– bruta *gross profit*
– en las existencias *stock profit*
– íntegra *gross return*
– líquida *clear profit*
– por hora *hourly earnings, earned rate*
– por unidad de tiempo *earned rate, hourly earnings*
– según libros *book profit*
– suplementaria *side profit*
– total *overall gain*
–, arrojar *to show a profit*
–, control automático de *automatic gain control*
–, curva de *earnings or wage curve*
–, denotar una *to show a profit*
–, escasa *small profit*
–, producir una *to yield a profit*
–, reportar una *to yield a profit*
ganancias *gains, profits, income*
– de capital *capital gains*
– íntegras *gross earnings or profits*
– o beneficios compensativos *offsetting gains*
– por intereses *interest earnings*
– potenciales *potential or expected earnings*
– previstas *expected or potential earnings*
– puestas a fondo común *pooled earnings*
–, cuenta de pérdidas y *profit and loss account*
–, cuentas de *income account*
–, estado de pérdidas y *profit and loss statement*
–, participación en las *profit sharing*
–, pérdidas y *revenue and expense, profit and loss*
ganar *to earn or gain*
–, precio de *bargain price*
ganga *strike*
garantía *warranty, security, surety, pledge*
– comercial *covering note*
– crediticia *credit guarantee*
– hipotecaria *mortgage*
– hipotecaria, bono sin *debenture bond*
– prendaria *collateral*
–, depositante de *pledger*
–, dinero en *earnest money*
–, ficha de *pledge card*
–, prestamista sobre *receiver*
–, préstamo con *loan against collateral*

–, prestar *to act as security*
–, valores dados en *pledged securities*
garantizado, negocio no *unsecured trade*
–, sueldo *guaranteed wage*
–, tiempo tipo *guaranteed standard time*
garantizar *to guarantee*
gastar *to spend*
–, poder para *spending power*
gastarse *to wear*
gasto *charge, expenditure, outlay, expense*
– accesorio *additional charge*
– adicional *additional expense*
– normal *design rate*
–, aprobación de un *allocation, allotment*
–, libre de todo *clear of all expenses*
gastos *expenses, costs*
– a bordo, libre de *free on board*
– a cargo del comprador *expenses at buyer's cost*
– a domicilio, libre de *delivered free*
– a prever *expenses involved*
– accesorios *incidental expenses*
– acumulados *accrued expenses*
– administrativos *administrative expenses*
– autorizables *allowable expenses*
– bancarios *bank charges*
– comprendidos, todos los *inclusive of all charges*
– cubiertos *clear expenses*
– centralizados, contabilidad de *expense-centre accounting*
– de administración *administration cost*
– de almacenaje *storage costs or charges, warehousing expenses*
– de capacitación *training expenses*
– de capital *capital charges or expenditure*
– de cobranza *collection expenses*
– de cobros *collection charges*
– de crédito y cobro *credit and collection expenses*
– de depósito *warehouse rent*
– de dirección *administrative expenses*
– de distribución *marketing expenses*
– de distribución, contabilidad de *distribution cost accounting*
– de embalaje *packing expenses*
– de embarque *shipping charges*
– de explotación *operating or working expenses*
– de fabricación *manufacturing expenses*

– de financiación *financial expenses*
– de funcionamiento *operating expenses*
– de inspección *surveying or superintending charges*
– de instalación *capital cost*
– de inversión *investment expenditure*
– de la venta directa *direct selling expenses*
– de manipulación *handling expenses*
– de manutención *living expenses*
– de operación *operating expenses*
– de promoción de ventas *sales promotion expenses*
– de publicidad *advertising expenses*
– de recaudación *collection fees*
– de transporte *transportation expenses*
– de viaje *travelling expenses*
– deficitarios *deficit spending*
– extraordinarios *after costs*
– familiares *family expenses*
– generales *general expenses, overhead costs*
– generales de distribución *general distribution expenses*
– gubernamentales *government expenditure*
– imprevistos *incidental expenses, incidentals*
– marginales *marginal expenses*
– menores *petty expenses*
– menores, caja para *petty cash*
– ocasionados *expenses incurred*
– ordinarios *current expenditure*
– ordinarios de operación *running expenses*
– permanentes *standing costs*
– reembolsables *expenses chargeable*
– suplementarios *additional charges*
– varios *sundry expenses*
–, comisión y *fees and expenses*
–, comprobante de *expenses voucher*
–, cubrir los *to pay expenses*
–, cuenta de *expense account*
–, cuenta de pérdidas y *account of outlays and costs*
–, cupo de *expense quota*
–, curva de *rating curve*
–, deducidos todos los *all charges deducted*
–, informe sobre los *expenses report*
–, ingresos y *income and expenditure*
–, sufragar los *to meet the costs*
generaciones, tabla de mortalidad de *generation life tables*
general de acciones, asamblea *meeting of shareholders*
– de depósito, almacén *bonded warehouse*
–, agente *general agent*
–, contador *general accountant*
–, estudio *overall study*
–, funcionamiento *overall operation*
–, gastos *general expenses, overhead costs*

–, huelga *general strike*
–, libro mayor *general ledger*
–, paro *general strike*
–, secretario *secretary-general*
generales, cuentas *general accounts*
género *feature*
– de negocio *line of business*
géneros de consumo corriente *staple commodities*
– en depósito *bonded goods*
– menudos *petty wares*
–, recepción de *receipt of goods*
–, saldar o liquidar *to clear goods*
gentes, derecho de *international law*
genuino *genuine*
geográfica, aérea *geographical area, land area*
geométrica de aumento o crecimiento, progresión aritmética o *arithmetic or geometric rate of growth*
gerencia *management, manager's office*
– de fabricación *production department*
– de ventas *sales department*
gerente *manager, administrator*
– de exportación *export manager*
– de ventas *sales department*
– interino *acting president (Am)*
– suplente *acting manager*
–, director *managing director*
gestión comercial *marketing, commercial service*
–, contabilidad de *management acounting*
gestor *administrator*
gestores para colocación de capitales *investors*
gira campestre *picnic*
girado *drawee*
girador *drawer*
girar *to draw*
– efectos comerciales *to trade*
– en descubierto *to overdraw*
– un cheque *to draw a cheque*
– una letra *to draw a draft*
giratorio, fichero *wheel-type filing system*
giro *draft*
– a la vista *sight draft*
– a plazo *time draft*
– bancario *bank draft*
– comercial *trade draft*
– de capital *capital turnover*
– de existencias *stock turnover*
– de existencias, promedio de *stock turnover rate*
– en descubierto *overdraft*
– o libranza postal *money order*
– sin documentos *clean draft*
–, protestar un *to protest a draft*
–, vencimiento del *draft maturity*

giros bancarios *bank draft*
– librados, registro de *draft register*
–, cuenta de *clearance account*
–, velocidad de *turnover*
global, autorización *overall authorization*
–, cifra *lumpsum*
–, importe *lumpsum*
–, suma *inclusive sum*
–, tiempo *overall time, observation period, elapsed time*
–, valor *aggregate value*
globales de distribución, costes *overall distribution costs*
–, datos *overall data*
gobierno *government*
–, junta de *steering committee*
goma, banda de *rubber band*
–, sello de *rubber stamp*
gracia, período de *grace period*
grado de salario *grade rate*
– de saturación *load factor, work opportunity, work loading*
– de solvencia *financial standing*
graduación *graduation, grading, grouping*
graduada, prima *sliding-scale premium*
–, tributación *graduated taxation*
gradual de salarios, escala *sliding scale*
–, clasificación *grading, grouping*
–, prueba *step-by-step test*
–, reajuste *rolling readjustment*
graduar *to graduate or classify*
gráfica *graph, chart*
– de dispersión *scatter chart*
gráfico de avance de una obra *progress chart*
– de procedimiento, diagrama *process diagram*
– de ventas *sales curve*
– del flujo de impresos *form flow diagram*
gran almacén *department store*
– consumo, de *consumer product, staple*
– establecimiento de venta *emporium*
– personaje o patrón *mogul*
grandes almacenes *department or general stores*
–, en letras *in block print*
granel, a *in bulk*
–, carga a *bulk cargo*
grano *grain*
grapas *staples*
gratificación *allowance*
– por desgaste de herramientas *tool allowance*
gratis *free*
gratuito *free*
–, comunidado *free publicity*
gravable *taxable*

–, ingreso *taxable income*
–, utilidad *taxable profit*
gravables, beneficios *taxable profits*
–, lista de bienes *tax roll*
gravado activo *pledged assets*
gravamen *lien, tax, encumbrance*
– por impuestos no pagados *tax lien*
– de factor *factor's lien*
–, libre de *free and clear*
–, primer *first lien*
gravar *to tax*
gravedad de los accidentes, porcentaje de *accident severity rate*
gremial, sindicato *trade guild*
gremio *guild, labour union*
– obrero *labour union*
– profesional *trade union*
– provisional *trade union*
–, delegado del *business agent, walking delegate (Am)*
–, tarjeta de afiliación a un *union card*
gremios obreros, oficiales de los *labour leaders*
grosero *vulgar*
grua *crane*
gruesa, avería *gross average*
–, utilidad (M) *gross earnings, gross profit*
grupo *group*
– de dirección, ficha para el *address group card*
– de edades determinadas *age group*
– de expertos *brains trust*
– de presión *pressure group*
– de trabajo *team, working group, equipment, means of production*
– director *steering group*
– humano *cohort*
–, póliza de *group policy*
grupos de usuarios *user groups*
– de presión *pressure groups*
– humanos, tabla de *cohort tables*
– representativos, sección cruzada *cross section*
–, variable entre *between groups variance*
guardatiempo *timekeeper*
gubernamentales, decisiones *governmental decisions*
–, gastos *government expenditure*
guerra de precios *price war*
– económica *economic warfare*
–, emprésito de *war loan*
–, impuesto de *war tax*
–, seguro de *war risk insurance*
guía comercial *trade directory*
– de carga *waybill, cargo receipt*

H

haber *credit*
–, debe y *debit and credit*
haberes *wages*
hábil *adroit*
–, día *business day*
habilidad *skill, proficiency*
– comercial *merchandising ability*
– para forzar las ventas *high-pressure
salesmanship*
–, prueba de *skill test*
habitante, consumo por *per capita
consumption*
–, renta por *per capita income*
hábito *custom*
hábitos de consumo *consumption habits*
hacendaria, política *financial policy*
hacendista *financier*
hacer *to make or do*
– bajar los precios *to force prices down*
– balance *to strike a balance*
– coincidir *to bring into line*
– cumplir *to enforce*
– efectivo *to cash, to collect*
– entrega *to deliver*
– inventario *to take account of stock*
– recuento de existencias *to take stock*
– saber *to notify*
– un pedido *to place an order*
hacienda o bienes *estate*
–, inspector de *tax inspector*
hambre, salario de *starvation wages*
hangar (A) *warehouse*
hecho en serie, artículo *mass-produced article*
hechura *workmanship*
heliográfica, copia *blue-print*
herramientas *tools*
–, cuarto de *tool store, tool crib*
higiene y seguridad *health and safety*
hinchadas, cuentas *accounts overcharged*
hipoteca *mortgage*
– colectiva *general mortgage*
– consolidada *unified mortgage*
–, escritura de *mortgage deed*
–, primera *first mortgage*
hipotecaria, bono sin garantía *debenture
bond*
–, cédula *mortgage bond*
–, compensación *foreclosure*

–, deuda *debt on mortgage*
–, obligación *mortgage bond*
hipotecario, acreedor *mortgagee*
–, banco *mortgage bank*
–, bono *mortgage bond*
–, préstamo *mortgage loan*
–, título *mortgage bond*
hipotecarios, valores *mortgage bonds*
hipótesis compuesta *composite hypothesis*
historia comercial *business history*
– de casos *case history*
– laboral *work history*
hoja *sheet*
– de balance *balance sheet*
– de cronometraje *time-observation or time-
study sheet*
– de datos técnicos *technical data sheet*
– de jornales devengados *time sheet*
– de repartición *work sheet*
– de servicios *statement of service*
– de trabajo *work sheet*
– para el estudio de tiempos *time-observation
or time-study sheet*
– volante u octavilla *leaflet*
–, pasar a otra *to carry forward*
hojas de instrucciones laborales *job
instruction sheet*
– de primas *posting sheet, bonus sheet*
– sueltas *loose leaf*
hojuela *apron, rider*
holding *holding company*
hombre anuncio *sandwich man*
– de negocios *dealer, trader, businessman,
merchant*
hombre-hora *manhour*
–, producción por *production per manhour*
honor, tribunal de *court of honour*
honorarios *fees, service fees*
– por cobros *collection fees*
– variables *variable fees*
honrado *honest*
hora *hour, time*
– absoluta *absolute time*
– de apertura *time on*
– legal *standard time*
– mano de obra *manhours*
– máquina *machine-hour*
– oficial *standard time*

–, avance de la *daylight saving*
–, ganancia por *hourly earnings, earned rate*
–, marcador de fecha y *time or clock stamp*
–, salario por *hourly wage*
horario *timetable*
– constante, jornal *straight time*
horas de asistencia normal *regular attendance hours*
– de comercio *business hours*
– de oficina *office hours*
– de oficina, después de las *after-office hours*
– de trabajo *working hours*
– de trabajo productivas *productive labour or work hours*
– disponibles *spare hours*
– extraordinarias *after hours, overtime*
– extras, trabajo a *overtime work*
– laborales *working hours*
– libres *spare hours*
– ordinarias *straight time*
– suplementarias *overtime*
horquilla, carretilla elevadora de *forklift truck*
hotel para motoristas *motel*
huelga *strike, walkout (Am)*

– de advertencia *token strike*
– de brazos caídos *sitdown strike*
– de patronos *lockout*
– de solidaridad *sympathetic strike*
– de trabajo lento *work to rule*
– general *general strike*
– loca *wildcat strike*
– patronal *lockout*
–, declarar una *to call a strike*
–, declararse en *to down tools*
–, derecho de *right to strike*
–, emplazamiento de *strike call*
–, fondo de *strike fund*
–, piquete de *picket*
–, seguro contra pérdidas de *strike insurance*
huelgas, rotura de *strike-breaking*
huelguista *striker*
–, cordón *picket line*
huelguistas, pago a *strike pay*
huída de capitales *flight of capital*
humano, factor *human factor*
–, grupo *cohort*
–, potencial *manpower*
humanos, recursos *human resources*

I

idea *idea, design, gimmick*
– publicitaria *advertising idea*
ideador *visualizer (Am), ideaman (Br)*
idealización *idealization*
idear *to devise*
– un sistema *to devise a method*
ideas mercadológicas *marketing ideas*
identificación *identification, empathy*
ignorancia económica *economic ignorance*
igual probabilidad, selección con *selection*
with equal probability
– remuneración por igual trabajo *equal pay*
for equal work
–, signo *equals sign*
igualar *to equalize or equate*
igualdad *equality, uniformity*
– de precios de oferta y demanda, mercado
con *close market*
ilegal *illegal*
–, interés *illegal interest*
ilimitada, responsabilidad *unlimited liability*
iliquidez *illiquidity*
ilusión *illusion*
imagen *image*
– de la marca *brand image*
impacto *impact*
impagable *unpayable*
implicación *implication*
implícita, función *implicit function*
implícito, contrato *implied agreement*
imponer derechos de aduana *to assess*
customs duty
– impuestos *to levy taxes*
imponibilidad *taxability*
imponible *taxable, rateable, dutiable, leviable*
–, activo no *tax liability*
–, ingreso *taxable income*
–, renta *taxable income*
–, utilidad *taxable income*
–, valor *taxable value*
importación *import, input*
–, artículos de *import goods*
–, comercio de *import trade*
–, cuota de *import allotment*
–, derechos de *import duties*
–, licencia de *import permit*
–, permiso de *import permit*
– sección de *import department*

importador *importer*
importadora, casa *import house*
importancia *importance, stress*
importar *to import*
importe *amount*
– a pagar *amount due*
– bruto *gross amount*
– global *lumpsum*
– líquido *net amount*
– marginal de ventas *marginal proceeds*
– neto *net amount*
– total *gross amount*
imposición *tax, taxation*
– de capitales *investment of capital*
– de la renta *income tax*
– fiscal *federal tax*
impositiva, base *tax base*
–, estipulaciones en política *canons of*
taxation
–, política *tax policy*
–, tasa *tax rate*
impositivo, criterio *system of taxation*
–, recargo *surtax*
–, sistema *system of taxation*
impracticable *unfeasible*
imprenta, tipo de *type, print character*
impresión *impression, printing*
–, calculadora con *printing calculator*
–, offset *impression offset*
impreso *in print*
impresos *printed matter*
– como salida de información, documentos
printed output for data
– de publicidad *trade or advertising literature*
–, diagrama del uso de *forms procedure chart*
imprevistas, pérdidas *windfall losses*
imprevistos *contingencies*
–, fondo para *contingency fund*
–, gastos *incidentals*
–, suplemento por *contingency allowance*
imprimir dinero *to print money*
–, máquina de *printing press*
improductivo *unproductive*
–, negocio *unsound business*
–, proyecto *unsound project*
–, tiempo *downtime*
improvisadas, compras *hand-to-mouth*
buying

impuesto *tax, duty, levy, assessment*
– a la exportación *export duty*
– a tanto alzado *composition tax*
– adicional *surtax*
– aduanal *customs duties*
– causado *tax incurred*
– compensatorio *compensatory duty*
– de guerra *war tax*
– estatal *state tax*
– fiscal *internal revenue tax*
– no pagado a tiempo *delinquent tax*
– personal *personal tax*
– por elaboración *processing tax*
– por persona *poll tax*
– predial *property or land tax*
– sobre beneficios extraordinarios *excess profits tax*
– sobre compraventa *sales tax*
– sobre donaciones *gift tax*
– sobre el precio de venta *sales tax*
– sobre espectáculos *admissions tax*
– sobre herencias *inheritance tax*
– sobre ingresos mercantiles *gross income tax*
– sobre la renta *income tax, revenue rate*
– sobre salarios *tax withheld on wages*
– sobre sueldos *wages tax*
– sobre transferencias de acciones *stock-transfer tax*
– sobre utilidades *profit tax*
– sobre ventas *excise tax*
– único *single tax*
–, base del *tax base*
–, causar *to be subject to tax*
–, manifestación de *tax return*
–, sujeto a *taxable*
–, tipo de *tax rate*
impuestos acumulados *accrued taxes, tax accruals*
– atrasados *back taxes*
– cobrados *taxes collected*
– de represalia *retaliatory tariff*
– directos *assessed taxes*
– estatales *state taxes*
– incobrables *irrecoverable taxes*
– indirectos *excise duties*
– no pagados, gravamen por *tax lien*
– no pagados, venta de bienes por *tax sale, tax title*
– sobre beneficios extraordinarios *excess profits tax*
–, alza de *increase of taxes*
–, aplicar *to impose taxes*
–, devolución de *tax refund*
–, evadir *to evade taxes*
–, evasión de *tax evasion, tax dodging*
–, exención de *tax exemption*

–, ingreso libre de *tax-free income*
–, libre de *tax free*
–, recaudador de *tax collector or receiver*
–, tipo de *tax rate*
–, utilidades antes de los *pre-tax earnings*
impugnada, cuenta *disputed account*
impulsadas, calculadora de teclas *key-driven calculator*
impulso *impulse, drive*
– aleatorio *random impulse process*
– de clasificación *sort impulse*
inaceptable *unacceptable*
inactiva, capacidad *idle capacity*
–, compañía *non-operating company*
–, máquina *idle machine*
inactividad, tiempo de *down time*
inactivo, archivador *storage file*
–, capital *idle capital*
–, fichero *storage file*
–, saldo *dormant balance*
–, tiempo *down time, idle time*
inacumulable *non-cumulative*
inadaptación *maladjustment*
inadecuado *inadequate*
inalienable *inalienable*
inamovible *non-removable*
inauguración, sesión de *opening session*
incapacidad *disability*
– absoluta permanente *permanent total disability*
– parcial permanente *permanent partial disability*
–, seguro contra *disability insurance*
incapacitado *disabled, disqualified*
incautación *seizure*
incendio, seguro contra *fire insurance*
incentivo *incentive, premium*
– amortiguador *weak or reduced incentive*
– para invertir *inducement to invest*
– reducido *reduced or weak incentive*
–, salario *incentive wage system*
incentivos monetarios *monetary inducements*
–, sistema de *bonus scheme, premium system*
incidencia *incidence*
inciso *clause*
incluído, con dividendo *cum dividend*
incluyendo impuestos indirectos *inclusive of indirect taxes*
incobrable *irrecoverable*
–, deuda *bad debt*
incobrables, créditos *bad debts*
–, cuentas *irrecoverable accounts*
–, impuestos *irrecoverable taxes*
incompleta, trabajador en jornada *part-time worker*
incondicional, venta *absolute sale*

inconsciente *unconscious*
inconvertible *unconvertible*
incorporación *incorporation*
incorporar *to incorporate or merge*
incrementar *to increase*
incremento *increase*
– del descuento *accrual of discount*
indagación *inquiry*
– sobre el mercado *market inquiry*
indefinida, contrato para suministro de cantidad *open-end contract*
indemnización *indemnity, compensation*
– doble *double damages*
– por averías *allowances for damages*
– por despido *dismissal or terminal wage*
– por desempleo *unemployment dole*
–, seguro de *indemnity insurance*
independientes, valores *independent values*
–, variables *independent variables*
indicador de cotizaciones *stock ticker*
– de mercado *market indicator*
– eléctrico, cinta del *ticker tape*
– electrónico, cinta del *ticker tape*
– financiero *financial index, stock market averages*
índice *index, ratio*
– alfabético *alphabetic index*
– anual *annual index*
– básico *basic index*
– completo *all-inclusive index*
– cruzado *cross reference*
– de acciones *accident rate*
– de archivadores *index filing*
– de aumento de población *population growth rate*
– de clasificación *sort index*
– de cobros *collection ratio*
– de costo unitario *index of unit cost*
– de crédito *credit rating*
– de la capacidad de compra *buying power index*
– de la producción física *index of physical production*
– de libros *accountant's index*
– de liquidez *liquidity ratio*
– de mercados *market index*
– de mortalidad *death rate*
– de población *population index*
– de precios *price index*
– de precios al consumidor *consumer price index*
– de precios de mercaderías *commodity price index*
– de precios de mercancías *commodity index*
– de producción *production or output index*
– de productividad *productivity index*

– de valores unitarios *unit value index*
– de ventas *sales ratio or index*
– del coste de vida *cost-of-living index*
– del poder adquisitivo *buying power index*
– no ponderado *weighted index*
–, número *index number*
índices de archivos *filing indexes*
indicitaria, cifra *index number*
indirecto, trabajo *indirect work or labour*
–, proceso *roundabout process*
indirectos, costos *indirect cost*
–, impuestos *excise duties*
individual, trabajo *individual working*
individuales, derechos *individual rights*
–, valorización de los méritos *merit rating*
individuo *individual*
indivisa, propiedad *joint property*
inductivo, método *inductive method*
industria *industry*
– naciente *infant industry*
–, automatización de la *industrial automation*
–, programa de capacitación en la *twin programme, training with industry programme*
industrial mixto, consejo *working council*
–, combinado *pool*
–, equipo *capital goods*
–, information *industrial information*
–, investigación *engineering research*
–, magnate *tycoon*
–, marca (M) *trademark*
–, norma *commercial standard*
–, obrero *factory worker*
–, paralización *tie-up*
–, producción *industrial output*
–, propiedad *industrial exclusive rights*
–, secreto *trade secret*
–, seguridad *industrial safety*
–, seguro *industrial insurance*
–, sociedad *industrial society*
–, socio *partner who furnishes service only*
–, valor *commercial value*
–, vitalidad *industrial health*
industriales, bienes de capital *industrial capital (goods)*
–, desperdicios *industrial waste*
–, fondo para accidentes *industrial insurance fund*
–, relaciones *industrial relations*
–, seguros *industrial insurance*
–, situaciones *industrial situations*
industrias *industries*
– básicas *key industries*
– clave *key industries*
– conexas *allied industries*
– esenciales *key industries*

ineficaz *ineffectual*
ineficiencia *inefficiency*
inelástico *inflexible*
inestabilidad *instability*
inestable *unstable*
–, moneda *unsound money, unsound currency*
–, moneda de valor *soft currency*
inevitable, espera *unavoidable delay*
–, retraso *unvoidable delay*
inexacto *incorrect, inaccurate*
inexperto *unskilled*
inexplotado *unworked*
infantil, trabajo *child labour*
inferior al normal, rendimiento *sub-standard performance*
inferiores, escalafones de mando *lower executive echelons*
inferioridad *inferiority*
inflación *inflation*
– de los costos *cost inflation*
– del crédito *credit inflation*
– lenta *creeping inflation*
–, controlar la *to curb inflation*
–, detener la *to check inflation*
inflacionario *inflationary*
inflacionistas, efectos *inflationary effects*
–, tendencias *inflationary trends*
inflado *inflated*
–, capital (M) *watered stock or capital*
inflexibilidad *affective rigidity*
influencia depresiva *depressing influence*
–, campo de *range of influence*
–, zona de *sphere of interest*
influjo y eflujo *input-output*
información *information*
– al día *factual information*
– anual *annual report*
– comercial *merchandising information*
– de crédito, requisitos de la *credit information requirement*
– de dirección *address information*
– de órdenes, ficha de *order information card*
– de ventas *sales information*
– directa *straight information*
– en la investigación de mercados *market research information*
– enviada *release*
– estadística *statistical information*
– industrial *industrial information*
– interesada *publicity*
– mercadológica *marketing information*
– mercantil *business information*
– publicitaria *publicity*
– publicitaria gratuita *free publicity*
– publicitaria, departamento de *publicity department*

–, cuadro de información *information desk*
–, documetos impresos como salida de *printed output for data*
–, ficha de *inquiry docket*
–, fuente de *information source*
–, oficina de *inquiry office*
–, registrar la *to file the information*
informaciones *inquiries*
– corrientes *current data*
–, archivo o lote de *file of information*
–, circuito de transferencia de *information path*
–, registro de *information record*
informada, opinión *informed opinion*
informante *informant*
informar *to report, to brief*
informe *report, information*
– anual *annual report*
– comercial *commercial report*
– de auditoría *audit report*
– de caja *cash report*
– de crédito *credit report*
– del avance de una obra *progress report*
– financiero anual *annual financial report*
– largo o detallado *long-form report*
– sobre los gastos *expenses report*
informes de entrevistas *interview reports*
– de investigación de mercados *market-research reports*
– de visitas y ventas *call and sales reports*
–, letrero de *inquiry docket*
–, mesa de *information desk*
–, petición de *information call*
–, posición de *information desk*
infracción *infringiment*
– de derechos de autor *copyright infringement*
– de patentes *patent infringement*
infrascrito *undersigned*
ingeniero *engineer*
– de normalización *standards engineer*
– encargado del estudio de métodos *methods engineer*
– encargados del planeamiento *planning engineer*
– proyectista *project engineer*
ingenio *device*
inglesa, semana *Monday morning to Saturday noon*
ingreso *revenue, income*
– bruto *gross revenue*
– de los factores de producción *factor income*
– del trabajo *labour income*
– diferido *deferred income*
– familiar *family income*
– gravable *taxable income*
– imponible *taxable income*

– libre de impuestos *tax-free income*
– medio *average earnings*
– nacional, análisis del *national income analysis*
– neto *net income*
– o renta anual *annual return*
– ordinario *current revenue*
– per cápita *per capita income*
– real *real income*
–, contribución sobre *income tax*
–, rasgo de *stroke*
ingresos *earnings, receipts*
– adicionales *additional income*
– aduana *customs receipts*
– brutos *gross receipts or earnings*
– acumulados *accrued income*
– íntegros *total receipts*
– mercantiles, impuesto sobre *gross income tax*
– por familia *income per family*
– totales *total receipts, gross proceeds*
– y gastos *income and expenditures*
–, cuenta de *income per family*
–, declaración de *income statement*
–, desembolsos de *revenue expenditures*
–, estado de *statement of income*
–, razón de paridad de *parity income ratio*
inhábil para los negocios *unbusinesslike*
inicial total al año, salario *gross initial annual salary*
–, capital *original capital*
–, costo *historical cost*
–, existencia *opening inventory*
–, inventario *opening inventory*
–, pedido *advance order*
–, salario *commencing salary*
–, sueldo *commencing salary*
injusta, competencia *unfair competition*
injusto *unfair, inequitable*
inmediata, carta de entrega *special-delivery letter*
–, entrega *special or spot delivery*
inmejorable, de control *topnotch*
inmigración *immigration*
inmobiliaria, compañía *real-estate company*
–, contribución *real-estate tax*
inmobiliario, bono *real-estate bond*
inmovilización del capital *lockup capital*
inmovilizado, activo *fixed assets*
inmovilizados, valores *fixed assets*
inmuebles *real estate*
–, bienes *real estate*
innegociable, conocimiento *straight bill of lading*
inquilino *tenant, lessee*
inscribir *to register, inscribe or enrol*

inscribirse *to enrol*
inscritas, acciones *listed stocks*
inscritos, compraventa de valores no *unlisted trading*
inseguridad *insecurity*
inserción *insertion*
insertar *to write in*
inserto *release*
insesgado *unbiased*
insinuación *insinuation*
insistencia *follow-up*
–, carta de *follow-up letter or reminder*
insoluto *unpaid*
insolvencia *insolvency, bankruptcy*
inspección *inspection*
– anual *annual survey*
–, gastos de *survey charges*
inspeccionar *to inspect*
inspector de contabilidades *chartered accountant*
– de hacienda *tax inspector*
– fiscal *tax examiner*
instalación, gastos de *capital cost*
instalaciones *fixtures*
–, coste de inversión de *plant investment cost*
instantáneas, método de observaciones *activity sample, observation ratio method, ratio delay method*
instinto *instinct, drive*
– de rebaño *herd instinct*
institución *institution*
instrucción *training, instruction, education*
– anual *annual training*
– técnica *technical instruction*
–, programa de *training schedule*
instrucciones laborales, hojas de *job instruction sheet*
– para embalaje *packing instructions*
instructivo *instruction sheet*
– de contabilidad *plan of accounts*
instructor *trainer*
– de vendedores *sales trainer*
instruir *to brief*
instrumento *instrument, tool*
instrumentos negociables *commercial paper, negotiable instruments*
insuficiente, producción *under-production*
insuficientes, fondos *no funds, insufficient funds*
insumo *input, investment, expenditure*
– corriente *current input*
– producto *input-output*
insumos y productos, análisis de *input-output analysis*
intangible, activo *intangibles*
intangibles *intangibles*

–, bienes *intangible assets*
íntegra, ganancia *gross return, gross earnings*
integralmente, asignar las acciones *to allot the shares in full*
integrante *integral*
íntegro *integral, complete*
–, pagado *paid in full*
–, precio *full price*
íntegros, ingresos *total receipts*
intelectual, leyes sobre propiedad *copyright laws*
–, protección de la propiedad *copyright protection*
inteligencia *intelligence*
–, prueba de *intelligence test*
intención *design*
intensidad *intensity*
intensivo, muestreo *intensive sampling*
intento *design*
interbloque, variancia *inter-block variance*
intercalar *to write in*
intercalarse *to merge*
intercambio *interchange*
– comercial *commercial intercourse*
interés *interest*
– a corto plazo *short-term interest*
– acumulado *accrued interest*
– bancario, tipo de *bank rate*
– compuesto *compound interest*
– corriente *current interest*
– establecido *absolute interest*
– fijo, bono a *active bond*
– ilegal *illegal interest*
– legal *interest at legal rate*
– mayoritario *majority interest*
– minoritario *minority interest*
– simple *simple interest*
– que se acumula *accruing interest*
–, colocar a *to place at interest*
–, conceder *to allow interest*
–, préstamos a *low interest loans*
–, tasa de *rate of interest*
–, tipo de *interest rate*
interés-dividendo *interest-dividend*
interesada, información *publicity*
Interesadas, partes *interested parties*
intereses creados *vested interests*
– devengados *interest income*
– económicos *financial interests*
– financieros *financial interests*
– vencidos *interest due*
–, capitalización de *compounding of interest*
–, fusión de *merger of interests*
–, ganancias por *interest earnings*
–, producir *to bear interest*
interestatal *inter-state*

–, comercio *inter-state commerce*
interferencia, suplemento por *interference allowance, synchronisation allowance*
interino, administrador *acting manager*
–, director *acting manager*
–, gerente (Am) *acting president*
–, jefe *acting manager*
–, presidente *acting president*
–, secretario *acting secretary*
interior, comercio *domestic or home trade*
–, deuda *domestic debt, internal debt*
–, emprésito *domestic loan*
–, mercado *home market*
–, página *inner page*
–, pedido *domestic order*
–, puerto *inner harbour*
intermediario *middleman, jobber*
– comercial *broker*
interna, auditoría *internal audit*
internacional de autor, derecho *international copyright*
–, organismo *international agency or institution*
interno, consumo *domestic consumption*
–, reglamento *bye-laws*
–, trabajo *internal or inside work*
intérprete *interpreter*
interrogado *respondent*
interrogador *interviewer*
interrogativo, método *questioning technique*
interrogatorio directo *direct interviewing*
interrupción *interruption, delay, stoppage*
intervalo *interval*
intervalos variables, pronóstico a *varying-interval prediction*
intervención de cuentas *audit, auditing*
intervenida, moneda no *uncontrolled money*
interventor *supervisor, auditor*
– de cuentas *auditor*
– general *comptroller*
intransferible *not transferable*
intrigante *lobbyist*
introducción *introduction*
introducido *staple*
introspección *introspection*
introversión *introversion*
introvertido *introvert*
intuición *intuition*
inútil *useless*
invalidez *disability, invalidity*
– total *total disability*
–, pensión de *disability benefit*
invención, prima de *patent*
inventarial, contabilidad *inventory accounting*
inventariar *to take stock*
inventario *inventory*

– de cierre *closing inventory*
– de mercancías *stocktaking*
– final *closing inventory*
– físico *physical inventory*
– inicial *opening inventory*
– por unidades *unit inventory*
–, cuenta de *inventory account*
–, hacer *to take account of stock*
–, libro de *stock book*
–, mermas en el *inventory shortage*
–, realización por *pre-inventory sale*
inventor *patentee*
inversión *investment, expenditure*
– básica *basic investment*
– bruta *gross investment*
– de capital *capital investment*
– de capitales, sociedad dedicada a la *investment trust*
– de instalaciones, coste de *plant investment cost*
– en el extranjero *foreign investment*
– en especie *investment in kind*
– excesiva *over-investment*
–, gastos de *investment expenditure*
–, multiplicador de *investment multiplier*
–, política de *investment policy*
inversiones, renta de *unearned income*
inversionista *investor*
– de capital limitado, empresa *closed-end investment company*
–, compañía *investing company*
–, sociedad *investment trust, opened trust*
invertido, capital *invested capital*
invertidos, fondos *investment funds*
invertir *to invest*
–, incentivo para *inducement to invest*
–, propensión a *propensity to invest*
investigación *research, inquiry*
– aplicada *applied research*
– científica *scientific research*
– comercial *commercial or business research*
– de gabinete *desk research*
– de la acción *action research*
– de la actividad *activation research*
– de la actividad comercial *business research*
– de la distribución *distribution or marketing research*
– de la opinión pública *public opinion research*
– de las ventas *sales research*

– de mercados *market research*
– de mercados, información en la *market research information*
– de mercados, informes de *market research reports*
– del mercado *market research*
– distributiva *marketing research*
– en la oficina *desk research*
– estadística *statistical research*
– experimental *experimental research*
– fundamental *basic research*
– industrial *engineering research*
– mercadológica *marketing research*
– metodológica *methodological research*
– operativa *operational or operations research*
– por encuesta *survey research*
– previa del mercado *pre-marketing research*
– prosecutiva o permanente *follow-up research*
– publicitaria *advertising research*
– sobre el consumidor *consumer research*
– sobre el mercado *market investigation*
– tecnológica *technological research*
–, medios de *research facilities*
–, proyectos de *research project*
–, técnicas de *research techniques*
–, trabajos de *research work*
investigaciones del mercado, director de *market research manager*
–, auxiliar en *research fellow*
investigador *investigator, researcher*
– científico *research scientist*
– colaborador *research associate*
– estadístico *statistical researcher*
–, analista *research analyst*
–, centro *research centre*
investigadora, actividad *research activity*
invisible, comercio *invisible trade*
invisibles, exportaciones *invisible exports*
–, operaciones *invisible transactions*
–, transacciones *invisible transactions*
involuntaria, desocupación *involuntary unemployment*
irredimible *irredeemable*
–, acción *debenture stock*
irregular, elemento *incidental or occasional element*
irrevocable *irrevocable*
–, carta de crédito *irrevocable letter of credit*
–, crédito *straight credit*

J

jefatura *leadership*
jefe *chief, boss, manager, head*
– actuante o accidental *acting chief*
– administrativo *overseer*
– auxiliar de ventas *assistant sales manager*
– comercial *market executive, market manager*
– de almacén *merchandise manager*
– de compras *buyer*
– de contabilidad *general accountant*
– de contrato *account executive*
– de créditos *credit manager*
– de cuadrilla *squad boss, labour foreman*
– de departamento *department chief or head or manager*
– de equipo *gang boss, leading hand, leadman, ganger*
– de escena *floor manager*
– de marca *brand man*
– de oficinas *office manager*
– de personal *personnel manager*
– de producción *production manager*
– de programación de productos *product planning manager*
– de promoción de ventas *sales promotion manager*
– de publicidad *advertising manager*
– de servicio *supervisor*
– de tienda *store manager*
– de tráfico *traffic director or manager*
– de ventas *sales manager*
– de ventas de zona *regional sales manager*
– de ventas en periódicos o revistas *circulation manager*
– de ventas para el exterior *foreign sales manager*
– de ventas para el interior *home sales manager*
– del departamento de anuncios *advertisement manager*
– ejecutivo del mercado *market manager, market executive*
– interino *acting manager*
–, contador en *chief accountant*
jerarquía *rank, order*
jerga comercial *commercialism*
– técnica *technical jargon*
jornada *day's work*
– doble *double shift*
– reducida *part-time employment*
jornadas-obrero *man-days*
jornal *wage, day rate, day-work rate*
– horario constante *straight time*
–, obra a *open work*
–, tiempo a *time on daywork, hours per day*
–, trabajador a *day labourer, wageworker*
–, trabajo a *journey work, day work, timework*
jornalero *labourer, journeyman*
jornales devengados, hoja de *time sheet*
–, junta ajustadora de *wage board*
–, libreta de *time book*
–, libretín de *time book*
jubilación *retirement, superannuation*
–, edad de *retirement age*
jubilar *to retire*
judicial, administración *receivership*
–, depositario *receiver*
–, sentencia *legal decision, court judgement*
–, venta *foreclosure sale*
juego de bolsa *stock speculation*
juicio *judgment, lawsuit, trial*
junta *committee, board, meeting*
– ajustadora de jornales *wage board*
– consultiva *advisory board*
– de accionistas *stockholder's meeting*
– de conciliación *conciliation board*
– de directores *board of directors*
– de gobierno *steering committee*
– del consejo *board meeting*
– directiva *board of directors*
–, citar a *to call a meeting*
jurado *jury*
jurados de empresa *employee participation in management*
justa, tarifa muy *tight rate, tight piecework price*
justicia, tribunal de *court of justice*
justificante *voucher*
justificantes de venta *sales vouchers*
justipreciar una persona *to size-up an individual*
justiprecio *appraisal, appraisement*
justo *correct, fair*
– del mercado, valor *fair market value*
–, beneficio *fair return*
–, precio *fair value*

L

labor productiva *productive labour*
–, tierra de *cultivated land*
laborable *workable, working*
laborables, compensación por accidentes *workmen's compensation*
–, condiciones *labour conditions*
–, datos *job data*
–, hojas de instrucciones *job instruction sheet*
–, horas *working hours*
–, leyes *labour laws*
–, relaciones *labour relations*
laboral, historia *work history*
–, legislación *labour laws, employment legislation*
–, manual *job manual*
–, paro *unemployment*
lado deudor *debit side*
lanzar al mercado *to put on sale*
lápiz tinta *copying pencil*
largo plazo *long term*
– plazo, obligaciones a *long-term liabilities*
– plazo, pasivo a *long-term liabilities*
–, informe *long-form report*
latente, análisis de la estructura *latent structure analysis*
–, plus valía *latent goodwill*
latifundio *large estate*
lavado cerebral *brain-washing*
leal, competencia *fair trade*
leales, precios *fair prices*
lealtad a la marca *brand loyalty*
lectura, punto de *break point, reading point*
–, sala de *reading room*
–, valor de *readership*
lecturas acumuladas, cronometraje por *cumulative timing continuous reading method*
legal *legal*
–, hora *standard time*
–, interés *interest at legal rate*
–, medida *standard measure*
–, moneda de curso *legal tender*
–, peso *standard weight*
legalizar *to legalize*
legislación *legislation*
– laboral *labour laws, employment legislation*
legítimo *legitimate, genuine*
lema o slogan *motto, slogan*

lenta, inflación *creeping inflation*
–, mercancía de venta *slow-selling merchandise*
lento, huelga de trabajo *working to rule*
leonino *unfair, one-sided*
letra *draft, bill*
– a corto plazo *short bill*
– a la vista *sight draft*
– a largo plazo *long bill*
– a plazo *usance or time bill*
– aceptada *accepted draft*
– bancaria *bank draft*
– de cambio *draft, bill of exchange*
– de favor *accommodation bill or draft*
– protestada *protested bill*
–, aceptación de una *acceptance of a draft*
–, cambiar una *to negotiate a bill*
–, girar una *to draw a draft*
–, protestar una *to protest a draft*
letras *bills*
– a cobrar *bills receivable*
– a pagar *bills payable*
– grandes, en *in black print*
letrero de informes *inquiry docket*
levantar la sesión *to adjourn the meeting*
ley *law, statute*
– de accidentes del trabajo *compensation act*
– de la oferta y la demanda *law of supply and demand*
– de los promedios *law of averages*
– de patentes *patent law*
– de rendimientos crecientes *law of increasing returns*
– de sociedades *corporation law, companies act*
– del trabajo *labour code*
– fiscal *tax law*
– mercantil *commercial code*
–, oro de *standard gold*
–, reforma de una *amendment*
leyes *laws*
– laborales *labour laws*
– sobre propiedad intelectual *copyright laws*
– suntuarias *sumptuary laws*
liberalización *liberalization*
libertad *liberty, right*
– de comercio *free trade*
– de empresa *free enterprise*

– de palabra *free speech*
– de prensa *free press*
libra *pound*
– esterlina *pound sterling*
librado *drawee*
librador *drawer*
libre *free, exempt*
– a bordo *free on board*
– al costado del vapor *free alongside*
– arbitrio *free will*
– cambio *free trade*
– de derechos *free duty*
– de derechos de aduana *customs-free*
– de elección *free choice*
– de impuestos *tax-free*
– de impuestos, ingreso *tax-free income*
– de gastos *free of charges*
– de gastos a bordo *free on board*
– de gastos a domicilio *delivered free*
– de gravamen *free and clear*
– de porte *postage-free*
– de todo gasto *clear of all expenses*
– empresa *free enterprise*
–, comercio *free trade*
–, mercado *open market or market*
–, método *open market*
–, puerto *free port*
–, trabajo *free labour, unrestricted work*
librecambista *free trader*
libres, horas *spare hours*
libreta de cheques *cheque book*
– de jornales *time book*
libro *book*
– borrador *daybook*
– de actas *minute book*
– de almacén *stock book*
– de balances de comprobación *trial balance book*
– de caja *cashbook*
– de caja chica *petty cash book*
– de compras *purchases journal*
– de cuentas *account book, ledger*
– de cheques *cheque book*
– de existencias *stock book*
– de facturas *invoice register, invoice book*
– de pedidos *order book*
– de primera entrada *book of original entry*
– de ventas *sales journal, sales book*
– diario *journal*
– mayor *ledger*
– mayor de compras *accounts payable ledger*
– mayor de devengos de empleados *employees' earnings ledger*
– mayor de ventas *accounts receivable ledger, sales ledger*
– mayor general *general ledger*

–, registrar un *to copyright*
libros auxiliares *subsidiary books*
–, cierre de los *closing the books*
–, clausura de los *closing the books*
–, ganancia según *book profit*
–, índice de *accountant's index*
–, llevar en los *to carry in the books*
–, tenedor de *book-keeper*
–, teneduría de *book-keeping accounting*
–, utilidades según *book profits*
–, valor según *book value*
licencia *licence, permit*
– de cambio *exchange permit*
– de exportación *export permit*
– de importación *import permit*
– de patente *patent licence*
–, derechos de *licence fees*
licenciado *lawyer, licensed*
– en economía *economist*
licitación *bidding, competitive bidding*
licitar *to bid*
lícito *legal*
líder *leader*
limitaciones, estatuto de *statute of limitations*
limitada, compañía de responsabilidad *limited liability company*
–, obligación *limited bond, limited liability*
–, póliza *limited policy*
–, responsabilidad *limited liability*
–, sociedad *limited partnership*
limitado *limited, restricted*
–, aval *qualified endorsement*
–, empresa inversionista de capital *closed-end investment company*
limitados, base de pagos *limited payment basis*
límite *limit*
– de crédito *line of credit, loan ceiling*
– de edad *age limit*
– de precio *price ceiling*
– del oro *gold point*
– superior al salario *wage ceiling, maximum wage*
–, precio *price line*
línea *line*
– de aceptación *acceptation line*
– de montaje *assembly or production line*
– de muestreo *sample line*
– de producción *production line*
– de productos *line of products*
lineal, estimación *lineal estimation*
–, operación *line operation*
–, organización *lineal organization*
–, programación *lineal programming*
líneas, muestreo de *line sampling*
lingote *ingot*

líquida, ganancia *clear profit*
–, utilidad *net profit*
liquidación *settlement, clearance, bargain sale, selling off*
– a precios reducidos *bargain sale*
– de balances *clearing*
– de comisiones *commission statement*
– de mercancías *clearing of goods*
– de sociedad *dissolution of partnership*
– de ventas *clearing line*
– por compensación *clearing*
– por o para los empleados *employees' settlement*
–, banco de *clearing bank, clearinghouse*
–, dividendo de *liquidating dividend*
–, estado de *liquidation statement*
–, precios de *clearance price*
–, valor en *breakup value*
–, venta de *clearing sale*
liquidar géneros *to clear goods*
– una cuenta *to settle an account*
liquidez *liquidity*
–, coeficiente de *current ratio*
–, escala de *scale of liquidity*
–, índice de *liquidity ratio*
–, patrón de *standard of liquidity*
–, preferencia por la *liquidity preference*
–, prima de *liquidity premium*
líquido *liquid*
–, activo *net value*
–, beneficio *clear benefit, net income, net profit*
–, importe *net amount*
–, lucro *net profit*
–, valor *net value*
líquidos, recursos *liquid resources*
lista *list*
– de artículos exentos de derecho *tax-free list*
– de bienes gravables *tax roll*
– de comprobación *check list*
– de contribuyentes *tax list*
– de direcciones *mailing list*
– de personas exentas de pago *tax-free list*
– de posibilidades *possibility list*
– de precios *price list*
– de precios al detalle *retail list price*
– de prospección *mailing list*

– de raya *payroll*
– negra *black list*
– provisional de precios *temporary price list*
–, pasar *to call the roll*
–, precio de *list price*
listas, muestreo por *sampling from files*
litigio *lawsuit*
litográfico offset, proceso *offset lithographic process*
–, procedimiento *offset*
loca, huelga *wildcat strike*
local *premises*
–, mercado *local market*
–, valor *local value*
locutor *announcer, speaker, commentator*
– de últimas noticias *newscaster*
logística, población *logistic population*
logotipo *logotype*
lonja de ventas *sales room*
lote *lot, share*
– al por mayor *wholesale lot*
– de informaciones *file of information*
– de saldo *job lot*
– o partida aislada *stray lot*
–, tamaño del *lot size, batch size*
lotes, clasificación por *block sorting*
–, producción por *batch production*
luces *lights*
– de aviso *warning lights*
lucrativa, corporación no *non-profit organization*
lucrativo *lucrative, profitable, revenue-earning*
– rentable *revenue earning*
lucro *profit*
– bruto *gross profit*
– líquido *net profit*
–, motivo *profit motive*
–, móvil del *profit motive*
–, perspectivas de *profit outlook*
lucha de clases *class struggle*
lugar de trabajo *work station*
– de venta *work station*
–, utilidad de *place utility*
lujo, artículos de *luxuries, luxury goods*
lumbrera *luminary*

LL

llegada, aviso de *arrival notice*
llegar a un convenio *to strike a bargain*
llenar una orden *to fill an order*
llevar *to carry*
– a cabo *to work out*
– cuentas *to keep accounts*
– en los libros *to carry on the books*
– un registro *to keep a record*

M

madrugada, trabajo de *lobster shift*
madurez *maturity*
maestro *foreman*
–, fichero *master file*
magazine *magazine, review*
– mensual *monthly magazine or review*
– trimestral *quarterly review*
magnate industrial *tycoon*
magnética del indicador electrónico, cinta
 ticker tape
–, cinta *magnetic tape*
magnetofónica, cinta *magnetic tape*
magro, año *lean year*
mala administración *mismanagement*
malversación *misappropriation,*
 embezzlement
malversados, fondos *misapplied funds*
mancomunada *joint*
–, concesión *pooled concession*
–, cuenta *joint account*
mancomunidad de empresas *pool*
mandato *mandate*
mando *leadership*
– de la dirección *steering control*
–, alto *top management*
–, capacidad de *leadership potential*
–, cualidades de *leadership qualities*
–, don de *leadership*
–, escalafones inferiores de *lower executive*
 echelons
mandos de una máquina *controls for*
 operating a machine
–, cuadro de *staffing*
manejo de datos, sistema de *data handling*
 system
manifestación de impuesto *tax return*
manifiesto *manifest*
maniobra *working*
maniobras de bolsa *stock speculation*
manipulación de pedidos *order handling*
– de precios *rigging of prices*
–, gastos de *handling expenses*
manipulada, moneda *managed currency*
mano de obra *manpower, workmanship*
– de obra contratada a largo plazo *indentured*
 labour
– de obra directa *productive labour*
– de obra especializada *skilled labour*

– de obra indirecta *indirect labour or work*
– de obra, distribución de la *allocation of*
 labour
– de obra, economía de *labour saving*
– de obra, economizador de *labour saving*
– de obra, hora *manhours*
– de papel *quire*
– disponible *available labour*
–, comprar de segunda *to buy second hand*
–, escritura a *handwriting*
–, máquina de sumar a *hand-operated adding*
 machine
mantener *to keep up*
mantenimiento *maintenance*
– anual *annual maintenance*
–, costes de *maintenance costs*
manual de detallistas *retailers' manual*
– de prácticas tipificadas *standard practice*
 manual
– del empleado *employee handbook or*
 manual
– laboral *job manual*
– para empleados *employee handbook*
–, obrero *blue-collar worker*
–, operación *manual operation*
–, tiempo *manual time*
–, trabajo *manual labour*
manufactura *manufacture*
– en proceso *work in process*
manufacturadas, mercancías *manufactured*
 goods
manufacturar *to manufacture or process*
manutención, gastos de *living expenses*
mapa *map, chart*
maqueta *template, model*
máquina *machine*
– alfabética de contabilidad *alphabetic*
 accounting machine
– calculadora, operador de *computer*
 operator, calculating machine operator
– contable, operador de *accounting machine*
 operator
– de calcular *computing or calculating*
 machine
– de dictar *dictating machine*
– de escribir *typewriter*
– de etiquetar *labelling machine*
– de facturar *billing machine*

– de fichas perforadas *punched-card machine*
– de fotocopias *photocopy machine*
– de imprimir *printing press*
– de perforación de fichas a gran velocidad *high-speed punched-card machine*
– de sumar a mano *hand-operated adding machine*
– de sumar y calcular *adding and calculating machine*
– de vender accionada por introducción de monedas *coin-operated vending machine*
– de venta automática *vending machine*
– eléctrica de contabilidad *electric accounting machine*
– electrónica de contabilidad *electronic book-keeping machine*
– electrónica de datos *electronic data machine*
– electrónica de dictado *electronic dictating machine*
– electrónica de elaboración de datos *electronic data-processing machine*
– franqueadora *franking machine*
– inactiva *idle machine*
– numérica de contabilidad *numerical accounting machine*
– o mecanismo electoral *machine*
– para envolver *wrapping machine*
– parada, tiempo de *idle machine time*
– registradora *cash register*
– registradora contable *cash register and book-keeping machine*
– sumadora *adder, adding machine*
– sumadora, cinta para *adding machine ribbon*
– sumadora, rollo de papel para *adding roll*
–, accesorio de *machine attachment*
–, aditamento de *machine attachment*
–, carga de *machine load*
–, cinta de *typewriter ribbon*
–, diagrama de procedimientos a *machine process chart*
–, mandos de una *controls for operating a machine*
–, tiempo de *machine or running time*
–, tiempo disponible de *available machine time*
maquinaria de equipo *machinery and equipment*
máquinas de oficina *business machines*
– de oficina, operario de *office-machine operator*
–, trabajo en varias *multiple machine work*
maquinista *engineer*
marasmo en los negocios *doldrums*
marbete *tag*
marca *brand*

– comercial *trade mark*
– corriente *standard make*
– de comercio *trade name*
– de consumo, producto de *consumer branded product*
– de fábrica *trade mark*
– industrial (M) *trade mark*
– registrada *brand or trade name*
– registrada, derecho de *trademark rights*
–, artículo de *trademark article*
–, dibujo de *brand image*
–, encuesta sobre tendencias de *brand trend survey*
–, imagen de la *brand image*
–, jefe de *brand man*
–, lealtad a la *brand loyalty*
–, nombre de la *brand or trade name*
–, nombre o dibujo registrado como *trade name*
–, productos de *brand products*
–, valor de aceptación de una *goodwill*
marcador de fecha y hora *time or clock stamp*
marcha del trabajo, cuadro de la *speed schedule*
–, en *in gear*
–, formación sobre la *on-the-job training*
–, paga de *severance pay*
margen *margin*
– bruto *gross margin*
– bruto del detallista *retailer's gross margin*
– comercial *mark-on*
– comercial acumulativo, cálculo del *cumulative markup calculation*
– comercial acumulativo, porcentaje del *cumulative markup percentage*
– comercial adicional neto *net additional markup*
– comercial efectivo *actual markup*
– comercial inicial *initial markup*
– comercial sostenido *gross margin, maintained markup*
– comercial, anulación *markup cancellation*
– comercial, promedio del *average markup*
– de beneficio bruto *gross profit margin*
– de preferencia *margin of preference*
– de seguridad *margin of safety*
– de utilidad *markup, margin of profit*
– del comerciante *dealer margin*
– del distribuidor *distributor margin*
– del dumping *margin of dumping*
–, rebaja de *markdown*
marginal *marginal*
– a consumir, propensión *marginal propensity to consume*
– de los factores, costo *marginal factor cost*
– de uso *marginal user cost*

– del capital, eficacia *marginal efficiency of capital*
–, producción *marginal production*
–, unidad *marginal unit*
–, utilidad *marginal utility*
marginales, gastos *marginal expenses*
marina, carta *chart, ocean chart*
marítima, carga *cargo, ocean freight*
–, conferencia *shipping conference*
marítimas, operaciones comerciales *shipping business or trade*
marítimo, comercio *shipping trade*
–, contrato *maritime contract*
–, flete *ocean freight*
marítimos, aseguradores contra riesgos *marine underwriter*
más, cobrar de *to overcharge*
masa *crowd*
– pasiva *liabilities*
–, comprar en *to buy up*
–, mercado de *mass-market measurement*
–, producción en *mass production*
masiva por muestreo, encuesta *massive sampling survey*
matemática de ganancias, previsión *mathematical expectation of gain*
–, prima *net premium*
materia *stuff*
– prima *raw material*
–, proceso de transformación de *processing*
material averiado *spoilage*
– de enseñanza *training aid*
– de escritorio, equipo de *stationery equipment*
– de explotación *working material*
– de promoción *promotional matter, dealer aids*
– de publicidad *advertising material*
– existente *existing material*
– para exposición de escaparates *window display material*
– para exposiciones *material for exhibitions*
– publicitario *advertising material*
– que no cumple con lo especificado *sub-specification material*
–, contabilidad de *material accounting*
–, cuadro demostrativo de situación de *status board*
materiales en curso de fabricación *in-process materials*
–, control de *material control*
–, daños *property damage*
–, movimientos de *materials handling*
–, tipificación de *material standardization*
–, valores *physical assets*
materias primas *raw materials*

– primas, cupo *allocation*
– y obras registradas *copyrighted material*
matiz *hue*
matrícula, puerto de *port of registration*
matriz *mat, matrix*
– de talón *stub mat*
–, casa *headquarters, main office*
–, compañía *parent or holding company*
–, empresa *parent company*
–, sociedad *parent company*
máxima admisible, carga *ultimate allowable stress*
–, producción *peak production*
máximas, ventas *peak sales*
máximo del concesionario, precio *distributor's maximum price*
– permitido, precio *ceiling price*
–, elevar al *to maximize*
–, esfuerzo *all-out effort*
–, precio *top price*
–, punto *peak*
–, salario *wage ceiling, maximum wage*
máximos legales, precios *price ceiling*
mayor *wholesale*
– de compras, libro *accounts payable ledger*
– de devengos de empleados, libro *employees' earnings ledger*
– de edad *of age*
– de ventas, libro *accounts receivable or sales ledger*
– estadístico *statistical ledger*
– general, libro *general ledger*
–, abastecedor de comestibles al por *wholesale grocer, supplier*
–, al por *at wholesale*
–, asiento del *ledger entry*
–, auxiliar del mayor *auxiliary ledger*
–, balance del *ledger balance*
–, comerciante al por *wholesale merchant, wholesaler*
–, comercio al por *wholesale, wholesale trade, wholesaling*
–, comprar al por *to buy wholesale*
–, empresa al por *wholesale enterprise or firm*
–, fuerza *force majeure, act of God*
–, libro *ledger*
–, lote al por *wholesale lot*
–, negocio al por *wholesale trade*
–, venta al por *wholesale, wholesale trade, wholesaling*
mayoreo *wholesale*
–, precio al *wholesale price*
–, vender al *to sell at wholesale*
mayoría de votos, gran *landslide*
mayorista *wholesale dealer*
–, almacén *wholesale store*

–, casa *wholesale concern*
–, comercio *wholesale trade*
–, mercado *wholesale market*
–, precio *wholesale price*
mayoritario, interés *majority interest*
mecanismo *device*
– electoral, máquina o *electoral machine*
mecanización *mechanization*
mecanizados, métodos de producción *assembly or flow or production line*
mecanógrafa *typist*
mecanografía *typewriting*
media aritmética ponderada *weighted arithmetic mean*
– de vencimiento, fecha *equated date*
– geométrica ponderada *weighted geometric mean*
– ponderada *weighted mean*
–, cuadrado de la desviación *variance*
–, ejecución *average performance*
–, producción *average output*
–, tasa *average rate*
–, tirada *average circulation*
mediador *conciliator, arbitrator*
medición *measurement, mensuration*
– de la productividad *productivity measurement*
– del rendimiento *performance measurement*
– del trabajo *work measurement*
medida *measure, size*
– de superficie *square measure*
– de tiempos por diferencia *differential timing*
– del trabajo *work measurement*
– legal *standard measurement*
– para altura de columnas *column inch*
–, patrón de *standard*
–, trabajo por *piecework*
medidas normalizadas *standardized dimensions*
medido, trabajo a jornal *measured daywork*
medio *medium, media*
– ambiente *environment, milieu*
– anual, aumento *average annual increase*
– de aumento, tipo *average of increase*
– de publicidad *advertising medium*
– ponderado *weighted average*
–, consumidor *average consumer*
–, error *mean error*
–, ingreso *average earnings*
–, precio *average price*
–, término *average*
–, tiempo *average time*
–, tiempo y *time and a half*
–, valor *median*
medios de comunicación *means of communication*

– de investigación *research facilities*
– de producción *means of production, production facilities, equipment, team*
– de transformación *processing equipment*
– publicitarios *advertising media*
medir *to measure*
mejor oferta *best bid*
mejora de métodos, análisis *methods engineering, production engineering*
mejoramiento comercial *business upswing*
mejorar *to improve*
mejoras *improvements*
mejoría de la instalación *plan improvement*
membrete *letterhead*
– comercial, carta *business letterhead*
memoria *memory, report statement*
– de quiebra *act of bankruptcy*
menaje, artículos de *household, home appliances*
mencionado antes *above-mentioned*
–, antes *above-mentioned*
menor de edad *minor*
–, cajero *petty cashier*
–, comercio al por *retailer*
–, comprobación en las tiendas al por *retail store audit*
–, negocio al por *retail trade*
–, socio *junior partner*
menores, caja para gastos *petty cash*
–, gastos *petty expenses*
menos, valuar en *to undervalue*
mensaje *message*
– nocturno *night message*
– ordinario *ordinary message*
– urgente *urgent message*
mensual *monthly*
–, cuota *monthly rate*
–, magazine *monthly magazine or review*
mensualidad *monthly payment*
mental, trabajo *mental work*
mente *mind*
menudeo *retail*
–, comercio al *retail trade*
–, método de precio de *retail method*
–, método del *retail method*
–, precio de *retail price*
–, vender al *to sell at retail*
menudos, géneros *petty wares*
mercader *merchant*
mercaderías *goods*
–, índice de precios de *commodity price index*
mercado *market*
– a término *time bargain*
– abierto *open market*
– alcista *bull market*
– bajista *bear market*

– bursátil de acciones *stock market*
– con igualdad de precios de oferta y demanda *close market*
– consumidor, análisis del *consumer market analysis or research*
– de abastecimientos *provision market*
– de cambios *exchange market*
– de competencia activa *active market price competition*
– de consumo *consumer market*
– de futuros *futures market*
– de gran consumo *thick market*
– de masa *mass market*
– de poco consumo *thin market*
– de productos disponibles *cash or spot market*
– de valores *stock market*
– del comprador *buyer's market*
– desanimado *idle market*
– encalmado *quiet market*
– estable *close market*
– extensible *expansible market*
– fácil *easy market*
– febril *feverish market*
– firme *strong or stiff market*
– flojo *weak or dull or sagging market*
– interior *home market*
– libre *open or free market*
– local *local market*
– mayorista *wholesale market*
– monetario *money market*
– nacional *domestic market*
– nacional, precios de *home market price*
– negro *black market*
– potential *potential market*
– saturado *saturated market*
– sostenido *steady market*
–, acaparar el *to corner the market*
–, adaptación de un producto a las necesidades de un *product planning*
–, analista del *market analyst*
–, baja del *drop in prices*
–, comprar a precio del *to buy at market price*
–, conducta del *market behaviour*
–, contracción del *business contraction*
–, dejar desprovisto el *to clear the market*
–, director de investigaciones del *market research manager*
–, en el *in the market*
–, encuesta sobre el *market survey*
–, estudio del *market study*
–, estrategia en la dirección del *market management strategy*
–, fluctuaciones del *market fluctuation*
–, indagación sobre el *market inquiry*
–, indicador de *market indicator*

–, investigación sobre el *market research*
–, jefe ejecutivo del *market executive*
–, lanzar al *to put on sale*
–, precio del *market price*
–, presentar en el *launch on the market*
–, pronóstico del *business forecast*
–, revista o informe del *market report*
–, tendencia expansionista del *increasing share of market*
–, tendencias del mercado *market trends*
–, tipo del *market rate*
–, valor justo del *fair market value*
mercadología *marketing*
–, analista de *marketing analyst*
mercadológica, esfuerzos de exploración *marketing efforts*
–, estrategia *marketing strategy*
–, función *marketing function*
–, información *marketing information*
–, investigación *marketing research*
–, procedimiento de investigación *marketing research procedures*
–, situación *marketing situation*
mercadológicas, ideas *marketing ideas*
mercadológico, enfoque *marketing approach*
mercadólogo *marketeer*
mercados, análisis de *market research or analysis*
–, índice de *market index*
–, información de la investigación de *market research information*
–, informes de investigación de *market research reports*
–, investigación de *market research*
mercadotecnia *marketing*
mercancía *merchandise, goods, product, article*
– compuesta *composite commodity*
– de consumo corriente *staple merchandise*
– de venta difícil o lenta *slow-selling merchandise*
– determinada, contrato de una *open-end contract*
–, dinero *money commodity*
–, fijación del precio de la *merchandise pricing*
–, merma de *item shortage or shrinkage*
–, remanente de una *carry over*
mercancías *goods*
– almacenadas *stock*
– de calidad *quality goods*
– de pacotilla *sale goods*
– en almacén *stock in hand*
– en depósito *bonded goods*
– en tránsito *goods in transit*
– exentas de derechos *free goods*

- manufacturadas *manufactured goods*
- pagaderas en dólares *dollar commodities*
- perecederas *perishable goods*
- vendidas, partida *bill of goods*
-, abarrotado de *overstocked*
-, contabilidad de *merchandise accounting*
-, cuenta de *goods or merchandise account*
-, exposición de *merchandise display*
-, fijación de precios de las *merchandise pricing*
-, índice de precios de *commodity index*
-, inventario de *stocktaking*
-, liquidación de *clearing of goods*
-, movimiento de *turnover*
-, política de *merchandising*
-, promedio de *stock average*
-, retirada de *withdrawal*
-, rotación de *merchandise turnover*
-, saldo de *clearing of goods*
-, surtido de *stock*
-, técnica de *merchandising*
mercantil *commercial, mercantile*
-, acto *commercial transaction*
-, casa *business house*
-, código *commercial law*
-, corporación *business corporation*
-, crédito *commercial standing*
-, derecho *commercial law*
-, efecto *trade bill*
-, información *business information*
-, ley *commercial code*
-, perito *expert accountant*
-, sociedad *commercial company*
mercantiles, obligaciones *commercial paper*
mercantilización *merchandising, commercialization*
mérito, calificación del *merit rating*
-, valorización del *merit rating*
meritorio *messenger*
méritos del obrero, formulario para valorar los *employee-rating form*
- individuales, valoración de los *merit rating*
merma *decrease, shrinkage, loss, abrasion*
- de mercancía *item shortage or shrinkage*
-, rebaja por *tret*
-, tara y *tare and tret*
mermas de las existencias *stock shortage*
- en el inventario *inventory shortage*
mes *month*
mesa de informes *information desk*
meta *goal*
metálico, anticipo en *cash advance*
-, dinero en *hard money*
-, premio en *cash price*
-, prima en *monetary incentive*
metódico *businesslike*

método *method*
- analítico *questioning technique*
- de amortización decreciente *declining balance method*
- de los componentes *method of selected points*
- de observaciones instantáneas *activity sample, observation ratio method, ratio delay method, snap-reading method*
- de porcentaje de terminación *percentage of completion method*
- de precio de menudeo *retail method*
- de prueba empírico *empirical test method*
- de tanteos *trial and error*
- de trabajo *working method, procedure*
- del menudeo *retail method*
- del precio de la última compra *price of last purchase method*
- del precio del mercado *market price method*
- del valor actual *actual value method*
- del valor de coste *cost value method*
- inductivo *inductive method*
- interrogativo *questioning technique*
- libre *open market*
- normalizado *standard method*
- numérico gráfico *graphico-numerical method*
metodológica, investigación *methodological research*
métodos de producción mecanizados *assembly or flow or production line*
- estadísticos *statistical methods*
-, análisis y mejora de *methods engineering, production engineering*
-, ingeniero encargado del estudio de *methods engineer*
métrica, tonelada *metric ton*
métrico, sistema *metric system*
microcopia *microcopy*
microcopiaje *microcopying*
microcopiar *to microcopy*
microficha *microcard*
microfilm *microfilm*
microfilmación *microfilming*
microfilmar *to microfilm*
microfotografiar en película *to microfilm*
micromuestra *microsample*
micromuestreo *microsampling*
micropelícula *microfilm*
miembro *member*
- que solo trabaja parte del día *part-time member*
- titular *regular member*
- vitalicio *life member*
miembros estatutarios *standing-request members*

migración permanente *permanent migration*
migraciones periódicas *periodic migrations*
migratorio, saldo *balance of migration*
milésimo *thousandth*
milla *mile*
– cuadrada *square mile*
millar *thousand*
millón *million*
mimeógrafo *mimeograph*
mina *mine*
minería *mining*
mínima, existencia *basic stock*
mínimo, precio *floor price*
–, salario *minimum wage*
–, sueldo *minimum wage*
minoría *minority*
minoritario, interés *minority interest*
minuta *draft*
minutas *minutes*
mitad *half*
mixta, comisión *joint committee*
–, muestra *composite sample*
mixtas, cuentas *mixed accounts*
mixto, modelo *mixed model*
–, muestreo *mixed sampling*
mobiliario y equipo *furniture and fixtures*
–, cuenta de *fixtures account*
mobiliarios, bienes *personal assets or estate*
moda *fashion*
–, artículos de *fashion goods*
–, tendencias de la *fashion trends*
–, último grito de la *up-to-the-minute*
modas, cambios en las *fashion changes*
–, exposición de *fashion show*
modelario *sampling*
modelo *pattern*
– de pruebas *test chart*
– mixto *mixed model*
–, póliza *sample policy*
–, según *after a pattern*
modelos registrados y patentes mundiales en trámite *designs registered and world patents pending*
–, exhibición de primeros *first sample showing*
modernización del equipo de fábrica *plant modernization*
módico, precio *moderate price*
modificación automática de dirección *automatic address modification*
– de costes *costs alteration*
modo de producirse el mercado *market behaviour*
módulos *standards*
moneda *currency*
– blanda *soft currency*
– convertible *convertible or hard currency*

– corriente *legal tender*
– de curso forzoso *compulsory currency, flat money*
– de curso legal *legal tender*
– de papel *paper money*
– de plata *silver coin*
– de valor constante *constant currency*
– de valor inestable *soft currency*
– deformada *coin biased*
– divisional *subsidiary money*
– en circulación *outstanding money*
– estable *sound money, hard currency*
– extranjera *foreign currency*
– extranjera, crédito en *credit in foreign exchange*
– falsa *counterfeit currency*
– fiduciaria *fiduciary or token money*
– inestable *unsound money or currency*
– manipulada *managed currency*
– no intervenida *uncontrolled money*
–, acuñación de *coining*
–, acuñar *to mint or coin*
–, casa de *mint*
–, depreciación de la *depreciation of currency*
–, papel *paper money*
monetaria, crisis *money crisis*
–, economía no *non-cash economy*
–, emisión *money issue*
–, recompensa *financial reward*
–, reforma *currency reform*
–, sistema de circulación *currency*
–, unidad *unit of currency*
monetarias, cuestiones *money matters*
monetario, coste *money cost*
–, mercado *money market*
–, patrón *standard of value*
–, premio *premium money*
–, salario *money wage*
monetarios, incentivos *monetary inducements*
–, temas *money matters*
monopolio *monopoly, trust, forestalling, engrossing*
–, precio de *monopoly prices*
–, regional *regional cartel*
monopolista *monopolist*
monopolizar *to monopolize*
– en cadena *in-line assembly*
montaje rotativo *rotary fixture*
–, cadena de *assembly line*
–, costo de *assembly cost*
–, línea de *assembly or production line*
–, planta de *plant*
montar *to assemble*
monto *amount*
– neto *net amount*
moratorias *moratorium*

moratorio *moratory*
mordida *graft*
morosas, cuentas *bad debts*
moroso *in arrears*
–, causante *delinquent taxpayer*
–, contribuyente *delinquent taxpayer*
–, deudor *delinquent taxpayer*
–, tasa de *death rate*
mortalidad *mortality, death rate*
– actual, tabla de *current life table*
– por accidentes, porcentaje de *accident death-rate*
– por profesionales, tasa de *occupational death-rate*
– prevista *expected mortality*
– real *actual mortality*
–, coeficiente de *death rate*
–, índice de *death rate*
mostrador de saldos *bargain counter*
–, exposición de *counter display*
motivación *motivation*
–, factor de *motivation factor*
motivo *motive*
– especulativo *speculative motive*
– lucro *profit motive*
– negocios *business motive*
– precaución *precautionary motive*
– transacción *transactions motive*
motivos de compra *buying motives*
móvil del lucro *profit motive*
–, archivo *mobile file*
–, escala *sliding scale*
movilidad del trabajo *mobility of labour*
movimiento *motion, movement*
– acelerado *accelerated motion*
– controlado *constrained movement*
– de alza *upward movement*
– de capital *capital turnover*
– de existencias *inventory turnover*
– de materiales, tiempo de *materials handling or transport time*
– de mercancías *turnover*
– de obreros *labour turnover*
– descendente *downward motion*
– elemental *elemental movement*
– general de la población *general population movement*
–, cuenta sin *inactive account*
–, fichero de *live file*
movimientos *movements*
– básicos, tiempo de *basic motion time*
– de capital *capital movements*
– de materiales *materials handling*
–, análisis de *motion analysis*
muebles, bienes *movable chattels, personal assets*

muelle, franco en el *free on dock*
muerta, carga *dead load*
muerto, peso *dead weight*
–, tiempo *dead time*
muestra *sample, specimen, model*
– al azar *random sample*
– científica *scientific sample*
– controlada *controlled sample*
– cruzada *cross sample*
– de autocorrección *self-correcting sample*
– mixta *composite sample*
– no aleatoria *non-random sample*
– no restringida al azar *unrestricted random sample*
– para ensayo *test sample*
– patrón *master sample*
– piloto *pilot sample*
– ponderada *weighted sample*
– representativa *representative sample*
– sin bias *unbiased sample*
– sin valor *sample without value*
– sucesiva *sequential sample*
– suelta *odd sample*
– tal como se recibe *as received sample*
–, comprar según *to buy by sample*
–, diseño de una *sample design*
–, ejemplar de *sample copy*
–, sacar una *to make a sample*
–, según *by sample*
–, según la *as per sample*
–, unidad de *sample unit*
muestral promedio, número *average sample number*
muestras concordantes *matched samples*
–, caja para *sample case*
–, cuarto de (Am) *showroom*
–, encuesta por *sample survey*
–, exposición de *sample display*
–, selección de *sample selection*
–, seleccionador de *sample selector*
muestrear *to sample*
muestreo *sampling*
– al azar *random sampling*
– aleatorio, error del *random sampling error*
– de líneas *line sampling*
– de probabilidad *probability sampling*
– estadístico *statistical sampling*
– intensivo *intensive sampling*
– mixto *mixed sampling*
– proporcional *proportional sampling*
– por cupos *quota sampling*
– por listas *sampling from files*
– restriccionista *restricted sampling*
– restringido *restricted sampling*
– sistemático *systematic sampling*
–, bias del *sample bias*

–, censo por *sample census*
–, diseño de *sampling design*
–, encuestas masivas por *massive sampling survey*
–, error de *sampling error*
–, error de azar en el *random sampling error*
–, error normal de *normal sampling error*
–, espacio de *sample space*
–, estructura del *sampling structure*
–, línea de *sample line*
–, operaciones de *sampling operations*
–, punto de *sample point*
–, técnica de *sampling technique*
–, tolerancia del *sample tolerance*
multa *fine, penalty*
multar *to fine*
multicopista *duplicator*
– de estarcio *duplicator stencil*
– de fluido *duplicator fluid*

multifásico *multiple-phase*
multilateral *multilateral*
múltiple *multiple*
–, actividad *multiple activity*
–, clasificación *multiple sorting*
multiplicación, signo de *multiplication sign*
multiplicador *multiplier*
– constante *constant multiplier*
– de inversión *investment multiplier*
– finito *finite multiplier*
multiplicar *to multiply*
múltiplo común *common multiple*
multitud *crowd*
– excitada *mob*
mundial, contrato *world contract*
municipal, concejo *city council*
mutua, ayuda *mutual assistant*
mutualista, fondo *mutual fund*

N

nacimiento, tasa de *birth rate*
naciente, industria *infant industry*
nación más favorecida, cláusula de la *most favoured nation clause*
nacional, análisis del ingreso *national income analysis*
–, carretera *national road*
–, comercio *home consumption*
–, corporación *domestic corporation*
–, deuda *national debt*
–, mercado *domestic market*
–, precios de mercado *home market price*
–, producción *national production*
–, producto *national product*
–, renta *national income*
nacionales, precios *home prices*
–, productos *domestic commodities*
nacionalidad *nationality*
nacionalizar *to nationalize*
natalidad, coeficiente *birth rate*
naturales, recursos *natural resources*
necesarias, compras *open to buy*
necesidad *need*
–, artículos de primera *primary or convenience goods*
necesidades de un mercado, adaptación de un producto a las *product planning*
– económicas *economic needs*
– personales, suplemento por *personal needs allowance, personal allownce*
–, formulario de *want slip*
negativa *refusal*
–, balanza de pagos *unfavourable balance of payments*
negativo, ahorro *non-saving*
–, balance *minus balance*
negligencia *negligence*
negociabilidad *marketability*
negociable *negotiable*
–, unidad *trading unit*
negociables, instrumentos *commercial paper, negotiable instruments*
negociado *division*
negociador *lobbyist*
negociante *commission merchant, trader*
– a comisión *commission merchant*
negociar *to trade, deal or negotiate*
–, capacidad de *merchandising ability*

–, poder para *bargaining power*
negocio *business, transaction*
– a plazo *business in futures, time bargain*
– al por mayor *wholesale trade*
– al por menor *retail trade*
– auxiliar *side business*
– improductivo *unsound business*
– no garantizado *unsecured trade*
–, género de *line of business*
–, ramo de *line of business*
–, seguro contra cese de *business interruption insurance*
negocios, agente de *middleman*
–, censo de *census of business*
–, cifra de *turnover*
–, entendido en *businesslike*
–, hombre de *dealer, trader, businessman, merchant, storekeeper*
–, inhábil para los *unbusinesslike*
–, marasmo en los *doldrums*
–, motivo *business motive*
–, oficina de *agency office*
–, papeles de *commercial or business papers or documents*
–, paralización de *business stagnation*
–, viaje de *business trip*
–, volumen de *business figure*
negra, bolsa *black market*
–, lista *black list*
negro, mercado *black market*
neta, pérdida *net loss*
–, tirada *net sales circulation*
–, utilidad *net profit*
netas, ventas *net sales*
neto *net*
– tangible, activo *tangible net worth*
–, activo *net value*
–, beneficio *clear benefit, net income, net profit*
–, bruto por *gross for net*
–, capital *net worth, proprietorship*
–, importe *net amount*
–, ingreso *net income*
–, monto *net amount*
–, precio *trade price*
–, valor *clear value*
nivel *level*
– de equilibrio *equilibrium level*

- de norma, al *up to standard*
- de precio *price level*
- de remuneración *compensation level*
- de rendimiento *performance index*
- de salarios *wage level*
- de significación *significance level*
- de sueldos *wage level*
- de vida *standard of living*
nivelación *levelling*
nivelar *to level*
no clasificado *unclassified*
- dividido *undivided*
- en forma *informal*
- entregado *undelivered*
- ganado *unearned*
- gravable *non-taxable*
- renovable *non-renewable*
- repartido *undistributed*
nocturno, mensaje *night message*
nombramiento *appointment*
nombrar *to appoint or designate*
nombre comercial *trade name*
- de marca *trade name*
- registrado *copyrighted name*
nomenclatura adoptada *adopted nomenclature*
nómina *payroll*
- de personal *personnel roster*
- de sueldos *payroll*
- devengada *accrued payroll*
-, datos de *payroll data*
-, semana de *payroll week*
nominal *nominal*
-, bono *registered bond*
-, precio *asking price*
-, salario *nominal wage*
-, valor *face value, nominal value*
nominativa, acción *registered share*
nominativo, título *personal or registered bond*
norma *norm, pattern, standard*
- altenativa *alternate standard*
- de calidad *quality standard*
- de producción *production standard*
- de rendimiento *performance standard*
- de trabajo *work standard*
- industrial *commercial standard*
- provisional *temporary standard, temporary work value*
- unificada *unified standard*
- variante *alternate standard*
-, al nivel de *up to standard*
-, proyecto de *standard project*
normal *standard*
- de muestreo, error *normal sampling error*
- de probabilidad, curva *normal probability curve*

- planeado, beneficio *planned normal profit*
-, actuación *normal performance*
-, capacidad *standard range*
-, distribución *normal distribution*
-, embalaje *packing*
-, envase *standard packing*
-, gasto *design rate*
-, horas de asistencia regular *attendance hours*
-, paso *standard gauge*
-, tiempo *normal time*
normalización *standardization*
- de equipos de oficina *office equipment standards*
- técnica *engineered standard*
-, ingeniero de *standards engineer*
normalizada, producción *standarized production*
normalizadas, cuentas *standardized accounts*
-, diferencias *standardized dimensions*
-, medidas *standardized dimensions*
-, piezas *standard parts*
normalizado, método *standard method*
-, procedimiento *standardized procedure*
-, tamaño *standard size*
normalizados, datos de tiempos *standard time data*
normas aprobadas *accepted standards*
- contables *accounting standards*
- cronometradas de producción *stopwatch production standards*
- cualitativas *qualitative standards*
- cuantitativas *quantitative standards*
- de aceptación *acceptance standards*
- de auditoría *auditing standards*
- de costos *cost standards*
- fiscales *tax regulations*
- publicitarias *advertising standards*
-, clasificación de normas *standard sort*
-, dentro de las *up to standard*
-, no sujeto a *informal*
-, oficina de *bureau of standards*
normativo, cuestionario *standardized questionnaire*
nota *note*
- de cargo *debit note*
- de compra *buying or purchase order*
- de crédito *credit note*
- de remisión *shipping note*
-, tomar *to take notice*
notaría *notary's office*
notario *notary*
- público *notary public*
noticia *notice, intelligence*
noticiario *newsreel, newcast*
noticias, emisión de últimas *newscast*

–, locutor de últimas *newscaster*
–, últimas *stop-press news*
notificar *to notify or advise*
nuevo, en estado de *in mint condition*
nula, cantidad *magnitude nil*
nulificar *to cancel*
nulo *null*
– y sin valor *null and void*
numérica de contabilidad, máquina *numerical accounting machine*
numérico gráfico, método *graphico-numerical method*
número *number, figure, digit*
– de acciones sin aumentar el capital, aumento el *stock split-up*

– de orden *serial number*
– de serie *serial number*
– entero *whole number*
– índice *index number*
– muestral promedio *average sample number*
– óptimo *optimum number*
– par *even number*
– rojo, en *in the red*
números al azar *random numbers*
– clave *key numbers*
– redondos *round numbers*
–, balance de *trial balance*

O

objetivo *goal, target*
objeto *object*
objetos de escritorio *office equipment*
obligación *debenture, debt, liability, indebtedness, bond*
– de rendir cuentas *accountability*
– emitida por bajo de la par *yield bond*
– hipotecaria *mortgage bond*
– limitada *limited bond, limited liability*
obligaciones *securities, liabilities, debentures*
– a corto plazo *short-term liabilities*
– a largo plazo *long-term liabilities*
– al portador *bearer paper*
– diferidas *deferred bonds*
– hipotecarias *mortgage bonds*
– mercantiles *commercial paper*
–, casa de valores, títulos u *security house*
–, emisión de *issue of bonds*
–, préstamo en *loan on debentures*
–, rendimiento de *bond yield*
obligacionista *debenture holder*
obligatoria, compensación *compulsory compensation*
obligatorio, seguro *compulsory or obligatory insurance*
obra *work*
– a jornal *open work*
– contratada a largo plazo, mano de *indentured labour*
– directa, mano de *productive labour*
– especializada, mano de *skilled labour*
– indirecta, mano de *indirect labour or work*
–, economía de mano de *labour saving*
–, gráfico de avance de una *progress chart*
–, informe del avance de una *progress report*
–, mano de *workmanship*
obras extras *variations*
– públicas *public works*
– registradas, materiales y *copyrighted material*
obrera en la dirección, participación *employee participation in management*
– en los beneficios, participación *industrial partnership*
–, asociación *labour union*
–, asociación profesional *trade union*
–, clase *working class*
–, cuestión *labour troubles*

obreras, directivos de organizaciones *labour leaders*
obrero *worker, labourer*
– calificado *skilled or qualified worker, craftsman*
– demostrador *demonstration worker, demonstrator*
– industrial *factory worker*
– manual *blue-collar worker*
– provisional *casual worker*
– reserva *standby man, spare man*
– semicalificado *semi-skilled worker*
–, contrato que prohibe afiliarse a sindicato *yellowdog contract*
–, derecho *labour*
–, formulario para valorar los méritos del *employee-rating form*
–, gremio *labour union*
–, paro *strike*
–, seguro *workmen's insurance*
–, sindicato *trade union*
obrero-hora *manhour*
obreros *workers*
– disponibles *labour market*
– y directivos, relaciones entre *labour-management relations*
–, bonificaciones de *employees' bonus*
–, compensación de los empleados y *employee cooperation*
–, cooperación entre patronos y *employee-employer cooperation*
–, despido temporal de *layoff*
–, explotación de *sweating*
–, explotar a *to sweat*
–, movimiento de *labour turnover*
–, primas de *employees' bonus*
–, sindicatos, fábrica con *closed shop*
obsequio *premium, bonus*
observación, período de *observation period, overall time, elapsed time*
obsesión *obsession*
obstáculo *handicap*
– en la marcha de la producción *bottleneck*
obtención de datos, proceso de *data processing*
ocasión, equipo de *used equipment*
–, precio de *bargain price*
ocasional, dividendo *irregular dividend*

ocioso *idle*
oculta, tendencia *undercurrent*
ocultación de utilidades *concealment of profits*
oculto, activo *concealed assets*
ocupación *occupation*
– total *full employment*
–, baja de la *decreasing employment*
ofensivo, dumping *obnoxions dumping*
oferta *bid, offer*
– de dinero *supply of money*
– de trabajo *employment offered*
– en baja *underbid*
– en firme *firm offer*
– mejor *best bid*
– sellada *sealed bid*
– y demanda *supply and demand*
– y demanda, diferencia entre los precios de *spread*
– y demanda, ley de la *law of supply and demand*
– y demanda, mercado con igualdad de precios de *close market*
–, cuadro de la *supply schedule*
–, precios de *bid and asked quotations*
–, elasticidad de la *elasticity of supply*
–, precio de *bid or offered price*
ofertas a precios unitarios *unit price bid*
– de empleos *advertisements by positions*
offset impresión *impression offset*
–, procedimiento *offset process*
oficial pagador *agent officer*
–, hora *standard time*
–, tasación *assessed valuation*
–, voto no *straw vote*
oficiales de los gremios o sindicatos obreros *labour leaders*
–, precios *official prices*
oficina *office, agency, bureau*
– central *main office, headquarters*
– comercial *business premises*
– de colocaciones *employment bureau, labour exchange*
– de correos *post office*
– de equipajes *receiving office*
– de información *inquiry office*
– de negocios *agency office*
– de normas *bureau of standards*
– de patentes *patent office*
– de registro de publicaciones *copyright receipt office*
– de tiempos *time-study department*
– de tipificación *bureau of standards*
– recaudadora de impuestos *tax office*
–, después de las horas de *after-office hours*
–, empleado administrativo de *office clerk*

–, empleado de *white-collar worker*
–, equipo de *office equipment*
–, horas de *office hours*
–, investigación en la *desk research*
–, jefe de *office manager*
–, máquinas de *business machine*
–, normalización de equipos de *office equipment standards*
–, operario de máquinas de *office-machine operator*
–, personal de *office force*
–, selección de empleados de *selection of office employees*
–, servicios de *office services*
–, trabajador de *office worker, white-collar worker*
–, trabajo de *office work, clerical work*
oficinas, automatización de las *office automation*
–, colocación en *office employment*
–, equipo de *office equipment*
–, jefe de *office manager*
–, supervisor de *office supervisor*
oficinista *office clerk, office worker, general clerk*
oficio *trade, craft*
–, prueba de capacidad en el *trade test*
oficios, buenos *good offices*
oficioso *informal*
omisión *omission*
–, salvo error u *errors and omissions excepted*
–, signo de *caret*
omitido, dividendo *passed dividend*
omitir *to omit*
onda corta *short wave*
–, extensión de *wave length*
opción de compra *option to purchase*
– del comprador *buyer's option*
operación *operation, phase*
– a término *business in futures*
– comercial *commercial transaction*
– de almacenar *storage operation*
– de personal *staff operation*
– lineal *line operation*
– manual *manual operation*
– normalizada, procedimientos de *standard operating procedures*
–, balance de *profit and statement*
–, beneficio de *revenue profit*
–, capital de *working capital*
–, costo de *operation cost*
–, costos de *operating expenses*
–, diagrama de *operation chart*
–, estado de *operation statement*
–, gastos de *operating expenses*
–, plan de *work schedule*

–, razón de *operating ratio*
–, utilidades de *operating profit*
operaciones bancarias *banking operations*
– comerciales marítimas *shipping business or trade*
– contables *accounting transactions*
– de muestreo *sampling operations*
– invisibles *invisible transactions*
– sucesivas, plantilla de *flow sheet*
–, análisis de *operational analysis or research*
–, orden de *sequence of operations*
operador de máquina calculadora *computer operator, calculating-machine operator*
– de máquina contable *book-keeping machine operator*
operante, función característica *operating characteristic function*
–, personal *task force*
operar *to operate, run, transact or act*
– en descubierto *sell short*
operario *workman, worker, operator*
– a destajo *pieceworker*
– de máquinas de oficina *office machine operator*
operarios, comisión de *works council*
operativa, investigación *operational or operation research*
opinión *advice, opinion*
– informada *informed opinion*
– pública *public opinion*
– pública, escrutinio de la *public opinion polls*
opiniones, encuesta de *opinion survey*
oportunidad, precio de *bargain*
–, venta de *bargain sale*
optativo *optional*
óptima, actuación *optimum performance*
–, población *optimum population*
óptimo, examen *quiz*
–, número *optimum number*
oral, comunicación *word-of-mouth*
–, publicidad *word-of-mouth advertising*
orden *order*
– de compra *purchase order*
– de embargo *distress warrant*
– de entrega *delivery order*
– de fabricación *factory or work order*
– de operaciones *sequence of operations*
– de pago *payment order, draft*
– de producción, comunicación de *notice of production*
– de trabajo *job, factory or works order*
– de, pagos a la *pay to the order of*
– del día *order of the day, agenda*

– para entrega y pago inmediato *spot order*
– vigente *standing order*
–, número de *serial number*
–, pagadero a la *payable to order*
órdenes al personal *personnel paging*
– de compra, receptor de *sales-order clerk*
– no despachadas *backlog*
– pendientes *backlog*
–, buscar *to canvass*
–, ficha de información de *order information card*
ordinaria, asamblea *regular meeting*
–, sesión *regular meeting*
ordinarias, acciones *common stock equities*
–, horas *straight time*
ordinario *regular*
–, acreedor *general creditor*
–, correo *regular mail*
–, ingreso *current revenue*
–, mensaje *ordinary message*
ordinarios de operación, gastos *running expenses*
–, gastos *current expenditure*
organismo internacional *international agency or institution*
organización, estructura de *organization structure*
– funcional *staff organization*
– lineal *lineal organization*
–, diagrama de *organization chart*
organizaciones obreras, directivos de *labour leaders*
organizar *to organize or constitute*
orientación *orientation*
– profesional *vocational guidance*
–, comité de *steering committee*
–, estudio de *pilot study*
origen *origin, source*
–, certificado de *certificate of origin*
–, datos de *primary data*
–, país de *source country*
original *original*
originales, comprobantes *supporting records*
oro *gold*
– de ley *standard gold*
– en barras *bar gold*
–, encaje de *gold reserve*
–, límite del *gold point*
–, patrón *gold standard*
–, patrón cambio *gold exchange standard*
–, punto *gold point*
–, talón *gold standard*
oscilaciones de ventas *sales fluctuations*

P

pacotilla, mercancías de *sale goods*
pacto *agreement, deal*
– de caballeros *gentlemen's agreement*
– de retroventa *agreement to resell*
padrón *register, list*
paga *fee, pay, payment, wages, salary*
– de marcha *severance pay*
–, sobre con la *pay envelope*
–, tarifa inicial de *starting rate of pay*
pagable a destino, flete *freight collect*
pagada, cuenta *account settled*
pagadera, cuenta *mature account*
pagaderas en dólares, mercancías *dollar commodities*
–, acumulaciones *accruals payable*
pagadero *payable*
– a la orden *payable to order*
– a la vista *due to demand*
– a plazos *payable in instalments*
– al entregar *cash on delivery*
– al portador *payable to bearer*
– en efectivo *payable in cash*
pagado *paid*
– a tiempo, impuesto no *delinquent tax*
– íntegramente *paid in full*
–, flete *freight prepaid*
pagador *payer, paying teller, paymaster, payroll clerk*
–, empleado *pay clerk*
–, oficial *agent officer*
pagar *to pay*
– a cuenta *to pay on account*
– a plazos *to pay by instalments*
– en efectivo *to pay cash*
– por completo *to pay in full*
– y despedir a un empleado *to pay off*
–, cuentas a *accounts payable*
–, dividendos por *dividends payable*
–, documentos por *notes payable*
–, efectos a *bills payable*
–, importe a *amount due*
–, letras a *bills payable*
pagaré *promissory note*
– a la vista *demand note*
– con opción de pago adelantado *acceleration note*
página de anuncios *advertising page*
– de la cubierta *cover page*

– interior *inner page*
– o recorte comprobante de anuncio *tear sheet*
–, primera *front page*
–, última *back page*
pago *payment*
– a cuenta *part payment, payment on account, down payment, advance cash*
– a huelguistas *strike pay*
– a plazos *instalment*
– adelantado *advance payment, cash in advance, prepayment*
– al contado *cash payment, prompt payment, cash and carry*
– anticipado *advance payment*
– aplazado *deferred payment*
– contra documentos *cash against documents*
– contra entrega *cash on delivery*
– contra reembolso *cash on delivery*
– de dividendos *payment of dividends*
– en especie *payment in kind*
– inmediato, orden para entrega y *spot order*
– parcial *partial payment, progress payment*
– por previsión social *social security payment*
– predial, boleta *real-estate tax receipt*
–, capacidad de *ability to pay*
–, carta de *acquittance*
–, coeficiente de carga del peso de *revenue weight load factor*
–, comprobante de *receipt*
–, con facilidades de *by easy payments*
–, condiciones de *usance*
–, cheque pendiente de *outstanding cheque*
–, descuento por pronto *cash or sales discount*
–, detener el *to stop payment*
–, día de *value date, pay day*
–, efectuar el *to effect payment*
–, exigir el *to enforce payment*
–, facilidades de *easy terms of payments, easy payments*
–, falta de *non-payment*
–, forma de *terms of payment*
–, lista de personas exentas de *tax-free list*
–, orden de *payment order, draft*
–, pendiente *unpaid*
–, pronto *prompt payment*
–, suspender el *to stop payment*
–, tipo básico de *base rate of pay*
pagos *payments*

- a la orden de *pay to the order of*
- al exterior, balanza de *balance of external payments*
- al portador *pay to the bearer*
- desfavorables, balanza de *adverse balance of payments*
- limitados, base de *limited payment basis*
- negativa, balanza de *unfavourable balance of payments*
- positiva, balanza de *favourable balance of payments*
-, balanza de *balance of payments*
-, déficit en la balanza de *deficit in the balance of payments*
-, detener *to stop payments*
-, suspender *to suspend*
-, suspensión de *suspension*
país de origen *source country*
-, compras en el *domestic purchases*
-, productos del *home goods*
-, valor de consumo en el *home consumption value*
palabra clave *code word*
-, libertad de *free speech*
-, sueldo por *straight time*
-, tomar la *to take the floor*
panel de consumidores *consumer panel*
-, prueba a través de un *test panel*
papel blanco *clean paper*
- carbón *carbon paper*
- cebolla *copying paper*
- de color *coloured paper*
- de embalaje *wrapping or packing paper*
- de envolver *wrapping paper*
- de estraza *kraft paper*
- fino para copias de cartas *copying paper*
- moneda *paper money*
- para máquina sumadora, rollo de *adding roll*
- secante *blotter, blotting paper*
-, mano de *quire*
-, moneda de *paper money*
-, punzadora para *paper punch*
papeleo *red tape*
- administrativo *red tape*
papelería *stationery*
-, tienda de *stationery store*
papeles *papers, documents*
- comerciales *commercial or business papers or documents*
- de negocios *commercial or business papers or documents*
papeletas, votación por *polls*
paquete *package*
- postal *parcel post*
paquetería *dry-goods store*

par, a la *at par*
-, bajo *below par*
-, cambio a la *exchange at par*
-, número *even number*
-, sobre *above par*
parada o desfile *parade, stoppage*
- de máquina, tiempo de *downtime machine*
-, tiempo de *downtime*
-, tiempo de máquina *idle machine time*
paralización de negocios *business stagnation*
- del trabajo *labour stoppage*
- industrial *tie-up*
paramétricas, pruebas no *non-parametric tests*
parámetro, punto *parameter point*
parcela *parcel of land*
parcial *part-time*
- permanente, incapacidad *permanent partial disability*
-, auditoría *partial audit*
-, dividendo *interim dividend*
-, pago *partial payment, progress payment*
parcialidad *bias*
paridad *parity, par*
- adquisitiva *parity in purchasing power*
- cambiaria *par of exchange*
- de ingresos, razón de *parity income ratio*
-, precio de *parity price*
paro *strike, shutdown, stoppage*
- forzoso *unemployment*
- general *general strike*
- laboral *unemployment*
- obrero *strike*
- patronal *lockout*
párrafo *paragraph*
parroquiano *customer*
parte de un socio, comprar la *to buy out*
- en, tomar *to take part in*
partes contratantes *contracting parties*
- interesadas *interested parties*
participación *share, interest*
- de control *controlling interest*
- en las ganancias *profit sharing*
- en los beneficios *profit sharing*
- obrera en la dirección *employee participation in management*
- obrera en los beneficios *industrial partnership*
-, cuenta en *joint account*
participantes *credits*
particular *private*
-, cuenta *private account*
-, secretaria *private secretary*
-, secretario *private secretary*
partida *lot, item*

– aislada, lote o *stray lot*
– de crédito *credit item*
– de saldo *job lot*
– del activo *asset*
– doble *double entry*
– doble, contabilidad por *double-entry book-keeping*
– mercancías vendidas *bill of goods*
– simple, contabilidad por *single-entry book-keeping*
– o asientos de cierre *closing entries*
–, asentar una *to make an entry*
–, masa *liabilities*
pasaporte *passport*
pasar *to pass*
– a otra hoja *to carry forward*
– al debe *to debit*
– la lista *to call the roll*
pasivas, deudas *accounts payable*
pasivo *passive, liabilities*
– a largo plazo *long-term liabilities*
– acumulado *accrued liabilities*
– asumido *assumed liabilities*
– comercial *current liabilities*
– consolidado *funded debt*
– contingente *contingent liabilities*
– de capital *capital liabilities*
– diferido *deferred liabilities*
– directo *direct liabilities*
– efectivo *actual liabilities*
– fijo *fixed liabilities*
– flotante *current liabilities*
– real *actual liabilities*
– social *company's liabilities*
– total *total liabilities*
–, activo y *assets and liabilities*
–, cuentas de *liability accounts*
–, fideicomiso *passive or dry trust*
paso normal *standard gauge*
pasta, cartera *millboard*
patentado *patented*
–, artículo *proprietary article*
patentar *to patent, to take out a patent*
patente *patent, licence, franchise*
– en tramitación *patent pending*
– primitiva *basic patent*
–, derechos de *patent royalties or rights*
–, infracción de *patent infringement*
–, licencia de *patent licence*
patentes mundiales en trámite, modelos registrados y designs *registered and world patents pending*
–, ley de *patent law*
–, oficina de *patent office*
–, poseedor de *patentee*
–, título de *letters patent*

–, y marcas *patent and trademark*
patrimoniales, valores *capital assets*
patrimonio *capital, net worth*
patrocinar *to sponsor*
patrón *pattern, template, employer*
– absoluto *absolute standard*
– cambio oro *gold exchange standard*
– de liquidez *standard of liquidity*
– de medida *standard*
– de vida *standard of living*
– doble *double standard, bimetallism*
– monetario *standard of value*
– oro *gold standard*
– plata *silver standard*
–, muestra *master sample*
–, peso *standard weight*
patronal, huelga *lockout*
–, paro *lockout*
–, sociedad *employers' association, employers' federation*
patronato *board of trustees*
patrono *employer*
–, responsabilidad del *employer's liability*
patronos, acuerdo entre el sindicato y los *union-employer agreement*
–, empleado que trabaja para varios *part-timer*
–, huelga de *lockout*
–, representante de *employer's representative*
peaje *toll*
peculado *peculation*
pedido *order*
– de compra *purchase order*
– de cotización *inquiry*
– de ensayo *trial order*
– en firme *firm order*
– hecho por correo *mail order*
– inicial *advance order*
– no preferente *unrated order*
– para el interior *domestic order*
– pendiente *standing order*
– urgente *rush order*
–, anotar un *to book an order*
–, colocar un *to place an order*
–, hacer un *to place an order*
–, surtir un *to fill an order*
–, suspender un *to hold up an order*
–, tomar un *to take an order*
pedidos a servir, envíos a cuenta de *advance payments on purchase obligations*
–, entrega de *order delivery*
–, facturación de *order invoicing*
–, formulario de *order form*
–, libro de *order book*
–, manipulación de *order handling*
–, volumen de *size*

–, volumen medio de *average order size*
pelados, precios *cut prices*
peligro, situación de *danger situation*
penal, cláusula *penalty clause*
pendiente *outstanding, pending, in abeyance, slope*
– de pago *unpaid*
– de pago, cheque *outstanding cheque*
–, cuenta *outstanding account*
–, deuda *unpaid debt or balance*
–, pedido *standing order*
pendientes, órdenes *backlog*
penosidad *stress*
pensamiento, sondeador del *scanner*
pensión *annuity*
– de invalidez *disability benefit*
– de retiro *retirement pension*
– diferida *deferred annuity*
– familiar *family allowance*
– vitalícia *life pension*
–, fondo de *pension fund*
pensiones de vejez, fondo de *superannuation fund*
–, plan de *pension plan*
pequeña exposición *show*
pequeño folleto *booklet*
percepción *perception*
pérdida *loss, waste*
– de actividad *activity loss*
– efectiva *actual or absolute total loss*
– neta *net loss*
– total *absolute total loss*
– total efectiva *absolute total loss*
– total real *actual total loss*
–, absorber la pérdida *to absorb the loss*
–, asumir la *to absorb the loss*
–, reportar una *to show a loss*
–, vender con *to sell at a loss*
pérdidas anuales *annual losses*
– de huelga, seguro contra *strike insurance*
– de la temporada *seasonal loss*
– imprevistas *windfall losses*
– por créditos fallidos *expenses for bad debts*
– y ganancias *revenue and expense, profit and loss*
– y ganancias, cuenta de *profit-and-loss account*
– y ganancias, estado de *profit-and-loss statement*
– y gastos, cuenta de *account of outlays and costs*
perdidas, formulario de ventas *lost-sale slip*
perdido, tiempo *lost time*
perecederas, mercancías *perishable goods*
perfil *outline, profile*
– de avance del trabajo *progress profile*

perforación alfabética *alphabetical punching*
– de datos alfabéticos al sumarizar *alphabetic summary punching*
– de fichas *punching*
– de fichas a gran velocidad, máquina de *high-speed punched-card machine*
– de fichas, equipo de *punched-card equipment*
perforadas, máquina de fichas *punched-card machine*
perforadora *perforator*
– alfanumérica *alphanumeric key punch*
–, cinta *punched tape*
perforar una ficha *to punch*
pericia *workmanship*
pericial, valoración *expert appraisal*
perímetro *perimeter*
periódicas, migraciones *periodic migrations*
periódico *newspaper, journal*
–, recorte de *newspaper clipping or cutting*
periódicos sensacionales *yellow press*
–, vendedor de *newsagent, newsboy*
periodismo *journalism*
periodístico *journalese*
período *period*
– agudo *peak period*
– contable *accounting period*
– de actividad *working life*
– de bonanza *boom*
– de gracia *grace period*
– de observación *observation period, overall time, elapsed time*
– de prueba *trial period*
– económico *accounting period*
– fiscal *accounting period*
períodos de capacitación *training periods*
– de descanso *rest periods*
perito *expert, appraiser*
– en mercadología *market expert*
– mercantil *expert accountant*
perjuicios, demanda por daños y *claim for damages*
permanente *permanent*
–, activo *permanent assets*
–, comisión *standing committee*
–, fichero *permanent card file*
–, incapacidad absoluta *permanent total disability*
–, incapacidad parcial *permanent partial disability*
–, migración *permanent migration*
permanentes, gastos *standing costs*
permeado de *permeated with*
permisible, utilidad *allowable return*
permiso *permit, licence*
– anual *annual leave*

– de exportación *export permit*
– de importación *import permit*
–, caducidad de un *expiry of a permit*
permuta *barter*
perpetuidad *perpetuity*
perpetuo *perpetual*
–, bono *annuity bond*
perseverancia *follow-up*
persona corporativa *corporate person*
–, comprar a una *to buy over*
–, coste anual por *annual cost per head*
–, impuesto por *poll tax*
–, justipreciar una *to size-up an individual*
personaje eminente *luminary*
–, gran *mogul*
personal *employees, personnel, force, clerical force, private*
– de estudios de proyectos *design engineering staff*
– de fábrica *plant personnel*
– de oficina *office force*
– de personal *employment, hiring*
– de proyectos *design staff*
– de reemplazo *labour turnover*
– de servicio de los detallistas, capacitación del *retail service training*
– de ventas *sales force*
– dirigente *supervisory staff*
– eventual *temporary workers*
– operante *task force*
–, analizador de *personnel analyst*
–, capacitación del *personnel training*
–, colocación de *allocation*
–, comité de dotación de *allocation committee*
–, departamento *personnel division*
–, dirección del *personnel management*
–, director de *personnel manager*
–, dotación de *allocation*
–, encuesta sobre *personnel survey*
–, enlace del *shop steward*
–, entrevista *oral interview*
–, escalas de clasificación de *personnel-rating scales*
–, fortuna *personal estate*
–, garantía *personal security*
–, impuesto *personal tax*
–, nómina de *personal roster*
–, operación de *staff operation*
–, órdenes al *personnel paging*
–, plantilla de *personnel allocation plan, staff establishment*
–, política respecto al *personnel policies*
–, préstamo *personal loan*
–, proceso de depuración del *clearance procedure*
–, pruebas de *personnel tests*

–, representante del *shop steward*
–, rotación del *turnover*
–, selección del *personnel selection*
–, traslado de *transfer of personnel*
personales, relaciones *personal acquaintances*
–, suplemento por necesidades *personal needs allowance*
personalidad *personality*
– compleja *complex personality*
– social *corporate personality*
personas exentas de pago, lista de *tax-free list*
perspectiva de la publicidad *advertising approach*
–, cliente en *prospective client*
perspectivas de lucro *profit outlook*
pesadez *heaviness*
pesar *to weigh*
peso *weight*
– bruto *gross weight*
– bruto, rebaja normalizada del *tare allowance*
– de pago, coeficiente de carga del *revenue weight load factor*
– legal *legal or standard weight*
– muerto *dead weight*
– patrón *standard weight*
– total *gross weight*
– total cargado *gross laden weight*
– unitario *unit weight*
–, exceso de *overweight*
–, falta de *short weight*
petición de informes *information call*
– de materiales *requisition for materials*
– de utillaje y herramientas, boletín de *tool ticket*
pie *foot*
pieza *art component, work-piece*
–, precio por *piecework price, price rate*
–, salario por *piece wage*
–, trabajo por *piecework*
piezas de recambio, servicio de *after-sales service*
– normalizadas *standard parts*
–, seguidor de *progress chaser*
pignorabilidad *pledgeability*
pignorable *pledgeable*
pignoradas, cuentas *pledged accounts*
piloto, encuesta *pilot survey*
–, etapa *pilot stage*
–, muestra *pilot sample*
–, precio *price leader*
–, proyecto *pilot project*
pinta *pint*
piquete de huelga *picket*
placer *satisfaction*
plagiario *plagiarist, plagiary*

plagio *plagiarism*
plan *plan, scheme, programme*
- de bonificaciones *bonus plan*
- de distribución *marketing plan*
- de operación *work schedule*
- de pensiones *pension plan*
- de remuneraciones *compensation plan*
- de retiro *retirement plan*
- de tareas *job planning*
- de trabajo *work schedule*
- del avance del trabajo *progress schedule*
- publicitario *advertising scheme or programme*
planeación económica *economic planning*
planeado, beneficio normal *planned normal profit*
planeamiento *planning*
-, ingeniero encargado del *planning engineer*
planificada, economía *planned economy*
plantilla de operaciones sucesivas *flow sheet*
plano *draft, drawing, map, chart*
planos y presupuestos *drafts and estimates*
planta *plant*
- de montaje *assembling plant*
- ensambladora *assembling plant*
plantilla de personal *personnel allocation plan, staff establishment*
-, según *according to pattern*
plásticos *plastics*
plata, moneda de *silver coin*
plataforma *pallet*
- de trabajo *step-plate*
- electoral *platform*
plaza, costo en *market price*
-, precio en *stop price*
-, valor en *market value*
plazo *time, term, instalment*
- anual *annual instalment*
- de entrega *time of delivery*
- fijo *fixed term*
- largo, bono de *long-term bond*
-, carta de crédito a *time letter of credit*
-, crédito a corto *short-term credit*
-, crédito a largo *long-term credit*
-, depósito a *time deposit*
-, deuda a corto *short-term debt*
-, giro a *time draft*
-, interés a corto *short-term interest*
-, largo *long term*
-, letra a *usance or time bill*
-, letra a corto *short bill*
-, letra a largo *long bill*
-, préstamo a *time loan*
plazos a cobrar *instalment receivables*
-, a *by instalments*
-, comprar a *instalment buying, hire purchase*

-, negocio a *business in futures*
-, pagadero a *payable in instalments*
-, pagar a *to pay by instalments*
-, pago a *instalment*
-, vender a *instalment or time selling*
plena actividad, en *in full swing*
- producción, en *in full swing*
plenaria, sesión *joint session*
pliego de peticiones *list of demands*
plural, acciones de voto *plural-voting stock*
pluralidad *plurality*
plus valía *goodwill, increased value, unearned increment*
- latente *latent goodwill*
población *population*
- abierta *open population*
- logística *logistic population*
- óptima *optimum population*
-, índice de *population index*
-, índice de aumento de *population growth rate*
-, movimiento general de la *general population movement*
pobreza *poverty*
poder *power, strength*
- adquisitivo *purchasing or buying power*
- adquisitivo, índice del *buying power index*
- amplísimo *full power*
- para gastar *spending power*
- para negociar *bargaining power*
-, carta *power of attorney*
-, por *by proxy*
poderes, conferir *to empower*
poderosa, prueba más *most powerful test*
política *policy*
- anticíclica *contra-cyclical policy*
- arancelaria *tariff policy*
- crediticia *credit policy*
- de austeridad *austerity programme, policy of restraint*
- de compras *purchasing policy*
- de coyuntura *business cycle policy*
- de crédito *credit policy*
- de existencias estabilizadoras *buffer-stock plan*
- de inversión *investment policy*
- de mercancías *merchandising*
- de precio único *one-price salary*
- de precios *price policy*
- de puerta abierta *open-door policy*
- de restricción de créditos *tight-money policy*
- de sostenimiento de precios *price-support policy*
- de ventas *sales policy or angle or approach*
- económica *economic policy*
- hacendaria *financial policy*

– impositiva *tax policy*
– impositiva, estipulaciones en *canons of taxation*
– respecto al personal *personnel policies*
– tributarias *tax policy*
– uniforme de precios *uniform price policy*
–, economía *political economy*
peticiones, pliego de *list of demands*
póliza *policy*
– a todo riesgo *all-risk policy*
– abierta *blanket policy*
– colectiva *group policy*
– de averías *average policy*
– de fidelidad *fidelity bond*
– de grupo *group policy*
– de seguro *insurance policy*
– del último superviviente *last-survivor policy*
– dotal *endowment policy*
– limitada *limited policy*
– modelo *sample policy*
–, tenedor de *policyholder*
ponderación *weighting*
–, función de *weight function*
ponderada, media *weighted mean*
–, media aritmética *weighted arithmetic mean*
–, media geométrica *weighted geometric mean*
–, muestra *weighted sample*
ponderado *weighted*
–, índice no *weighted index*
–, medio *weighted average*
–, promedio *weighted average*
–, valor *weighted value*
ponderar *to weigh*
ponencias de trabajo *working parties*
poner en servicio *to put in service*
pontazgo *bridge toll*
por *per*
– cabeza *per capita*
– ciento *per cent, percentage*
– cobrar *receivable*
– debajo de los costos *below the line*
– día *per diem, per day*
– encima de los costos *above the line*
– mayor *wholesale*
– mayor, negocio al *wholesale trade*
– menor *retail*
– menor, negocio al *retail trade*
– pagar *payable*
– persona *per capita*
– poder *by proxy*
– saldo de cuentas *in full*
porcentaje *percentage, rate, ratio, per cent*
– anual de aumento *annual percentaje of increase*
– anual constante, depreciación por *straight-line depreciation*

– de accidentes *accident rate*
– de gravedad de los accidentes *accident severity rate*
– de mortalidad por accidentes *accident death rate*
– de terminación, método de *percentage of completion method*
– de utilidades *percentage of profits*
– elevado de cambios de personal *high turnover rate*
– elevado de cambios de surtido *high turnover rate*
–, coste más *cost plus*
pormenorizar *to detail or itemize*
portacopia *copyholder*
portador *bearer*
–, acciones al *bearer shares*
–, al *to bearer*
–, bonos al *coupon bonds*
–, cheque al *cheque to bearer*
–, obligaciones al *bearer paper*
–, pagaderos al *payable to bearer*
–, pagos al *pay to the bearer*
–, título al *bearer instrument*
–, títulos al *active bond*
portafolio *portfolio*
porte *freight, carriage*
– de correos *postage*
–, carta de *waybill, railway bill*
–, franco de *postage-free*
–, libre de *postage-free*
portuarios, derechos *port duties*
posdata *postscript*
poseedor *holder, possessor, owner*
– de patente *patentee*
posfechado *postdated*
–, cheque *postdated cheque*
posibilidad comercial *commercial feasibility*
posibilidades fiscales *financial resources*
–, lista de *possibility list*
posición *position*
– comercial *commercial standing*
– de informes *information desk*
– de la herramienta, preparación y puesta en *indexing tool*
– de la máquina, preparación y puesta en *indexing machine*
– del utilaje, preparación y puesta en *indexing jig*
positiva, balanza de pagos *favourable balance of payments*
positivos, valores *assets*
posponer *to postpone or extend*
postal *postal*
–, dirección *mailing address*
–, encomienda *parcel post*

–, giro *money order*
–, paquete *parcel post*
–, talón *postal receipt*
–, tarifa *postal rates*
–, timbre *postage stamp*
--, zona *postal zone*
postor más bajo *low bidder*
postura *bid*
postventas, servicio de *after-sales service*
potencia, a toda *all-out*
potencial de comercio, zona *potential trading area*
– de compra, capacidad *potential buying power*
– de producción *productive potential*
– de ventas *sales potential*
– humano *manpower*
–, cliente *prospective client*
–, consumidor *potential consumer*
–, densidad *potential density*
–, mercado *potential market*
potenciales, ganancias *potential or expected earnings*
–, ventas *potential sales*
potencialidad económica *economic possibilities*
práctica comercial *commercial usage, trading custom*
– contable *accounting practice*
–, prueba *test run*
–, regla *working rule*
prácticas normalizadas, procedimiento de *standard practice procedure*
– tipificadas, manual de *standard practice manual*
precaución, motivo *precautionary motive*
precautorios, derechos *preventive rights*
precifrado *pre-coding*
precio *price, worth*
– a destajo *flat rate*
– actual *market or current price*
– al contado *cash price*
– al detalle *retail price*
– al mayoreo *wholesale price*
– alzado, contrato a *lumpsum contract*
– bajo *low price*
– bajo costo *below cost price*
– base o básico *base price*
– comercial *trade price*
– competitivo *competitive price*
– con descuento *discount price*
– convenido *agreed price*
– corriente *market price*
– de avalúo *assessed valuation*
– de cierre *closing quotation or rate*
– de competencia *competitive price*

– de compra *buying or purchase price*
– de costo *cost price*
– de detallista *retail price*
– de emisión *issue price*
– de exportación *export price*
– de fábrica *factory price*
– de factura *invoice price*
– de factura, rebaja del *sales allowance*
– de ganga *bargain price*
– de la mercancía, fijación del *merchandise pricing*
– de la última compra, método del *price of last purchase method*
– de lista *list price*
– de menudeo *retail price*
– de menudeo, método de *retail method*
– de ocasión *bargain price*
– de oferta *bid or offered price*
– de oportunidad *bargain*
– de paridad *parity price*
– de primera oferta *upset price*
– de rebaja *markdown price*
– de reventa *resale price*
– de subasta *upset price*
– de tasa *standard price*
– de venta *selling price*
– de venta al contado *cash price*
– de venta al detalle *retail selling price*
– de venta al público *gross price, gross sale price*
– de venta, impuesto sobre *sales tax*
– del mercado *market price*
– del mercado, comprar a *to buy at market price*
– del mercado, método *market price method*
– determinado, contrato a *fixed-price contract*
– dominante *prevailing price*
– en alza *rising price*
– en plaza *spot price*
– estable *close price*
– fijo de venta *fixed selling price*
– fuerte *published price*
– íntegro *full price*
– justo *fair value*
– límite *price line*
– máximo *top price*
– máximo del concesionario *distributor's maximum price*
– máximo permitido *ceiling price*
– mayorista *wholesale price*
– medio *average price*
– mínimo *floor price*
– módico *moderate price*
– muy rebajado *knockout price*
– neto *trade price*
– nominal *asking price*

– piloto *price leader*
– para venta interior *domestic price*
– ponderado *average price*
– por pieza *piecework price, piece rate*
– predominante *ruling price*
– probable *prospective price*
– redondo *all-round price*
– reducido *reduced price*
– regulador *standard price*
– revisable, contrato de *sliding-scale contract*
– según contrato *price as provided in the contract*
– sin beneficio *close price*
– sostenido *support price*
– techo *ceiling price*
– tirado, comprar a *to buy dirt cheap*
– tope *ceiling price*
– único, política de *one-price salary*
– unitario *unit price*
– y el costo, diferencia entre el *markup price*
–, aumento de *increased price*
–, cambios de *price changes*
–, diferencia de *markup*
–, factor determinante del *price determining factor*
–, límite de *price ceiling*
–, nivel de *price level*
–, sostener el *to keep up the price*
–, subida de *price advance*
–, vender a bajo *undersell*
–, venta bajo *underselling*
precios al consumidor, índice de *consumer price index*
– al detalle, lista de *retail list price*
– al cierre *closing prices*
– al menudeo *retail prices*
– ascendentes escalonados, compras a *upscale buying*
– bursátiles *stock-exchange quotations*
– constantes *constant prices*
– de apertura *opening prices*
– de fábrica *manufacturer's price*
– de liquidación *clearance prices*
– de mercado nacional *home market prices*
– de mercancías, índice de *commodity index*
– de monopolio *monopoly prices*
– de oferta y demanda *bid and asked quotations*
– de oferta y demanda, diferencia entre los *spread*
– de oferta y demanda, mercado con igualdad *close market*
– de venta *selling prices*
– descendentes *falling prices*
– estables *stable prices*
– firmes *steady prices*

– leales *fair prices*
– máximos legales *price ceiling*
– mínimos *floor prices*
– nacionales *home prices*
– oficiales *official prices*
– pelados *cut prices*
– reducidos, liquidación a *bargain sale*
– totales *all-in prices*
– únicos, tienda a *limited price store*
– unitarios, contrato a *unit-price contract*
– unitarios, oferta a *unit-price bid*
–, ajuste de *price adjustment*
–, alza de *boom*
–, baja de *price decline*
–, caída de *drop in prices*
–, cartel de *cartel for price fixing*
–, comportamiento de los precios *price behaviour*
–, conducción de *price leadership*
–, desplome de *price collapse*
–, directivo que fija los *pricing executive*
–, espiral de costos y *cost-price spiral*
–, estabilidad de *price steadiness*
–, estabilización de *price strengthening*
–, fijador de *price leader, price setter*
–, guerra de *price war*
–, hacer bajar los *to force prices down*
–, índice de *price index*
–, lista de *price list*
–, manipulación de *rigging of prices*
–, política de *price policy*
–, política de sostenimiento de *price-support policy*
–, rebaja de *short rates*
–, rebaja desleal de *underselling, price-cutting*
–, reducción de *price-cutting*
–, reglamentación de *price-fixing*
–, requisición de *demand*
–, resistencia contra los altos *price resistance*
–, subsidio de *price subsidy*
precisar *to set, fix or compel*
precisión, cronómetro de *calibrated stopwatch*
predial, boleto de pago *real-estate tax receipt*
–, impuesto *property or land tax*
predispuesto *set*
predominante, precio *ruling price*
preestreno *preview*
prefabricación *prefabrication*
preferencia por la liquidez *liquidity preference*
–, margen de *margin of preference*
preferencial *preferential*
–, tarifa *preferential tariff*
preferente *preferential*
–, dividendo *preferred dividend*
–, pedido no *unrated order*

preferentes participantes, acciones *participating stock*
–, acciones *preferred stock*
preferida, apreciación *preferred rating*
preferidas, acciones *preferred stock*
preferido *preferred*
prefijados, costes *standard costs*
pregunta de respuesta libre *open question*
– directa *open-ended question*
– dirigida *leading question*
prejuicio *bias*
preliminar, estudio *preliminary study or investigation*
premeditada, compra *premeditated purchase*
premio *bonus, premium, prize*
– de cobranza *collection fee*
– de seguro *insurance premium*
– en efectivo *cash award*
– en metálico *cash price*
– monetario *premium*
prenda *security, collateral*
–, dinero en *earnest money*
prendaria, garantía *collateral*
prendas, prestamista sobre *pledge holder*
–, tenedor de *receiver*
prendatario *receiver*
prensa sensacionalista *yellow press*
–, circulación de la *press circulation*
–, comunicado de *press release*
–, conferencia de *press conference*
–, libertad de *free press*
–, publicidad en la *newspaper or press advertising*
–, recorte de *press clipping or cutting*
preparación *preparation, set-up*
– de cuentas *accountancy, accounting*
– de ventas *accountancy, accounting*
– del cuestionario *questionnaire design*
– del trabajo *planning*
– y puesta en posición de la herramienta *indexing tool*
– y puesta en posición de la máquina *indexing machine*
– y puesta en posición del utillaje *indexing jig*
–, tiempo de *make ready time, set-up time*
preparada, entrevista no *non-structured interview*
prescribir *to prescribe*
prescripción *prescription*
prescrito, error *prescribed error*
presencia, tiempo de *attendance time, all-in time*
presentación *statement*
– de datos, sistema de *data display system*
– del producto *product design*
–, carta de *covering letter, letter of*

introduction
presentar al pago *to present for payment*
– en el mercado *to launch on the market*
– una comunicación *to read a paper*
– una economía *to show a saving*
presidente *chairman, president*
– en funciones *acting president*
– interino *acting president*
presidir la asamblea *to preside over the meeting*
presión *pressure*
–, grupos de *pressure groups*
presiones sociales *social pressures*
prestación social *social service*
prestaciones *benefits*
– adicionales al sueldo *fringe benefits*
– por vejez *old-age benefits*
prestamista *moneylender*
– sobre garantía *receiver*
– sobre prendas *pledge holder*
préstamo *loan*
– a corto plazo *short-term loan*
– a descubierto *unsecured loan*
– a plazo *time loan*
– bancario *bank loan*
– con garantía *loan against collateral*
– de consumo *loan for consumption*
– de un día *clearance loan*
– de uso *loan for use*
– en obligaciones *loan on debentures*
– hipotecario *mortgage loan*
– personal *personal loan*
– pignoraticio *pledge loan*
– reembolsado *refunded loan*
– sin caución *unsecured loan*
– sobre títulos *advances on securities*
–, conceder un *to grant a loan*
–, deudor de un *pledger*
–, sociedad de ahorro y *savings and loan association*
–, solicitante de *loan applicant*
–, solicitud de *loan application*
–, tomar a *to borrow*
préstamos a bajo interés *low-interest loans*
–, sección de *loan department*
prestar *to lend*
– con respaldo colateral *to lend on collateral*
– garantía *to act as security*
– sobre hipoteca *to lend on mortgage*
prestigio de una empresa, valor *goodwill*
–, propensión al *prestige bias*
presupuestados, costos *estimated cost*
presupuestar *to estimate*
presupuesto *budget, estimate*
– aproximado *rough estimate*
–, balancear el *to balance the budget*

–, comprobación del *budgetary control*
–, planos y *drafts and estimates*
–, reducciones en el *cuts in the budget*
–, revisión de *budgetary control*
presupuestos, fiscalización del *budgetary control*
pretendido, tiempo *target time*
prever, gastos a *expenses involved*
previa deducción de gastos *expenses deducted*
–, con cita *by appointment*
–, prueba *pre-test, pre-testing*
previsión *expectation, foresight*
– de ventas *forecasting sales, sales forecast*
– de ventas a largo plazo *long-range sales forecast*
– de ventas, especialista en *sales forecaster*
– matemática de ganancias *mathematical expectation of gain*
– social *social security, welfare*
– social, pago por *social security payment*
–, fondo de *provident or emergency fund*
previsiones *expectations*
prevista de terminación, fecha *due date*
–, mortalidad *expected mortality*
previstas, compras *planned purchases*
–, ganancias *expected or potential earnings*
–, rebajas *planned markdowns*
–, ventas *planned sales*
previsto *foreseen*
–, tiempo *design time*
prima *premium, bonus*
– cien por cien *hundred per cent incentive, straight piecework*
– de compensación *lien bonus, timeworker's bonus*
– de emisión *stock premium*
– de exportación *drawback*
– de liquidez *liquidity premium*
– de producción *incentive wage, production bonus*
– de riesgo *risk premium*
– en metálico *monetary incentive*
– escalonada *stepped bonus*
– estipulada *stipulated premium*
– graduada *sliding-scale premium*
– matemática *net premium*
– total *gross premium*
– única *single premium*
–, materia *raw material*
primado, tiempo *allowed time, incentive time*
primario, coste *prime cost*
–, producto *primary commodity, commodity product*
primarios, datos *primary data*
–, derechos *primary rights*
primas de obreros *employees' bonus*

–, boletín de *bonus sheet, earnings sheet*
–, cupo de materias *allocation*
–, hojas de *posting sheet, bonus sheet*
–, materias *raw materials*
–, sistema de *incentive system or plan, bonus plan, premium system*
primer gravamen *first lien*
primera clase, correo *first-class mail (Br)*
– de cambio *first of exchange*
– especie, error de *error of first kind*
– entrada, libro de *book of original entry*
– necesidad, artículos de *primary or convenience goods*
– oferta, precio de *upset price*
– página *front page*
primeros modelos, exhibición *first sample showing*
primitivas, acciones *original stock*
primo, costo *prime cost*
principal *principal, capital, staple*
–, abastecimiento *main supply*
–, cajero *head teller*
–, casa *headquarters*
–, socio *senior partner*
principales, carreteras *highways*
principio *principle*
– de aceleración *acceleration principle*
principios *code*
prioridad *priority*
privada, auditoría *internal audit*
–, banca *private banking*
privado, secretario *private secretary*
privilegiada, deuda *preferred debt*
privilegiadas, acciones *preference shares*
privilegiado, acreedor *preferred creditor*
–, bono *priority bond*
privilegio *privilege*
– de invención *patent*
probabilidad *probability*
– arbitraria, selección con *selection with arbitrary probability*
– completa de vida *complete expectation of life*
– condicional *conditional probability*
– de sobrevivencia *probability of surviving*
– de vida *life expectancy*
– proporcional al tamaño, selección con *selection with probability proportional to size*
– total *overall probability*
–, curva normal de *probability normal curve*
–, función de *probability function*
–, muestreo de *probability sampling*
–, selección con igual *selection with equal probability*
–, superficie de la *probability surface*
–, tasa de *probability rate*

probable *prospective*
–, cliente *prospective client*
–, error *probable error*
–, precio *prospective price*
probador *tester*
problema de archivos *filing problem*
procedimiento *procedure, working method*
– de arbitraje *arbitration process*
– de archivo *file procedure*
– de distribución *marketing process*
– de fabricación *manufacturing process*
– de facturación *invoice procedure*
– de formularios, diagrama de *forms or papers procedure chart*
– de prácticas normalizadas *standard practice procedure*
– litográfico *offset*
– normalizado *standardized procedure*
– offset *offset process*
– tipificado de investigación *standard procedure*
–, diagrama gráfico de *process diagram*
procedimientos a máquina, diagrama de *machine process chart*
– de investigación mercadológica *marketing research procedures*
– de operación normalizada *standard operating procedures*
– de verificación de ventas *sales control procedures*
–, diagrama de *process diagram*
procesar *to process or manufacture, to prosecute*
proceso *process, processing*
– clave *key process*
– contencioso *lawsuit*
– de circulación, diagrama del *flow process chart*
– de datos *data processing*
– de depuración del personal *clearance procedure*
– de elaboración *processing order*
– de fabricación *factory process*
– de obtención de datos *data processing*
– de transformación de la materia *processing*
– de valoración *appraisal process*
– de ventas *selling or sales process*
– económico *economic process*
– indirecto *roundabout process*
– litográfico offset *offset lithographic process*
– o procedimiento clave *key process*
–, diagrama del *process chart*
–, en *work in process*
–, fabricación en *goods in process*
–, manufactura en *work in process*
–, productos en *goods in process*

–, suplemento del *process allowance*
–, tiempo auxiliar del *auxiliary process time*
–, tiempo del *process time*
–, tiempo disponible de *available process time*
producción *production, output, yield*
– bruta *gross output*
– contínua *straight-line or continuous production*
– de fábrica *plant output*
– de series completas *full line production*
– de utilidad máxima *best profit outfit*
– diaria *stock*
– disminuida *down-rated output*
– efectiva *actual attainment or output*
– en cadena *assembly-line production, line or flow production*
– en escala comercial *commercial-scale production*
– en masa *mass production, stock production*
– en pequeñas series o lotes *small batch production*
– en proceso *work in process*
– en serie *mass production, series or regular production*
– en un tiempo determinado *turnout*
– industrial *industrial output*
– insuficiente *under-production*
– marginal *marginal production*
– máxima *peak production*
– mecanizados, métodos de *assembly or flow or production line*
– media *average output*
– nacional *national product*
– normalizada *standardized production*
– o rendimiento de planta *plant output*
– por hombre hora *production or output per manhour*
– por lotes *batch production*
– sin aumento de sueldo, aumento de *speed-up*
–, aumento de *increased production*
–, cadena de *assembly or flow or production line*
–, capacidad de *productive capacity*
–, capital de *production capital*
–, circuito de *workflow*
–, comunicación de orden de *notice of production*
–, contabilidad de costes de *production cost accounting*
–, contable de costes de *production cost accountant*
–, control de la *production control*
–, coste de *production cost*
–, costo de *operating cost*
–, curva de *output or production curve*

–, depreciación a base del coste unitario de unit cost depreciation
–, elementos de capital goods
–, en plena in full swing
–, estadísticas de production statistics
–, exceso de glut
–, factor de output factor
–, factores de production factors
–, freno a la restriction of output
–, índice de output index
–, ingreso de los factores de factor income
–, jefe de production manager
–, línea de production line
–, medios de means of production, production facilities
–, métodos mecanizados de assembly or flow or production line
–, norma de production standard
–, normas cronometradas de stopwatch production standards
–, obstáculo en la marcha de la bottleneck
–, potencial de productive potential
–, prima de incentive wage, production bonus
–, programas de production schedule
–, registro de production record
–, restricción de la restriction of output
–, serie de assembly or flow line
–, tiempo de production time
producir to produce or yield
– intereses to bear interest
– una ganancia to yield a profit
productiva, labor productive labour
productivas, horas de trabajo productive labour or workhours
productividad productivity
– decreciente diminishing productiveness
–, coeficiente de productivity index
–, escala de sueldos según incentive wages
–, índice de productivity index
–, medición de la productivity measurement
–, promedio de productivity average
–, prueba de productivity test
productivo productive, profitable
–, tiempo productive time
–, trabajo productive work
–, unidad de valor unit production value
producto product, production
– a las necesidades de un mercado, adaptacion de un product planning
– básico staple, consumer product
– bruto gross proceeds
– bruto nacional gross national product
– corriente consumer product, staple
– de consumo consumer product, staple
– de desecho waste product
– de marca de consumo consumer branded

product
– de una fábrica en un tiempo dado turnout
– decreciente diminishing return
– final end product
– hecho en serie mass-produced article
– nacional national product
– primario primary commodity, commodity product
– social social product
–, coeficiente insumo input-output coefficient
–, crear un to develop a product
–, factor input-output
–, insumo input-output
–, presentación del product design
–, prueba del product testing
–, rendimiento del product performance
productor producer
productos goods, products
– alimenticios foodstuffs
– básicos staple commodities
– de consumo consumer goods
– de marca branded goods
– del país home goods
– disponibles, mercado de cash or spot market
– domésticos home goods
– en proceso goods in process
– entregables contra contratos, falta de squeeze
– extranjeros foreign products
– nacionales domestic commodities
– para entrega futura commodity futures
– por clases o tamaños, clasificación de grading
– residuales waste products
– semiacabados goods partly processed
– terminados finished products
–, análisis de insumos y input-output analysis
–, calidad de los quality of products
–, depreciación de downgrading
–, diseño de product design
–, jefe de programación de product planning manager
–, línea de productos product line
–, serie de line of products
profesional obrera, asociación trade union
–, conducta professional conduct
–, enfermedad occupational disease
–, formación vocational training
–, fotografía professional photography
–, gremio trade union
–, orientación vocational guidance
–, riesgo occupational hazard
proforma pro forma
prognosis prognosis
programa programme, schedule
– a beneficio de los empleados y obreros

employee benefit programme
- abierto *open-end programme*
- básico *master schedule*
- de atenciones *requirements schedule*
- de capacitación *training programme*
- de capacitación de oficinas *office training programe*
- de capacitación en la industria *twin programme, training with industry programme*
- de fabricación *manufacturing schedule*
- de instrucción *training schedule*
- de pruebas laborales de aptitud *aptitude jobtest programme*
- de tiempo *time schedule*
- de trabajo *work schedule or programme*
-, comunicación de retraso en el *behindschedule*

programación *programming, planning*
- anticipada *programming*
- económica *economic planning*
- de productos, jefe de *product planning manager*
- de trabajo *working schedule*
- lineal *linear programming*

programada, reunión *scheduled meeting*
-, tarea *programmed job*

programado, según lo *according to schedule*

programador *programmer*

programas de adiestramiento *training programmes*
- de conservación *conservation programme*
- de producción *production schedule*

progresión aritmética o geométrica de aumento o crecimiento *arithmetic or geometric rate of growth*
- por categorías *bracket progression*

progresiva, compensación *set-off*
-, disminución *set-off*
-, tarifa *progressive tariff*
-, tributación *progressive tax*

progresivo, salario *progressive wage*

progreso, trabajo en *work in progress*

prohibición de importación *import ban*

promedio *average, mean*
- anual *annual average*
- aritmético *arithmetical mean or average*
- compensado *weighted average*
- compuesto *composite average*
- de ejecución *average performance*
- de existencia al detalle *average retail stock*
- de giro de existencias *stock turnover rate*
- de mercancías *stock average*
- de pedidos, volumen *average order size*
- de productividad *productivity average*
- de ventas brutas *average gross sale*

- de vida futura *average life expectancy*
- del margen comercial *average markup*
- directo *straight average*
- global, escala de *scale of global progression*
- ponderado *weighted average*
- variable *variable average*
-, arrojar un *to strike an average*
-, costo variable *average variable cost*
-, escala de *scale of progression*
-, número muestral *average sample number*
-, variable del *variance from the average*
-, valor *average*

promedios, ley de los *law of averages*

promesa de crédito *credit commitment*

promesas *commitments*

prominente *staple*

promisorio *promissory*

promoción *promotion*
- de ventas *sales promotion*
- de ventas, gastos de *sales promotion expenses*
- de ventas, jefe de *sales promotion manager*
-, material de *promotion material, dealer aids*

promover *to promote*

pronóstico *forecast*
- a intervalos variables *varying-interval prediction*
- de los productores *producer's forecast*
- del mercado *business forecast*

pronto pago *prompt payment*
- pago, rebaja por *cash discount*

propagación, tiempo de *transmit time*

propagador *spreader*

propaganda *advertising, publicity, propaganda*

propagandista *propaganda agent*

propensión *propensity, bias*
- a ahorrar *propensity to save*
- a atesorar *propensity to hoard*
- a consumir *propensity to consume*
- a invertir *propensity to invest*
- a sobrevalorar el prestigio *prestige bias*
- al prestigio *prestige bias*
- marginal a consumir *marginal propensity to consume*

propiedad *ownership*
- corporativa *corporate property*
- indivisa *joint property*
- industrial *industrial exclusive rights*
- inmueble *real estate*
- intelectual, leyes sobre *copyright laws*
- reservados, derechos de *all rights reserved*
- literaria *copyright*
-, capacidad de la *real-estate record office*
-, derechos de *property rights*
-, título de *title deed*

–, traspaso de título de *change of title*
propietaria, compañía *close corporation*
propietario *proprietor*
proporción de accidentes *accident rate*
– entre existencias y giro *stock-turnover ratio*
– entre existencias y ventas *stock-sales ratio*
proporcional, depreciación *straight-line depreciation*
–, muestreo *proportional sampling*
propósito *purpose*
propuesta *bid*
propuestas selladas *sealed bids*
prorrata *pro rata*
prorratear *to pro-rate*
prorrateo *apportioning*
prórroga *postponement, respite*
prorrogar el vencimiento *to extend the time*
prosecución *follow-up*
prosecutiva, investigación *follow-up research*
–, cuantificación *quantifying follow-up*
prospección, carta de *sales letter*
–, lista de *mailing list*
prospecto *prospectus, handbill, loose sheet*
– desplegable *folder*
– publicitario pequeño *advertising leaflet*
prosperidad *prosperity*
– comercial *boom*
próspero *prosperous, successful*
protección arancelaria *tariff protection*
– de la propiedad intelectual *copyright protection*
proteccionista *protectionist*
–, arancel *protective tariff*
–, tarifa *protective tariff*
protectora de cheques *cheque writer*
proteger *to protect*
protesta *protest*
protestada, letra *protested bill*
protestar un giro *to protest a draft*
– una letra *to protest a draft*
protesto *protest*
–, aviso de *notice of protest*
–, verificar el *to protest*
prototipo *master sample*
– de envase *standard packing*
– de vendedor *sales type*
provechoso *useful, profitable*
proveedor *supplier, caterer*
proveedores, anticipo del estado a sus *imprest*
–, cuenta de *accounts payable*
–, fichero de *resource file*
proveer *to supply*
provisión *stock*
provisional *provisional, temporary*
– de precios, lista *temporary price list*

–, gremio *trade union*
–, norma *temporary standard, temporary work value*
–, obrero *casual worker*
provisiones *supplies, produce*
provocador, agente *agent provocateur*
provocar *to trigger-off*
proyectar *to plan or lay out*
proyectista, ingeniero *project engineer*
–, técnico *development engineer*
proyecto *project, plan, designation*
– de anuncio compuesto *advertising display, layout*
– de contrato *draft contract or agreement*
– de convenio *draft convention*
– de especificación *draft specification*
– de investigación *research project*
– de norma *standard project*
– de publicidad *advertising programme*
– de tipificación *standard project*
– improductivo *unsound project*
– piloto *pilot project*
proyectos, agencia de *design agency*
–, director de equipo de *project leader*
–, personal de *design staff*
–, personal de estudios de *design engineering staff*
prudencial, cálculo *estimate*
prueba *test, proof, slip*
– a través de un panel *test panel*
– acelerada de duración *accelerated life test*
– acelerada de fatiga *accelerated fatigue test*
– administrativa general *general clerical test*
– de accidentes, a *accident proof*
– de aptitudes diferenciales *differential aptitude test*
– de capacidad *aptitude test*
– de capacidad mental *mental ability test*
– de cotejo *call back proof*
– de eficacia *efficiency test*
– de ensayo *prediction test*
– de estabilidad *stability test*
– de habilidad *skill test*
– de inteligencia *intelligence test*
– de productividad *productivity test*
– de significado *significance test*
– del producto *product testing*
– empírico, método de prueba *empirical test method*
– gradual *step-by-step test*
– más poderosa *most powerful test*
– práctica *test run*
– previa *pre-test, pre-testing*
– simétrica *symmetrical test*
– unilateral *one-sided test*
–, balanza de *trial balance*

–, campaña de *test campaign, try-out campaign*
–, colocación a *trial employment*
–, período de *trial period*
pruebas de ajuste *test pattern*
– aceleradas de destreza *accelerated performance tests*
– de aceptación *acceptance tests*
– de contabilidad *accounting evidence*
– de personal *personnel tests*
– de recepción *acceptance tests or trials*
– laborales de aptitud, programa de *job-aptitude test programme*
– no paramétricas *non-parametric tests*
–, dispositivos de *testing devices*
–, encargado de *tester*
–, modelo de *test chart*
psicograma *profile*
psicológica, capacitación *psychological training*
psiquis *psyche*
pública, asistencia *public welfare work*
–, auditoría *public audit*
–, escrutinio de la opinión *public opinion polls*
–, investigación de la opinión *public opinion research*
–, opinión *public opinion*
publicación comercial *business publication*
publicaciones, registro de *production record*
públicas, director de relaciones *public relations manager*
–, obras *public works*
–, relaciones *public relations*
publicidad *publicity, advertising*
– directa *direct advertising*
– directa por correo *mail order advertising*
– en la prensa *press or newspaper advertising*
– oral *word-of-mouth advertising*
– redaccional *publicity*
–, analista de *advertising analyst*
–, archivos de *advertising record*
–, campaña de *advertising campaign*
–, circular de *advertising circular, circular letter*
–, departamento de *advertising publicity*
–, enfoque de la *advertising approach*
–, esfuerzos de *advertising efforts*
–, factura de *advertising bill or invoice*
–, gastos de *advertising expenses*
–, impresos de *trade literature advertising*
–, jefe de *advertising manager*
–, medio de *advertising medium*
–, promoción de *advertising material*
–, proyecto de *advertising programme*
–, tarifas de *rate card, advertising rates*

publicitaria gratuíta, información *free publicity*
–, eficacia *advertising effectiveness*
–, frase central *slogan*
–, idea *advertising idea*
–, información *publicity*
–, investigación *advertising research*
publicitarias, normas *advertising standards*
–, televisión *commercial television*
publicitario pequeño, prospecto *advertising leaflet*
–, dólar *advertising dollar*
–, material *advertising material*
–, plan *advertising scheme or programme*
–, texto *advertising copy*
publicitarios, comunicados *publicity releases*
–, medios *advertising media*
público *public*
– titulado, contable *certified public accountant*
–, aceptación del *consumer acceptance*
–, el *community*
–, notario *notary public*
–, servicio *public utility*
públicos, bienes *public goods*
–, fondos *government bonds, stock*
–, valores *public securities*
puente, derechos de *bridge toll*
puerta abierta, política de *open door policy*
– en puerta, ventas de *door-to-door selling*
puerto *port, harbour*
– de destino *port of destination*
– de embarque *port of origin, port of shipment*
– de emergencia *distress port*
– de escala *port of call*
– de matrícula *port of registration*
– interior *inner harbour*
– libre *free port*
– terminal *port of delivery*
–, derechos de *harbour duties*
puesta a punto, duración de la *adjustment time*
– en posición y reparación de la herramienta *indexing tool*
– en posición y reparación de la máquina *indexing machine*
– en posición y reparación del utillaje *indexing jig*
puestas a fondo común, ganancias *pooled earnings*
puesto a bordo *free on board*
– a domicilio *delivered free*
– al costado *free alongside*
– clave *key position*
– de trabajo *workbench, work place, work station*
– expositivo interior *floor stand*

- o empleo a cargo vacante o libre *vacant post or situation*
- sobre vagón *free on rail*
- vacante *vacant post or situation*

pujante *strong*

pujar *to outbid*

punto *point, score*
- crítico, cláusula de *peril point clause*
- de arranque *starting point*
- de desvanecimiento *vanishing point*
- de equilibrio *break-even point*
- de lectura *break point, reading point*
- de muestreo *sample point*
- de referencia *bench mark*
- de reposo *resting point*
- de separación *break point, reading point*
- de utilidad máxima *best profit point*
- de vista *standpoint, angle, point of view*
- focal *focal point*
- máximo *peak*
- oro *gold point*
- parámetro *parameter point*
- -, duración de la puesta a *adjustment time*

puntuación *bracket, punctuation, scoring*
- -, alta *high rating*

punzadora para papel *paper punch*

purga *purge*

Q

quebrar *to fail, to become bankrupt*
queja *complaint, grievance*
querella *dispute, complaint*
quiebra *bankruptcy, failure*
– comercial *bankruptcy*
– fraudulenta *fraudulent bankruptcy*
–, memoria de *act of bankruptcy*

–, sindicato de una *receiver in bankruptcy*
quiebras, código de *bankruptcy laws*
quimera *delusion*
quincena *fortnight*
quincenal *bi-weekly, fortnightly*
quinquenio *five-year period*

R

racial *racial*
racionalización *rationalization*
racionamiento *rationing*
racionar *to ration*
radicar una causa *to bring a suit*
radio, comunicado por *radio release*
–, emisión de *radio broadcast*
radiodifusión *broadcasting, broadcast*
radiodifusora *broadcasting station*
raíces, bienes *real assets, realty*
–, certificado de compra de bienes *tax certificate*
raiz cuadrada *square root*
rama, en *raw, crude*
ramo *line of business*
– de negocio *line of business*
rango de salarios *wage range or spread*
rapidez *speed*
– de la distribución, tiempo o *rate or speed of turnover*
rasgo *trait*
– de ingenio *stroke of genius*
raspadura *erasure*
ratificar *to approve*
ratio *ratio*
raya, lista de *payroll*
rayador (Am) *timekeeper*
razón *ratio*
– de depreciación *depreciation rate*
– de operación *operating ratio*
– de paridad de ingresos *parity income ratio*
– social *firm or trade name, business house*
reacción *reaction*
– automantenida *self-sustaining reaction*
– en cadena *chain reaction*
reaccionar entre sí *to interact*
reaccionario *reactionary*
reaceptación *re-acceptance*
reajuste *readjustment*
– de salarios *salary adjustment*
– gradual *rolling readjustment*
real *real, actual*
– de la depreciación, factor *effective depreciation factor*
–, capacidad *actual capacity*
–, capital *capital assets*
–, costo *actual cost*
–, depreciación *actual depreciation*

–, pago *true discount*
–, ingreso *real income*
–, mortalidad *actual mortality*
–, pasivo *actual liabilities*
–, salario *real wages*
–, tara *actual tare*
–, tasa *effective rate*
–, tiempo *actual or clock time, time taken or used*
–, valor *actual value*
realidad *reality*
realizable, activo *circulating assets*
realizables, valores *liquid assets*
realización por inventario *pre-inventory sale*
realizadas, utilidades *realized profits*
–, utilidades no *paper profits*
rearrendar *to re-lease*
reasegurador *reinsurance underwriter, reinsurer*
reaseguradora, compañía *reinsuring company*
reaseguro *reinsurance*
reavalúo *reappraisal, reassessment*
rebaja *rebate, reduction, discount*
– de margen *markdown*
– de precios *short rates*
– de venta *sale discount*
– del precio de fuera *sales allowance*
– desleal de precios *dumping*
– efectiva *actual markdown*
– normalizada del peso bruto *trade allowance*
– o deducción por merma *tret*
– por cantidad *quantity discount*
– por merma *tret*
– por pronto pago *cash discount*
– total *gross markdown*
–, comprar con lo *to buy at discount*
–, precio de *markdown price*
–, tarifa reducida por *cut rate*
rebajada para detallista, tarifa *open retail rate*
rebajado, precio muy *knockout price*
rebajar *to abate*
– el valor *write down*
– sueldo *to cut a salary*
rebajas en cadena *chain discount*
– previstas *planned markdowns*
–, cancelación de *markdown cancellation*
–, revocación de *markdown cancellation*

–, tienda de *discount house*
rebaño, instinto de *hard instinct*
recambio, servicio de piezas de *after-sales service*
recargar *to overcharge*
recargo *surcharge, surtax*
– impositivo *surtax*
recaudación *collection*
–, gastos de *collection fees*
recaudador *collector*
– de impuestos *tax collector or receiver, collector of taxes*
recaudadora de impuestos, oficina *tax office*
recepción de géneros *receipt of goods*
–, pruebas de *acceptance tests or trials*
recepcionista *receptionist*
receptor *set*
– de órdenes de compra *sales order clerk*
receso económico *business depression*
rechazar *to reject*
recibe, muestra tal como se *as received sample*
recibido, valor *value received*
recibidor, cajero *receiving teller*
recibir *to receive or accept*
–, valores a *receivables*
recibo *receipt*
– de expedición *forwarding receipt*
– sin reservas *clean receipt*
–, acusar *to acknowledge receipt*
–, acuse de *acknowledgement of receipt*
–, al *on receipt*
recipiente *receptacle, bin*
reciprocidad comercial *reciprocal trade*
recíproco *reciprocal*
reclamación *claim*
reclamado, dividendo no *unclaimed dividend*
reclamar por daños *to claim damages*
–, sin *unclaimed*
reclamo, artículo de *loss leader*
–, venta de *bargain sale*
reclutar *to recruit*
recogida de datos, técnicas de *data-collection techniques*
recolección de datos *data collection, collecting data*
recomendación, carta de *letter of recommendation*
recomendar *to recommend*
recompensa *amends, reward, compensation*
– colectiva *collective reward*
– monetaria *financial reward*
recompensar *to remunerate*
reconocer *to acknowledge, recognize or honour*
reconocido *staple*
reconversión *reconversion*

recordativa, ficha *reminder card*
recorte *cutting, dip*
– de periódico *newspaper clipping or cutting*
– de prensa *press clipping or cutting*
– de un aumento *tear sheet*
recorrido *flow path*
rectificación de defectuosos *rectification of rejects*
rectificar *to correct or rectify*
–, factor para *calibrating factor*
recuadro *box*
recuento *re-count*
– de existencias, hacer *to take stock*
– físico *physical inventory*
recuperación *recuperation, recovery*
– económica *business recovery*
recurrente *recurring*
recurso *device*
recursos *resources*
– económicos *financial resources*
– financieros *financial resources*
– humanos *human resources*
– líquidos *liquid resources*
– naturales *natural resources*
red *network*
– de distribución *distributing or distribution network, supply network*
– de televisión *television network*
– de tranmisiones *communication network*
– o cadena de emisoras de televisión *television network*
redacción, servicio de *copy department*
redaccional, publicidad *publicity*
redactor *editor*
redimible *redeemable*
–, bono *callable bond*
redimir *to redeem*
rédito *return, interest*
redituar *to produce or yield*
– interés *to bear interest*
redondo, precio *price in round figures*
–, viaje *round trip*
redondos, números *round numbers*
reducción *reduction, cutback, abatement*
– básica *basic abatement*
– de costes *cost reduction*
– de precios *price cutting*
– de tarifas *rate cutting*
– de tipos *variety reduction, simplification, limiting variety*
reducciones en el presupuesto *cuts in the budget*
reducida, jornada *part-time employment*
–, tarifas *trim rates*
reducido, costo *low or reduced cost*
–, empleo *part-time employment*

–, incentivo *reduced or weak incentive*
–, precio *reduced price*
reducidos, liquidación a precios *bargain sale*
reducir *to reduce*
reducirse *to abate*
redundancia *redundancy*
reeducación *re-training*
reembolsables, anticipos *returnable advances*
–, gastos *expenses chargeable*
reembolsado, préstamo *refunded loan*
reembolsar *to refund or repay*
reembolso, contra *against payment*
–, entrega contra *cash on delivery*
–, envío contra *c.o.d. shipment, cash on delivery shipment*
–, pago contra *cash on delivery*
reemplazo *replacement*
–, personal de *labour turnover*
reestreno *revival*
refaccionar *to finance*
refacción *financing*
referencia *reference*
– bancaria *bank reference*
– comercial *trade reference*
–, punto de *bench mark*
reforma *reform*
– agraria *land reform*
– arancelaria *tariff reform*
– de una ley *amendment*
– monetaria *currency reform*
regalía *bonus, royalty*
regalo *present, gift*
regatear *to bargain*
régimen de almacenes generales de depósito *bonded warehouse*
– de financiación *financial arrangement*
regimentación *regimentation*
regional *regional, local*
–, monopolio *regional cartel*
–, cartel *regional cartel*
registrada, derecho de marca *trademark rights*
–, marca *brand or trade name*
registrado como marca, nombre *trade name*
–, nombre *copyrighted name*
–, seudónimo *copyrighted name*
registrador *controller*
– de datos *data recorder*
– de tiempo *time recorder*
registradora *register*
– contable, máquina *cash register and book-keeping*
– sumadora, máquina *cash registering and adding machine*
–, caja *cash register*
–, máquina *cash register*

registrados y patentes mundiales en trámite, modelos *designs registered and world patents pending*
–, datos *recorded information*
–, derechos *copyrighted*
–, temas *copyrighted material*
registrar *to register*
– la información *to file the information*
– un libro o una obra *to copyright*
registro *record, file, register*
– acumulativo, ficha de *accumulative record card*
– alfanumérico *alphanumerical record*
– de acciones *stock register*
– de caja (C) *cash book*
– de colocaciones *employment register*
– de comprobantes *voucher register*
– de datos o informaciones *information record*
– de devoluciones *returns record*
– de direcciones *address register*
– de existencias *stock record*
– de facturas *invoice register*
– de giros librados *draft register*
– de informaciones *information record*
– de la capacidad de compra *buying power survey*
– de la propiedad *real-estate record office*
– de producción *production record*
– de publicaciones *production record*
– de publicaciones, oficina de *copyright receipt office*
– de publicidad *advertising record*
– de ventas *sales record*
– de verificación de existencias *stock control record*
– demográfico *registry of vital statistics*
– estadístico de ventas *sales record*
– sumador *adding register*
–, derechos de *registration fee*
–, elevar un *to keep a record*
regla *rule*
– de cálculo *slide rule, computing rule*
– fija *standard*
– práctica *work rule*
–, cuenta en *clear account*
–, en *in order*
reglamentación *regulation*
– de precios *price fixing*
– del trabajo *labour regulations*
– para contratos colectivos de trabajo *collective bargain provisions*
reglamento *rules, regulations*
– interno *bye-laws*
reglas de contabilidad *accounting measures*
regresión *regression*
regulación *regulation*

regulador, precio *standard price*
rehacer *to re-make*
reinvertidas, utilidades *reinvested profits*
reinvertir *to reinvest*
reiterativo, elemento *repetitive or cyclic element*
reivindicación *claim*
relación *report, list, statement, ratio*
relaciones *relations*
– comerciales *business connections*
– con los clientes *consumer relations*
– crediticias *credit relations*
– del trabajo *labour relations*
– entre empresario y empleado *employer-employee relations*
– entre obreros y directivos *labour management relations*
– humanas *human relations*
– industriales *industrial relations*
– laborales *labour relations*
– personales *personal acquaintances, commerce, social relations*
– públicas *public relations*
– públicas, director de *public relations manager*
– públicas, encargado de las *public relations officer*
– públicas, especialista en *public relations specialist*
– suplementarias *supporting schedules*
relato *statement*
reloj de control de entrada *time clock*
– de control de tiempo de trabajo *job time recording clock*
– fechador *time or clock stamp*
– registrador *time clock*
–, fecha de *clock or time card*
remanente de una mercancía *carry over*
–, saldo *remaining balance*
rematador *auctioneer*
remate *auction*
–, vender en *to auction*
remesa *shipment, remittance*
remisión *remittance*
–, nota de *shipping note*
remitente *shipper, sender*
rémora *drag, hindrance*
remuneración *remuneration, salary, wage*
– complementaria hasta el salario garantizado *make-up pay*
– equitativa *adequate compensation*
– por igual trabajo, igual *equal pay for equal work*
–, nivel de *compensation level*
remuneraciones, plan de *compensation plan*
remunerar *to remunerate or compensate*

rendimiento *output, output rate, yield, return, effectiveness, performance*
– anterior, análisis del *past performance analysis*
– bajo, bono *low-yield bond*
– bruto *gross return*
– comercial *coefficient of efficiency*
– continuo *continuous rating*
– creciente *increasing returns*
– de capital *return on capital*
– de obligaciones *bond yield*
– de planta *plant output*
– decreciente *diminishing returns*
– del producto *product performance*
– del trabajo *job performance*
– económico *commercial efficiency*
– efectivo *actual output*
– fijo *fixed income*
– inferior al normal *sub-standard performance*
– total *throughput*
– total o bruto *gross efficiency, gross output, overall performance*
–, alto *high yield*
–, mención del *performance measurement*
–, nivel de *performance index*
–, norma de *performance standard*
–, tabla de *yield table*
–, tasa de *rate of returns*
rendimientos crecientes, ley de *law of increasing returns*
rendir cuentas *to be accountable*
– interés *to bear interest*
renglón *item, line of business*
renombrado *top notch*
renovable *renewable, replaceable*
–, fondo *revolving fund*
renovación de capital *capital turnover*
renovar *to renew or replace*
renta *income, rent, annuity*
– acumulada *accrued income*
– anual *yearly or annual income, annuity*
– anual, ingreso o *annual return*
– de inversiones *unearned income*
– de retiro, contrato *income bond*
– del capital *interest, return on capital*
– económica *economic profit*
– fija, valores de *fixed-income securities*
– imponible *taxable income*
– nacional *national income*
– por habitante *per capita income*
– variable, valores de *common stocks*
– vitalicia *life annuity*
–, imposición de la *income tax*
–, impuesto sobre la *income or revenue tax*
rentabilidad *profitability*
– efectiva *income basis*

–, análisis de la curva de la *break-even analysis*
–, curva de *break-even curve*
rentable, espacio *revenue-producing space*
–, lucrativo *revenue earning*
rentar *to rent*
rentas *income*
– públicas *revenue*
–, administración de *collector's office*
–, colector de *collector of internal revenue*
renuncia *resignation*
renunciar *to resign*
reordenar *to reorder*
reorganizar *to reorganize*
reparación *amends, reward, compensation*
– de la herramienta, puesta en posición y *indexing tool*
– de la máquina, puesta en posición *indexing machine*
– del utillaje, puesta en posición *indexing jig*
reparaciones, taller de *workroom*
reparar *to repair*
repartición de costos *distribution of costs*
– de utilidades *profit sharing*
–, coeficiente de *coefficient of apportionment*
–, depósito de *warehouse*
–, escala de *scale of apportionment*
–, hoja de *work sheet*
repartibles, utilidades *distributive profits*
repartidas, utilidades no *undistributed profits*
reparto, zona de *distributing zone*
repasar *to review*
repetición de accidentes *accident sequences*
repetitivo, elemento *repetitive or cyclic element*
reponer *to replace or restore*
reportar *to obtain, to report*
– una pérdida *to show a loss*
reporte *report*
– anual *annual report*
– de auditoría *auditor's report*
reposición *replacement*
– de almacenes *replenishment of stores*
–, costo de *replacement cost*
reposo *relaxation time*
–, punto de *resting point*
–, tiempo de *resting time*
represalia, impuestos de *retaliatory tariff*
representación *representation*
representante *representative agent*
– de los patronos *employers' representative*
– del personal *shop steward*
representar *to represent*
representativa, muestra *representative sample*
representativas, seleccción de muestras

representative sample selection
representativo, corte *cross section*
representativos, grupos *cross sections*
represión *repression*
reproducción de documentos, servicio de *documentary reproduction service*
reproducir *to reproduce*
reprogramar *to re-programme*
repudiar *to repudiate*
repuesto, almacén de *stockroom*
repuestos *spares, spare parts*
reputación comercial *commercial standing*
requisición de precios *inquiry*
requisitos *requirements, requisites, qualifications*
– de la información de crédito *credit information requirements*
– del trabajo *job requirements*
– educacionales *educational requirements*
resaca *redraft*
resarcir *to indemnify*
rescate *redemption*
rescindir *to rescind*
reserva *reserve*
– bancaria *bank reserve*
– de contigencia *contingent reserve*
– en efectivo *cash reserve*
– monetaria *currency reserve*
– obligatoria en metálico *compulsory cash reserve*
– para accidentes industriales *industrial accident fund reserve*
– para agotamiento *reserve for depletion*
– para amortización *sinking-fund reserve*
– para auxilio a empleados *benefit-fund reserve, relief-fund reserve*
– para bonificaciones *allowances reserve*
– para cuentas incobrables *reserve for bad debts*
– para fluctuaciones en cambios de moneda *reserve for exchange fluctuations*
– para impuestos *reserve for taxes*
– para participación de utilidades *profit-sharing reserve*
– para pensiones *pension-fund reserve*
– para primas no devengadas *unearned premium reserve*
– para renovación y reposición *reserve for renewals and replacements*
– secreta *secret reserve*
– superior a lo normal *reserve above normal*
– técnica *unearned premium reserve*
–, capital de *uncalled capital*
–, cuenta de *allowance or provision account*
–, fondo de *reserve fund*
–, obrero *spare or standby man*

–, territorio *exclusive territory*
reservas *reserves, spares*
– de oro *gold reserve*
– de tasación *offset reserves, valuation reserves*
–, aceptación sin *general acceptance*
–, recibo sin *clean receipt*
resguardo *acquittance*
residencia *domicile*
residencial, zona *residential neighbourhood*
residente *resident*
residual, saldo *residual balance*
residuales, productos *waste products*
resignación *resignation*
resistencia *resistance*
– a comprar *sales resistance*
– contra los altos precios *price resistance*
resolver *to resolve*
respaldado, banco no *non-member bank*
respaldo colateral, prestar con *to lend on collateral*
– económico *financial backing*
responder *to answer or reply*
– por *to vouch for*
responsabilidad *responsibility, accountability*
– comercial *business responsibility*
– del patrono *employer's liability*
– directa *primary liability*
– económica *financial liability*
– ilimitada *unlimited liability*
– limitada *limited liability*
– limitada, compañía de *limited liability company*
– limitada, sociedad de *limited liability company*
– solidaria *joint liability*
–, doble *double liability*
responsable *responsible, accountable*
respuesta *answer, reply*
– libre, pregunta de *open question*
–, curva de *overall response curve*
–, sin *non-response, non-respondent*
resta *subtraction*
–, signo de *subtraction sign*
restituir *to pay back or refund*
restos, venta de *remainder sale*
restricción *restriction, curtailment*
– de créditos, política de *tight-money policy*
– de la producción *restriction of trade*
– del comercio *restraint of trade*
– del crédito *credit restriction*
restriccionista *restrictionist*
–, muestreo *restricted sampling*
restringida al azar, muestra no *unrestricted random sample*
restringido, muestreo *restricted sampling*

restringir *to restrain*
resultado *result*
resultar *to result*
resumen *summary, abstract, scoring*
– de asientos *abstract of posting*
– semanal *weekly summary*
resúmenes, boletín de *abstract bulletin*
resumida, cuenta *bulk account*
resumir *to summarize, to sum up or abridge*
retardo *delay*
retasar *to reappraise*
retención *conservation, retention*
retenidas, sumas *amounts withheld*
retenido *withheld*
retirada de mercancías *withdrawal*
retirar *to withdraw*
– de la circulación *to withdraw from circulation*
– efectivo *to draw cash*
– el crédito *to cancel credit*
– fondos *to withdraw funds*
retirarse *to withdraw or retire*
retiro *withdrawal, retirement*
– en efectivo *cash withdrawal*
– forzoso *compulsory retirement*
–, contrato renta de *income bond*
–, pensión de *superannuation*
–, plan de *retirement plan*
retiros, caja de *retiring fund*
retorno, carga de *return cargo*
–, flete de *home or return freight*
retrasar *to delay*
retraso *time out, delay, stoppage, interruption*
– evitable *avoidable delay*
– en el programa, comunicación de *behind-schedule notice*
retrasos *arrears*
retribución *fee, compensation, wages, allowance*
retribuir *to pay or remunerate*
retroactivo *retroactive*
retroventa *buying back*
–, pacto de *agreement to resell*
reunión *meeting*
– del consejo de administración *board meeting*
– programada *scheduled meeting*
revalidar *to re-validate*
revaluación *revaluation*
revaluar *to reappraise or revalue*
revendedor *middleman*
reventa *resale*
–, precio de *resale price*
reversión *reversion*
– de cuentas, sección de *auditing department*
revisable, contrato de precio *sliding-scale*

contract
revisar *to inspect, audit or check*
revisión *inspection, review*
– de cuentas *audit*
– de precios, cláusula de *variation clause*
– de presupuestos *budgetary control*
– del coste de ventas *cost auditing of sales*
– o ajuste interior de cuentas *internal audit*
revisor *supervisor*
– de cuentas *auditor*
revista del mercado *market report*
– trimestral *quarterly magazine or review*
revocable *revocable*
revocación o cancelación de rebajas *markdown cancellation*
revocar *to revoke, repeal or abrogate*
revolvente, fondo *rotary fund*
riego, tierra de *irrigated farm land*
riesgo *risk, hazard*
– de accidentes *accident risk*
– del comprador *buyer's risk*
– del transportador *carrier's risk*
– del vendedor *seller's risk*
– profesional *occupational hazard*
–, cantidad en *amount at risk*
–, función del *risk function*
–, póliza a todo *all-risk policy*
–, prima de *risk premium*
–, seguro contra todo *all-risk insurance*
–, sin *devoid of risk*
–, todo *all-risk*

riesgos asegurables *insurable risk*
– marítimos, aseguradores contra *marine underwriters*
–, diversificación de los *spread of risk*
rigidez *rigidity*
riqueza *wealth, worth*
ritmo *pace, speed, tempo*
robo, seguro contra *burglary insurance*
rodillo *platen*
rojos, en números *in the red*
rollo de papel para máquina sumadora *adding roll*
rompehuelga *strike-breaker*
rotación *rotation*
– de cultivos *crop rotation*
– de existencias en almacén *stock turnover*
– de trabajos *job rotation*
– del personal *turnover*
– del surtido *stock turnover*
rotativo, crédito *revolving credit*
–, montaje *rotary fixture*
rotular *to label, address or docket*
rótulo *sign, docket*
– o etiqueta engomada *sticker*
rotura de huelgas *strike-breaking*
rúbrica *flourish after signature, title*
ruta *route, routing*
–, ficha de *route or batch card, work or route label*
–, venta en *road selling*
rutina *routine*

S

saber, hacer *to notify*
sabotaje *sabotage*
sacapunta *pencil sharpener*
sacar una muestra *to take a sample*
sagacidad *general ability, cleverness*
sala de control *control room*
– de lectura *reading room*
sala o local de exhibición *showroom*
salarial, tarifa *wage rate*
salario *salary, remuneration, wages*
– a destajo *taskwork wages*
– base *base pay, base rate, basic wage, wage floor*
– de hambre *starvation wages*
– deseado *expected salary*
– diario *daily wage*
– diferencial por piezas *differential piecework*
– establecido *stated salary*
– garantizado, remuneración complementaria hasta el *make-up pay*
– igual por trabajo igual *equal pay for equal work*
– incentivo, sistema de *incentive wage system*
– inicial total al año *gross initial annual salary*
– máximo *wage ceiling, maximum wage*
– mínimo *minimum wage*
– monetario *money wage*
– nominal *nominal wage*
– por hora *hourly wage*
– por pieza *piece wage*
– por pieza, sistema de *piecework system*
– progresivo *progressive wage*
– real *real wages*
– tipo *standard wage*
– tope *wage ceiling, maximum wage*
–, grado de *grade rate*
–, límite superior del *wage ceiling, maximum wage*
salarios, alza de *wage rise*
– por hora *hourly wages*
–, categorías de *salary ranges*
–, curva de *wage or earnings curve*
–, departamento de *wages department*
–, escala de *salary range*
–, escala gradual de *sliding scale*
–, estipulaciones de *salary stipulations*
–, estructura de *wage structure*
–, impuesto sobre *tax withheld on wages*

–, nivel de *wage level*
–, rango de *wage scale*
–, reajuste de *salary adjustment*
–, sistema de *salary plan*
–, tarifa de *wage rate*
saldada, cuenta *account settled*
saldados, beneficios *paid-up benefits*
saldar *to settle, to balance*
– o liquidar géneros *to clear goods*
– los libros *to balance the books*
– una deuda *to discharge a debt*
saldo *balance, settlement, payment in full, clearance*
– acreedor *active balance*
– de apertura *opening balance*
– deudor *debit balance*
– en caja *cash balance*
– en efectivo *cash balance*
– inactivo *dormant balance*
– migratorio *balance of migration*
– o liquidación de mercancías *clearing of goods*
– remanente *remaining balance*
– residual *residual balance*
–, arrastrar el *to strike a balance*
–, arrojar un *to show a balance*
–, lote de *job lot*
–, partida de *job lot*
saldos *sale goods*
– negativos, verificación o control de *minus balance control*
–, mostrador de *bargain counter*
–, vendedor de *job merchant*
–, venta de *clearance sale*
salida *outlay*
– de información, documentos impresos como *printed output for data*
– de almacén, ficha de *stores issued card*
salida-entrada, curva de *output-input curve*
salidas *expenditures*
– de caja *cash disbursements*
–, entradas y *input-output*
saliente *outgoing*
salud, póliza *health insurance*
salvo error u omisión *errors and omissions excepted*
sanciones *sanctions*
– económicas *economic sanctions*

satisfacción *satisfaction*
– en el trabajo *job satisfaction*
satisfacer la demanda *to meet the demand*
saturación *load*
–, grado de *load factor, work opportunity, work loading*
saturado, mercado *saturated market*
–, no *underloaded*
se renta *for rent*
– vende *for sale*
seca, carga *dry cargo*
secante, papel *blotter, blotting paper*
sección *section, división*
– comercial *business district*
– cruzada, datos de *cross section data*
– cruzada, muestreo por *cross section sampling*
– de anuncios *advertising department*
– de cambio extranjero *foreign exchange department*
– de compras *purchasing department*
– de crédito *credit department*
– de exportación *export department*
– de importación *import department*
– de préstamos *loan department*
– de publicidad *advertising department*
– de revisión de cuentas *auditing department*
– de ventas *sales department*
– o lugar de venta *selling floor, ground floor*
secretaria *secretary*
– particular *private secretary*
secretaría *secretary's office*
– comercial *commercial secretary*
– de estado *ministry*
secretariado *secretariat*
secretario *secretary*
– adjunto *assistant secretary*
– auxiliar *assistant secretary*
– comercial *commercial secretary*
– ejecutivo *executive secretary*
– general *secretary-general*
– interino *acting secretary*
– particular *private secretary*
– privado *private secretary*
secreto industrial *trade secret*
sector de consumo *consumer sector*
secuencia *sequence*
– cíclica *timed sequence*
– cronizada o temporizada *timing sequence*
secundarios, datos *secondary data*
sede *headquarters*
– central *headquarters*
segregación *segregation*
seguidor de piezas *progress chaser*
según comprobante *as per voucher*
– factura *as per invoice*

– contrato, precio *price as provided in the contract*
– lo programado *according to schedule*
– modelo *after a pattern*
– muestra *according to pattern*
– plantilla *according to pattern*
segunda clase, correo de *second-class mail (Br)*
– mano, comprar de *to buy second hand*
seguridad *reliability, safety, guarantee*
– colectiva *collective security*
– en sí mismo *self-confidence*
– industrial *industrial safety*
– social *social security*
–, caja de *safe, safe-deposit box*
–, coeficiente de *factor of safety*
–, dispositivo de *safety device*
–, factor de *safety factor*
–, higiene y *health and safety*
–, margen de *margin of safety*
seguro *insurance, safe*
– a término *term insurance*
– aéreo *airplane insurance*
– colectivo *group insurance*
– contra accidentes *casualty insurance*
– contra cese de negocio *business interruption insurance*
– contra compensación legal por accidentes de *compensation insurance*
– contra compensación de trabajo *workmen's compensation insurance*
– contra daño por choque *collision insurance*
– contra desfalco *embezzlement insurance*
– contra el desempleo *unemployment insurance*
– contra incapacidad *disability insurance*
– contra incendio *fire insurance*
– contra pérdidas de huelga *strike insurance*
– contra robo *burglary insurance*
– contra todo riesgo *all-risk insurance*
– cumulativo *accumulation insurance*
– de compensación *compensation insurance*
– de contingencia *casualty insurance*
– de cumplimiento *performance bond*
– de enfermedad *health insurance*
– de fidelidad *fidelity insurance*
– de guerra *war-risk insurance*
– de indemnización *indemnity insurance*
– de salud *health insurance*
– de transporte *transportation insurance*
– de vejez *old age insurance*
– de vida ordinario *ordinary life insurance*
– dotal *endowment insurance*
– familiar *family insurance*
– industrial *industrial insurance*
– obligatorio *compulsory or obligatory*

insurance
- obrero *workmen's insurance*
- propio, fondo de *insurance fund*
- social *social insurance, social security*
- y fianza *insurance and bond*
-, flete y cambio, costo, *cost, insurance, freight and exchange*
-, póliza de *insurance policy*
-, prima de *insurance premium*
seguros industriales *industrial insurance*
- sociales *social insurance*
-, agente de *insurance broker*
-, compañía de *insurance company*
-, corredor de *insurance broker*
selección *selection*
- al azar *random selection*
- con igual probabilidad *selection with equal probability*
- con probabilidad arbitraria *selection with arbitrary probability*
- con probabilidad proporcional al tamaño *selection with probability proportional to size*
- de empleados de oficina *office employees selection*
- de muestras *sample selection*
- de muestras representativas *representative sample selection*
- del personal *personnel selection*
seleccionador de muestras *sample selector*
seleccionar *to select, to pick out*
selectiva de precios, fijación *discriminatory pricing*
-, ayuda no *non-discriminatory assistance*
-, enfoque de la distribución *selective distribution approach*
selectivo *selective*
sellada, oferta *sealed bid*
selladas, propuestas *sealed bids*
sello *seal, stamp*
- comercial *business die*
- o timbre de goma *rubber stamp*
sellos, fechador de *date stamp*
semana *week*
- básica de trabajo *basic work week*
- comercial *business week*
- de nómina *payroll week*
- inglesa *Monday morning to Saturday noon*
- laborable *work week*
semanal *weekly*
-, resumen *weekly summary*
semanario *weekly paper*
semestral *semi-annual*
semiacabado *semi-finished*
semiacabados, productos *goods partly processed*

semicalificado, obrero *semi-skilled worker*
semimayoreo *jobbing*
semimayorista *jobber*
sencillo, viaje *one-way trip*
sensacionales, periódicos *yellow press*
sensacionalista, prensa *yellow press*
sensato *sensible*
sentencia judicial *legal decision, court judgement*
sentido de la responsabilidad *dependability*
- común *common sense*
sentimiento *feeling*
sentimientos *feelings*
señal *signal, pledge*
- de entrada *cue*
separación de empleo *dismissal*
-, punto de *break point, reading point*
separata *reprint*
seriado *serial*
serie alfabética *alphabetical sequence*
- de artículos *article series, line of goods*
- de frecuencias *frequency series*
- de producción *assembly or flow or production line*
- de productos *line of products*
- o línea de artículos *line of goods*
-, artículo hecho en *mass produced article*
-, en *assembly-line, mass production*
-, fabricación en *mass production, series production*
-, número de *serial number*
-, producción en *mass production, series production*
-, producto hecho en *mass produced article*
-, trabajo en *production work*
series completas, producción de *full line production*
- de tiempos, análisis de *time series analysis*
- o lotes, producción en pequeñas *small batch production*
servicio *service*
- de asesoramiento *advisory service*
- de ayuda después de vender *after-sales service*
- de documentación *documentation service*
- de expediciones *distribution department*
- de piezas de recambio *after-sales service*
- de postventas *after-sales service*
- de redacción *copy department*
- de reproducción de documentos *documentary reproduction service*
- detallista, capacitación o formación del personal de *retail service training*
- para los clientes *customer service*
- público *public utility*
- público, empresa de *utility*

– social *social work*
–, departamento de *service department*
–, jefe de *supervisor*
–, poner en *to put in service*
servicios administrativos *administrative services*
– de abastecimiento *supply services*
– de oficina *office services*
– públicos *public service utilities*
–, bienes y *goods and services*
–, hoja de *statement of service*
servida, zona *coverage*
servir, envíos a cuenta de pedidos a *advance payments on purchase obligations*
–, contrato de *agreement of services*
sesgo por defecto *downward bias*
sesión *session, meeting*
– de clausura *closing session*
– de inauguración *opening session*
– extraordinaria *special meeting*
– ordinaria *regular meeting*
– plenaria *joint session*
sesionar *to hold a meeting*
sesiones, clausura de *adjournment*
seudónimo registrado *copyrighted name*
shock *shock*
siglas *initials*
signatario *signatory*
significación, nivel de *significance level*
significado, prueba de *significance test*
signo *sign, mark*
– de división *division sign*
– de interrogación *question mark*
– de multiplicación *multiplication sign*
– de por ciento *percentage sign*
– de omisión *caret*
– de resta *subtraction sign*
– de sumar *addition sign*
– igual *equals sign*
signos taquigráficos *stenographic symbols*
sigue carta *letter follows*
–, suma y *amount carried forward*
símbolo *symbol*
simétrica, prueba *symmetrical test*
simpatía *sympathy*
simpático *sympathetic*
simple, contabilidad por partida *single-entry book-keeping*
–, interés *simple interest*
simplificación *limiting variety, simplification, variety reduction*
simultánea, actividad *multiple activity*
sin *without*
– compromiso *without obligation*
– demora *without delay*
– fecha *undated*

– riesgo *devoid of risk*
– reclamar *unclaimed*
– respuesta *non-response, non-respondent*
– valor *worthless*
sindicados, fábrica con obreros *closed shop*
sindical, delegado *business agent*
– gremial *trade guild*
sindicalizado, trabajador no *non-union workman*
sindicato de trabajadores *labour union*
– obrero *trade union, labour union*
– obrero, contrato que prohibe afiliarse a *yellow-dog contract*
– y los patronos, acuerdo entre el *union-employer agreement*
síndico de una quiebra *receiver in bankrupcy*
–, administrador *receiver*
siniestro *accident, disaster, damage*
sinóptico, balance *working sheet*
síntoma *symptom*
sistema *system*
– abierto *open system*
– automático *automatic system*
– bancario *banking system*
– cerrado *closed system*
– comercial *business system*
– contable *accounting system*
– de archivos *filing system*
– de cartas *card system*
– de circulación monetaria *currency*
– de compensación *balanced system*
– de comunicación directa *public address system*
– de conjunto *overall system*
– de contabilidad *accounting system*
– de continuidad *follow-up system*
– de depósitos *warehousing system*
– de fichas *filing system*
– de incentivos *bonus scheme, premium system*
– de manejo de datos *data handling system*
– de presentación de datos *data display system*
– de prima *incentive system or plan, bonus plan or scheme premium system*
– de salario incentivo *incentive wage system*
– de salario por pieza *piecework system*
– de salarios *salary structure*
– de tarifas *rate structure*
– de ventas *sales policy*
– de ventas, característica del *selling points*
– económico *economic system*
– financiero *financial system*
– impositivo *system of taxation*
– métrico *metric system*
– social *social system*
– tributario *tax system*

–, actuación del *system performance*
–, idear un *to devise a method*
sistemático, enfoque *systematic approach*
–, esquema *systematic structure*
–, muestreo *systematic sampling*
sistematización de datos *data processing*
sistematizar *to systematize*
sitio *site*
–, comprobación en el *spot check*
situación *condition, location*
– de fondos *remittance payment*
– de material, cuadro demostrativo de *status board*
– de peligro *danger situation*
– financiera *financial standing*
– mercadológica *marketing situation*
situaciones industriales *industrial situations*
slogan *slogan*
sobornar *to buy over, to bribe*
soborno *graft*
sobrante *surplus*
sobre con la paga *pay envelope*
– la par *above par*
sobrecarga *overload, additional load*
sobrecargadas, cuentas *accounts overcharged*
sobrecosto *additional charge*
sobreflete *freight surcharge*
sobregiro *overdraft*
sobreimpuesto *surtax*
sobreinversión *overinvestment*
sobrepeso *overweight*
sobreprecio *surcharge, excess price*
sobrepujar *to outbid*
sobreseer *to supersede*
sobrestante *foreman*
sobretasa *surtax*
sobretiempo *overtime*
sobreutilidad *excess profits*
sobrevalorar el prestigio, propensión a *prestige bias*
sobrevivencia, probabilidad de *probability of surviving*
social, activo *company's assets*
–, asistencia *relief, social welfare*
–, capial *capital stock, joint stock*
–, clase *class*
–, domicilio *place of business*
–, pasivo *company's liabilities*
–, personalidad *corporate personality*
–, prestación *social service*
–, previsión *social security, welfare*
–, producto *social product*
–, razón *company or trade name*
–, seguridad *social security*
–, seguro *social insurance, social security*
–, servicio *social work*

–, sistema *social system*
–, valor *social value*
sociales, activos *corporated assets*
–, conflictos *social conflicts*
–, presiones *social pressures*
–, relaciones *social acquaintances, social relations*
socialismo *socialism*
sociedad *society, association, partnership*
– anónima *chartered company, corporation*
– bancaria anónima *joint-stock company, stock company*
– civil *civil partnership*
– comercial *trade association*
– cooperativa *cooperative society*
– de ahorro y préstamo *savings and loan association*
– de crédito *credit institution, credit company*
– de crédito comercial *commercial credit company*
– de socorros mutuos *benefit society*
– dedicada a la inversión de capitales *investment trust*
– en comandita *joint company, limited partnership*
– en comandita por acciones *joint-stock company*
– familiar *family partnership*
– filial *subsidiary company*
– financiera *finance company, commercial credit company*
– industrial *industrial society*
– inversionista *investment trust, open trust*
– limitada *limited partnership*
– matriz *parent company*
– mercantil *commercial company*
– patronal *employer's association, employer's federation*
– por acciones *joint-stock company, stock company*
– responsabilidad limitada *limited-liability company*
–, contrato de *partnership contract, incorporation papers*
–, escritura de *incorporation papers*
–, liquidación de *dissolution of partnership*
sociedades anónimas, deudas de *corporate debts*
–, contabilidad de *corporation accounting*
–, ley de *corporation law, companies act*
socio *member, partner*
– activo *active partner*
– capitalista *partner who furnishes capital only*
– comanditario *dormant partner, sleeping-partner*
– industrial *partner who furnishes service only*

– menor *junior partner*
– principal *senior partner*
–, comprar la parte de un *to buy out*
socios fundadores *founding stockholders*
socorros mutuos, sociedad de *benefit society*
solicitado, empleo *employment wanted*
solicitante *applicant*
– de préstamo *loan applicant*
solicitar *to apply for*
– empleo *to look for a job*
solicitud *application, petition*
– de cotización *request for quotation*
– de empleo *application for employment*
– de préstamo *loan application*
– de trabajo *employment wanted*
solidaria, responsabilidad *joint liability*
solidaridad, huelga de *sympathetic strike*
solución *solution, settlement*
solvencia *ability to pay, solvency*
– económica *financial responsibility*
–, grado de *financial standing*
solvente *solvent, sound*
someter *to submit*
sondeador del pensamiento *scanner*
sondeo, técnicas de *survey techniques*
sostener el precio *to keep up the price*
sostenido, mercado *steady market*
–, precio *support price*
sostenimiento *support, maintenance*
– de precios, política de *price-support policy*
subagencia *sub-agency*
subalterno *subordinate*
subarrendar *to sublet*
subarriendo *sub-lease*
subasta *auction*
–, comprar por *to buy at auction*
–, precio de *upset price*
–, vender a *to set up*
subcomisión *subcommittee*
subconsciente *subconscious*
subdelegado *sub-delegate*
subdesarrollado *underdeveloped*
subdirector *assistant manager, associate director*
subdividir *to subdivide*
subfase *sub-operation*
subida de precio *price advance*
subíndice *sub-index*
sublimación *sublimation*
sublimal, estímulo *sublimal stimulus*
submontaje *sub-assembly*
submuestra *sub-sample*
subnormal *subnormal, substandard*
subproducto *by-product, residual product*
subprueba *sub-test*
subrayar *to underscore or underline*

subsanar *to adjust*
subsidiar *to subsidize*
subsidiaria, compañía *underlying company*
–, cuenta *sub-account*
subsidio *subsidy*
– anual *annual subsidy*
– de precios *price subsidy*
subsidios para la exportación *export subsidies*
subtotal *subtotal*
subunidad *sub-unit*
subvención *bounty*
sucursal, director de *branch manager*
sucesión *succession, estate*
sucesiones, contabilidad de *estate accounting*
sucesiva, muestra *sequential sample*
sucesivas, plan de operaciones *flow sheet*
sucesivos, entre empleos *between jobs*
sucesores *successors*
sucursal *branch*
–, director de *branch manager*
sueldo *salary, wages*
– base *base pay or rate or wage*
– completo *full pay*
– constante *straight time*
– después de deducciones *take-home pay*
– garantizado *guaranteed wage*
– inicial *starting salary*
– mínimo *minimum wage*
– uniforme por hora *straight time*
–, a *on a salary*
–, aumento de *raise in salary*
–, prestaciones adicionales al *fringe benefits*
–, rebajar *to cut a salary*
–, trabajador a *salaried employee*
sueldos acumulados *accrued salaries*
– según productividad, escala de *incentive wages*
–, ajuste automático *automatic wage adjustment*
–, controversia sobre *wage dispute*
–, escala de *wage scale*
–, impuesto sobre los *wage tax*
–, nivel de *wage level*
–, nómina de *payroll*
–, tabulador de *wage scale*
suelos, conservación de *soil conservation*
suelta, muestra *odd sample*
sueltas, hojas *loose leaf*
sueltos, artículos *piece goods*
sueño *dream*
– diurno *daydream*
sufragar los gastos *to meet the costs*
sugerencias de los empleados *employee suggestion*
sujetarse a condiciones *to meet conditions*
sujeto *person, subject*

– a aprobación *on approval*
– a impuesto *taxable*
– a normas, no informalte de un *to buy out*
suma *addition, amount*
– a la vuelta *carry over*
– exacta *amount certain*
– global *inclusive sum*
– total *grand total*
– y sigue *amount carried forward*
sumador, registro *adding register*
sumadora *adding machine*
– algebraica *algebraic adder*
– electrónica *electronic adder*
–, cinta para máquina *adding machine ribbon*
–, máquina *adder, adding machine*
–, máquina registradora *cash registering and adding machine*
–, rollo de papel para máquina *adding roll*
sumar *to add*
– a mano, máquina de *hand-operated adding machine*
– y calcular, máquina de *adding and calculating machine*
–, signo de *addition sign*
sumario *summary, abstract, syllabus*
sumas retenidas *amounts withheld*
suministrar *to furnish*
suministro *supply*
– de cantidad indefinida, contrato para *open-end contract*
suntuarias, leyes *sumptuary laws*
superabundancia *glut*
superación *sublimation*
superar *to surpass or exceed*
superávit *surplus*
– adquirido *acquired surplus*
– bloqueado *restricted surplus*
– corriente *current surplus*
– de capital *capital surplus*
superficialmente *perfunctorily*
superficie de la probabilidad *probability surface*
–, medida de *square measure*
superintendente *superintendent, supervisor*
– auxiliar *assistant superintendent*
superior del salario, límite *wage ceiling, maximum wage*
supermercado *supermarket*
superposición *overlapping*
superproducción *overproduction*
supervisar *to supervise*
supervisión *supervision*
– de los archivos *filing supervision*
supervisor *overseer, supervisor*

– de capacitación *training supervisor*
– de oficinas *office supervisor*
supervivencia *survival*
superviviente, póliza del último *last-survivor policy*
suplementaria, ganancia *side profit*
suplementarias, horas *overtime*
–, relaciones *supporting schedules*
suplementario, trabajo *supplementary work*
suplementarios, gastos *additional charges*
suplemento *supplement, extra, allowance*
– de crédito *supplementary approriation*
– del proceso *process allowance*
– por aprendizaje *learner's allowance, training allowance*
– por fatiga *fatigue allowance*
– por imprevistos *contingency allowance*
– interferencia *interference allowance, synchronisation allowance*
– por necesidades personales *personal needs allowance, personal allowance*
suplente *substitute*
–, gerente *acting manager*
suplir *to supplement, to substitute*
Suprema, Corte *Supreme Court*
supresión *abatement*
suprimible *abatable*
suprimir *to cancel or abolish, to suppress or abate*
supuesto *assumption*
surtido de mercancías *stock*
–, rotación del *stock turnover*
surtir sus almacenes *to lay in a stock*
– un pedido *to fill an order*
suscribir *to subscribe, to underwrite*
– valores *to underwrite*
suscriptor *subscriber, signer*
suscritas, acciones *subscribed capital stock*
suscrito *undersigned, subscribed*
susodicho *above-mentioned*
suspender *to discontinue or interrupt*
– el pago *to stop payment*
– pagos *to suspend payments*
– un pedido *to hold up an order*
suspensión *abeyance*
– de pagos *suspension of payments*
–, cuenta de *clearing account*
suspenso, en *in abeyance*
sustento *support, maintenance*
sustitución, costo de *replacement cost*
sustituir *to substitute*
sustituto *substitute, surrogate*
sustracción *subtraction*
sustraer *subtract*

T

tabla *table*
- de contingencias *contingency table*
- de la demanda *demand schedule*
- de mortalidad actual *current life table*
- de rendimiento *yield table*

tablas *tables*
- de grupos humanos *cohort tables*
- de mortalidad de generaciones *generation life tables*

tabulación cruzada *cross tabulation*
- de datos *tabulation of data*

tabulador de sueldos *wage scale*

tabular *to tabulate*

tachar *to strike out or delete*

táctica financiera *financial policy*

taller *shop, workshop*
- de fabricación de utillaje *tool room*
- de reparaciones *workroom*

talleres para determinación de costes, contabilidad de *shop and cost accounting*

talón *stub, coupon*
- oro *gold standard*
- postal *postal receipt*
-, matriz *stub mat*

talonario *stub book*
- de cheques *chequebook*

tamaño *size*
- corriente *stock size*
- del anuncio *ad size*
- del lote *lot size, batch size*
- normalizado *standard size*
-, clasificación por *grading*

tamaños, clasificación de productos por clases o *grading*

tambor de direcciones *address drum*

tangible, activo *tangible assets, tangibles*
-, activo neto *tangible net worth*

tangibles, bienes *tangible property*

tanteo *score, approximate estimate*

tanteos, método de *trial and error*
-, por *by trial and error*

tanto alzado, comprar a *to buy outright*
-, impuesto a *composition tax*

taquidactilógrafo *stenographer-typist*

taquigrafía *shorthand, stenography*
-, cuaderno de *stenographer's notebook*

taquigráficos, signos *stenographic symbols*

taquígrafo *stenographer*

taquimecanógrafo *stenographer-typist*

tara *tare*
- real *actual tare*
- según factura *invoice tare*
- tasada *estimated tare*
- y merma *tare and tret*
-, determinación de la *taring*
-, escala de *tare bar*

taraje *tare weight*

tarar *to tare, to weigh before loading*

taras, escala de *tare bar*

tarea *task, work, piecework, job*
- programada *programmed job*
- tipificada *standard job*
-, trabajo a *piecework*

tareas, plan de *job planning*

tarifa *rate, tariff*
- amplia *loose rate, loose piece rate*
- arancelaria *schedule of customs duties*
- base *base rate*
- constante *straight rate*
- de contribuciones *tax rate*
- de salarios *wage rate*
- de valoración *evaluated rate*
- del cambio *rate of exchange*
- escalonada *step rate, sliding scale, scale of discounts*
- estrecha *tight rate, tight piece rate*
- fiscal *schedule of import duties*
- inicial de paga *starting rate of pay*
- muy justa *tight rate, tight piecework price*
- por tiempo *time rate, time wage*
- postal *postal rates*
- preferencial *preferential tariff*
- progresiva *progressive tariff*
- proteccionista *protective tariff*
- rebajada para detallistas *open retail rate*
- reducida por rebaja *cut rate*
- salarial *wage rate*
- única *flat rate*

tarifas aéreas *air fares*
- de aeropuerto *airport tariffs*
- de publicidad *rate card, advertising rates*
- reducidas *trim rates*
-, ficha de *rate card*
-, fijación de *rate fixing, rate setting*
-, reducción de *rate cutting*
-, sistema de *rate structure*

tarjeta *card*
- de afiliación a un gremio *union card*
- registradora de horas trabajadas *timecard*
tasa *tax, rate*
- básica *base rate*
- de crecimiento *rate of growth*
- de depreciación *depreciation rate*
- de descuento *discount rate*
- de interés *rate of interest*
- de mortalidad *death rate*
- de mortalidad por profesiones *occupational death rate*
- de nacimiento *birth rate*
- de probabilidad *probability rate*
- de rendimiento *rate of return*
- impositiva *tax rate*
- media *average rate*
- real *effective rate*
- uniforme *flat rate*
-, precio de *standard price*
tasable *rateable*
tasación *appraisal, assessment, rating*
- oficial *assessed valuation*
-, depreciación por *appraisement method of depreciation*
tasada, tara *estimated tare*
tasador *appraiser*
- aduanero *appraiser*
-, técnico *valuation engineer*
tasar *to appraise or assess*
techo, precio *ceiling price*
tecla *key*
- de arranque automático *auto-start key*
teclado, calculadora accionada por *key-drive calculator*
teclas impulsadas, calculadora de *key-driven calculator*
-, calculadora de *digital computer*
técnica *technique*
- comercial *marketing*
- contable *expert accountancy*
- de diseños *design technique*
- de mercancías *merchandising*
- de muestreo *sampling technique*
-, asistencia *technical assistance*
-, formación *technical training*
-, instrucción *technical instruction*
-, jerga *technical jargon*
-, reserva *unearned premium reserve*
técnicas de investigación *research techniques*
- de muestreo *sampling techniques*
- de recogida de datos *data-collection techniques*
-, consultas *technical queries*
tecnicismo *technicality, techniques*
técnico *expert, technician*

- comercial *comercial practitioner*
- de un editor, consultor *reader*
- electrónico *electronic engineer*
- proyectista *development engineer*
- tasador *valuation engineer*
-, asesor *technical adviser*
-, director *technical director*
técnicos, hoja de datos *technical data sheet*
tecnocracia *technocracy*
tecnológica, investigación *technological research*
tecnológico *technological*
tela, en *in cloth boards*
teléfono, entrevista por *telephone interview*
teletipo *teletype, tape printer*
televisar *to teleview, televise or telecast*
televisión *television*
- comercial *commercial television*
- publicitaria *commercial television*
-, red de *television network*
televisivo *televising*
televisor *televiser, television receiver, television set*
televisual *televising*
temas monetarios *money matters*
- registrados *copyrighted material*
temperamento *temperament*
-, analisis de *temperament analysis*
temporada, artículos de *seasonal goods*
-, derechos arancelarios de *seasonal duties*
-, pérdidas de la *seasonal loss*
-, ventas fuera de *off-season sales*
temporal de obreros, despido *lay-off*
-, tierra de *unirrigated farmland*
temporero *temporary*
tendencia *trend*
- a la baja *downward trend*
- al alza, con *strong*
- alcista *upward trend*
- demográfica *population trend*
- expansionista del mercado *increasing share of market*
- oculta *undercurrent*
tendencias *tendencies, trends*
- de la moda *fashion trends*
- de marca, encuesta sobre *brand*
- del mercado *market trends*
- económicas básicas *basic economic trends*
- en conflicto *conflicting tendencies*
- inflaccionistas *inflationary trends*
tenedor *holder*
- de acciones *stockholder*
- de libros *book-keeper*
- de póliza *policyholder*
- de prendas *receiver*
- de títulos *security holder*

– ficticio de acciones de otros *dummy stockholder*
teneduría de libros *book-keeping, accounting*
tenencia *holding, possession*
tener en cartera *to have on file*
tensión *tension*
tentativo, balance *tentative balance sheet*
teoría *theory*
– de costos *theory of comparative costs*
– de los valores internacionales *theory of international values*
– tercería *arbitration, intervention*
terminación, fecha prevista de *due data*
–, método de porcentaje de *percentage of completion method*
terminados, productos *finished products*
terminal, puerto *port of delivery*
término *term, deadline*
– de entrega *time of delivery*
– medio *average*
–, depósito a *time deposit*
–, mercado a *time bargain*
–, operación a *business in futures*
–, seguro a *terms insurance*
terminología *terminology*
términos comerciales *commercial terms*
– de venta *terms of sale*
terrateniente *landholder, landowner*
terreno *land, ground, lot*
–, encuestas sobre *field surveys*
territorio reservado *exclusive territory*
tesorería *treasury*
tesorero *treasurer*
tesoro *revenue*
test *test*
– de aptitud *aptitude test*
– de ensayo *prediction test*
testificar *to witness or testify*
testigo *witness, specimen, sample*
texto *text, copy*
– comercial *comercial*
– corregido *revised text*
– de aviso (M, C, A) *advertising copy*
– publicitario *advertising copy*
–, tipo de *body type*
ticket *ticket, docket, slip*
tiempo *time, term*
– a jornal *time on daywork, hours per day*
– auxiliar del proceso *auxiliary process time*
– básico *basic time*
– concedido *allowed time, incentive time*
– dado, producto de una fábrica en un *turnout*
– de adaptación *adjustment time*
– de aprendizaje *learning or training time*
– de ausencia *absent time*
– de cambio de trabajo *changeover time*

– de descanso *relaxation or rest time*
– de espera *waiting time*
– de fabricación *task or production time*
– de inactividad *down time*
– de máquina *machine, machining or running time*
– de máquina parada *idle machine time*
– de movimiento de materiales *materials handling time transport time*
– de movimientos básicos *basic motion time*
– de parada *down time*
– de parada de máquina *down-time machine*
– de preparación *make-ready time, set-up time*
– de presencia *attendance time, all-in time*
– de producción *production time*
– de propagación *transit time*
– de reposo *rest or relaxation time*
– de trabajo *job time*
– de trabajo, reloj de control de *job time recording clock*
– de transporte *transport or handling or materials handling time*
– del proceso *process time*
– desocupado *spare time*
– determinado, producción en un *turnout*
– disponible de máquina *available machine time*
– disponible de proceso *available process time*
– doble *double time*
– estimado *estimated time*
– extra *overtime*
– global *overall time, observation period, elapsed time*
– improductivo *down time*
– inactivo *down time, idle time*
– manual *hand time, manual time*
– medio *average time*
– muerto *dead time*
– normal *normal time*
– o rapidez de la distribución *rate or speed of turnover*
– perdido *lost time*
– por diferencia *subtracted time*
– por diferencias, medida de *differential timing*
– pretendido *target time*
– previsto *design time*
– primado *allowed time, incentive time*
– productivo *productive time*
– real *actual or clock time, time taken or used*
– tipo *standard time*
– tipo garantizado *guaranteed standard time*
– total de fabricación *total process time*
– trabajado, ficha de *attendance card*
– transcurrido *elapsed time, observation period, overall time*

– unitario *time per unit*
– y medio *time and a half*
–, anotador de *timekeeper*
–, control de ciclo de *time cycle control*
–, economía de *time saving*
–, ganancia por unidad de *earned rate*
–, registrador de *time recorder*
–, tarifa por *time rate or wage*
–, utilidad de *time utility*
tiempos normalizados, datos de *standard time data*
– por cronómetro, estudio de *stopwatch time study*
– y deberes, hoja para el estudio de *time observation sheet, time study sheet*
–, ficha de *clock or time card*
–, oficina de *time study department*
tienda a precios únicos *limited price store*
– al detalle *retail store*
– al por mayor *wholesale enterprise*
– de comestibles *grocer's shop, grocery*
– de papelería *stationer's*
– de rebajas *discount house*
– de ultramarinos *retail grocery store*
– de ventas al contado *cash store*
–, administrador de *store manager*
–, director de *store manager*
–, encargado de *store manager*
–, jefe de *store manager*
tiendas al por menor, comprobación en las *retail storeaudit*
– de autoservicio *self-service stores*
– en cadena *chain stores*
tierra *earth, land*
– de labor *cultivated land*
– de riego *irrigated farmland*
– de temporal *unirrigated farmland*
– virgen *virgin soil*
timar *to swindle*
timbre *stamp, seal*
– de goma *rubber stamp*
– fiscal *revenue stamp*
– postal *postage stamp*
–, tributación por *stamp tax*
tinta, lápiz *copying pencil*
típico, error *standard error*
tipificación *standardization*
– absoluta *absolute standard*
– de materiales *material standardization*
– de rendimiento *output standardization*
–, oficina de *bureau of standards*
–, proyecto de *standard project*
tipificada, tarea *standard job*
tipificadas, manual de prácticas *standard practice manual*
tipificado de investigación, procedimiento

standard procedure
tipificador *standardizer*
tipo *standard, type, kind*
– bancario *bank rate*
– básico *normal rate*
– básico de pago *base rate of pay*
– corriente *current rate*
– de cambio *conversion rate*
– de comisión progresiva o en escala ascendente *progressive or stepped-up commission rate*
– de descuento *discount rate*
– de imprenta *type, print character*
– de impuesto *tax rate*
– de interés *interest rate*
– de interés bancario *bank rate*
– de texto *body type*
– del mercado *market rate*
– garantizado, tiempo *guaranteed standard time*
– medio de aumento *average of increase*
–, actuación *standard performance*
–, costes *standard costs*
–, embalaje *standard packing*
–, envase *standard packing*
–, formulario *standard blank, standard form*
–, salario *standard wage*
–, tiempo *standard time*
–, variable del *variation from standard*
tipos cruzados *cross rates*
– de imprenta *printing types*
–, reducción de *variety reduction, simplification, limiting variety*
tirada *press-work, circulation*
– aparte *off-print*
– media *average circulation*
– neta *net sales circulation*
tiradas, control de las *circulation control*
tirado *dirt cheap*
tiraje *edition, issue*
tiro *edition, circulation*
titulado, contable público *certified public accountant*
titular, miembro *regular member*
título *title, right, article*
– al portador *bearer instrument*
– constitutivo *charter*
– de compraventa *bill of sale*
– de patente *letters patent*
– de propiedad *title deed*
– de propiedad, traspaso de *change of title*
– hipotecario *mortgage bond*
– nominativo *registered bond*
títulos *securities, documents*
– al portador *active bonds*
– fiduciarios *bonds*

– u obligaciones, casa de valores *security house*
–, tenedor de *security holder*
todo riesgo *all risks*
todos los gastos comprendidos *inclusive, inclusive of all charges*
tolerancia *admissible error, tolerance, allowance*
– de fabricación *factory limits*
– del muestreo *sample tolerance*
–, factor de *tolerance factor*
tomador de tiempo *timekeeper*
tomar *to take*
– a préstamo *to borrow*
– dictado *to take dictation*
– en arriendo *to lease or rent*
– la palabra *to take the floor*
– nota *to take notice*
– parte en *to take part in*
– un pedido *to take an order*
tonel *barrel*
tonelada *ton*
– corta *short ton*
– larga *long ton*
– métrica *metric ton*
tonelaje *tonnage, turnover*
tope, precio *ceiling price*
–, salario *wage ceiling, maximum wage*
tormenta de cerebros *brainstorm*
total al año, salario inicial *gross initial annual salary*
– cargado, peso *gross laden weight*
– de capital, cantidad *aggregate principal amount*
– de fabricación, tiempo *total process time*
– de ventas *turnover*
– efectiva, pérdida *absolute total loss*
– real, pérdida *actual total loss*
–, bruto *gross*
–, coste *all-in or gross cost*
–, curva *overall curve*
–, empleo *full employment*
–, ganancia *overall gain*
–, importe *gross amount*
–, ocupación *full employment*
–, pasivo *total liabilities*
–, pérdida *total loss*
–, peso *gross weight*
–, prima *gross premium*
–, probabilidad *overall probability*
–, rebaja *gross markdown*
–, rendimiento *throughput*
–, suma *grand total*
–, valor *aggregate value*
totalidad *full amount*
totalizador *totalizer*

totalizar *to add up, to total*
trabaja parte del día, miembro que solo *part-time member*
trabajadas, tarjeta registradora de horas *time card*
trabajado, ficha de tiempo *attendance card*
trabajador *worker, labourer, workman*
– a domicilio *homeworker*
– a jornal *wageworker*
– a sueldo *salaried employee*
– calificado *skilled tradesman, craftsman, skilled worker*
– de oficina *office worker, white-collar worker*
– del campo *farm hand*
– en jornada incompleta *part-time worker*
– eventual *casual worker*
– no sindicalizado *non-union workman*
trabajadores eventuales *casual workers*
–, sindicato de *labour union*
trabajo *work, job, task, labour, activity*
– a destajo *piecework, taskwork*
– a horas extras *overtime work*
– a jornal *daywork, timework*
– a jornal medido *measured daywork*
– a tarea *piecework*
– a trato (Ch) *taskwork*
– a turnos *shift work*
– agotador *sweat, fatigue*
– clave *key job*
– consumido *expended work*
– contable *accounting work*
– continuo *non-stop work, work round the clock*
– controlado *controlled work, restricted work*
– de equipo *group or team work*
– de investigación *research work*
– de madrugada *lobster shift*
– de oficina *office or clerical work*
– de urgencia *rush job*
– de ventas, carga de *sales workload*
– deficiente *substandard work*
– diario *daywork*
– directo *straight or direct work*
– diurno *daytime work*
– en cadena *assembly-line operation*
– en campaña *fieldwork*
– en colaboración *combined work*
– en equipo *team work*
– en progreso *work in progress*
– en serie *production work, assembly-line operation*
– en varias máquinas *multiple machine work*
– experimental *experimental work*
– externo *outside or external work*
– extraordinario *overtime work*
– igual, salario igual por *equal pay for equal*

work
- indirecto *indirect work or labour*
- individual *individual work*
- industrial de niños *child labour*
- infantil *child labour*
- interno *internal or inside work*
- lento, huelga de *work to rule*
- libre *free labour, unrestricted work*
- manual *manual labour*
- mental *mental work*
- o servicio social *social work*
- por medida *piecework*
- por pieza *piecework*
- por unidad de tiempo *time work*
- productivas, horas de *productive work hours*
- productivo *productive work*
- suplementario *supplementary work*
-, abandono del *stop work*
-, accidente de *industrial accident, occupational injury*
-, activo de *working assets*
-, adiestramiento en el *job instruction or training*
-, ahorro de *labour saving*
-, análisis del *job analysis*
-, bono de *job card, job ticket*
-, calificación del *job rating*
-, cantidad de *work load*
-, carga de *load factor, work opportunity, work load*
-, cesación del *downing of tools*
-, cesar en el *to down tools*
-, ciclo de *work cycle*
-, clasificación del *job classification*
-, código del trabajo *labour laws*
-, coeficiente de *stress, work coefficient*
-, comité de *task group*
-, condiciones de *working conditions*
-, conflicto de *labour dispute*
-, conseguir a fuerza de *to work out*
-, contrato de *employment contract*
-, contrato colectivo de *collective bargaining agreement*
-, convenio de *collective agreement, work agreement*
-, convenios colectivos de *collective bargaining*
-, cooperación de un *team work*
-, cuadro de la marcha del *speed schedule*
-, demanda de *labour demand*
-, descripción del *labour layoff*
-, día de *working day*
-, diagrama de distribución del *work distribution chart*
-, diagrama de flujo del *work flow charting*

-, división del *division of labour*
-, ejecución del *job performance*
-, elemento de *work element*
-, encuesta sobre el análisis del *work analysis survey*
-, escala de valoración del *job evaluation scale*
-, especificación del *job or work specification*
-, estudio del *work study*
-, factor de *job or work factor*
-, falta de asistencia al *absence from work*
-, fuerza de *work force*
-, grupo de *team, working group, equipment, means of production*
-, hoja de *work sheet*
-, horas de *working hours*
-, ingreso del *labour income*
-, ley de accidentes del *compensation act*
-, ley del *labour code*
-, lugar de *work station*
-, medición del *work measurement*
-, medida de *work measurement*
-, método de *method of working*
-, movilidad del *mobility of labour*
-, norma de *work standard*
-, oferta de *employment offered*
-, orden de *job or work order, factory or manufacturing order*
-, paralización del *labour stoppage*
-, plan de *work schedule*
-, plan de avance del *progress schedule*
-, plataforma de *step-plate*
-, ponencias de *working parties*
-, preparación del *planning*
-, programa de *work schedule*
-, programación de *work schedule*
-, puesto de *workbench, work place, work station*
-, reglamentación del *labour regulations*
-, reglamentación para contratos colectivos de trabajo *collective bargaining provisions*
-, relaciones del *labour relations*
-, rendimiento del *job performance*
-, satisfacción *job satisfaction*
-, semana básica de *basic working week*
-, sencillo *straight or direct work*
-, solicitud de *employment wanted*
-, tiempo de *market rate*
-, tiempo de cambio de *changeover time*
-, unidad de *work or labour unit*
-, valor del *work value, job standard*
-, valores unitarios de *work unit value*
-, valuación del *job evaluation*
trabajos *works*
-, rotación de *job rotation*
-, valoración de *job evaluation or rating*
traducción *translation*

– fiel *close translation*
traducir *to translate*
traductor *translator*
tráfico *traffic*
– de aeropuertos, control del *airport traffic control*
–, volumen de *traffic flow*
tramitación burocrática *clerical routine*
– de facturas *invoice procedure*
–, patente en *patent pending*
tramitar *to carry out, to negotiate*
trámite *step, procedure*
–, en *pending*
–, fichero de *suspense file*
transacción *transaction, settlement*
–, motivo *transaction motives*
transacciones comerciales *commercial transactions*
– consumadas *completed transactions*
– invisibles *invisible transactions*
transar *to settle, to compromise*
transbordar *to tranship*
transcribir *to transcribe*
transcripción *copying*
transcurrido, tiempo *elapsed time, observation period, overall time*
transferencia *transfer*
– bancaria *bank transfer*
– de informaciones, circuito *information path*
transferencias de acciones, impuesto sobre *stock-transfer tax*
transferible *transferable*
–, bono no *registered bond*
tranformación, medios de *processing equipment*
– de la materia, proceso *processing*
transigir *to compromise*
tránsito *transit, traffic*
– aéreo, control de *air traffic control*
–, mercancías en *goods in transit*
transitorio *temporary*
transmisión de datos *data transmission*
transmisiones, red de *communication network*
transmitir *forward*
transportación *transportation*
transportador *carrier, conveyor*
transportadora, cinta *belt conveyor*
transportar *to carry*

transporte *transportation*
– en carga *transport loaded*
–, gastos de *transportation expenses*
–, seguro de *transportation insurance*
–, tiempo de *transport or handling time, materials handling time*
traslado de personal *transfer of personnel*
traspasar *to assign, to transfer*
traspaso *assignment, cession*
– de título de propiedad *change of title*
–, asiento de *transfer entry*
tratado *treaty, agreement*
– comercial *trade agreement*
tratante *trader*
trato *deal, agreement*
– colectivo *collective bargaining*
–, cerrar un *to strike a bargain*
–, trabajo a (Ch) *taskwork*
tregua *cooling-off period*
tren de ensamblaje *assembly or flow or production line*
tribunal *court*
– de honor *court of honour*
– de justicia *court of justice*
tributación *taxation*
– fiscal *federal tax*
– graduada *graduated taxation*
– por timbre *stamp tax*
– progresiva *progressive taxation*
–, base de *tax basis*
–, doble *double taxation*
tributaria, bonificación *tax rebate*
–, capacidad *tax-paying capacity*
–, política *tax policy*
tributario, sistema *tax system*
–, valor *taxable value*
tributarios, bienes *taxable income*
tributo *tax, contribution*
trimestral, magazine *quarterly magazine or review*
–, revista *quarterly magazine or review*
trimestre *quarter*
triplicado *triplicate*
trueque *barter, trade-in*
trust *trust*
–, administrador de un *trustee*
turno, cambio de *shift changeover*
–, duración del *shift time*
turnos, trabajo a *shift work*

U

ubicación *site, location*
última página *back page*
últimas noticias *stop-press news*
– noticias, emisión de *newcast*
– noticias, locutor de *newcaster*
último *ultimate*
– grito de la moda *up-to-the-minute*
ultramar *overseas*
ultramarinos, tienda de *retail grocery store*
unánime *unanimous*
única, prima *single premium*
–, tarifa *flat rate*
único, impuesto *single tax*
únicos, tienda a precios *limited price store*
unidad *unity, unit*
– administrativa *administrative unit*
– de costo *cost unit*
– de cuenta *accounting unit*
– de desarrollo de un producto *product development unit*
– de muestra *sample unit*
– de tiempo, trabajo por *time work*
– de trabajo *work or labour unit*
– de valor productivo *unit production value*
– marginal *marginal unit*
– monetaria *unit of currency, monetary unit*
– negociable *trading unit*
–, costo por *unit cost*
unidades de consumo *consumer units*
– de las existencias, comprobación en *unit stock control*
–, inventario por *unit inventory*
unificación *standardization*
unificada, norma *unified standard*
uniformar *to standardize*
uniforme de precios, política *uniform price policy*
– por horas, sueldo *straight time*
–, tasa *flat rate*
uniformidad *consistency, steadiness*
unilateral *unilateral*
–, prueba *one-sided test*
unitaria, banca *unit banking*
–, utilidad *unit profit*
unitario de producción, depreciación a base del coste *unit cost depreciation*
–, coste *unit cost*
–, peso *unit weight*

–, precio *unit price, piece rate, piecework price*
–, tiempo *time per unit*
unitarios de trabajo, valores *work unit value*
–, contrato de precios *unit-price contract*
–, oferta a precios *unit-price bid*
universal *universal*
–, feria *world fair*
universitaria, formación *academic training*
universo *universe*
urgencia, trabajo de *rush work*
–, venta de *distress selling*
urgente, mensaje *urgent message*
–, pedido *rush order*
usanza *usance*
uso *use, custom, practice*
– de imperios, diagrama del *forms-procedure chart*
– final *end use*
– y desgaste *wear and tear*
–, préstamo de *loan for use*
–, valor de *value in use*
usuario *user*
usuarios, grupos de *user groups*
usufructo *usufruct*
usurero *usurer*
útil, carga *useful load*
–, vida *working life*
utilaje *fixture, jig, tooling*
utilidad *profit, usefulness*
– accidental *casual income*
– bruta *gross profit*
– creciente *increasing returns*
– de forma *form utility*
– de lugar *place utility*
– de tiempo *time utility*
– decreciente *diminishing returns*
– gravable *taxable profit*
– gruesa (M) *gross earnings, gross profit*
– imponible *taxable income*
– líquida *net profit*
– marginal *marginal utility*
– máxima, producción de *best profit outfit*
– máxima, punto de *best profit point*
– neta *net profit*
– permisible *allowable returns*
– unitaria *unit profit*
–, margen de *markup, margin of profit*
utilidades *earnings, profits*

– acumuladas *accumulated profits*
– antes de los impuestos *pre-tax earnings*
– anticipadas *anticipated profits*
– aparentes *book profits*
– brutas *gross profits*
– contingentes *contingent profits*
– de las empresas *corporate earnings*
– de operación *operating profits*
– devengadas *accrued income*
– diferidas *deferred income, deferred credits*
– esperadas *anticipated profits*
– excedentes *excess profits*
– netas *net profits*
– no realizadas *paper profits*
– no repartidas *undistributed profits*
– realizadas *realized profits*

– reinvertidas *re-invested profits*
– repartibles *distributive profits*
– según libros *book profits*
–, impuesto sobre *profit tax*
–, ocultación de *concealment of profits*
–, participación de *profit sharing*
–, porcentaje de *percentage of profits*
–, reparto de *profit sharing*
–, tributación por *income tax*
utilización de datos *information handling*
– de mercancías, ciclo de *turnover*
–, coste de *user cost*
utillaje y herramientas, boletín de petición de *tool ticket*
–, taller de fabricación de *tool room*

V

vacante *vacancy, vacant*
–, puesto *vacant post or place*
–, puesto a cargo *vacant post or situation*
vacilación *hesitation*
vagón, puesto sobre *free on rail*
vale *bonus, voucher, promissory note*
– de caja chica *petty-cash voucher*
valer *to cost, to be worth*
vales a pagar *bills payable*
valía *worth, value*
validar *to validate*
validez *validity*
válido *valid*
valioso *valuable*
valor *value, price*
– a la par *par value*
– absoluto *absolute value*
– actual, método del *actual value method*
– acumulativo *accumulative value*
– agregado *value added*
– al cobro *value for collection*
– al vencimiento *value at maturity*
– asegurado *amount value*
– asignado *rating*
– capitalizado *capitalized value*
– catastral *assessed valuation*
– convenido *agreed value*
– constante, moneda de *constant currency*
– de aceptación de una marca *goodwill*
– de consumo en el país *home consumption value*
– de coste *cost value*
– de coste, método del *cost value method*
– de emisión *issue price*
– de equilibrio *equilibrium value*
– de factura *invoice value*
– de la clientela *goodwill*
– de lectura *readership*
– de prestigio de una empresa *goodwill*
– de venta *selling price, trade value*
– de uso *value in use*
– declarado *declared value*
– del trabajo *work or job value*
– depreciado *depreciated value*
– efectivo *cash value*
– en cambio *exchange value*
– en cuenta *value in account*
– en libros *book value*

– en liquidación *breakup value*
– en plaza *market value*
– entendido *value agreed upon*
– entregado *surrender value*
– equitativo *fair value*
– estable, divisas de *hard currency*
– fiduciario *fiduciary value*
– global *aggregate value*
– imponible *taxable value*
– industrial *commercial value*
– justo del mercado *fair market value*
– líquido *net value*
– local *local value*
– medio *median, average*
– neto *clear value*
– nominal *face or nominal value*
– nominal, capital declarado de acciones sin *stated capital*
– ponderado *weighted value*
– productivo, unidad de *unit production value*
– real *actual value*
– recibido *value received*
– según libros *book value*
– social *social value*
– total *aggregate value*
– tributario *taxable value*
– variable *average*
–, al *ad valorem*
–, bajar de *to decline in value*
–, muestra sin *sample without value*
–, nulo y sin *null and void*
–, rebajar el *write down*
–, sin *worthless*
valoración *evaluation, appraisal, rate, rating*
– correlativa *appraisal, rate, rating*
– de funciones *function evaluation*
– de la actuación *rating, speed or performance rating*
– de los méritos individuales *merit rating*
– de trabajos *job evaluation*
– de trabajos, encargado de la *job evaluator*
– del mérito *merit rating*
– del trabajo *job rating*
– estimada de la actuación *flat ratings*
– pericial *expert appraisal*
–, escala de *rating scale, scale of rating*
–, proceso de *appraisal process*
valorador *appraiser*

valores *securities, assets*
- a recibir *receivables*
- al cobro *receivables*
- bancarios *bank paper*
- bursátiles *stock-exchange securities, listed securities*
- dados en garantía *pledged securities*
- de especulación *equity securities*
- de renta fija *fixed-income securities*
- de renta variable *common stocks*
- del estado *government bonds*
- disponibles (A) *available assets*
- en cobranza *bills for collection*
- fiscales *government bonds*
- hipotecarios *mortgage bonds*
- independientes *independent values*
- inmovilizados *fixed assets*
- internacionales, teoría de los *theory of international values*
- materiales *physical assets*
- no inscritos, compraventa de *unlisted trading*
- no vendidos, compromiso para comprar *standby underwriting*
- patrimoniales *capital assets*
- positivos *assets*
- públicos *public securities*
- realizables *liquid assets*
- unitarios de trabajo *work unit value*
- unitarios, índice de *unit value index*
-, adelanto sobre *advance upon collateral*
-, afijación de *value allocation*
-, bolsa de *stock exchange*
-, cotización de *listing securities*
-, escala de *range of values*
-, mercado de *stock market*
-, suscribir *to underwrite*
-, títulos u obligaciones, casa de *security house*
valorización de los méritos individuales *merit rating*
- del mérito *merit rating*
- del trabajo *job rating*
-, tarifa de *evaluated rate*
valorizar *to appraise or value*
valuable *rateable, appraisable*
valuación *valuation, appraisal*
- del trabajo *job evaluation*
valuador *appraiser*
valuar en menos *to undervalue*
valla anunciadora *posting, bill posting*
- de anuncios *posting, bill posting*
- de carretera *highway billboard*
vapor, entregado al costado del *delivered alongside*
variable *variable, open-ended*

- aleatoria *aleatory variable, random variable*
- aleatoria continua *continuous random variable*
- de, capital *open-end capital*
- dependiente *dependent variable*
- promedio, costo *average variable cost*
- vectorial aleatoria *vector random variable*
-, promedio *variable average*
variables independientes *independent variables*
-, costes *variable costs*
-, honorarios *variable fees*
-, pronóstico a intervalos *varying-interval prediction*
variación *variation*
- admitida *allowable variation*
- del promedio *variation from the average*
- del tipo *variation from standard*
- entre grupos *between-groups variance*
variaciones estacionales *seasonal changes*
variancia, norma *alternate standard*
varianza *variance*
varios, gastos *sundry expenses*
vectorial aleatorio, variable *vector random variable*
vejez, prestaciones por *old-age benefits*
-, seguro de *old-age insurance*
velocidad *speed, tempo, pace*
- de giro *turnover*
-, apreciación de la *speed rating, performance rating*
vencer *to mature or expire*
vencida, anualidad *annuity due*
-, cuenta *mature account*
vencido *overdue*
vencidos, intereses *interest due*
vencimiento *maturity, maturity date, expiration*
- del giro *draft maturity*
-, fecha de *maturity or due date*
-, prorrogar el *to extend the time*
-, valor al *value at maturity*
vende por correo, firma que anuncia y *mail order house*
vendedor *salesman, seller, consultant, merchandiser*
- a domicilio *canvasser, peddler*
- ambulante *street hawker, street seller*
- de periódicos *newsagent, newsboy*
- de saldos *job merchant*
- mayorista *wholesaler*
- viajero *travelling salesman (Br)*
-, dependiente *salesperson*
-, prototipo de *sales type*
-, riesgo del *seller's risk*
-, viajante *travelling salesman (Br)*

vendedores, adiestramiento de agentes
   training of salesmen
–, instructor de *sales trainer*
vender *to sell*
– a bajo precio *to undersell*
– a comisión *to sell on commission*
– a subasta *to auction*
– accionada por introducción de moneda,
   máquina de *coin- operated vending machine*
– al contado *to sell for cash*
– al mayoreo *to sell at wholesale*
– al menudeo *to sell at retail*
– con pérdida *to sell at a loss*
– en descubierto *to sell short*
– en remate *to auction*
–, aptitud para *sales ability*
–, capacitación para *sales ability*
vendibilidad *saleability*
vendible *saleable*
vendidas, partida mercancías *bill of goods*
vendidos, compromiso para comprar valores
   no *stand-by underwriting*
–, devolución de artículos *sales return*
venta *sale*
– a bajo precio *underselling*
– a crédito *credit sale, sales to date*
– a plazos *instalment or time selling*
– al contado *cash sale*
– al contado, precio de *cash price*
– al descubierto *short selling*
– al detalle, precio de *retail selling price*
– al por mayor *wholesale trade*
– al público, precio de *gross price, gross sale
   price*
– anual *annual sale*
– automática *automatic vending*
– automática, máquina de *vending machine*
– bajo precio *underselling*
– de balance *inventory sale*
– de bienes embargados *distress sale*
– de bienes por impuestos no pagados *tax
   sale, tax title*
– de liquidación *clearance sale*
– de oportunidad *bargain sale*
– de reclamo *bargain sale*
– de restos *remainder sale*
– de saldos *clearance sale*
– de urgencia *distress selling*
– de ventas *sales policy*
– difícil *close bargain*
– difícil, mercado de *slow-selling merchandise*
– directa, gastos de la *direct selling expenses*
– en almoneda *auction sale*
– en kioscos *news-stand sales*
– en ruta *road selling*
– forzosa *forced sale*

– incondicional *absolute sale*
– interior, precio para *domestic price*
– judicial *foreclosure sale*
– por concesionario *concession sale*
– por correo *mail order business*
– por correspondencia *mail order business,
   mail order selling*
–, comprobante de *bill of sale*
–, condiciones de *sales terms*
–, costes de *sales cost*
–, contable de costes de *sales cost accountant*
–, en *in print*
–, en estado de *in saleable condition*
–, especialista en previsión de *sales forecaster*
–, factura de *bill of sale*
–, fichero de condiciones de *term-card file,
   term-discount file*
–, fuerza de *sales force*
–, gran establecimiento de *emporium*
–, justificantes de *sales vouchers*
–, lugar de *work station*
–, precio de *published price*
–, precio fijo de *fixed selling price*
–, previsión de *forecasting sales, sales forecast*
–, rebaja de *sale discount*
–, sección o lugar de *selling floor*
–, términos de *terms of sale*
–, valor de *selling price, trade value*
ventaja *advantage*
ventanilla, cheque con *counter cheque*
ventas a cuenta *account sales*
– a largo plazo, previsión de *long-range sales
   forecast*
– al contado, tienda de *cash store*
– al descubierto, compra para cubrir *short
   covering*
– al detalle *retail sales*
– al extranjero *foreign sales*
– brutas *gross sales*
– brutas, promedio de *average gross sale*
– continuadas *follow-up sales*
– de cuentas combinadas *combined account
   deals*
– de puerta en puerta *door-to-door selling*
– de zona, director o jefe de *regional sales
   manager*
– efectivas *actual sales*
– en abonos *instalment sales*
– en expectativas *expected sales*
– en firme, contratos de *contracts of sale*
– en periódicos y revistas, jefe de *circulation
   manager*
– fuera de temporada *off-season sales*
– máximas *peak sales*
– netas *net sales*
– para el exterior, director o jefe de *foreign*

sales manager
- para el interior, director o jefe de home
  sales manager
- pérdidas, formulario de lost-sale slip
- pérdidas, volante de lost-sale slip
- por compensación compensation sales
- potenciales potential sales
- previstas planned sales
-, agente de sales agent
-, análisis de sales analysis
-, área de sales territory or area
-, bonificaciones sobre sales discounts
-, campaña de sales campaign
-, característica del sistema de selling points
-, centro de shopping centre
-, cifra de sales figure
-, contabilidad de sales accounting
-, control de sales control
-, corredor de sales broker
-, crear to build sales
-, cuenta de sales account
-, cupo de sales quota
-, curva de las sales curve
-, datos sobre las sales data
-, departamento de sales department
-, diario de sales journal
-, dirección de sales management
-, disolución de clearing line
-, efectividad de las selling effectivenes
-, enfoque de sales approach
-, equipo de sales equipment, sales team
-, escritura de bill of sale
-, esfuerzo de selling effort
-, fiscalización de sales control
-, fuerza de sales force
-, gerencia de sales department
-, gerente de sales department
-, gráfico de sales curve
-, habilidad para forzar las high-pressure
  salesmanship
-, importe marginal de marginal proceeds
-, impuesto sobre excise tax
-, índice de sales index
-, información de sales information
-, informes de visitas y call and sales reports
-, investigación de las sales research
-, jefe auxiliar de assistant sales manager
-, jefe de sales manager
-, jefe de promoción de sales promotion
  manager
-, libro de sales book
-, libro mayor de accounts receivable ledger,
  sales ledger
-, lonja de sales room
-, oscilaciones de sales fluctuations
-, personal de sales force

-, política de sales policy or approach
-, potencial de sales potential
-, proceso de selling or sales process
-, promoción de sales promotion
-, registro de sales record
-, registro estadístico de sales record
-, sección de sales department
-, total de turnover
-, volúmen de sales volume
-, zona de sales territory
verdadero, coste actual cost
verificación check, control
- de carteles emplazados traffic audit
- de ficheros files auditing
- de existencias, registro de stock control
  record
- de saldos negativos minus balance control
- de ventas, procedimientos de sales control
  procedures
-, boletín de inspection card
verificador de ventas sales controller
verificar to verify or check
- el protesto to protest
- un censo to take a census
versalita small capital
vertical, expansión vertical expansion
vetar to veto
vía route, way
viajante comercial commercial traveller (Am),
  travelling salesman (Br)
- comisionista commission traveller
- vendedor travelling salesman (Br)
viaje travel, trip
- comercial business trip
- de negocios business trip
- redondo round trip
- sencillo one-way trip
- sin escala non-stop trip
-, gastos de travelling expenses
viajero passenger, traveller
- comerciante travelling salesman (Br)
-, agente travelling salesman (Br),
  commercial traveller (Am)
-, cheque de traveller's cheque
-, vendedor travelling salesman (Br)
viajes, agente de travel agent
viáticos travelling expenses
vicio defect, flaw
vida económica economic life
- futura, promedio de average life expectancy
- útil working life
-, duración media de life expectancy
-, estandard de standard of life, standard of
  living
-, índice del coste de cost-of-living index
-, nivel de standard of living, standard of life

–, patrón de *standard of living*
–, probabilidad completa de *complete expectation of life*
–, probabilidad de *life expectancy*
vigencia *duration*
vigente *standing*
–, orden *standing order*
vigilante *foreman, floorwalker*
violación de contrato *breach of contract*
violenta, baja *crash*
virgen, tierra *virgin soil*
visible de comercio, balanza *visible balance of trade*
–, archivo *visible file*
visibles de comercio, elementos *visible items of trade*
visión *video*
visitas y ventas, informes de *call-and-sales reports*
–, volante de *call slip*
vista de aduana *customs inspector*
–, cambio a la *sight rate, sight exchange*
–, efecto a la *sight draft*
–, letra a la *sight draft*
–, pagadero a la *due to demand*
–, pagaré a la *demand note*
–, punto de *angle, point of view, approach*
vitales, estadísticas *vital statistics*
vitalícia, anualidad *life annuity*
–, pensión *life pension*
–, renta *life annuity*

vitalício, miembro *life member*
vitalidad industrial *industrial health*
vitrina *showcase, glass case*
víveres, almacenista de *wholesale grocer*
viviendas, escasez de *housing shortage*
vocación *vocation*
vocal *member of a board*
volante o formulario *slip*
– de ventas perdidas *lost-sale slip*
– de visitas *call slip*
–, hoja de *leaflet*
volumen *volume*
– de los negocios *business figure turnover*
– de pedidos *order size*
– de tráfico *traffic flow*
– de ventas *sales volume*
– medio de pedidos *average order size*
– promedios de pedidos *average order size*
volver a comprar *to buy back*
votación *voting*
– por papeletas *polls*
voto *vote*
– de calidad *deciding vote*
– de confianza *vote of confidence*
– no oficial *straw vote*
– plural, acciones de *plural-voting stock*
–, acciones con derecho a *voting stock*
–, acciones sin derecho a *non-voting stock*
vuelo *flight*
vuelta de correo, a *by return mail*
–, de la *brought forward*

Z

zona *zone, district, area*
- aduanera *customs area*
- comercial *business district, shopping centre*
- de abastecimiento *distribution zone*
- de difusión *circulation area*
- de error *error band*
- de influencia *sphere of interest*
- de reparto *distributing zone*
- de ventas *sales territory*
- del dolar *dollar area*
- enfocada *coverage*
- postal *postal zone*
- potencial de comercio *potential trading area*
- residencial *residential neighbourhood*
- servida *coverage*

LISTA SELECTA DE ABREVIATURAS Y ACRONIMOS
ESPAÑOL

acept.	aceptación	acceptance	acc.
admón.	administración	administration	admin.
ad.val.	ad valorem, conforme a su valor	according to value	ad.val.
AELI	Asociación Europea de Libre Intercambio	European Free Trade Association	EFTA
AID	Asociación Internacional de Desarrollo	International Development Association	IDA
AIE	Agencia Internacional de la Energía	International Energy Agency	IEA
ALALC	Asociación Latino-Americana de Libre Cambio	Latin American Free Trade Association	ALALC
a.m.	antes del mediodía	before noon	a.m.
BEBS	Basura entra, basura sale	Garbage in, garbage out	GIGO
BIP	Banco Internacional de Pagos	Bank for International Settlements	BIS/BIZ
BIRF	Banco Internacional de Reconstrucción y Fomento	International Bank for Reconstruction and Development/World Bank	IBRD
c/c	cuenta corriente	account current	a/c
c.c.	centímetro cúbico	cubic centimetre	cc
CAEM	Consejo de Asistencia Económica	Council for Mutual Economic Assistance	CMEA
CCI	Cámara de Comercio Internacional	International Chamber of Commerce	ICC
CFI	Corporación Financiera Internacional	International Finance Corporation	IFC
CEE	Comunidad Económica Europea	European Economic Community	EEC
CEPAL	Comisión Económica para América Latina	Economic Commision for Latin America	ECLA
cf.	comparar	compare, confer	cf.
Cía.	compañía	Company	Co.
cl.	centilitro	centilitre	cl.
cm.	centímetro	centimetre	cm.
C.O.D.	Entrega contra reembolso, Cobrar a la entrega	Cash on delivery, Collect on delivery	COD
C.S.F.	coste, seguro y flete	Cost, insurance and freight	C.I.F.
cta.	cuenta	account	a/c
cte.	corriente	current	
ch/	cheque	cheque, sight draft	
doc.	docena	dozen	doz.
dto.	descuento	discount	dis
d/v	días vista	Days after sight	D/S
f.a.b.	franco a bordo	Free on board	F.O.B.
FIDA	Fondo Internacional de Desarrollo	International Fund for Agricultural Development	IFAD
FIFO	Primero en entrar, primero en salir	First in, first out	FIFO

FMI	Fondo Monetario Internacional	International Monetary Fund	IMF
GATT	Acuerdo General sobre Tarifas y Comercio	General Agreement on Tariffs and Trade	GATT
h.	hora	hour	hr.
IVA	Impuesto sobre el valor añadido	Value Added Tax	VAT
Kg.	Kilogramo	Kilogram(me)	Kg.
Kl.	Kilolitro	Kilolitre	Kl.
Km.	Kilómetro	Kilometre	Km.
l.	litro	litre	l.
l.a.b.	libre a bordo	Free on board	f.o.b.
lb.	libra	pound	lb.
m.	metro	metre	m.
MCCA	Mercado Común Centroamericano	Central American Common Market	CACM
OEA	Organización de Estados Americanos	Organization of American States	OAS
OIEA	Organismo Internacional Energía Atómica	International Atomic Energy Commission	IAEC
OIT	Organización Internacional del Trabajo	International Labour Organization	ILO
ONU	Organización de las Naciones Unidas	United Nations Organization	UNO
OPAEP	Organización de los Países Arabes Exportadores de Petróleo	Organization of Arab Petroleum Exporting Countries	OAPEC
OPEP	Organización de los Países Exportadores de Petróleo	Organization of Petroleum Exporting Countries	OPEC
OTAN	Organización del Tratado del Atlántico Norte	North Atlantic Treaty Organization	NATO
OUA	Organización de la Unidad Africana	Organization of African Unity	OAU
P.D.	posdata	Postscript	P.S.
p.ej.	por ejemplo	for example	e.g.
p.m.	tarde	post meridiem, afternoon	p.m.
PNB	Producto nacional bruto	Gross National Product	GNP
S.A.	Sociedad Anónima	Stock Company, Corporation, Private Limited Company	PLC
S. en C.	Sociedad en Comandita	Silent partnership, commandite, partnership in commendam	
s.e.u.o.	salvo error u omisión	Errors and omissions excepted	E.&.O.E.
S.L./Sdad. Lda.	Sociedad Limitada	Limited Company	Ltd.
TIJ	Tribunal Internacional de Justicia	International Court of Justice	ICJ
u.e.p.s.	último en entrar, primero en salir	Last in, first out	LIFO